Ubuntu® Linux®
Secrets

Ubuntu® Linux® Secrets

Richard Blum

Wiley Publishing, Inc.

Ubuntu® Linux® Secrets

Published by
Wiley Publishing, Inc.
10475 Crosspoint Boulevard
Indianapolis, IN 46256
www.wiley.com

Copyright © 2009 by Wiley Publishing, Inc., Indianapolis, Indiana

Published simultaneously in Canada

ISBN: 978-0-470-39508-0

Manufactured in the United States of America

10 9 8 7 6 5 4 3 2 1

Library of Congress Cataloging-in-Publication Data
Blum, Richard, 1962–
  Ubuntu Linux secrets / Richard Blum.
    p. cm.
  Includes index.
  ISBN 978-0-470-39508-0 (paper/website)
  1. Ubuntu (Electronic resource) 2. Linux. 3. Operating systems (Computers) I. Title.
  QA76.76.O63B5984 2009
  005.4'32—dc22
                    2009005635

To my family. "By wisdom a house is built, and through understanding it is established; through knowledge its rooms are filled with rare and beautiful treasures."

—Proverbs 24:3–4 (NIV)

About the Author

Richard Blum has worked in the IT industry for over 20 years as both a systems and network administrator. During that time he has administered UNIX, Linux, Novell, and Microsoft servers, as well as helped manage desktop workstations on a 3,500-user network. He has used Linux since the days of loading the system from floppy disks and has utilized Ubuntu workstations and servers in his environment.

Rich has a bachelor of science degree in electrical engineering and a master of science degree in management, specializing in management information systems, from Purdue University. He is the author of several Linux books, including *Linux Command Line and Shell Script Bible, Professional Assembly Language Programming, Network Performance Open Source Toolkit, sendmail for Linux, Running qmail, Postfix,* and *Open Source E-mail Security.* He's also a coauthor of *Professional Linux Programming,* and *Linux for Dummies, 8th Edition.* When he's not being a computer nerd, Rich plays bass guitar for his church worship band and enjoys spending time with his wife, Barbara, and their two daughters, Katie Jane and Jessica.

Credits

Acquisitions Editor
Jenny Watson

Senior Development Editor
Tom Dinse

Technical Editor
Warren Wyrostek

Production Editor
Rebecca Coleman

Copy Editor
Publication Services, Inc.

Editorial Manager
Mary Beth Wakefield

Production Manager
Tim Tate

Vice President and Executive Group Publisher
Richard Swadley

Vice President and Executive Publisher
Barry Pruett

Associate Publisher
Jim Minatel

Project Coordinator, Cover
Lynsey Stanford

Compositor
Maureen Forys,
Happenstance Type-O-Rama

Proofreader
Word One

Indexer
Robert Swanson

Cover Designer
Ryan Sneed

Acknowledgments

First, all glory and praise go to God, who through His Son makes all things possible and gives us the gift of eternal life.

Many thanks go to the great team of people at Wiley Publishing for their outstanding work on this project. Thanks to Jenny Watson, the acquisitions editor, for offering me the opportunity to work on this book. Also, thanks to Tom Dinse, the development editor, for keeping things on track and making this book more presentable. The technical editor, Warren Wyrostek, did an amazing job of double-checking all the work in this book, plus making suggestions to improve the content. Thanks, Warren, for your hard work and diligence. I would also like to thank Carole McClendon at Waterside Productions, Inc. for arranging this opportunity for me and for helping out in my writing career.

Finally, I would like to thank my parents, Mike and Joyce Blum, for their dedication and support while raising me, and my wife, Barbara and daughters, Katie Jane and Jessica, for their love, patience, and understanding, especially while I was writing this book.

Contents at a Glance

Contents

Introduction

Welcome to *Ubuntu Linux Secrets*. Like all books in the *Secrets* series, you can expect to find both hands-on tutorials and real-world practical application information, as well as reference and background information that provides a context for what you are learning. This book is a fairly comprehensive resource on the Ubuntu Linux distribution. By the time you have completed *Ubuntu Linux Secrets* you will be well-prepared to utilize your Ubuntu workstation or server to its fullest.

Who Should Read This Book

If you're new to the Linux world, you'll benefit greatly from this book's hands-on approach. The book walks through all of the steps required for setting up an Ubuntu Linux system, guiding you through the pitfalls and offering practical advice for getting your Ubuntu workstation up and running. It then walks through all of the applications you'll find on your new system, showing you how to use the office productivity software; work with images, audio and video clips on your desktop; run CDs and DVDs; and interact with the Internet.

If you're an advanced Linux enthusiast, you'll also benefit from *Ubuntu Linux Secrets*. Nowadays it's easy to get lost in the graphical world of prebuilt desktop packages. Most desktop Linux distributions try their best to hide the Linux system from the typical user. However, there are times when you have to know what's going on under the hood. This book shows you how to use the Ubuntu administration features to manage your system, including monitoring programs, users, and disk space. It shows how to access the Linux command-line prompt and what to do once you get there. It also explains how to use your Ubuntu system as a complete program development platform, discussing how to program using shell, Perl, and Python scripts; the C, Java, and Ruby programming languages; and the PHP web-scripting language.

Ubuntu Linux Secrets also walks the seasoned system administrator through how to use the various server software packages included in the Ubuntu server distribution. It discusses how to set up a complete web server using both the LAMP and Tomcat web servers and a database server using the popular MySQL or the feature-rich PostgreSQL database package, how to interact on a Microsoft Windows network using the Samba software, and how to create an email server for your home or organization.

How This Book Is Organized

This book is organized to lead you through the basics of the Ubuntu Linux distribution features, from installing your system to using the installed applications. The book is divided into five parts, each one building on the previous parts.

Part 1 starts you out on your Ubuntu Linux journey by helping you get your Ubuntu system running. Chapter 1, "What Is Ubuntu?" walks through the complicated world of Linux distributions, describing why there are so many distributions and what the Ubuntu

Linux distribution has to offer. After explaining the basics of the Ubuntu system, Part 1 continues with

◆ Downloading and working with the Ubuntu LiveCD (Chapter 2)
◆ Installing Ubuntu on your PC (Chapter 3)
◆ Exploring the features of the GNOME desktop (Chapter 4)

In Part 2, the book takes you through the features you'll find in the Ubuntu workstation:

◆ Working with files and folders in Ubuntu (Chapter 5)
◆ Working with text files using the Ubuntu text editors (Chapter 6)
◆ Using the OpenOffice.org office productivity suite (Chapter 7)
◆ Becoming familiar with the Ubuntu Network applications (Chapter 8)
◆ Accessing your email with the Evolution email software (Chapter 9)
◆ Working with image files (Chapter 10)
◆ Playing and ripping CDs (Chapter 11)
◆ Playing DVDs and watching video clips from the Internet (Chapter 12)

Part 3 shows you how to manage your Ubuntu system:

◆ Installing and updating software packages (Chapter 13)
◆ Configuring network access (Chapter 14)
◆ Installing and using external devices such as printers and scanners (Chapter 15)
◆ Configuring your display and setting up multiple monitors (Chapter 16)
◆ Adding new users (Chapter 17)
◆ Controlling running programs and monitoring the system (Chapter 18)
◆ Using the Ubuntu command line (Chapter 19)

In Part 4, you'll see how to install and configure the Ubuntu server packages:

◆ Creating a domain name server (DNS) (Chapter 20)
◆ Maintaining a web server for dynamic web applications (Chapter 21)
◆ Using Samba to interact with other devices on a Microsoft Windows network (Chapter 22)
◆ Managing a complete email server (Chapter 23)
◆ Running a full-featured database server using either MySQL or PostgreSQL (Chapter 24)

The last section of the book, Part 5, demonstrates how to use your Ubuntu workstation as a complete programming development environment:

◆ Writing and running shell scripts from the Ubuntu command line (Chapter 25)
◆ Working with Perl and Python scripts to manipulate data (Chapter 26)
◆ Using the C programming language to create professional applications (Chapter 27)
◆ Installing the Java programming environment to write applications (Chapter 28)
◆ Installing Ruby to write local and web applications (Chapter 29)
◆ Using PHP on the Ubuntu LAMP server to write dynamic web applications (Chapter 30)

Conventions and Features

There are many different organizational and typographical features throughout this book designed to help you get the most of the information.

Secrets

When the author wants to provide additional information to help you get the most out of your Ubuntu system, the information will appear in a Secrets sidebar, separate from the main chapter material.

Secret

The information in the Secrets sidebars is important and is set off in a separate paragraph with a special icon. Secrets provide additional information about things to watch out for, tips on how to better use a feature, or background information that helps in understanding a topic.

Minimum Requirements

To get the most from the Ubuntu workstation software you must have a PC with at least a 700-MHz processor, 384 MB of system memory (RAM), 8 GB of disk space, and a graphics card capable of at least 1024 × 768 resolution. It also helps to have a sound card if you plan on working with audio and video, and a network card if you plan on interacting with a local network or the Internet.

Where to Go from Here

Once you've completed *Ubuntu Linux Secrets* you'll be well on your way to being an Ubuntu Linux guru. In the ever-changing world of Linux, it's always a good idea to stay in touch with new developments. The Ubuntu Linux distribution comes out with a new version every 6 months, adding new features and removing some older ones. To keep your knowledge of Ubuntu fresh, it's important to stay well informed. Find a good Linux forum on the web and monitor what's going on in the Linux world. There are many popular sites, such as Slashdot and Distrowatch, that provide up-to-the-minute information about advances in Linux. It's also a good idea to keep an eye on the Ubuntu distribution site itself. Each new release goes through a series of beta releases, which are a great way to be introduced to new features before they're released in the next version.

Part 1

Starting Out with Ubuntu

What is Ubuntu?

♦ ♦

Secrets in This Chapter

The Linux Kernel

The GNU Utilities

The Linux Desktop Environments

Linux Distributions

Ubuntu Linux

♦ ♦

One of the most confusing features of Linux is the concept of a distribution. Many novice Linux users get confused about what a distribution is and why there are so many of them.

Before diving into the world of Ubuntu, it often helps to have an understanding of what Linux is and how it relates to Ubuntu. This will help you understand where Ubuntu came from, and you'll have a better idea of which flavor of Ubuntu is right for you. With that in mind, this chapter explains what Linux and Linux distributions are, then it explains the pieces that specifically make up the Ubuntu Linux distribution. It finishes by walking through different Ubuntu distributions and discussing what each provides.

What Is Linux?

If Ubuntu is your first experience with Linux, you may be confused about why there are so many different versions of it. I'm sure you have heard various terms such as "distribution," "LiveCD," and "GNU" when looking at Linux packages—and have been confused.

Trying to wade through the world of Linux for the first time can be a tricky experience. Even for experienced Linux users, trying to figure out the features that distinguish different distributions can be tricky. This section walks through exactly what Linux is and describes each of its components.

For starters, there are four main parts of a Linux system:

- ◆ The Linux kernel
- ◆ The GNU utilities
- ◆ Windows management software
- ◆ Application software

Each of these four parts has a specific job in the Linux system. However, each of the parts by itself isn't very useful. You need all of them in one package to have a Linux system. Figure 1-1 shows a basic diagram of how the parts fit together to create the overall Linux system.

This section describes these four main parts in detail and gives you an overview of how they work together to create a complete Linux system.

The Linux Kernel

The core of the Linux system is the kernel. The kernel controls all of the hardware and software on the computer system, allocating hardware when necessary, and executing software when required.

If you've been following the Linux world at all, no doubt you've heard the name Linus Torvalds. Linus is the person responsible for creating the first Linux kernel software, when he was a student at the University of Helsinki. He intended it to be a copy of the UNIX system, at the time a popular operating system used at many universities.

After developing the Linux kernel, Linus released it to the Internet community and solicited suggestions for improving it. This simple process started a revolution in the world of computer operating systems. Soon Linus was receiving suggestions from students as well as professional programmers from around the world.

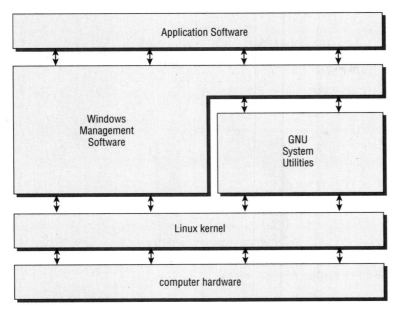

Figure 1-1: The Linux system.

Allowing anyone to change programming code in the kernel would result in complete chaos. Therefore, to simplify things, Linus acted as a central point for all improvement suggestions. It was ultimately Linus's decision whether or not to incorporate suggested code in the kernel. This same concept is still in place with the Linux kernel code, except instead of Linus controlling the kernel code alone, a team of developers has taken on the task.

The kernel is primarily responsible for four main functions:

- ◆ System memory management
- ◆ Software program management
- ◆ Hardware management
- ◆ Filesystem management

The following sections explore each of these functions in more detail.

System Memory Management

One of the primary functions of the operating system kernel is *memory management*. Not only does the kernel manage the physical memory available on the server, it can also create and manage *virtual memory*, or memory that does not actually exist.

It does this by using space on the hard disk, called the *swap space*. The kernel swaps the contents of virtual memory locations back and forth from the swap space to the actual physical memory. This process allows the system to think there is more memory available than what physically exists (as shown in Figure 1-2).

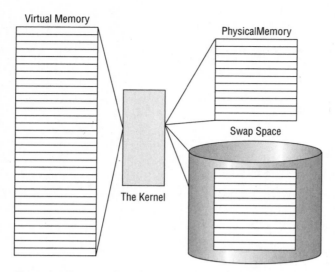

Figure 1-2: The Linux system memory usage.

The memory locations are grouped into blocks called *pages*. The kernel locates each page of memory in either the physical memory or the swap space. It then maintains a table of the memory pages that indicates which pages are in physical memory and which pages are swapped out to disk.

The kernel keeps track of which memory pages are in use and automatically copies memory pages that have not been accessed for a period of time to the swap space area (called *swapping out*). When a program wants to access a memory page that has been swapped out, the kernel must make room for it in physical memory by swapping out a different memory page and swap in the required page from the swap space. Obviously, this process takes time, and it can slow down a running process. The process of swapping out memory pages for running applications continues for as long as the Linux system is running.

You can see the current status of the memory on a Ubuntu system by using the System Monitor utility, as shown in Figure 1-3.

The Memory graph shows that this Linux system has 380.5 MB of physical memory. It also shows that about 148.3 MB is currently being used. The next line shows that there is about 235.3 MB of swap space memory available on this system, with none in use at the time.

By default, each process running on the Linux system has its own private memory pages. One process cannot access memory pages being used by another process.

The kernel maintains its own memory areas. For security purposes, no processes can access memory used by the kernel processes. Each individual user on the system also has a private memory area used for handling any applications the user starts.

Often, however, related applications run that must communicate with each other. One way to do this is through data sharing. To facilitate data sharing, you can create *shared memory pages*.

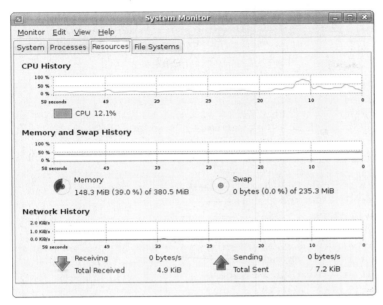

Figure 1-3: The Ubuntu System Monitor utility, showing the current memory usage.

A shared memory page allows multiple processes to read and write to the same shared memory area. The kernel maintains and administers the shared memory areas, controlling which processes are allowed access to the shared area.

The special `ipcs` command allows us to view the current shared memory pages on the system. Here's the output from a sample `ipcs` command:

```
test@testbox:~$ ipcs -m

------ Shared Memory Segments --------
key shmid owner perms bytes nattch status
0x00000000 557056 test 600 393216 2 dest
0x00000000 589825 test 600 393216 2 dest
0x00000000 622594 test 600 393216 2 dest
0x00000000 655363 test 600 393216 2 dest
0x00000000 688132 test 600 393216 2 dest
0x00000000 720901 test 600 196608 2 dest
0x00000000 753670 test 600 393216 2 dest
0x00000000 1212423 test 600 393216 2 dest
0x00000000 819208 test 600 196608 2 dest
0x00000000 851977 test 600 393216 2 dest
0x00000000 1179658 test 600 393216 2 dest
0x00000000 1245195 test 600 196608 2 dest
0x00000000 1277964 test 600 16384 2 dest
0x00000000 1441805 test 600 393216 2 dest

test@testbox:~$
```

Each shared memory segment has an owner that created the segment. Each segment also has a standard Linux permissions setting that sets the availability of the segment for other users. The key value is used to allow other users to gain access to the shared memory segment.

Software Program Management

The Linux operating system calls a running program a *process*. A process can run in the foreground, displaying output on a display, or it can run in the background, behind the scenes. The kernel controls how the Linux system manages all the processes running on the system.

The kernel creates the first process, called the *init* process, to start all other processes on the system. When the kernel starts, it loads the init process into virtual memory. As the kernel starts each additional process, it allocates to it a unique area in virtual memory to store the data and code that the process uses.

Most Linux implementations contain a table (or tables) of processes that start automatically on boot-up. This table is often located in the special file /etc/inittabs. However, the Ubuntu Linux system uses a slightly different format, storing multiple table files in the /etc/event.d folder by default.

The Linux operating system uses an init system that utilizes *run levels*. A run level can be used to direct the init process to run only certain types of processes, as defined in the /etc/inittabs file or the files in the /etc/event.d folder. There are seven init run levels in the Linux operating system. Level 0 is for when the system is halted, and level 6 is for when the system is rebooting. Levels 1 through 5 manage the Linux system while it's operating.

At run level 1, only the basic system processes are started, along with one console terminal process. This is called *Single User mode*. Single User mode is most often used for emergency filesystem maintenance when something is broken. Obviously, in this mode only one person (usually the administrator) can log into the system to manipulate data.

The standard init run level is 3. At this run level most application software, such as network support software, is started. Another popular run level in Linux is 5. This is the run level where the system starts the graphical X Window software and allows you to log in using a graphical desktop window.

The Linux system can control the overall system functionality by controlling the init run level. By changing the run level from 3 to 5, the system can change from a console-based system to an advanced, graphical X Window system.

Later on, in Chapter 19, "The Command Line," you'll see how to use the ps command to view the processes currently running on the Ubuntu system. Here are a few lines extracted from the output of the ps command:

```
test@testbox~$ ps ax
PID TTY STAT TIME COMMAND
1 ? Ss 0:01 /sbin/init
2 ? S< 0:00 [kthreadd]
3 ? S< 0:00 [migration/0]
4 ? S< 0:00 [ksoftirqd/0]
5 ? S< 0:00 [watchdog/0]
4708 ? S< 0:00 [krfcommd]
```

```
4759 ? Ss 0:00 /usr/sbin/gdm
4761 ? S 0:00 /usr/sbin/gdm
4814 ? Ss 0:00 /usr/sbin/atd
4832 ? Ss 0:00 /usr/sbin/cron
4920 tty1 Ss+ 0:00 /sbin/getty 38400 tty1
5417 ? Sl 0:01 gnome-settings-daemon
5425 ? S 0:00 /usr/bin/pulseaudio --log-target=syslog
5426 ? S 0:00 /usr/lib/pulseaudio/pulse/gconf-helper
5437 ? S 0:00 /usr/lib/gvfs/gvfsd
5451 ? S 0:05 gnome-panel --sm-client-id default1
5632 ? Sl 0:34 gnome-system-monitor
5638 ? S 0:00 /usr/lib/gnome-vfs-2.0/gnome-vfs-daemon
5642 ? S 0:09 gimp-2.4
6319 ? Sl 0:01 gnome-terminal
6321 ? S 0:00 gnome-pty-helper
6322 pts/0 Rs 0:00 bash
6343 ? S 0:01 gedit
6385 pts/0 R+ 0:00 ps ax
$
```

The first column in the output shows the process ID (or PID) of the process. Notice that the first process is our friend, the init process, which is assigned PID 1 by the Ubuntu system. All other processes that start after the init process are assigned PIDs in numerical order. No two processes can have the same PID.

The third column shows the current status of the process. The first letter represents the state the process is in (S for sleeping, R for running). The process name is shown in the last column. Processes that are in brackets have been swapped out of memory to the disk swap space due to inactivity. You can see that some of the processes have been swapped out, but the running processes have not.

Hardware Management

Still another responsibility for the kernel is hardware management. Any device that the Linux system must communicate with needs driver code inside the kernel code. The driver code allows the kernel to pass data back and forth to the device, acting as a intermediary between applications and the hardware. Two methods are used for inserting device driver code in the Linux kernel:

- ◆ Drivers compiled in the kernel
- ◆ Driver modules added to the kernel

Previously, the only way to insert a device driver code was to recompile the kernel. Each time you added a new device to the system, you had to recompile the kernel code. This process became even more inefficient as Linux kernels supported more hardware. Fortunately, Linux developers devised a better method to insert driver code into the running kernel.

Programmers developed the concept of kernel *modules* to allow you to insert driver code into a running kernel without having to recompile the kernel. Also, a kernel module can be removed from the kernel when the device is finished being used. This improvement greatly simplified and expanded the use of hardware with Linux.

The Linux system identifies hardware devices as special files, called *device files*. There are three classifications of device files:

- ◆ Character
- ◆ Block
- ◆ Network

Character device files are for devices that can handle data only one character at a time. Most types of modems and terminals are created as character files. *Block files* are for devices that can handle data in large blocks at a time, such as disk drives.

The *network file types* are used for devices that use packets to send and receive data. These devices include network cards and a special loopback mechanism that allows the Linux system to communicate with itself using common network programming protocols.

Linux creates special files, called *nodes,* for each device on the system. All communication with the device is performed through the device node. Each node has a unique number pair that identifies it to the Linux kernel. The number pair includes a major and a minor device number. Similar devices are grouped into the same major device number. The minor device number is used to identify a specific device within the major device group. This is an example of device files on a Linux server:

```
test@testbox~$ ls -al sda*
brw-rw---- 1 root disk 8, 0 2008-05-07 11:42 /dev/sda
brw-rw---- 1 root disk 8, 1 2008-05-07 11:42 /dev/sda1
brw-rw---- 1 root disk 8, 2 2008-05-07 11:42 /dev/sda2
brw-rw---- 1 root disk 8, 5 2008-05-07 11:42 /dev/sda5
test@testbox~$ ls -al ttyS*
crw-rw---- 1 root dialout 4, 64 2008-05-07 11:42 /dev/ttyS0
crw-rw---- 1 root dialout 4, 65 2008-05-07 11:42 /dev/ttyS1
crw-rw---- 1 root dialout 4, 66 2008-05-07 11:42 /dev/ttyS2
crw-rw---- 1 root dialout 4, 67 2008-05-07 11:42 /dev/ttyS3
test@testbox~$
```

The sda device is the first SCSI hard drive, and the ttyS devices are the standard IBM-PC COM ports. The list shows all of the sda devices that were created on the sample Ubuntu system. Similarly, the list shows all of the ttyS devices created.

The fifth column is the major device node number. Notice that all of the sda devices have the same major device node, 8, while all of the ttyS devices use 4. The sixth column is the minor device node number. Each device within a major number has a unique minor device node number.

The first column indicates the permissions for the device file. The first character of the permissions indicates the type of file. Notice that the SCSI hard drive files are all marked as block (b) device, while the COM port device files are marked as character (c) devices.

Filesystem Management

Unlike some other operating systems, the Linux kernel can support different types of filesystems to read and write data to hard drives. Besides having over a dozen filesystems of its own, Linux can read and write to filesystems used by other operating systems, such as Microsoft Windows. The kernel must be compiled with support for all types of filesystems that the system will use. Table 1-1 lists the standard filesystems that a Linux system can use to read and write data.

Table 1-1: Linux Filesystems

Filesystem	Description
ext	Linux Extended filesystem—the original Linux filesystem
ext2	Second extended filesystem; provided advanced features over ext
ext3	Third extended filesystem; supports journaling
hpfs	OS/2 high-performance filesystem
jfs	IBM's journaling file system
iso9660	ISO 9660 filesystem (CD-ROMs)
minix	MINIX filesystem
msdos	Microsoft FAT16
ncp	Netware filesystem
nfs	Network filesystem
ntfs	Support for Microsoft NT filesystem
proc	Access to system information
reiserFS	Advanced Linux filesystem for better performance and disk recovery
smb	Samba SMB filesystem for network access
sysv	Older UNIX filesystem
ufs	BSD filesystem
umsdos	UNIX-like filesystem that resides on top of MS-DOS
vfat	Windows 95 filesystem (FAT32)
xfs	High-performance 64-bit journaling filesystem

Any hard drive that a UNIX server accesses must be formatted using one of the filesystem types listed in Table 1-1.

The Linux kernel interfaces with each filesystem using the virtual file system (VFS), which provides a standard interface for the kernel to communicate with any type of filesystem. VFS caches information in memory as each filesystem is mounted and used.

The GNU Utilities

Besides having a kernel to control hardware devices, a computer operating system needs utilities to perform standard functions, such as controlling files and programs. Although Linus Torvalds created the Linux system kernel, he had no system utilities to run on it. Fortunately for him, at the same time he was working, a group of people were working together on the Internet trying to develop a standard set of computer system utilities that mimicked the popular UNIX operating system.

The GNU organization (GNU stands for GNUs Not UNIX) developed a complete set of UNIX utilities but had no kernel system to run them on. These utilities were developed under a software philosophy called open-source software (OSS).

The concept of OSS allows programmers to develop software and release it to the world with no licensing fees attached. Anyone can use the software, modify it, or incorporate it into his or her own system without having to pay a license fee. Uniting Linus's Linux kernel with the GNU operating system utilities created a complete, functional, free operating system.

Secret   Although the bundling of the Linux kernel and GNU utilities is often just called Linux, you will see some Linux purists on the Internet refer to it as the GNU/ Linux system to give credit to the GNU organization for its contributions to the cause.

The Core GNU Utilities

The GNU project was mainly designed for UNIX system administrators to have a UNIX-like environment available. This focus resulted in the project porting many common UNIX system command line utilities. The core bundle of utilities supplied for Linux systems is called the *coreutils* package.

The GNU coreutils package consists of three parts:

- ✦ Utilities for handling files
- ✦ Utilities for manipulating text
- ✦ Utilities for managing processes

These three groups of utilities each contain several utility programs that are invaluable to the Linux system administrator and programmer.

The Shell

The GNU/Linux shell is a special interactive utility. It provides a way for users to start programs, manage files on the filesystem, and manage processes running on the Linux system. The core of the shell is the command prompt. The command prompt is the interactive part of the shell. It allows you to enter text commands, then it interprets the commands and executes them in the kernel.

The shell contains a set of internal commands that you use to control things such as copying files, moving files, renaming files, displaying the programs currently running on the system, and stopping programs running on the system. Besides the internal commands, the shell also allows you to enter the name of a program at the command prompt. The shell passes the program name off to the kernel to start it.

There are quite a few Linux shells available to use on a Linux system. Different shells have different characteristics; some are more useful for creating scripts, and some are more useful for managing processes. The default shell used in all Linux distributions is the *bash* shell.

The bash shell was developed by the GNU project as a replacement for the standard UNIX shell, called the Bourne shell (after its creator, Stephen Bourne). The bash shell name is a play on this wording, referred to as the Bourne-again shell.

Besides the bash shell there are several other popular shells that Ubuntu supports. Table 1-2 lists the more popular shells available in Ubuntu.

Table 1-2: Linux Shells

Shell	Description
ash	A simple, lightweight shell that runs in low-memory environments but has full compatibility with the bash shell
korn	A programming shell compatible with the Bourne shell, but supporting advanced programming features such as associative arrays and floating-point arithmetic
tcsh	A shell that incorporates elements from the C programming language into shell scripts
zsh	An advanced shell that incorporates features from bash, tcsh, and korn, providing advanced programming features, shared history files, and themed prompts

Most Linux distributions include more than one shell, although usually they pick one of them as the default. Ubuntu installs only the bash shell by default, but the others are available to download and install (see Chapter 13, "Software Installs and Updates").

The Linux Desktop Environment

In the early days of Linux (the early 1990s), all that was available was a simple text interface to the Linux operating system. This text interface allowed administrators to start programs, control program operations, and move files around on the system.

With the popularity of Microsoft Windows, computer users expected more than the old text interface to work with. This expectation spurred more development in the OSS community, and the advent of Linux graphical desktops emerged.

Linux is famous for being able to do things more than one way, and no place is this feature more relevant than graphical desktops. You can choose from a plethora of graphical desktops in Linux. The following sections describe a few of the more popular ones.

The X Windows System

There are two basic elements that control your video environment—the video card in your PC and your monitor. To display fancy graphics on your computer, the Linux software needs to know how to talk to both of them. The X Windows software is the core element in presenting graphics.

The X Windows software is a low-level program that works directly with the video card and monitor in the PC. It controls how Linux applications can present fancy windows and graphics on your computer.

Linux isn't the only operating system that uses X Windows; there are versions written for many different operating systems. In the Linux world, only two software packages can implement X Windows.

The XFree86 software package is the older of the two, and for a long time it was the only X Windows package available for Linux. As its name implies, it's a free, open-source version of the X Windows software.

Recently, a new package called X.org has come onto the Linux scene. It too provides an open-source software implementation of the X Windows system. It is becoming increasingly popular, and many Linux distributions are starting to use it instead of the older XFree86 system. Ubuntu uses the X.org package to implement the X Windows system.

Both packages work the same way in controlling how Linux uses your video card to display content on your monitor. To do that, they have to be configured for your specific system. That is supposed to happen automatically when you install Linux.

When you first install Ubuntu, it attempts to detect your video card and monitor, then creates an X Windows configuration file that contains the required information. During installation you may notice a time when the installation program scans your monitor for supported video modes. Sometimes this causes your monitor to go blank for a few seconds. Because many different types of video cards and monitors are out there, this process can take a little while to complete.

Secret

Unfortunately, sometimes the installation can't autodetect what video settings to use, especially with some of the newer, more complicated video cards, and some Linux distributions will fail to install if they can't find your specific video card settings. Others will ask a few questions during installation to help manually gather the necessary information. Still others default to the lowest common denominator and produce a screen image that is not customized for your video environment.

To complicate matters more, many PC users have fancy video cards, such as 3-D accelerator cards, so that they can play high-resolution games. In the past, these video cards caused a lot of problems if you tried to install Linux. But lately, video card companies are helping to solve this problem by providing Linux drivers, and many customized Linux distributions now include drivers for specialty video cards.

The core X Windows software produces a graphical display environment but nothing else. While this is fine for running individual applications, it is not too useful for day-to-day computer use. There is no desktop environment to allow users to manipulate files or launch programs. To do that, you need a desktop environment on top of the X Windows system software.

The GNOME Desktop

The GNU Network Object Model Environment (GNOME) is the default desktop environment used in Ubuntu. First released in 1999, GNOME has become the default desktop environment for many other Linux distributions (including the popular Red Hat commercial Linux distribution).

Although GNOME chose to depart from the standard Microsoft Windows look and feel, it incorporates many features that most Windows users are comfortable with:

- ◆ A desktop area for icons
- ◆ Two panel areas
- ◆ Drag and drop capabilities

Figure 1-4 shows the standard GNOME desktop used in Ubuntu.

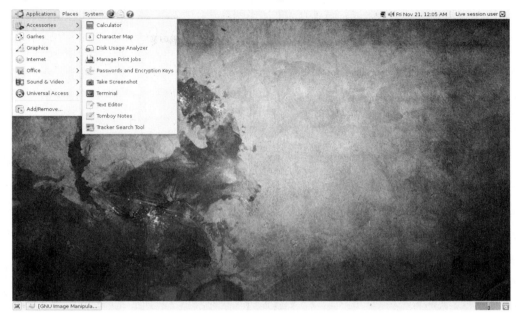

Figure 1-4: The default GNOME desktop in Ubuntu 8.10.

GNOME developers have produced a host of graphical applications that integrate with the GNOME desktop. These applications are shown in Table 1-3.

Table 1-3: GNOME Applications

Application	Description
epiphany	Web browser
evince	Document viewer
gcalc-tool	Calculator
gedit	GNOME text editor
gnome-panel	Desktop panel for launching applications
gnome-nettool	Network diagnostics tool
gnome-terminal	Terminal emulator
nautilus	Graphical file manager
nautilus-cd-burner	CD-burning tool
sound juicer	Audio CD-ripping tool
tomboy	Note-taking software
totem	Multimedia player

As you can see, quite a few applications are available for the GNOME desktop. Some of these applications are included in Ubuntu by default, while others you have to install from the Ubuntu repository. Besides all of these applications, other Linux applications use the GNOME library to create Windows-based applications that run on the GNOME desktop.

The KDE Desktop

The K Desktop Environment (KDE) was first released in 1996 as an open-source project to produce a graphical desktop similar to the Microsoft Windows environment. The KDE desktop incorporates all of the features you are probably familiar with if you are a Microsoft Windows user. Figure 1-5 shows a sample KDE desktop running on Kubuntu Linux.

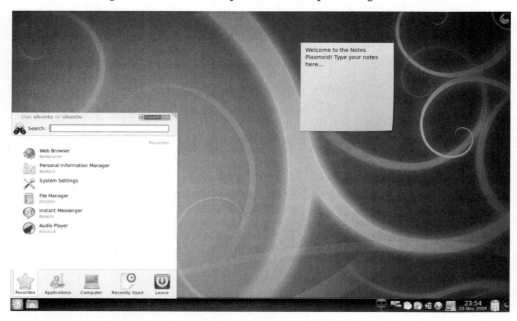

Figure 1-5: The default KDE desktop in Kubuntu 8.10.

Just like in Microsoft Windows, the KDE desktop allows you to place application and file icons on the desktop area. Unlike Windows, if you single-click an application icon, the KDE system starts the application. If you single-click on a file icon, the KDE desktop attempts to determine what application to start to handle the file.

The bar at the bottom of the desktop is called the *panel*. The panel consists of four parts:

- ◆ **The K menu:** similar to the Windows Start menu; contains links to start installed applications
- ◆ **Program shortcuts:** quick links to start applications directly from the panel
- ◆ **The taskbar:** shows icons for applications currently running on the desktop
- ◆ **Applets:** small applications that have an icon in the panel that often can change depending on information from the application

All of the panel features are similar to what you would find in Microsoft Windows.

Besides the desktop features, the KDE project has produced a wide assortment of applications that run in the KDE environment. These applications are shown in Table 1-4.

Table 1-4: KDE Applications

Application	Description
amaroK	Audio file player
digiKam	Digital camera software
K3b	CD-burning software
Kaffeine	Video player
Kmail	Email client
Koffice	Office applications suite
Konqueror	File and web browser
Kontact	Personal information manager
Kopete	Instant messaging client

You may notice the trend of using a capital K in KDE application names. This is only a partial list of applications produced by the KDE project. Many more applications are part of the KDE project. Similar to the GNOME environment, Kubuntu doesn't include all of the KDE project software by default, but you can easily install anything using the software repository.

Other Desktops

The downside to a fancy graphical desktop environment is that it requires a fair amount of system resources to operate properly. In the early days of Linux, a hallmark and selling feature of Linux was its ability to operate on older, less powerful PCs that the newer Microsoft desktop products couldn't run on. However, with the popularity of KDE and GNOME desktops, this hallmark has changed, and it can take almost as much memory to run a KDE or GNOME desktop as the latest Microsoft desktop environment (the minimum requirements for Ubuntu is 384 MB of memory).

If you have an older PC, don't be discouraged. The Linux developers have banded together to take Linux back to its roots. They've created several low-memory-oriented graphical desktop applications that provide basic features that run perfectly fine on older PCs.

Although those graphical desktops don't have a plethora of applications designed around them, they still run many basic graphical applications that support features such as word processing, spreadsheets, databases, drawing, and, of course, multimedia applications.

Table 1-5 shows some of the smaller Linux graphical desktop environments that can be used on lower-powered PCs and laptops.

Table 1-5: Other Linux Graphical Desktops

Desktop	Description
xfce	A lightweight desktop that packages components separately so you can pick and choose which features you want to implement
fluxbox	A bare-bones desktop that doesn't include a panel—only a pop-up menu to launch applications
fvwm	Supports some advanced desktop features such as virtual desktops and panels, but runs in low-memory environments
fvwm95	Derived from fvwm, but made to look like a Windows 95 desktop

These graphical desktop environments are not as fancy as the KDE and GNOME desktops, but they provide basic graphical functionality. Figure 1.6 shows what the xfce desktop used in the Xubuntu distribution looks like.

Figure 1-6: The default xfce desktop as seen in the Xubuntu 8.10 distribution.

If you are using an older PC, try a Linux distribution that uses one of these desktops and see what happens. You may be pleasantly surprised.

Linux Distributions

Now that you have seen the four main components required for a complete Linux system, you may be wondering how you are going to put them all together to make a Linux system. Fortunately, there are people who have already done that for us.

A complete Linux system package is called a *distribution*. Many different Linux distributions are available to meet almost any computing requirement you have. Most distributions are customized for a specific user group, such as business users, multimedia enthusiasts, software developers, or normal home users. Each customized distribution includes the software packages required to support specialized functions, such as audio and video editing software for multimedia enthusiasts, or compilers and Integrated Development Environments (IDEs) for software developers.

The Linux distributions are often divided into three categories:

◆ Full-core Linux distributions
◆ Specialized distributions
◆ LiveCD test distributions

The following sections describe these different Linux distributions and show some examples of Linux distributions in each category.

Core Linux Distributions

A core Linux distribution contains a kernel, one or more graphical desktop environments, and just about every Linux application that is available, precompiled for the kernel. It provides one-stop shopping for a complete Linux installation. Table 1-6 shows some of the more popular core Linux distributions.

Table 1-6: Core Linux Distributions

Distribution	Description
Slackware	One of the original Linux distribution sets, popular with Linux geeks
Red Hat	A commercial business distribution used mainly for Internet servers
Fedora	A spin-off of Red Hat, but designed for home use
Gentoo	A distribution designed for advanced Linux users, containing only Linux source code
Mandriva	Designed mainly for home use (previously called Mandrake)
openSuSe	Different distributions for business and home use (now owned by Novell)
Debian	Popular with Linux experts and commercial Linux products

In the early days of Linux, a distribution was released as a set of floppy disks. You had to download groups of files and then copy them onto disks. It would usually take 20 or more disks to make an entire distribution! Needless to say, it was a painful experience.

These days, with home computers commonly having CD and DVD players built in, Linux distributions are released as either a CD set or a single DVD. This makes installing Linux much easier.

However, beginners still often run into problems when they install one of the core Linux distributions. To cover just about any situation in which someone might want to use Linux, a single distribution has to include lots of application software. Distributions include everything from high-end Internet database servers to common games. Because of the quantity of applications available for Linux, a complete distribution often takes four or more CDs.

Although having many options available in a distribution is great for Linux geeks, it can become a nightmare for beginning Linux users. Most distributions ask a series of questions during the installation process to determine which applications to load by default, what hardware is connected to the PC, and how to configure the hardware. Beginners often find these questions confusing. As a result, they often either load too many programs on their computer or don't load enough and later discover that their computer won't do what they want it to.

Fortunately for beginners, there's a much simpler way to install Linux.

Specialized Linux Distributions

Over the past few years a new subgroup of Linux distributions has started to appear. These are typically based on one of the main distributions but contain only a subset of applications that would make sense for a specific area of use.

Besides providing specialized software (such as only office products for business users), customized Linux distributions also attempt to help beginning Linux users by autodetecting and autoconfiguring common hardware devices, which makes installing Linux a much more enjoyable process.

Table 1-7 shows some of the specialized Linux distributions available and what they specialize in.

Table 1-7: Specialized Linux Distributions

Distribution	Description
Linspire	A commercial Linux package configured to look like Windows
Xandros	A commercial Linux package configured for beginners
SimplyMEPIS	A free desktop distribution for home use
Ubuntu	A free desktop and server distribution for school and home use
PCLinuxOS	A free distribution for home and office use
dyne:bolic	A free distribution designed for audio and MIDI applications
Puppy Linux	A free, small distribution that runs well on older PCs

Table 1-7 contains just a small sampling of specialized Linux distributions. There are hundreds of specialized Linux distributions, and more are popping up all the time on the Internet. No matter what your specialty, you'll probably find a Linux distribution made for you.

Many of the specialized Linux distributions (including Ubuntu) are based on the Debian Linux distribution. They use the same installation files as Debian but package only a small fraction of a full-blown Debian system.

The Linux LiveCD

A relatively new phenomenon in the Linux world is the bootable Linux CD distribution, which lets you see what a Linux system is like without actually installing it. Most modern PCs can boot from a CD instead of the standard hard drive. To take advantage of this capability, some Linux distributions create a bootable CD that contains a sample Linux system (called a Linux LiveCD). Due to the size limitations of a single CD, the sample can't contain a complete Linux system, but you'd be surprised at all the software they can cram in there. The result is, you can boot your PC from the CD and run a Linux distribution without having to install anything on your hard drive.

It's is an excellent way to test various Linux distributions without having to make changes to your PC. Just pop in a CD and boot! All of the Linux software will run directly off the CD. There are many Linux LiveCDs that you can download from the Internet and burn onto a CD to test-drive.

Table 1-8 shows some popular Linux LiveCDs.

Table 1-8: Linux LiveCD Distributions

Distribution	Description
Knoppix	A German Linux, the first Linux LiveCD developed
SimplyMEPIS	Designed for beginning home Linux users
PCLinuxOS	Full-blown Linux distribution on LiveCD
Ubuntu	A worldwide Linux project, designed for many languages
Slax	A live Linux CD based on Slackware Linux
Puppy Linux	A full-featured Linux designed for older PCs

You may notice something familiar in Table 1-8. Many specialized Linux distributions also have a Linux LiveCD version. Some Linux LiveCD distributions, such as Ubuntu, allow you to install the Linux distribution directly from the LiveCD. You can boot with the CD, test drive the Linux distribution, and, if you like it, install it onto your hard drive. This feature is extremely handy and user friendly.

As with all good things, Linux LiveCDs have a few drawbacks. Because you access everything from the CD, applications run more slowly, especially if you're using older, slower computers and CD drives. Also, because you can't write to the CD, any changes you make to the Linux system will be gone the next time you reboot.

But there are advances being made in the Linux LiveCD world that help to solve some of these problems. These advances include the ability to

  ♦ Copy Linux system files from the CD to memory
  ♦ Copy system files to a file on the hard drive
  ♦ Store system settings on a USB Memory Stick
  ♦ Store user settings on a USB Memory Stick

Some Linux LiveCDs, such as Puppy Linux, are designed with a minimum number of Linux system files and copy them directly into memory when the CD boots, which allows you to remove the CD from the computer as soon as Linux boots. Not only does it make your applications run much faster (because applications run faster from memory), but it frees up your CD tray for ripping audio CDs or playing video DVDs from the software included in Puppy Linux.

Other Linux LiveCDs use an alternative method that allows you to remove the CD from the tray after booting. It involves copying the core Linux files onto the Windows hard drive as a single file. After the CD boots, it looks for that file and reads the system files from it. The Ubuntu Wubi project uses this technique to move the LiveCD contents to a single file stored in the Windows drive on the PC. From there you can boot directly into Ubuntu (more on this in Chapter 2, "Playing with the LiveCD").

Secret

A popular technique for storing data from a live Linux CD session is to use a USB Memory Stick (also called a flash drive and a thumb drive). Just about every Linux LiveCD can recognize a plugged-in USB Memory Stick (even if the stick is formatted for Windows) and read and write files from it. This capability allows you to boot a Linux LiveCD, use the Linux applications to create files, store them on your Memory Stick, then access them from your Windows applications later (or from a different computer).

What Is Ubuntu?

Now that you've seen what's behind a Linux distribution, it's time to turn our attention to the Ubuntu Linux distribution. Even within Ubuntu, there are several features that you have to choose from before running your system. This section walks through the different versions and choices available.

Ubuntu Versions

The Ubuntu Linux distribution is based on Debian Linux. As was discussed in the Core Linux Distributions section, the Debian distribution contains a variety of software and features. The Ubuntu developers created two subsets of the main Debian Linux system for specialized use:

- ◆ Ubuntu workstation
- ◆ Ubuntu server

The Ubuntu workstation distribution includes only the software that's most commonly used in a desktop environment:

- ◆ The OpenOffice.org office productivity suite
- ◆ The Firefox web browser software
- ◆ The Evolution email and calendar software
- ◆ Tomboy note-taking software
- ◆ F-spot digital image editing
- ◆ Totem video player
- ◆ Rhythmbox music player

The Ubuntu workstation distribution provides a complete home, school, and even office desktop environment, all in one package and all for free.

The Ubuntu server distribution includes only software that's most commonly used in a computer data center environment:

- ◆ The Postfix email server
- ◆ The Samba file and print-sharing server for Windows
- ◆ The Apache web server
- ◆ The MySQL database server

The Ubuntu server distribution can support any size of server environment, from the small home network to the larger corporate data center.

Ubuntu Release Schedule

The Linux world is constantly evolving, and, for any Linux distribution to keep up with new advances, new versions of the software must be released on a regular schedule. The Ubuntu distribution does an excellent job of scheduling releases and sticking to the schedule.

Ubuntu releases new versions every six months. Some releases are tagged as long-term support (LTS). For these releases, Ubuntu provides security and patch updates for up to 3 years.

The current list of Ubuntu releases is shown in Table 1-9.

Table 1-9: Ubuntu Releases

Release	Date	Name
4.10	10/20/2004	Warty Warthog
5.04	04/08/2005	Hoary Hedgehog
5.10	10/13/2005	Breezy Badger
6.06	06/01/2006	Dapper Drake (LTS)
6.10	10/26/2006	Edgy Eft
7.04	04/19/2007	Feisty Fawn
7.10	10/18/2007	Gutsy Gibbon
8.04	04/24/2008	Hardy Heron (LTS)
8.10	10/30/2008	Intrepid Ibex

Each Ubuntu release is assigned a code name. You'll often see the Ubuntu releases referred to by their code names instead of their release numbers.

The 6.06 and 8.04 releases are LTS releases and are slightly different from the others. LTS support distributions are intended for users who don't want to constantly upgrade to new versions of software but who want to maintain the existing software packages as new bug and security patches are released. LTS distributions are often handy in places such as schools or offices that don't want to constantly upgrade the workstation operating system but want to keep current on security and bug patches.

Ubuntu Cousins

The Ubuntu workstation distribution uses only the GNOME desktop environment. Consequently, other Ubuntu distributions have been developed to offer customers a choice (because that's what Linux is all about).

In addition to the main Ubuntu distribution, Ubuntu also supports specialized distributions that are based on the Ubuntu code base but that use alternative desktops:

- ◆ **Kubuntu:** uses the KDE desktop environment
- ◆ **Xubuntu:** uses the xfce desktop environment
- ◆ **Edubuntu:** uses the GNOME desktop to provide specialized educational software

All of the Ubuntu distributions and features are based on the same basic ideas and principles of open-source software. The Kubuntu distribution contains the same core group of workstation software packages as Ubuntu, such as OpenOffice.org and Firefox, but it also provides the common KDE desktop utilities, including Dolphin for filesystem browsing, KMail as an email client, and the KDE desktop utilities for managing your graphical environment.

The Xubuntu distribution is designed for less-powerful workstations. Besides using the xfce desktop, it uses the AbiWord word processor, as well as the Firefox web browser. It can run on systems with as little as 128 MB of memory.

The Edubuntu distribution is something of a mix-and-match distribution. It uses the GNOME desktop but includes the KDE education software suite. That suite includes educational games for school-aged children and activities for pre-school aged children to get them used to the Linux environment.

Summary

This chapter discussed the origins of Linux system came and how it works. The Linux kernel is the core of the system, controlling how memory, programs, and hardware interact. The GNU utilities are also an important piece in the Linux system. The Linux shell is part of the GNU core utilities.

The chapter also discussed the final piece of a Linux system, the Linux desktop environment. Things have changed over the years, and Linux now supports several graphical desktop environments.

Next, the chapter talked about the various Linux distributions. A Linux distribution bundles the various parts of a Linux system into a simple package that you can easily install on your PC. The Linux distribution world consists of full-blown Linux distributions that include nearly every application imaginable, as well as specialized Linux distributions that include applications focused on a special function. The Linux LiveCD craze has created another group of Linux distributions that allow you to easily test drive Linux without installing it on your hard drive.

Finally, the chapter discussed the Ubuntu Linux distribution and showed how the different versions and releases of Ubuntu fit together.

In the next chapter we'll look at the Ubuntu LiveCD. We'll walk through how to test-drive Ubuntu on your PC without having to load anything, and we'll see how to install it directly on your current Windows PC without having to make changes to your hard drive.

Playing with the LiveCD

Chapter
2

One of the coolest features in the Linux world is the invention of the LiveCD. Ubuntu uses this feature to allow you to test-drive Ubuntu on your PC without having to commit to installing it. This chapter walks you through the things you'll need to do to get a LiveCD running on your system, and it takes you through some of the features of the LiveCD so you can get the most from your LiveCD experience. It also discusses a new feature of the LiveCD, Wubi, which lets you create a bootable Ubuntu partition right in your existing Windows system.

The Ubuntu LiveCD

As discussed in Chapter 1, "What Is Ubuntu?," the Ubuntu distribution provides a LiveCD that you can boot from your PC to run Ubuntu without having to install it. The Ubuntu operating system runs directly from the LiveCD and memory without affecting the hard drive setup. This is a great way to quickly determine whether Ubuntu will run on a specific desktop PC or laptop.

Before you can run the Ubuntu LiveCD, you'll need a copy of it. The Ubuntu project provides three ways for you to obtain the Ubuntu distribution LiveCD:

+ Purchase it from Canonical Ltd.
+ Request a free copy to be sent in the mail.
+ Download it via the Internet.

Canonical Ltd. is a European company committed to providing software and hardware support for Ubuntu. You can purchase copies of the Ubuntu LiveCD from Canonical via the Ubuntu web site (www.ubuntu.com).

Canonical also provides single copies of Ubuntu that you can download for free. If you don't have a high-speed Internet connection, you can purchase or request a free copy of the LiveCD. If you're going the free CD route, be prepared to wait. Free copies of the LiveCD can take up to 10 weeks for delivery.

Of the three options, downloading the LiveCD via the Internet is the quickest way to get Ubuntu up and running on your PC. If you have a high-speed Internet connection, downloading the CD takes only an hour or so, depending on your connection bandwidth.

note Because Ubuntu is so popular, you'll often find Ubuntu LiveCDs for sale in online and brick-and-mortar computer bookstores. If you frequent a particular computer bookstore, check out the Linux section and see if it's there. However, it's not unusual for it to take a month or so after the release of a new version for it to appear for sale in bookstores.

If you decide to download the LiveCD file, the next section walks you through the process to perform the download.

Downloading Ubuntu

The popularity of LiveCD Linux distributions has triggered a new interest in creating and using CD image files. A CD image file places the contents of the entire data CD in a single archive file. This file is called an *ISO image file*, which usually ends with a .iso file extension. The ISO image file contains a byte-for-byte copy of all the data on the LiveCD. After downloading the ISO image file, all you need to do is use a CD-burning software package to convert the ISO image file into a CD.

Ubuntu makes the process of downloading and creating the LiveCD fairly easy, but there are still a few things you should watch out for, especially if you've never done it before.

Once you decide to download the LiveCD image file, you have to decide which method to use to download the file via the Internet. The following sections walk through the different methods for downloading the LiveCD file.

Downloading from the Web

These days just about everything you can do on the Internet can be done from your trusty web browser. This includes downloading large ISO image files. Downloading the Ubuntu LiveCD image file is as simple as clicking a few links on the Ubuntu web site. Unfortunately, there are a few choices you need to make here. This section discusses what you need to know to determine which LiveCD version is right for you.

Finding the Right Version

If you go to the Ubuntu web site (`www.ubuntu.com`), you'll see several links and buttons that get you to the download page. Clicking any of them takes you to the express download page, which includes a form that you must fill out to determine the correct file to download.

The first step to downloading the LiveCD is to figure out which LiveCD you need. The Ubuntu download page has a three-step process you follow:

1. Select the workstation or server LiveCD.
2. Select your hardware platform (32 or 64 bits).
3. Select a download location.

As discussed in Chapter 1, there are two versions of Ubuntu—the workstation version and the server version. Each version is distributed on a separate LiveCD. The first step is to select which one you want to download.

note   Although the Ubuntu server software comes on a LiveCD, this description is somewhat misleading. You can't boot the Ubuntu server software directly from the LiveCD and run it. The Ubuntu server LiveCD allows you only to install the server software onto a system.

The second decision in your download selection is the hardware platform you intend to run the LiveCD on. There are two options:

♦ 32-bit Intel and AMD processors
♦ 64-bit Intel and AMD processors

If you're working with an older PC, you may not know what processor you have. There are a few ways to find out. If your system is currently running a version of Microsoft Windows, you can use the System Properties dialog box to display what processor is in the system. Here are the steps for doing so on a Windows XP or Vista workstation:

1. Right-click on either the *My Computer* desktop icon or the *My Computer* entry in the Start menu.

2. Select *Properties* from the menu list.
3. Find the CPU information in the System Properties dialog box.

The CPU information will tell you what type of processor is in the PC. Figure 2-1 shows a sample Properties dialog box from a Windows Vista workstation.

Figure 2-1: The *My Computer* System Properties dialog box in Windows Vista.

If you have a 64-bit processor in your PC, it'll say so in the CPU information section.

The final decision you need to make before your download can start is which server to use to download the LiveCD image file. Ubuntu LiveCD images are available on many different servers (called *mirrors*) worldwide. The idea is to prevent a single server from overloading with download requests, as well as to help distribute network traffic. If you can find a location that's close to you, it will speed up the download process.

Once you've made your selections, click the Start Download button to begin the download.

caution   As a security feature, some web browsers (such as Internet Explorer version 7.0) block automatic file downloads. When this happens, a warning banner appears at the top of the web page viewing pane. Just click the banner to continue with the download.

Starting the download isn't usually a problem. Often the problem is keeping the download running. The LiveCD ISO image file (usually 700 MB or more) takes a while to download, even on high-speed Internet connections. During that time many things can happen. It helps if you have a download manager that allows you to interrupt and restart the download process.

Interrupting and Restarting the Download

When you're downloading a large ISO image file, things can (and often do) go wrong with your Internet connection before the entire file makes its way to your PC. Some browsers allow you to recover from an interrupted download, while others require that you start all over again.

The Firefox browser uses a download manager that's a great tool for downloading large files. The Firefox download manager keeps track of the file download and allows you to stop and restart the download as often as you want (as long as you keep the same browser window open). It also allows you to resume a previous download that failed, starting from the point of failure. This is a great feature if you're on an Internet connection that is subject to failure. Figure 2-2 shows the Firefox download manager window in action.

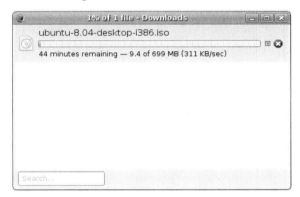

Figure 2-2: The Firefox web browser download manager.

The download manager provides controls for pausing the download so you can resume it later. Once the download is complete, the download manager keeps a record of the download for future reference.

Using BitTorrent to Download

Peer-to-peer (P2P) network sharing has become a popular way to distribute large files on the Internet. Instead of hosting the file as a single download on a single FTP server, a P2P system has clients register on the P2P server, which then splits the file into many small pieces for download.

As different clients retrieve the different pieces of the file, they advertise which pieces they have and offer them to other clients for downloading. Before long, an individual client can retrieve pieces of the download directly from multiple clients instead of having to go to the main server. As the client program retrieves the individual pieces, it recreates the original file. When it's retrieved all of the pieces, you've got your copy of the original file.

Although P2P has gotten a bad rap lately because some users post material that violates copyright laws, it's still a valid way to distribute large files, as long as they're legal. The Ubuntu project fully supports using P2P to distribute the various Ubuntu LiveCD versions. It's perfectly legal to use P2P to download the Ubuntu ISO image file.

Installing P2P Software

The protocol behind the P2P network is called *BitTorrent.* The BitTorrent protocol uses a central server that advertises which connected clients have which parts of the available download files controlled by the server.

Before you can join the P2P fray, you'll need to install a BitTorrent client package on your PC. Several commercial and free versions are available for different operating systems.

For Mac OS X and Linux systems, the Transmission Open Source software package, shown in Figure 2-3, is a popular free BitTorrent client.

Figure 2-3: The Transmission client used in Ubuntu.

To get the transmission package go to the Transmission main Web page (www .transmissionbt.com), then click the download link at the top of the page.

On the download page you can find a binary distribution for Mac OS X systems or the source code package for Linux systems. You'll need to use your Linux distribution's C compiler system to compile the source code into the binary package.

If you're using a Microsoft Windows system (such as XP or Vista), you can download the free µTorrent client package, shown in Figure 2-4.

The µTorrent package downloads as a Microsoft installer file. Just download the file, then double-click it to start the installer. Once the µTorrent program installs, you can run it from the Start menu.

Start the Download Process

Downloading a file via the BitTorrent process is a little different from the web download method. Instead of directly finding the ISO image file to download, you must first obtain a special file (called a *torrent file*) that provides the information about the BitTorrent server hosting the download and the specific ISO image file to download. Each image file uses a separate torrent file.

Ubuntu provides torrent files in a separate location from its web site's main download area. Instead of going to the download page on the Ubuntu web site, go to http://releases. ubuntu.com.

On this page is a list of all the supported Ubuntu releases available for download. When you select the version you want, it takes you to a download page with links for the various LiveCD files, plus links to other types of files available.

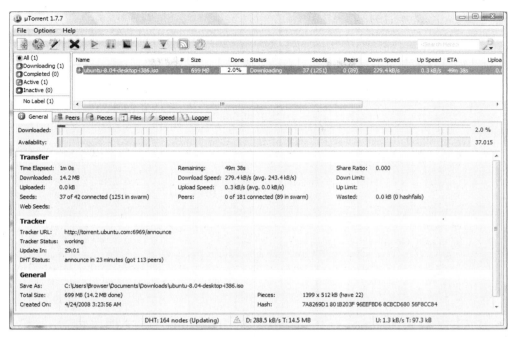

Figure 2-4: The µTorrent client used in Microsoft Windows.

If you scroll to the bottom of the page, you'll see the BitTorrent files intermixed with the other files. The BitTorrent files all end in .torrent. You'll see torrent files for each of the different types of Ubuntu LiveCDs available:

- ubuntu-8.04-server-i386.iso.torrent
- ubuntu-8.04-server-amd64.iso.torrent
- ubuntu-8.04-desktop-i386.iso.torrent
- ubuntu-8.04-desktop-amd64.iso.torrent

The filenames tell you which version each one is. For example, the 32-bit desktop version is the ubuntu-8.04-desktop-i386.torrent file.

Depending on which web browser you're using, you may be able to start the BitTorrent application automatically by selecting the appropriate .torrent file. Microsoft Internet Explorer requires that you first download the .torrent file to your PC, then double-click the file from Windows Explorer to start the µTorrent program.

Once you start the .torrent file from your BitTorrent client package, it automatically contacts the BitTorrent server to start the download. It may take a few minutes for the BitTorrent server to connect your client with the other clients sharing the appropriate ISO image file, so be patient. Once your client finds the other clients, they start communicating with each other to determine which client has which parts of the overall file, and the download begins.

The BitTorrent client software can download multiple parts from multiple clients at the same time. This often provides a quicker way to download a file than the traditional FTP method.

As your BitTorrent client is downloading parts of the file, other BitTorrent clients connect to your PC to download the parts that you've already retrieved. There's no need to worry about that, though, because all of the interaction is happening within the confines of the BitTorrent client software. Your PC is protected from these remote connections doing any harm.

Once the BitTorrent software completely downloads the ISO image file, it continues to offer it for download to other clients. Proper BitTorrent etiquette dictates leaving your BitTorrent client running for a while so that you share your file parts with at least as many clients as you've used to retrieve them (called the *share ratio*).

Verifying the File

After retrieving the entire LiveCD ISO image file, don't celebrate just yet—there's still one more step before you create your CD. With large file downloads, it's quite possible that something somewhere along the way became corrupted. It's a good idea to ensure that the file you're about to use to install your operating system is valid.

Besides file corruption, there's another thing you have to worry about. When you download an ISO image file from a server (especially a mirror server), you're trusting that the people who created that file are trustworthy. Unfortunately, that's not always the case. There are plenty of stories about attackers modifying ISO image files with malicious code and posting them on download servers.

The bottom line is that it's a good idea to verify that the ISO image file you downloaded is the same as the original file posted by Ubuntu. Fortunately, there's an easy way to do this.

Using MD5 Sums

One way to verify the authenticity of a large file is with math. You can use a mathematical formula to evaluate the contents of the file before the download and compare those results with the results of the same formula after the download. If the results match, there's a good chance that the file downloaded correctly and without modification.

The most common mathematical formulas used for this purpose are the *MD5* and *SHA1 hash algorithms.* Hash algorithms compute a unique, fixed-size result from any amount of data. If anything in the data changes, the hash algorithm result is different.

The MD5 algorithm generates a 128-bit value, usually represented as a 32-character hexadecimal value, often referred to as the *MD5 sum.* The SHA1 algorithm is more complex and generates a 160-bit value, represented as a 40-character hexadecimal value.

Ubuntu posts the MD5 sums for each of its download files in the general release page (`http://releases.ubuntu.com/8.04`) as the file `MD5SUMS`. These values are also kept on the web page `https://help.ubuntu.com/community/UbuntuHashes`. (Note that this is a secure https web site, and not a standard http site.)

The Ubuntu BitTorrent files each contain their own signed SHA1 sum. This file automatically downloads with the ISO image file from the BitTorrent site.

Once you've downloaded the hash files, you'll want to perform the hash algorithm on your downloaded ISO image file and compare the values. The next section discusses just how to do this.

Calculating MD5 Sums

After you've downloaded the large ISO image file, you'll need to perform the MD5 or SHA1 hash algorithm on it. Most BitTorrent client packages automatically compare the SHA1 sum against the downloaded one. However, if you use the MD5 sum, you'll have to compute that yourself. How you do this mostly depends on the operating system you're using.

Mac OS X and Linux

The Mac OS X operating system and most Linux distributions contain a MD5 hash algorithm program by default. You can easily use it to compute the MD5 sum of the downloaded ISO image file. On the Mac OS X system, you do that with the md5 command:

```
$ md5 ubuntu-desktop-8.04-i386.iso
MD5 (ubuntu-desktop-8.04-i386.iso) =
8895167a794c5d8dedcc312fc62f1f1f
$
```

The MD5 program computes the MD5 hash value for the file, then displays it. You can then compare that value to what Ubuntu publishes as the correct value. If they match, then you've got a valid ISO image file.

Secret

On Linux systems, the MD5 program is called md5sum. If you're upgrading from an existing Ubuntu installation, Ubuntu doesn't install the MD5 program by default and doesn't include it in the list of standard packages to install. To install the MD5 program, you need to install the sleuthkit package, which isn't listed in the Add/Remove programs groups. To install it, start a command prompt, and use the command:

```
sudo apt-get install sleuthkit
```

This command installs the MD5 application (along with some other cryptographic applications) onto your system.

Windows

If you're using Microsoft Windows, you'll have to download a separate MD5 program to calculate the MD5 sum of your ISO image files. A common open source MD5 program is the winmd5sum application, available for free download at www.nullriver.com/products/winmd5sum.

Just download the installation file from the link and install it on your Windows system. Figure 2-5 shows the winmd5sum program in action.

Figure 2-5: The winmd5sum program calculating an MD5 sum.

Not only does the winmd5sum program calculate the MD5 sum of the ISO image file, but you can also cut and paste the real MD5 sum value directly from the Ubuntu web site into the winmd5sum window, and it'll compare the two values for you.

Creating the LiveCD

Now that you've got the ISO image file for the Ubuntu LiveCD on your PC, it's time to make a CD out of it. A host of different CD-burning software packages are available, both commercial and free. The problem is that many of the free CD-burning software packages supplied by PC vendors don't include an option for burning CD image files.

Burning the CD image file is somewhat different from burning regular files from your hard disk to a CD. The ISO image file represents the entire CD, not just a single file on it. It requires a special CD-burning feature to extract all of the files and folders contained within the ISO image file.

Depending on the operating system you're using, burning a new CD can be either a simple or complicated process. This section explains how to burn CDs on different operating systems.

Burning CDs in Linux

The Linux environment contains two powerful CD-burning tools that both fully support burning ISO image files:

- ◆ K3b for the KDE desktop environment
- ◆ Brasero for the GNOME desktop environment

With both of these tools, burning an ISO image file is as easy as selecting the Burn Image to CD option, then selecting the ISO image file to burn.

You can get to K3b in Kubuntu from the K menu. Just select Multimedia, then K3b CD & DVD Burning. The main K3b window, shown in Figure 2-6, appears.

Select the Burn CD Image button from the main window, select the ISO image file, insert a blank CD, and click the Start button.

GNOME-based desktops (like Ubuntu) use the Brasero CD-burning tool. Figure 2-7 demonstrates using the Brasero utility in Ubuntu.

To start Brasero in Ubuntu, select Applications ➪ Sound & Video ➪ Brasero Disc Burning. When the main Brasero window appears, select the Burn Image option.

Burning CDs in Mac OS X

The Mac OS X operating system has built-in CD-burning software, so there's nothing else you need to download. You can burn CDs using the Disk Utility tool, which is located in the Utilities folder within the Applications folder.

After you start the Disk Utility tool, select the ISO image file you want to burn from the left-side finder area, then click the Burn icon in the top toolbar.

The Disk Utility tool burns the ISO image file to the CD, then compares the CD to the ISO image file to verify that the burn was successful.

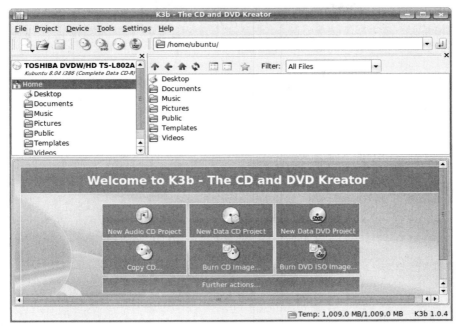

Figure 2-6: The main K3b CD-burning window.

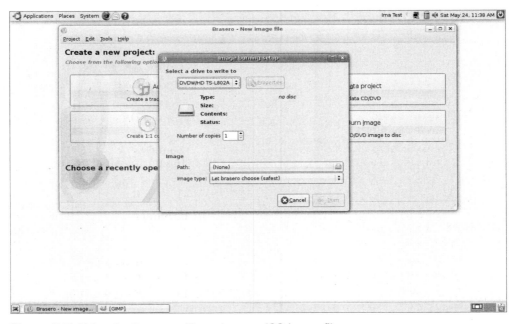

Figure 2-7: Using the Brasero utility to burn an ISO image file.

Burning CDs in Windows

The Windows environment doesn't contain CD-burning software by default. Many free and commercial packages are available, but not all of them include an option for burning ISO image files.

If your particular CD-burning software package doesn't burn CD images, Ubuntu recommends a free CD image-burning software package called InfraRecorder. The InfraRecorder package can be found at the popular SourceForge web site (infrarecorder.sourceforge.net).

Just download the InfraRecorder package and install it on your PC. After you start InfraRecorder, click the Actions menu bar item, then select Burn Image. You'll see a dialog box to select the image to burn, then another dialog box will appear (shown in Figure 2-8), waiting for you to insert a blank CD to start the burning.

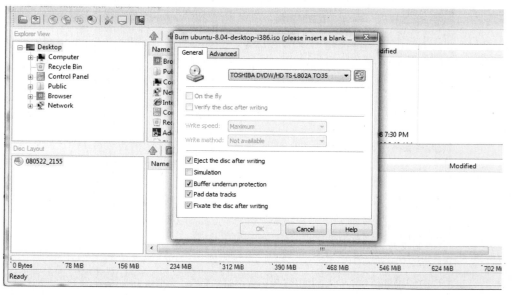

Figure 2-8: The InfraRecorder CD burning tool for Microsoft Windows.

Once you insert a blank CD, InfraRecorder burns the ISO image file onto it. After you have the LiveCD ISO image on a CD, it's time to start playing around with Ubuntu!

Booting the LiveCD

The beauty of the Ubuntu LiveCD is that it offers you a real taste of what running Ubuntu on your PC is like, without the hassle of going through the installation process. When you boot the LiveCD from your PC, Ubuntu goes through all of the normal boot processes as if it were actually installed on the PC hard drive. This includes detecting your PC hardware and trying to load the appropriate drivers (called *modules* in Linux) to interact with the detected hardware.

The following sections walk through the Ubuntu LiveCD boot process and how to use Ubuntu once you get it started from the LiveCD.

The Boot Process

The first step in booting the LiveCD is to determine whether and how your PC can boot from its CD drive. Many PCs can do so by default. Just place the Ubuntu LiveCD in your CD tray and restart your PC. If your particular PC doesn't boot from the CD, there are a couple of things you can try before giving up.

First, go into your PC BIOS and see whether it's set to allow booting from the CD drive. Different PC motherboard manufacturers use different BIOS software, and there are a multitude of ways to configure this setting. Figure 2-9 shows the boot sequence section in a sample BIOS setup.

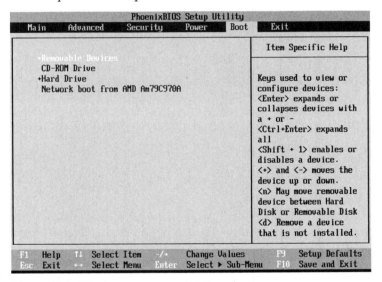

Figure 2-9: The boot sequence BIOS settings.

Once you find the boot sequence section, ensure that the CD is higher up in the list than the hard drive. This forces the PC to check for a bootable CD before trying to boot from the hard drive.

Another trick that many PC manufacturers use is a hot key during the boot process to select the boot device. On some PCs, hitting the F12 key during the boot splash-screen brings up a boot menu, allowing the user to select which device to boot from. The user selects the CD/DVD device, and the system boots from the CD.

Using Ubuntu

After you start the Ubuntu boot process, you should see the main Ubuntu boot screen, shown in Figure 2-10.

Figure 2-10: The Ubuntu boot menu.

The LiveCD allows you to perform four functions other than booting Ubuntu:

+ Install Ubuntu to the hard drive.
+ Check the validity of the LiveCD.
+ Test the memory on the PC.
+ Boot from the PC's hard drive.

The last option can be a lifesaver in an emergency. There may be a time when the boot sector on your hard drive becomes corrupt, and the Linux OS won't boot. Just pop in your trusty Ubuntu LiveCD, select the option to boot from the hard drive, and you might be able to save your data!

If you choose to boot from the CD image, Ubuntu goes through all of the hardware detection processes as if it were booting from an installed image.

You'll notice that you can access several options from the boot menu using the keyboard F keys. Table 2-1 shows what each of these keys are for.

Table 2-1: The Ubuntu LiveCD Boot Menu Keys

Key	Description
F1	Display a Help screen that lists the F key options.
F2	Select the default language used for the Ubuntu menus.
F3	Select the keyboard mapping used for Ubuntu.
F4	Select the boot mode for video devices.
F5	Enable special accessibility features, such as screen magnifiers or on-screen keyboards.
F6	Provide additional boot parameters to the GRUB (boot loader)

The F6 key allows you to add any specific boot options required for special hardware on your PC. This feature is extremely handy when trying the LiveCD from laptops, which often have issues with special hardware devices.

The LiveCD Desktop

Once the boot process finishes, you have a complete Ubuntu system running on your PC, shown in Figure 2-11.

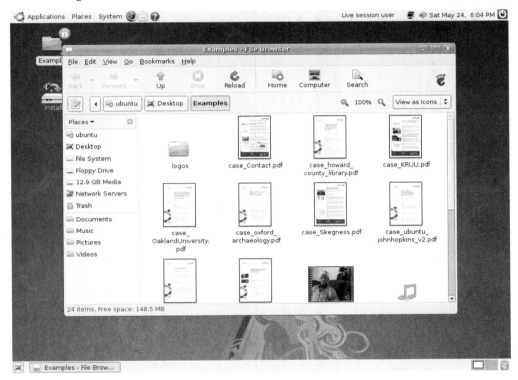

Figure 2-11: The Ubuntu LiveCD desktop.

The LiveCD desktop includes all of the features of a normal Ubuntu workstation desktop, including all of the installed software. You can test-drive any of the applications—as if you had installed Ubuntu on your PC.

note   Depending on the speed of your PC, running some of the applications from the LiveCD could be slow.

The LiveCD desktop includes two desktop icons that aren't available on the normal Ubuntu desktop. One is a folder with example files using the various document and multimedia files Ubuntu supports by default. Just click on a file to launch the application that Ubuntu uses to handle that type of file. The examples include word-processing documents, spreadsheets, audio files, and video clips. These files will give you a pretty good indication of how things would run in a real Ubuntu installation.

The other desktop icon is labeled *Install*. As you can probably guess, clicking that icon starts the Ubuntu installation program. We'll walk through the details of that in Chapter 3, "Installing Ubuntu."

Although you can run all of the applications from the LiveCD, as you go through the various applications, you may notice one problem: When you're running Ubuntu from the LiveCD there's no place to store your files for future use.

When Ubuntu runs from the LiveCD, the operating system is running in memory. The home folder for the default user (called *ubuntu*) exists only in memory. Any files you save will be lost when you reboot your PC. The next section shows how you can change that.

Storing Files

Even though you don't have direct access to your hard drive from the LiveCD, you still have plenty of options available for saving files. This section discusses some ways to store your files as you work from the LiveCD.

Using the Windows Partition

One of the great features of Ubuntu is that it comes with support for all Microsoft filesystems. This feature allows you to read and write files from your Ubuntu system directly from or to any drive formatted for DOS or Windows (including the newer NTFS format, which Windows XP and Vista use).

You can view the hard drives on your PC directly from the LiveCD desktop. Click the Places menu item. You'll notice a list of different places you can view, shown in Figure 2-12.

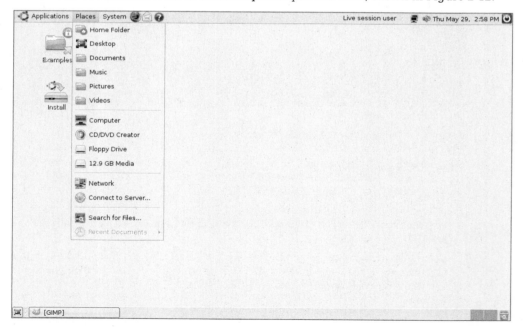

Figure 2-12: Accessing Microsoft Windows partitions from the LiveCD.

Your PC hard drive is identified either by its volume name or the generic size of the disk if it doesn't have a volume name assigned to it. Select the hard drive volume, and Ubuntu will open your hard drive directory structure within the Nautilus disk management utility (discussed in Chapter 5, "File Management"). You can browse through your Windows hard drive folders just as if you were in Windows itself. Not only can you access all of your files, but you can write new files in the folders.

Using USB Devices

Inexpensive USB memory sticks are a popular form of storage these days. These devices are like miniature hard drives. Any data you store on memory sticks remain until you delete the data, even after unplugging the memory stick from your PC.

The Ubuntu LiveCD will automatically detect a USB memory stick if you plug it into your PC while it's running. It'll create a desktop icon for the device and open it up using the Nautilus disk manager, shown in Figure 2-13.

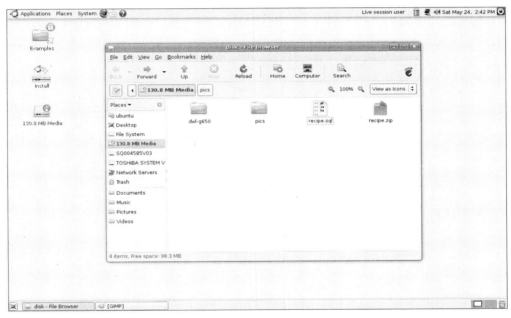

Figure 2-13: Accessing a USB memory stick from the LiveCD.

Just save or copy your files to the USB memory stick. To remove the stick, right-click on the device icon on the desktop and select Unmount Volume. You must unmount the device before removing it, or your files may become corrupted.

note Some USB memory stick devices use a light to indicate whether the device is in use. Ubuntu may or may not be able to use this light. In some situations, the light works fine until you unmount the volume, but it stays lit.

Using Network Shares

If you have a Windows network, you can connect to any shared folders available on the network. If Ubuntu detects your network card properly, it'll automatically attempt to connect to your network. It detects any Windows networks that appear on the network.

You can access your network shared folders from the LiveCD by selecting the Places menu item, then selecting either Network (to browse your Windows network) or Connect to Server (to connect directly to a specific server share). In either case, you'll see the server and shares, as shown in Figure 2-14.

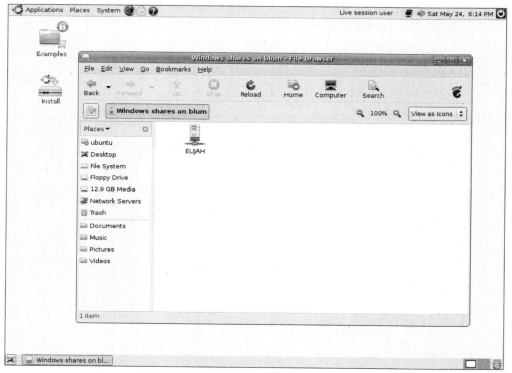

Figure 2-14: Browsing the Windows network from the Ubuntu LiveCD.

Just double-click on your server, then Share, and you can access files and folders (and write to files and folders) just like on any other Windows network device.

Running Ubuntu in Windows

The main drawback to running Ubuntu directly from the LiveCD is that it's slow. Sometimes it's hard to get a good feel for how the software will run on a particular system because the LiveCD distorts how Ubuntu would run from the hard drive. Ubuntu has a solution for this.

The Wubi Project

The Windows Ubuntu Installer (Wubi) project was created as an alternative to running Ubuntu from the LiveCD. Wubi creates a complete Ubuntu disk partition as a single file on a Windows operating system, then creates an entry in the standard Windows boot program that enables your PC to boot directly from the Ubuntu file.

This means that you can have a complete, bootable Ubuntu system by installing a single program on your Windows PC. Currently, Wubi supports Windows 95, 98, 2000, XP, and Vista.

Installing in Windows

The main goal of Wubi is to make installing Ubuntu on an existing Windows PC easy, and they've accomplished their task. There are two ways to get Wubi:

- Install it directly from the Ubuntu workstation LiveCD.
- Download it from the Wubi web site.

If you have the Ubuntu workstation LiveCD, you already have the Wubi software. While in Windows, insert the LiveCD into your CD tray and either let the CD autorun or click the Autorun file. The Ubuntu LiveCD menu appears, allowing you to either restart your PC to boot from the LiveCD or to run the Wubi program. Running the Wubi program produces the Wubi setup window, shown in Figure 2-15.

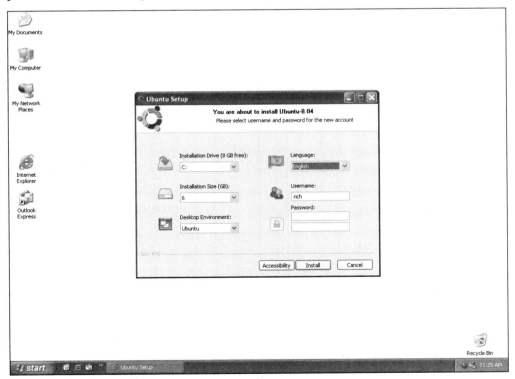

Figure 2-15: The Wubi setup window.

The Ubuntu setup window allows you to select the hard drive to install the Ubuntu files onto and how much disk space to use for your Ubuntu system. You'll want to allow at least 4 GB of space for your Ubuntu distribution files.

If you haven't already downloaded the Ubuntu LiveCD, there's a great feature in Wubi that you can take advantage of. You can download the Wubi installation file from the Wubi web site and install Ubuntu in Windows without having to burn the LiveCD.

The Wubi web site (`http://wubi-installer.org`) provides a link to download just the Wubi setup program. Once you download the Wubi setup program and start it, it'll automatically contact the Ubuntu web site and download the appropriate desktop LiveCD ISO image file for your PC. After the download completes, Wubi will mount the ISO image file—just as if it were on a CD—and start the Ubuntu installation.

Running Ubuntu in Windows

After Ubuntu installs as a Windows application, you'll see a new menu when you start your Windows PC, as shown in Figure 2-16.

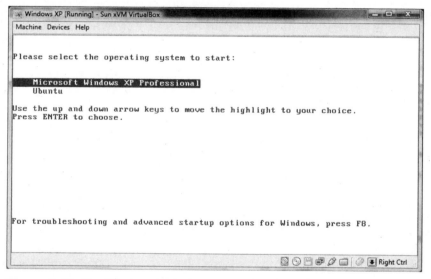

Figure 2-16: The Windows boot menu with Ubuntu installed.

The default menu item is your original Windows operating system. Selecting this option (or doing nothing and letting the counter count down) starts your Windows system, just as it always did before you installed Ubuntu. If you select the Ubuntu menu option, Ubuntu boots from the installed Ubuntu image file installed on your Windows system.

After the boot-up you'll get the Ubuntu login window, as if Ubuntu were installed on a hard drive partition. When you log in with the account you specified in the Wubi setup program, you'll be at the Ubuntu desktop, with the entire application available for you to use. If you have a network interface card installed on your PC (and Ubuntu detected it), the Ubuntu software update program (discussed in Chapter 13, "Software Installs and Updates") will automatically connect to the Ubuntu software repository and offer software updates for you.

All of the Ubuntu files required to run Ubuntu are located on your Windows hard drive in the Ubuntu folder. If you want to remove Ubuntu from your Windows drive, don't just delete the folder. Go to the Add/Remove Software tool in the Windows Control Panel and select the Ubuntu software to uninstall. Ubuntu will remove all of the files, including the Ubuntu option from the Windows boot menu, restoring your PC to the way it was before Ubuntu was installed.

Although running Ubuntu from your Windows partition is faster than using it on the LiveCD, there's still a performance penalty. To get the full benefit of Ubuntu, you should install it as a separate partition on a hard drive. That's exactly what we'll do in the next chapter.

Summary

The Ubuntu LiveCD distribution allows you to get a feel for how Ubuntu would run on your PC without having to go through a full installation. This chapter walked through the steps of downloading and creating a LiveCD, then booting and using the LiveCD.

Several versions of the LiveCD are available. The standard Ubuntu workstation installation is available on the desktop-i386 LiveCD image. After downloading the image, you'll want to verify that the image isn't corrupted or has been tampered with. Ubuntu uses both MD5 and SHA1 hashes to verify the authenticity and accuracy of the downloaded file. Mac OS X and Linux systems include MD5 hash programs to calculate the hash value of the downloaded image. The winmd5sum program is a free utility you can download for Windows to calculate MD5 hashes.

After explaining how to download and verify the LiveCD ISO image file, the chapter discussed how to burn the image onto a CD. Mac OS X includes a CD-burning utility in the Disk Utilities package. Most Linux distributions include either the K3b or Brasero CD-burning packages. For Windows PCs, some free CD-burning tools don't provide the option of burning an ISO image file to CD. You can download the InfraRecorder package for free. This package can burn ISO image files to CDs from Windows.

After creating the LiveCD the chapter covered how to boot from it on your PC. Some PCs are configured to automatically detect a CD in the CD tray and boot, while others require a change to the system BIOS settings or hitting a special key at boot time.

Once booted into the Ubuntu LiveCD you'll be able to run the Ubuntu desktop directly from the CD. This is an excellent way to check out hardware compatibilities before trying to install Ubuntu.

Finally, the chapter discussed the Wubi project. The Wubi project provides an interface within Windows to load Ubuntu as a file on the Windows hard drive partition and boot the file from the Windows boot loader. This enables you to install Ubuntu directly on top of an existing Windows PC without having to repartition the hard drive.

The next chapter walks through the official Ubuntu installation process. This includes installing Ubuntu on an existing Windows PC as a second partition, as well as converting an entire PC into an Ubuntu workstation.

Installing Ubuntu

Chapter

3

Once you've decided that Ubuntu is the Linux distribution for you, and that it'll work properly on your PC, you should install it on your hard drive to get its full benefits. Although the Ubuntu installation process has become fine tuned and streamlined over the years, there are still a few things you need to be concerned about when installing the system. This chapter discusses what you should think about before you start the installation, then walks through the process step by step to ensure that your Ubuntu installation experience is a happy one.

Preparing Your PC

Before you start the installation process, you should take some time to analyze the workstation or server you're going to use for your Ubuntu system. Although the Linux world has made great advances in hardware support, there are still a few things you need to watch out for. This section describes some of the things you should look at while analyzing your hardware.

System Requirements

In the old days of Linux (the 1990s), one of the selling points of the Linux operating system was that it could run on just about any old piece of computer hardware you had lying around. Unfortunately, with the popularity of fancy graphical desktop environments, those days are mostly over (see Chapter 1, "What Is Ubuntu?").

To get the most from your Ubuntu desktop experience, you'll want to have a fairly decent hardware configuration. Although Ubuntu may not require quite as many resources as some other operating systems, it still requires some effort to run.

Here's a list of the minimum hardware components suggested for an Ubuntu desktop installation:

♦ **CPU:** In the past, determining the CPU in a workstation was a simple task. It was easy to tell whether you had a 286, 386, or 486 processor. These days a plethora of processors are available, and it's not always easy to figure out which ones are better or faster. Ubuntu supports all of the 32-bit AMD and Intel families of processors, including the i386 platform and the newer multicore processors that are popular in workstations and server-oriented Xeon processors. Ubuntu also supports 64-bit AMD and Intel processors. With these processors you can use either the 32-bit desktop Ubuntu installation or the 64-bit Ubuntu installation customized for the 64-bit environment. The minimum recommendation for a graphical desktop environment is a 1.2 GHz x86-class processor. Slower processors might work, but you might not be happy with the results. Note that Ubuntu also supports the Intel x86 Macintosh hardware platforms, including newer Mac desktop and notebook workstations.

♦ **Memory:** The minimum amount of memory suggested depends on what you want to do with your Ubuntu system. To properly run the GNOME desktop environment plus the advanced applications, you'll want at least 384 MB of memory. However, as with any advanced graphical operating system, if you intend to use the desktop applications to their fullest, I'd suggest having more memory. For server environments, it depends mostly on the load you expect your server to undertake. For a basic server environment Ubuntu requires only 64 MB of memory (because there aren't any graphics requirements on the server), but for high-volume web, database, or mail servers, you'll want at least 2 GB of memory available. The Ubuntu operating system also uses *swap space,* which is a special area reserved on the hard drive for virtual memory (see Chapter 1). Swap space helps increase the amount of memory available to the system, although with a performance penalty. When Ubuntu runs out of physical memory, it swaps out memory blocks to the swap area. When the memory blocks are needed, Ubuntu must swap them back into the physical memory. This process obviously takes more time than accessing data directly from the physical memory.

✦ **Hard drive:** The minimum hard drive space suggested for a typical Ubuntu installation is 1.8 GB; however, if you want to be able to do anything with your system after you install Ubuntu, you'll probably want to have more disk space. Remember also to factor in the swap space area when determining your total hard disk size requirements. The minimum suggested by Ubuntu is 4 GB, although you could possibly survive with less. Ubuntu recognizes most types of hard drive installations, such as secondary disks and USB disks. The way you get more disk space depends on your system and your budget.

✦ **CD/DVD drive:** These days just about every PC comes with some type of CD and/or DVD drive. However, many older systems don't have them. If you're planning on using the LiveCD, you'll need some type of CD/DVD drive in your PC. Be careful when purchasing a new CD/DVD drive because there are generally two types available. The type you need depends on the disk controller used in your system. The majority of workstation-oriented systems use the integrated device electronics (IDE) controller, while many server-oriented systems use the small computer system interface (SCSI) controller (see the "Installing a Hard Drive" section in this chapter). You must purchase the CD/DVD drive appropriate for your disk controller. If you decide to use the Wubi installer to install Ubuntu, you can use your network card to download the ISO image file and install directly from that without using a CD or DVD. With this method you should be able to avoid purchasing a CD/DVD drive (unless, of course, you want to use the CD/DVD for playing audio CDs or video DVDs).

✦ **Keyboard:** A keyboard is a basic requirement for most workstations. Even if you run a hands-off server, some systems require a connected keyboard to boot. Ubuntu supports different types of keyboards, as well as different language keyboards. When you run the LiveCD installation, Ubuntu will prompt you for the type of keyboard you're using. Take note if you're using a special keyboard so you can select the proper keyboard during the installation process.

✦ **Mouse:** In a graphical desktop environment, having a mouse is almost a necessity (although Ubuntu does include support for nonmouse navigation). Mouse technology has come a long way since the early days of PCs. You can purchase all types of mouse devices, from the standard rolling-ball mouse to an optical mouse to a wireless mouse. There are also different places for the mouse to connect, such as a serial port, a PS/2 port, and a USB port. Ubuntu has the ability to automatically detect most mouse devices. If your mouse requires special drivers for special buttons or features, such as scroll wheels, it may or may not work in Ubuntu. Many newer laptops use a touchpad to provide control of the mouse pointer as well as scrolling and clicking features. Ubuntu can handle these features.

✦ **Sound card:** If you intend to use any of the multimedia features available in Ubuntu, such as playing music CDs, watching DVDs, or listening to downloaded audio files, you'll need to have a sound card installed in your workstation. Ubuntu can automatically detect most sound cards without requiring any additional drivers. Ubuntu also detects and installs drivers for some proprietary sound cards. However, these drivers are considered unsupported, and, if you experience any problems, you're on your own.

♦ **Video card:** A video card can make or break a workstation system. Ubuntu can automatically detect and use most standard video cards. Due to the graphical-oriented environment used by the Ubuntu desktop, you'll want to use a VGA graphics card capable of at least 1024 × 768 resolution. With the popularity of PC gaming, many workstations use advanced 3-D accelerator video cards. Ubuntu provides support for many standard 3-D video cards, such as ATI, Intel, and NVIDIA, and can use customized drivers for cards that provide them. Some of the more exotic video cards may be a problem, especially if they don't include a Linux driver. Similar to sound cards, Ubuntu can use unsupported drivers for video cards, but be wary of using these drivers because other things can break when installed.

♦ **Printer:** Ubuntu has the ability to automatically detect and configure most common desktop and network printers. This ability also applies to many of the newer all-in-one printers that can scan documents. However, you may have to choose the correct driver for your particular brand and model. Make a note of what brand and model of printer you're using and how you'll need to connect to it (parallel printer cable, USB cable, or network address).

♦ **Modem:** Ubuntu supports using modems to dial remote computer systems and as a way to access the Internet. Ubuntu can automatically detect and use most standard modems, including external and internal modems. One type of modem to be careful about is *Winmodems*. Winmodems are popular in laptops and require special software (usually found in Microsoft Windows) to operate. Many Winmodems are now supported in the Linux world. However, if you can avoid a Winmodem, do so.

♦ **Network card:** With the popularity of home networks, many workstations come with some type of network connectivity interface built into the motherboard. Ubuntu does an excellent job of detecting most wired and even wireless network interfaces. If your network is connected to the Internet, Ubuntu will automatically configure itself to retrieve software and security patches from the Ubuntu servers across the network. Depending on your network environment, you may have to customize the network configuration settings for the network device.

If you are unsure about the hardware in your system, the following web sites can provide information about hardware configuration that work with Ubuntu (or Linux in general):

https://wiki.ubuntu.com/HardwareSupport

https://help.ubuntu.com/community/Hardware

http://www.tldp.org/HOWTO/Hardware-HOWTO

These sites provide updated information about what devices work and often explain how to get them working in an Ubuntu environment.

Secret

Laptops often pose a problem for Linux distributions. Many older laptops use proprietary hardware devices that aren't supported by Linux. On some of these laptops, Ubuntu may not even be able to run the LiveCD. Older laptops with proprietary video systems are especially prone to fail in the Linux environment.

However, most newer laptops use more standard hardware that Ubuntu can detect and use without any problems. Pay special attention to the video, modem, and wireless network cards used in your laptop because these devices cause the most problems. A great resource for working with Linux and laptops is www. linux-laptop.net. It provides valuable guidance from users who've successfully loaded specific Linux distributions on specific laptops.

If you're purchasing a new laptop, you should check it for Ubuntu compatibility, either by booting it using the Ubuntu LiveCD or by verifying its hardware on the various Ubuntu and Linux hardware web sites.

Often the hardest part of an Ubuntu installation is finding enough disk space on a system to install it. If you're converting a workstation into an Ubuntu-only workstation, that shouldn't be an issue. However, if you want to keep your existing Windows workstation setup and add Ubuntu, that can take some work.

Because it is a common setup, the next section discusses how to prepare your Windows PC for installing Ubuntu in a dual-boot environment.

Creating a Place for Ubuntu

To install Ubuntu permanently on your PC, you'll need to have a hard disk area set up for it. There are three common options for this setup:

- ♦ Replace the existing operating system on your hard drive with Ubuntu.
- ♦ Install Ubuntu on a second hard drive.
- ♦ Partition an existing hard drive to include Ubuntu.

Obviously, the easiest solution for installing Ubuntu on a PC is to replace the existing operating system installed on the hard drive. The Ubuntu installation easily guides you through this process. Just remember that when you're done, you won't have the original files from your previous operating system. If you want to keep any files, you'll need to back them up yourself to media that you can read from Ubuntu.

Secret

With the popularity of virtual server programs such as VMWare and Sun VirtualBox, many Linux enthusiasts load Ubuntu within a virtual environment running inside a Windows operating system. If you're trying to do that, just follow the Ubuntu installation method to replace the existing operating system on the hard drive. Just make sure that you're inside your virtual server environment before doing that!

The other two methods require a *dual-boot* scenario. In a dual-boot scenario, both Ubuntu and another operating system (often Windows) reside on hard drives in the computer. When you boot the computer, a menu appears, asking you which operating system you want to boot, as shown in Figure 3-1.

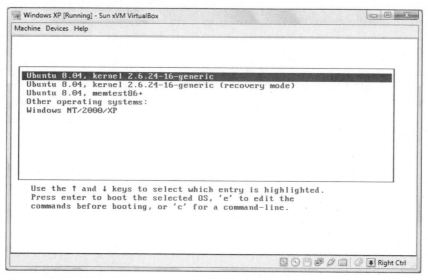

Figure 3-1: The Ubuntu and Windows dual-boot menu.

You'll need to take some special precautions when setting up your workstation in a dual-boot environment. This section walks through some of the things to watch for in each of these two scenarios.

Installing a Second Hard Drive

Next to replacing the existing operating system, the second easiest way to get Ubuntu onto a workstation is to install a second hard drive. Many workstations support multiple hard drives by either chaining two hard drives together on the same disk controller or providing multiple disk controllers to handle hard drives.

The most common disk controller used in workstation PCs is the integrated device electronics (IDE) controller. The IDE controller allows up to two devices per channel. Workstations often will have more than one IDE channel installed on the motherboard.

Secret

The serial advanced technology attachment (SATA) controller is a technology that's becoming more popular in newer PCs. This technology emulates an IDE controller but with much faster response times. Ubuntu has full support for SATA devices, so you can easily use them for your Ubuntu installation.

Usually you can determine your disk controller configuration by looking at the BIOS setup screen for your PC. Figure 3-2 shows an example of the disk controller area on a BIOS screen.

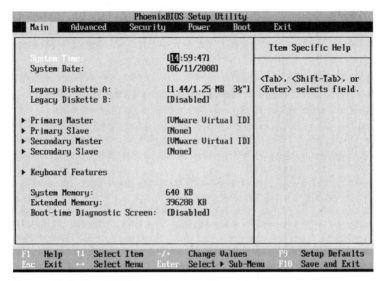

```
                        PhoenixBIOS Setup Utility
   Main      Advanced      Security      Power      Boot      Exit

                                                    Item Specific Help
      System Time:            [14:59:47]
      System Date:            [06/11/2008]
                                                   <Tab>, <Shift-Tab>, or
      Legacy Diskette A:      [1.44/1.25 MB  3½"]  <Enter> selects field.
      Legacy Diskette B:      [Disabled]

   ▶ Primary Master          [VMware Virtual ID]
   ▶ Primary Slave           [None]
   ▶ Secondary Master        [VMware Virtual ID]
   ▶ Secondary Slave         [None]

   ▶ Keyboard Features

      System Memory:          640 KB
      Extended Memory:        396288 KB
      Boot-time Diagnostic Screen:  [Disabled]


   F1   Help    ↑↓  Select Item   -/+    Change Values    F9   Setup Defaults
   Esc  Exit    ↔   Select Menu   Enter  Select ▶ Sub-Menu F10  Save and Exit
```

Figure 3-2: The BIOS hard drive configuration area.

This example shows two controllers (a primary and a secondary), with each supporting two devices (a master and a slave). This configuration allows you to connect a total of four separate devices to the workstation. Besides the hard drive, IDE controllers also support connecting CD/DVD devices, so you'll need to be careful when evaluating your disk controller situation.

If your motherboard contains only one disk controller and uses it for the hard drive and the CD/DVD device, you won't be able to add a second hard drive on that controller. Usually you can find plug-in disk controller cards to add a second controller to the workstation. You'll need to do that if you want to add another hard drive.

If your motherboard contains two disk controllers, you can purchase a second hard drive and easily connect it to one of the controllers to use for Ubuntu. The Ubuntu installation process detects the empty hard drive and will format it for Ubuntu.

If both of the disk controllers already contain one device, you'll need to use a master/slave configuration to add the second hard drive. This process requires a controller cable that has three plugs—one for connecting to the motherboard and two connectors to plug devices into.

The devices themselves must also be specially configured for this setup. Each device uses a jumper setting to determine where in the chain it's located. One hard drive must be set as the master hard drive, and one must be set as the slave.

Many advanced server systems use a small computer system interface (SCSI) hard drive controller instead of an IDE controller. SCSI controllers typically allow up to seven devices per controller channel (although some newer ones allow 16 devices). These controllers are popular in servers that support multiple hard drives in a redundant array of inexpensive disk (RAID) configuration. RAID systems use multiple hard drives to emulate a single hard drive for fault-tolerance purposes. There are several formats of RAID support:

- RAID0: Divides data among multiple hard drives but without redundancy.
- RAID1: Writes all data to two or more drives (called *mirroring*).
- RAID2: Incorporates error detection codes within stored data.
- RAID3: Stores data across several drives at the byte level, reserving one drive to store a parity bit. The parity bit is used to rebuild an individual drive if it fails.
- RAID4: Stores data across several drives at the block level, reserving one drive to store a parity bit.
- RAID5: Stores data across several drives at the block level; also writes a parity bit for each block on the drives.

RAID1 is common when only two hard drives are present. One hard drive is the primary, and the other is a hot backup. The disk controller performs all disk write requests from the operating system on both hard drives. RAID3 and RAID5 are the most popular methods of RAID disk support and usually require three or more hard drives. Both of these methods can recover data from a complete failure of any one disk in the system.

Despite the "inexpensive" part of its name, RAID technology can be expensive, and it is used primarily for high-availability server environments. The Ubuntu server installation can detect and use most SCSI controllers and RAID configurations.

However, don't confuse a hardware RAID environment with a software RAID. Many Windows servers allow you to emulate a RAID environment using standard disk hardware. This is called a *software RAID* because there aren't multiple disks, but the operating system acts as if there are. Ubuntu will work with standard disk drives, but it won't emulate a RAID environment using them.

Partitioning an Existing Hard Drive

Partitioning an existing hard drive is the most complicated method for installing Ubuntu on an existing workstation. Normally, if you have an existing operating system on your workstation (such as Windows XP or Vista), it uses the entire hard drive installed on the PC. During installation, Ubuntu allows you to split the hard drive into multiple sections, called *partitions.* It will then install the operating system on the new partition. The original operating system still resides on the first partition, allowing you to run it, just as before, in a dual-boot configuration.

Before you run the Ubuntu installation, you'll want to know what your particular hard drive setup is, so you'll know how much space you can allocate for Ubuntu. Here are the steps in preparing your existing hard drive for the Ubuntu installation.

Examining the Current Hard Drive Setup

Before diving into partitioning your existing hard drive, it's a good idea to know what you have to work with. If you already have Microsoft Windows running on the existing hard drive, you can use the utilities included in Windows to examine your system.

The Windows Computer Manager provides a graphical tool for looking at the hard drives installed on your workstation. This tool is available in Windows 2000 Workstation, XP, and Vista. You can get to it by following these steps:

1. Right-click on the My Computer desktop icon or the My Computer entry in the Start menu.
2. Select Manage from the resulting menu. This starts the Computer Management tool window.
3. From the Computer Management tool window, select the Disk Management entry.

The Disk Management tool, shown in Figure 3-3, appears, showing the current hard drives installed on the PC.

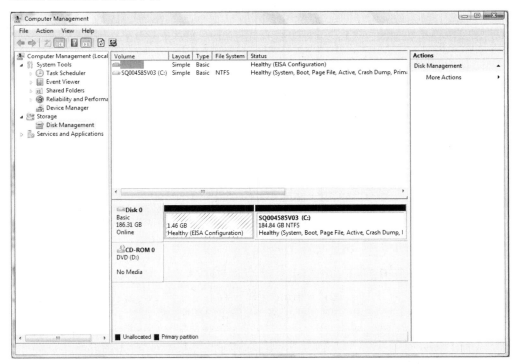

Figure 3-3: The Windows Vista Disk Management tool.

The Disk Management tool displays all of the hard drives recognized by Windows and shows whether they are formatted and used. Each hard drive appears as a separate line in the list and is shown with the partitions and format types identified.

Many newer workstations utilize a *hidden partition* to store important recovery information. A hidden partition is a section of the hard drive that's partitioned, but not assigned a drive letter, by the operating system. Even if you see only a C: drive on your Windows setup, your hard drive may still contain two partitions, as shown in the example in Figure 3-3. The hidden partition can't be used for Ubuntu, or you'll lose the ability to restore your Windows system if it crashes.

If you see an area on the hard drive marked *unallocated,* that means the hard drive has free space that's not part of the Windows partition. You can use this as part of the Ubuntu partition. If it's 4 GB or larger, then you don't have to do anything to your existing Windows partition. You can install Ubuntu directly into the unallocated hard drive areas without having to alter the existing Windows partition.

If you see only a single partition that's allocated for Windows on your hard drive, you'll need to continue with the partitioning process to free up space for Ubuntu.

Determining Free Space

The next step in the partition process is to determine how much free space you have on your existing hard drive. Remember, you'll need at least 4 GB of free space for Ubuntu, plus you'll probably want to keep some extra free space for the original operating system.

To find out how much free space is available on your Windows partition, you can turn again to the Windows Computer Management tool. The top portion of the Disk Management window shows detailed statistics for each hard drive partition.

The statistics shown include the total size of the partition and the amount of free space available. Make note of the free space available on the partition. That's the amount of space you'll have available to divvy up between the existing Windows partition and the new Ubuntu partition.

Secret

A common mistake is to assign all of the free space on a hard drive to the new Ubuntu partition. You'll want to keep some free space assigned to the Windows partition; otherwise, the Windows operating system installed might not boot properly. It's always a good idea to have at least 1 GB of free space available on the Windows partition, even if you're not planning on adding any new software or data.

Once you've determined the amount of space you have available for Ubuntu, the next step is to ensure that the space on the disk is really empty.

Defragmenting Files

During the normal course of using your workstation, Windows tends to write files at random places on the hard drive. This can spread data over the entire disk space area. When you split the hard drive into partitions, you'll want to ensure that you don't lose any of the data used in the Windows system, including system and data files.

To make a clean partition of the hard drive, you'll need to make sure that all of the Windows data are moved toward one end of the hard drive. This process is commonly done with a *defragmenting* tool.

Defragmenting is a common process in the Windows world. It's the process of realigning how files are stored on the hard drive. As Windows creates and removes files, file data get split into various blocks scattered around the hard drive. Defragmenting reassembles all of the blocks for each file into a contiguous area near the beginning of the hard drive.

All versions of Windows include a utility for defragmenting the hard drive. You can get to the defragment utility from the Computer Management window. Just select the Disk Defragmenter option.

In Windows Vista, disk defragmenting happens behind the scenes, without any indication of what's going on. Windows XP provides a handy defragmenter window that shows the progress as files are moved about. Figure 3-4 shows the Windows XP defragmenter window.

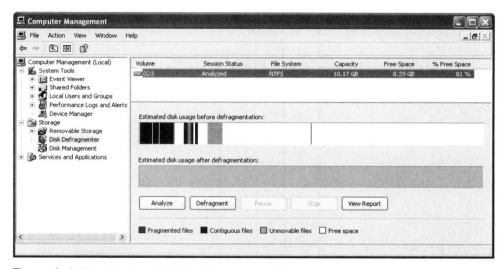

Figure 3-4: The Windows XP disk defragment utility.

Often it takes more than one pass to get all of the files into a common area. After defragmenting moves the files to a contiguous area at the beginning of the disk space, you're ready to partition the hard drive as part of the Ubuntu installation.

Installing from the LiveCD

The Ubuntu installation process is one of the simplest in the Linux world. Ubuntu guides you through all of the steps to setup the system, then installs the entire Ubuntu system without prompting you for too much information.

You can start the installation process from two locations in the LiveCD:

♦ Directly from the boot menu without starting Ubuntu
♦ From the Install desktop icon after you start the Ubuntu system

Both options initiate the same installation process, which guides you through seven steps of options. These options are discussed in the following sections.

Select a Language

When you start the Ubuntu installation, the first window you get is the Language window, shown in Figure 3-5.

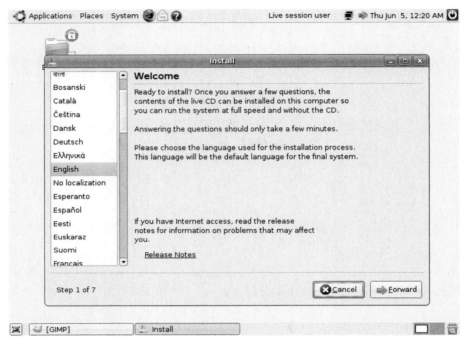

Figure 3-5: The Ubuntu language selection window.

This window asks you to select the language Ubuntu uses to display text messages during the installation process, and it sets the default language used when the operating system runs. However, this doesn't necessarily mean that all of the applications running on the system will use that language. Individual applications may or may not detect the default language configured in Ubuntu.

Select a Time Zone

The second window in the installation process, shown in Figure 3-6, allows you to select the time zone for your area.

This window allows you to select your location via map or a drop-down list. Although selecting the time zone from the map sounds like a good idea, it can often be a challenge, depending on how many cities Ubuntu recognizes near your particular city.

Select a Keyboard

Next in the installation process is identifying the keyboard you'll use with the Ubuntu system. Although this may sound like a simple option, it can get complicated if you have a keyboard that includes special keys. Ubuntu recognizes hundreds of keyboard types and lists them all in the Keyboard Configuration window, shown in Figure 3-7.

Figure 3-6: The time zone configuration window

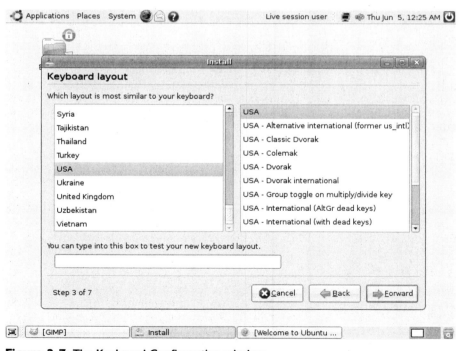

Figure 3-7: The Keyboard Configuration window.

The Keyboard Configuration window lists the types of keyboards commonly used, based on your country. The list on the left contains countries, and the list on the right shows the known keyboard types used in the country selected. First, select your country from the list on the left, then select your keyboard type from the list on the right (you can click in the keyboard list and type the name of your keyboard to quickly jump to it).

Beneath the two lists is an area where you can test the keyboard selection. Just type any special or unique characters available on your keyboard to see whether the setting you selected produces the proper characters.

Prepare the Disk Space

This step in the installation is possibly the most important—and also the most complicated. Here's where you need to tell the Ubuntu installer where to place the Ubuntu operating system on your computer. One bad move here can really ruin your day.

The exact partition window you get during the installation depends on your hard drive configuration. Figure 3-8 is an example of what this looks like.

The Ubuntu Disk Partition window starts out with at least two selections:

- ◆ A guided partition to install Ubuntu on the entire hard drive
- ◆ A manual partition to create your own partitions

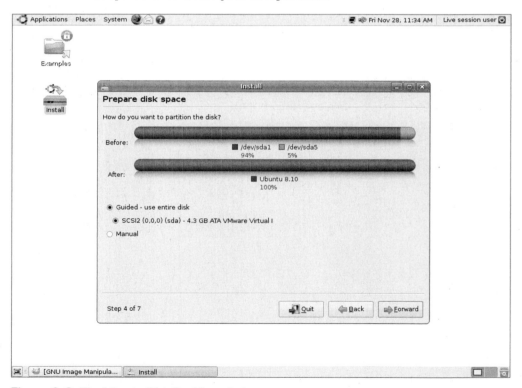

Figure 3-8: The Ubuntu Disk Partition window.

By default, Ubuntu offers a guided partition where it automatically reformats the entire hard drive on the system for Ubuntu. If you want to run an Ubuntu-only workstation, this is the quickest and easiest way to go.

caution **If you choose to install Ubuntu on the entire hard drive, any previously installed operating system (and data) will be removed. Be sure to back up any important files before you begin the Ubuntu installation.**

If Ubuntu detects an existing operating system on your hard drive, it'll offer an additional option to the Guided Partition option. Besides offering to install on the entire hard drive, Ubuntu will offer to automatically partition the hard drive to retain the existing operating system, plus create a partition for the Ubuntu installation.

In this case, Ubuntu allows you to select how much disk space to allocate for the new Ubuntu partition. You can drag the partition separator to redistribute disk space between the original operating system and the new Ubuntu partition. Keep in mind the disk space requirements determined earlier in the "Determining Free Space" section to use here.

caution **If you choose to partition an existing operating system, remember that bad things can (and often do) happen. Even if you plan to keep the existing operating system, it's a good idea to make a complete backup of that operating system before performing the partition process.**

If you select the manual partition process, Ubuntu turns control of the partition process over to you. It provides a great partition utility, shown in Figure 3-9, for you to use to create, edit, or delete hard drive partitions.

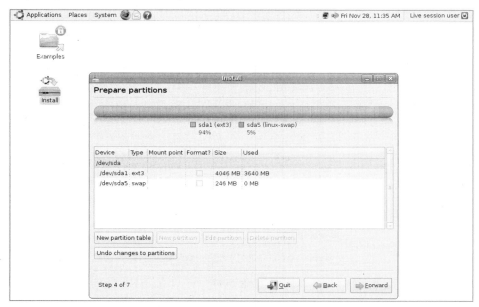

Figure 3-9: The Ubuntu Manual Partition utility.

The Manual Partition utility displays the current hard drives, along with any existing partitions configured in them. You can manually remove, modify, or create individual partitions on any hard drives installed on the system.

Part of the manual partition process is to assign a filesystem to each partition. A filesystem is a method used for storing and accessing files on the partition. Many filesystem formats are available. Unlike some other operating systems, Ubuntu supports several filesystems. You can select any of the available filesystems for any of the partitions Ubuntu will use. Table 3-1 shows the filesystem types available for you when creating disk partitions in Ubuntu.

Table 3-1: Ubuntu Partition Filesystem Types

Partition Type	Description
ext3	A popular Linux journaling filesystem that is an extension of the original Linux ext2 filesystem
ext2	The original, nonjournaling Linux filesystem
ReiserFS	The first journaling filesystem supported in Linux
JFS	The journaled file system, created by IBM and used in AIX UNIX systems
XFS	A high-performance journaling filesystem created by Silicon Graphics for the IRIX operating system
FAT16	Older Microsoft DOS filesystem
FAT32	Newer Microsoft DOS filesystem compatible with Microsoft Windows
Swap area	Virtual memory area
Do not use	Ignore the partition

The most common partition type (and the default used by the Ubuntu guided methods) is the ext3 format. This filesystem format provides a journaling filesystem for Ubuntu. A journaling filesystem saves file changes to a log file before attempting to commit them to the disk. If the system should crash before the kernel can properly commit the data, the journal log file is used to complete the pending file commits and return the disk to a normal state. Journaling filesystems greatly reduce file corruption in Linux.

After you've selected a filesystem for the partition, Ubuntu will want to know where to mount the partition in the virtual filesystem (see Chapter 5, "File Management"). The Ubuntu virtual filesystem handles hard drives by plugging them into specific locations in the virtual filesystem. Table 3-2 lists the locations where you can mount a partition.

Table 3-2: Mount Point Locations

Location	Description
/	The root of the Linux virtual filesystem
/boot	The location of the Linux kernel used for booting the system

Table 3-2: *(continued)*

Location	Description
/home	User directories for storing personal files and individual application setting files
/tmp	Temporary files used by applications and the Linux system
/usr	A common location for multi-user application files
/var	The variable directory, commonly used for log files and spool files
/opt	Optional package installation directory for third-party applications
/usr/local	A common alternative location for optional multi-user package installations

If you create just one partition for Ubuntu, you must mount it at the root mount point (/). If you have additional partitions available, you can mount them in other locations within the virtual filesystem.

If you're using the manual partition method, don't forget to allocate a partition for the swap area, even if you already have lots of physical memory installed on your system. The standard rule of thumb is to create as large of a swap area as you have physical memory. Thus, if you have 2 GB of physical memory, create a 2 GB partition and assign it as the swap area.

Secret

One problem with Linux is that if the root mount point hard drive becomes full, the system will be unable to boot. To prevent this from happening, many Linux administrators create a separate partition for the /home mount point, where user files are normally stored.

This keeps user files separate from the operating system files. With this technique, a user who tries to store many large files won't take up all of the disk space and crash the system. Even if the installation is just for a single-user personal workstation, this technique can prevent you from accidentally using up all the disk space and crashing your system.

Once you've created the partition settings (either manually or via the Ubuntu guided method) you're ready to move on to the next step in the installation process.

Create a Login ID

Up next in the installation process is selecting a Login ID, shown in Figure 3-10.

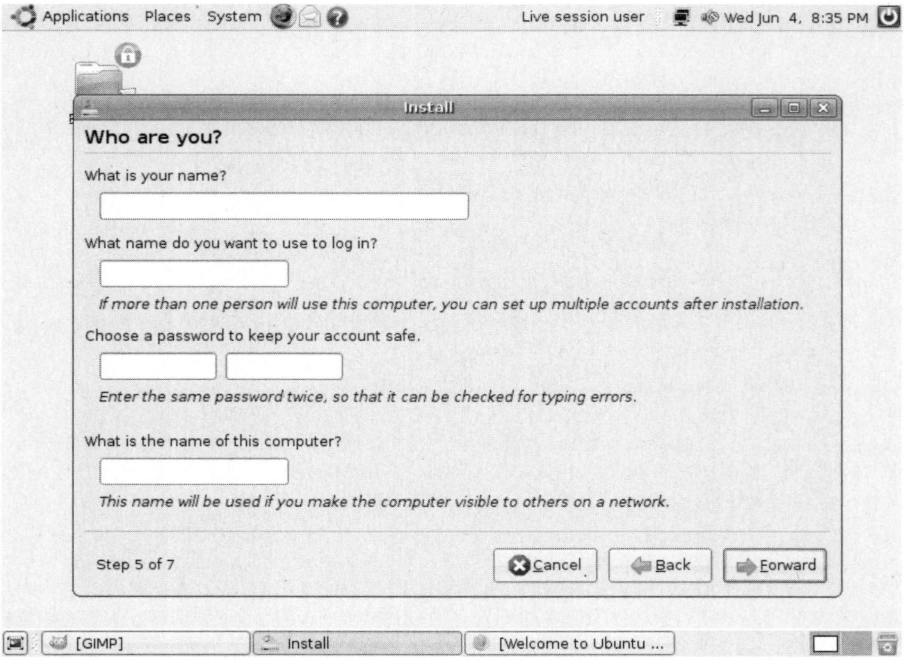

Figure 3-10: The Login ID window.

The userID you create in this process is important. Unlike some other Linux distributions, the Ubuntu distribution doesn't use an administrator login account (usually called *root* in the UNIX/Linux world). Instead, Ubuntu provides the ability for normal user accounts to belong to an administrators group. Members in the administrators group have the ability to become temporary administrators on the system (see Chapter 17, "Users and Groups").

Having an account with administrative privileges is important because the administrator is the only account allowed to perform most system functions, such as changing system features, adding new devices, and installing new software. Without an administrative account, you won't be able to do much of anything new on the system.

The final step in this window is assigning the computer name. Ubuntu uses this name when advertising its presence on the network, as well as when referencing the system in log files. You should select a computer name that's unique on your network.

Migrate Documents and Settings

A relatively new feature in the Ubuntu installer is the Migrate Documents and Settings window, which may or may not appear next in your installation process, depending on your original system before you installed Ubuntu. The main Migrate Documents and Settings window is shown in Figure 3-11.

The Migrate Documents and Settings window appears if you're transitioning a Windows partition to an Ubuntu partition. The goal of the Ubuntu Migrate Documents and Settings feature is to enable a seamless transition from a Microsoft Windows workstation to an Ubuntu workstation.

Figure 3-11: The Ubuntu installer's Migrate Documents and Settings window.

In this step the installer looks in the hard drive partitions you're replacing for any existing Windows partitions. If it finds them, it offers to help migrate any Windows user accounts to the Ubuntu environment.

This tool looks for the Documents and Settings folder in an existing Microsoft Windows installation, then attempts to duplicate that environment in Ubuntu. If any Windows users configured, the Migrate Documents and Settings displays the individual user names, along with folders containing data for that user. The tool allows you to select which users to migrate, along with which folders to migrate. Currently, the Windows user features Ubuntu will attempt to migrate are

- Internet Explorer bookmarks
- Files in the My Documents folder
- Files in the My Pictures folder
- Files in the My Music folder
- Wallpaper saved by the user

The Migrate Documents and Settings feature is an aggressive feature in Ubuntu that allows current Windows users an easy way to migrate to Ubuntu.

caution   Although the Migrate Documents and Settings feature is useful, don't rely on it to work properly. If you're migrating a Windows workstation to an Ubuntu workstation, it's always a good idea to make a copy of your important data before starting the migration process.

Review Options

The final step in the installation process requires you to review and confirm all of the features you selected in the previous installation steps. You can backtrack to a previous installation option window and modify your selections. Pay close attention to the disk partition settings because once you click the Install button those settings become permanent.

There is an additional element that you can tweak in this window. Clicking the Advanced button produces the Advanced Options window, shown in Figure 3-12.

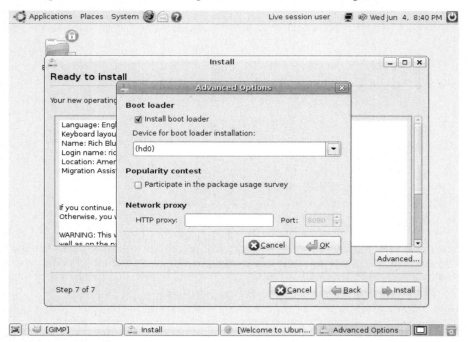

Figure 3-12: The Advanced Options window.

The Advanced Options window allows you to customize three additional features in Ubuntu:

- ◆ The boot loader
- ◆ The package survey
- ◆ The network proxy

When Ubuntu installs on a workstation, it has the ability to provide its own boot loader. The boot loader is responsible for starting the operating system. When you have a Windows operating system installed, Windows provides its own boot loader.

Ubuntu can replace the Windows boot loader with the grand unified boot loader (GRUB) program. GRUB is the standard boot loader used in Linux systems; it can start Linux systems, as well as many other operating systems, including Windows.

GRUB can be loaded in either the master boot record (MBR) of the first hard drive (called hd0 in Ubuntu) or, in a multiple hard drive system, it can reside on the hard drive that contains the Linux partition.

The Advanced Options window allows you to configure this feature. By default, Ubuntu enables GRUB and installs it in the MBR of the first hard drive.

Secret

You may also notice that you can uncheck the check box for installing the boot loader. This option won't install any boot loader and will just create the partitions and install Ubuntu. Use this feature if you already have Linux installed in another partition and want to add an Ubuntu partition. You can then manually configure the existing GRUB boot menu to include the new Ubuntu partition.

The GRUB boot menu is stored in the /boot/grub/menu.1st file.

The second step in the Advanced Options window is a package usage survey. The package usage survey retrieves some nonpersonal information about your setup (such as the CPU type, amount of memory, amount of hard drive space, and installation method you used) and sends it to a central repository for statistical purposes. You can view the current package usage survey results by going to the web site http://popcon.ubuntu.com, where several different tables and graphs show current survey totals.

The final step in the Advanced Options window is to set a network proxy server. Some local networks (especially those in businesses) must filter any outgoing network traffic to restrict what web sites employees can access. This is done using a network proxy.

The firewall blocks all normal HTTP access from the network, but the network proxy can receive HTTP requests, then block the unacceptable ones and forward the allowed ones. This capability gives a company total control over what its employees can and can't access on the Internet from the corporate network.

If your Ubuntu workstation is on a network that uses a network proxy, you must configure that feature for your Internet access to work properly.

When you've finished setting any advanced options, you're ready to start the installation. After starting the installation there's nothing more for you to do other than sit back and watch things happen. The Ubuntu installer takes over, creating the disk partitions you specified and installing the entire Ubuntu operating system.

Installing from the Alternate Install CD

If your workstation can't run the LiveCD, you can possibly install Ubuntu using the alternate install CD. The alternate install CD performs a text-based installation of the Ubuntu system instead of the GUI-oriented LiveCD install. This installation requires less memory and a less advanced video card.

If you use the alternate install CD, you can still install the Ubuntu GUI desktop environment. Often you can run the Ubuntu GUI desktop just fine after installing the applications and customizing the graphics for your specific video environment.

For the most part, the alternate install CD requests the same information for the installation as the LiveCD, but it uses text-oriented menus instead of graphical GUI menus. You'll be prompted to select the installation language, the time zone, the keyboard type (the alternate install CD can even autodetect most standard types of keyboards), and the default userID and host name information.

The alternate install CD provides something that's not available in the LiveCD, and that feature appears in the disk partitioning section. Linux systems can use a feature called *logical volume management* (LVM), which allows you to create dynamic partitions on your system. You can add and remove disk space from LVM partitions at any time, providing a flexible way to allocate disk space on your system.

The follow sections describe how to use LVM in both the guided and manual partition methods when using the alternate install CD.

Guided Partitions

When you get to the Partition Disks section of the alternate install CD process, you'll see a slightly different configuration from what the LiveCD presents. Figure 3-13 shows the main Partition Disks window that appears when performing an installation from the alternate install CD.

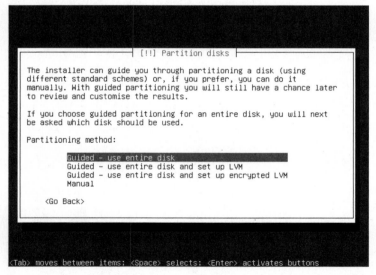

Figure 3-13: The Partition Disks window in the alternate CD installation.

Notice that there are two additional guided options available for you to use:

- ◆ Use the entire disk and set up LVM.
- ◆ Use the entire disk and set up encrypted LVM.

When you select one of these options, the Ubuntu installer will automatically create a logical volume on your hard drive for Ubuntu. Once the logical volume is created, you can use Linux utilities to modify it at any time (see Chapter 18, "Basic Administration").

Secret

Disk space management is a tricky business, and the Linux logical volume management (LVM) feature is a great tool designed to help solve some of the basic problems of disk management, but it has been known to cause other problems.

When designing the layout of a system, often it's difficult to predict exactly how much disk space will be required for applications and user data. With standard filesystems such as ext3, if you need to add space you must back up the data, create a completely new partition, then restore the data on the new partition.

With LVM, instead of associating a location in the virtual filesystem to a partition, you assign it to a logical volume group. You can add any physical disk partition you wish to the logical volume group. If the logical volume group runs out of space, you can add a new hard drive, then dynamically add space to the existing logical volume group.

LVM maintains its own table so it knows which partitions are part of which logical volume group. It's not uncommon for a logical volume group to become corrupt, even though the data on the hard drive partition are just fine. Data corruption can cause catastrophic problems on a Linux system, especially if it happens to the root partition.

Therefore, administrators for large Linux systems often use a combination of dedicated partitions and LVM partitions. They'll use a dedicated partition for the root partition, then create LVM partitions for the /opt and /home portions of the virtual filesystem. This configuration allows you to add disk space as new applications are installed or when users start running out of space, while maintaining the integrity of the root filesystem.

Manual Partitions

Besides the guided LVM partitions, you can manually create LVM partitions on your Ubuntu installation from the alternate install CD. If you select the Manual Partition option from the Partition Disks window, you'll get the second-level Partition Disks window, shown in Figure 3-14.

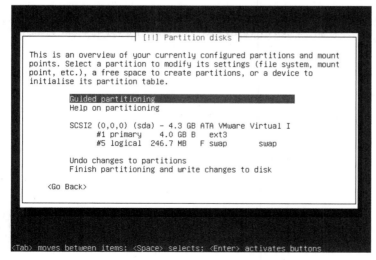

Figure 3-14: The second-level Partition Disks window.

In this window you can manually select a partition to modify or delete, or you can add a new partition. The first entry shows the actual hard drive device detected. The indented entries under that show the free space on that hard drive, plus any existing partitions on that hard drive, and their information.

Select the free space area you want to work on, and hit the Enter key. The Partition Disks window for the next level appears, shown in Figure 3-15.

Figure 3-15: The individual partition configuration window.

When you select the Use As entry, a menu appears, allowing you to select which filesystem to install on the partition. Besides the standard filesystems available in the LiveCD install (see "Prepare the Disk Space" section earlier in this chapter), you'll see three additional entries—the two LVM options (regular and encrypted) and an option to create a software RAID volume.

Once you've created the partition with the filesystem of your choice, you can save the settings and continue with the installation.

Server Installation

If you're interested in installing a Linux server, the Ubuntu server LiveCD is probably the easiest way to go. The Ubuntu server installs many popular server packages automatically for you, without any configuration required.

This section walks through the Ubuntu server installation process, showing how to configure your server.

Main Installation

The Ubuntu server LiveCD installation is very similar to the workstation alternate CD installation process. The server installation uses a text-based approach because servers often don't have (or need) fancy video cards.

The first few steps in the Ubuntu server installation are the same as the alternate CD installation. You'll be asked to select a language, then the Ubuntu installer will ask whether you want it to detect your keyboard. Selecting the Yes option initiates a series of questions about special keys on your keyboard. After the dust settles, Ubuntu will show the recommended keyboard setting. If you don't think the keyboard selection is correct, you can start over.

The next step in the process is the network configuration. Because you're installing a server, Ubuntu assumes that the server will need to be connected to a network. Ubuntu first attempts to acquire an IP address for your network using the dynamic host configuration protocol (DHCP).

This method requires a server on the network that's responsible for assigning and maintaining IP addresses for the network. Many routers provide this feature.

Secret

The problem with acquiring an IP address using DHCP is that you're not guaranteed to keep the same IP address. For workstations, that is no big deal, but for a server, it can be a huge problem because clients need a consistent, reliable way to reach the server.

There are two ways to solve this problem. Most DHCP servers (even routers that perform DHCP server functions) allow you to dedicate an IP address to a specific host. If your DHCP server provides this feature, find the MAC address of your Ubuntu server system and add it to the DHCP server for a static IP address assignment.

The other method is to keep the Ubuntu server off your network during this part of the installation process. If the DHCP query fails, the Ubuntu installation program will query you for specific IP address information.

The Ubuntu server installation also allows you to partition the hard disk for the server. The installer provides four guided methods for partitioning the hard disk:

- ◆ Using the existing hard drive partitions
- ◆ Using the entire hard disk
- ◆ Using a logical volume manager (LVM) to allow you to easily add more disk to the same logical volumes later on
- ◆ Using an encrypted LVM system to safeguard your server data

Besides these four guided methods you can create the hard disk partitions manually. Once you have set up your hard disk environment, you can select which server programs the installer should install for you.

Server Programs

The most important part of the Ubuntu server installation process is determining which server programs you need to run on your server. Table 3-3 shows the server packages that you can automatically install from the server installation process.

Table 3-3: The Ubuntu Server Packages

Package	Description
DNS server	The BIND domain name server package
LAMP server	The Linux Apache web server with PHP programming language support and the MySQL database server
Tomcat	The Apache Java servlet application web server
Mail server	The Postfix email server
OpenSSH server	Provides secure socket shell (SSH) access to the server
PostgreSQL server	The PostgreSQL open-source database server
Print server	The common UNIX print server (CUPS)
Samba file server	Provides file sharing services for Windows networks

Each of these server packages is discussed in more detail later in this book. The following sections provide a brief overview of each of the servers to give you an idea what they're used for.

The DNS Server

The Berkeley Internet Name Domain (BIND) package is a popular server that provides domain name service (DNS) for networks. Every network on the Internet must have a domain name server. Many networks employ the services of an Internet service provider (ISP) to handle the DNS server for their network. However, you can use the Ubuntu server software to run your own DNS server. See Chapter 20, "DNS Server," for details on how to set up and install a DNS server on your network.

The LAMP Server

The Linux-Apache-MySQL-PHP (LAMP) server is a popular web programming environment. Many sites use LAMP technology to support online stores, blogs, and content management systems (CMS). A LAMP server environment is often difficult to configure, due to the multitude of packages that need to be synchronized. The Ubuntu server takes all of the hassle out of installing a LAMP server by preconfiguring all of the individual components to operate properly.

If you install the LAMP server, the installation process displays an additional query window, shown in Figure 3-16.

The MySQL server uses user accounts to access databases contained within the server. The main administrative user account is the root user. By default this user account doesn't have a password, which could be a dangerous thing, especially if your Ubuntu server is on an open network.

You can select a password for the root MySQL user account from this window.

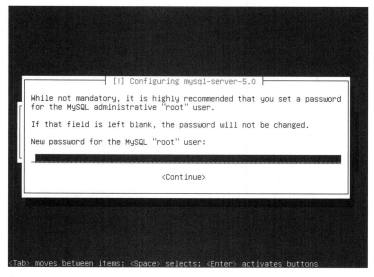

Figure 3-16: The MySQL root user window.

Secret

The default empty root password for MySQL has become security issue for many sites. If the system administrator forgets to assign a password, anyone can get into the MySQL server and perform administrative functions. For that reason Ubuntu goes out of the way to ensure that you assign a password to the MySQL root account.

Of course the flipside to this problem is setting a root password then forgetting it. Chapter 21, "Web Server," explains how to get out of this predicament.

The Tomcat Server

If you've done any work in the Java environment, you've no doubt heard about Java server pages (JSP) and Java servlets. These programming languages allow you to produce dynamic web applications using Java and HTML code. The Apache project has spun off a sister project called Tomcat, which provides a web server along with JSP and a Java servlet processor, all in one application.

The Ubuntu server installation allows you to install a complete Tomcat server by selecting it from the installation menu. There's nothing to configure—just load the package and you're ready to start hosting JSP or Java servlet applications from your Ubuntu server.

The Mail Server

Several popular email server packages available for the Linux environment. The Ubuntu server installation package installs the Postfix email server. If you choose to install a mail server, yet another configuration window appears, shown in Figure 3-17.

```
┤ [!] Postfix Configuration ├
Please select the mail server configuration type that best meets your
needs.

 No configuration:
 Should be chosen to leave the current configuration unchanged.
 Internet site:
 Mail is sent and received directly using SMTP.
 Internet with smarthost:
 Mail is received directly using SMTP or by running a utility such
 as fetchmail. Outgoing mail is sent using a smarthost.
 Satellite system:
 All mail is sent to another machine, called a 'smarthost', for
delivery.
 Local only:
 The only delivered mail is the mail for local users. There is no
network.

General type of mail configuration:

                    No configuration          ↑
                    Internet Site             ▪

      <Go Back>

<Tab> moves between items; <Space> selects; <Enter> activates buttons
```

Figure 3-17: The Postfix configuration window.

There are lots of different configuration issues for the Postfix server (see Chapter 23, "Email Server"). The Ubuntu server uses defaults for all of the configuration options but must have one piece of information for the email server to run properly on your network.

There are several ways to setup an email server, so you'll need to tell the Ubuntu installer script your email server environment:

- ♦ **No Configuration:** Use the default Postfix configuration.
- ♦ **Internet Site:** Configure Postfix to receive and deliver mail directly with remote mail servers.
- ♦ **Internet with SmartHost:** Configure Postfix to receive mail directly from remote mail servers, but deliver all outbound mail to a single remote server to forward for delivery.
- ♦ **Satellite System:** Configure Postfix to receive and deliver mail through a single remote server.
- ♦ **Local Only:** Configure Postfix to receive and deliver mail only for local users on the system.

Select the option that matches your network environment. The installation will prompt you for additional information, depending on the option you select.

The OpenSSH Server

The OpenSSH server uses the secure shell (SSH) protocol to communicate with remote clients and other servers from the network using encrypted communications. The OpenSSH package contains two programs:

- ♦ **sshd:** a secure shell server program that listens for incoming connections
- ♦ **ssh:** a secure shell client program that allows you to connect to remote sshd servers

The OpenSSH environment uses a command line interface (see Chapter 19, "The Ubuntu Command Line") where you can submit Linux commands to the remote server and view the responses.

The PostgreSQL Server

Although the LAMP server uses the popular MySQL Open Source database, the Ubuntu server also supports another popular open source database, PostgreSQL. The PostgreSQL server is often considered more powerful than MySQL in high-volume environments, and it contains some features found in expensive commercial database servers. You can install the LAMP server and the PostgreSQL server to provide both database server environments on your server.

The PostgreSQL server is discussed in more detail in Chapter 24, "Database Server."

The Print Server

The Ubuntu print server package uses the common UNIX print server (CUPS) to advertise any connected printers on the network. This feature provides a great way to share printers among other UNIX systems on the network. See Chapter 22, "Samba and Print Servers," for details on how to set up a CUPS server using the Ubuntu server.

The Samba File Server

The Samba file server is a powerful package that allows the Ubuntu server to interact on a Microsoft Windows network. It provides shared folders and shared printers for Windows workstations and other Windows servers. The Samba software turns your Ubuntu server into a full-featured Windows server, even allowing it to join a Windows domain.

Not only does the Samba software provide Windows server features, but it also provides a client mode. In the Samba client mode you can connect to remote Windows server shares and retrieve files, or print to remote Windows network printers. Chapter 22 provides details on how to configure and use your Samba software.

Upgrading Ubuntu

If you already have a version of Ubuntu running on your system, Ubuntu allows you to upgrade to a new version fairly painlessly. There are three methods of performing upgrades to Ubuntu systems:

- ◆ A sequential upgrade from one version to the next
- ◆ A long-term support (LTS) upgrade from one LTS version to the next LTS version
- ◆ A clean upgrade of any version to a new version

A sequential upgrade allows you to upgrade to the next available Ubuntu version. For example, you can directly upgrade version 7.10 to 8.04, 8.04 to 8.10, and 8.10 to 9.04.

Ubuntu also provides special versions called long-term support (LTS). Ubuntu supports these versions with security patches and software updates for up to 3 years. The LTS versions come out at odd intervals between regular Ubuntu version releases, so they aren't directly connected to the latest available version. However, you can directly upgrade one LTS version to the next LTS version. Thus, you can directly upgrade 6.06 LTS to 8.04 LTS.

Before you upgrade you should download and install all of the available patches and updates to the existing Ubuntu version. If your Ubuntu workstation is connected to the Internet, the Update Manager automatically notifies you when a new version of Ubuntu is available, as shown in Figure 3-18.

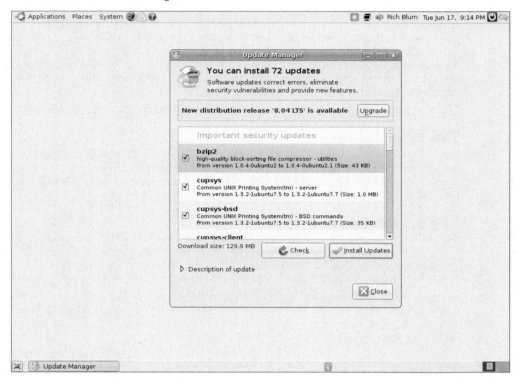

Figure 3-18: The Ubuntu Update Manager showing a new version available.

Selecting that option automatically downloads the files necessary to perform a complete upgrade to the new version of Ubuntu.

For Ubuntu server versions, you must use the command line software package updater called *apt-get* (see the section titled "Command Line Package Management" in Chapter 13, "Software Installs and Updates") to obtain the new Ubuntu installation. Just as with the Ubuntu workstation distribution, you can upgrade an Ubuntu server version with the next direct version or the next LTS version.

Secret

If you don't have access to the Internet from your Ubuntu workstation or server, you can upgrade using the alternate install CD but not the LiveCD. When you boot from the alternate install CD it prompts you if the installation is an upgrade of an existing system, and it attempts to maintain your existing documents and settings located in the /home directory structure.

Summary

This chapter walked through the processes required to install Ubuntu on your workstation or server system. The main way to install an Ubuntu workstation or server is via the LiveCD.

Before trying to install Ubuntu, you should take an inventory of the hardware devices installed on your PC so you can be prepared for any installation problems. If you intend to keep an existing operating system on your PC, you'll need to determine how you'll install Ubuntu. If you plan on partitioning a single hard drive, you'll need to defragment the Windows partition before running the Ubuntu installation. You'll also need to determine how much disk space you can allocate for the Ubuntu installation.

The LiveCD guides you through all of the requirements for setting up the Ubuntu software. As part of the installation process, it'll examine the installed hard drives and offer to automatically guide you through the necessary setup. You can choose to allow Ubuntu to use the entire hard drive, partition an existing hard drive for a new Ubuntu partition, or use a second hard drive for Ubuntu.

Besides the guided partition you can manually alter the partitions on your PC during the installation. If you decide to manually create and edit partitions, don't forget to create a swap area at least the same size as the amount of physical memory in the PC.

The Ubuntu workstation distribution also provides an alternate install CD, which performs the same installation process as the LiveCD install (plus a few additional features) in a text-oriented environment. You can use the alternate install CD to setup logical volume management (LVM) partitions, which allow you to freely add and remove disk space from partitions.

The Ubuntu server installation is a text-oriented installation that provides installation options to install several preconfigured software packages, including a DNS server, an email server, a LAMP server, a print server, and a Samba server.

The next chapter looks at the Ubuntu desktop. It describes the individual features of the desktop and provides in-depth information about how to configure your desktop just the way you want it.

Exploring the Desktop

Chapter
4

♦ ♦

Secrets in This Chapter

The Desktop Layout

Exploring the Panel

Panel Menus

Multiple Desktops

♦ ♦

Now that you have Ubuntu installed on your workstation, it's time to go exploring. The default desktop used in Ubuntu is GNOME. If you've never used the GNOME desktop before, things might seem a little different. Although GNOME borrows many of the same windowing ideas from Microsoft Windows and Apple Macintosh, it does have some unique features of its own. This chapter walks through the basics of the GNOME desktop, providing you with a detailed tour of how to utilize the desktop to its fullest.

Desktop Features

When you first log in to the Ubuntu workstation system, you're greeted by the default GNOME desktop, shown in Figure 4-1.

Figure 4-1: The default Ubuntu GNOME desktop.

The GNOME desktop layout used in Ubuntu consists of three sections:

- ◆ A bar at the top of the screen containing menus and icons
- ◆ A blank desktop area in the middle of the screen
- ◆ A bar at the bottom of the screen containing a trash can and a couple of desktop icons

The bars at the top and bottom of the screen are called *panels*. Each panel has a different function on the desktop. The panels can contain menus for selecting applications and utilities, icons to launch applications, and special programs called *panel applets*.

The following sections describe each of the three sections in the Ubuntu workstation desktop.

The Top Panel

Ubuntu divides the panel at the top of the desktop into three areas:

- ◆ A menu area
- ◆ A quick-launch icon area
- ◆ An applet area

Each of these areas serves a different function on the desktop. The following sections describe each of these three areas and what they contain.

The Menu Area

The far left side of the top panel contains the menu area. The menu area contains links that allow you easy access to all of the applications and utilities installed on the Ubuntu system. There are three top-level menu links that appear directly on the top panel:

- ◆ **The Applications menu**: Contains links that launch application programs available on the Ubuntu system.
- ◆ **The Places menu**: Contains links to locations in the Ubuntu virtual filesystem, plus links to additional hard drives, floppy disks, CD/DVD drives, and USB drives, and for connecting to remote filesystems.
- ◆ **The System menu**: Contains links to utilities for changing user and system settings.

Each top-level menu link provides additional links that are menus (entries that have an arrow next to them) or individual links that directly launch applications or utilities. When you hover the mouse pointer over a submenu link, the submenu automatically appears next to the main menu, showing the links it contains, as depicted in Figure 4-2.

Figure 4-2: The Applications ⇨ Accessories submenu.

The purpose of each of the top-level menus is explained in the following sections.

The Applications Menu

The Applications menu contains links to standard applications installed on the Ubuntu system. Table 4-1 describes the items you'll find in the Applications menu.

Table 4-1: The Applications Menu

Menu Item	Description
Accessories	A submenu containing small utilities for everyday functions. Contains items such as a calculator and dictionary
Games	A submenu full of fun, graphical games that you can use instead of doing real work
Graphics	A submenu with applications for creating and manipulating different types of graphic images, including importing images from scanners and digital cameras
Internet	A submenu supporting applications for use on the Internet, including web browsing, email, and instant messaging
Office	A submenu containing applications for word processing, spreadsheets, and presentation graphics
Sound and Video	A submenu with applications for playing audio files, audio CDs, video DVDs, and burning your own audio CDs and video DVDs
Add/Remove	Launches the Ubuntu Update Manager

The Applications menu is the go-to place for launching most of the applications you'll use in your Ubuntu workstation. If you add other applications using the Software Installer (see Chapter 13, "Software Installs and Updates"), those applications also appear in the Applications menu.

The Places Menu

The next top-level menu selection is the Places menu, shown in Figure 4-3.

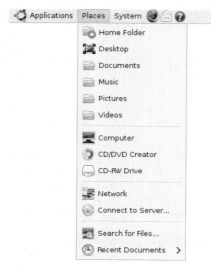

Figure 4-3: The Places menu.

The Places menu provides links to common locations within the virtual filesystem, plus quick links to removable drives and external network systems. These items are listed in Table 4-2.

Table 4-2: The Places Menu

Menu Item	*Description*
Home Folder	The main folder for the user
Desktop	Access to the files that appear on the desktop
Documents	Direct access to the Documents folder contained in the user's home folder
Music	Direct access to the Music folder contained in the user's home folder
Pictures	Direct access to the Pictures folder contained in the user's home folder
Videos	Direct access to the Videos folder contained in the user's home folder
Computer	Links to the Nautilus file manager software package
CD/DVD Creator	Launches the Brasero CD-burning software
Floppy Drive	Direct access to the floppy drive
Network	Launches the network browser application, which scans the network for available Windows servers
Connect to Server...	Provides direct access to various types of network servers
Search for Files...	Provides access to the Nautilus file manager search feature
Recent Documents...	Provides a list of documents you've opened recently using the OpenOffice.org software packages

Notice that one of the locations in the Places menu is your desktop. GNOME treats your desktop just like any folder in the system (in fact, it is a folder in your home directory). You can access files stored on your desktop, as well as any desktop shortcuts you create (discussed in the "Adding Desktop Icons" section).

The Connect to Server menu option allows you to specify a remote server for Ubuntu to connect to and retrieve files from. Ubuntu can connect to several types of servers to access files and folders:

- ♦ **SSH:** Connect to a remote server using the secure shell protocol, which uses an encrypted network connection.
- ♦ **FTP (with login):** Connect to a remote file transfer protocol (FTP) server using a specific login account.
- ♦ **Public FTP:** Connect to an FTP server using an anonymous account to access publicly posted files.
- ♦ **Windows share:** Connect to a Windows server or workstation advertising a share.

- ◆ **WebDAV (HTTP):** Connect to web-based distributed authoring and versioning sites to collaboratively edit files with others.
- ◆ **Custom location:** Use a uniform resource identifier (URI) to define the location of a server and file or folder to access.

When you select a server type, the Connect to Server window provides text boxes for you to specify any required information for connecting to the server, such as the server hostname, ports, and login information.

The System Menu

The last top-level menu is the System menu, shown in Figure 4-4.

Figure 4-4: The System menu.

The System menu contains items for managing your Ubuntu workstation. The items in this menu are shown in Table 4-3.

Table 4-3: The System Menu

Menu Item	*Description*
Preferences	A submenu containing utilities for setting your workstation features
Administration	A submenu containing utilities for changing your workstation settings and managing the workstation
Help and Support	The installed Ubuntu Help menu, along with links to various sections in the Ubuntu web site
About GNOME	Brief information about the GNOME version and a link to the GNOME web site
About Ubuntu	Information about the Ubuntu version and a link to the Ubuntu web site
Shut Down…	A link to the Ubuntu Shut Down menu, providing options for ending your workstation session

The Quit menu provides several options for how to exit the system. There are two options for ending your current GNOME desktop session:

- ◆ Leave the current desktop session with the system running.
- ◆ Shut down the Ubuntu workstation.

The first option allows you to close the current user session but keep the Ubuntu system running. There are three ways to do this:

- ◆ **Log Out:** Terminate the session for the currently logged-in user account, and return to the login screen.
- ◆ **Lock Screen:** Keep the current user logged in, but lock the screen so only that user can enter a password to get to the desktop.
- ◆ **Switch User:** Return to the login screen to allow another user to log in, but keep the current user session active.

There are also three options for shutting down the Ubuntu workstation:

- ◆ **Hibernate:** Store the current session state in a temporary file and blank the screen.
- ◆ **Restart:** Reboot the Ubuntu system and start over.
- ◆ **Shut Down:** Stop all running processes and, if possible, turn off the PC.

The Hibernate feature is especially interesting. In Hibernate mode Ubuntu writes any information about your system state, such as the windows you have open and the applications running, to a temporary file on the hard drive. It then shuts down the desktop but keeps the PC powered up. The PC (and Ubuntu) is still running but not processing anything. When you press a key, Ubuntu wakes up, reads the system state file it created, and quickly restores the session to its previous state.

Secret

If you're using Ubuntu workstation on a laptop computer, Hibernate mode can quickly drain your battery. Instead of Hibernate mode, Ubuntu provides the Suspend mode for laptops. In Suspend mode the system state is stored in memory, and the system goes into a low-power consumption mode. This state allows the laptop to stay in Suspend mode for longer, if running on battery power.

For most laptops, Ubuntu also has the ability to detect when you close the laptop lid and automatically go into Suspend mode. However, this is not a recommended way to end your Ubuntu session if your laptop is not plugged in because your laptop eventually will run out of battery power and lose the saved session.

The Quick-launch Area

Next to the menu area is the quick-launch icon area. This section of the panel contains three quick-launch icons that Ubuntu provides by default. Clicking an icon once launches the specific application. The applications installed by default in the Ubuntu quick-launch icon area are

- ◆ **Firefox:** the default web browser software installed in Ubuntu
- ◆ **Evolution:** the default email client package installed in Ubuntu
- ◆ **Help Center:** a link to the Ubuntu Help Center, which provides instructions for performing basic tasks on the system

The idea behind the quick-launch area is to provide a quick way to start commonly used applications, so you don't have to go hunting through the Applications menu for them. Later, in the "Adding Panel Applets" section, you'll see how to add quick-launch icons for your favorite applications.

The Applet Section

At the far right of the top panel you'll find several icons and information. These are *panel applets.* Panel applets are small utilities that run in the background and appear on the panel as icons to show real-time information. Depending on the type of system you're using to run Ubuntu (laptop or desktop) and the features you have installed (such as network cards, modems, and proprietary video cards), you'll see different applets on the panel. Some of the most common applets that you may find running are

- ◆ **Update Manager:** monitors the state of the software packages installed on your system and announces whether updates are available from the Ubuntu repository
- ◆ **Proprietary Devices Manager:** lets you know whether you have hardware installed that required Ubuntu to install a proprietary device driver (non-open source)
- ◆ **Network Manager:** monitors network connectivity, as well as resources available for wireless network cards
- ◆ **Power Manager:** if you're running Ubuntu on a laptop, this applet displays whether the laptop is on battery power and, if so, estimates how much time is left on the battery charge
- ◆ **Date/Time Calendar:** displays the date and time and provides quick access to the Evolution calendar feature
- ◆ **User Switcher:** displays the current user and allows you to switch between users if more than one user is logged in to the system
- ◆ **Log Off:** provides quick access to the Log Out/Shut Down menu

The Update Manager applet shows the status of the Update Manager software that's running in background on the system (see Chapter 12). It automatically informs you when there are updates to install on the Ubuntu system. It also displays a different icon depending on what updates are available.

The other important icon is the Network Manager. If you have a wireless network card, this applet is crucial to setting up your network. Clicking the applet displays the wireless access points detected by Ubuntu. Clicking on an individual access point brings up the Wireless Network Configuration window, allowing you to set your configuration settings (see Chapter 13, "Networking").

Secret   You can control which applets start automatically with the Session Preferences tool, available in the menu by selecting System ➾ Preferences ➾ Session. The Startup Programs tab shows all of the applets configured to start automatically. You can uncheck the check box of any applets you don't want to start and add any of your own programs that you want to start automatically when you log in.

The Desktop Workspace

As mentioned in "The Places Menu" section in this chapter, the GNOME desktop workspace is a normal folder in each user's home folder. There are three basic types of objects you can have on your desktop:

- ◆ Shortcuts to launch applications

◆ Files for documents
◆ Folders

Ubuntu developers have changed their thinking on the desktop workspace area. In the past, Ubuntu had provided a few default desktop icons for each user, such as an icon linked to the user's home folder (called *Home*) and an icon (called *Computer*) that linked to the root of the virtual filesystem directory.

These icons are still in the LiveCD Ubuntu desktop, but once you install Ubuntu the desktop workspace changes. In the last few releases of Ubuntu, the Ubuntu developers have taken a different approach to the desktop. Now there's nothing in the workspace area! The default Ubuntu desktop starts out as a blank slate.

You're free to add your own desktop icons, as described in the "Adding Desktop Icons" section.

The Bottom Panel

The bottom panel is configured slightly different from the top panel. It contains four elements:

◆ The Desktop Viewer icon
◆ The taskbar area
◆ The Workspace Switcher icon
◆ The Trash icon

The following sections explain each of these items in more detail.

The Desktop Viewer

The Desktop Viewer is the icon located at the far left of the bottom panel. Clicking this icon minimizes all open active windows to reveal the desktop workspace. This is a great way to get back to your desktop workspace if you've got lots of windows open.

Once all of the windows are minimized, clicking the icon a second time maximizes all of the currently active windows, placing them back the way they were before you minimized them.

The Taskbar Area

The taskbar area provides icons for applications as they run on the system. You can change the status of an application's window using its icon in the taskbar. There are three actions you can take with an application:

◆ Click the underscore icon in the upper-right corner of the application window to minimize it to the taskbar.
◆ Click the application icon in the taskbar of a minimized application to open the application window.
◆ Click the application icon in the taskbar of an open application to bring it to the top of other windows that are opened on the desktop.

Right-clicking the taskbar icon for an application produces the same menu as clicking the icon in the top-left corner of the application window. This menu allows you to move, resize, and close the application window, as well as move it to another workspace, which is next in the bottom panel.

The Workspace Switcher

The workspace switcher changes the active *workspace*. A workspace is an instance of your Ubuntu desktop. You can have multiple workspaces active at the same time and use the workspace switcher to switch between them. Each workspace shares the same top and bottom panels, as well as desktop, but allows you to have separate application windows open in separate workspaces.

With this feature you can run an application in one workspace, then switch to another workspace to start other applications. When you need to return to the first application, instead of looking for it in your taskbar, you just switch to the first workspace.

By default, Ubuntu creates two workspaces. Each workspace appears as a square icon in the lower right of the bottom panel. Clicking on the workspace icon switches you to the appropriate workspace.

Secret   If you have a mouse device that supports horizontal scrolling, you can switch between workspace areas by scrolling horizontally when on the desktop. Many laptop touchpads support horizontal scrolling by moving your finger sideways across the touchpad, either near the top or bottom of the touchpad.

The Trash Icon

The Trash icon works just like the Recycle Bin in Windows, or the Trash on a Macintosh. To delete, drag and drop files, folders, and shortcut links either from your desktop or from a Nautilus window directly into the Trash Can applet on the panel.

When you drag a file or folder to the Trash icon, Ubuntu doesn't delete it; puts it in a special place in the filesystem. Don't expect your disk space to clear up after you've placed a file or folder in the trash.

Click the Trash icon in the panel to open the trash using the Nautilus File Manager (see Chapter 5), as shown in Figure 4-5.

In the Nautilus window you can take items out of the trash by dragging and dropping them into another folder on the system, you can permanently delete a file by right-clicking on it and selecting Delete from Trash, or you can click the Empty Trash button to permanently delete everything in the trash from your system.

Secret   In case you're wondering where files and folders go when you place them in the trash, Ubuntu creates a folder in your home folder area called `.local/share/Trash`. This is where it places any items you put in the trash can. The `.local` folder is a hidden folder in your home folder, so you'll need to enable the Show Hidden Files feature in Nautilus to see it.

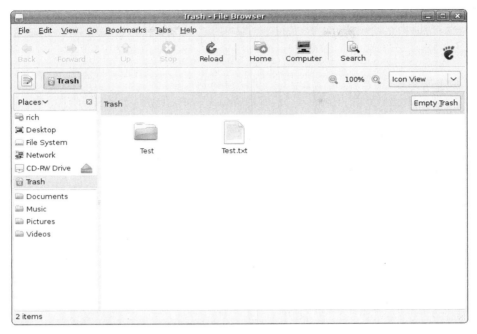

Figure 4-5: Opening the Trash applet.

Modifying the Desktop

The top and bottom panels are completely configurable. There are plenty of ways to customize your desktop panels. This section walks through the things you can do to alter the panels on your desktop.

Adding to the Panel Menus

You can customize the default menus Ubuntu provides on the top panel, adding links to your own applications or sites. If your Ubuntu workstation is used by more than one user, all users can have their own unique menu configuration without affecting the other users' configuration.

Right-clicking on one of the three existing menus in the top panel produces a menu with five options:

- ♦ **Help:** displays a quick tutorial on how to use the GNOME menus
- ♦ **Edit Menus:** allows you to select what items appear in the default menus
- ♦ **Remove from Panel:** allows you to completely remove the menu from the panel
- ♦ **Move:** if the panel isn't locked, allows you to move the menu to a different location on the same panel
- ♦ **Lock to Panel:** prevents changes to the panel layout

The Edit Menus option provides a graphical editor that allows you to add and remove individual items from three separate menus on the system:

◆ The Applications menu

◆ The System ⇨ Preferences submenu

◆ The System ⇨ Administration submenu

The menu editor lists the three menus on the left side of the window, as shown in Figure 4-6.

Figure 4-6: The GNOME menu editor.

As you select an individual menu, the items or submenus in that menu appear in the right side of the window. Items and submenus that are active contain a check mark in the check box next to them. If the check box is empty, that item or submenu won't appear on the menu.

You can add new submenus as well as new item links to the menus. To add a new submenu, select the parent menu location from the left side of the window, then click the New Menu button. After you name the new menu, it appears in the window on the right. Make sure you check the check box next to the new submenu or it won't appear in your final menu.

Once the new submenu appears in the list on the right, you can move it around in the menu list using the Move Up and Move Down buttons. You can also use the New Separator button to add a horizontal bar in the menu list to help separate item groups.

To add a new item link in the menu or submenu, select the menu or submenu in the left window, then click the New Item button. The Create Launcher dialog box appears, as shown in Figure 4-7.

You can create three different types of links in the Create Launcher dialog box:

◆ A link to launch an application

◆ A link to launch an application that runs in the Terminal session

◆ A link to a specific location on the local filesystem or on a remote system

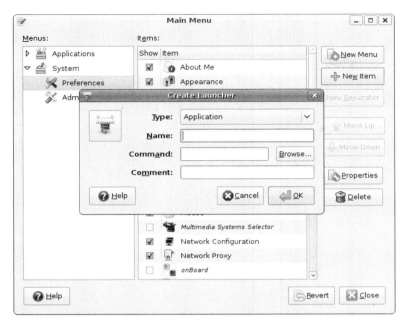

Figure 4-7: The Create Launcher dialog box for creating a new menu item.

Once you've created a new submenu or item, you can edit it by right-clicking on the item and selecting Properties from the resulting menu. Likewise, if you decide to remove a submenu or item, just right-click on it and select Delete from the menu.

Secret

The GNOME desktop uses the XDG menu specification, which for each menu defines a single global menu file for all users, plus individual menu files for each individual user. This feature enables you to set a global menu structure, and it allows individual users to customize their own menu settings without affecting the menus of other users. The menu files use text HTML tags to define menus, submenus, and items.

The global menu files for the three top-level menus are located in the /etc/xdg/menus folder. The three menu files are

- applications.menu
- preferences.menu
- settings.menu

Each menu file is a text file that contains the formatted definitions of the menus and items. These menu items appear for all users (although a user can still elect to disable an individual item).

Each user has a separate menu folder, located in his or her home folder in the .config/menus folder. Any additions made to the menu by the user are placed in this folder, using the same menu filenames as the global menu files. These changes apply only to that user and are not seen by other users.

If you completely mess up your menu system, you can return to the default setup by simply clicking the Revert button (as seen in Figure 4-6). However, if you've made many changes, you might want to avoid that solution because you'll lose all of the customizing you've done.

Adding Panel Applets

Besides the default applets that appear in the top panel, you can add applications to both the top and bottom panels. This capability provides easy access to quick utilities and commonly used applications.

To add a new applet, right-click on an empty space on either panel, then select the Add to Panel option in the menu that appears. Table 4-4 shows the different applet options available.

Table 4-4: The Add to Panel Menu Options

Applet	Description
Custom Application Launcher	Creates a launcher icon for a new application
Application Launcher	Copies an existing application launcher
Address Book Search	Searches the Evolution address book
Battery Charge Monitor	Displays the estimated time until discharge for a laptop battery
Brightness Applet	Adjusts the brightness of a laptop display
Character Palette	Inserts special characters into your documents
Clipboard Text Encryption	Encrypts, decrypts, or signs text in the clipboard
Clock	Displays the current time and date
Connect to Server	Connects to a remote server for file access
CPU Frequency Scaling Monitor	Displays the frequency at which the CPU is running. Frequency scaling is used in laptops to conserve power
Deskbar	Provides a single search interface for searching data in multiple files and applications
Dictionary Lookup	Returns dictionary definitions for words
Disk Mounter	Graphically accesses local hard disks and USB devices
Drawer	A convenient location to store documents and other files
Dwell Click	Sets default click type for the mouse for assistive technologies
Eyes	They follow your mouse!
Fish	A fishbowl for your amusement
Force Quit	Terminates a stuck application

Table 4-5: *(continued)*

Applet	Description
Inhibit Applet	Blocks automatic power-saving features from enabling
Invest	Tracks your investments
Keyboard Accessibility Status	Displays status of the keyboard accessibility features
Keyboard Indicator	Displays the type of keyboard detected and provides a menu for easily setting keyboard features
Lock Screen	Runs a password-protected screen saver
Main Menu	Adds a consolidated menu icon
Menu Bar	Adds a complete Ubuntu panel menu
Modem Monitor	Activates and displays the status of a dial-up modem network connection
Notification Area	Creates an area for notification icons
Pilot Applet	Interfaces with a connected Palm Pilot device
Pointer Capture	Provides a region that, when clicked, locks the mouse pointer device to prevent unintended mouse clicks
Quit	Provides a Log Out/Shut Down menu
Run Application	Allows you to quick-start an application by typing it in or selecting it from a list of known applications
Search for Files	Searches filenames and file contents for words
Separator	Places a vertical bar on the panel to separate icons
Show Desktop	Minimizes all maximized applications, or maximizes all minimized applications when clicked
Sticky Notes	Places an electronic sticky note on your desktop
System Monitor	Provides basic system load information in a handy graph
Terminal Server Client Applet	Connects to a remote server session using terminal server software
Tomboy Notes	Organizes note taking
Trash	Puts unneeded files and folders in the trash area. Must be manually emptied to delete the files
User Switcher	Suspends the logged-in user and allows logging in to another user account
Volume Control	Changes the volume of the PC speakers
Weather Report	Connects to Internet weather sites and displays current conditions
Window List	Provides a group of buttons to easily switch between open windows on the desktop
Window Selector	Provides a simple menu to easily switch between open windows on the desktop
Workspace Switcher	Switches between desktop workspaces

That's quite a lot of applets to choose from! The following sections give a brief overview of some of the more common applets.

Application Launchers

There are two types of application launchers you can place on the panels. The generic Application Launcher option allows you to copy an existing application launcher from the three main menu areas (see the "Adding to the Panel Menus" section earlier in this chapter) to create an icon in the panel.

This is a great way to easily place a commonly used application on the panel for quick access. When you select this option, a drop-down menu appears, allowing you to browse the menus to select the application or utility to place on the panel.

The Custom Application Launcher option allows you to create your own application launcher for an application that doesn't appear in the menus. It uses the same dialog box as when you add a new launcher in the menu (see Figure 4-7) and allows you to select an application, a terminal session, or a specific location.

Secret

Once you place an application launcher icon in the panel, you can right-click on the icon to access a list of options for handling both the application and the application launcher icon. The Properties menu item allows you to change the command used to launch the application, such as add command line options. The Move menu item allows you to move the icon to another location on the same panel (if you want to move it to the other panel you'll need to delete it and re-create it on the other panel). You can also lock the icon into its current location on the panel by selecting the Lock to Panel menu item. Finally, you can remove the application launcher icon from the panel by selecting the Remove from Panel menu item.

The only limit to the number of application launcher icons you can have is space on the panel. Some people like to fill up the top panel with applications, while others prefer the clean look.

The Deskbar

The Deskbar applet is possibly the most useful tool in the GNOME desktop (in fact, many other Linux distributions place it in the panel by default). With this interface you can search a wealth of locations. Just a few of the items you can search are filenames, folder names, file contents, application names, web site names, and the dictionary. The Deskbar applet even allows you to link to the Yahoo! search engine to provide search results.

The Deskbar is a comparatively comprehensive search utility. If you're looking for something on your system, the Deskbar applet search utility is the way to find it. The Deskbar accomplishes all of this using plug-in extensions. Each extension adds a new location for the Deskbar to search.

After you add the Deskbar applet to your panel, just click it to bring up the search interface, shown in Figure 4-8.

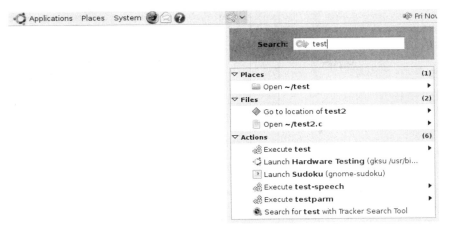

Figure 4-8: The Deskbar search applet.

Typing a word or phrase in the search text box automatically produces locations that contain that text. Clicking the entry in the results area automatically takes you to that location, either by launching the application, displaying the web site in Firefox, or opening Nautilus to display the file or folder.

Secret

You can change the order in which the Deskbar searches extensions. Right-click the Deskbar icon and select the Preferences menu item. The Deskbar Preferences dialog box appears, allowing you to disable extensions for places you don't want to search and change the order in which Deskbar uses the extensions in the search. This feature allows you to customize your searches based on what you search for the most. If you search mostly for files, then it's a waste of time having to wait for a web search to complete.

Creating a New Menu

Besides modifying an existing panel menu using the GNOME menu editor, you can create a new menu of your own for your panel. Two applets provide this feature:

- ◆ Main Menu
- ◆ Menu Bar

The Main Menu applet creates a single icon on the panel. This single icon contains the entire GNOME menu system (see "The Menu Area" section earlier in this chapter). The submenus in the Applications top-level menu are listed, along with the Places and System menus.

Once you create the main menu, you can use the GNOME menu editor to customize it. Using the techniques explained earlier in "The Menu Area" section, you can add and remove individual menu items from this panel menu.

The Menu Bar applet creates a duplicate of the default GNOME top-level menus (Applications, Places, and System). When the Menu Bar applet appears on the panel, you can customize the menu items using the menu editor.

Adding Desktop Icons

The default Ubuntu desktop workspace is empty, with no icons. Some people prefer a clean desktop, while others like the convenience of having a place to quickly access files and launch applications.

You can easily add icons for files, folders, and application launchers (shortcuts) to your desktop workspace. Right-clicking on an empty place in the workspace produces a menu that provides a few different desktop options, shown in Table 4-5.

Table 4-5: Desktop Options

Option	Description
Create Folder	Create a new folder for storing additional items
Create Launcher	Create an application launcher (shortcut) for an application or terminal session
Create Document	Create a document and place it in the desktop workspace
Clean Up by Name	Rearrange the desktop icons
Keep Aligned	Automatically align desktop icons by rows and columns
Paste	Paste a cut file or folder from Nautilus on the desktop workspace
Change Desktop Background	Change the desktop image or color

You can place new icons anywhere on the desktop you choose. The Clean Up by Name feature reorganizes the desktop to place folder icons first, then arranges application launcher and document icons alphabetically by name. If the Keep Aligned option is selected, Ubuntu aligns any icons placed near other icons using the same spacing as when it cleans up the desktop.

Secret

The Ubuntu default Create a Document feature allows you only to create a text document to place in the desktop workspace. You can add other document types by creating templates and placing them in the Template folder in your home folder.

The easiest way to do this is with the OpenOffice.org application. In OpenOffice.org you can open a blank Writer document, then save it as an ODF text document template file (with the extension .ott) in the Templates folder. Make sure you name the file using a descriptive name, because that's what appears in the Create a Document menu. When you select the template from the Create a Document menu, Ubuntu creates a new file using the template file.

After you create a file, folder, or application launcher icon on the desktop workspace, you can open the object by double-clicking it. For documents, Ubuntu automatically opens the appropriate editor for the document type. Ubuntu opens folder using the Nautilus file manager (see Chapter 5), and, for application launchers, Ubuntu starts the application.

Right-clicking a desktop icon produces a menu with several options:

- **Open:** Open the item using the default application.
- **Open with Other Application:** Select an application other than the default to open the file or folder.
- **Cut:** Remove the item from the desktop to place in another location.
- **Copy:** Copy the item to place in another location.
- **Make Link:** Create an application launcher icon pointing to the item.
- **Rename:** Assign a new name to the item.
- **Move to Trash:** Place the item in the trash for deletion.
- **Stretch Icon:** Resize the icon to make it larger.
- **Restore Icon's Original Size:** Return the icon to its normal size.
- **Send to:** Email the item using the Evolution email client.
- **Encrypt:** Use another user's public encryption key to encrypt the document or folder.
- **Sign:** Sign the document or folder using your private encryption key.
- **Create Archive:** Build an archive file including the file or folder.
- **Sharing Options:** Create a Windows share for a folder (if Windows networks sharing is installed).
- **Properties:** Display the features of the file or folder or the settings of an application launcher icon.

These options are covered in more detail in Chapter 5.

Desktop Appearance

Besides choosing objects for the desktop, you can configure the way the desktop appears. Ubuntu allows you to change several desktop features.

The main tool for controlling the look and feel of your desktop is Appearance Preferences. Start the Appearance Preferences tool by selecting System ➪ Preferences ➪ Appearance. The Appearance Preferences tool is shown in Figure 4-9.

The Appearance Preferences tool provides five tabs for controlling the look and feel of your desktop:

- Desktop Theme
- Background
- Fonts
- Interface
- Visual Effects

This section walks through how to customize your desktop to your liking using this tool.

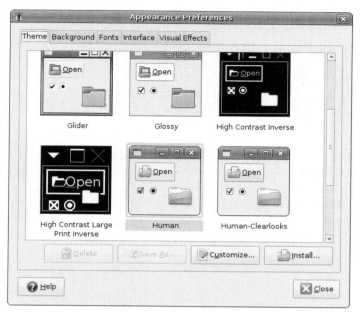

Figure 4-9: The Appearance Preferences tool.

The Desktop Theme

The Desktop Theme controls the appearance of objects on your desktop, such as check boxes, radio buttons, folder icons, and window color schemes. Ten themes are provided in Ubuntu, including high-contrast themes for people with visual impairments.

The default theme set by Ubuntu is called *human*. This produces a relaxing orange window theme on the desktop. You can select any of the themes to test and easily switch back if you decide you don't like it.

Once you select a theme, you can make additional changes to the look and feel of it. Clicking the Customize button starts the Customize Theme dialog box, shown in Figure 4-10.

The Customize Theme dialog box allows you to change the appearance of individual items such as check boxes and radio buttons, windows, windows borders, icons used for folders and documents, and the mouse pointer.

You're not stuck with only the themes provided by Ubuntu. There are several clearinghouses on the Internet for GNOME themes. One such site is http:// themes.freshmeat.net. Once there, select the GTK link to view themes available for the GNOME desktop. You'll see a plethora of creative themes available for your GNOME desktop. Just download the archived theme files to your home folder, then click the Install button on the Theme tab.

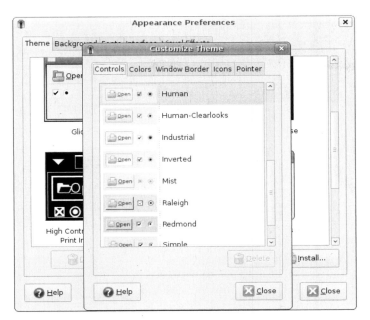

Figure 4-10: Customize a desktop theme.

The Background

The background on the desktop is an important feature because it's the thing you end up staring at the most! Ubuntu allows you to use an image as the background (called *wallpaper*) or use a color background.

The Background tab controls what's on the background of your desktop. You'll see a few images loaded by default that you can use, along with the option to select a color for the background.

You can load your own wallpaper image by following these steps:

1. Click the Add button.
2. Use the file browser to find your image file.
3. Click the Open button.

The image is imported into the backgrounds list and automatically selected as the background wallpaper.

The No Wallpaper option allows you to select a single color for the background or a gradual shading from one selected color to another color (either horizontally or vertically). GNOME has a cool color wheel that you can use to select the color, as shown in Figure 4-11.

Just click the base color from the outside wheel, then select the shading from the inner triangle.

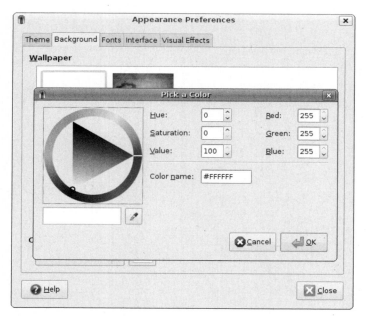

Figure 4-11: The color selection wheel.

Fonts

The Fonts tab allows you to customize the fonts Ubuntu uses for various functions within the desktop. As expected, Ubuntu provides a variety of fonts to choose from. However, one nice feature is the ability to customize how the fonts are rendered on the screen.

Clicking the Details button at the bottom of the Fonts tab page produces the Font Rendering Details dialog box, shown in Figure 4-12.

Here you can really get down to the basics of rendering fonts on your screen. Remember, though: The more detailed you make the fonts, the nicer they appear but the more processing time and power are required to display your text.

Interface

The Interface tab provides a few settings for customizing the way menus and toolbars appear in windows:

- ◆ **Show Icons in Menus**: Display icons in the menu alongside the text menu item.
- ◆ **Editable Menu Shortcut Keys**: Enable use of shortcut keystrokes to select menu options.
- ◆ **Toolbar Button Labels**: Set how toolbar items appear, either as text only, icon only, icon with text below it, or icon with text next to it.

These window settings apply to any window that uses the GNOME interface. They don't apply to applications that don't use the GNOME library, such as applications built on the KDE desktop library.

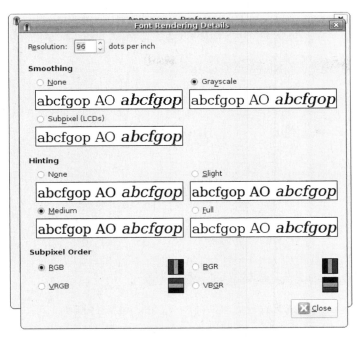

Figure 4-12: The Font Rendering Details dialog box.

Visual Effects

The Visual Effects tab allows you to select how creatively your desktop handles windows. There are three levels of effects:

- None
- Normal
- Extra

At the None level, windows appear and disappear without any special effects. At the Normal level, windows fade in when opened and fade out when closed or minimized.

If you have an advanced graphics card in your PC, you can select the Extra level of effects. This setting provides fancier effects, such as windows that melt when minimized.

Accessibility Features

Section 508 of the U.S. Rehabilitation Act specifies that all computing devices must be accessible for people with disabilities to operate. Ubuntu includes several features that enable people with disabilities to operate the desktop and applications on the workstation.

These features include screen magnifiers (enlarge areas of the screen), screen readers (read text on the screen), and keyboard and mouse assistive features (such as sticky keys and slow mouse clicks). You can enable the individual features as necessary.

Before you can use the individual accessibility features, you need to enable the accessibility features in Ubuntu. This is done using the Assistive Technologies dialog box, shown in Figure 4-13.

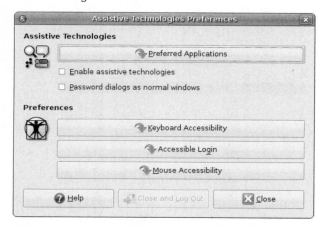

Figure 4-13: The Ubuntu Assistive Technologies dialog box.

Follow these steps to enable using the assistive technologies packages:

1. Select System ⇨ Preferences ⇨ Assistive Technologies.
2. Check the Enable Assistive Technologies check box.
3. Click the Close and Log Out button.

Ubuntu enables the assistive technologies features when you log back into the system. Once the assistive technologies features are enabled, you can start configuring the functions you require. The following sections describe the different assistive technology features you can configure.

Preferred Applications

Clicking the Preferred Applications button produces the Preferred Applications dialog box. Clicking the Accessibility tab produces two settings for features:

♦ **Visual:** tools for reading and/or magnifying the screen
♦ **Mobility:** tools for assisting in typing

There are multiple selections for each feature, and you can set the features to start automatically when the user logs in to the desktop.

Visual Tools

The two main software packages used in Ubuntu for people with visual impairments are Orca and the GNOME magnifier.

The Orca project (http://live.gnome.org/Orca) provides several options for accessing data on the screen:

♦ An audio screen reader
♦ A Braille interface
♦ A screen magnifier

When you start Orca, the screen magnifier starts and displays an enhanced version of the desktop screen, shown in Figure 4-14.

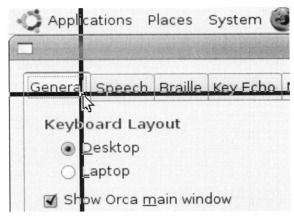

Figure 4-14: The Orca screen magnifier in action.

The screen magnifier reproduces the mouse as a large pointer in the middle of the crosshairs. You can pan the screen by moving the mouse. To select a button or other window object, place it in the crosshairs, then click the mouse button.

Secret

Orca is completely configurable. By default it uses keyboard key sequences to enable and disable features. Hitting the `Insert-spacebar` key combination produces the Orca Configuration window, where you can customize all of the Orca settings and features. To try out Orca, press the `Insert-h` key combination. This action starts the Learn Mode feature. In Learn mode, instead of performing functions, Orca displays information on what specific input events would do had Orca been activated. To exit the Learn mode, just hit the Esc key.

Typing Tools

The Ubuntu assistive technologies feature includes two types of typing helpers:

- ◆ Onboard
- ◆ Dasher

The Onboard package provides a graphical keyboard on the desktop, allowing you to use your mouse or other pointing device to select keys to type.

The Dasher package is an advanced tool that looks almost space-aged. A window appears, with letters streaming by. The idea is to click on a letter to select it. As you click on letters, Dasher uses predictive technology along with a built-in dictionary to stream letters that are most likely to appear next in line with the letters you've already selected. The creators of Dasher claim that an experienced user can "type" with a pointing device as fast as an experienced typist.

Keyboard Features

The accessibility features in the GNOME desktop also include special keyboard handling features:

- ◆ **Accessible Feature Keys:** Enable and disable the accessibility features via the keyboard.
- ◆ **Sticky Keys:** Simulate multikey presses by typing one key at a time.
- ◆ **Slow Keys:** Accept only long key presses to prevent stray key presses.
- ◆ **Bounce Keys:** Ignore duplicate key presses.

You can access the keyboard accessibility features in two ways. The first method uses the Assistive Technologies window. Just click the Keyboard Accessibility button.

The second method is to use the Keyboard Configuration tool by clicking System ⇨ Preferences ⇨ Keyboard from the Panel menu. Either way, you get the Keyboard Preferences dialog box, shown in Figure 4-15.

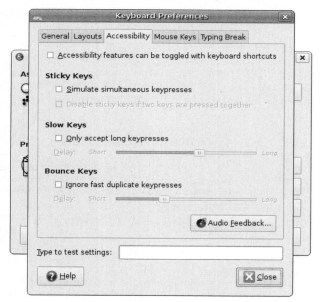

Figure 4-15: The GNOME Keyboard Preferences dialog box.

The Accessibility tab provides the settings for configuring your keyboard.

Mouse Features

To access the accessibility features for the mouse, go to the Mouse Preferences dialog box. Select System ⇨ Preferences ⇨ Mouse to produce the dialog box shown in Figure 4-16.

In the Mouse Preferences dialog box you can implement two handy features:

- ◆ **Simulated Secondary Click:** Simulate a double click by clicking once and holding down the mouse button.
- ◆ **Dwell Click:** Simulate a mouse click by stopping the mouse pointer at a location.

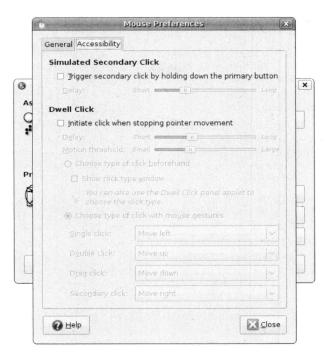

Figure 4-16: The Mouse Preferences dialog box.

The Dwell Click is ingenious. When you stop the mouse pointer, the mouse pointer turns into a crosshair. The click event that GNOME sends to the desktop (or the application) depends on how you move the mouse. The possible moves are shown in Table 4-6.

Table 4-6: Dwell Click Moves

Action	Result
Move left	Single primary click (a left-click on a right-handed mouse)
Move right	Single secondary click (a right-click on a right-handed mouse)
Move up	Double primary click
Move down	Click and drag the item

This feature allows you to control the mouse clicking without pressing any buttons.

Secret

As you might recall from the "Adding Panel Applets" section, there's a panel applet called Dwell Click. This panel applet allows you to set the Dwell Click features using buttons on the panel instead of the Mouse Preferences dialog box.

Summary

This chapter discussed the GNOME desktop used by Ubuntu. It walked through the three different sections of the desktop. The top panel contains the main GNOME menu, providing easy access to all of the applications and utilities installed on the Ubuntu workstation. The desktop workspace provides a location for you to place icons for quick access to files, folders, and shortcuts to start applications.

The bottom panel provides the desktop viewer, which allows you to quickly minimize and maximize running application windows; and the taskbar area, which displays an icon for each window application running on the desktop. You can control an application from its taskbar icon. Finally, the workspace switcher provides an easy way to change between the two workspaces provided by Ubuntu.

You can change all of the default desktop settings in Ubuntu. The chapter showed how to add menu items to the menus and add panel items such as panel applets. A variety of panel applet utilities are available and provide just about any type of information you might need directly on the panel.

The next section in the chapter discussed the desktop appearance and showed how to modify the basic appearance of your desktop. It showed how to change the background to your favorite image, as well as how to change the look and feel of the windows and window objects used on the desktop.

Finally, the chapter discussed the accessibility features in the GNOME desktop. There are quite a few advanced features that you can use, such as the Orca screen reader and magnification and the Dasher visual keyboard. The chapter closed by showing how to set the accessibility features on the mouse to provide for buttonless clicking to simulate any type of mouse click required in an application window.

The next section gets into the actual applications installed on the Ubuntu workstation. In the next chapter you'll see how to use the default file management package, Nautilus, to navigate around your Ubuntu system and manage your files and folders.

Part 2

Starting Out with Ubuntu

File Management

Chapter
5

◆ ◆

Secrets in This Chapter

The Linux Filesystem

Using Nautilus

Handling Files

File Properties

◆ ◆

Ⅰf you've never used Linux before, trying to understand and manage the file structure can be a bit of a challenge. The Ubuntu workstation includes some tools to help with handling files, which makes life easier for novices and advanced users alike. The first part of this chapter discusses how Ubuntu handles hard drives and files so that you can figure out where your files and folders are. The second part of the chapter walks through Nautilus, the graphical file management tool provided in Ubuntu. The Nautilus application helps you navigate through the complicated Ubuntu filesystem and makes working with your files and folders much easier.

The Linux Filesystem

If you're new to the Linux system, you may be confused by how it references files and directories, especially if you're used to the way the Microsoft Windows operating system does that. Before exploring the Linux system, it helps to have an understanding of how it's laid out.

Filepaths

The first difference you'll notice is that Linux does not use drive letters in pathnames. In the Windows world, the physical drives installed on the PC determine the pathname of the file. Windows assigns a letter to each physical disk drive, and each drive contains its own directory structure for accessing files stored on it.

For example, in Windows you may be used to seeing filepaths such as `C:\Documents and Settings\Rich\My Documents\test.doc`.

This indicates that the file `test.doc` is located in the directory `My Documents`, which is under the directory `Rich`, which is contained under the directory `Documents and Settings`, which is located on the hard disk partition assigned the letter `C` (usually the first hard drive on the PC).

The Windows filepath tells you exactly which physical disk partition contains the file named `test.doc`. If you want to save a file on a floppy disk, you would click the icon for the `A` drive, which automatically uses the filepath `A:\test.doc`. This path indicates that the file is located at the root of the drive assigned the letter `A`, which is usually the PC's floppy disk drive.

This is not the method used by Linux. Linux stores files within a single directory structure, called a *virtual directory*. The virtual directory contains filepaths from all the storage devices installed on the PC, merged into a single directory structure.

The Linux virtual directory structure contains a single base directory, called the *root*. Directories and files beneath the root directory are listed based on the directory path used to reach them, similar to the way Windows does it.

Secret   You'll notice that Linux uses a forward slash (/) instead of a backward slash (\) to denote directories in filepaths. The backslash character in Linux denotes an escape character and causes all sorts of problems when you use it in a filepath. This may take some getting used to if you're coming from a Windows environment.

For example, the Linux filepath /home/rich/Documents/test.doc indicates that the file test.doc is in the directory Documents, under the directory rich, which is contained in the directory home. It doesn't provide any information about which physical disk on the PC the file is stored on.

The tricky part about the Linux virtual directory is how it incorporates each storage device. The first hard drive installed in a Linux PC is called the *root drive*. The root drive contains the core, or root, of the virtual directory. Everything else builds from there.

On the root drive, Linux creates special directories called *mount points*. Mount points are directories in the virtual directory structure where you assign additional storage devices.

The virtual directory causes files and directories to appear within these mount point directories, even though they are physically stored on a different drive.

Often the system files are physically stored on the root drive, while user files are stored on a different drive, as shown in Figure 5-1.

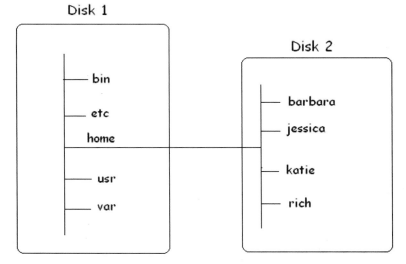

Figure 5-1: The Linux file structure.

As shown in Figure 5-1, there are two hard drives on the PC. One hard drive is associated with the root of the virtual directory (indicated by a single forward slash). Other hard drives can be mounted anywhere in the virtual directory structure. In this example, the second hard drive is mounted at the location /home, which is where the user directories are located.

The Linux filesystem structure has evolved from the UNIX file structure. Unfortunately, the UNIX file structure has been convoluted over the years by different flavors of UNIX. These days it seems that no two UNIX or Linux systems follow the same filesystem structure. However, a few common directory names are used for the same functions. Ubuntu makes use of many of the common UNIX directory names. Table 5-1 lists the directories you'll see by default in the Ubuntu virtual filesystem.

TABLE 5-1: Ubuntu Directory Names

Directory	Usage
/	The root of the virtual directory. Normally, no files are placed here
/bin	The binary directory, where many GNU user-level utilities are stored
/boot	The boot directory, where boot files are stored
/dev	The device directory, where Linux creates device nodes
/etc	The system configuration files directory
/home	The home directory, where Linux creates user directories
/initrd	Location of files used during the boot process if a RAM disk is required
/lib	The library directory, where system and application library files are stored
/lost+found	Directory where lost filesystem nodes are stored. If your disk crashes, look here for missing files
/media	Mount point used to mount external disks in the virtual directory
/mnt	The mount directory, a common place for mount points used for removable media
/opt	The optional directory, often used to store optional software packages
/proc	Controlled by the kernel, this special directory provides information about internal kernel processes and can be used to send information to the kernel
/root	The root home directory
/sbin	The system binary directory, where the GNU admin-level utilities are stored
/srv	Used as a base directory on the Ubuntu server platform for data that is served to others, such as web pages
/sys	Similar to the /proc directory, used by the newer Linux kernel to communicate with plug-in kernel modules
/tmp	The temporary directory, where temporary work files can be created and destroyed
/usr	The user-installed software directory
/var	The variable directory, for files that require write privileges, such as log files

In addition to the way it handles pathnames, Ubuntu has a way of handling filenames that might differ from what you might be used to in Windows. The next section discusses this feature of Ubuntu.

Filenames

In the old days of Windows (such as in the popular versions 3.0 and 3.1), there were strict limitations on what you could name your files. The standard in Windows was called the *8.3 format*. This format prescribed

♦ An eight-character name that couldn't use spaces or many special characters

♦ A period

♦ A three-character file extension, usually consisting of letters

In Windows the file extension determined the type of file the filename referred to. Application files that could be run on the system had to have file extensions of .exe or .com. Text script files used a file extension of .bat. Data files for individual applications also had their own file extension. If you used the Microsoft Office productivity software suite, Word documents ended in .doc, Excel documents ended in .xls, and PowerPoint documents ended in .ppt.

Newer versions of Windows did away with the 8.3 file naming format. You can now use any length of filename and almost about any characters you wish. However, Windows did retain the three-character file extension as part of the filename. The extension still indicates the type of file so that Windows knows how to handle it.

Ubuntu (and Linux in general) doesn't require file extensions on files per se, but it does utilize them. Executable files in Ubuntu are marked by a permissions setting on the file (see Chapter 17, "Users and Groups"). They don't require any special file extension on the filename.

There is one special category of files in Ubuntu that's important to know. Files that begin with a period are called *hidden files*. Hidden files are configuration files used for various applications, as well as the Linux operating system itself. They're called *hidden* because the default way of handling the files, whether using graphical or command line tools, is to ignore files that begin with a period. To view hidden files you need to set your file management program to display them (see Chapter 19, "The Ubuntu Command Line").

In the Windows world you're used to using graphical tools to manage files and folders. Ubuntu also contains a graphical tool, called Nautilus, that you can use to manage your files and folders. The next section describes the Nautilus tool and how to use it.

Nautilus

The Nautilus application is a GNOME utility that provides access to files and folders using a graphical interface. Ubuntu uses Nautilus for all desktop file management functions. To get the most out of your Ubuntu desktop, you'll need to know how to use Nautilus. The following sections describe Nautilus and how to perform most common file management features with it.

Nautilus Window Components

The default Nautilus mode used by Ubuntu is Browser mode. In Browser mode, Nautilus operates much like a web browser. Figure 5-2 shows viewing a folder in Browser mode.

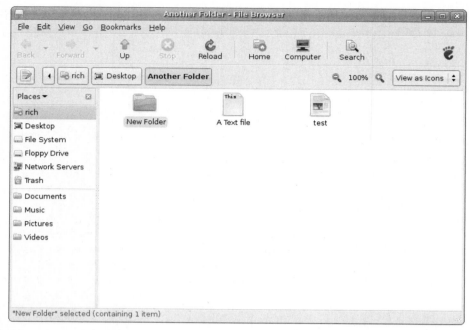

Figure 5-2: Viewing a folder in Nautilus Browser mode.

The main window in Browser mode contains six separate sections:

- ◆ A menu bar at the top
- ◆ A toolbar
- ◆ A location bar
- ◆ A left pane
- ◆ The View pane
- ◆ A status bar at the bottom

Let's do a quick review of each of these areas to become familiar with Nautilus.

The Top Menu Bar

The top menu bar contains menu links to various functions in Nautilus. It consists of the following items:

- ◆ **File:** Contains links to functions related to handling files and folders in the folder window. The links are divided into five sections:
  - • Functions that create new files and folders
  - • Functions that open a folder using either spatial or Browser mode, or open a file using an application
  - • Functions that open the parent folder or a new location
  - • Functions that display the properties of the file or folder
  - • Functions that close the parent folder, all folders, or the entire Spatial Mode window

◆ **Edit:** Contains links to functions that modify existing files and folders in the folder window. These links are divided into seven categories that allow you to
  - Implement the cut/copy/paste feature to manage files and folders
  - Select all or a subset of files and folders in the folder
  - Create a new link to the file or folder or rename an existing file or folder
  - Delete the selected files or folders by moving them to the trash
  - Manage icon size
  - Perform additional functions on the files and folders
  - Configure the Nautilus Spatial Mode window environment

◆ **View:** Sets the viewing features in the Spatial Mode window. These links let you
  - Refresh (reload) the items in the window
  - Reset the Spatial Mode window settings or view hidden files
  - Modify how Nautilus displays files in the window
  - Modify the size of items in the window
  - Select Icon or List View mode via radio buttons

◆ **Go:** Provides links to jump to specific locations in the virtual filesystem, as well as to remote locations, just like the Places menu item on the panel (see Chapter 4, "Exploring the Desktop"). It also contains a history list of past folder locations you've visited so you can quickly move between folders.

◆ **Bookmarks:** Like a web browser, Nautilus allows you to bookmark locations in the virtual filesystem. Jumping back to a specific location is as easy as selecting the bookmark.

◆ **Help:** Provides links to the Nautilus Help window.

Under the top menu area, there's a toolbar area that provides quick access to several features.

The Toolbar

The toolbar used in Nautilus Browser mode allows you to quickly navigate around the virtual filesystem by selecting individual tool buttons. There are three standard navigation buttons used on the toolbar:

◆ **Back:** Navigate to a previous folder that you've accessed.

◆ **Forward:** Navigate forward to a folder you've accessed but then moved back from.

◆ **Up:** Navigate to the parent folder of the current folder.

Besides these quick navigation buttons that can move you relative to your current location, the toolbar also includes two location-specific navigation buttons:

◆ **Home:** Jump to your home folder.

◆ **Computer:** View individual filesystems on the computer, such as hard drives, USB Memory Sticks, floppy disks, and CD/DVD drives.

The Reload button is used to refresh the window area if you've just copied a new file or folder to the area and it hasn't shown up yet. The Stop button allows you to stop Nautilus from inventorying files and folders in the folder. This button is handy if you accidentally navigate to a folder with many files and folders.

The Search button uses the quick search feature in Nautilus. A search bar appears in the location bar area, allowing you to enter a file or folder name for Nautilus to look for. Figure 5-3 shows the results of performing a search for a file named test.

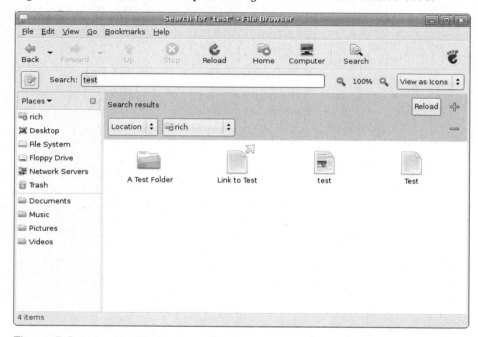

Figure 5-3: Using the Nautilus search feature to find a file.

Notice that the search returned not only the file called test, but also a file called Test, a link with Test in the name, and a folder with Test in the name.

The Location Bar

The location bar normally contains two items. The first item is a graphical representation of the filepath, called the *button bar*. Each folder in the filepath of your current location is represented as a separate button. Click the individual buttons to jump to the corresponding folder in the path.

Secret The buttons in the button bar are also draggable. You can click and drag a folder button to a new location (in the same or a different Nautilus window) to copy that folder.

The Toggle button on the far left side of the location bar allows you to toggle the path display between the button bar and the *text location bar.* The text location bar displays the path using text, such as /home/rich/Desktop.

In the text location bar you can enter a specific path in the virtual filesystem to jump directly to that location. This feature allows you to type a location to view instead of having to browse your way there.

As you learned in "The Toolbar" section, if you click the Search button in the toolbar, the location bar turns into the search bar.

On the right side of the location bar are two items, Zoom buttons, and the View-as drop-down list.

The View-as drop-down list allows you to select the viewing mode Nautilus uses in the Browser View pane to display files and folders. There are two viewing modes:

♦ **Icon view:** displays files and folders as icons
♦ **List view:** displays files and folders as a text list

In Icon view, objects appear as large icons with labels beneath them. There is an icon for folders and another one for files. The folder icon is the same design for all folders, but file icons can differ.

Nautilus attempts to detect what application to use to open a file and displays an icon accordingly. For text documents, Nautilus actually displays part of the text content from the file directly on the icon. For image files, Nautilus displays a thumbnail of the image. This feature allows you to easily browse through documents and images in Nautilus without having to open the files to see what's inside.

In List view, Nautilus displays files and folders as a list, similar to what you're used to seeing if you use Windows Explorer. Figure 5-4 demonstrates viewing a folder in List view.

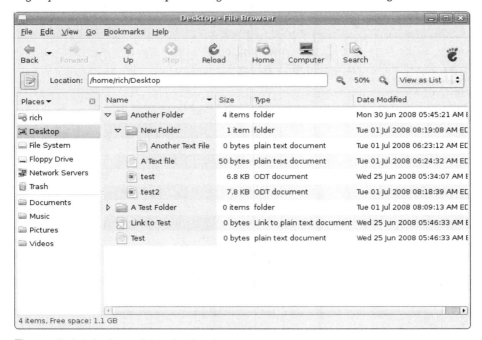

Figure 5-4: Viewing a folder in List view.

One neat feature in List view that you won't see in Windows Explorer is the ability to expand each folder in List view to see its contents. The contents appear in the list under the parent folder, slightly indented from other files and folders. You can continue expanding subfolders the same way.

In List view, Nautilus displays additional information about the file that doesn't appear in Icon view. By default, the size, type of file, and modification date are shown in the list. You can easily change what information appears in List view (discussed in the "Modifying Nautilus Windows" section later in this chapter).

Secret   Use the Zoom buttons to increase the size of the file icons to get a better glimpse of what's inside the files. The Zoom buttons also work when in List view, making the font larger for the file and folder names.

The Left Pane

The left pane in Browser mode provides a few different features for working with files and folders. The top drop-down bar in the left pane allows you to select the specific feature to use. The features available in the left pane are shown in Table 5-2.

Table 5-2: Nautilus Left Pane Features

Feature	Description
Places	Provides links to specific places in the virtual filesystem
Information	Provides information about the current folder level displayed in Nautilus
Tree	Displays a drop-down tree of folders in the path
History	Displays a list of past folders you've viewed
Notes	Allows you to set notes for a particular folder level
Emblems	Allows you to select emblems that tag folders for easy identification

The default feature is the Places feature. It provides quick links to specific places in the virtual filesystem, much like the Places menu in the top panel (see Chapter 4).

The Tree feature makes Nautilus look similar to Windows Explorer. You can select folders from the Tree view, and they expand to show any subfolders contained within. Clicking a folder brings the folder contents up in the window area.

The Emblems feature allows you to assign special icons to a folder from a list of more than 40 icons. Emblem icons help you easily identify special folders, as well as tag folders that have special features, such as shared folders.

The Status Bar

The status bar in Nautilus Browser mode, located at the bottom of the window, provides information about the files in the folder being viewed. The status bar displays the number of files and folders in the current folder, along with the amount of disk space remaining on the system.

You can hide any of the Nautilus Browser mode components (with the exception of the main View pane) to expand your viewing area. Just click the View menu bar item, then click the component you want to hide. Components that are active have a check mark next to them. To show a component, just select it from the menu.

Browser Versus Spatial Mode

In the default Browser mode used in Ubuntu, Nautilus displays all of the file and folder information in the same window, much like a web browser. In Spatial mode, Nautilus uses a single window for each folder, creating a new window each time you open a new folder.

tip To use Nautilus in Spatial mode, you need to change the behavior setting. Select Edit from the menu bar, then select Preferences from the Edit menu. In the Preferences dialog box, select the Behavior tab at the top, then remove the check mark from the box labeled Always Open in Browser Window.

In Spatial mode, Nautilus doesn't provide much in the way of help or navigation. If you click on a folder, a separate Nautilus Spatial Mode window opens, with the contents of the folder. Because the parent window remains open, navigating through a series of folders and subfolders in Spatial mode can quickly fill up your desktop.

It's called *Spatial mode* because Ubuntu places each new window in a specific location (space) on the desktop. If you move a Spatial mode window to a new location (space) on the desktop, the next time you open that same folder level, the Spatial mode window opens in that same space. This feature allows you to arrange windows on the desktop as you prefer, and they'll always return to the same location when you open a folder.

The Spatial mode window contains only a menu bar, the View pane, and the status bar, as shown in Figure 5-5.

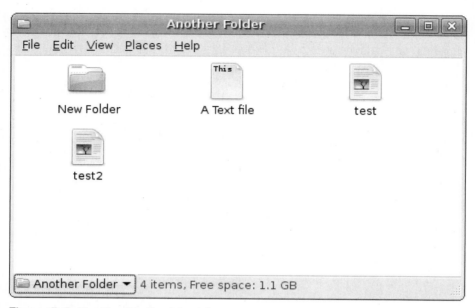

Figure 5-5: The Nautilus Spatial mode.

The menu bar in Spatial mode contains most of the same entries as in Browser mode. However, instead of the Go and Bookmark entries used in Browser mode, the Spatial mode menu bar uses the Places menu entry. The Places menu entry works exactly as the Places menu item in the Panel menu.

You'll notice that the bottom status bar in the Spatial mode window contains two items:

- ◆ A drop-down list of parent folders. You can select any of the parent folders in the list and jump to that location.
- ◆ Status information on the number of items and the amount of free space available in the folder.

The drop-down list is similar to the location bar in Browser mode. Clicking on the drop-down list produces a list of folders in the path of the current folder, starting at the root folder. You can select any of the folders to open a new Spatial mode window at that location.

Although Spatial mode doesn't include the View-as options, you can still switch between Icon and List view using the View menu bar item. Just select the Icon or List view items from the menu. There are also options for changing the icon or font size, just like the Zoom button in the Browser Mode window.

Modifying Nautilus Windows

You can easily customize the look and feel of Nautilus to suit your needs. Simply select Edit ⇨ Preferences from the top menu. The main Preferences dialog box appears, as shown in Figure 5-6.

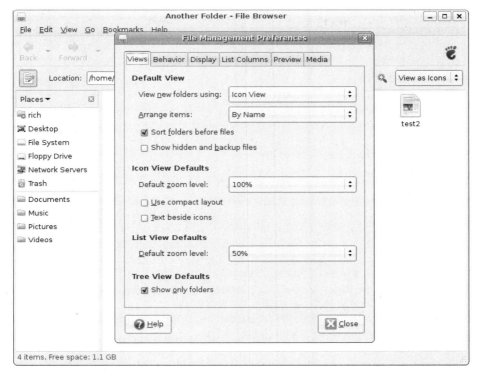

Figure 5-6: The Nautilus Preferences dialog box.

There are six tabs in the Preferences dialog box for altering how Nautilus displays file and folder information. The following sections describe each of these tabs and the settings available on them.

The Views Tab

The Views tab contains settings for how items appear in the View pane. It includes settings for both Icon and List views:

◆ **View New Folders:** Sets the default view to Icon or List view.
◆ **Arrange Items:** Sets how Nautilus displays icons in the View pane, either by name, size, type, modification date, or emblems added to the icon.
◆ **Sort Folders Before Files:** When checked, folders are sorted first in the View pane, by the Arrange Items setting, then files are sorted. When not checked, all items are sorted by the Arrange Item setting.
◆ **Show Hidden and Backup Files:** Displays files starting with a period or with a .tarfile extension.
◆ **Icon Default Zoom Level:** Sets the default icon size in Icon view. Set to 100 percent by default.
◆ **Use Compact Layout:** When checked, reduces the amount of space between icons in Icon View mode.

◆ **Text Beside Icons:** Places filename and other information next to the file or folder icon instead of beneath the icon.

◆ **List Default Zoom Level:** Sets the default font size in List view. Set to 50 percent by default.

◆ **Show Only Folders:** In the left pane in Tree mode, displays only folders in the tree, not files.

These settings affect the Nautilus window, as well as the desktop file and folder icons. Changing these settings has an immediate effect on the existing icons.

The Behavior Tab

The Behavior tab controls how Nautilus responds to actions when clicking file icons or text in the View pane and on the desktop. The options available to set in this tab are

◆ **Single-Click to Open Items** and **Double-Click to Open Items:** Radio buttons indicate whether files open using a single-click or a double-click.

◆ **Always Open in Browser Windows:** When checked, Nautilus windows open in Browser mode. When not checked, Nautilus windows open in Spatial mode.

◆ **Run Executable Text Files When They Are Opened:** When clicking on a text file, run the file as a shell script using Terminal.

◆ **View Executable Text Files When They Are Opened:** When clicking on a shell script text file, open the file in a text editor.

◆ **Ask Each Time:** When clicking on a shell script text file, ask whether you want to run the file or open it in a text editor.

◆ **Ask Before Emptying the Trash or Deleting Files:** When clicking the Empty Trash button, ask before deleting files in the trash folder.

◆ **Include a Delete Command That Bypasses Trash:** Adds an item to the right-click menu to delete the file instead of sending to trash.

Secret

The single-click option allows you to launch applications and open files by single-clicking rather than double-clicking. This mode can be dangerous, and you must be careful when selecting a file for copying or deleting. To select a file without opening it, hold down the Ctrl key before clicking the file.

The Display Tab

The Display tab controls how Nautilus displays file and folder information when in Icon View mode. When Icon view is at 100 percent zoom level, by default all you see is the name of the file or folder. If you use the Zoom button (or View ⇨ Zoom from the menu bar) to zoom in closer, you see additional information about the file at different zoom values. There are three zoom levels at which Nautilus provides information about the icon item:

◆ The 50 percent zoom level

◆ The 150 percent zoom level

◆ The 400 percent zoom level

When the View pane reaches these zoom levels, Nautilus displays the file or folder information set for that level. On the Display tab you specify which information displays at each of these zoom levels. There are three drop-down boxes used to specify what information is shown at what zoom level. The file information you can display is shown in Table 5-3.

Table 5-3: Zoom-Level Information

Setting	Description
None	Don't display any additional information
Size	Display the file size or total folder size using bytes, KB, MB, or GB units, depending on the size
Type	Display the basic file type as detected by Nautilus
Date Modified	Display the date and time the file was last modified
Date Accessed	Display the date and time the file was last accessed by a user
Owner	Display the owner setting
Group	Display the group setting
Permissions	Display the file access permissions using text format
Octal Permissions	Display the file access permissions using a four-digit octal number
MIME type	Display the full MIME-compatible type format
SELinux Context	Display the Secure Linux context assigned to the file or folder

You can set up any of these information items at any of the three zoom levels. The Display tab also allows you to set the format Nautilus uses to display the date and time (if those options are selected for display) using three formats:

- ◆ Wed 02 Jul 2008 06:04:34 AM EDT
- ◆ 2008-07-02 06:04:34
- ◆ today at 6:04:34 AM

The first format is the standard UNIX date and time format. The second format uses a more compact date and time format. The last format uses standard text nomenclature to indicate the age of the file. It uses the language setting for the Ubuntu system to display terms such as today, yesterday, and last week.

The List Columns Tab

The List Columns tab contains settings used in the List View mode. You can control what file and folder information appears in the List View display. These settings are the same as listed in Table 5-3 for zoom level. The default settings that appear in List View mode are

- ◆ Name
- ◆ Size
- ◆ Type
- ◆ Date modified

You can create any combination of information settings to appear in List View mode by selecting the appropriate values in this tab.

The Preview Tab

The Preview tab controls how files are previewed in Icon View mode. In Icon View mode, Nautilus can show the contents of the file within the icon. This feature is helpful (unless it takes an inordinate amount of time for Nautilus to show the contents, as explained in the Preview Settings option list that follows). Preview settings allow you to change how Nautilus handles different types of files in Icon View mode. There are three preview options for each file type:

- ◆ **Always:** Always display the contents in the icon, even on a slow media such as a remote network server.
- ◆ **Local Files Only:** Display contents in the icon only if the file or folder is on the local system.
- ◆ **Never:** Never display the contents in the icon.

The file types for which you can configure Preview settings are

- ◆ **Text files:** Files that Nautilus identifies as containing only text
- ◆ **Other previewable files:** Used primarily for OpenOffice.org files and image files. You can also set a size limit, because you might not want to display a thumbnail of an image file that could take a long time to load.
- ◆ **Sound files:** Any type of audio file, such as `.ogg`.
- ◆ **Folders:** Calculates the number of files in the folder.

Secret

If you have lots of files and folders on remote network servers, it's usually not a good idea to allow Nautilus to preview them in the Icon view. Doing so can unnecessarily use network bandwidth, as well as take a long time.

The Media Tab

The Media tab controls how Nautilus launches applications for various types of media disks placed in the CD/DVD drive. Nautilus can automatically detect the media type and launch an application based on the type of media inserted.

You can specify which applications to run when you insert a specific type of CD or DVD into your CD/DVD drive, saving you the hassle of finding the application yourself.

For each category of media you can select one of four actions:

- ◆ **Ask What to Do:** Always display a dialog box prompting you for an action.
- ◆ **Do Nothing:** Ubuntu doesn't do anything when you insert media into the CD/DVD drive.
- ◆ **Open Folder:** Open the media contents in a new Nautilus window.
- ◆ **Open Using a Specific Application:** Assign an application to open the inserted media.

For each media type, Nautilus provides you with the applications you can use to open it. You can select the application you want to use for the various CD and DVD media types. Table 5-4 lists the different media types and their default applications.

Table 5-4: Default Applications for Opening Media Types

Media Type	Application
Audio CD	Open Rhythmbox music player
Video DVD	Open movie player
Music CD or DVD	Open Rhythmbox music player
Photo CD or DVD	Open F-Spot photo manager
Software CD or DVD	Open autorun prompt
Blank Blu-Ray Disc	Open CD/DVD Creator
Blank CD Disc	Open CD/DVD Creator
Blank DVD Disc	Open CD/DVD Creator
Blank HD-DVD Disc	Open CD/DVD Creator
Blu-Ray Video	No applications installed
DVD Audio	Open Rhythmbox music player
HD DVD Video	Open movie player
Picture CD	Open F-Spot photo manager
Super Video CD	Open movie player
Video CD	Open movie player

Table 5-4 shows, for example, that if you place any type of blank CD or DVD media in the drive, Ubuntu will start the CD/DVD Creator application (see "Burning Files to CD" later in this chapter).

Handling Files

In addition to its use for viewing and accessing files, Nautilus provides a graphical interface for just about all your file management needs. The following sections walk you through how to work with files and folders using the Nautilus graphical interface.

Creating New Files and Folders

At some point you'll want to quickly create a new text file or a new folder on your Ubuntu system. To create a file in Nautilus,

1. Navigate to the folder where you want to create the file or folder.

You must have the folder in your View pane before you can create the file or new folder there.

2. Right-click on an empty space in the View pane.

   Be careful not to click on an existing object in the View pane. If you do, the Object menu appears rather than the menu to create a new object.

3. Select Create Folder or Create Document.

4. Type the name of the item you want to create.

Selecting the Create Document option opens a submenu that lists the types of files you can create. The list includes any template files you have in your Templates folder (see Chapter 4) for creating a specific type of file, plus an option to create an empty text file.

Copying and Moving Files

There are three ways to copy or move a file in Nautilus. If you're familiar with Microsoft Windows or the Apple Macintosh you'll know about dragging and dropping. Nautilus supports these methods to copy and move files:

♦ Drag and drop to move a file or folder from one location to another. Hold down the primary mouse button over the item's icon (in Icon view) or name (in List view) and move the mouse pointer while continuing to hold down the mouse button. Release the mouse button when the file or folder is in the new location. You can do this within the same Nautilus window or between separate windows. You can also move a file or folder from a Nautilus window to the desktop area.

♦ If you're using Nautilus in Browser mode, you can open Tree view in the left pane to drag and drop files and folders to any folder listed in the tree.

♦ Hold the Ctrl key and drag and drop the file icon or name to create a copy of the file or folder in the new location, keeping the original in place. As when moving a file or folder, you can copy the file to any folder in the same Nautilus window or between Nautilus windows (including the desktop).

Nautilus also supports cut and paste or copy and paste for handling files from the File menu. Here are the steps required to perform a cut or copy:

1. Right-click on file or folder.

2. Select Cut to move the file or Copy to copy the file.

   If you select Cut, the file doesn't disappear from the View pane until you've placed it in the new location. Don't expect the file to disappear immediately from the original location.

3. Navigate to the folder where you want to place the file.

   As with the drag and drop method, you can right-click on a folder in the Nautilus window, a folder in the left pane in Tree view, or on the desktop.

4. Right-click in an empty space and select Paste.

Nautilus provides a quick and easy way to perform all of your file management functions.

Running Programs

Nautilus gives you the ability to launch applications directly from the files you have in your folders. Ubuntu configures Nautilus to automatically detect the most common file types used and to launch the appropriate application.

To launch an application for a known file type, just single- or double-click the file (depending on the Nautilus setting). You can also right-click on a file to open the Action menu and choose one of the following:

  ♦ **Open with Default Program:** launches the application associated with the file type, as if you had clicked the file
  ♦ **Open with Other Application:** allows you to select another application to launch to open the file

If you choose to open the file using another application, a dialog box appears with a list of the installed applications that Ubuntu knows about, as shown in Figure 5-7.

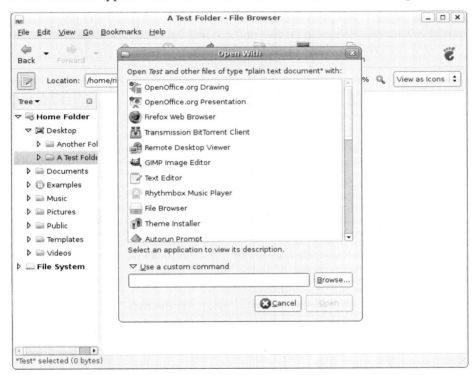

Figure 5-7: The Nautilus Open With dialog box.

If you don't find the application you want to use in the list, click the Use a Custom Command arrow, and a text box and button appear. You have two options for selecting the application:

  ♦ Type the full pathname of the application in the text box.
  ♦ Click the Browse button to browse the filesystem for the application file.

Once you select an application, click the Open button to launch the selected file in that application.

Deleting Files

Eventually you'll want to remove files from your system. Here's how to delete files and folders using Nautilus:

1. Navigate so that the file or directory you want to delete is in the View pane.
2. Select the item:

   To delete an individual file or folder, single-click on the item to select it.

   To delete a sequential group of files or folders, hold down the Shift key and select the first file, then while still holding the Shift key select the last file.

   To delete a random group of files or folders, hold down the Ctrl key and select the individual files or folders you want to delete.
3. Press the Delete key or right-click and select Move to Trash

Secret

If you find yourself moving items to the trash only to just turn around and immediately empty the trash, you can add the Delete item to the list of actions by setting that feature in the Nautilus Preferences dialog box. See "The Behavior Tab" section in this chapter for instructions.

File Properties

Ubuntu keeps track of specific properties for each file and folder on the system. Nautilus provides an easy interface to view and modify these properties. When you right-click on a file or folder in Nautilus, select the Properties menu to access the Properties dialog box, shown in Figure 5-8.

You can view and set most of the properties directly from this dialog box. Five separate tabs provide access to various properties:

- Basic
- Emblems
- Permissions
- Open With
- Notes

The following sections discuss each of these tab areas.

Basic Properties

The Basic Properties tab shows the core properties associated with the file or folder. All of the standard information related to the file is shown on this page:

- The filename
- The type of the file as detected by Nautilus

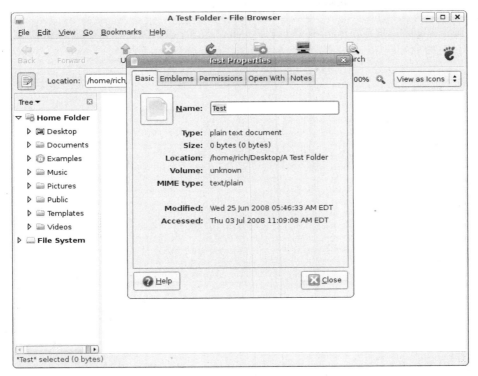

Figure 5-8: The Properties dialog box from Nautilus.

- ◆ The size of the file
- ◆ The full path of the file
- ◆ The disk volume that contains the file
- ◆ The MIME type of the file
- ◆ The date and time the file was last modified
- ◆ The date and time the file was last accessed

Of these elements, the filename is the only thing you can change. The rest of the properties are detected by Nautilus and displayed on the page.

Emblems

The Emblems tab produces a list of various icons you can associate with the file, as shown in Figure 5-9.

As you select an emblem, it appears on top of the icon in Nautilus or on the desktop if the file or folder icon is on the desktop. Emblems help you tag special files and folders so you can easily recognize them as you browse through your virtual filesystem.

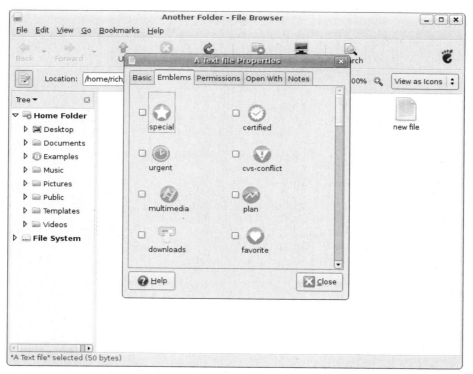

Figure 5-9: The Emblems tab in the Properties dialog box.

Permissions

No discussion of file management in Linux is complete without talking about *file permissions.* The Ubuntu system uses file permissions to restrict access to files and folders. This feature allows you to keep others from viewing or deleting your files and folders, and it also provides a way for you to share files and folders with others.

Chapter 17, "Users and Groups," goes into great detail about how to create the permissions to control and share files or folders. However, in our discussion of Nautilus we should take a quick peek at how Nautilus displays file and folder permissions.

The Permissions tab, shown in Figure 5-10, shows the current settings for the file or folder.

As discussed in Chapter 17, Ubuntu uses three permissions groups for controlling access to files and folders:

- ◆ The owner of the file or folder
- ◆ A group assigned to the file or folder
- ◆ Anyone else on the system (others)

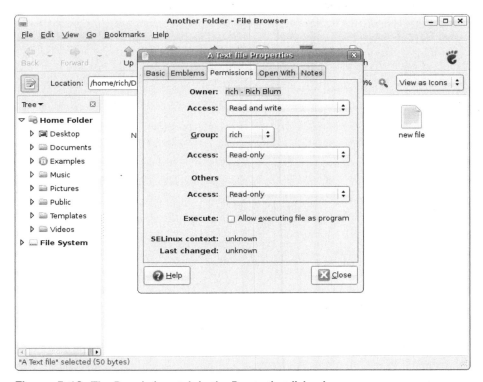

Figure 5-10: The Permissions tab in the Properties dialog box.

For each of these three permission groups there are three settings for control:

- ◆ None (not allowed for the file owner)
- ◆ Read-only
- ◆ Read and write

By default, the owner of the file has read and write permissions, and the group and others are set to read-only. You can easily change the default group for the file or folder, as well as the permission settings, in the Permissions tab.

Secret

The Permissions tab also contains a check box to indicate when the file is an executable script program file. By checking this box you can run the script file by simply double-clicking it in Nautilus. However, even when the executable program check box is checked, Nautilus asks you whether you want to view the file or run it, as shown in Figure 5-11.

continues

continued

Figure 5-11: The View or Run dialog box.

The dialog box also gives you the option of running the script file inside a Terminal session or directly from the desktop.

Open With

Nautilus uses file extensions to identify some types of files, and the application it uses to open them. However, this doesn't always work. Nautilus also attempts to detect the file type by reading the first few bytes contained in the file.

Ubuntu uses file extensions to identify some types of files, but Nautilus attempts to detect the file type by reading the first few bytes contained in the file.

The Open With tab allows you to change the default application Nautilus uses or to add other options for opening the file. Just click the Add button, then either scroll through the list of installed applications or select the command textbox drop-down arrow and enter your own program.

Notes

The Notes section is a convenient place for you to add notes about a file or folder. Ubuntu keeps the notes with the file or folder properties; you can display them by going to the Properties dialog box. When you create a note for a file or folder, Nautilus adds a note emblem to the file or folder icon and activates the Urgent emblem, as shown in Figure 5-12.

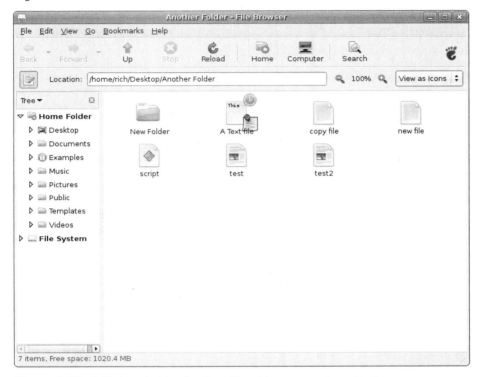

Figure 5-12: A file icon in Nautilus for a file with a note assigned to it.

You can edit or remove the note using the Notes section.

Summary

This chapter walked through the world of file management in Ubuntu. Ubuntu uses the Linux filesystem, which combines all storage devices into a single virtual filesystem. You can mount devices anywhere in the virtual filesystem as directories. Ubuntu provides a / media directory for mounting external storage devices, such as floppy disks, USB Memory Sticks, and CD/DVD drives.

The default file management tool in Ubuntu is Nautilus. Nautilus provides a graphical way to manage files by creating, copying, deleting, moving, and renaming files and folders. Nautilus can display files and folders using either a graphical Icon View mode or a more text-oriented List View mode. You can perform the same functions in either mode.

The Nautilus window itself can also be customized. You can use Nautilus in Browser mode, which works like a web browser, to navigate through the virtual filesystem, double-clicking folders to open them and view their contents. Nautilus also supports the Spatial mode, which is a more bare-bones operation. In Spatial mode you view the files and folders in a single window without many bells and whistles. Double-clicking a folder in Spatial mode opens a new Nautilus window that contains the contents of the folder.

The next chapter deals with the topic of text files. Text files are a crucial part of any operating system, whether they are configuration files, log files, program script files, or just data files. It's important to know how to handle text files to get the most out of your Ubuntu experience. In the next chapter you'll see the various ways Ubuntu allows you to work with text files.

Working With Text

Chapter
6

◆ ◆ ◆ ◆ ◆ ◆ ◆ ◆ ◆ ◆ ◆ ◆ ◆ ◆ ◆ ◆ ◆ ◆ ◆ ◆

Secrets in This Chapter

◆ ◆ ◆ ◆ ◆ ◆ ◆ ◆ ◆ ◆ ◆ ◆ ◆ ◆ ◆ ◆ ◆ ◆ ◆ ◆

Working with text files is a necessity in just about every computer environment. Tasks such as viewing system logs, modifying configuration files, and writing programs require the ability to work with text files. Ubuntu offers a few different ways to work with text files. This chapter walks through two graphical text editors, the gedit text editor and the emacs editor, as well vim, an old-fashioned text-based editor you can use when working in a command line session. The chapter ends by discussing the Tomboy Notes application, which, although not specifically a text editor, allows you to organize your world by creating text notes that do much more than just sit in a folder.

The gedit Editor

If you're working in the Ubuntu GNOME desktop environment, there's a graphical text editor that supports most of your text editing needs already installed. The gedit program is a basic text editor with a few advanced graphical features thrown in for fun. This section walks through the features of gedit and demonstrates how to get the most out of it for all your text processing needs.

Starting gedit

You can access the gedit text editor in the Ubuntu desktop environment using three different methods:

- ◆ Select the Text Editor entry in the Accessories menu, under the Applications Panel menu item.
- ◆ Double-click a text file from the desktop or within Nautilus (see Chapter 5, "File Management").
- ◆ From a command line prompt in a Terminal session (see Chapter 19, "The Ubuntu Command Line"), run the gedit command:

```
$ gedit mytest.txt
```

Whether you start a new file or start gedit with a specific file (such as when you double-click a file in Nautilus), gedit creates an editor buffer space and is ready for you to start editing text, as shown in Figure 6-1.

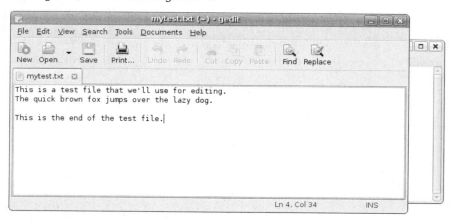

Figure 6-1: The gedit main editor window.

If you're editing an existing file, the name of the file you're editing appears in the tab for the Edit pane. If you hover your mouse pointer over the tab, a dialog box appears, showing the full pathname of the file, the MIME type of the file, and the character set encoding it uses. You can perform most common text editing features within the Edit pane, such as cutting, copying, and pasting text, as well as deleting blocks of text by highlighting the text with the mouse and hitting the Delete key.

Secret

You can edit multiple files at the same time using gedit. From the gedit command line prompt, enter each file separately on the command line:

```
$ gedit mytest.txt mytest2.txt
```

If you already have a gedit session open, just select File then either **New** or **Open** to open another file in the same gedit window session.

Each file opens in a separate window pane and in a separate editor buffer. You can easily switch between files by clicking on the pane tab for the file you want to edit.

The tab on the Edit pane also provides quick access to common editor functions. Right-clicking on the tabbed pane allows you to

- ◆ Start a gedit window session using that file
- ◆ Save the file using the current filename
- ◆ Save the file using a new filename
- ◆ Print the file
- ◆ Close the window pane

The tabbed mini-menu provides easy access to most of the common functions you'll need to perform with the text file without having hunt through the menu bar menus.

Basic gedit Features

Besides the tabbed editor window panes, gedit uses both a menu bar and tool bar that allow you to set features and configure settings. The tool bar provides quick access to the most common features contained in the menu bar. The menu bar items available are

- ◆ **File:** for creating new files, opening existing files, saving existing files, and printing files
- ◆ **Edit:** for manipulating text in the active buffer area and setting the editor preferences
- ◆ **View:** for setting the editor features to display in the window and for setting the text highlighting mode
- ◆ **Search:** for finding and replacing text in the active editor buffer area
- ◆ **Tools:** provides access to features for plug-in tools installed in gedit
- ◆ **Documents:** for managing files open in the buffer areas
- ◆ **Help:** provides access to the complete gedit user manual

One interesting feature in the File menu is Open Location, which allows you to open a file from the network using the standard uniform resource identifier (URI) format popular throughout the World Wide Web. This format identifies the protocol used to access the file (such as HTTP or FTP), the server where the file is located, and the complete path of the server to access the file.

The Edit menu contains the standard cut, copy, and paste functions, along with a neat feature that allows you to easily enter the date and time in several different formats in the text.

The View menu allows you to customize what elements appear in the gedit window, as well as define how gedit formats the text in the Edit pane. You can use the View menu to disable the tool bar, status bar, or the side pane for the window. The status bar appears at the bottom of the window, showing the current line and column where the cursor is, the current edit mode (Insert or Overwrite), and the status when opening or saving files. The side pane produces a list of all the files opened in the gedit session.

The Highlight mode in the View menu allows you to specify what type of text file is in the editor buffer. Gedit has the ability to use a different color scheme to identify different elements in a text file. For example, in programming files, gedit can use different colors for keywords, function names, and constants.

Gedit determines the type of content contained in a text file by examining the filename extension. Many programming languages use specific filename extensions to identify files, such as .c for C language programs, .sh for shell script programs, and .php for PHP programs. When gedit detects that in a filename, it automatically sets the appropriate file type.

The Search menu provides a standard find function, which produces a dialog box where you can enter the text to find and select how the find should work (matching case, matching the whole word, and the search direction). It also provides an incremental search feature, which works in real-time mode, finding text as you type characters of the word.

Setting Preferences

The Edit menu contains a Preferences item, which produces the gedit Preferences dialog box, shown in Figure 6-2.

This is where you can customize the operation of the gedit editor. The Preferences dialog box contains five tabbed areas for setting the features and behavior of the editor.

View

The View tab provides options for how gedit displays the text in the editor window:

- ◆ **Text Wrapping:** This option determines how to handle long lines of text in the editor. The Enable Text Wrapping option wraps long lines to the next line of the editor. The Do Not Split Words over Two Lines option prevents auto-inserting dashes in long words that can be split between two lines.
- ◆ **Line Numbers:** This option enables display of line numbers in the left margin of the editor window.
- ◆ **Current Line:** This option enables highlighting of the line of the current cursor position, which helps you to easily find the cursor position.
- ◆ **Right Margin:** This option enables the right-side margin, and allows you to set how many columns should be in the editor window. The default value is 80 columns.
- ◆ **Bracket Matching:** When the option is enabled, bracket pairs in programming code are highlighted, allowing you to easily match brackets in if-then statements, for and while loops, and other coding elements that use brackets.

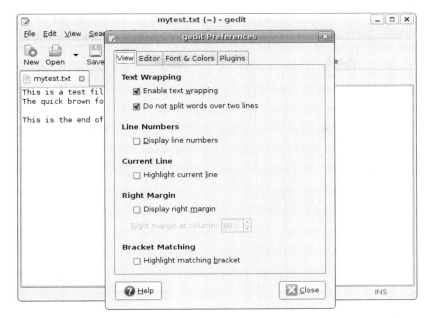

Figure 6-2: The gedit Preferences dialog box.

The line numbering and bracket matching features provide an environment for programmers to troubleshoot code—a feature not often found in some text editors.

Editor

The Editor tab provides options for how the gedit editor handles tabs and indentation, along with how files are saved:

- ◆ **Tab Stops:** This option sets the number of spaces skipped when you press the Tab key. The default value is eight. This feature also includes a check box that, when checked, inserts spaces instead of a tab skip.
- ◆ **Automatic Indentation:** When this option is enabled, gedit automatically indents lines in the text for paragraphs and code elements (such as if-then statements and loops).
- ◆ **File Saving:** This option provides two features for saving files: whether to create a backup copy of the file when opened in the editor window, and whether to automatically save the file at a preselected interval.

The auto-save feature is a great way to ensure that your changes are saved on a regular basis to prevent catastrophes due to crashes or power outages.

Font & Colors

The Font & Colors tab allows you to configure (not surprisingly) two items:

- ◆ **Font:** This option allows you to select the default font (Monospace 10) or a customized font and font size from a dialog box.
- ◆ **Color Scheme:** This option allows you to select the default color scheme used for text, background, selected text, and selection colors, or to choose a customized color for each category.

The default colors for gedit match the standard Ubuntu desktop theme selected for the desktop. These colors will change to match the scheme you select for the desktop.

Plug-ins

The Plug-ins tab provides control over the plug-ins used in gedit. Plug-ins are separate programs that can interface with gedit to provide additional functionality. The Plug-ins tab is shown in Figure 6-3.

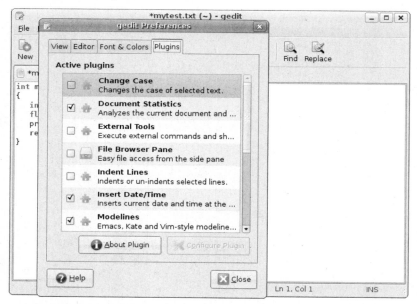

Figure 6-3: The gedit plug-ins Preferences tab.

Several plug-ins are available for gedit, but not all of them are installed by default. Table 6-1 describes the plug-ins that are currently available in gedit.

Table 6-1: Gedit Plug-ins

Plug-in	Description
Change Case	Changes the case of selected text
Document Statistics	Reports the number of words, lines, characters, and nonspace characters
External Tools	Provides a shell environment in the editor to execute commands and scripts
File Browser Pane	Provides a simple file browser to make selecting files for editing easier
Indent Lines	Provides advanced line indentation and un-indentation
Insert Date/Time	Inserts the current date and time in several formats at the current cursor position

Table 6-1: *(continued)*

Plug-in	Description
Modelines	Provides emacs-style message lines at the bottom of the editor window
Python Console	Provides an interactive console at the bottom of the editor window for entering commands using the Python programming language
Snippets	Allows you to store often-used pieces of text for easy retrieval anywhere in the text
Sort	Quickly sorts the entire file or selected text
Spell Checker	Provides dictionary spell checking for the text file
Tag List	Provides a list of commonly used strings you can easily enter into your text
Text Encryption	Provides encryption services, such as signing a file, encrypting text, and decrypting encrypted text
User Name	Inserts the current user's login name at the current cursor position

Plug-ins that are enabled show a check mark in the check box next to their name. Some plug-ins also provide additional configuration features after you select them, such as the External Tools plug-in. It allows you to select a shortcut key to start the terminal, where gedit displays output from the terminal, and the command to start the shell session.

Secret

There are lots of additional plug-ins for gedit besides what Ubuntu installs by default. The clearinghouse for gedit plug-ins is located at

http://live.gnome.org/Gedit/Plugins

This site contains official gedit plug-ins, along with a wealth of plug-ins developed by others. You can download additional plug-ins from there and install them in your gedit setup.

Unfortunately, not all plug-ins are installed in the same place in the gedit menu bar. Some plug-ins appear in the Tools menu bar (such as the Spell Checker and External Tools plug-ins), while others appear in the Edit menu bar (such as the Change Case and Insert Date/Time plug-ins).

The Character Map

If you're using the gedit editor to compose text, you might need to enter a special character in your document, such as a mathematical symbol or a non-English character. Gedit doesn't directly provide a way to insert special characters, but Ubuntu provides another program that will help.

The Character Map application provides a wealth of special characters, from various non-English characters to a host of special symbols used in science, mathematics, and engineering.

Start the Character Map application by clicking the Applications Panel menu, then Accessories, then Character Map. The Character Map main window appears, as shown in Figure 6-4.

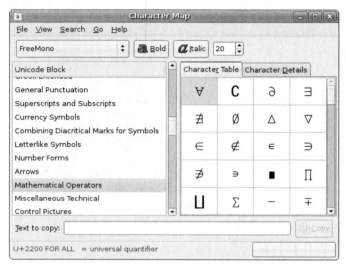

Figure 6-4: The Character Map application window.

The Character Map window consists of four areas:

- A font and formatting selection area at the top
- The character set list on the left side
- A grid block on the right side, containing the characters in order of their character code values
- A text box beneath the character set list for copying and pasting characters from the grid block
- A status bar indicating the character name selected in the grid block

The character set list can show character sets based on their Unicode location (similar character sets appear sequentially in the Unicode) or by language (called *script*). When you select a Unicode block or script from the left pane, the characters contained within that character set appear in the right pane grid block.

You can see information about an individual character by selecting it in the grid block, then clicking the Character Details tab at the top of the grid block pane. When you find the character you want to use, just drag and drop it into the Text to Copy box. You can add as many characters to the text box as you like.

Once you have the characters you need in the text box, click the Copy button to copy them into the clipboard area. From there, you can paste the characters into a gedit session Edit pane. When you are working in the gedit Edit pane, you can place the characters wherever you need within the text document.

The vim Editor

If you're working in Command Line mode, you may want to become familiar with at least one text editor that operates directly within the command line environment. The vi editor is the original text editor used on UNIX systems. It uses the Console Graphics mode to emulate a text editor window, allowing you to see the lines of your text file, move around within the file, and insert, edit, and replace text.

Although vim may possibly be the most complicated editor in the world (at least in the opinion of those who hate it), it provides many features that have made it a staple for UNIX administrators for decades.

When the GNU Project ported the vi editor to the open-source world, they chose to make some improvements to it. Because it no longer resembled the original vi editor, they renamed it *vim* (which stands for *vi improved*).

Ubuntu installs vim by default. It also creates an alias program named vi to point to vim so that you can use either command, vi or vim, to start the vim editor from the command line prompt.

This section walks you through the basics of using the vim editor to edit your text files without having to leave the command line environment.

The Basics of vim

The vim editor works with data in a memory buffer. To start the vim editor, just type the vim command (or the vi alias) and the name of the file you want to edit:

```
$ vim mytext.txt
```

If you start vim without a filename, or if the file doesn't exist, vim opens a new buffer area for editing. If you specify an existing file on the command line, vim will read the entire contents of the file into a buffer area, and makes it ready for editing, as shown in Figure 6-5.

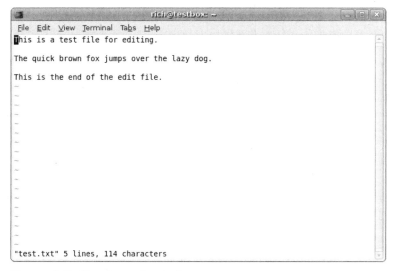

Figure 6-5: The vim main window.

The vim editor operates in Full-Screen mode, using the entire console window for the editor area.

The initial vim editor window shows the contents of the file (if any), along with a message line at the bottom of the window. If the file contents don't take up the entire screen, vim places a tilde on lines that are not part of the file (as seen in Figure 6-5).

The message line at the bottom provides information about the edited file, depending on the status of the file, and the default settings in your vim installation. If the file is new, the message [New File] appears.

The vim editor has two modes of operation:

   ◆ Normal mode
   ◆ Insert mode

When you first open a file (or start a new file) for editing, the vim editor enters Normal mode. In Normal mode the vim editor interprets keystrokes as commands (more on those later).

In Insert mode, vim inserts every key you type at the current cursor location in the buffer. To enter Insert mode, press the i key. To get out of Insert mode and return to Normal mode, press the Esc key on the keyboard.

Secret

In Normal mode you can move the cursor around the text area using the arrow keys (as long as your terminal type is detected properly by vim). If you happen to be on a flaky terminal connection that doesn't have the arrow keys defined, hope is not lost. The vim commands include keyboard commands for moving the cursor:

   • h to move left one character
   • j to move down one line (the next line in the text)
   • k to move up one line (the previous line in the text)
   • l to move right one character

Moving around within large text files line by line can get tedious. Fortunately, vim provides a few commands to help speed things along:

   ◆ Page Down (or Ctrl-f) to move forward one screen of data
   ◆ Page Up (or Ctrl-b) to move backward one screen of data
   ◆ G to move to the last line in the buffer
   ◆ *num* G to move to line number *num* in the buffer
   ◆ gg to move to the first line in the buffer

The vim editor has a special feature within Normal mode called *Command Line mode*. Command Line mode provides an interactive command line where you can enter additional commands to control the actions in vim. To get to Command Line mode, hit the colon character from Normal mode. The cursor moves to the message line and a colon appears, waiting for you to enter a command.

Within the Command Line mode are several commands for saving the buffer to the file and for exiting vim:

- ♦ q to quit if no changes have been made to the buffer data
- ♦ q! to quit and discard any changes made to the buffer data.
- ♦ w *filename* to save the file under a different filename
- ♦ wq to save the buffer data to the file and quit

After seeing just a few basic vim commands you might understand why some people absolutely hate the vim editor. To be able to use vim to its fullest, you must know plenty of obscure commands. However, once you get a few of the basic vim commands down, you can quickly edit files directly from the command line, no matter what type of environment you're in.

Editing Data

While in Insert mode, you can insert data into the buffer; however, sometimes you need to add or remove data after you've already entered it into the buffer. While in Normal mode, the vim editor provides several commands for editing the data in the buffer. Table 6-2 lists some common editing commands for vim.

Table 6-2: vim Editing Commands

Command	Description
x	Delete the character at the current cursor position
dd	Delete the line at the current cursor position
dw	Delete the word at the current cursor position
d$	Delete to the end of the line from the current cursor position
J	Delete the line break at the end of the line at the current cursor position
a	Append data after the current cursor position
A	Append data to the end of the line at the current cursor position
r *char*	Replace a single character at the current cursor position with *char*
R *text*	Overwrite the data at the current cursor position with *text*, until you press Esc

Some of the editing commands also allow you to use a numeric modifier to indicate how many times to perform the command. For example, the command 2x deletes two characters starting from the current cursor position, and the command 5dd deletes five lines starting at the line from the current cursor position.

Secret

Be careful when trying to use the PC keyboard Backspace or Delete keys while in the vim editor. The vim editor usually recognizes the Delete key because of the functionality of the x command, which deletes the character at the current cursor location. Usually, the vim editor doesn't recognize the Backspace key for deletions but instead uses it as a back arrow key.

Copy and Paste

A standard feature of modern editors is the ability to cut or copy data, then paste it elsewhere in the document. The vim editor provides a way to do this.

Cutting and pasting is relatively easy. You've already seen the commands in Table 6-2 that can remove data from the buffer. However, when vim removes data, it actually stores it in a separate register. You can retrieve that data by using the p command.

For example, you can use the dd command to delete a line of text, then move the cursor to the location in the buffer where you want to place it, then use the p command. The p command inserts the text after the line at the current cursor position. You can do this with any command that removes text.

Copying text is a little bit trickier. The copy command in vim is y (for yank). You can use the same second character with y as with the d command (yw to yank a word, y$ to yank to the end of a line). After you yank the text, move the cursor to the location where you want to place the text and use the p command. The yanked text now appears at that location.

Yanking is tricky. You can't see what happened, because you're not affecting the text that you yank. You never know for sure what you yanked until you paste it somewhere.

Secret

There's another feature in vim that helps us out with yanking.

Visual mode highlights text as you move the cursor. You can use Visual mode to select text to yank for pasting. To enter Visual mode, move the cursor to the location where you want to start yanking, then press v. You'll notice that the text at the cursor position is now highlighted. Next, move the cursor to cover the text you want to yank (you can even move down lines to yank more than one line of text). As you move the cursor, vim highlights the text in the yank area. After you've covered the text you want to copy, press the y key to activate the yank command. Now that you've got the text in the register, just move the cursor to where you want to paste, and use the p command to insert it.

Search and Substitute

You can easily search for data in the buffer using the vim search command. To enter a search string, hit the forward slash (/) character. The cursor goes to the message line, and vim displays a forward slash. Enter the text you want to find, and press the Enter key. The vim editor responds with one of three actions:

  ◆ If the word appears after the current cursor location, it jumps to the first location where the text appears.

  ◆ If the word doesn't appear after the current cursor location, it wraps around the end of the file to the first location in the file where the text appears (and indicates so with a message).

  ◆ It produces an error message that the text was not found in the file.

To continue searching for the same word, hit the forward slash character, then hit the Enter key.

The substitute command allows you to quickly replace (substitute) one word for another in the text. To get to the substitute command you must be in Command Line mode. The format for the substitute command is

`:s/old/new/`

The vim editor jumps to the first occurrence of the text *old* and replaces it with the text *new*. There are a few modifications you can make to the substitute command to substitute more than one occurrence of the text:

- `:s:/old/new/g` to replace all occurrences of *old* in a line.
- `:#,#s/old/new/g` to replace all occurrences of *old* between two line numbers.
- `:%s/old/new/g` to replace all occurrences of *old* in the entire file.
- `:%s/old/new/gc` to replace all occurrences of *old* in the entire file but prompt for each occurrence.

As you can see, for a command line text editor, vim contains quite a few advanced features. Because every UNIX and Linux distribution includes it, it's a good idea to know the basics of the vim editor so that you can always edit files, no matter where you are or what you have available.

The emacs Editor

The emacs editor is an extremely popular editor that appeared before UNIX was around. Developers liked it so much that they ported it to the UNIX environment, and now it's been ported to the Linux environment. The emacs editor started out as a console editor, much like vi, but it has migrated to the graphical world.

The emacs editor still provides the original Console Mode editor, but it now also has the ability to use graphical X Windows to allow editing text in a graphical environment. Normally, when you start the emacs editor from a command line, it'll determine whether you have an available X Window session. If so, it will start in Graphical mode. If not, it'll start in Console mode.

Although the emacs editor isn't installed by default in Ubuntu, you can easily add it to your text editing toolbelt by using the Add/Remove feature in Ubuntu (see Chapter 13, "Software Installs and Updates") and searching for emacs22. You can also find it listed in both the All and Accessories categories.

After installing the Ubuntu emacs22 package and restarting your system, you'll see two new entries in the Accessories section of the Applications menu:

- emacs22 (client)
- emacs22 (X11)

The emacs22 client entry starts an emacs session if you have an emacs server running on the system. Because we didn't install the emacs server, this entry won't be of any use now.

The emacs22 X11 entry starts a windows-based emacs session for you to use. Alternatively, you can use a console-based emacs session from the Ubuntu command line prompt.

This section describes both the Console mode and Graphical mode emacs editors so that you'll know how to use either one if you want (or need) to.

Using emacs on the Console

The Console mode version of emacs is another editor that uses lots of key commands to perform editing functions. The emacs editor uses key combinations involving the Control key (the Ctrl key on a PC keyboard) and the Meta key. In most PC terminal emulator packages, the Meta key is mapped to the PC's Alt key. The official emacs documents abbreviates the Ctrl key as `C-` and the Meta key as `M-`, Thus, to enter a `Ctrl-x` key combination, the document shows `C-x`. I'll do the same here so as not to confuse you.

Secret

> If you try to use the Alt key for the emacs Meta key in the Ubuntu Terminal application, you'll run into a problem with the Terminal menu keys (for example, `Alt-f` is an emacs command, but it also opens the File menu in Terminal).

To avoid this problem you can use the Esc key as the Meta key in emacs. The only difference is that you don't hold down the Esc key as a key combination. Instead, you press and release the Esc key first, then press the required key to perform the function.

The Basics of emacs

To start a console-based version of emacs, open a Terminal session and, at the command prompt, type

```
$ emacs -nw mytest.txt
```

When emacs starts, it displays a basic information and help screen, shown in Figure 6-6.

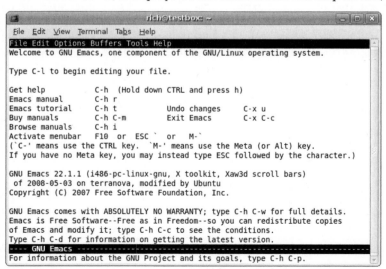

Figure 6-6: The emacs console window screen.

Pressing any key displays the contents of the text file. You'll notice that the top of the Console Mode window shows a typical menu bar. Unfortunately, you won't be able to use the menu bar in Console mode. You can use the menu bar only in Graphical mode.

Secret

Unlike the vim editor, where you have to move in and out of Insert mode to switch between entering commands and inserting text, the emacs editor has only one mode. If you type a printable character, emacs inserts it at the current cursor position. If you type a command, emacs executes the command.

To move the cursor around the buffer area, you can use the arrow keys, and the Page Up and Page Down keys, assuming emacs detected your terminal emulator correctly. If not, you can use these command keys for moving the cursor around:

- ◆ C-p moves up one line (the previous line in the text).
- ◆ C-b moves left (back) one character.
- ◆ C-f moves right (forward) one character.
- ◆ C-n moves down one line (the next line in the text).

There are also commands for making longer jumps with the cursor within the text:

- ◆ M-f moves right (forward) to the next word.
- ◆ M-b moves left (backward) to the previous word.
- ◆ C-a moves to the beginning of the current line.
- ◆ C-e moves to the end of the current line.
- ◆ M-a moves to the beginning of the current sentence.
- ◆ M-e moves to the end of the current sentence.
- ◆ M-v moves back one screen of data.
- ◆ C-v moves forward one screen of data.
- ◆ M-< moves to the first line of the text.
- ◆ M-> moves to the last line of the text.

There are several commands you should know for saving the editor buffer back into the file and exiting emacs:

- ◆ C-x C-s saves the current buffer contents to the file.
- ◆ C-z exits emacs but keeps it running in your session so you can come back to it.
- ◆ C-x C-c exits emacs and stops the program.

You'll notice that two of these features require two key commands. The C-x command is called the *extend command*. This provides yet another whole set of commands to work with.

Editing Data

The emacs editor is pretty robust with inserting and deleting text in the buffer. To insert text, just move the cursor to the location where you want to insert the text and start typing.

To delete text, use the Backspace key to delete the character before the current cursor position and the Delete key to delete the character at the current cursor location.

The emacs editor also has commands for killing text. The difference between deleting text and killing text is that when you kill text, emacs places it in a temporary area where you can retrieve it (see the "Copying and Pasting" section). Deleted text is gone forever.

There are a few commands for killing text in the buffer:

- ◆ M-Backspace kills the word before the current cursor position.
- ◆ M-d kills the word after the current cursor position.
- ◆ C-k kills from the current cursor position to the end of the line.
- ◆ M-k kills from the current cursor position to the end of the sentence.

Secret The emacs editor also includes a fancy way of mass-killing text. Just move the cursor to the beginning of the area you want to kill, and hit either the C-@ or C-SPACEBAR keys. Then move the cursor to the end of the area you want to kill and use the C-w command. All of the text between the two locations is killed.

If you make a mistake when killing text, the C-u command will undo the kill command and restore the data.

Copying and Pasting

You've seen how to cut data from the emacs buffer area. Now it's time to see how to paste it somewhere else. Unfortunately, if you use the vim editor, this process might confuse you when using the emacs editor.

In an unfortunate coincidence, pasting data in emacs is called *yanking*. In the vim editor, copying is called *yanking*, which is can be confusing if you happen to use both editors.

After you kill data using one of the kill commands, move the cursor to the location you want to paste the data and use the C-y command. This command yanks the text out of the temporary area and pastes it at the current cursor position. The C-y command yanks the text from the last kill command. If you've performed multiple kill commands, you can cycle through them using the M-y command.

To copy text, just yank it back into the same location you killed it from, then move to the new location and use the C-y command again. You can yank text back as many times as you desire.

Searching and Replacing

Searching for text in the emacs editor is done using the C-s and C-r commands. The C-s command performs a forward search in the buffer area from the current cursor position to the end of the buffer, while the C-r command performs a backward search in the buffer area from the current cursor position to the start of the buffer.

When you enter either the C-s or C-r command, a prompt appears in the bottom line, querying you for the text to search. Emacs can perform two types of searches.

In an *incremental* search the emacs editor performs the text search in real-time mode as you type the word. When you type the first letter, it highlights all of the occurrences of that letter in the buffer. When you type the second letter, it highlights all of the occurrences of the two-letter combination in the text, and so on until your complete the text you're searching for.

In a *non-incremental* search, hit the Enter key after the C-s or C-r commands. This action locks the search query into the bottom line area and allows you to type the search text in full before searching.

To replace an existing text string with a new text string, use the M-x command. This command requires a text command, along with parameters.

The text command is replace-string. After typing the command, hit the Enter key, and emacs will query you for the existing text string. After entering that, hit the Enter key again, and emacs will query you for the new replacement text string.

Using Buffers in emacs

The emacs editor has multiple buffer areas, which allows you to edit multiple files at the same time. You can load files into a buffer and switch between buffers while editing.

To load a new file into a buffer while you're in emacs, use the C-x C-f key combination. This is the emacs Find a File mode. It takes you to the bottom line in the window and allows you to enter the name of the file you want to edit. If you don't know the name or location of the file, just hit the Enter key to bring up a file browser in the editor window, as shown in Figure 6-7.

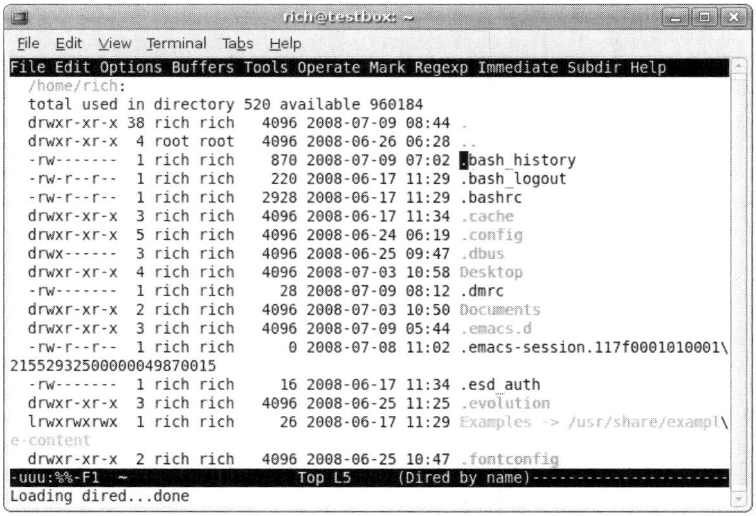

Figure 6-7: The emacs find a file browser.

From here you can browse to the file you want to edit. To traverse up a directory level, go to the double dot entry and hit the Enter key. To traverse down a directory, go to the directory entry and hit the Enter key. When you've found the file you want to edit, just hit the Enter key, and emacs will load it into a new buffer area.

You can list the active buffer areas by hitting the C-x C-b extended command combination. The emacs editor splits the editor window and displays a list of buffers in the bottom window. There are always two buffers that emacs provides besides your main editing buffer:

- A scratch area called *Scratch*
- A message area called *Messages*

The scratch area allows you to enter LISP programming commands, as well as enter notes to yourself. The message area shows messages generated by emacs while operating. If any errors occur while using emacs, they will appear in the message area.

Secret

There are two ways to switch to a different buffer area in the window:

- C-x o to switch to the buffer listing window. Use the arrow keys to move to the buffer area you want to use, and hit the Enter key.
- C-x b to type in the name of the buffer area you want to switch to.

When you switch to the buffer listing window, emacs will open the buffer area in the new window area. The emacs editor allows you to have multiple windows open in a single session. The following section discusses how to manage multiple windows in emacs.

Using Windows in Console Mode emacs

The Console Mode emacs editor was developed many years before graphical windows appeared. However, it was advanced for its time, in that it could support multiple editor windows within the main emacs window.

You can split the emacs editor window into multiple windows using one of two commands:

- C-x 2 splits the window horizontally into two windows.
- C-x 3 splits the window vertically into two windows.

To move from one window to another, use the C-x o command. You'll notice that when you create a new window, emacs uses the buffer area from the original window in the new window. Once you move into the new window you can use the C-x C-f command to load a new file or use one of the commands to switch to a different buffer area in the new window.

To close a window, move to it and use the C-x 0 (that's a zero) command. If you want to close all of the windows except the one you're in, use the C-x 1 (that's a numerical one) command.

Using emacs in GNOME

If you select the emacs22 (X11) entry from the Accessories menu or run emacs from the command line prompt without the -nw option, emacs will automatically start in Graphical mode, shown in Figure 6-8.

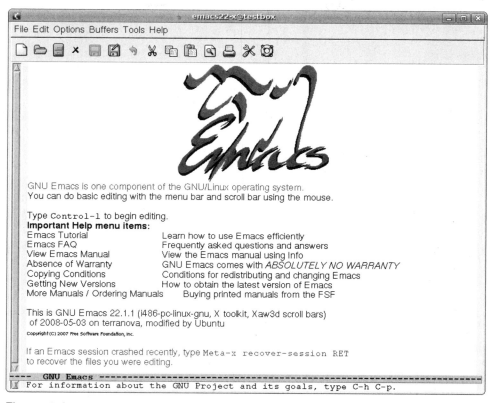

Figure 6-8: The emacs graphical window.

If you've already used emacs in Console mode, you should be fairly familiar with the X Windows mode. All of the key commands are available as menu bar items. The emacs menu bar contains the following items:

- ◆ **File:** allows you to open files in the window, create new windows, close windows, save buffers, and print buffers
- ◆ **Edit:** allows you to cut and copy selected text to the clipboard, paste clipboard data to the current cursor position, search for text, and replace text
- ◆ **Options:** provides settings for many emacs features, such as highlighting, word wrap, cursor type, and setting fonts
- ◆ **Buffers:** lists the current buffers available and allows you to easily switch between buffer areas
- ◆ **Tools:** provides access to the advanced features in emacs, such as the command line interface access, spell checking, email, a calculator, a calendar, and comparing text between files (called *diff*)
- ◆ **Help:** opens the emacs online manual for help with specific functions

Besides the menu bar, the graphical version of emacs also provides a tool bar for easy access to common menu bar items for cutting and pasting text and printing or saving a file.

Secret

The emacs program can also automatically detect file types based on file extensions. Along with the normal graphical emacs menu bar items, there is often a separate item specific to the file type in the editor buffer. For example, if you open a C program in emacs, it provides a C menu item, allowing advanced settings for highlighting C syntax, and compiling, running and debugging the code from a command prompt. You can do all of your program development directly from the emacs window!

The Tomboy Notes Application

To round out the discussion on handling text in Ubuntu, let's take a look at the Tomboy Notes application. While not necessarily a text editor per se, it's becoming a popular tool for text manipulation in the Ubuntu environment.

The Tomboy Notes application allows you to create a series of notes to organize your thoughts. The neat thing about the notes is that you can link notes together based on linking words, much like links on web sites. You can write a note about remembering to mow the lawn next week and make a link in it to another note reminding you about the brand of fertilizer to use. You can also embed email and web links within your notes. Clicking the link automatically starts the email client or web browser and goes to that link. That really moves your note-taking to the next level!

This section walks through how to start and use the Tomboy Notes application.

Starting Tomboy Notes

You start the Tomboy Notes application from the Applications Panel menu item. Just select Applications ➪ Accessories ➪ Tomboy Notes, and you'll see the Tomboy Notes Search window, along with a special Start Here note, as shown in Figure 6-9.

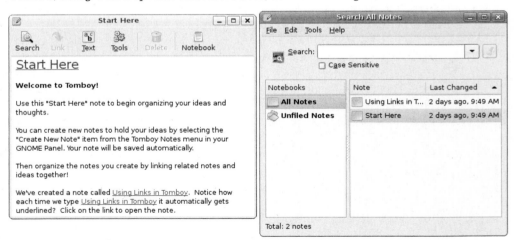

Figure 6-9: The Tomboy Notes search window and Start Here note.

Notice that when you start Tomboy Notes, a yellow paper pad and pencil icon appears on the top panel in the applets area. This icon allows you to directly access the Tomboy Notes application without having to wade through the Panel menu.

Secret   You can add the Tomboy Notes applet to your panel as a permanent icon. Just use the Add to Panel feature for either the top or bottom panel (see Chapter 4, "Exploring the Desktop," for how to do that).

Once you have the Tomboy Notes applet running, left-click on the applet to produce the mini menu, shown in Figure 6-10.

Figure 6-10: The Tomboy Notes mini menu.

The mini menu allows you to create a new note, display a notebook, or search for a note directly from the Applet menu.

When the Tomboy Notes applet is running in the panel, you can also access the mini menu by pressing the Alt-F12 key combination at any time.

Creating Notes

To create a new Note, select the File ⇨ New option from the Search window, or select Create a New Note from the Applet mini menu. The new note template, shown in Figure 6-11, appears.

At the top of the new note is the note title. This is what identifies your note in the Notes system. You can change the title of your note to whatever you want it to be.

Under the title is a text area. Here's where you can start writing your note.

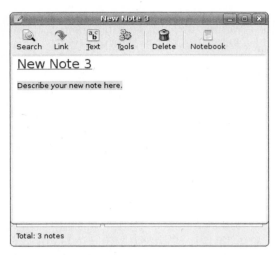

Figure 6-11: The Tomboy Notes new note template.

Editing Notes

When writing the note, you're not limited to ordinary text. The tool bar area in the Notes editor window provides some functions to help you with your note-taking:

- ◆ **Search:** Takes you back to the Search window to look for other notes.
- ◆ **Link:** Allows you to highlight text and select Link to create a new note using the text as the title.
- ◆ **Text:** Lets you set special text features, such as bold, italic, strikethrough, and highlights, as well as set the size of the text font and create a bullet list.
- ◆ **Tools:** Provides simple tools for synchronizing your note with a server, exporting your note to HTML format, and seeing what other notes link to the current note.
- ◆ **Delete:** Removes the current note.
- ◆ **Notebook:** Allows you to select a notebook to place the note in.

The Text menu bar item allows you to customize your note text by using special text formatting and adding bullet lists. Tomboy Notes also provides some automatic features, such as creating HTML and email links when it detects web and email addresses in your note. This feature is demonstrated in Figure 6-12.

You'll notice in the example shown in Figure 6-12, when I enter a web page URL or an email address, Tomboy Notes automatically creates an active link to the object. Clicking the links opens the web browser (for the URL link) or the email client (for the mail address) for that location.

The editor window also checks spelling, underlining words that it thinks are incorrectly spelled.

To create a new note, linked to text in an existing note, highlight the text words for the link title and select the Link button. As shown in Figure 6-12, a new note appears, ready for editing.

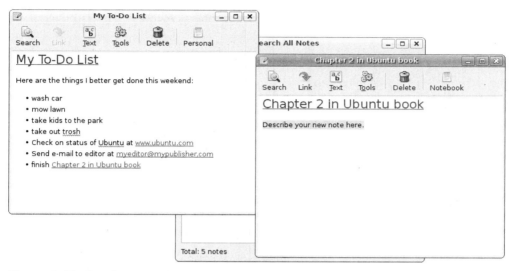

Figure 6-12: Creating a note with a bullet list and links.

Organizing Notes

Once your notes get scattered around, things can get disorganized. To help manage the chaos, Tomboy Notes provides notebooks for you to store your notes. A notebook contains a set of notes that are related.

You can create a new notebook by either selecting File ➪ Notebooks ➪ New Notebook from the Search window or by clicking the Tomboy Notes applet in the panel and selecting Notebooks ➪ New Notebook. After naming the new notebook, it appears in the Search window notebook list.

You can drag and drop notes from the All Notes list and the Unfiled Notes list into your new notebook.

Changing Preferences

The Search window provides access to change the preference settings used in Tomboy Notes. Select Edit ➪ Preferences to access Tomboy Preferences, shown in Figure 6-13.

The Preferences dialog box contains four tabs:

- ♦ **Editing:** Allows you to enable or disable spell checking, automatically highlight wiki words to create new notes, enable automatic bullet lists, and select a custom font.
- ♦ **Hotkeys:** Allows you to select special keys that activate Tomboy Notes windows when the applet is running. By default, Alt-F12 displays the Search window and Alt-F11 displays the Start Here note.
- ♦ **Synchronization:** Allows you to specify a Tomboy Notes server to sync your notes with. This option allows you to access your notes from any device that has access to the server.
- ♦ **Add-ins:** Tomboy add-ins provide additional functionality within Tomboy.

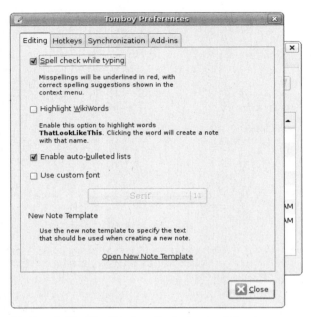

Figure 6-13: The Tomboy Preferences dialog box.

The Synchronization feature enables you to store your Tomboy notes in a location other the default location that Ubuntu uses for Tomboy Notes (located in the `.tomboy` folder under your home folder). Usually you would want to use a location that you can access from the network, such as a WebDAV folder or a shared folder on a server.

When you synchronize your Tomboy Notes, Tomboy scans the notes available in the remote folder and updates the local Tomboy files with notes contained in the Remote Synchronize folder, then updates the Remote Synchronize folder with any new notes added to the local files.

Secret

The wiki words feature allows Tomboy to monitor your text and attempt to determine when you want to create a new note link in your text. Wiki words are multiple words put together with no spacing, such as ThisIsAnExample. When Tomboy detects wiki words in the text it creates a link.

Clicking the link creates a new note using the wiki word as the note title. This feature allows you to easily type a note and set aside new notes as you type. Then, when you're ready to add content to the new notes, you just click on the wiki word links in the main note.

Tomboy add-ins, discussed in the next section, provide additional features to Tomboy.

Tomboy Add-ins

Ubuntu includes a default set of Tomboy add-ins, but not all of them are enabled by default. Table 6-3 shows the add-ins installed in Ubuntu, as well as which ones are enabled by default.

Table 6-3: Tomboy Add-ins in Ubuntu

Add-in	Default Status	Description
Backlinks	Enabled	Displays what notes link to the current note
Export to HTML	Enabled	Saves note in HTML format
Sticky Notes Importer	Enabled	Converts notes created with the Sticky Notes application in Tomboy Notes format
Insert Timestamp	Disabled	Adds a date/time value to your note
Note of the Day	Disabled	Creates a new note using today's date as the title. If you don't add anything to the note, Tomboy automatically deletes it
Bugzilla links	Disabled	Allows you to create a link to a Bugzilla bug report URL by dragging the URL from a browser into the note
Evolution Mail Integration	Enabled	Allows you to drag and drop an email message from Evolution into a note as a mail icon. Clicking the icon opens the message in Evolution
Printing Support	Enabled	Formats a note for printing
Local Directory Sync Service	Enabled	Synchronizes the note with a local Tomboy server
SSH Sync Service	Disabled	Synchronizes the note with a remote Tomboy server using SSH
WebDAV Sync Service	Enabled	Synchronizes the note with a remote Tomboy server using WebDAV
Fixed Width	Enabled	Uses a fixed-width font when creating text in notes

You can enable a disabled add-in from the Tomboy Preferences dialog box's Add-In tab. Just select the add-in you want and click the Enable button.

Summary

In this chapter we explored the applications available in Ubuntu for working with text files. By default, Ubuntu uses the gedit text editor to handle text files. You can open a text file in Nautilus by double-clicking the file icon or name. Nautilus automatically opens the file in the gedit program.

The gedit program provides lots of features, such as cutting and copying text, searching for text, and color-coding text in program code. Gedit also provides plug-ins, which can extend the functionality of the text editor by providing features such as spell checking, encryption, and inserting the current date and time.

If you must work in a command line environment, Ubuntu provides the vim command line editor by default. The vim editor creates a graphical environment within the text command line environment by using the Terminal text graphics features. You can view multiple lines of the text file and cut, copy, and paste text just as in a graphical editor.

For advanced editing features, a common editor in the UNIX environment is the emacs editor. Ubuntu provides this editor, but you must install it from the software repository. After installing emacs, you can use it either from the command line or the GNOME desktop environment. The emacs editor provides advanced editing features, including the ability to run and debug programming code from within the editor.

The chapter finished by discussing the Tomboy Notes application. Tomboy Notes allows you to create notes within small windows and store them in notebooks. You can link related notes to easily access a note referenced in another note. You can also create links to web sites and email addresses within notes that automatically start the appropriate application. Tomboy Notes provides an interesting environment for organizing your thoughts and projects.

The next chapter dives into the work of office productivity software. These days, just about everyone needs access to a full-featured word processing, spreadsheet, and presentation program. Ubuntu includes the popular OpenOffice.org office suite of software to solve all of your office productivity needs.

The OpenOffice Suite

Chapter 7

Without a doubt, the Microsoft Office product has revolutionized the world of office software. It has become the de facto standard in word processing, spreadsheet, and presentation graphics programs. Computer users compare all other office software packages to Microsoft Office products. Unfortunately, there's not a version of Microsoft Office that runs directly on Ubuntu. If you want Microsoft Office products in Linux, you have to use an open-source look-alike package.

In Ubuntu, that package is the OpenOffice.org suite of software, which contains packages that replicate each of the programs in Microsoft Office. This chapter discusses how to build your perfect office software environment, then walks through how to use the individual packages contained in OpenOffice.org.

The OpenOffice.org Suite

The OpenOffice.org suite of software packages includes several packages to provide office automation functionality to your desktop. The full OpenOffice.org suite contains the software components shown in Table 7-1.

Table 7-1: The OpenOffice.org Software Components

Package	Description
Base	Graphical database
Calc	Spreadsheets
Draw	Drawing
Impress	Presentation graphics
Math	Mathematics
Writer	Word processing

Ubuntu only installs the Calc and Writer packages during the default installation process. After the programs have been installed, you can access them by selecting the Applications panel menu item, then selecting the Office submenu.

If your Ubuntu workstation has access to the Internet, you can easily install the other OpenOffice.org components from the Add/Remove application (see Chapter 13, "Software Installs and Updates").

When you open the Add/Remove application, you'll see the following entries:

- ◆ OpenOffice.org Database
- ◆ OpenOffice.org Formula
- ◆ OpenOffice.org Office Suite
- ◆ OpenOffice.org Presentation
- ◆ OpenOffice.org Spreadsheet
- ◆ OpenOffice.org Word Processor

To install all of the remaining pieces, just select the OpenOffice.org Office Suite option. This downloads all of the files to the entire OpenOffice package.

The following sections describe each of these applications and show how to use them.

Word Processing

Word processors are a crucial·element for any home or office workstation. From writing letters to creating marketing brochures, word-processing software allows you to customize your documents with far more control than a plain text editor could ever provide. OpenOffice.org Writer has all the best features you expect in a word processor.

Writer Features

Before you proceed, let's take a look at the layout of the Writer window, shown in Figure 7-1.

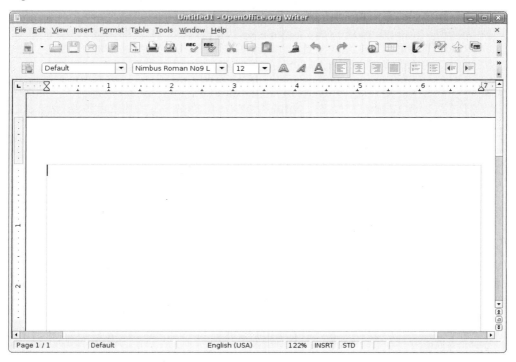

Figure 7-1: The OpenOffice.org Writer window.

The basic window that appears when you start Writer contains several elements to assist you in your word processing. These elements are discussed in the following sections.

The Menu Bar

At the top of the window is the menu bar. If you've ever used Microsoft Word, this should look familiar to you. The menu bar options are:

- **File:** Contains the Open, Save, Save As, Print, and Page Preview (called Print Preview in other word processors) commands. There is also a set of wizards that help guide you through creating common types of documents, and you can send documents through email, create templates, create web pages, and export the document into different formats.
- **Edit:** Contains the normal Cut, Copy, and Paste commands, along with the Select All and Find commands. You can also change tracking, merge documents, and compare documents.
- **View:** Contains Zoom functions and toolbar options, along with the options to show or hide formatting characters and to see what the document would look like as a web page.
- **Insert:** Includes options to add page breaks and special characters, along with indexes, tables, bookmarks, headers, footers, and cross-references to your documents.
- **Format:** Contains character, paragraph, and page settings, along with styles, autoformatting capabilities, and columns.
- **Table:** The table control options allow you to insert, delete, and select cells, convert between tables and text, and more.
- **Tools:** Contains the spell checker and thesaurus, along with hyphenation, auto-correction, an image gallery, and a bibliography database.
- **Window:** Includes options for creating a new window for a new document or selecting from a list of existing open documents.
- **Help:** Provides options to view instructions from the installed manual and the OpenOffice.org online help manual. Also provides links to report bugs and volunteer to translate OpenOffice.org into another language.

The individual menus have more features than what is listed here. In fact, the Writer menu bar contains most of the features that you're used to using in Microsoft Word.

Secret

Writer supports accessibility shortcut keys that allow you to select menu bar options from the keyboard. Press the Alt key and select the underlined letter from the desired top-level menu to open the menu (such as Alt-f to open the File menu). Then press the underlined letter key for the menu item you want to use.

The Standard Toolbar

Beneath the menu bar is the standard toolbar. Each icon in this bar represents a different function, which is detailed in Table 7-2.

Table 7-2: The Writer Standard Toolbar

Button	Description
New	Create new documents of various types. Click the down arrow to select a particular type of document to create from among any of the OpenOffice.org types.

continues

Table 7-2: *(continued)*

Button	Description
Open	Open an existing file for reading or editing.
Save	Save the current document. If you haven't saved this document before, the Save As dialog box opens.
Document as E-mail	Open a Compose email window in the preferred email program and automatically attach this document.
Edit File	Edit the displayed web page.
Export Directly As PDF	Open a Save As dialog box with PDF selected as the file type.
Print File Directly	Send a file to the default printer.
Page Preview	Show this page as it would look if you printed it. To return from Preview mode, click Close Preview.
Spellcheck	Run the spell checker on your entire document or the selected text.
AutoSpellcheck On/Off	Activate or turn off the automatic spell checker feature.
Cut	Remove the selected text from the document and save it in memory.
Copy	Make a copy of the selected text and save it in memory.
Paste	Place the text from memory into the document at the cursor's current location. Click the down arrow to see options for how the text can be pasted.
Format Paintbrush	Pick up the formatting of the first text you click and apply it to the second text you click.
Undo	Undo the last change you made to the document. Click the down arrow to choose how far you want to back up.
Redo	Reinstate the last change to the document after first using Undo to cancel it. Click the down arrow to choose how far back you want to redo.
Hyperlink	Open or close a dialog box that you can use to build complex hyperlinks.
Table	Insert a new table. Click the down arrow to drag and choose how many rows and columns the table should have.
Show Draw Functions	Access the many OpenOffice.org drawing utilities.
Find and Replace	Open or close the Find and Replace dialog box.
Navigator	Open or close the Navigator window, which allows you to jump to specific features within your document.
Gallery	Open or close a pane along the top of the document that provides access to clip art. Click this button again to close the pane.

continues

Table 7-2: *(continued)*

Button	Description
Data Sources	Select an external data source from which to retrieve data for the document.
Nonprinting Characters On/Off	Show all spaces, returns at the ends of paragraphs, and other characters that you don't normally see in your documents.
Zoom	Alter how large the document shows on your screen.
Visible Buttons	Select which toolbar buttons appear on the toolbar.
Help	Open the OpenOffice.org Help dialog box.

You may notice that there isn't enough room on the standard toolbar to display icons for all of the features. Clicking the double arrow icon on the right side of the standard toolbar displays the features that didn't fit. You can customize the standard toolbar to select which features are present and which are hidden. Just select the Visible Buttons feature in the extended area.

The Formatting Bar

The formatting toolbar is directly below the standard toolbar. The default series of icons allows you to select word-processing functions to format your text, such as styles, fonts, font sizes, and special layout formatting instructions.

The features on this bar are identical to what you see in most modern word processors.

Secret

The formatting toolbar changes depending on what you're doing. If your cursor is within a table, for example, the formatting toolbar contains buttons useful for working with tables.

The Ruler

Below the formatting toolbar is the ruler. This feature marks the margins and tabs of your document in the measuring units of your choice. To change which measurements units you want to use, right-click the ruler to open the Measurements pop-up dialog box. The available measurement units are

- ♦ Millimeter
- ♦ Centimeter
- ♦ Inch (the default)
- ♦ Point
- ♦ Pica

This feature helps you line up text in the document as you type, creating a uniform look for your documents.

The Document Pane

Beneath the ruler is the document pane. Just click in the pane and start typing. As with any word processor, the Writer document pane allows you to cut and paste text by highlighting sections and either selecting the function from the Edit menu bar or by using the quick keyboard shortcuts.

Secret

Writer provides lots of shortcut keys to help you perform simple functions without having to leave the keyboard. Some of the more common ones are

- `Ctrl-a` **to select all text in the document**
- `Ctrl-x` **to cut selected text to the clipboard**
- `Ctrl-c` **to copy selected text to the clipboard**
- `Ctrl-v` **to paste text from the clipboard**
- `Ctrl-j` **to justify text**
- `Ctrl-d` **to double underline text**
- `Ctrl-e` **to center text**
- `Ctrl-f` **to find and replace text**
- `Ctrl-Shift-p` **to use superscript**
- `Ctrl-l` **to align text to the left**
- `Ctrl-r` **to align text to the right**
- `Ctrl-Shift-b` **to use subscript**
- `Ctrl-Enter` **to insert a manual page break**

To see a complete list of the shortcut keys available, look at the help manual for Writer under the Help menu bar option.

You can also access a formatting shortcut menu by right-clicking in the document section. This action gives you quick access to the items in the formatting toolbar.

Working with Writer Files

One of the great things about Writer is that it can work with many file types. This capability allows you to create documents that can be used with various types of word-processing systems.

Not only can you save new documents in various formats, but you can also read documents created in other word-processing programs. Here's a list of the document types you can use with OpenOffice.org Writer:

- ◆ **OpenDocument (.odt) format:** a proposed open standard that may one day be supported by all word-processing programs
- ◆ **OpenOffice.org 1.0 (.sxw) format:** the original OpenOffice document format
- ◆ **Microsoft Word 97/2000/XP (.doc) format:** yes, you can read and write Word documents using Writer

- ◆ **Microsoft Word 95 (.doc) format:** even some of the older Word formats
- ◆ **Microsoft Word 6.0 (.doc) format:** and even some of the really old Word formats
- ◆ **Rich Text (.rtf) format:** a standard format for saving basic font and document information
- ◆ **StarWriter 3.0–5.0 (.sdw) format:** Sun's StarOffice word processor (a close cousin to OpenOffice.org)
- ◆ **Text format (.txt):** plain text that doesn't use special formatting characters or fonts
- ◆ **HTML (.html):** the standard HyperText Markup Language used for web publishing
- ◆ **Microsoft Word 2003 (.xml) format:** an attempt by Microsoft to create a standard word-processing document format using the XML standard language

The versatility of Writer is one of its primary features. You're not locked into a specific document format or style when you use Writer.

Secret

Although the option is not available in the Save As dialog box, the OpenOffice. org Writer toolbar allows you to export any format of document to the PDF document format. You can create PDF documents from your Writer documents by pressing the Export Directly as PDF button. This generates a PDF document that is completely compatible with the Adobe Acrobat software package format.

Spreadsheets

In the accounting world, spreadsheets are king. These days, however, many home users have discovered the benefits of using spreadsheet software. From balancing checkbooks to keeping track of budgets, having all the numbers at your fingertips can come in handy.

The Microsoft Excel spreadsheet is the most popular package used in the Windows world. In the OpenOffice.org suite, the spreadsheet package is called Calc.

Although not a direct replacement for Excel, Calc can perform most of the functions of Excel. The following sections take a look at OpenOffice.org Calc so that you can get to work.

The OpenOffice.org Calc Layout

Between OpenOffice.org Writer and other spreadsheet programs you might have used, much of what you see in OpenOffice.org Calc should look familiar. Take a look at the layout shown in Figure 7-2.

If you've used spreadsheet programs before, Calc should be familiar to you. Calc uses the common spreadsheet grid layout, with increasing numbers identifying the rows and increasing letters identifying the columns. The following sections describe the individual elements of Calc.

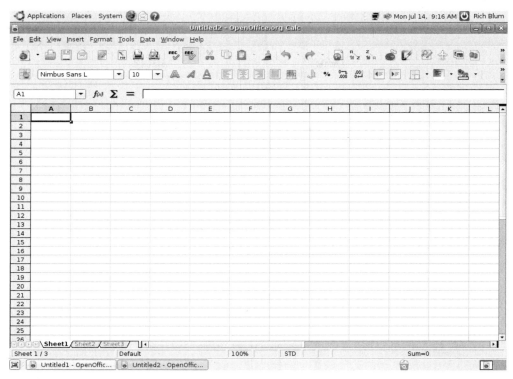

Figure 7-2: The OpenOffice.org Calc layout.

The Menu Bar

Along the top of the window is the menu bar. Calc has all the features you expect from a modern spreadsheet system. It has too many menu options to cover in depth, so, instead, here's a summary of what you find on each menu:

- ♦ **File:** the Open, Save, Save As, Print, and Page Preview (called Print Preview in other spreadsheets) commands, along with a set of wizards and options for sending documents through email, creating templates, and creating web pages

- ♦ **Edit:** the Select All and Find commands, along with change tracking, headers and footers, and plug-in loading

- ♦ **View:** the Zoom functions and toolbars, along with options for showing or hiding column and row headers

- ♦ **Insert:** commands for adding page breaks and special characters, along with cells, rows, functions, and external data to your spreadsheets

- ♦ **Format:** cell and row formatting, cell merging, and page settings, along with conditional formatting and specifying the format to identify data in a cell (explained in further detail below)

- ♦ **Tools:** spell checker and thesaurus, along with hyphenation, autocorrection features, an image gallery, and a macro creator and editor

- ♦ **Data:** data selection, sorting, and grouping routines

If you've used Excel or any other spreadsheet application, you should recognize these functions.

By default, Calc attempts to detect the format of the data you enter into a cell. However, sometimes it guesses wrong, and other times you may want to select another format, such as the format used to display a date or numeric value. Calc provides formatting for

- Numbers
- Percentages
- Currency
- Date
- Time
- Scientific numbers
- Fractions
- Boolean values
- Text

Each category of cell data has several options for how Calc presents it. There's even a user-defined option to allow you to customize how the data appears in the cells.

The Standard Toolbar

Beneath the menu bar is the standard toolbar. Each icon in this series represents a different function, as shown in Table 7-3.

Table 7-3: The Calc Standard Toolbar

Button	Description
New	Create new documents of various types. Click the down arrow to select a particular type of document to create from among any of the OpenOffice.org types.
Open	Open an existing file for reading or editing.
Save	Save the current document. If you haven't saved this document before, the Save As dialog box opens.
Document as E-mail	Open a Compose email window in your preferred email program and automatically attach this document.
Edit File	Edit the displayed spreadsheet.
Export Directly as PDF	Open a Save As dialog box with PDF selected as the file type.
Print File Directly	Send a file to the default printer.
Page Preview	Show this page as it would look if you printed it. To return from Preview mode, click Close Preview.
Spellcheck	Run the spell checker on your entire document or the selected text.
AutoSpellcheck	Activate or turn off the automatic spell checker feature.

continues

Table 7-3: *(continued)*

Button	Description
Cut	Remove the selected text from the document and save it in memory.
Copy	Make a copy of the selected text and save it in memory.
Paste	Place the text from memory into the document at the cursor's current location. Click the down arrow to see options for how the text can be pasted.
Format Paintbrush	Pick up the formatting of the first text you click and apply it to the second text you click.
Undo	Undo the last change you made to the document. Click the down arrow to choose how far you want to back up.
Redo	Reinstate the last change to the document after first using Undo to cancel it. Click the down arrow to choose how far back you want to redo.
Hyperlink	Open or close a dialog box that you can use to build complex hyperlinks.
Sort Ascending	Reorder the selected data in ascending order.
Sort Descending	Reorder the selected data in descending order.
Insert Chart	Create a chart based on the selected data.
Show Draw Functions	Access the many OpenOffice.org drawing utilities.
Find and Replace	Open or close the Find and Replace dialog box.
Navigator	Open or close the Navigator window, which allows you to jump to specific features within your document.
Gallery	Open or close a dialog box that provides access to clip art.
Data Sources	If you have the OpenOffice.org Base database package installed, this option allows you to import data from tables and queries into Calc.
Zoom	Alter how large the document shows on your screen.
Help	Open the OpenOffice.org Help dialog box.

If your monitor doesn't allow you to enlarge the Calc window to display all of the standard toolbar buttons, an icon appears at the far right, allowing you to see the icons that didn't fit. The standard toolbar allows you to customize which buttons appear on the toolbar, so you can select the features you use most often. Just select the Visible Buttons entry and check the buttons you want to appear on the standard toolbar.

The Formatting Bar

The formatting bar is directly below the standard toolbar. This series of icons allows you to click buttons and expand drop-down list boxes that represent standard spreadsheet functions, such as styles, fonts, font sizes, and number formatting instructions. Most features on this bar are identical to what you see in modern spreadsheets.

The Formula Bar

Directly below the formatting bar in a default OpenOffice.org Calc setup is the formula bar. Table 7-4 lays out what you find in this short collection of entries. The formula bar actually changes depending on what you're doing, offering you buttons for particular tasks.

Table 7-4: The Calc Formula Bar

Button or Item	Description
Name Box	Displays the current cell name. This can be in either the generic ColumnRow format (such as A1 or B5) or a text name that you specify for a specific cell.
Function Wizard	Click to open the Function Wizard dialog box and browse to find the particular spreadsheet function you're looking for.
Sum	Click to start a SUM (addition) function in the input line.
Formula Textbox	Click to place an = in the input line to signal that you're about to enter a function.
Input Line	Assign values or enter functions to fill a spreadsheet cell.

The Function wizard is a great tool for seeing the functions available in Calc and for getting a bird's eye view of your own formulas as you enter them into cells.

The Document Pane

The document pane is where you work on your spreadsheet. Just pick a cell and start typing. You can also access a formatting shortcut menu by right-clicking in the document section.

Each cell contains data, in the form of a numerical value, a text value, or a formula. Formulas reference cells by their column and row location. For example, cell A1 is the cell in the first column (A) and the first row (1). Cell B1 is the cell in the second column (B) and the first row (1).

Formulas can contains both equations and built-in Calc functions. An equation uses standard mathematical operations (use the asterisk for multiplication and the forward slash for division):

```
=(A1 * B1) / A2
```

This equation multiplies the values in cells A1 and B1, then divides that total by the value stored in cell A2.

Calc provides a wealth of built-in functions for data manipulation. Fortunately, you don't need to memorize all of the functions. Pressing the Function button on the formula bar produces a dialog box listing the available functions.

Selecting a cell that contains a formula and clicking the Function button in the formula bar produces a graphical representation of the formula, shown in Figure 7-3.

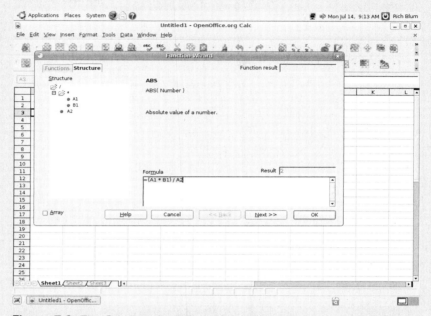

Figure 7-3: The Calc Function Wizard Structure window.

The Structure tab shows the relationship between cells in the formula. Notice that it also shows the structure of the mathematical operations as folders containing the individual operands (cells). This is a great tool for breaking down complex formulas into simple pieces.

Working with Calc Files

Just like the Writer package, the Calc package allows you to read and write various spreadsheet formats:

- **OpenDocument Spreadsheet (.ods) format:** a proposed standard spreadsheet document format
- **OpenOffice.org 1.0 Spreadsheet (.ots) format:** the older OpenOffice 1.0 spreadsheet format
- **Data Interchange Format (.dif):** a text file format used to import and export spreadsheets between dissimilar spreadsheet programs
- **dBase (.dbf):** exports the spreadsheet data into a dBase database file
- **Microsoft Excel 97/2000/XP (.xls) format:** the standard Microsoft Excel spreadsheet formats used by the most popular versions of Excel

+ **Microsoft Excel 95 (.xls) format:** and even the older Excel spreadsheet format
+ **Microsoft Excel 5.0 (.xls) format:** and older Excel spreadsheet formats
+ **StarCalc 3.0–5.0 (.sdc) format:** Sun's StarOffice spreadsheet format (a close cousin of the OpenOffice.org suite)
+ **SYLK (.slk) format:** the symbolic fink format, used to exchange data between spreadsheets and other applications, such as databases
+ **Text CSV (.csv) format:** the comma-separated text values, often used to export data to databases
+ **HTML (.html) format:** formats spreadsheet data as an HTML web page
+ **Microsoft Excel 2003 (.xml) format:** a standard proposed by Microsoft for using the Internet XML standard for defining spreadsheet data

Just like with Writer, the advantage to using Calc is its versatility. You can work with just about all of the popular spreadsheet types, as well as save your spreadsheets as those types.

Secret Also, similar to Writer, the Calc standard toolbar provides a button for you to export the spreadsheet directly as a PDF document. This is a great feature for creating reports directly from your spreadsheets.

Presentations

These days it's almost impossible to attend a business meeting that doesn't use Microsoft PowerPoint to present information. PowerPoint has quickly become the de facto tool used for presentations.

The OpenOffice.org equivalent to PowerPoint is the Impress package. Impress allows you to create slides using the same techniques found in PowerPoint, and you can even process existing PowerPoint slides. This section walks through the components of Impress and demonstrates how to create a new presentation using Impress.

Using the Presentation Wizard

When you open Impress from the Applications ➪ Office menu, the first thing that launches is the Presentation wizard, shown in Figure 7-4.

If you don't want this wizard to show up the next time you open Impress, click the Do Not Show This Dialog Again box.

To use the wizard to create a new presentation, follow these steps:

1. Leave the Empty Presentation option selected (unless you have a template you need to work from) and click Next.

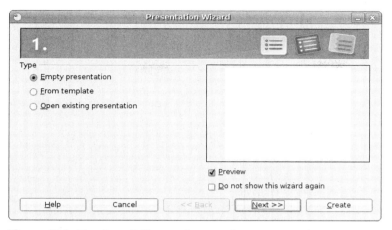

Figure 7-4: The OpenOffice.org Impress Presentation wizard.

2. To select one of the default slide backgrounds that come with Impress, you can do so by looking to the Select a Slide Design drop-down list box, choose Presentation Backgrounds, then click the various options to see what the design looks like, to the right of the dialog box.

3. To select a presentation (content) layout template that was designed specifically for the template you chose in this dialog box's screen 1, you can do so by looking to the Select a Slide Design drop-down list box, choose Presentation(s), then select the presentation type you want to use.

4. If your presentation will ultimately appear on something other than a computer screen, adjust the Select an Output medium to match its intended setting.

The choices are Screen, Overhead Sheet, Slide, and Paper.

5. Click Next to proceed to the next section.

6. Under Select a Slide Transition, experiment with the various options in the Effect and Speed drop-down list boxes to narrow down how you want to transition from one slide to another. Impress animates these transitions for you if the Preview box is checked.

7. To navigate manually from one slide to the next (the default option) while you give your presentation, skip to Step 10. If you want to have your presentation advance automatically, click the Automatic option.

8. In Duration of Page, set how long you want each slide to stay up.

9. In Duration of Pause, set how long of a gap you want between slides.

If you have Show Logo checked, the OpenOffice.org logo appears during the blank pauses.

10. After you have your settings selected, click Create to proceed.

This will open OpenOffice.org Impress, as shown in Figure 7-5. You may find it useful to click the X in the upper right of the Slides pane to clear up the window by closing extra panes.

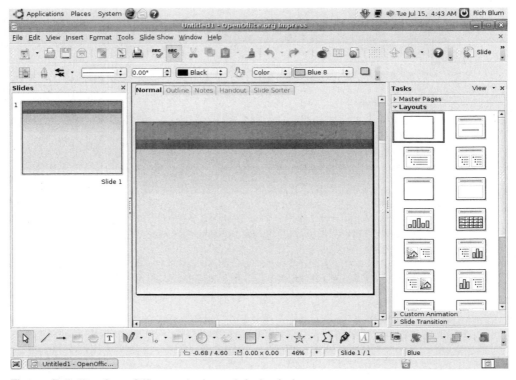

Figure 7-5: The OpenOffice.org Impress default window.

The next section walks through the components used in Impress.

Taking a Tour of OpenOffice.org Impress

The Impress software package is one thing in the OpenOffice.org suite that doesn't mimic its Microsoft Office counterpart. Although you will find some similar features, Impress generally has its own way of doing things. The following sections describe the components used in Impress to assist you in creating your presentation.

Before you proceed, take a look at the window layout shown in Figure 7-5. The default window layout in Impress contains three sections:

- A Slides view on the left side
- A Tasks view on the right side
- The main slide pane in the middle

The Slides and Tasks views, while helpful, might look like clutter if you're trying to concentrate on creating your slide. If you don't need them, just click the X in the upper-right corner of each pane. You can bring them back at any time by choosing View ⇨ Slide Pane and/or View ⇨ Task Pane from the menu bar.

The Menu Bar

Just as with the other OpenOffice.org packages, at the top of the Impress window is the menu bar. Impress has many of the same features as commercial presentation software packages. Here's a brief rundown of the menu items:

- ◆ **File:** Contains the standard Open, Save, Save As, and Print commands, along with a set of standard OpenOffice.org wizards for creating various types of documents. There's also the ability to send documents through email and create templates.
- ◆ **Edit:** Offers the normal Cut, Copy, and Paste functions, along with the Select All and Find commands. One nice feature here is the ability to quickly duplicate a slide.
- ◆ **View:** Contains the Zoom functions and toolbars, along with the ability to select whether you're looking at slides, notes, or another section such as the Slide or Tasks panes.
- ◆ **Insert:** Allows you to insert a new slide, along with charts, frames, graphics, movies, and spreadsheets.
- ◆ **Format:** Includes the usual text-formatting features, along with layout, graphics, and style formatting.
- ◆ **Tools:** Has utilities for spell checking and enabling the autocorrect feature. Also includes functions to create and organize macros, along with an image gallery.
- ◆ **Slide Show:** The slide show controller menu for testing your presentation.

These menus have more features than just those listed here. Half the fun of working with Impress is exploring the features available for creating your presentations.

The Standard Toolbar

Along the top of the window is the standard toolbar, which you can remove at any time by choosing View ⇨ Toolbars ⇨ Standard from the menu bar. Each icon in this toolbar represents a different function and is described in Table 7-5.

Table 7-5: The Impress Standard Toolbar

Button or Item	Description
New	Create new documents of various types. Click the down arrow to select a particular type of document to create from among any of the OpenOffice.org types.
Open	Open an existing file for reading or editing.
Save	Save the current document. If you haven't saved this document before, the Save As dialog box opens.
Document as E-mail	Open a Compose email window in your preferred email program and automatically attach this document.
Edit File	Edit the displayed file.
Export Directly as PDF	Open a Save As dialog box with PDF selected as the file type.
Print File Directly	Send a file to the default printer.

continues

Table 7-5: *(continued)*

Button or Item	Description
Spellcheck	Run the spell checker on your entire document or the selected text.
AutoSpellcheck	Activate or turn off the automatic spell checker feature.
Cut	Remove the selected text from the document and save it in memory.
Copy	Make a copy of the selected document text and save it in memory.
Paste	Place the text from memory into the document at the cursor's current location. Click the down arrow to see options for how the text can be pasted.
Format Paintbrush	Pick up the formatting of the first text you click and apply it to the next text you click.
Undo	Undo the last change you made to the document. Click the down arrow to choose how far you want to back up.
Restore	Reinstate the last change to the document after first using Undo to cancel it. Click the down arrow to choose how far back you want to redo.
Chart	Insert a chart into the presentation by using the selected data.
Spreadsheet	Insert a spreadsheet into the presentation.
Hyperlink	Open or close a dialog box that you can use to build complex hyperlinks.
Display Grid	Display or remove the line-up grid from the slide.
Navigator	Open or close the Navigator window, which allows you to jump to specific features within your document.
Zoom	Alter how large the document shows on your screen.
Help	Open the OpenOffice.org Help dialog box.
Slide	Insert a new slide after the current one.
Slide Design	Open the Slide Design dialog box.
Slide Show	Start a slide show.

As with the other packages in the OpenOffice.org suite, many icons are available in the standard toolbar. You can select which icons appear by clicking the Expand Toolbar button on the far right side of the standard toolbar and selecting the Visible buttons option.

The Line and Filling Bar

The line and filling toolbar is directly below the standard toolbar. This series of icons allows you to select features for the standard items in your slides, such as arrow styles, colors, line styles, and other formatting instructions. Most features on this bar are identical to what you see in modern presentation programs.

The Document Pane

The tabbed pane contains your slides and related information. In Normal view, that document is your slide. Click one of the tools in the drawing bar (discussed in the next section) to enter any content. To add more slides before or after that one, right-click over the document area and select Slide ➪ New Slide. For each slide, you can use the layouts in the Tasks pane on the right to change their setup.

Just above your document you'll see a series of tabs, each of which takes you to a particular view of your slides. Table 7-6 outlines the views and what you find in them.

Table 7-6: Available Impress Views

View	Description
Normal	Individual slide view in which you can edit the slides one by one.
Outline	All-slides view with the slides listed in order for easy reviewing. Along the side, the slides are shown in thumbnail mode in a separate window as you navigate.
Notes	Individual slide view in which you can see a small version of the slide and write notes about that slide.
Handout	Six slides per page, as you might print for handouts.
Slide Sorter	All-slides view with as many slides packed in as possible in columns and rows. You can reorder slides by dragging them where you want them to appear, then dropping them.

These features provide a wealth of opportunities to edit and evaluate your presentation.

Secret

There's one more view that doesn't appear as a tab in the slide area. The Master view is available by selecting View ➪ Master from the menu bar. You have the option in the Master submenu of choosing either Slide Master to view the Master slide, Notes Master to view the Master note page, or Master Elements to assign the information that is available in the Master views.

The Drawing Bar

Beneath the document window is a drawing toolbar, which allows you to select lines, arrows, shapes, and more for your presentation creation needs. Most of these buttons have down arrows that allow you to select additional features for each item.

Working with Impress Files

The Impress application doesn't support as many file types as Writer and Calc do. This limitation is mostly due to a lack of standards in the presentation graphics environment.

The formats that Impress does support are

- **OpenDocument Presentation (.odp) format:** a standard presentation graphics format proposed by OpenOffice.org
- **OpenOffice.org 1.0 Presentation (.otp) format:** the original OpenOffice.org presentation graphics file format
- **Microsoft PowerPoint 97/2000/XP (.ppt) format:** possibly the most popular presentation graphics tool used in business. You can use Impress to read and write most PowerPoint slide presentations
- **OpenOffice.org 1.0 Drawing (.sxd) format:** an older, rudimentary graphics drawing format
- **StarDraw 3.0–5.0 (.sda) format:** Draw's commercial cousin from Sun
- **StarImpress 4.0 and 5.0 (.sdd) format:** Impress' commercial cousin from Sun
- **OpenOffice.org Drawing (.odg) format:** rudimentary graphics drawing format

Although Impress can work with OpenOffice.org Draw files, the default file format for Impress files is the ODP format. As with the other packages in the OpenOffice.org suite, Impress also provides a toolbar icon for you to save your slides as PDF files.

Database

Those who are used to using Microsoft Access to store and organize data might be initially disappointed with Ubuntu, because, by default, there's no database package installed. However, by using the Add/Remove software application you can easily have a full-featured database program at your fingertips. OpenOffice.org Base provides an interface for working with data that is very similar to Microsoft Access.

Getting Help from the Wizard

The Base package provides a graphical interface for many types of databases. The basic use of Base is to create and use a database from scratch in a file on your system. However, Base also allows you to connect to database servers using the Java Database Connectivity (JDBC) and Open Database Connectivity (ODBC) protocols. These options provide a graphical environment for working with just about any type of database.

The first interface you encounter when starting Base is the Database wizard (Figure 7-6).

The wizard guides you through the basics of opening an existing Base database file, creating your own database using the Base database format, or connecting to an existing database server.

Base provides direct access to various database servers, including

- MySQL
- Oracle
- Adabas D
- Spreadsheets
- dBase
- Text files
- Any database using a JDBC driver
- Any database using an ODBC driver

Figure 7-6: The OpenOffice.org Base Database Wizard.

The JDBC and ODBC protocols provide you the ability to connect to any database using industry-standard database drivers.

The following sections describe how to create a new database and open an existing database.

Creating a New Database File in the Database Wizard

In the Database wizard dialog box, do the following to create a new database file:

1. Select the Create a New Database radio button.
2. Click Next. The Decide How to Proceed after Saving the Database dialog box appears.
3. If you want to register this database as a data source in OpenOffice.org, leave Yes, Register the Database for Me selected; otherwise, select the No, Do Not Register the Database radio button. A registered database is accessible by all of your OpenOffice.org applications rather than just OpenOffice.org Base.
4. If you want to immediately open this file for editing, leave the Open the Database for Editing check box checked; otherwise, uncheck the box.
5. If you want to immediately create a new table in the database by using the Table wizard, select the Create Tables Using the Table Wizard check box.
6. Click Finish. The Save As dialog box opens.
7. Either select the directory you want to save the document to in the Save In Folder drop-down list box or click the right-facing arrow next to Browse for Other Folders to navigate to where you want to save the document.
8. Enter the name for your document in the Name text box.
9. Click the Save button.

Whatever you specified should happen. If you chose to immediately open the database, you see something equivalent to Figure 7-7.

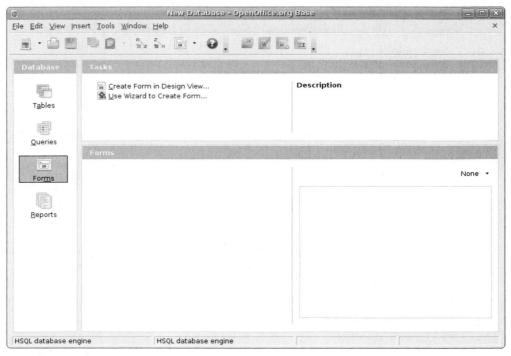

Figure 7-7: A database open in OpenOffice.org Base.

The Base window allows you to work with several types of database objects:

- ◆ **Tables:** Store data into separate tables to organize related data elements.
- ◆ **Queries:** Create queries to extract data based on requirements.
- ◆ **Forms:** Create forms for easily entering new data records.
- ◆ **Reports:** Create reports for displaying data in easy-to-understand formats.

The "Working with Tables" section later in this chapter walks through using data in a Base database.

Opening an Existing File in the Database Wizard

If you have a Microsoft Access file that you want to open in OpenOffice.org Base, do the following from the initial Database wizard dialog box:

1. Select Open an Existing File.

2. If the file is in the Recently Used drop-down list box, select the file there. Otherwise, click the Open button. If you click the Open button, the Open dialog box appears. You can browse to locate the existing database file.

3. Navigate to the file you want to open and select the file.

4. Click Open.

The file opens in a window similar to that shown in Figure 7-7.

Taking a Tour of Base

Before you proceed, let's walk through the basic Base window layout shown in Figure 7-7. The following sections describe what each element does.

The Menu Bar

Along the top of the window is the menu bar. Base gives you access to many of the features you would expect in a database interface:

- **File:** the usual Open, Save, and Save As commands, along with a set of wizards and the ability to send documents through email
- **Edit:** the Cut, Copy, and Paste commands, along with access to database properties, advanced settings, and the Form and Report wizards
- **View:** access to toolbars and database objects, along with preview and sort features
- **Insert:** the ability to create forms, queries, and more
- **Tools:** the ability to assign relationships between tables, filter tables, run SQL queries, create macros, and more

The menu bar provides access to all of the features in Base. Besides the menu bar, Base provides other ways to access the same features.

The Standard Toolbar

Beneath the menu bar is the standard toolbar. Each icon in this series represents a different function, as described in Table 7-7.

Table 7-7: The Base Standard Toolbar

Button or Item	Description
New	Create new documents of various types. Click the down arrow to select a particular type of document to create from among any of the OpenOffice.org types.
Open	Open an existing file for reading or editing.
Save	Save the current document. If you haven't saved this document before, the Save As dialog box opens.
Copy	Make a copy of the selected text and save it in memory.
Paste	Place the text from memory into the document at the cursor's current location. Click the down arrow to see options for how the text can be pasted.
Sort Ascending	Sort the entries in the lower-right pane in alphabetical order.
Sort Descending	Sort the entries in the lower-right pane in reverse alphabetical order.
Form	Create a form.
Help	Open the OpenOffice.org Help dialog box.
Open Database Object	Open the selected item in the lower-right pane.
Edit	Open the Design view for the selected item in the lower-right pane.
Delete	Delete the selected item in the lower-right pane.
Rename	Rename the selected item in the lower-right pane.

You probably know the drill by now: You can modify the standard toolbar to include the items you most commonly use. Just select the Expand Toolbar button at the far right side of the toolbar, then select the Visible Buttons entry to select the buttons you want to appear.

The Database Pane

To the left of the main window area is the Database pane. In this pane you see four icons for the main database objects you can work with: Tables, Queries, Forms, and Reports.

Select these icons to determine what appears in the two rightmost panes. For example, to work with your tables, select the Tables icon. You can manually create your own database object, use the Base Wizard to guide you through creating an object, or select an existing object to view or edit.

The Tasks Pane

The upper-right pane is the Tasks pane. In that pane, you see what types of things you can do for a particular selection in the Database pane. The description to the right of the pane explains what each feature can do for you.

The Tables/Queries/Forms/Reports Pane

The lower-right pane shows the tables, queries, forms, and reports that already exist. You can open any of these files to work in by double-clicking them in this pane.

Working with Tables

Tables are the core of the database system. They hold your data and allow you to quickly access the information. It's a good idea to understand how tables are organized in Base and how you can use them to hold and display your data.

To create a new table, you can use the Base Table Wizard if you want a standard table, or you can create your own table in Design View. Figure 7-8 shows the Table Design View dialog box.

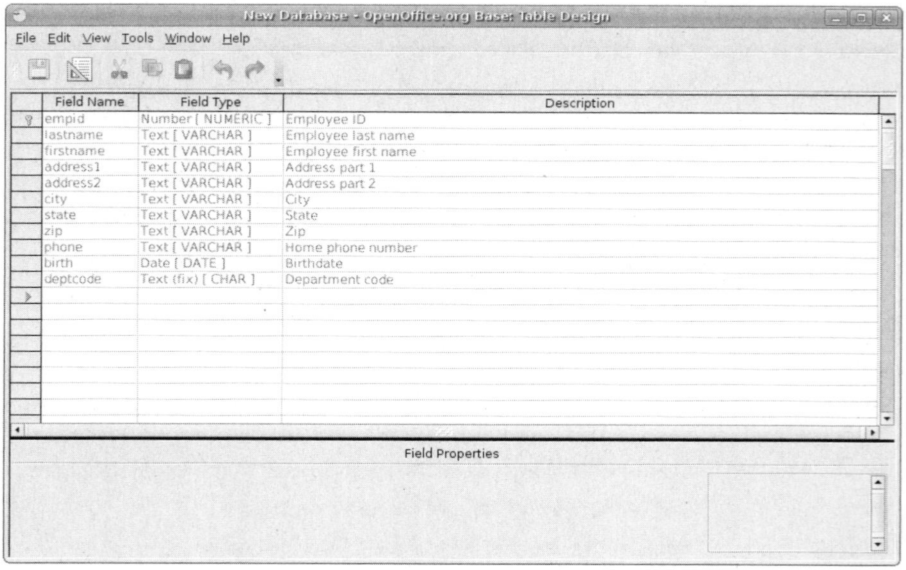

Figure 7-8: The Table Design View dialog box in Base.

Each row in the Table Design box represents a data field in the table. Each field must have a unique field name and be assigned a field type. Field type defines the type of data present in the field (characters, numbers, dates, and so on). The description area allows you to write a brief description describing the meaning of the data field.

Creating a new table is easy:

1. Enter a text name describing the data in the Field Name box.
2. Select a Field Type from the drop-down menu.
3. Enter a brief description in the description text area.
4. If the field is a primary key, right-click on the left of the row and select Primary Key.

   A table's primary key is a data field that can uniquely identify each record in the table. In the example in Figure 7-8, each employee is identified by a unique employee ID because more than one employee can have the same last name.
5. Repeat steps 1 through 4 for any other data elements in the table.
6. Select File ⇨ Save As to save the table with a unique table name.

The new table now appears in the main Base window under the Tables area. Double-clicking the new table brings up the Data Viewing and Entry window, shown in Figure 7-9.

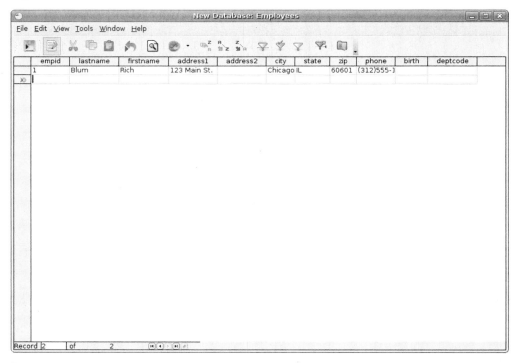

Figure 7-9: The Data Viewing and Entry window in the Base application.

If you are familiar with Microsoft Access, you should feel right at home here. This window allows you to view the existing data records in the table and easily add new data records.

Drawing

Whether you're an aspiring graphic artist or just need a tool that lets you generate simple graphics for use on their own, in a presentation, or elsewhere, OpenOffice.org Draw provides a host of drawing functions. If nothing else, it's a whole lot of fun to play with!

Taking a Tour of OpenOffice.org Draw

To start Draw, don't look in the Office menu. The Draw application appears instead in the Graphics menu under OpenOffice.org Drawing. The main Draw window is shown in Figure 7-10.

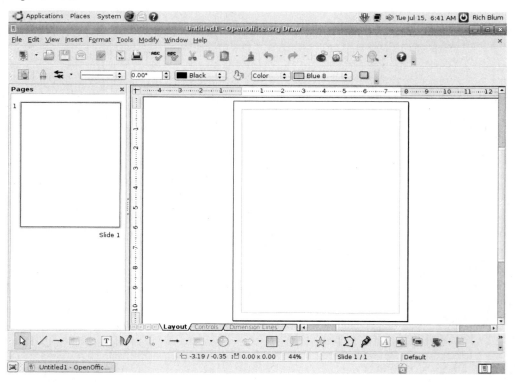

Figure 7-10: The Draw main window area.

Similar to Impress, Draw has some extra windows cluttering up the main window area. If you find the Pages pane on the left too much clutter, click the X in its upper right to get rid of it. You can bring it back any time by selecting View ⇨ Page Pane.

Let's take a walk through the features in the Draw main window.

The Menu Bar

Along the top of the window is the usual menu bar. Draw is a typical "vector" graphics program, meaning that it relies on lines rather than dots or other techniques. (See Chapter 10, "Image Manipulation" for a discussion of software for editing photographs and other heavy-detail graphics work.)

Draw is a fairly extensive drawing application, and it has too many menu options to cover in depth. The following is a summary of what you'll find on each menu:

- **File:** Contains the standard Open, Save, Save As, Print, and Export commands, along with a set of wizards to help create new documents. As with the other OpenOffice.org packages, Draw has the ability to send documents through email and create templates.
- **Edit:** Offers the Cut, Copy, and Paste functions, along with the Find, Replace, and other commands. The unique function here is Image Map, which allows you to create a hotspot on your drawing and link it to a specific URL.
- **View:** Includes the usual Zoom functions and toolbars, along with the ability to select which tools appear in the main Draw window.
- **Insert:** Contains the usual collection of charts, frames, graphics, and spreadsheets, along with options for adding pictures and even movies.
- **Format:** Includes line, text, and graphics formatting, along with layers and style formatting.
- **Tools:** Has utilities for spell checking, as well as hyphenation, autocorrection, an image gallery, and an eyedropper for grabbing colors.
- **Modify:** Contains various options for altering the appearance of an object, such as rotating, aligning, and converting lines to arcs, and images to 3-D.

Secret

The key to the Draw program is its specialized toolbars. Draw provides toolbars for various features you can use in your drawing. You can lay out as many specialized toolbars as you need to perform your work. Select View ⇨ Toolbars to see a list of the specialized toolbars you can use in your project. These toolbars include options for 3-D effects, forms, inserting media, and text formatting.

The Standard Toolbar

Beneath the menu bar is the standard toolbar, which you can remove at any time by choosing View ⇨ Toolbars ⇨ Standard. Each icon in this series represents a different function, as described in Table 7-8.

Table 7-8: The Draw Standard Toolbar

Item	Description
New	Create new documents of various types. Click the down arrow to select a particular type of document to create from among any of the OpenOffice.org types.
Open	Open an existing file for reading or editing.
Save	Save the current document. If you haven't saved this document before, the Save As dialog box opens.
Document as E-mail	Open a Compose email window in your preferred email program and automatically attach this document.
Edit File	Edit the document.
Export Directly as PDF	Open a Save As dialog box with PDF selected as the file type.
Print File Directly	Send a file to the default printer.
Spellcheck	Run the spell checker on your entire document or the selected text.
AutoSpellcheck	Activate or turn off the automatic spell checker feature.
Cut	Remove the selected text from the document and save it in memory.
Copy	Make a copy of the selected text and save it in memory.
Paste	Place the text from memory into the document at the cursor's current location. Click the down arrow to see options of how the text can be pasted.
Format Paint-brush	Pick up the formatting of the first item you click and apply it to the second item you click.
Undo	Undo the last change you made to the document. Click the down arrow to choose how far you want to back up.
Restore	Reinstate the last change to the document after first using Undo to cancel it. Click the down arrow to choose how far back you want to redo.
Chart	Insert a chart using the selected data.
Hyperlink	Open or close a dialog box that you can use to build complex hyperlinks.
Navigator	Open or close the Navigator window, which allows you to jump to specific features within your document.
Zoom	Alter how large the document shows on your screen.
Help	Open the OpenOffice.org Help dialog box.

Draw uses the same basic standard toolbar as the other OpenOffice.org products, so there aren't any surprises here. As with the other products, you can pick and choose which toolbar icon appears by default.

The Line and Filling Bar

The line and filling bar is directly below the standard toolbar. As usual, you can remove the line and filling bar at any time by using the View menu. This series of icons allows you to click buttons and expand drop-down list boxes that represent standard presentation software functions, such as arrow styles, colors, line styles, and other formatting instructions.

The Ruler

Directly below the line and filling bar are the rulers. These items mark the margins and tabs, for example, of your document in the measuring units of your choice. To change which measurement units you want to use, right-click the ruler and change the Measurements to your preferences.

The Document Pane

Click in the big white space and start drawing. You can access the formatting menu by right-clicking in the document pane.

You don't have to start out with a blank canvas. Draw allows you to work with most popular image file types. Just use the File ⇨ Open menu selection to choose any standard graphics format file (such as BMP or JPG) to work with. After the file is opened in Draw, you can use all of the standard Draw tools available to work on the image.

The Drawing Bar

Beneath the document window is a drawing toolbar, which allows you to select lines, arrows, shapes, and more for your drawing creation needs. Most of these buttons have down arrows, which allow you to see the full range of features they offer.

Working with Draw Files

When you attempt to open or save a file, you'll notice that Draw appears to have limited support for different file types. The only file formats you can save a document as are

- ◆ **OpenDocument Drawing (.odg) format:** the OpenOffice.org proposed standard for graphics files
- ◆ **OpenOffice.org 1.0 Drawing (.sxd) format:** the older OpenOffice.org graphics format
- ◆ **StarDraw 3.0 (.sdd) format:** the older Sun StarDraw format
- ◆ **StarDraw 5.0 (.sda) format:** the newer Sun StarDraw format

That's not much to work with, especially when dealing with picture files. Fortunately, Draw has an alternative way to save images. You can save images to a format other than the standard formats by using the Export feature in the File menu.

This produces a host of supported graphics formats: BMP, EMF, EPS, GIF, JPG, MET, PBM, PCT, PGM, PNG, PPM, RAS, SVG, SWF (Flash), TIFF, WMF, and XPM. That range of formats should satisfy any artist.

Math

One of the limitations of Writer is its inability to work with mathematical symbols. If you work in an environment that uses math symbols in reports, you either have to use multiple lines to show your equations (which never looks right!) or write them by hand.

The OpenOffice.org Math package is a great solution to this problem. You can lay out complex mathematical equations using proper symbols in the Math editor workspace, then insert them into any of your OpenOffice.org documents. Whether you're a middle school student or a professional engineer, Math is a great tool to have installed in your OpenOffice.org environment.

Starting Math

The Math application differs somewhat from other OpenOffice.org applications installed in Ubuntu. You can search the Panel menus for hours and you won't find the entry for Math.

Instead, you must start a Math session from within another OpenOffice.org application. In each of the OpenOffice.org applications, when you select File ⇨ New from the menu bar, you get a list of new documents you can start. One of those options is Formula.

Selecting a new Formula document starts a new Math window, shown in Figure 7-11.

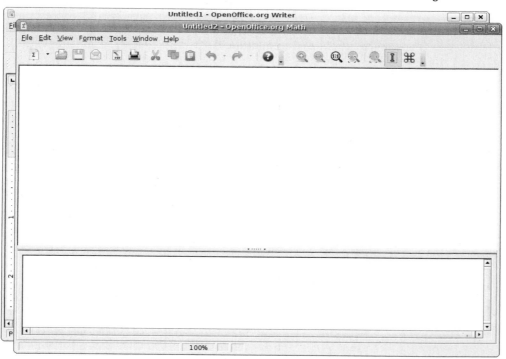

Figure 7-11: The OpenOffice.org Math main window.

There's not all that much to the Math window. Let's take a walk through the various sections.

The Math Layout

Many OpenOffice.org Math functions are different from other OpenOffice.org programs. However, in many ways this program is less complex than some, thanks to its special-purpose nature. Remember that it's not a calculation program. It's for laying out complex formulas on paper or the screen.

The Menu Bar

Along the top of the window is the menu bar, just the same as the other OpenOffice.org applications:

- ◆ **File:** the standard Open, Save, Save As, and Print commands that you find in most OpenOffice.org programs, along with a set of wizards and the ability to send documents through email
- ◆ **Edit:** the Cut, Copy, and Paste commands, along with Select All, and the ability to move to set markers in the formula
- ◆ **View:** the usual Zoom functions and toolbars, along with screen update features
- ◆ **Format:** settings to change the font type, font size, spacing, and alignment features. Also contains an entry to convert the formula into text mode as best as possible
- ◆ **Tools:** the standard Customize and Options entries for customizing Math's setup and behaviors, in addition to formula importing and access to the symbol catalog

The Standard Toolbar

Beneath the menu bar is the standard toolbar. Each icon in this series represents a different function. You're likely to find this toolbar quite different from those in the other OpenOffice.org programs. Mostly, it's just smaller with fewer options. Each icon is described in Table 7-9.

Table 7-9: The Math Standard Toolbar

Item	Description
New	Create new documents of various types. Click the down arrow to select a particular type of document to create from among any of the OpenOffice.org types.
Open	Open an existing file for reading or editing.
Save	Save the current document. If you haven't saved this document before, the Save As dialog box opens.
Document as E-mail	Open a Compose email window in your preferred email program and automatically attach this document.

continues

Table 7-9: *(continued)*

Item	*Description*
Export Directly as PDF	Open a Save As dialog box with PDF selected as the file type.
Print File Directly	Send a file to the default printer.
Cut	Remove the selected text from the document and save it in memory.
Copy	Make a copy of the selected text and save it in memory.
Paste	Place the text from memory into the document at the cursor's current location. Click the down arrow to see options for how the text can be pasted.
Undo	Undo the last change you made to the document. Click the down arrow to choose how far you want to back up.
Restore	Reinstate the last change to the document after first using Undo to cancel it. Click the down arrow to choose how far back you want to redo.
Help	Open the OpenOffice.org Help dialog box.
Zoom In	Show the image larger.
Zoom Out	Shrink the image.
I	Show the image at its actual size.
Show All	Show the whole formula in the largest size that will fit on the screen.
Update	Update the formula shown in the document window.
Formula Cursor	Turn on or shut off the formula cursor.
Catalog	Open the Symbols dialog box.

There are fewer things you can do with the formulas in Math, so there are fewer features in its standard toolbar.

The Document Pane

This is where all the action occurs. There are two sections in the document pane:

- The main (upper) window
- The Commands (lower) window

You can't type anything in the main (upper) document window in Math. Instead, you type in the Commands (lower) window. As you enter the formula in the Commands window, the text appears in the main window. Right-clicking in the Commands window opens a shortcut menu. The shortcut menu provides standard formulas that you can use in your formula. Select a specific formula from the shortcut menu, and a template appears in the Commands window, along with the real output in the main window. The best way to see how this works is to experiment. That's what we'll do in the next section.

Working with Math

If you have never used software like this, it helps to work through a simple example to see what is involved in creating a mathematical formula you can export to your Writer document.

Here's a simple exercise you can do to get a feel for using Math:

1. Right-click in the Commands window. The main shortcut menu opens.
2. Select a submenu to open. We'll select the Formats submenu for this exercise.
3. Select a formula component within this submenu. To follow along with this exercise, choose the matrix {…} entry. The template for the matrix code that's needed in order to add a matrix to the formula appears in the Commands dialog box. It uses the <?> symbol to indicate an entry in the matrix equation that you must replace. Also, the actual matrix layout appears in the main window. The combination is shown in Figure 7-12.

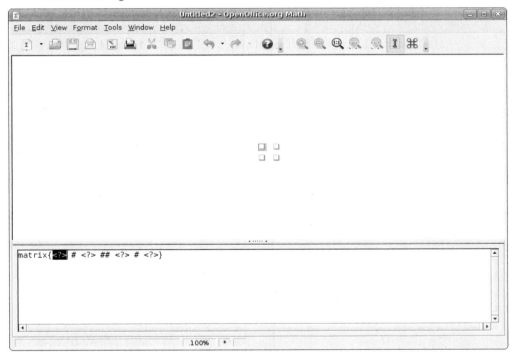

Figure 7-12: Starting to add a matrix in Math.

Secret

If you prefer to select the mathematical symbols visually rather than by their names, select the View ⇨ Selection option from the menu bar. This produces the Selection dialog box with two sections. The top section contains buttons for each of the symbol categories. As you select a symbol category, the symbols contained in that category appear in the bottom section of the dialog box.

Just click on the symbol you want to use, and it appears in the command window.

4. Replace each of the <?> entries with the proper letters and numbers for your formula.

   When you change matrix{<?> # <?> ## <?> # <?>} to matrix{A # B ## C # D}, Math automatically places the variables in the main window output.

5. Continue adding components to the formula until you're finished.

   Suppose that you want to multiply the matrix by 3. To find out the proper format for multiplication, press Enter to go down to the next line in the Commands window (to use as "scratch paper"), right-click to display the pop-up menu, and choose Unary/Binary Operators ▷ a Times b. This choice adds the phrase <?> times <?> beneath the matrix code. Now you know how to format a multiplication, so erase this phrase and use it as a guideline to change your formula to:

   ```
   3 times matrix{A # B ## C # D}
   ```

   This line gives the result shown in Figure 7-13.

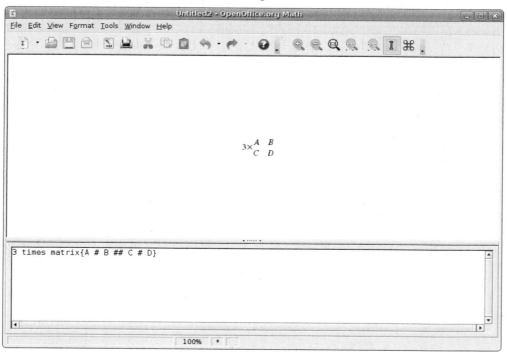

Figure 7-13: A complete formula in OpenOffice.org. Math.

Once you've created your formula you can save it using OpenDocument format (.odf), the StarOffice format (.sxm), and MathML 1.01 (.mml) format. The MathML format is a standard similar to HTML for working on the Web. You can also use the Export to PDF button in the standard toolbar to create a PDF document with your new formula.

Summary

This chapter walked through the world of OpenOffice.org, the standard office productivity suite used in Ubuntu. OpenOffice.org provides several applications to help with your office automation needs. The Writer application provides word-processing capability and can be used to read and save documents in Microsoft Word format. Likewise, the Calc program is a spreadsheet application that can read and save documents in Microsoft Excel format.

The Impress application provides presentation graphics capabilities to Ubuntu. Although it can read PowerPoint files, it currently has limited functionality, so you might be restricted in what you can do. The Draw application provides additional graphic capabilities that allow you to create and manipulate image files using many common image formats.

The Base application provides personal database services. You can create tables, queries, forms, and reports in a graphical environment, using a local database file or by connecting to a remote network database server.

Finally, the chapter walked through the Math application. Math allows you to create complex mathematical formulas to insert into your Writer documents.

In the next chapter we'll dive into the world of Internet software. These days, just about everyone uses the Internet, so having software to interact on the Internet is a must. Ubuntu provides several Internet applications by default, plus it provides some extended applications that are easy to install. We'll walk through the most popular ones for various Internet functions.

Network Applications

Chapter
8

♦ ♦

Secrets in This Chapter

Talking with Ekiga

Browsing with Firefox

IM'ing with Pidgin

Accessing Other Workstations with Remote Desktop Viewer

Accessing Windows Servers with Terminal Server Client

File Sharing with BitTorrent

File Retrieval with gFTP

♦ ♦

These days, working on the Internet has become almost a necessity of life. Whether you are researching school projects or working on job proposals, the Internet provides a vast wealth of information at your fingertips. The key to tapping into that information is having the correct software tools available. Ubuntu is no slouch when it comes to providing software applications to access the Internet. There's a software package for just about anything you'd want to do on the Internet. This chapter walks through the basic Internet software packages you can use in your Ubuntu installation.

The Ubuntu Internet Software Suite

The Ubuntu distribution supports a wide variety of software that allows you to interact on the Internet. A core group of Internet packages is part of the standard installation. You can access this software by selecting Applications ⇨ Internet from the Panel menu. The standard software packages you'll find are

- Ekiga Softphone
- Evolution email
- Firefox web browser
- Pidgin instant messenger
- Remote Desktop Viewer
- Terminal Server Client
- Transmission BitTorrent Client

This chapter looks at all of these applications but one. We'll save discussing the Evolution email software package for Chapter 9, "Evolution," because email is such an important topic.

Ekiga

The world of Internet phone service has exploded with the popularity of broadband Internet connectivity in the home. Being able to reliably place and receive phone calls to anywhere around the world from your Internet connection is pretty cool and can save you some money. Ubuntu includes the Ekiga Internet phone software to turn your Ubuntu workstation into a telephone that can reach the world!

The default Ekiga Internet phone software is a redesign of the old GNOME GnomeMeeting package for Internet voice and video conferencing applications. Ekiga was expanded to provide the same basic functions as the more popular Skype software, along with compatibility with Microsoft NetMeeting. This compatibility allows you to join in conferences with your Microsoft friends.

To start Ekiga, click on Applications ⇨ Internet ⇨ Ekiga Softphone. The first time you start Ekiga, you get a series of configuration windows to help you set up your system.

Follow these steps to configure your Ekiga software:

1. Click Forward to start the wizard.

    The Ekiga wizard may skip to step 3 automatically if it detects your full username in your Ubuntu username configuration.

2. If prompted, type the name you want to be identified by on the network.

Other Ekiga users see you listed by the name you enter here.

3. Click Forward to continue.

The wizard proceeds to the Ekiga Account page.

4. Type your Ekiga account username and password where prompted.

If you don't have an account yet, click the button to go to the Ekiga web site (www. ekiga.net) and register for a free account. If you prefer, you can use the Ekiga Softphone with other Internet phone providers and skip this step. After installing Ekiga you'll need to refer to your specific provider's instructions for configuring the software.

5. Click Forward to continue.

6. In the resulting Connection Type window, select the type of Internet connection your system uses, then click Forward.

The configuration wizard goes through a series of windows to automatically determine hardware and software specifics of your system.

7. For each subsequent window, click Forward after the relevant determination or detection is completed.

The series of windows includes the following:

- **NAT Type:** Determines whether a network address translation (NAT) server is in place between your system and the Internet. Remote Ekiga users who want to call to you must be able to access your system from the Internet. If you use a NAT for Internet connectivity, your network address is the address of the NAT, not your system. You'll need to connect to a remote server for them to access you directly. Ekiga takes care of this for you.

- **Audio Manager:** Detects the software that controls your audio applications. For Ubuntu, this software is called ALSA.

- **Audio Devices:** Detect the audio input and output devices on your system. The Ekiga software will most likely succeed in detecting these devices with no intervention on your part. If you have more than one audio input or output device, you can select which one to use for Ekiga.

- **Video Manager:** Detects the video manager software on your system. For most Ubuntu, this software is Video4Linux (V4L2).

- **Video Devices:** Determines whether a video input device (webcam) is connected to your system.

8. Click the Apply button to accept the settings and start Ekiga.

After finishing the configuration, the main Ekiga window (shown in Figure 8-1) appears, listening for incoming calls and waiting for you to place a call.

When you don't want the Ekiga window on your desktop, you can close it and keep Ekiga running in the background. It appears on your desktop panel as an icon, indicating that it's still running. Click the icon for the main Ekiga window to appear. Right-clicking the icon allows you to perform several functions, such as place a new call, set your availability status, or look up a phone number in your phone book. When a new call comes in, the icon will light up and you'll hear a sound.

Figure 8-1: The main Ekiga window.

Secret

After you're registered you can participate via four communication types:

● **Softphone-to-Softphone:** Communicate with remote SIP users via their SIP address—even with users on different SIP servers. The Ekiga SIP server will forward SIP calls to the remote server and accept calls from remote SIP servers. You can make and receive SIP calls at no cost with your Ekiga account.

● **Softphone-to-Real Phone:** Place calls to regular telephone numbers using your Ekiga Softphone. You must register a separate account at the Ekiga website and pay any relevant charges you accrue for your calls.

● **Real Phone-to-Softphone:** Receive calls from regular telephones using a phone number you purchase from Ekiga. The phone number can be located in any country! When the number receives an incoming call, Ekiga will route the call to your SIP connection.

● **Text messaging:** Send instant messages to any SIP address on any SIP server via the Chat window in the Ekiga Softphone.

Firefox

Many people attribute the explosive growth of the Internet to the graphical web browser. The Internet had been around for a long time before the invention of the browser, but the graphical browser allowed the common PC user easy access to the Internet.

The most popular browser for the Linux platform is *Firefox*. Firefox is actually just one component in the Mozilla suite of Internet software packages that provides web browsing, email, and newsfeed reading. However, in Ubuntu it's automatically installed by and is the default web browser.

This section walks through the features of Firefox, plus shows you how to customize Firefox for your own browsing pleasure.

Walking Through Firefox

Firefox's primary purpose is to fetch web pages, download their content, and render the page for your interactive viewing pleasure. It does this via internal and external software modules. Knowing how to use and configure these modules is crucial for your web pages to display properly.

If you're used to using Microsoft's Internet Explorer or Apple's Safari web browsers, the basic functions in Firefox should be familiar. The main layout of the Firefox browser window is shown in Figure 8-2.

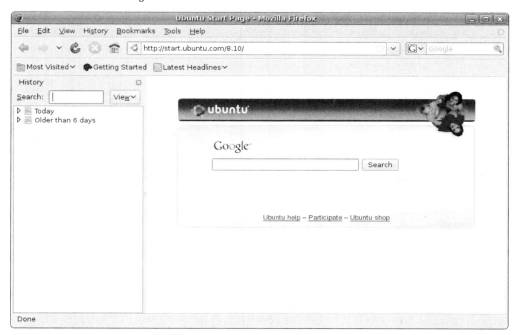

Figure 8-2: Firefox with the History sidebar open.

I'm sure you'll recognize some, if not all, of the features in the Firefox browsing window. The following sections walk through the individual features you'll find in the Firefox browser.

The Menu Bar

The menu bar at the top of the window provides easy access to all of the features of Firefox. The menu bar contains the following menu items:

- ◆ **File:** Open local HTML files and remote URLs, save web pages to local files, and print web pages.
- ◆ **Edit:** Cut, copy, and paste text within web pages, search within web pages, and set your Firefox preferences (setting preferences is discussed in detail in the "Configuring Firefox" section later in this chapter).
- ◆ **View:** Enable and disable individual toolbars, change the font size and type used for text, and view the HTML source code used to create the web page.

♦ **History:** Navigate forward and backward through recently viewed web pages by single-stepping through them or jumping directly to a recently viewed page listed.

♦ **Bookmarks:** Set a link to a viewed page and select previously saved links.

♦ **Tools:** Access downloaded files, search the web for terms, and customize Firefox add-ons.

♦ **Help:** Access the online Firefox manual and report bugs and broken web sites.

The Navigation Toolbar

The next area in the browser window is the navigation toolbar. This toolbar provides items to help you navigate among web pages:

♦ **Back arrow:** Single step backward through recently viewed web pages.

♦ **Forward arrow:** Single step forward through recently viewed web pages.

♦ **Recent pages button:** Lists the recently viewed web pages so you can jump directly to a particular page.

♦ **Refresh:** Requests that the web site resend the page content.

♦ **Stop:** Stops loading data from a web site.

♦ **Home:** Goes to the home page setting in the preferences.

♦ **Address textbox:** Manually enter a URL to display; displays the URL of the web site currently being viewed.

♦ **Google search text box:** Links directly to the Google search web site and sends data entered for the search.

The Google search text box is a great feature to have handy in the navigation toolbar. It allows you to perform Google searches without having to go to the Google site.

Secret

The address text box in Firefox does lots more than just allow you to type in a URL. If you type a URL, the address text box becomes a drop-down list that lists sites matching the characters in the URL as you type. The drop-down list also displays titles of web pages, which is a great help in identifying sites.

Once you connect to a web site, you'll notice that icons appear next to the URL in the address text box. If the web site supports newsfeeds, Firefox allows you to subscribe to the newsfeed by clicking the orange signal icon (the radiating circles). There's also a star icon next to the URL. Clicking that icon bookmarks the page.

The Bookmark Toolbar

The bookmark toolbar consists of three buttons:

♦ **Most Visited:** Arranges links to the web pages you visit the most, sorted in order of visits.

♦ **Getting Started:** Takes you directly to the Firefox web page, which contains tutorials and an online manual.

♦ **Latest Headlines:** Combines output from several newsfeeds into one list. You can click on a single news topic to view the entire story.

You can add new bookmarks and folders for bookmarks to the bookmark toolbar. Right-click on an empty space in the bookmark toolbar, then select New Bookmark or New Folder to add bookmarks, or New Separator to add a separator bar between entries.

Secret You can also work with your bookmarks from a sidebar in the main window area. Select View ⇨ Sidebar ⇨ Bookmarks to open the Bookmarks sidebar. From here you can list all of the bookmarks in the Bookmark toolbar, your Bookmark menu area, or all of the bookmarks at once.

The Browser Window

The meat and potatoes of Firefox is the browser window area, which is where you'll see web site content appear. Firefox displays both text and images, and it attempts to handle multimedia content such as audio clips and video if it has the appropriate plug-ins (more on that in the "Configuring Firefox" section later in this chapter).

Firefox supports tabbed browsing. Tabbed browsing enables you to open several web sites in the same Firefox window. Tabbed browsing is a relatively new feature in web browsers, so you may not have run into it yet. It's a great feature to use if you have to jump between several sites comparing information.

After you start the Firefox web browser, the web site defined as your home page appears in a tabbed page. You can keep that page open and open another web site in a new tabbed page by pressing Ctrl-t. The new web page appears within the same Firefox window as a tabbed page. You can switch between the two tabbed pages by simply clicking the appropriate tab at the top of each page.

You can also open web links as new tabbed pages by right-clicking the link and selecting Open Link in New Tab. This feature is great for navigating through complex web sites where you need to refer back to previous pages.

Configuring Firefox

Using the default settings in Firefox, you can start surfing right away without having to customize your browser. However, you may want to take a moment to look over the various Firefox preferences, such as the default web site to show when it starts up, what font sizes to use, what colors to use, and many other options.

The following steps show how to access the Preferences window, where the Firefox configuration parameters are stored:

1. Start Firefox.

   Ubuntu provides two ways for you to start Firefox. You can use the standard menu entry by clicking Applications ⇨ Internet ⇨ Firefox, or you can just click the globe icon in the top panel.

2. Choose Edit ⇨ Preferences.

   The Preferences window appears, as shown in Figure 8-3. This dialog box contains all of the settings you'll need to personalize your web browsing experience.

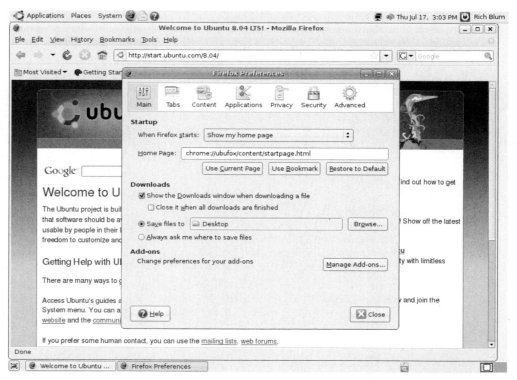

Figure 8-3: The Firefox Preferences window.

3. Click the icons along the top of the Preferences window to access the various preferences categories.

The Advanced category is complex enough to offer tabs for various subcategories. We'll explore these individual tabs as well.

4. Click Close to close the Preferences dialog box and get back to surfing.

The following sections walk though each of the preference categories you can set.

Main Preferences

Selecting the *Main* icon allows you to determine how you want Firefox to look and act when it runs. This dialog box contains three separate sections:

◆ **Startup:** This section allows you to choose what Firefox shows you immediately upon starting. You can type a URL directly into the Home Page text box or click one of the following buttons:

• **Use Current Page:** Navigate to the page you want to use for your default web page, then click this button. The URL for this page appears in the Location(s) text box.

- **Use Bookmark:** Click this button to open the Set Home Page dialog box, which contains all of your bookmarks. Select the bookmark you want to use, then click OK to add the URL for this page to the Location(s) text box.
- **Restore to Default:** Click this button to have Firefox open with an empty window.

◆ **Downloads:** This section allows you to set how Firefox performs file downloads. You can specify where you want Firefox to download files, as well as indicate whether the Downloads window appears while a file is downloading.

◆ **Add-ons:** You can add and manage additional utilities for Firefox. The section "Working with Add-ons" later in this chapter describes these options in more detail.

Tabs

This Preferences section provides a few options that control how Firefox handles tabbed browsing:

◆ **Set new pages to open in a tabbed window or a new window:** Many web sites configure links to open in a separate window so that the original web page stays visible. This setting allows you to open these links in a tabbed window rather than start a new Firefox session.

◆ **Warn when closing Firefox if multiple tabs are open:** When closing Firefox, it's easy to forget you have multiple tabs open. This feature causes Firefox to warn you that web sites are open in other tabs.

◆ **Warn when using multiple tabs might affect the performance of Firefox:** Using multiple tabs takes extra processing power, so use tabs with caution if you're running on a slower system. If this option is enabled, Firefox will attempt to notify you when things start getting sluggish.

◆ **Always show the tab bar at the top, even if there's only one page:** By default Firefox doesn't show a tab if there's only one page open.

◆ **Switch to a new tab page immediately when it's opened:** Rather than switch to a new page, you might prefer to stay on the original page when you open a new tab. If this check box *isn't* selected, Firefox will keep the current tabbed window open instead of switching to the newly opened tab.

Secret

Be careful when using tabbed browsing on sites that use an authentication method such as a user login. Tabbed browsers are notorious for sharing sessions between tabbed windows, so if you log into a site in one tabbed window, you can access the site in another tabbed window with the same login without logging in. Unfortunately, if you log out from one window, sometimes the other window is still logged into the site. Be especially careful of this "feature" when using Firefox in a shared workstation environment.

Content Settings

Selecting the *Content* icon brings you to the Content section of the Firefox Preferences dialog box, shown in Figure 8-4.

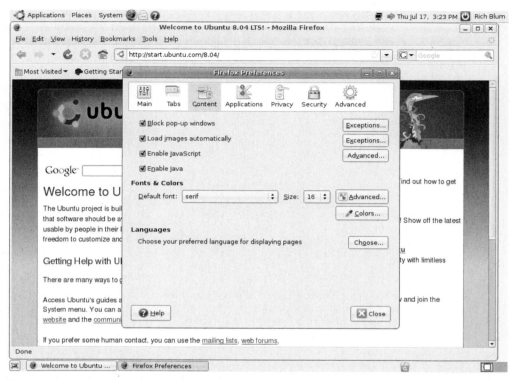

Figure 8-4: The Firefox Content Preferences window.

This section lets you control how Firefox handles various types of content on web pages. The settings at the top allow you to process or block particular items. Notice that each of these options has a button to its right that offers additional control:

♦ **Block Popup Windows:** Tells Firefox to block new windows that appear automatically from web sites. Be careful of this feature though, because some sites have functionality that requires the ability to open additional windows, such as a login window. You can click the Allowed Sites button to make exceptions for them. If you don't configure this feature, a yellow bar appears in the browser window when a pop-up is blocked, allowing you to access the pop-up settings if you wish to change them.

♦ **Load Images Automatically:** Lets you block all images in a web site. This is a useful feature for people who are sight impaired or who are trying to speed up browsing by blocking pictures. Selecting the option For the Originating Web Site Only blocks many ads. That's because ads are often loaded from other sites and appear on the one you're viewing, but that option can also block legitimate graphics. The Exceptions button helps you manage what to see and what not to see.

♦ **Enable JavaScript:** This option, when unchecked, prevents web sites from running JavaScript on your browser. If you visit unfamiliar sites, disabling JavaScript may prevent bad things from happening, but some sites rely on it to provide fancy features, such as pop-up menus. The Advanced button opens the Advanced

JavaScript Settings dialog box, which you can use to choose what you will allow this scripting language to do. In this dialog box, you can set what you'll allow JavaScripts to do and not do.

◆ **Enable Java:** Enabling this feature allows Firefox to run any Java applet code that's sent by a web site. There are checks in Java applet code to prevent unauthorized access to your system, but, again, if you visit a lot of unfamiliar sites, disabling Java may prevent bad things from happening.

The middle section of the Content settings box is Fonts & Colors. These features include

◆ **Default Font:** Click this drop-down list box to select the font you want to use.

◆ **Size:** Click this drop-down list box to choose the font size you want to use.

◆ **Advanced:** Click this button to open the Fonts dialog box, which lets you choose the default fonts and sizes to use for various font classes, along with other visual settings. Here you can also specify that pages can use their own fonts rather than your overrides.

◆ **Colors:** Click this button to open the Colors dialog box and change the default colors assigned to text, the background, and links.

At the bottom is the Languages section, along with a Choose button. Some web sites offer content in more than one language. Setting this value to a specific language tells Firefox which language to select if there's a choice.

Secret

If you want to change the font size of a web page, hold down the Ctrl-+ (plus) keys to make the fonts bigger or the Ctrl-- (minus) keys to make the fonts smaller. (The + and - refer to the keys on your number keypad, not the main keyboard.)

Applications

The *Applications* section shows the application Firefox will launch when it detects various multimedia file types in web pages. For each multimedia file type, you can select from several options:

◆ **Always ask:** Provides a dialog box that allows you to pick which application Firefox should use to open the content.

◆ **Save file:** Provides a Save As dialog box to save the file on your hard drive.

◆ **Use an external application:** Lets you select a specific external program to run the content from the web site, while leaving Firefox running.

◆ **Use a Firefox plug-in:** Allows you to select an internal Firefox plug-in to run the content inside the Firefox browser window.

Plug-ins are small utilities that run inside Firefox to render multimedia content within the Firefox window. Firefox provides several default plug-ins, along with additional plug-ins developed by other programmers. We'll examine plug-ins more closely in the "Working with Add-ons" section later in this chapter.

Privacy

There's plenty of information that Firefox stores on your workstation while you're browsing. The *Privacy* icon section provides some level of control on how Firefox handles that information. These options are shown in Figure 8-5.

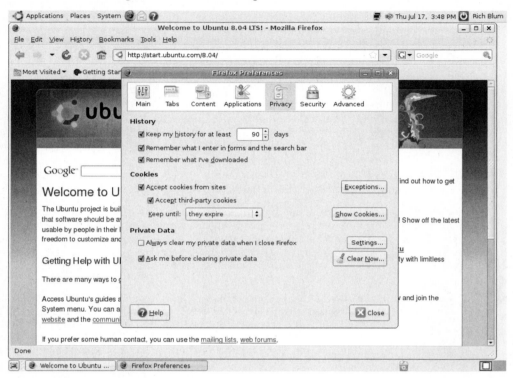

Figure 8-5: The Firefox Privacy Preferences window.

The privacy-setting options are

◆ **History:** The History section lets you designate how many days you want your browser to remember where you've been. You can also choose to let Firefox remember text you've entered into forms and the search bar. If you use this feature, Firefox will attempt to autocomplete words you've already typed before in those forms. You can also allow Firefox to remember the files you've downloaded so you can easily review them to avoid inadvertently downloading a file you've already downloaded.

◆ **Cookies:** Cookies have become a sensitive topic in the Internet world. Cookies are small files a web site stores on your machine so that data you've accumulated on the site can be accessed again when you return. A web site can read only the cookies that it sets, so one site can't tell what other sites you've been to. To prevent cookies from being stored, uncheck the Accept Cookies from Sites box. You can also only allow certain sites to set cookies by clicking the Exceptions button and adding the sites into the list.

♦ You can view every cookie you currently have by clicking the Show Cookies button, and can either remove them individually (select the cookie you want to remove, then click Remove Cookie) or click the Remove All Cookies button to toss out all of your cookies immediately. For the Keep Until drop-down list box, choose how often you want Firefox to dump cookies:

- **Until they expire:** Most cookies have an automatic expiry date. This setting allows Firefox to delete cookies when they expire.

- **I close Firefox:** If you are using a shared workstation or just don't want the computer storing cookies after you're done using the browser, choose this option.

- **Ask me every time:** If you want to be ultra-paranoid about cookies or to see how often they are actually used, choose this option.

♦ **Private Data:** This section allows you to specify which stored items (such as cookies, temporary files, history items, and stored form data) are cleared and how they are cleared. Select the Always Clear My Private Data When I Close Firefox check box if you want to clear all of your stored files every time you exit Firefox.

♦ You can select specific items to clear by clicking the Settings button and choosing the individual items you want cleared. To prevent accidental clearing of your data, the Ask Me Before Clearing Private Data check box is selected by default.

Secret

The private data also include cached web pages that Firefox stores as temporary files while you browse. Firefox stores each site you visit as a file in the cache area. The next time you visit the site, Firefox determines whether the page is the same, and, if it is, automatically displays the cached page to save network bandwidth.

These cached pages take up space on your hard drive and can slow down your browsing experience when you get too many. It's always a good idea to periodically clear the cache on a regular basis. Instead of digging down into the Preferences menu to do that, you can hit the Ctrl-Shift-Del key combination on the keyboard while Firefox is running or select Tools ⇨ Clear Private Data from the menu bar.

Security

The *Security* section provides settings that control your well-being while browsing the web. This option is divided into three sections:

♦ **Phishing settings:** The first three check boxes specify actions that Firefox should take when it thinks it's encountered a rogue web site. Such sites include those that try to automatically download add-ons to Firefox (either with or without your knowledge), sites that are on a list of suspected attack sites, and sites whose IP address doesn't resolve to the hostname they claim they are.

♦ **Passwords:** Firefox allows you to store in a local file any passwords that you commonly use while on the web. This feature helps you remember and type your passwords in web site forms. However, storing passwords can be a risky practice, so Firefox also provides a master password you can set to gain access to your stored passwords.

◆ **Warning messages:** Firefox can warn you when you're about to embark on risky activity on the Internet. This includes sending data to an unencrypted page, leaving an encrypted page to go to an unencrypted page, and visiting encrypted pages that use older encryption algorithms.

Secret

Phishing (trying to obtain personal data by trickery) has become a huge problem on the Internet. It usually appears as a two-pronged attack. First, someone sends you an email message pretending to be from a bank or other trusted source. That email message includes a link that redirects you to a web site to "verify" your account information.

The second prong in the attack is in the web site that the link takes you to. These web sites may look official, but they have nothing to do with the actual bank or trusted source you think they are. The anti-phishing settings in Firefox can detect and warn you when a web site attempts to disguise itself as a trusted web site.

Advanced Preferences

This section provides four tabbed sections of settings for more advanced features in Firefox that you probably won't need to change:

◆ **General:** The General tab lets you set up features for movement-impaired users, implement additional browser control features, and ensure that another program doesn't replace Firefox as the default browser on the system.

◆ **Network:** Click the Settings tab in the Connections section if you must use a proxy server on your network to access the Internet. The Cache section allows you to set how much disk space Firefox is allowed to consume when storing visited web page content. This setting allows Firefox to display the pages faster the next time you visit them. You can clear the cache by clicking the Clear Now button. The cache data is also part of the private data that you can set to clear automatically when you exit Firefox.

◆ **Update:** The Update tab tells Firefox how to handle checking for updates, both for itself and for any add-ons you have installed.

◆ **Encryption:** The Encryption tab has settings for security protocols Firefox uses and for any special encryption certificates for encrypted web sites. Usually, you can leave these settings alone.

Working with Add-ons

Firefox includes some pretty advanced features for web browsing. However, you can extend the features available in Firefox with two methods:

◆ Plug-ins
◆ Extensions

A *plug-in* provides functionality to Firefox for handling different types of multimedia. A plug-in displays the results directly in the Firefox browser window, instead of using an external program that runs outside the browser. When browsing you often may be prompted by Firefox to install a particular plug-in to view content on a web page. Firefox can detect which plug-in is required for a specific type of multimedia content. Chapter 11, "Using Audio," and Chapter 12, "Using Video," explain how to add popular plug-ins (such as Macromedia's Flash plug-in) to your system.

Firefox also supports a concept called *extensions,* which refers to extra features that aren't included in the main Firefox browser. Extensions allow you to pick and choose advanced features that can enhance your browsing experience.

Select Tools ⇨ Add-ons to open the Add-ons dialog box, shown in Figure 8-6.

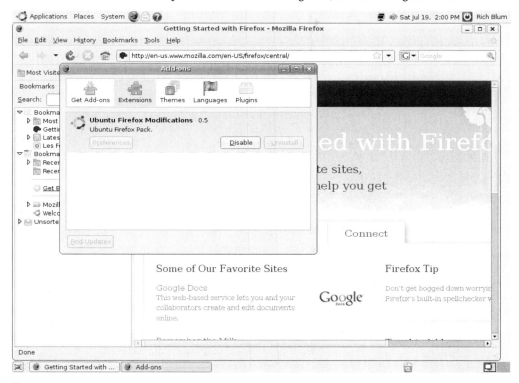

Figure 8-6: The Firefox Add-ons dialog box.

The Extensions section shows the currently installed extensions. The only extension Ubuntu installs by default is the Ubuntu Firefox pack, a customized set of features for Ubuntu.

Click the Get Add-ons link (if you are connected to the Internet) to open a web page that lets you browse to see what extensions are available. You'll see a list of common extensions that are recommended to install, plus a link to get Ubuntu-specific extensions. When you click the Ubuntu extensions link, the Ubuntu Install/Remove Extensions dialog box appears, shown in Figure 8-7.

You can peruse a list of extensions you can add to Firefox and select the ones you think might come in handy.

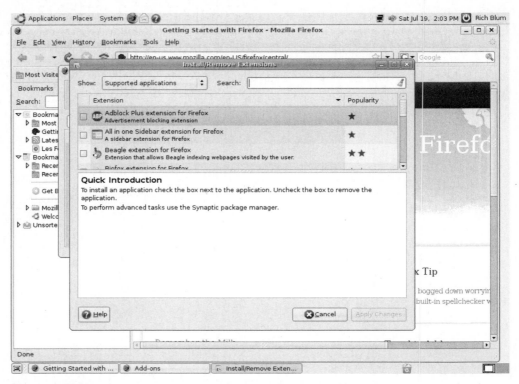

Figure 8-7: The Ubuntu Install/Remove Extensions dialog box for Firefox.

Secret Clicking the Browse All Add-ons link takes you to the main Firefox Add-ons web page. You can search through all of the available add-ons here. Be careful, though, because there's no guarantee that all of the add-ons will work properly in the Ubuntu Firefox environment. All you can do is download and try them out.

Pidgin

Instant messaging (IM) has become the new killer app for the younger generation. America Online (AOL) provided one of the first popular instant messaging services, named AOL Instant Messenger, or AIM. Others include ICQ, MSN, Yahoo!, and Google. A wide variety of computer operating systems, including Linux, support these various services.

Ubuntu uses the *Pidgin* instant messenger client software. Pidgin allows you to connect to a host of instant messaging services to interact in your favorite IM environment.

Secret

Not that long ago, the Pidgin application was called GAIM, but copyright litiga-
tion forced the GAIM Open Source project to change its name, and they came
up with Pidgin. You may still find documentation on the Internet and in books
referring to the GAIM package. Don't get confused by the name change; they're
the same product.

Using the Pidgin Instant Messenger

To start Pidgin, choose Applications ➪ Internet ➪ Pidgin Instant Messenger. The first
time you start Pidgin it detects that there are no accounts configured, so the Accounts
Management dialog box appears. To configure a new IM account in Pidgin, follow these
steps:

1. Click the Add button in the Accounts dialog box.

The Add Account dialog box, shown in Figure 8-8, appears.

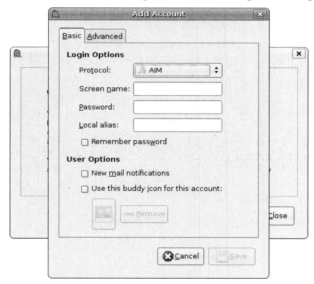

Figure 8-8: The Pidgin Add Account dialog box.

2. In the Protocol drop-down list box, select the IM network you want to use.

Your options are AIM, bonjour, Gadu-Gadu, Google Talk, GroupWise, ICQ, IRC,
MSN, MySpaceIM, QQ, Simple, Sametime, XMPP, Yahoo, and Zephyr.

3. In the Screen Name textbox, enter the login name for your IM account.

4. In the Password textbox, enter your IM password for this account.

5. In the Local Alias textbox, enter the name you actually want to show in people's
IM clients, unless you want to use your screen name.

Often people prefer to appear as alias names rather than use their login name in IM sessions.

6. Check the Remember Password check box so that you don't have to enter your password every time you connect to this IM service.

Remember to log out or use the Lock Screen option if you walk away from your computer, just in case someone gets it into his or her head to go play a trick and send messages to people by using your IM client.

7. If you get email through the selected IM service and want to know when new mail has arrived, check the New Mail Notifications check box.

If mail arrives while Pidgin is running, you'll get a notification about the new mail.

8. If you want to use a tiny picture as a buddy icon, click the Open button next to the Buddy Icon label and navigate to the picture you want to use.

If you don't assign a picture for the buddy icon, Pidgin will use a blank image icon.

9. If you want access to the more advanced options for this IM service, click the Advanced tab.

This tab provides additional options depending on your IM service, such as alternative servers and TCP ports.

10. When you finish entering your information, click Save to add this IM account to your accounts list.

Go through this process for each IM account you want to use with Pidgin (Pidgin can monitor multiple IM accounts). When you finish, the Accounts dialog box shows all of the IM accounts you've configured, and the Buddy List window appears, as shown in Figure 8-9.

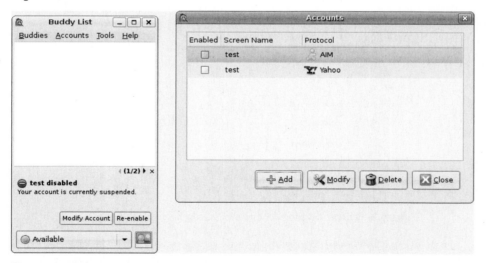

Figure 8-9: The Pidgin Accounts and Buddy List windows.

In the Accounts dialog box, click the box in the Enabled column for the accounts you want to automatically log into when Pidgin starts.

You can modify the account settings at any time by selecting the account in the Accounts dialog box and clicking the Modify button.

After you start a session, the Buddy List window displays your active connections. If you close the Buddy List window, the Pidgin icon appears on your panel as the program runs in background. You can open the Buddy List window by right-clicking this icon.

Secret
When you right-click the Pidgin icon in the panel, a menu appears, allowing you to open the Buddy List, open the Accounts dialog box, install new plug-ins for Pidgin, and set the Pidgin Preferences.

Pidgin Preferences

You can customize several features in Pidgin. Access the Pidgin Preferences dialog box by starting Pidgin from the Panel menu, then right-clicking the Pidgin icon in the Panel System area and selecting Preferences. The Preferences dialog box, as shown in Figure 8-10, appears.

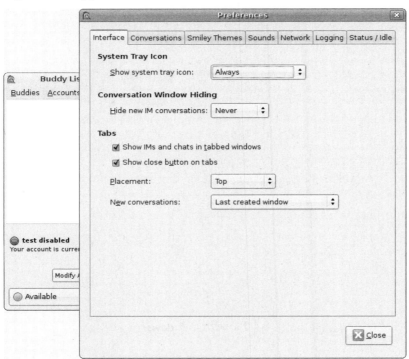

Figure 8-10: The Pidgin Preferences dialog box.

The Preferences dialog box contains seven tabbed pages of settings you can customize:

◆ **Interface:** Select how Pidgin interfaces with the desktop by specifying when the Panel icon should appear, how new IM conversation windows appear, and whether to use tabbed windows or separate windows for multiple conversations.

◆ **Conversations:** Set features for your conversations, such as formatting, fonts, and notifying buddies when you start typing a message.

◆ **Smiley Themes:** Manage multiple themes for inserting smiley icons in your messages.

◆ **Sounds:** Configure how you want Pidgin to notify you of conversation events, such as when buddies log in or log out, when you're offered a new message, and when others talk.

◆ **Network:** Set additional TCP properties for a specific network, along with any specialized settings for network proxy servers you may need to go through.

◆ **Logging:** Select whether you want Pidgin to log your IM conversations and, if so, how to log them.

◆ **Status/Idle:** Configure how Pidgin detects when you're away from the workstation and change your IM status.

Make your IM life easier by taking a few minutes to customize how you want Pidgin to work in your particular environment.

Remote Desktop Viewer

The *Remote Desktop Viewer* application allows you to eavesdrop on another workstation (with their permission, of course). You can see everything on the other workstation, and if the workstation owner allows it, you can even take control of the mouse and keyboard to interact with the remote desktop as if you were sitting there yourself!

To start the Remote Desktop Viewer, select Applications ⇨ Internet ⇨ Remote Desktop Viewer from the Panel menu. Click the Connect button on the taskbar, and either enter the IP address or hostname of the remote workstation or click the Find button to search for available workstations on your network.

When you've established a connection, a dialog box appears on the remote workstation, asking whether it's okay for you to establish the connection, as shown in Figure 8-11.

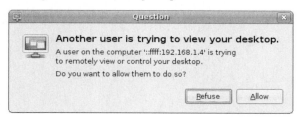

Figure 8-11: The Question dialog box for the Remote Desktop Viewer.

After the remote desktop user allows the connection, the entire desktop appears in the control window, shown in Figure 8-12.

You can now fully interact with the remote desktop, selecting items from the panel, starting applications, and using its applications.

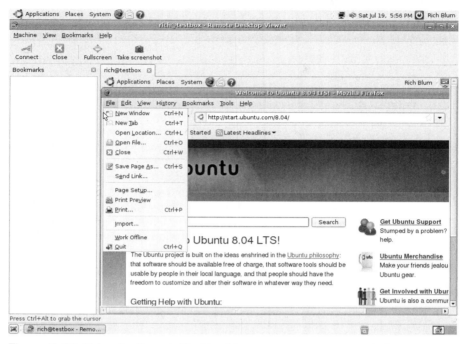

Figure 8-12: Using the Remote Desktop Viewer to access a remote desktop.

Secret

To enable other workstations to use Remote Desktop Viewer to connect to your Ubuntu workstation, select System ⇨ Preferences ⇨ Remote Desktop. The Remote Desktop Preferences window, shown in Figure 8-13, appears.

Figure 8-13: The Remote Desktop Preferences window.

continues

continued

Select the Allow Other Users to View Your Desktop check box. If you want to allow others to control your desktop in the session, keep the Allow Other Users to Control Your Desktop box checked. If you want to allow them only to view your desktop, remove the check mark.

By default, Ubuntu requires that you give permission for a remote user to connect to your desktop. You can set up a security feature that requires the remote user to enter a password that you select.

Terminal Server Client

If you live in a Microsoft Windows environment, you may have to work with remote Windows servers. One feature that Microsoft Windows provides for Windows clients is the *Terminal Services Client* application.

The Terminal Services Client application allows remote Windows clients to connect to a Windows server and interact with the server desktop as if they were on the server console. This feature allows clients to run applications on the server without having to physically be at the server. This is a great way to share server applications for clients, as well as give system administrators easy access to remote Windows servers.

Believe it or not, Ubuntu also contains software that allows you to connect as a client to a Microsoft Windows terminal server. The *Terminal Server Client* package works just like the Windows version, allowing you to connect to Windows servers and interact with the server desktop.

Click Applications ➪ Internet ➪ Terminal Server Client to see the Settings window, as shown in Figure 8-14.

In the Settings window you can start a new session by following these steps:

1. Enter the address of the remote Windows server.

   This can be a host address if you're on a Windows network, or the IP address of the server.

2. Select the protocol to use. Terminal Server uses the remote desktop protocol (RDP) to connect to Microsoft Windows servers. There are two common versions, RDP 4.0 (which is called RDP) supported in Windows NT servers and later, and RDP 5.0 (called RDP5) used in Windows 2000 servers and later. The RDP5 protocol provides additional features, so use it if possible. The Terminal Server Client also supports the X Windows display manager protocol (XDMCP), the virtual network computing (VNC) protocol, and the independent computing architecture (ICA) protocols if they're installed on your system. These protocols allow you to connect to remote UNIX, Linux, and Citrix servers.

3. Enter the username to log in with.

   This can be either a domain name if the server is in a Windows domain or a local username for the server.

Figure 8-14: The Terminal Server Client Settings window

4. Enter the password for the username.

5. Optionally, enter the domain.

If the server is part of a domain and you're using a domain user account to log in with, you'll need to notify the server which domain to use.

6. Optionally, enter a client hostname.

If you want to emulate accessing the server from a specific client hostname, enter it here. Otherwise, leave this field blank.

7. Select a protocol file, if available.

The protocol file allows you to save settings related to the connection for use in later connections.

8. Save the connection settings.

You can save the connection settings by clicking the Save As button, then recall them for another session using the Open button.

9. Click the Connect button to start the session.

The Terminal Server Client software attempts to establish a connection with the remote Windows server, then logs in with the login information you provided. When the login is complete, the server desktop appears in a window, as shown in Figure 8-15.

Figure 8-15: The Terminal Server Client window with an active session.

The entire desktop window for the server session appears within the Terminal Server Client window. You have full control of the session on the desktop. You can move the mouse to launch applications and type on the keyboard to enter commands. When you close the session, log out from the server but do not shut it down. The remote session works as if you were logged in from the server console. Selecting the shutdown menu item will indeed shut down the server!

Transmission

Internet file sharing has become a controversial topic these days in the copyright world. However, networks such as BitTorrent (www.bittorrent.com) have found legitimate use among software companies and other content distributors as a way to offer downloads for larger files without carrying the brunt of the bandwidth use themselves. In fact, Ubuntu distributions themselves are offered as BitTorrent files for quicker downloading.

BitTorrent file transfers work by connecting to a central server and posting information about the file to download, along with your current upload and download speeds. The central server doesn't transfer the file. It is more of a clearinghouse for information on the file download. Each file is divided into multiple pieces. Individual BitTorrent clients download the individual pieces from other clients who've already downloaded them, then advertise which pieces they have to offer to other clients.

This means that clients contact other clients to download the file pieces, rather than downloading directly from the server. This process is called *peer-to-peer networking,* and it saves bandwidth for the server because clients download directly from each other.

While you're downloading pieces of the file, other BitTorrent clients may be downloading the pieces you have from your client! This is all perfectly harmless because the BitTorrent software restricts the access that clients have to your system.

The key to a BitTorrent download is the `.torrent` file. The `.torrent` file contains the file to download and the location of the central server that coordinates the downloads.

The standard Ubuntu installation includes the *Transmission* BitTorrent client. You start it by selecting Applications ➪ Internet ➪ Transmission BitTorrent Client.

When you find out that a file is available over BitTorrent, you first download the `.torrent` file for the item. After you have this file downloaded, follow these steps to get the actual file:

1. Start your BitTorrent client.
2. Select Torrent ➪ Add.

   A file browser window appears, allowing you to look for the `.torrent` file that controls the BitTorrent session.
3. Navigate to and select the `.torrent` file for the document you want to download, then click OK.

   The file appears in the Transmission list window, along with some status information. It can take a minute or so for Transmission to fully synchronize with the central server. Figure 8-16 demonstrates a BitTorrent download in action.

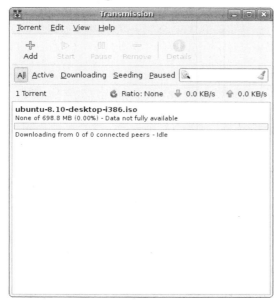

Figure 8-16: The Transmission window with a file downloading.

4. After the download completes, keep Transmission running in background for a while.

Proper net etiquette dictates that you allow Transmission to continue running so that other BitTorrent clients can retrieve pieces of the download file from you. They have access only to the files you offer in your Transmission session and nothing else on your workstation. The Ratio status for the file indicates how much of the file remote clients have uploaded from you compared to what you've downloaded. It's polite to keep Transmission running at least until you obtain a 1:1 ratio.

5. Stop Transmission and halt the BitTorrent connection by selecting Torrent ⇨ Quit from the menu.

Transmission places the downloaded file in the same folder as the .torrent file.

Secret

Both Nautilus and Firefox recognize .torrent files and can automatically start Transmission when you select the .torrent file, either from your local filesystem (in Nautilus) or from a web site link (in Firefox).

gFTP

Although BitTorrent is the wave of the future, plenty of Internet sites still require you to download files using the file transfer protocol (FTP). You will often find file repositories for applications, utilities, and other neat stuff on FTP sites. Unfortunately, Ubuntu doesn't include a graphical FTP client by default, but you can easily add one.

The *gFTP* program is a popular FTP client for the GNOME desktop environment. It contains a host of advanced features that make it a popular file download program and allow you to

* Download files simultaneously
* Interrupt and resume transfers
* Download entire directories with a single command
* Choose passive or active downloading
* Drag and drop files between Nautilus and gFTP
* Transfer files securely with SSH and SSH2

You can use the Ubuntu Add/Remove application (discussed in Chapter 13, "Software Installs and Updates") to download and install the gFTP package. Just go to the Internet section of the Add/Remove application, and you'll see it listed.

After you install gFTP, you can easily download files from FTP repositories on the Internet. Just follow these steps:

1. Click Applications ⇨ Internet ⇨ gFTP.

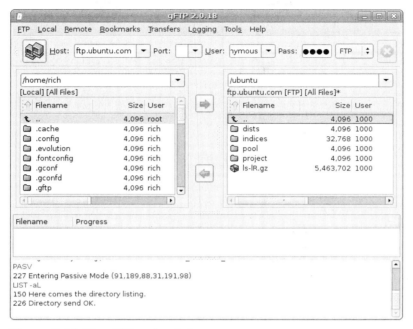

Figure 8-17: The gFTP main window.

When you install gFTP, Ubuntu creates a link in the Internet menu for it. Clicking the link produces the main gFTP window, shown in Figure 8-17. By default, gFTP points to your home directory as the local directory (shown in the list box on the left).

2. Enter the hostname of the remote FTP server in the Host drop-down box, the username in the User drop-down box, and the password in the Pass drop-down box.

If you've connected to a host previously, its hostname and user login name appears in the drop-down boxes. You can select these from the list.

3. When the remote FTP session starts, a list of files and folders available appears in the list box at the right.

4. Find and select the file(s) you want to download by clicking in the list box on the right.

Double-clicking a folder opens it and displays the contents of the folder. From the list box on the left, select the folder to download the file(s) to, then click the left-pointing arrow to transfer them.

5. When finished, click the icon next to the hostname to disconnect and end the FTP session.

It's as simple as that. Using a graphical FTP client makes transferring lots of files via FTP almost painless.

Secret

Although it's true that Ubuntu doesn't include a graphical FTP client by default, it does provide a command-line FTP client in the default installation. Open a Terminal session by selecting Applications ⇨ Accessories ⇨ Terminal, then type *ftp* at the command prompt. The `ftp>` command-line prompt appears, waiting for you to enter commands.

The command-line FTP client allows you to send FTP commands directly to a remote FTP server. The most common commands you'll need to use are

- `open`: **establishes a connection with a remote host**
- `binary`: **sets the transfer mode for binary (application) files**
- `ascii`: **sets the transfer mode for text files**
- `cd`: **changes directories on the remote host**
- `put`: **sends a file to the remote host**
- `get`: **retrieves a file from the remote host**
- `close`: **closes the connection with the remote host**
- `exit`: **stops the FTP command line client and returns to the command prompt**

You can also write scripts to use the FTP command-line client automatically. This feature allows you to schedule a file download for late at night when network bandwidth might not be at a premium.

Summary

This chapter walked through the various Internet applications that Ubuntu provides. Ubuntu installs a wealth of applications by default, and there are more available in the Add/Remove application.

The Ekiga Softphone application allows you to use your workstation to make and receive phone calls. You must sign up with an Internet phone service to use your software on the Internet. Ekiga also includes a server you can register with for free.

For web browsing, Ubuntu includes the Firefox browser. It has all of the features of Microsoft Internet Explorer and Apple Safari, plus a few extras. You can customize Firefox by downloading and installing add-ons, such as plug-ins to handle multimedia content and extensions to provide additional functionality.

The Pidgin software provides an interface to common instant messaging (IM) services. You can keep in touch with your IM partners while using your Ubuntu workstation.

Ubuntu provides two software packages for remote desktop control. The Remote Desktop Viewer allows you to connect to another Linux desktop using the Remote Desktop server software. Ubuntu includes this software, but you must activate it to allow others to connect to your desktop remotely. Once the server software is active, another user can use the Remote Desktop Viewer to access your desktop and, if you allow, interact with your computer via mouse and keyboard.

The Terminal Server Client software included with Ubuntu allows you to connect to Microsoft Windows servers on a network that support Terminal Services. This software allows you to access and use a Windows server desktop directly from your Ubuntu workstation.

Ubuntu also includes the Transmission software, which allows you to download large files using the BitTorrent protocol. BitTorrent provides a central server to manage a file download, and it allows clients to interact with each other, downloading pieces of a large file from other clients as they become available. Many Linux distributions are turning to BitTorrent as a means of efficiently distributing Linux releases.

Although not included as part of the default Ubuntu installation, the gFTP software package is another important piece of Internet software that you can easily install. It provides a graphical interface for advanced FTP capabilities, such as downloading entire folders of files and using newer encrypted FTP protocols such as secure FTP (SFTP). FTP repositories are still popular on the Internet, and it's a good idea to have a graphical tool handy.

You'll notice one Internet application that's not discussed in this chapter. With the popularity of Internet email, Ubuntu now includes the Evolution email client package. Because Internet email is a complex topic, the entire next chapter is devoted to configuring and using Evolution.

Evolution

Chapter
9

◆ ◆ ◆ ◆ ◆ ◆ ◆ ◆ ◆ ◆ ◆ ◆ ◆ ◆ ◆ ◆ ◆ ◆ · · · · · · · · · · · · ·

Secrets in This Chapter

Configuring Evolution

Sending Mail

Organizing Mail

Address Book

Calendar

◆ ◆ ◆ ◆ ◆ ◆ ◆ ◆ ◆ ◆ ◆ ◆ ◆ ◆ ◆ ◆ ◆ · · · · · · · · · · · ·

Although web surfing has become a popular activity on the Internet, quite possibly the most crucial feature of the Internet is email. From high-power businesspeople working on multimillion-dollar projects to grandmothers trying to organize the next family get-together, email has changed the way people communicate. Ubuntu provides one of the most popular email client packages available on the Linux platform. The Evolution package is much more than just a simple email client. It's a full-featured, personal organizer that helps simplify your life. This chapter digs into the workings of Evolution and shows you how to configure and use it to your advantage.

The Evolution Suite

The GNOME project supports the *Evolution* software suite of personal organization software. Personal organization software has become a popular way to help organize your life on a workstation. The software suite includes

- ◆ An email client for interacting with an email server
- ◆ A calendar for setting appointments
- ◆ A task manager for keeping to-do lists
- ◆ An address book for storing contact information
- ◆ A memo taker for storing important memos for future reference

Evolution integrates all of these elements into a single desktop interface, allowing you to easily switch among them and combine information (such as using addresses from the address book in the email client and posting to-do list tasks in the calendar).

The following sections walk through the process of configuring and using the Evolution software suite on your Ubuntu workstation.

Starting Evolution

The first time you start Evolution on your Ubuntu installation, it walks through a setup wizard. The wizard attempts to help you configure settings in the email client to communicate with your remote ISP mail server so you can send and receive mail from Evolution.

Secret

Evolution stores all of its information in the .evolution folder in your home folder. If you don't have an .evolution folder, Evolution wizard automatically creates one.

If you had already configured Evolution and get the setup wizard, that means that something bad happened to your .evolution folder. Hopefully you have a good backup handy (as discussed in the "Backing Up Evolution" section later in this chapter).

The following sections walk through the Evolution setup process.

Obtain Email Client Info

Before you start the Evolution wizard, it'll help if you have several pieces of information handy. Most of this information you should be able to obtain from your email Internet Service Provider (ISP):

♦ **Your email address:** This should be assigned by your ISP, with a format such as me@myhost.com.

♦ **The type of email server your ISP uses for incoming mail:** There are several protocols used by ISP email servers to communicate with email clients. The two most popular are POP and IMAP. You may need to check your ISP documentation or ask your ISP's help desk to determine which server they support.

♦ **The name or IP address of your ISP's incoming mail server:** Your ISP should provide a hostname or IP address for you to connect to receive your mail, such as pop.isp.com.

♦ **The type of email server your ISP uses for outbound mail:** Sending outbound messages requires a different protocol than retrieving inbound messages. Most ISP email servers use SMTP for sending mail from clients.

♦ **The name or IP address of your ISP's outbound mail server:** Some ISPs use a separate server for outbound mail than inbound mail. Check with your ISP and enter the server hostname, such as smtp.isp.com.

♦ **Any special ports or passwords needed for authentication or an encrypted session:** These days many ISPs require that you establish an encrypted connection for both inbound and outbound messages. If this isn't a requirement of your ISP, you should consider using it if your ISP supports it. Usually you'll need to use an alternative TCP port, instead of the default POP, IMAP, or SMTP ports, as well as use your email address and password for authentication.

The most confusing option you'll need to deal with is the two types of incoming email servers supported by ISPs:

♦ Post office protocol (POP, often called POP3)

♦ Interactive mail access protocol (IMAP)

The main difference between these two protocols is that POP usually requires you to download all of your incoming messages from the ISP's server to your local workstation. IMAP allows you to create folders on the ISP's server and store all of your messages there. IMAP servers usually allow you a specific amount of storage space on the server, so you must be careful how much mail you accumulate.

The nice feature about IMAP is that by keeping all of your messages on the server, you can access them from any workstation on the Internet. With POP, once you download a message to your workstation, it's gone from the server and can't be accessed from any other workstation.

Run the Wizard

Start the Evolution wizard by selecting either Applications ➪ Internet ➪ Evolution Mail, or Applications ➪ Office ➪ Evolution Mail and Calendar from the Panel menu, or just by single-clicking the Evolution mail client launcher icon (the open envelope) on the panel.

The wizard organizes the Evolution configuration into a series of several dialog boxes. Each dialog box asks questions about a particular feature of the configuration. The first wizard dialog box is a simple welcome message. After that, the configuration questions start.

This section walks through the various dialog boxes you'll need to complete in the configuration process to get your email running.

Restore from Backup

The Restore from Backup dialog box allows you to rebuild your Evolution setup from a backup (see the "Backing Up Evolution" section later in this chapter). If your Evolution setup becomes corrupt or you lose important email messages, you can completely restore your Evolution system from a previous backup.

Select the check box to restore Evolution from a backup file, then select the Evolution archive file to restore. Restoring from a backup archive file resets all of your settings and restores all of your stored mail messages and folders from the time the archive file was created, so don't restore unless you know you have a problem.

Identity Information

If you're not restoring a backup archive file, click the Forward button to proceed to the Identity dialog box, shown in Figure 9-1.

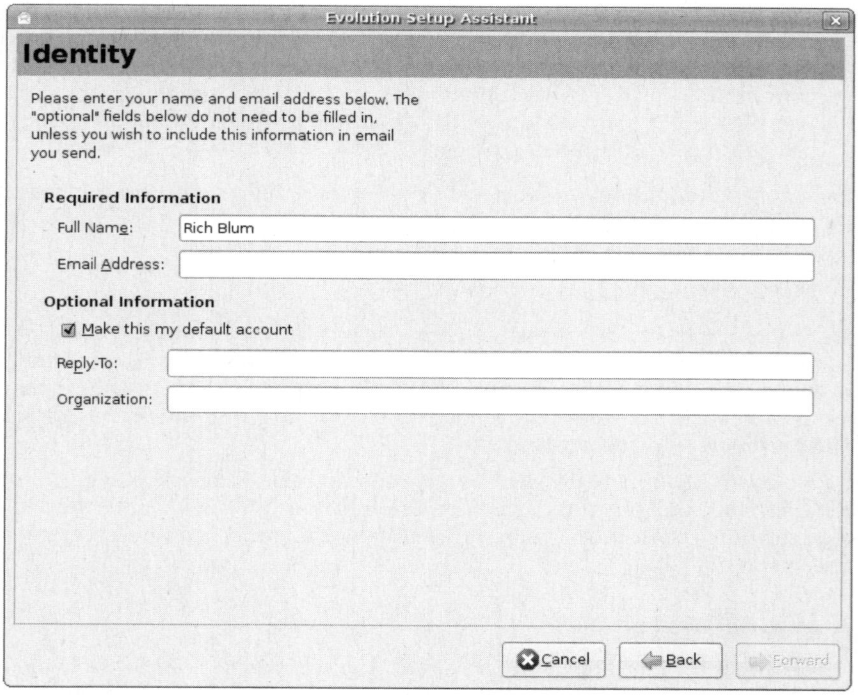

Figure 9-1: The Evolution Identity wizard dialog box.

This form starts the process of creating a new account on the Evolution system. To complete this form, follow these steps:

1. Check the Full Name field. By default, Ubuntu uses the full name you used when you created your system user account. You can change this value, if necessary. This information is what Evolution uses as your full name in email messages (such as identifying you in the From line in email messages).

2. Enter your ISP email address in the Email Address field. This is the email address that appears as the default return email address in all of your messages.

3. If you want to use this account as your default email account, check the Make This My Default check box. Evolution allows you to maintain multiple email accounts in the client configuration, but only one can be set as the default.

4. Enter a Reply-To email address. Enter a different email address here if you want your emails to show a different email address in the Reply-To message heading. When people use the Reply button to respond to your emails, the system sends the reply to this address rather than the address you used to send the message.

5. Enter an organization name. Enter an organization name if you want to identify your organization in your emails, such as if you're using this account as a business account or wish to identify yourself with something other than your full name.

6. Click the Forward button to move to the next dialog box.

The Receiving Email dialog box appears next.

Receiving Email

The Receiving Email dialog box can be tricky because it dynamically changes based on the type of incoming email server you select. Table 9-1 lists the types of email servers from which Evolution can retrieve mail messages.

Table 9-1: Evolution Host Email Servers

Server Type	Description
None	Sets up Evolution but doesn't set up an individual email account
Hula	A remote Hula server
IMAP	A remote ISP server using mail folders on the remote server
Microsoft Exchange	A local Microsoft Exchange email server
Novell Groupwise	A local Novell Groupwise email server
POP	A remote ISP server using mail folders on the local workstation
Usenet news	News digests from Usenet newsgroups
Local delivery	Removes mail from the local email directory to your home directory

continues

Table 9-1: *(continued)*

Server Type	Description
mh-format mail directories	Reads mail from a local mh mail system
maildir-format mail directories	Reads mail from a maildir-formatted mail system (such as qMail)
Standard UNIX mbox spool directory	Reads mail from an mbox directory (such as Postfix)
Standard UNIX mbox spool file	Reads mail from a standard mbox file (such as sendmail)

If you're connecting to an internal corporate email server, such as Novell or Microsoft, check with your technical support personnel to determine the mail server type and the appropriate settings. Chapter 23, "Email Server," describes how to set up Evolution to connect to an Ubuntu email server running the default Postfix mail system.

As mentioned, if you're connecting your Ubuntu workstation to a remote ISP mail server, you'll most likely use either POP or IMAP to connect. Both of these protocols use the same Receive Email dialog box format, shown in Figure 9-2.

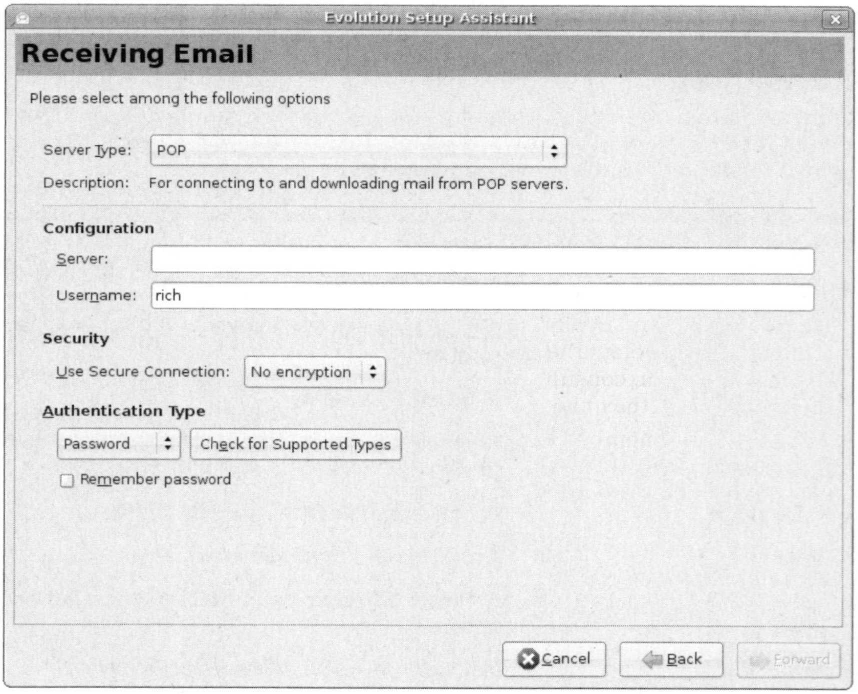

Figure 9-2: The Evolution Receive Email wizard dialog box for POP and IMAP accounts.

Here are the instructions for setting up a POP or IMAP server account in the Evolution wizard:

1. Select POP or IMAP as the type of incoming server your ISP uses in the Server Type list box. The Receive Email dialog box stays the same for both of these email server types.

2. Enter the hostname of your email server. You can specify the hostname or the IP address of the remote ISP server.

Secret

If your POP or IMAP server requires that you use a TCP port other than the standard TCP port (110 for POP and 143 for IMAP), you must enter it here as part of the server hostname. Just place a colon between the server hostname and the alternative port value, like this:

```
pop.isp.com:600
```

Evolution will automatically detect that new port and use it instead of the default.

3. Enter the username of your email account. Most likely you'll need to enter your full email address here. Check with your ISP's tech support if that doesn't work.

4. If your email server uses encryption, select the type. These days most ISPs support some type of encryption to safeguard messages sent across the Internet. The SSL and TLS encryptions are the most common, and both are supported in Evolution.

5. Select the authentication type if your email server uses it. Many ISPs use authentication to ensure you're a valid customer before allowing you to connect to the POP or IMAP server. This helps cut down on spamming problems. Several authentication options are used, including a plain text password, APOP, login, NTLM/SPA, GSSAPI, DIGEST-MD5, and CRAM-MD5. You can click the Check for Supported Types button, and Evolution will attempt to connect to your ISP's email server and automatically detect the best authentication method to use. If you have problems with this option, consult your ISP's tech support to find out what (if any) authentication option they use.

6. Check the Remember Password check box if you want Evolution to remember your password. If you allow Evolution to remember your password, it can automatically log into your ISP's email server to retrieve mail. If you're using a shared workstation, doing so could be dangerous because others could read your email and send messages using your name and email account. If you don't select this option, Evolution will prompt you for your ISP password each time it connects.

7. Click Forward to go to the next set of options.

The next dialog box is Receiving Options. At this point, the POP and IMAP server configurations diverge a bit, so I'll discuss each in a different section.

POP

Follow these steps to continue the configuration if you're using a POP email server:

1. The POP Receiving Options dialog box, shown in Figure 9-3, appears.

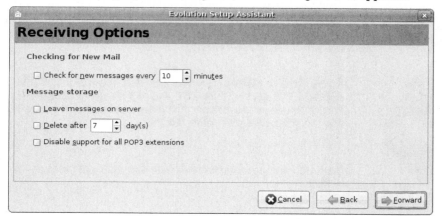

Figure 9-3: The Evolution POP Receiving Options wizard dialog box.

2. Set how often Evolution checks the ISP's email server for new mail. If you're using a broadband Internet connection, you can set Evolution to check your incoming mail at a regular interval. If you've set it to remember your password in the previous wizard dialog box, it happens behind the scenes. If you're using a dial-up Internet connection, you should probably leave this check box blank and manually check your messages.

3. Set how you want Evolution to handle messages on the POP server. With the POP system, you can read your messages and leave them on the server, but be careful with this option. Many ISPs don't allow POP messages to stay on the server for long and may clean out previously downloaded messages without warning. Alternatively, you can set Evolution to delete read messages from the server after a specific number of days. If your ISP's server doesn't support the newer POP3 extensions, you can disable them so Evolution won't try to use them.

4. Click the Forward button to go to the Sending Email options.

This completes the POP mail receiving options. Skip to the "Sending Email" section to continue your setup.

IMAP

Follow these steps to continue the configuration if you're using an IMAP email server:

1. The IMAP Receiving Options dialog box, shown in Figure 9-4, appears.

2. Set how often Evolution checks the ISP's email server for new mail. If you're using a broadband Internet connection, you can set Evolution to check your incoming mail at a regular interval. If you've set it to remember your password in the previous wizard dialog box, it happens behind the scenes. If you're using a dial-up Internet connection, you should probably leave this check box blank and manually check your messages.

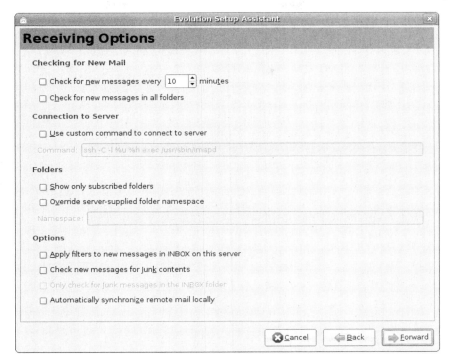

Figure 9-4: The Evolution IMAP Receiving Options wizard dialog box.

3. Set a custom command to access the IMAP server. Some IMAP servers require an encrypted connection that uses the secure shell (SSH) protocol. This option allows you to start your IMAP session within an SSH environment.

4. Define how Evolution handles server folders. If you have lots of folders on your IMAP server, you can subscribe and unsubscribe to them to organize which folders are active at any time. Using this feature allows you to see only the folders you currently subscribe to. It also allows you to alter the naming hierarchy used on the server.

5. Set options for the way Evolution handles your mail messages. The problem with accessing mail on IMAP servers is that the message isn't processed by Evolution. This means that if you're using spam filtering in Evolution, mail stored in your server's IMAP folders won't be filtered. The options in this section allow Evolution to peek at the messages in your IMAP folders and process them through the spam filters. This topic is discussed in greater detail in the "Mail Filtering" section later in this chapter.

6. Click the Forward button to go to the Sending Email options.

This completes the IMAP mail receiving options. Next, it's time to configure Evolution for outbound email messages.

Sending Email

The Evolution wizard provides two methods for sending mail from the Ubuntu workstation:

- ◆ SMTP
- ◆ Sendmail

The SMTP method connects to a remote email server (usually supplied by your ISP) to forward messages to others on the Internet. This method is called a *smart host.* Your local workstation doesn't have to connect to each remote mail server for every destination email address you use. Instead, it connects to a single server that forwards messages to the proper destination server. This is most likely the method you'll use if you're using your ISP for your email service.

The sendmail method uses the internal mail server software running on the workstation to send messages directly from your workstation to remote email servers on the Internet. This method requires running an email server on your Ubuntu workstation, which is not a common practice. See Chapter 23 for more information on running an email server on an Ubuntu server.

Selecting the SMTP method produces the wizard dialog box shown in Figure 9-5.

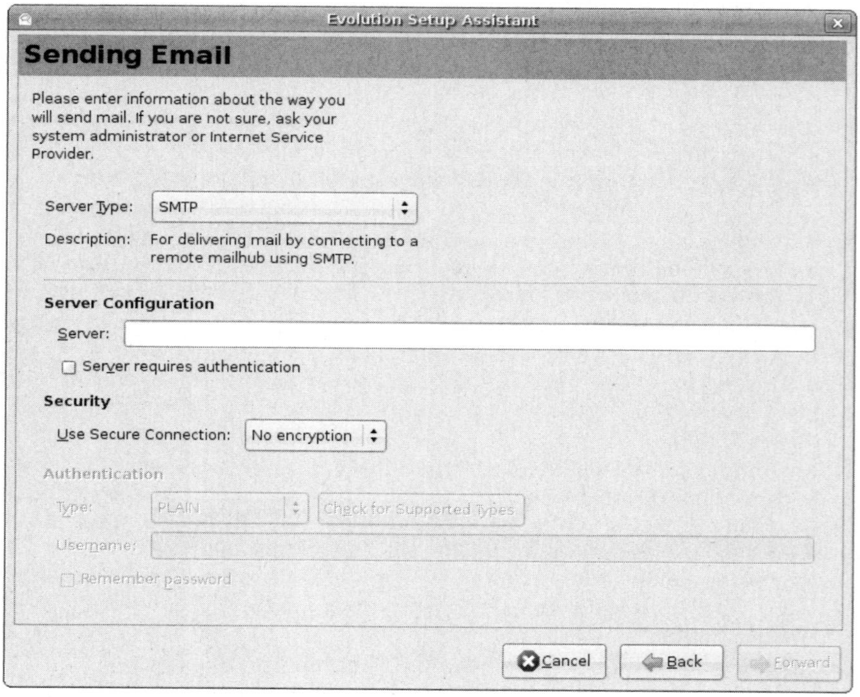

Figure 9-5: The Evolution Send Mail wizard dialog box.

The steps for configuring Evolution using SMTP with your ISP are as follows:

1. Enter the server hostname or IP address for your remote ISP server. Often an ISP will provide a separate hostname for outbound SMTP service, even if a single server provides both inbound and outbound mail service. This makes it easier for the ISP if it decides to switch to a two-server setup.

2. Select the check box if your ISP's server requires authentication. Because of spamming problems, most ISP servers now allow only their customers to send mail messages. Spammers often look for *open relays* that forward messages from any client to any destination. SMTP authentication requires that you use some type of authentication method to validate who you are before the server accepts your messages for forwarding.

3. Select the encryption method your ISP's email server uses. Encryption allows you to help keep your messages secure as they traverse the network between your workstation and your ISP. If your ISP supports encrypted sessions, select either TLS or SSL.

4. Select the authentication method supported by your ISP's email server, and enter your login information. If you've determined that your ISP requires authentication, Evolution prompts you for the authentication type and your login information.

5. Click the Forward button to continue with the configuration.

Secret

Novice users often confuse authentication and encryption. Authentication is the process of identifying yourself to your ISP so that it allows you to forward outbound messages. It doesn't protect the email message or verify your identity to the remote mail recipient. Digital signatures authenticate your identity for the recipient.

The Encryption option doesn't encrypt the message itself. TLS and SSL encrypt only the communication link between your workstation and the ISP's server. Evolution still sends the message as plain text, so once the message gets to the ISP's server, it's sent to the remote destination as plain text. If you want to send an encrypted message that stays encrypted for the duration of the mail delivery process, you must manually encrypt the message itself using an encryption tool such as GnuPG. This option can be added using the Synaptic software installer, discussed in Chapter 13, "Software Installs and Updates."

Final Configuration

That finishes the bulk of the configuration required for your email. There are just a few housekeeping dialog boxes left:

◆ The Account Management dialog box allows you to assign a name to the configuration settings. By default it uses your email address.

◆ The Time Zone dialog box allows you to select the time zone used in your email address time and date stamps. This option is convenient if you want to use a time stamp different from the system time when you're traveling.

◆ The Done dialog box allows you to go back and review your settings, or you can click the Apply button to start the configuration process using your settings.

After the configuration completes, Evolution starts the main window, ready for you to interact with your ISP's mail server.

The Evolution Window

The Evolution window provides lots of information and can easily get confusing. Several areas in the window provide easy access to all of the features within the Evolution software suite, as shown in Figure 9-6.

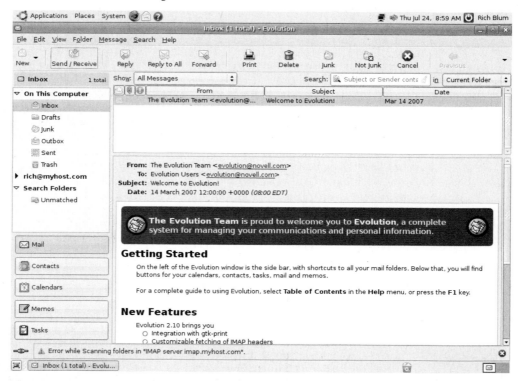

Figure 9-6: The default Evolution window in Ubuntu.

This section walks though each of the window areas and discusses how to use them.

The Menu Bar

The top menu bar in Evolution provides menu access to all of the features in Evolution. Let's walk through the main features in each top-level menu:

◆ **File:** Contains menu items for opening a new Evolution window, communicating with the remote mail server, backing up and restoring settings, importing messages and addresses from other mail systems, printing a message, and working offline.

◆ **Edit:** Allows you to delete a message, select text in a message, and search for words in a message. It also allows you to set synchronizing options for handheld devices, set spam filtering, add plug-ins, and modify the configuration settings.

◆ **View:** Allows you to set how the main pane area lists messages:
- By message
- As Sent folder
- By subject
- By sender
- By status
- By follow-up flag
- Wide view
- As Sent folder for wide view
- Define your own view

The View section also allows you to select which Evolution product to view (email, address book, calendar, memos, or task list), which window bars to display, whether to display the Message Preview pane, and how to display messages.

The View options allow you to customize the look of your Evolution desktop to suit your needs. You can change the sort method for the message list on the fly to organize your messages however you want.

◆ **Folder:** Manages folders on the local workstation. You can create a new folder, copy or move messages to folders, subscribe to IMAP folders on the server, and modify or delete folders.

◆ **Message:** Offers individual message-handling functions, such as reply and forward, copy or move to another folder, compose a new message, or view an existing message.

◆ **Search:** Allows you to search messages for words or phrases.

◆ **Help:** Provides links to the Evolution manual, a quick reference guide, and online help and bug reporting.

Secret

Emails often go back and forth among multiple people conversing about a topic. In those situations, one of the best ways to follow the conversation is to use the *Thread view* in Evolution. Click View ⇨ Group by Threads to sort messages based on the message threads. This option groups message threads in a hierarchical format, showing which messages are replies or forwards from other messages, so that you can easily follow the conversation from start to end.

The Toolbar

The toolbar provides icons for quick access to specific features in the menu bar. The default icons provided are

◆ **New:** Click the envelope icon to start a new message. Click the down arrow next to it to start a new message, folder, appointment, contact, meeting, memo, or task.

◆ **Send/Receive:** Connect to the mail server to send any messages queued for sending and retrieve any messages sent to you.

◆ **Reply:** Start a new message to the sender of the original message and include the original message in the new message body.

- ◆ **Reply to All:** Start a new message to the sender with a copy to all recipients of the original message and include the original message in the new message body.
- ◆ **Forward:** Send the original message to a new recipient.
- ◆ **Print:** Send the message to a printer.
- ◆ **Delete:** Remove the current message from the folder.
- ◆ **Junk:** Mark the message as junk mail for the spam blocker software to block.
- ◆ **Not Junk:** Mark the message as normal mail for the spam blocker software.
- ◆ **Cancel:** Abort the current process.
- ◆ **Previous:** Go to the previous message in the message list.
- ◆ **Next:** Go to the next message in the message list.

At the end of toolbar menu, you can click to view tool icons that don't fit in the current window.

The Junk and Not Junk buttons are described in more detail in the "Mail Filtering" section later in this chapter.

The Search Tool

The Search tool allows you to quickly search the contents of your stored email messages. The Search tool appears directly above the message list area in the Evolution window.

Enter the text you want to find, then select the range for the search:

- ◆ The current folder shown in the message list
- ◆ All folders in the current account
- ◆ All folders in all accounts configured in Evolution

Click on the magnifying glass icon at the left side of the search window to select which message header field to search. You can also search for words in the message body, but be careful—the search could take a long time if your mailbox is full.

If you select the Advanced Search option from the list, the dialog box shown in Figure 9-7 appears.

The Advanced Search option allows you to create complex searches based on multiple words in multiple locations in the message headers and body.

The Message List

The Message List pane displays the messages in any folder selected from the sidebar list. The column headings at the top of the message list are clickable buttons that sort the messages based on the heading you click.

The three icons at the far left of the message list indicate the status of the mail message:

- ◆ **Message Status:** Indicates whether the message has been read or is unread.
- ◆ **Attachment:** Indicates whether a file is attached to the message and, if so, whether it's a text or binary file.
- ◆ **Message Tag:** Indicates whether the message is tagged as important or urgent. Also supports custom message tags.

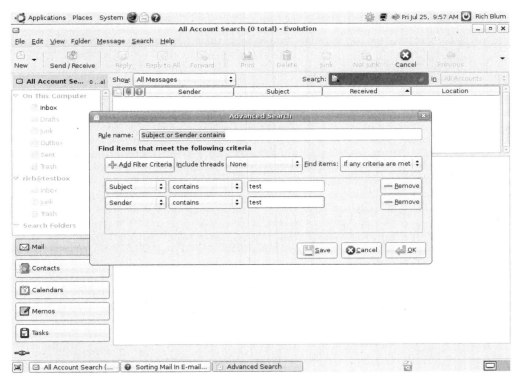

Figure 9-7: The Advanced Search dialog box.

The remaining columns in the Message List pane show standard email header information about the message, including the sender, the subject, the size, and the time sent.

There are three ways to sort messages in the message list:

- From the View menu bar, by selecting Current View
- From the message list headers, by clicking on the column heading
- From the message list headers, by right-clicking and selecting the sort order

By right-clicking on the column headings you can add and remove columns to help fit the message header information you're most interested in seeing in the display line.

If the Preview pane is enabled you can single-click a message in the message list and view the message body in the Preview pane. Double-click a message in the message list to bring the message up in a new window.

The Sidebar

The sidebar provides a quick look at all of the folders managed by the Evolution session. Each email account that you create is shown as a drop-down menu item, with the individual folders for the account beneath it. Most accounts have at least three folders:

- **Inbox:** the folder for all new incoming messages
- **Junk:** if mail filtering is enabled, contains mail that Evolution detects as spam
- **Trash:** temporary location to store deleted messages

You create new folders for an account by right-clicking on the account and selecting New Folder from the resulting menu. After creating new folders, move mail messages simply by dragging and dropping them from the message list to the folder where you want to store them.

The Switcher

The Switcher provides a graphical way to switch between the various software packages in the Evolution suite. Clicking the button for a package brings the package up in the main viewing window.

The Preview Pane

If enabled, the Preview pane displays the contents of the currently selected email message from the message list. This feature provides a quick way to scan an email message without having to open the message itself. You can quickly click through messages in the message list and view the contents of each message in the Preview pane.

Using Evolution

Now that you have Evolution configured to interact with your ISP, you can start sending and receiving email messages from your Ubuntu workstation.

Sending Messages

The following steps outline how to create a new email message and send it:

1. Click New. The Compose Message window opens, as shown in Figure 9-8. If you want to create another item, such as a new contact list entry or a calendar appointment, click the down arrow next to New to open the list of options to choose from.

2. Type the recipient's email address (such as rich@myhost.com) or a list of addresses separated by commas (such as rich@myhost.com, barbara@herhost.com) in the To text box.

3. If you want to add a carbon copy (CC) or blind carbon copy (BCC) to the list of recipients, click the View menu item in the Compose Message window and select the desired field (CC or BCC) to appear, then enter the appropriate addresses into those fields.

4. Type the topic of your email into the Subject text box.

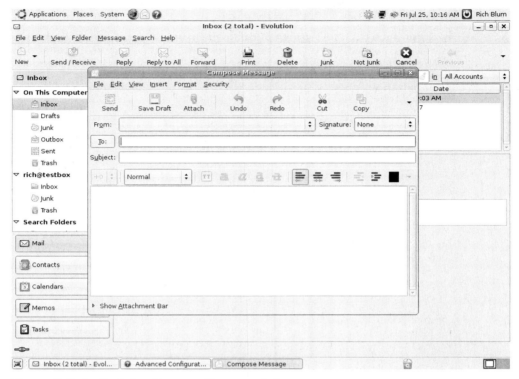

Figure 9-8: An Evolution Compose Message window.

5. In the lower window, type the body of your email. The Compose Message window provides basic editing and some word-processing features. The message text area automatically checks the spelling of your text. If you want to use advanced formatting features such as fonts, colors, and styling, select Format from the menu bar and then choose HTML. This creates an HTML-formatted message and enables the font control features in the toolbar.

6. If you want to add a signature to the bottom of your email, click the drop-down list box next to Signature and select Autogenerated. To create a custom signature block for your messages, go back to the main Evolution window and choose Edit ⇨ Preferences to open the Evolution Preferences dialog box. See the "Changing the Configuration" section later in the chapter for details on how to set a signature block.

7. If you want, add a attachment to your file. Click the arrow next to the Show Attachment Bar text at the bottom of the Compose Message window. Right-click in the new text area and select Add Attachment, then use the file browser to select the file to attach.

8. When you finish typing your message, click the Send button.

Evolution places the new message in the Outbox folder, either waiting for the next scheduled connection to the remote server or until you click the Send/Receive button on the toolbar.

Changing the Configuration

You're not stuck with the settings you entered during the setup wizard phase. At any time you can alter the individual accounts you created, as well as make changes to the overall setup in Evolution. You do this by selecting Edit ➪ Preferences from the menu bar, which produces the Evolution Preferences dialog box, shown in Figure 9-9.

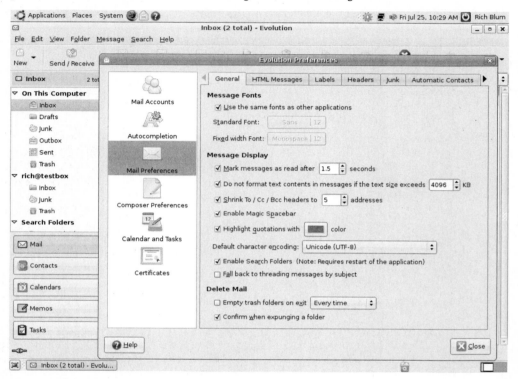

Figure 9-9: The Evolution Preferences dialog box.

The Evolution Preferences dialog box contains categories of preferences as icons along the left side of the box, with specific settings for each category listed on the right side. Each category has several preferences you can set to customize your Evolution client.

Mail Accounts

When you select this category you'll see the email account you created in the setup wizard. You can select the account and click the Edit button to modify any of the settings.

You can also create new accounts by clicking the Add button. This button starts the Mail Configuration wizard, which is the same wizard that walked you through steps to set up your original email account.

Evolution allows you to maintain multiple email accounts. You can also keep an account but disable it from appearing in the Evolution sidebar area. Just unselect the Enabled check box next to the account to disable it.

Autocompletion

The autocompletion feature determines how Evolution recognizes email addresses as you type them in the To, CC, and BCC lines in a new message. By default, Evolution peeks inside your personal address book at existing addresses and tries to match possible entries as you type addresses.

Evolution also has the ability to connect to a remote lightweight directory access protocol (LDAP) server. LDAP servers provide a common directory for storing data, including address books. If your network supports an LDAP server, you can allow Evolution to access those entries.

Mail Preferences

The Mail Preferences section provides a wide array of settings to customize your Evolution client. The settings are further divided into tabbed sections:

- ◆ **General:** Set default fonts for messages, set how Evolution displays messages, and specify whether it should automatically empty the Trash folder.
- ◆ **HTML Messages:** Set HTML message features to disable images, and disable HTML messages by showing only the plain text portion of a message.
- ◆ **Labels:** Define color codes and names for message tags. You can create message tags to organize messages in the message list.
- ◆ **Headers:** Select which message headers appear in the displayed message.
- ◆ **Junk:** Select which spam filter to use and what to do with messages marked as spam.
- ◆ **Automatic Contacts:** Choose to automatically add the recipients of replied messages to your address book.
- ◆ **Calendar and Tasks:** Select which calendars to check when receiving meeting requests via email.

Secret

HTML messages are often a problem with spam mail. Spammers can create customized HTML messages that display images from remote sites or redirect you to a specific web page that can identify that you read the message.

The HTML Messages section allows you to decide the level of HTML support you want to have while reading your messages. Disabling all HTML messages is the safest policy.

Composer Preferences

The Composer Preferences section provides settings to customize how the Compose Messages window operates. There are three tabs in this section:

- ◆ **General:** Set message body features for your email. This option contains three sections of settings:
  - • **Default Behavior:** Specify the format (plain text or HTML) of the message, whether to request a read receipt, how to forward messages (inline or as an attachment), whether to include the text of a replied message in the new message, and the character set for the message.

- **Top-Posting Option:** Indicate where to place the signature block when replying to a message. This option places your signature block above the original message, which is considered bad etiquette in some Internet forums.
- **Alerts:** Set alerts for Evolution to warn when you attempt to send a message with a blank subject line or have no direct recipient other than blind carbon copy recipients.
- **Signatures:** Create one or more signature blocks that you can add to the bottom of your messages.
- **Spell Checking:** Define the spelling language to use and indicate whether to check spelling as you're typing.

The Evolution message composer works like any standard word processor. You can cut and paste text and even format text if you use the HTML-formatted mail option.

Calendar and Tasks

In this section you can alter the settings for the calendar and tasks software in Evolution. This section contains five tabs of settings:

- **General:** Set the time zone and time format used in the calendar and specify how you want the weekdays displayed on the calendar.
- **Display:** Set how to display the time interval for blocks of time, plus define color codes used in the calendar.
- **Alarms:** Specify where Evolution should look to produce alarms for events. The default is to produce an alarm for scheduled events in the calendar and events stored in the address book.
- **Free/Busy:** Define a server to access for determining other peoples' schedules.
- **Calendar Publishing:** Define one or more locations to publish your calendar so that others can determine your availability.

The calendar and tasks features of Evolution are discussed in more detail in the "Accessing the Calendar and Tasks" section later in this chapter.

Certificates

These days, security is a huge concern in the Internet world. Many sites require that you either encrypt your messages or digitally sign them to ensure that they were sent by you.

The Certificates section allows you to define encryption certificates you use to digitally sign your messages and for others to use to send you an encrypted message. You can also store certificates for others so that you can send them encrypted messages.

 **Secret**

Certificates consist of two parts, a public key and a private key. You keep your private key but share your public key with people who communicate with you. Likewise, you can collect public keys from people you communicate with.

When you send an encrypted message, you must use the recipient's public key to encrypt the message. This step ensures that your intended recipient, using his or her private key, is the only one who can decrypt the message.

When you digitally sign a message, you use your private key. The recipient can then use your public key to verify that you did, in fact, use your private key to sign the message.

Mail Filtering

In the busy world of the Internet, it's not uncommon to receive dozens of email messages a day. Trying to sort through a stack of messages in your inbox can be a difficult task.

Evolution provides a way to help you out with this problem. *Mail filtering* allows you to set Evolution to sort incoming messages based on keywords and phrases, then store the sorted messages in separate folders.

This section discusses the two popular methods of sorting mail, filtering messages and filtering spam.

Filtering Messages

Evolution allows you to set message filters for your inbox. To view, create, and modify message filters, select the Edit menu option, then select Message Filters. The Message Filters dialog box, shown in Figure 9-10, appears.

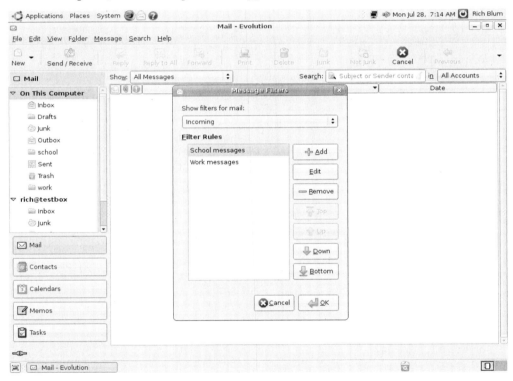

Figure 9-10: The Evolution Message Filters dialog box.

Each message filter is called a *rule*. Each rule defines one or more conditions for Evolution to check in a message. If the rule conditions are met in a message, Evolution handles the message as directed by the rule, usually storing it in a separate folder on the system.

Rules are applied in the order they appear in the Message Filters list. As soon as a message matches a rule, Evolution handles the message according to the rule definition, and the rule processing stops. You can alter the order of rules from the Message Filter dialog box by selecting a rule and clicking the Top, Up, Down, or Bottom buttons.

You define new rules by clicking the Add button. The Add Rule dialog box appears, shown in Figure 9-11.

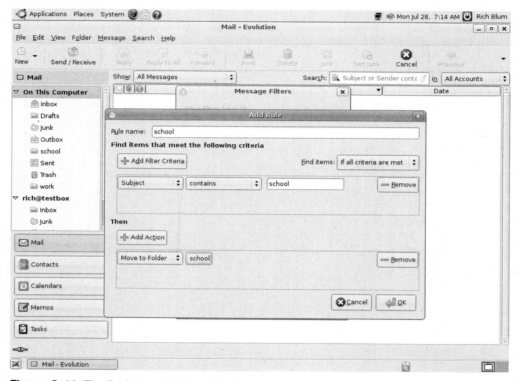

Figure 9-11: The Evolution Add Rule dialog box.

After assigning the new rule a unique name, you select filters to apply to the messages. The filter can be applied against message headers, such as sender, recipient, subject, date sent, date received, and the body of the message, or against features of the message, such as the message size and status.

You can add as many filters in a single rule as are necessary to uniquely identify messages for the rule. You can also set how filters are combined to satisfy the rule:

♦ All filters must match.
♦ At least one filter matches.

Once you define the filter(s) used, you must define the action the rule takes with the message. Some of the more popular actions you can take are

♦ Move message to a specific folder.
♦ Place the message in the inbox but put a copy in a specific folder.
♦ Delete the message.
♦ Assign a color to the message to make it stand out in the message list.

◆ Set a specific status for the message.
◆ Play a sound or beep when the message appears.
◆ Forward the message to an external program.

After setting the features of the rule, click the OK button to save it in the Message Filters list.

Filtering Spam

The world of Internet email has been plagued with unsolicited commercial email (UCE), also known as spam. It's not uncommon to receive more spam messages than valid messages in a day. Evolution attempts to help this situation by providing access to two spam filter programs for you to integrate with your mailbox.

◆ SpamAssassin
◆ Bogofilter

These filter programs use Bayesian technology to dynamically adjust to incoming spam messages. They read messages and learn different features of messages marked as spam. They can then use that knowledge to help block spam messages that have those features. The downside to this technique is that you must train the program to recognize spam messages.

To access the spam message filter options in Evolution, go to the Preferences window (select Edit ➪ Preferences from the menu bar), select the Mail Preferences icon on the left side, then select the Junk tab at the top. The Junk settings dialog box is shown in Figure 9-12.

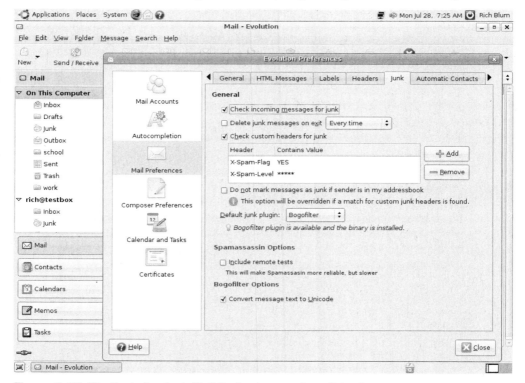

Figure 9-12: The Evolution Junk Mail Preferences settings dialog box.

Ubuntu installs the BogoFilter plug-in as the default system spam filter program for Evolution to help eliminate spam. You can install SpamAssassin as a separate plug-in using the Synaptic Package Manager (see Chapter 13, "Software Installs and Updates").

Secret

The Bogofilter Bayesian spam-filtering process works best when it has many data samples to learn from. As spam messages come into your inbox, don't delete them. Take the extra time to mark those messages as spam by clicking the Junk button in the Evolution toolbar. This step helps expand the Bayesian data model for Bogofilter and block future spam messages.

Likewise, if Bogofilter should mark any valid messages as junk, you'll want to click the Not Junk button in the toolbar so that Bogofilter doesn't make the same mistake on future messages.

Backing Up Evolution

As you can tell from this chapter, there are plenty of customized settings involved in a well-running Evolution setup. You'll want to ensure that you have a good backup of your Evolution environment so you don't have to configure all of those settings again should you lose your Evolution installation.

The easiest way to save your Evolution settings is to use the Backup Settings feature in the File menu. The backup feature creates an archive file that contains the system settings for your Evolution accounts, along with all email messages, contacts, tasks, and appointments you have stored. To create the archive file, Evolution must first be shut down so that it can access all of the files necessary for the backup process. A Notice dialog box appears, asking whether that's all right and whether you want to restart Evolution after the backup completes. Once you create the backup archive file, it's a good idea to remove it from your system and store it in a safe place, such as on a USB Memory Stick.

If you lose your Evolution settings or data, you can easily restore them by using the Restore Settings feature in the File menu or by selecting the backup archive file in the setup wizard.

Using the Address Book

The address book in Evolution provides a great place to keep contact information for all your personal and business needs. The Evolution email program can access the address book to add recipients of email messages.

To access the address book, click the Contacts button in the Switcher section of the Evolution window. The main Contacts window appears, shown in Figure 9-13.

The address book window displays a brief entry for each address in the book. If you double-click on an individual entry, the Contact Editor dialog box appears, shown in Figure 9-14.

In the Contact Editor dialog box you can assign names, email addresses, instant messaging accounts, phone numbers, mailing addresses, and other information about the contact. To start a new contact, just click the New button in the toolbar area. A Contact Editor for a new contact appears.

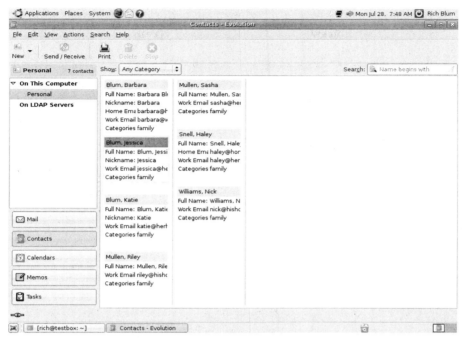

Figure 9-13: The Evolution Address Book Contacts window.

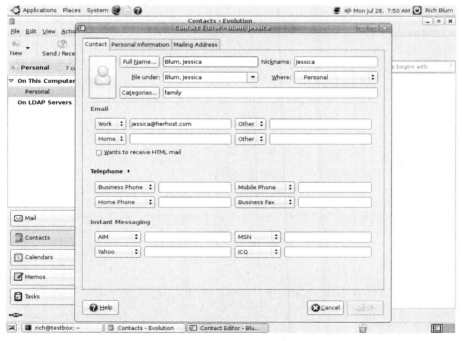

Figure 9-14: The Evolution Address Book Contact Editor dialog box.

The Contact Editor is a great tool for organizing all of your contact information, plus it makes that information readily available when you create email messages.

Accessing the Calendar and Tasks

The Calendar and Tasks features of Evolution provide ways for you to manage your time more efficiently. This section walks through the features available in each of these tools.

Calendar

To access the calendar, click the Calendar icon in the Evolution Switcher area. The main Calendar window appears, shown in Figure 9-15.

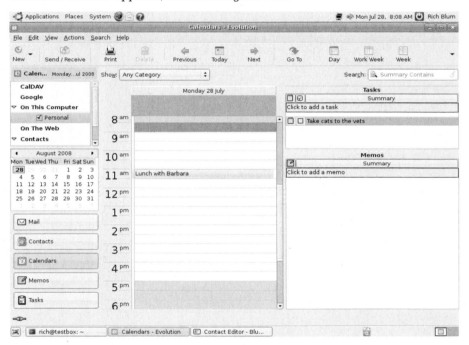

Figure 9-15: The Evolution Calendar window.

The default view shows the calendar for a single day. Work times are highlighted in the calendar (as set in the Edit ⇨ Preferences settings). Notice that the Day view also contains panes showing any tasks and memos created.

Secret

You can also access the calendar by clicking the Date applet running in the top panel (see Chapter 4, "Exploring the Desktop"). When you click the date on the panel, a calendar for the month appears. Clicking any date on the calendar starts Evolution, using that date as the default calendar day.

To schedule a new appointment, follow these steps:

1. Right-click on the calendar in the time block the appointment starts. This action produces a menu prompting you to schedule the new event. You can select a new appointment, a new meeting, a new task, or a new all-day event.

2. Select New Appointment from the menu. The Appointment dialog box appears.

3. Select the calendar to place the appointment in. Evolution allows you to maintain separate calendars and keep appointments in each one separate.

4. Enter a summary of the appointment that will appear on your calendar, as well as a location for the appointment.

5. Enter the start time and duration of the appointment. By default Evolution uses the start time of the time block you right-clicked in and sets the duration of the event to the default time division set in the Preferences.

6. Enter a full description of the appointment, plus any notes you may need.

7. Select the Alarms button if you want an alarm to notify you of the event.

8. Select the Recurrence button if you want to schedule this appointment for a recurring time and day. You can create regularly scheduled appointments, and Evolution will automatically enter them into your calendar, such as once a day, once a week, once a month, or once a year. You can also specify when the recurring appointments stop.

9. Save the appointment by clicking the Save button.

After you save the appointment, it appears in your calendar.

Secret

You can reschedule an appointment simply by dragging and dropping the appointment entry in the calendar. To move the appointment to another day, change the Calendar view to a weekly or monthly view, then drag the appointment to the new day.

You can also change the duration of an appointment or meeting by dragging the boundaries of the appointment to an earlier or later time in the calendar.

Tasks

Start the Tasks tool by selecting the Tasks button in the Evolution Switcher. The main Tasks window, shown in Figure 9-16, appears.

The window shows tasks that you've created and the status of each task (a check mark next to a task indicates that it has been completed). You can start a new task by clicking the Click to Add a Task bar. You can view details of an individual task by double-clicking on the task line.

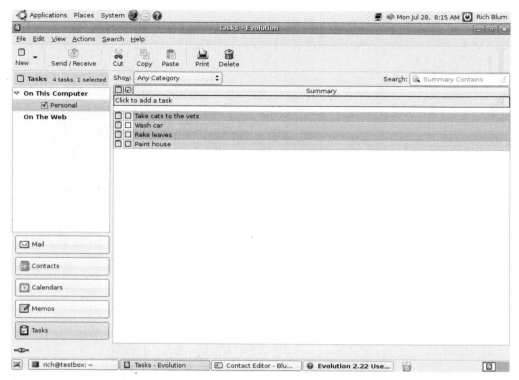

Figure 9-16: The Evolution Tasks main window.

Summary

This chapter walked through the features of the Evolution software package. Evolution is much more than a simple email program. It is a full-featured personal organizer, containing email, a calendar, an address book, a memo taker, and a task scheduler.

Evolution is a popular email program for the GNOME desktop environment. It allows you to manage mail from local and remote email accounts. You can easily manage multiple email accounts from the single Evolution desktop.

After explaining how to configure your email accounts, the chapter walked through how to send messages and how to organize your mail using mail filtering. Evolution interfaces with the Bogofilter spam program to help spot spam and redirect it to a separate folder on your system.

Next, the chapter discussed other features of Evolution. It showed how to use the address book in Evolution to store your contact information, the calendar to mark appointments, and the task scheduler to store and track important tasks you need to remember.

In the next chapter we'll take a look at the graphics programs included with Ubuntu. Programs are available for most of the graphics processing you'll need to do.

Image Manipulation

Chapter
10

◆ ◆

Secrets in This Chapter

Eye of GNOME Image Viewer

GIMP Image Editor

F-Spot Photo Manager

◆ ◆

In this visual world, handling images is almost a daily task. From working with images exported from digital cameras to modifying graphics for a new web site, software for creating and manipulating images is vital to any desktop environment. Ubuntu provides an excellent set of software packages for creating and handling images. This chapter dives into those three packages. The Eye of GNOME Image Viewer is a behind-the-scenes package that most people don't think about, at least not until they double-click on an image file. The second package covered is GIMP, which stands for GNU Image Manipulation Program. The GIMP application is a full-featured image-editing package. Finally, the chapter walks through the features of the F-Spot Photo Manager, which is more than just a simple way to export images from your digital camera.

Eye of GNOME Image Viewer

The Eye of GNOME Image Viewer is a standard package for the GNOME desktop. Its main duty is to display image files stored in folders and on removable media such as CDs and USB Memory Sticks.

This section walks through how to use the Image Viewer software while you're perusing your image files.

Using the Image Viewer

The Image Viewer software is unique in that you usually don't start it by itself. There's no entry for it in the default Ubuntu Applications menu. Instead, it's usually started by some other application, such as Nautilus, when you want to view image files. If you're viewing a folder in Nautilus and double-click on an image file, the Image Viewer main window appears with the image inside, as shown in Figure 10-1.

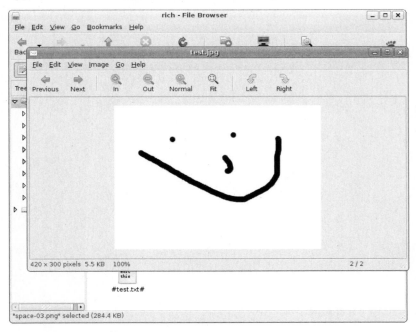

Figure 10-1: The Image Viewer window in action.

Just as you would expect from any other GNOME application, the Image Viewer window includes a menu bar, a toolbar, a viewing area, and a status bar at the bottom of the window. Let's take a look at the various features included in these sections.

The Menu Bar

The menu bar is somewhat sparse by most application standards. There aren't a whole lot of things you can do in the Image Viewer. The main menu options are the following:

- **File:** Open a new file in the Image Viewer window or open the file with another application, such as GIMP, F-Spot Photo Manager, or Firefox. You can also save the image in another image format or send the image to a printer. The Properties entry displays the standard image file properties, such as the size and resolution of the image, along with any metadata embedded in the image file.
- **Edit:** Send the image file to the Trash, edit the toolbar items, or edit the preferences for the Image Viewer settings.
- **View:** Enable and disable the toolbar and status bar and alter the size of the image by zooming in or out from the normal size. The View menu area also allows you to work in Image Collection mode, which displays thumbnails of all images in the current folder at the bottom of the window, allowing you to easily browse all of the image files.
- **Image:** Flip the image horizontally or vertically, rotate the image clockwise or counterclockwise, or set the image as the current desktop background wallpaper.
- **Go:** Move among images in a folder by single-stepping forward or backward or jumping to the first or last image.
- **Help:** Display the Image Viewer manual or, if you're connected to the Internet, retrieve online help or post a bug report.

The Image Collection view is a great way to shuffle through multiple images in a folder, as shown in Figure 10-2.

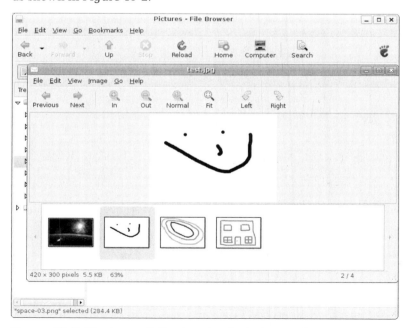

Figure 10-2: The Image Collection view in the Image Viewer application.

When you click on an image in the Image Collection area, Image Viewer displays that image in the main viewing area in the window. If there are more image files in the collection than fit in the Image Collection area, you can click the scroll arrows at the left and right ends to scroll through the images.

Secret

A great way to change the image file types for a large group of images is to use the Image Collection view. Select all of the images you want to change in the Image Collection area by holding down the Ctrl key and selecting each image (or holding down the Shift key and selecting the first and last images in a series). Then click File ⇨ Save As from the menu bar. A Save As template dialog box appears, allowing you to change the filenames (using a common template) and the file image type.

The Toolbar

The toolbar provides quick access to individual features of the Image Viewer. The default icons in the toolbar are

- ♦ **Previous:** View the previous image in an image collection.
- ♦ **Next:** View the next image in a image collection.
- ♦ **In:** Zoom in on the image in the viewer by increasing the magnification.
- ♦ **Out:** Zoom out from the image in the viewer by decreasing the magnification.
- ♦ **Normal:** Reset the image to normal size in the viewer (undo a zoom in or out function).
- ♦ **Fit:** Alter the image size so the entire image appears in the viewer window.
- ♦ **Left:** Rotate the image counterclockwise 90 degrees.
- ♦ **Right:** Rotate the image clockwise 90 degrees.

You can add other icons to the Image Viewer toolbar. Select Edit ⇨ Toolbar to display the Toolbar Editor, show in Figure 10-3.

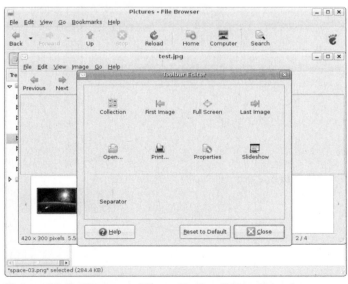

Figure 10-3: The Image Viewer Toolbar Editor dialog box.

You can drag and drop icons from the Toolbar Editor directly to the toolbar area to add those functions.

The Window

The window area in the Image Viewer is obviously where the image appears. However, in Image Collection mode (see "The Menu Bar" section earlier in this chapter), the window area is divided into two sections.

The top section shows the current image, and the bottom section contains thumbnails of other images in the same folder. Click on any thumbnail image to display it in the top section of the window area.

Secret

You can right-click on the image displayed in the viewer window and select from an additional menu of options:

- Open the image with either the GIMP Image Editor or the F-Spot Photo Manager.
- Save the image as another image file type.
- Print the image.
- Send the image to the Trash.
- Display the properties of the image.

The image Properties dialog box displays the image properties, such as type of image, its width and height, file size, and location, as shown in Figure 10-4.

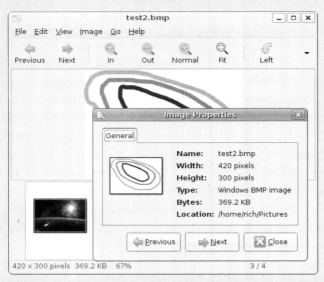

Figure 10-4: The Image Properties dialog box in Image Viewer.

The Status Bar

The status bar at the bottom of the Image Viewer window shows basic information about the image that's displayed. The information displayed in the status bar area is

- ◆ The image width and height (as *width × height*)
- ◆ The image file size
- ◆ The zoom level of the current display (as a percentage of the original image size)
- ◆ The image number in the collection (as an *image/total* value)

You can disable the status bar from the View menu bar area. Doing so provides a little more room for viewing the image in the window area.

Supported File Types

The Image Viewer supports quite a handful of image file types, listed in Table 10-1.

Table 10-1: Image Viewer File Types

File Type	Description
SVG	Scalable vector graphics
XPM	X pixmap for X Windows
XBM	X bitmap for X Windows
WBMP	Wireless application protocol bitmap
TGA	Truevision Targa file format
RAS	Sun raster image
PNM	Portable any map format
PCX	PC Paintbrush format
ICNS	Icon image format
ANI	Atari image format
GIF	Graphics interchange format
BMP	Bitmap format
ICO	Icon format for Microsoft Windows
JPEG	Joint Photographic Experts Group compressed image file
PNG	Portable network graphics format
TIFF	Adobe tagged image file format

One of the great features of Image Viewer is that you can use the Save As function in the File menu bar to convert an image from one image type to another.

You can also launch Image Viewer from the command-line prompt in Terminal. The program is called *eog* (for Eye of GNOME). If you run the eog program by itself, the Image Viewer window opens with no image in it. You can view a specific image using the command

```
eog imagefile
```

There are also a host of command-line parameters you can use with the eog program. Some of the more useful ones are

- `--disable-sound`: **Don't allow access to the sound server from the image.**
- `--display=DISPLAY`: **Change the default X Window server for displaying the Image Viewer.**
- `--enable-sound`: **Allow access to the sound server from the image.**

For additional information, see Chapter 19, "The Ubuntu Command Line."

The GIMP Image Editor

The GIMP Image Editor is a popular open-source graphics program in the Linux world. It's similar to Adobe Photoshop in that it allows you to edit images using various techniques. The following sections walk through the features of GIMP and include a demonstration of how to use GIMP.

Starting GIMP

Start GIMP from the Panel menu by selecting Applications ➪ Graphics ➪ GIMP Image Editor. When you start GIMP for the first time, it opens a user setup wizard. The average user can just click Continue in each dialog box in the wizard for a standard setup. If you're a graphics guru who has a particular reason to change the default settings, you can do so within the setup wizard dialog boxes.

After you've worked through all the wizard dialog boxes, one or more dialog boxes pop up containing the main dialog box (see Figure 10-5) and two additional tool dialog boxes. You can close the box that contains the layer, channel, path, and undo functions. The Toolbox dialog box and the main dialog box are somewhat incorporated. You can't close the Toolbox dialog box, but you can move it to another display workspace by right-clicking on the title bar and selecting the Move to Workspace Right option.

The following sections explain how to use GIMP for standard image-editing tasks.

GIMP Basic Tools

The beauty of GIMP is that all of the tools you need to edit images appear in separate dialog boxes, allowing you to lay out multiple tools as you draw and have easy access to them while working. The main dialog box allows you to switch among the various tool dialog boxes while editing an image.

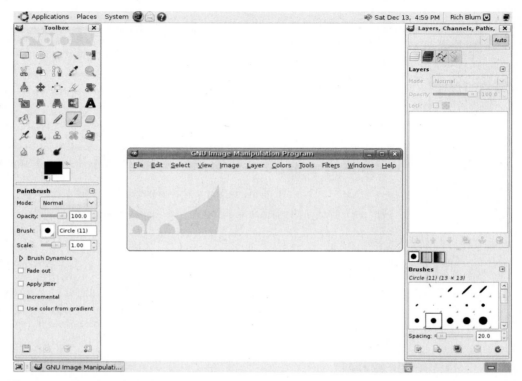

Figure 10-5: GIMP's main dialog box.

The File menu item in the main dialog box allows you to open or acquire an image to work with. GIMP allows you to edit images by

- Starting a new image from scratch on a blank canvas
- Loading an existing image from your computer
- Retrieving an image from a remote location using a uniform resource identifier (URI)
- Retrieving an image from a scanner connected to your computer
- Producing a screenshot of your desktop or a single application window on the desktop

GIMP supports all of the standard image types, such as GIF, JPG, TIFF, and others.

When you open an image, it appears in the main dialog box within an editing window area. If you open more than one image at a time, each image opens in a new dialog box in its own editing window. This feature allows you to work on several images at the same time without having to switch between images in a single window.

The Toolbox dialog box contains all of the image-editing tools. The Toolbox consists of tools for selecting image areas, reorienting the image (such as flipping); drawing using a pencil, paintbrush, ink, or airbrush; filling colors, and adding basic special effects.

For each tool you select, the bottom section of the Toolbox dialog box shows detailed settings for the tool. In Figure 10-5, the Paintbrush tool is selected, so settings related to the paintbrush (such as brush size and opacity of the color) appear in the bottom section.

You can also keep detailed settings for multiple options open as separate dialog boxes. The menu bar in the main dialog box allows you to select the editing features to open. Choosing Tools from the menu bar produces a list of the Toolbox dialog boxes you can have open on your desktop, as shown in Figure 10-6.

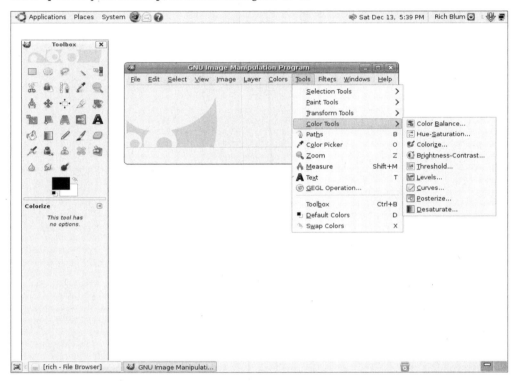

Figure 10-6: The GIMP Toolbox dialog box list.

Below the tools in the Toolbox dialog box is an area for selecting the foreground and background colors (depicted as a black and a white square). Double-click the black square to set the foreground color for the image, and double-click the white square to set the background color. Next to that area is an icon you can click to easily change the Drawing tool shape and size.

To demonstrate the abilities of the GIMP, let's get an image and play with it.

Using GIMP

The best way to explain the features available in GIMP is to demonstrate how to edit an image. This section walks through the process of obtaining an image and using various features in GIMP to manipulate it.

Taking a Screenshot

GIMP provides a method for capturing screen images. You can capture a single application window, an area that you specify, or the entire desktop.

Follow these steps to create a screenshot image:

1. Open GIMP by choosing Applications ⇨ Graphics ⇨ GIMP Image Editor.
2. From the GIMP menu bar, choose File ⇨ Create ⇨ Screen Shot. The Screen Shot dialog box appears, as shown in Figure 10-7.

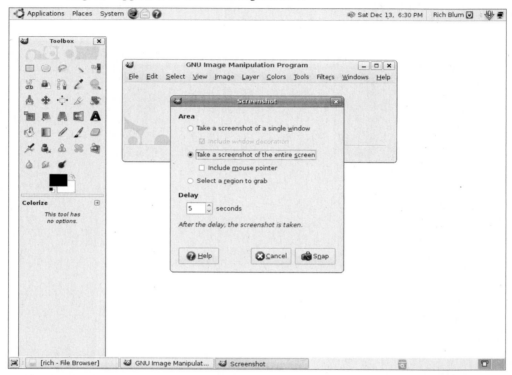

Figure 10-7: The GIMP Screen Shot dialog box.

You can select to capture either a single application window or the entire desktop. You can also set a delay for when GIMP takes the screenshot, allowing you time to set up the window the way you want before taking the picture.

3. When the screenshot is taken, GIMP opens the image in an image editing window. Select File ⇨ Save As to save the image file. GIMP allows you to save the image in most common image formats. All you need to do is place the proper image format extension on the filename (such as .jpg, .tiff, .gif, or .bmp). After you click OK, GIMP may produce another dialog box with options specific to the image file type you saved the image as.

You now have a saved image file that you can play with in GIMP. Let's see what we can do to it.

Editing the Image File

Now let's open our saved image file and play around with GIMP's image-editing features.

1. Select File ⇨ Open and select the image file you saved from your screenshot. GIMP opens the file in an image-editing window, as shown in Figure 10-8.

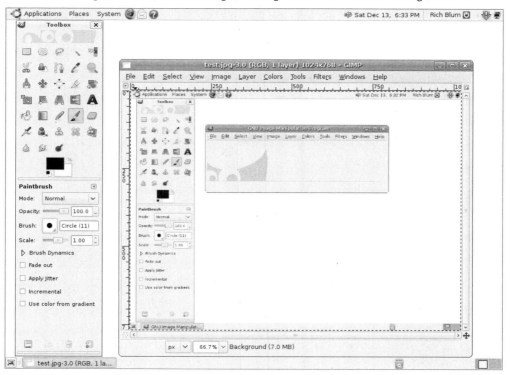

Figure 10-8: The GIMP Image Editing window.

2. From the toolbox, choose one of the selection tools (such as the rectangular box) and select an area on your image.

3. Again from the toolbox, choose the Rotate tool, then click in the selected area on the image. The Rotate dialog box appears, allowing you to specify the details of the rotation. As you increase or decrease the amount of rotation, you'll see the selected image area actually rotate in the editor. When you get to just the right spot, click the Rotate button to apply the rotation.

4. From the toolbox, select the drawing instrument of your choice (paintbrush, pencil, etc.) and do some doodling in your image. By default, your drawing color is set to black. To change the color, double-click the foreground area in the toolbox. The Change Foreground Color dialog box appears, as shown in Figure 10-9.

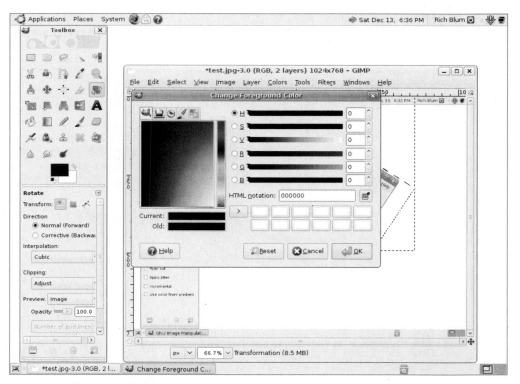

Figure 10-9: The GIMP Change Foreground Color dialog box.

> This tool provides an easy way to select just the right color for your drawings. You can point and click to select the color you're looking for.

5. Save your creation with either the same filename or a new filename to create a separate image file.

These steps demonstrate the basic image-editing capabilities of GIMP. If you're familiar with basic image-editing tools like Microsoft Paintbrush, you're probably happy with these results.

However, if you're used to more advanced image-editing tools, you're probably not all that impressed yet. Fortunately, there are still more features in GIMP we can play with. GIMP includes a set of prebuilt filters that can apply special effects to your image.

You can find the filters in the Filters menu bar. There are eight groups of filters you can choose from, including filters to blur the image, enhance the colors in the image, distort the image, and add noise and shadow effects.

Now follow along with these steps to add some effects to your image:

1. If you've closed your image file, open it using File ➪ Open so it's in a new image-editing window.

2. Click the Filters menu item and select a special effect from the menu list. The Filters section contains lots of special effects to enhance the look of your image. Figure 10-10 shows the result of the Distorts ➪ Whirl and Pinch effect.

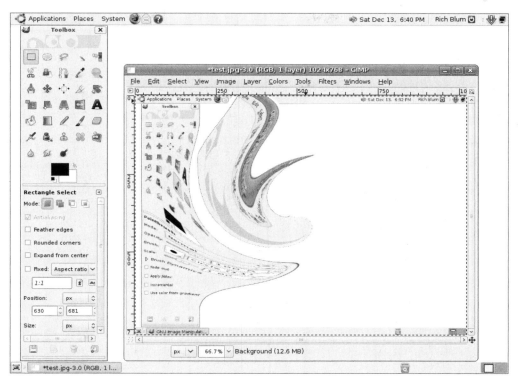

Figure 10-10: The image after applying the Whirl and Pinch effect.

Now you're starting to see some of the fancier features of GIMP. But wait, there's even more.

Using GIMP Scripts

For those of us who lack artistic ability, GIMP tries to help out as best as it can. Many artistic people have contributed scripts to GIMP that provide more special effects than you'll see in a Hollywood action movie.

The key is being able to apply a series of special effects to create an overall effect on the image. GIMP allows you to string special effects together using a scripting language. Ubuntu includes both the Python-Fu and Script-Fu GIMP scripting languages.

The Python-Fu and Script-Fu scripts are accessible from the Filters menu bar area, directly below the Filters list. GIMP incorporates the Python-Fu and Script-Fu scripts directly in the filter categories. When you run a script, it'll produce a dialog box so you can set the parameters to alter the effect of the script.

Secret

You'll need to be a little patient when working with GIMP scripts. Because scripts apply several layers of special effects to an image, they often take a while to complete. Don't think that GIMP has locked up your workstation and shut things down in the middle of a script.

The prebuilt scripts included with GIMP produce some amazing effects. Figure 10-11 demonstrates the Weave effect on the saved desktop image.

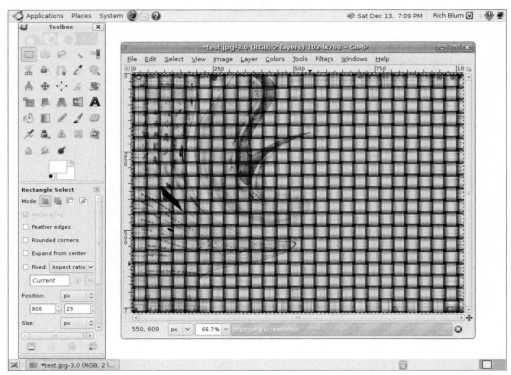

Figure 10-11: The sample image after applying the Weave Script-Fu effect.

The result looks quite professional for a simple open-source program! Take the time to play around with the various script effects available in GIMP. You'll be surprised at the quality of the special effects. As the GIMP manual states, most of the effects can be reversed using the Edit ➪ Undo menu item, so feel free to play.

F-Spot Photo Manager

Digital cameras have pretty much taken over the consumer photography world. People are taking digital pictures of nearly every event in their lives.

The downside to the popularity of digital cameras is that now everyone wants software for handling digital images from cameras. Ubuntu includes the F-Spot Photo Manager application for this purpose.

The F-Spot Layout

Start the F-Spot application by selecting Applications ➪ Graphics ➪ F-Spot Photo Manager from the Panel menu. If this is the first time you've opened F-Spot, an Import window appears. If you're importing photos from a digital camera, the Import window allows you to select which images to import, as shown in Figure 10-12.

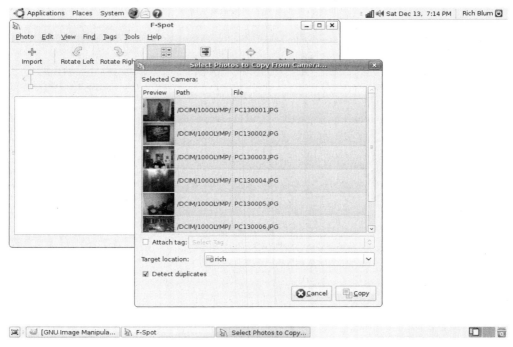

Figure 10-12: The F-Spot Import window.

From the Import window you can import images from folders and from external devices such as digital cameras and USB Memory Sticks into the F-Spot database.

Secret

When you plug a digital camera into the USB port, Ubuntu automatically launches F-Spot Photo Manager and asks whether you want to import all of the images from the camera.

Ubuntu also mounts the camera as a removable media device and displays an icon on the desktop. When you're done importing the images, you should right-click the removable media icon and select Unmount Volume before disconnecting the camera.

Browse to the folder or device that contains your images, then click the Open button.

F-Spot examines the images on the device (or in the folder) and provides three options:

- ◆ Attach a tag to identify the group of images.
- ◆ Copy the image to the Photo folder or work with the image from its original location.
- ◆ Search subfolders for additional images.

When importing, F-Spot allows you to specify a tag to identify all of the photos as a group. You can use this tag to easily find the photos in your album.

To complete the import, click the Import button.

Secret

When you import images from a digital camera or external storage device, F-Spot always copies the image and leaves the original. Likewise, when you import images from a folder, F-Spot copies the image and leaves the original, but you can change that in the Preference settings.

F-Spot stores images in the Photos folder under your home folder. F-Spot keeps photo information (such as file location and tags) in a separate database file, also located in your home folder. Look for the file .gnome2/f-spot/photos.db in your home folder. You can access this database using the sqlite3 command-line program in a Terminal window, but be careful not to delete or modify the file— F-Spot won't be able to track the photo information.

Once you've imported the images, they appear as an *import roll* in the main F-Spot viewing window, shown in Figure 10-13.

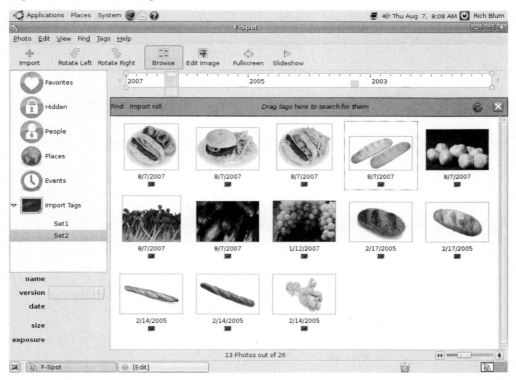

Figure 10-13: The main F-Spot viewing window.

The F-Spot viewing window consists of five areas:

- The menu bar
- The toolbar
- The sidebar
- The viewing area
- The status bar

The following sections walk through each of these areas in F-Spot.

The Menu Bar

The menu bar contains all of the options for you to view, manage, and manipulate images in the F-Spot library. It consists of the following menu items:

- **Photo:** Import new images, manage image versions, export images to another application, print them, or send them via email.
- **Edit:** Modify a selected image in the viewing area. You can rotate, adjust the color, change the timestamp of the image, add or remove tags assigned to the image, and delete the image from the F-Spot library. This menu also contains entries to set the preferences for F-Spot and to install additional plug-in modules.
- **View:** Start a slideshow of the current images, view images in Full-Screen mode, alter the layout of the images in the viewer, and zoom in on or out from the image. You can also set what image elements appear in the viewing window, as well as what window areas appear.
- **Find:** Find a specific image or group of images based on tags, assigned ratings, dates, or when imported.
- **Tags:** Add and remove tags from individual images or groups of images, as well as create new tag names.
- **Help:** Display the help manual for F-Spot.

F-Spot allows you to easily print images or send them via email from the Photo menu area. You can also select the Export To option to export selected images to a CD for burning or to any of several online image-storage applications, such as Flickr, PicasaWeb, and 23hq.

The Toolbar

The toolbar provides quick access to several common features in F-Spot:

- **Import:** Retrieve images from a folder or external digital camera and place them in the F-Spot library.
- **Rotate Left:** Rotate the selected image or images counterclockwise 90 degrees.
- **Rotate Right:** Rotate the selected image or images clockwise 90 degrees.
- **Browse Mode:** The default mode. Display thumbnails of all the images in the library, or all of the images selected by a specified filter.
- **Edit Image:** Open an image in the Image Editor, which allows you to crop the image and apply effects to it.
- **Switch to Full-Screen Mode:** Display the image in Full-Screen mode.
- **Switch to Slideshow Mode:** Single-step through the images one at a time as a slideshow.

The Slideshow mode allows you to automatically display all of the images in the Browse window in order, which is perfect for presentations or displaying your photos to others. In Full-Screen mode, F-Spot enlarges the image to fill the entire screen.

The Sidebar

The sidebar area contains two sections:

- ◆ The Tag Selector area
- ◆ The Image Information area

The Tag Selector allows you to quickly view all images with a specific tag. F-Spot includes several default tags that you can apply to your images, such as favorites, hidden, people, places, and events.

If you assign tags when you import a group of images, F-Spot adds those tags to the Tag Selector area so you can easily and quickly access those images.

The Image Information area provides basic information about the image selected in the viewer window. If there are multiple versions of the image available (see "Using the F-Spot Editor" later in this chapter), you can select which version of the image to view.

The Viewing Area

The viewing area is divided into two sections. The top section contains the Arrange By tool. The Arrange By tool allows you to quickly locate an image based on one of two criteria:

- ◆ The image date
- ◆ The image location

You can toggle the criteria used by the View menu bar option. Just select the Arrange By item and select either month or folder.

Under the Arrange By tool is the main viewing area. F-Spot opens in Browse mode, which displays thumbnails of all the images in the library. You can specify which images appear in the Browse mode by selecting a tag from the Tag Selector area in the sidebar. When you do that, the find bar appears at the top of the viewing area, shown in Figure 10-14.

You can combine tags in the find bar by simply selecting another tag from the Tag Selector. You can also right-click on the tag in the find bar to remove it from the find filter or negate it in the find filter. Negating a tag displays all images in the library that do *not* have a specific tag.

The Status Bar

The status bar, located at the bottom of the F-Spot display window, shows the status of the photos displayed in the viewing area. If F-Spot displays all of the photos from the library, the status bar shows the total number of images. If you select images, the status bar indicates how many images have been selected. If you use the find bar to filter images, the status bar indicates how many images are being displayed of the total number of images in the library.

The other element in the status bar is the Quick Zoom tool. This tool allows you to change the zoom level in the viewing area. You can quickly increase or decrease the size of the thumbnail images using this tool.

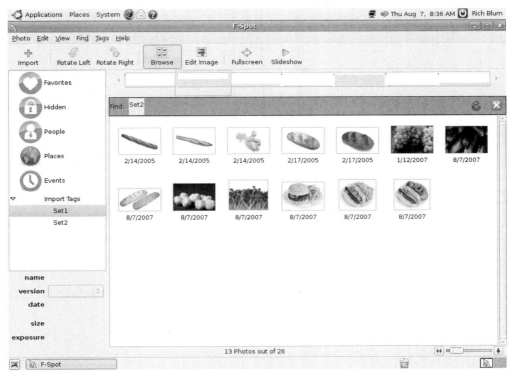

Figure 10-14: The find bar used in the F-Spot viewing area.

Using the F-Spot Editor

Not only can F-Spot organize your photos, but it also provides an image editor with some advanced features to help you clean up your photos. After importing an image, you can use the image editor to apply various effects. Follow these steps to work with an image:

1. Open an image for editing from the browse window. You can open an image for editing by double-clicking on the image or by single-clicking the image and then clicking the Edit Image button in the toolbar. The selected image appears enlarged, and the other images in the library appear in a scroll area across the top, as shown in Figure 10-15.

2. Enter a comment for the image in the Comment text box. You can store comments, which are hidden in normal view but appear when you edit the image. This feature is great for adding notes about things you need to change or what the image is for.

3. Select an editing constraint from the Crop tool's drop-down box. Editing constraints allow you to specify guidelines for the image size, ensuring that you don't crop the image too large or too small. The available editing constraints are

    - **No Constraint:** Allows you to set any size for the crop area.
    - **Same as Photo:** Maintains the current dimension ratio of the image.

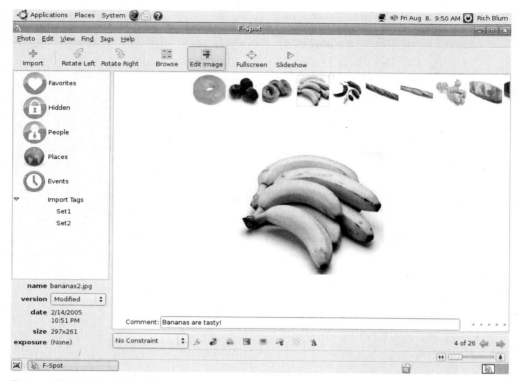

Figure 10-15: The F-Spot Edit Image window.

- **4 × 3 (Book):** Sets the dimension ratio to 4 × 3, a common size used in photo books.
- **4 × 7 (Postcard):** Sets the dimension ratio to 4 × 7, the size of a postcard in the United States.
- **5 × 7 (L, 2L):** Sets the dimension ratio to 5 × 7, commonly used for mid-sized photos.
- **8 × 10:** Sets the dimension ratio to 8 × 10, a common size for larger photos.
- **Square:** Restricts the crop area to a perfect square.
- **Custom Ratios:** Allows you to set your own custom dimensions to ensure you don't crop outside those dimensions.

The editing constraints prevent you from changing the image dimensions beyond the specified size. This ensures that your image will fit as desired.

4. Select an area of the image you want to work with. When you click and drag inside the image area, the total image becomes grayed out and the selection area becomes brighter. The image selection area is constrained by the editing constraint, if selected.

5. Click the Crop icon (the first icon in the bottom row of buttons). This action removes the excess image area from around the selected crop area. The new image area should now correspond to the editing constraint size you selected in step 3.

6. Edit the image using the Edit buttons in the bottom area. The image editing tools that F-Spot offers are

- **Redeye Removal:** Select the area around eyes and click this button to help reduce the redeye effect from flashes.
- **Manually Adjust Colors:** Alter the image shade and color.
- **Convert Image to Black and White:** Change the image to black and white (grayscale).
- **Convert Image to Sepia Tones:** Change the image to a brown-tone image, similar to old-style photographs.
- **Adjust the Image Angle:** Align the image with the background.
- **Create a Soft-Focus Visual Effect:** Slightly blur the image to produce the effect of using a soft lens in photography.
- **Automatically Adjust Colors:** Allow F-Spot to determine the best color shading for the image.

When you select the Manually Adjust Colors tool, the Adjust Color window, shown in Figure 10-16, appears.

You can adjust common photo features such as exposure, saturation, and brightness of the image.

7. Exit the Edit Image window by clicking the Browse button in the toolbar.

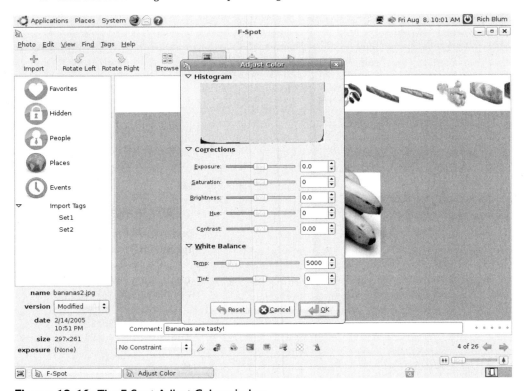

Figure 10-16: The F-Spot Adjust Color window.

When you edit an image in F-Spot, it automatically saves the original and creates a copy of the edited image. The version setting in the Image Information area indicates that you're viewing a modified version of the original image. This setting continues when you return to Browse mode.

You can reset back to the original image by selecting the image in Browse mode, clicking the Version drop-down list in the lower-left corner of the screen, and selecting the original entry. Each time you edit an image you create another modified copy of the image. F-Spot maintains all of the modified copies and allows you to easily switch among them using the Version drop-down list.

 **Secret**

You can assign a specific name to a version by creating the new version before editing it. Select the image, then select Photo ⇨ Create New Version from the menu bar. A dialog box appears, asking you to name the new version. Once you assign a name to the version, you can use the Edit Image feature to edit that version. All edits to the image remain in that version.

Summary

This chapter discussed the image-handling and manipulating packages installed in Ubuntu by default. You won't find the Eye of GNOME Image Viewer in the menus. Instead, it is opened automatically by the Nautilus file manager when you double-click on an image file. Image Viewer allows you to perform basic image viewing features with an image.

The GIMP Image Editor is a full-featured tool for acquiring and editing images. GIMP performs many of the complex image-editing functions available in commercial image-editing packages. GIMP also provides advanced image effects created by other artists, so you're not limited by your own abilities.

The F-Spot Photo Manager is the default photo-handling application in Ubuntu, but it can also be used for handling other types of images as well. F-Spot uses a database system to manage photo libraries and assist you in finding photos. You can assign tags to individual and groups of photos, then easily retrieve them based on their assigned tag. F-Spot also provides basic image-editing features such as removing redeye, enhancing color, and cropping.

The next chapter dives into the world of Ubuntu audio support. Unfortunately, audio support in Linux is not a pretty sight, and it has many pitfalls. The next chapter tries to dig through the mess and present the information you need for working with audio files. It also explains how to work around the Ubuntu limitations on restricted audio file types.

Using Audio

Chapter
11

◆ ◆

Secrets in This Chapter

Using Sound Files

Ubuntu and Sound

Playing CDs with Rhythmbox

Burning CDs with Brasero

Playing Audio Files from Nautilus

◆ ◆

I t wasn't all that long ago that sound on a computer just meant a series of beeps and blips coming out of a tiny computer speaker. Over the past few years the computer world has exploded with audio features. From playing and extracting songs on a CD to listening to streaming radio stations on a web site, there are plenty of reasons to have audio software on your workstation. Ubuntu doesn't disappoint the audiophile with its basic installation packages. Plenty of audio features are built into Ubuntu, and you can download additional packages to provide even more audio features. This chapter walks through the basics of using your Ubuntu workstation to process audio files and CDs.

Audio File Basics

Before diving into the software packages, it's a good idea to first cover some of the basics of the open-source audio world. Unfortunately, the audio world is full of legal and ethical issues that cause problems for the open-source software enthusiast. You'll need to know what to expect, or you might be disappointed.

First, let's take a quick look at the popular audio file formats used on computers, portable music players, and the Internet. These formats are shown in Table 11-1.

Table 11-1: Common Audio File Formats

Extension	Name	Description
.aac	Advanced audio coding	An ISO standard audio compression format made popular as the default format for Apple iPod music players
.flac	Free lossless audio codec	An open-source, lossless audio format that doesn't use compression
.ogg	Ogg Vorbis	An open-source audio compression format equivalent to MP3 compression and quality
.mp3	MPEG-1 audio layer 3	A patented audio compression format requiring licensing rights
.wav	Waveform audio format	A Microsoft and IBM standard for uncompressed audio
.wma	Windows media audio	A proprietary audio compression format created by Microsoft and controlled by strict licensing requirements

For each specific audio file format, Ubuntu must use software that can play the audio file. These programs are called *codecs*. Each codec specializes in a specific audio file format. Ubuntu includes codecs for the FLAC, OGG, and WAV audio file formats by default. There are reasons why it doesn't contain codecs for the others by default.

By far the most controversial audio file format is MP3. Despite the widespread popularity of the MP3 audio format (or maybe because of it), MP3 has been the subject of numerous legal battles over the past few years based on patent infringement. Because of this legal problem, many Linux distributions shy away from supporting MP3 files by default.

Instead, the Ogg Vorbis audio file format has slowly become the de facto standard for compressed audio files in the open-source audio world. Just about all Linux distributions, including Ubuntu, have full support for .ogg files. Ogg Vorbis is the recommended audio file format for handling most audio files in Linux. Many portable music devices also support the Ogg Vorbis audio file format, allowing you to use the same music files on your Ubuntu workstation and portable music player.

Secret

Ubuntu doesn't include support for Microsoft audio files due to licensing issues. A couple of options are available if you require support for Microsoft audio files on your workstation. You can purchase commercial Linux audio packages that provide support for Microsoft audio file formats. These packages are properly licensed to use the Microsoft audio format.

The Linux world also contains a library of reverse-engineered Microsoft audio codecs that can be installed on any Linux platform, including Ubuntu. Be warned, though, because the legality of these libraries is still in question in some countries.

Controlling Sound in Ubuntu

When you install Ubuntu, it attempts to automatically detect and configure the sound environment on your workstation. Usually it's successful in this attempt, although it's possible that you may have to install modules for special sound cards, especially if you have an exotic one. If so, consult the sound card manufacturer's web site and look for instructions on loading Linux drivers.

Secret

Many posts have been made to Ubuntu online forums about how to solve sound card issues. Try scanning the forums (available at http://ubuntuforums.org) to see whether your particular sound card problem has already been resolved by someone else.

There are a few commands you can enter from the command line (see Chapter 19, "The Ubuntu Command Line") to evaluate the sound situation on your system:

aplay -l lists the sounds cards that Ubuntu detected on your system. It's possible that Ubuntu detected your sound card but has it in a muted state.

lspci -v lists all of the hardware devices recognized on your Ubuntu system. If Ubuntu sees your sound card but didn't install it, you have a driver issue. If your sound card is not listed, then Ubuntu didn't recognize the hardware. Try reseating your sound card or check your system BIOS settings.

To find a driver for your sound card, try the Advanced Linux Sound Architecture (ALSA) project web site:

http://www.alsa-project.org/main/index.php/Matrix:Main

The ALSA web site includes drivers and specific instructions for installing them on your Ubuntu system.

Once Ubuntu recognizes your sound card and loads the drivers, it uses a *front-end* package to interface with your sound card. The front-end package provides a common interface between audio applications and your sound card. This way, audio application developers don't have to worry about interacting with hundreds of different sound cards. They just code to use the front-end applications.

You set your sound environment front end using two utilities in Ubuntu:

♦ The Sound Preferences dialog box
♦ The ALSA Mixer applet

The following sections describe how to use each of these utilities.

Sound Preferences

Start the Sound Preferences dialog box by selecting System ⇨ Preferences ⇨ Sound from the top Panel menu. The Sound Preferences utility starts, as shown in Figure 11-1.

The Sound Preferences dialog box has two tabs of settings:

♦ **Devices:** Allows you to select which sound system to use for specific audio functions.
♦ **Sounds:** Allows you to select specific sounds for specific system functions.

Each tab controls the settings for specific features of the sound environment.

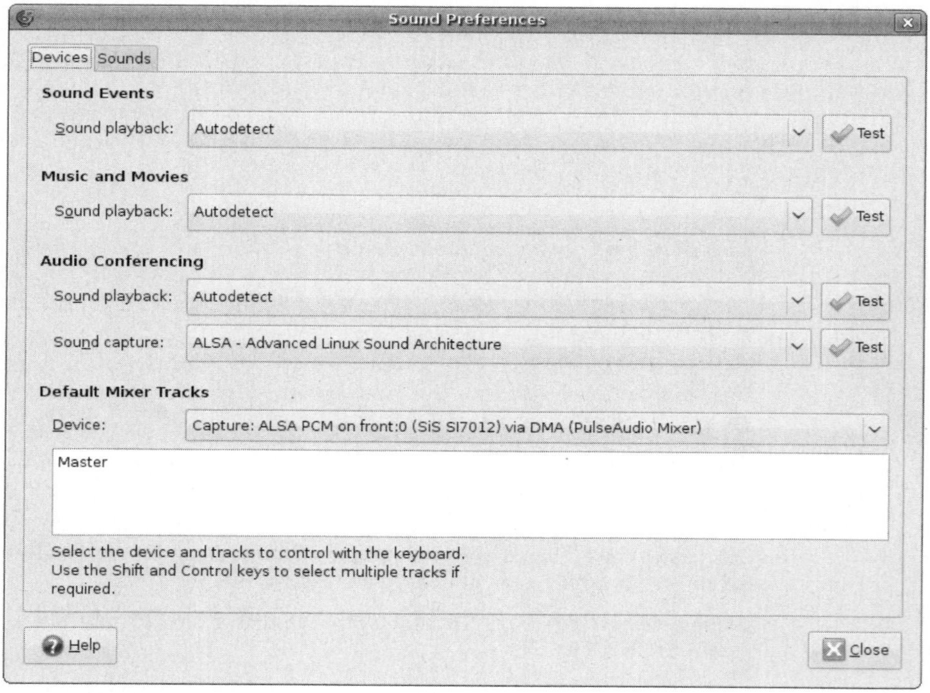

Figure 11-1: The Sound Preferences dialog box.

The Devices Tab

The Devices tab sets the default front-end sound system used for the different types of sound generated on the workstation, shown in Table 11-2.

Table 11-2: Sound Generation in Ubuntu

Method	Description
Sound Events	Sounds created by the operating system when events occur, such as mouse clicks, warning messages, and logging out of the system
Music and Movies	Sounds created by playing audio and video files in an application
Audio Conferencing	Sounds created by a conferencing software package, such as the Ekiga Softphone

For each category of sounds, you can select the front-end sound management system to use. Ubuntu includes three software sound management packages:

- ♦ The Advanced Linux Sound Architecture (ALSA)
- ♦ The Open Sound System (OSS)
- ♦ The PulseAudio Sound Server

By default Ubuntu will set the values to autodetect the best sound system for your workstation. You can change the selected sound management system by clicking the drop-down box for the sound generation method and selecting the sound management system you want to use.

The Audio Conferencing setup allows you to select separate sound management systems for playing received sound and recording sound to send.

Secret

The ALSA sound management software is newer and more advanced than the other two systems. It's by far the most robust of the three packages, providing the most options and support for the most sound cards. You should select the ALSA system whenever possible, if it supports your particular sound card.

The Sounds Tab

The Sounds tab provides an interface for you to select various sounds for Ubuntu to play for specific system events. Figure 11-2 shows the events that you can define sounds for.

For each event you can select to play the default sound, disable the sound, or select a custom sound from a sound file. The only restriction is that the sound file must be in WAV format.

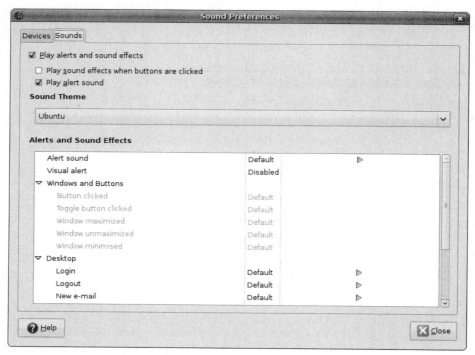

Figure 11-2: The Sounds tab in the Sound Preferences window.

Secret

From the Sounds tab you can also disable all sounds generated from the operating system, which can come in handy sometimes. Just remove the check from the Play Alerts and Sound Effects check box, and your desktop will be quiet!

The Sound Applet

When Ubuntu detects a sound card in your workstation at installation time, it automatically places the *Sound applet* in your panel (see Chapter 4, "Exploring the Desktop"). The Sound applet appears as a speaker icon in the right side of the top panel. When you click it, the master volume control appears, as shown in Figure 11-3.

Figure 11-3: The Sound applet master volume control.

The slider allows you to set the overall volume level of the workstation speakers. For more detailed volume control, double-click the Sound applet icon, and the ALSA mixer window, shown in Figure 11-4, appears.

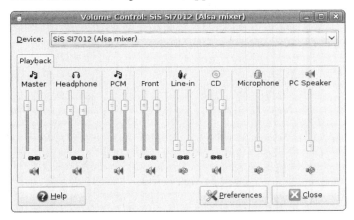

Figure 11-4: The ALSA mixer window.

The ALSA mixer contains eight sets of sliders for detailed control of the sound environment:

- **Master:** Controls the overall volume level of the mixer (this is the same as the master volume control that appears if you single-click the icon).
- **Headphone:** Controls the volume level for the headphone jack on the workstation.
- **PCM:** Controls the volume level for audio CDs and music files when played from the system.
- **Front:** Controls the volume level for the speakers on the workstation, either internal or external.
- **Line-in Boost:** Sets the recording level for an external microphone plugged into the microphone jack on the workstation.
- **CD:** Sets the left and right channel volume when playing audio CDs.
- **Microphone:** Sets the recording level for the built-in microphone on the workstation.
- **PC Speaker:** Sets the volume for the built-in speaker on the workstation.

Using these sliders you can customize the sound volume for playing and recording audio from all applications on your workstation.

Rhythmbox

Playing music on your computer workstation is a great way to entertain yourself while doing mundane work, such as creating spreadsheets and writing reports. The Ubuntu workstation installs the Rhythmbox package mainly for playing CDs, but it also

- ◆ Plays streaming audio from Web radio stations
- ◆ Plays podcasts from Web podcast stations
- ◆ Plays songs stored on an external music device, such as an MP3 player
- ◆ Allows you to purchase and play songs from online music stores
- ◆ Allows you to create playlists of stored music files to customize your listening

The following sections walk through the various features available in Rhythmbox to help you get the most out of your music listening.

Playing Audio CDs

When you place an audio CD in the CD tray of your workstation, Ubuntu automatically launches Rhythmbox. You can manually launch Rhythmbox from the Panel menu by selecting Applications ➪ Sound & Video ➪ Rhythmbox Music Player.

Rhythmbox scans the CD and displays the tracks and track lengths of the CD in the main window (you may have to click on the CD in the Devices section in Rhythmbox first). If your workstation is connected to the Internet, Rhythmbox also contacts a remote CD database to extract information about the CD, including the CD title, individual track song titles, and the album cover art for the CD, if available. Figure 11-5 shows the Rhythmbox window after opening an audio CD.

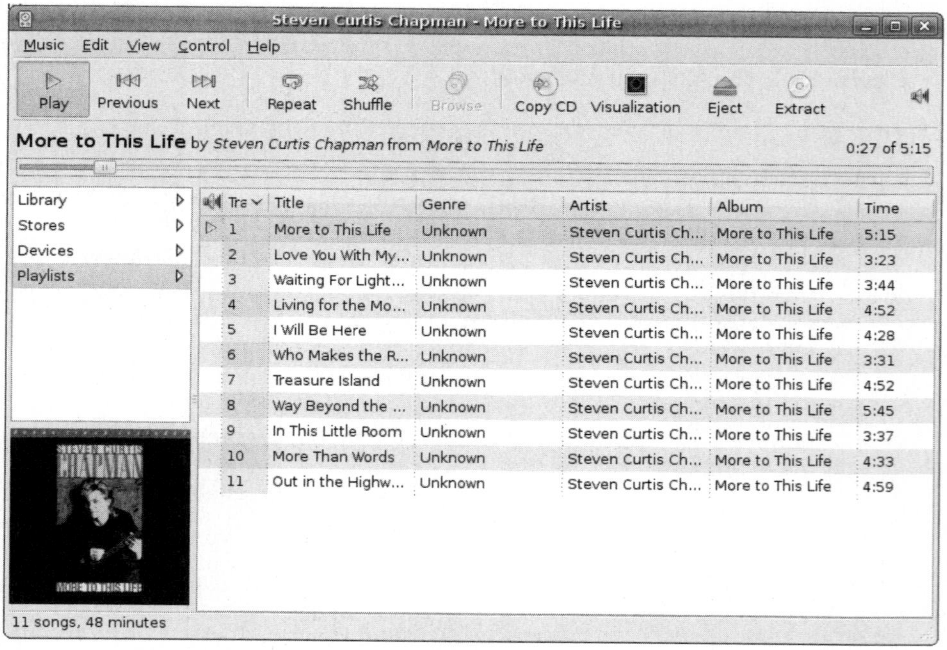

Figure 11-5: Starting an audio CD using Rhythmbox.

The main Rhythmbox interface is fairly straightforward. It lists the individual CD tracks in the main window area, along with the basic track information it retrieved. The toolbar provides buttons for the basic functions you'd expect for interacting with a CD player, plus a couple of extras:

- ♦ **Play:** Start the current track.
- ♦ **Previous:** Jump to the previous track in the song list.
- ♦ **Next:** Jump to the next track in the song list.
- ♦ **Repeat:** Repeat the current track.
- ♦ **Shuffle:** Randomly play the tracks in the song list.
- ♦ **Browse:** Browse through the music tracks.
- ♦ **Visualization:** Display a screensaver image while playing the track.
- ♦ **Eject:** Remove the CD from the CD tray.
- ♦ **Extract:** Convert the tracks on the CD to audio files and store them in the music library.

The Extract feature enables you to copy tracks from the CD to audio files on your workstation (called *ripping*). Once you rip the songs from a CD to your workstation, Rhythmbox stores them in a library so you can play them without the CD!

caution The CD music world is full of licensing restrictions. It's generally considered unacceptable to copy tracks from a CD and return the CD to the store. Once you purchase a CD you're more than welcome to copy tracks to audio files for your own use. However, it's unacceptable to share ripped audio files with others while you are still using them on your system.

You can set the location and audio file format used for storing the resulting audio files in the Rhythmbox Preferences window, shown in Figure 11-6. You get there by selecting Edit ⇨ Preferences from the menu bar.

Select the Music tab to view the settings for ripping CDs. The default location for storing music files is the Music folder under your home folder. You can change that to another folder if you desire. Just remember that you'll need the proper file permissions to store them there.

The Preferences window allows you to organize your music library any way you want. The default setting is for Rhythmbox to create a top-level folder named after the artist, then a subfolder named after the album. Rhythmbox places the individual files, named by track title and number, in the subfolder. If you don't like this organization method, the drop-down boxes for the folder hierarchy and filename provide several options to customize your music library layout.

The last drop-down box in the Preferences section allows you to select the audio file type used to store the track:

- ♦ CD-quality, lossless (FLAC audio)
- ♦ CD-quality, lossy (Ogg multimedia)
- ♦ Voice, lossless (WAV audio)
- ♦ Voice, lossy (Speex audio)

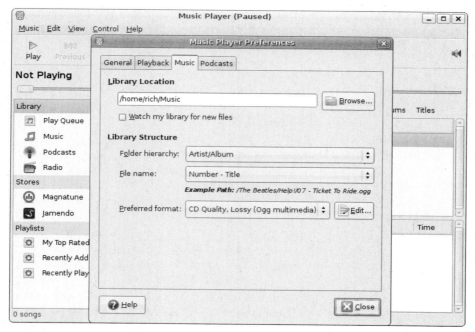

Figure 11-6: The Rhythmbox Preferences window.

The default is the Ogg multimedia format, which is an open-source audio format that has a relatively small file size and an excellent quality of playback. Most portable music players also recognize the Ogg format, so you can copy these files to your portable music player and listen to them there, as well.

Secret

If you've installed additional audio codec programs on your workstation, you can add them to the default list. Just click the Edit icon, select the audio format, then select the codec application to handle the file conversion.

After you've set the ripping preferences, you can copy any or all of the tracks to the music library from the main window.

Playing Audio Files

Rhythmbox can play audio files stored in the music library. The main Rhythmbox library area is the Music folder under your home folder. When you select the Music link in the Library section of the main page, Rhythmbox displays the files it finds in your library.

If you attempt to play an audio file that Ubuntu doesn't have a codec for, it displays a warning message, shown in Figure 11-7.

Figure 11-7: The Ubuntu audio file codec warning message.

If your workstation is connected to the Internet, click the Search button for Ubuntu to attempt to locate an appropriate codec for the audio file type in its package repositories. If it finds one or more codec packages that can handle the audio file format, it displays them in an selection box, shown in Figure 11-8.

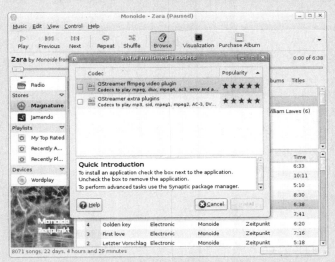

Figure 11-8: The Ubuntu audio codec installation window.

Just select a codec program to automatically install it to add support for the audio file format on your workstation.

Listening to Internet Audio

If you have a high-speed connection to the Internet, you can use Rhythmbox to listen to streaming music and *podcasts*. A podcast is an audio file available for easy downloading or playing directly from a web site. The name *podcast* originally referred to files compatible with the popular Apple iPod portable music player, but the name now applies to any multimedia file distributed over the Internet for playback on a portable audio device or personal computer.

Clicking the Radio link in the Library section displays a list of Internet radio sites configured for playback in Rhythmbox, as shown in Figure 11-9.

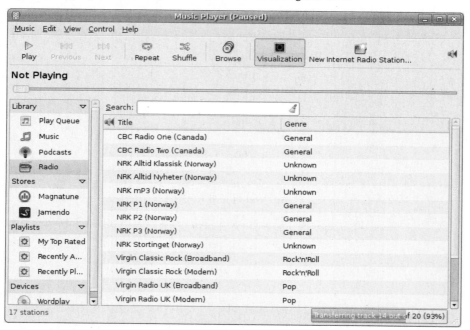

Figure 11-9: The Internet radio station list in Rhythmbox.

You can add more Internet radio sites by clicking the New Internet Radio Station button that appears in the toolbar when you're in the Radio mode. Just enter the URL of the radio site, and Rhythmbox attempts to make the connection.

Similarly, clicking the Podcast link in the Library section displays a list of Internet podcast sites configured for playback in Rhythmbox. You can add more Internet podcast sites by clicking the New Podcast Feed button.

Many news and entertainment programs release podcasts at regular intervals, such as once a week. By *subscribing* to a podcast you can have Rhythmbox update the podcast with the latest episode by simply clicking the individual podcast entry. You can also click the Update All Feeds button to update all of the podcasts configured on your system.

Secret

Rhythmbox can automatically download new podcasts from podcast sites that you subscribe to. Open the Preferences window, then click the Podcasts tab. Set the Check for New Episodes drop-down box to specify the frequency (for example, weekly) at which you expect new podcasts to appear. Rhythmbox will automatically connect to your subscribed podcasts and check for new episodes.

Ripping Audio CDs

The world has not been the same since the invention of the Apple iPod. The ability to carry around an entire music library in a miniature device has revolutionized the way people listen to music. Consequently, a common requirement for workstations is the ability to extract song tracks from a CD to load onto a portable music device. Rhythmbox has the ability to extract song tracks from an audio CD and create music files.

To rip all of the tracks on the CD, just select the Extract icon from the toolbar, as shown in Figure 11-10.

The Rhythmbox program rips the tracks to audio files and places them in your music library.

You can specify in the Preferences window how Rhythmbox stores the ripped audio tracks (see the "Playing Audio CDs" section of this chapter).

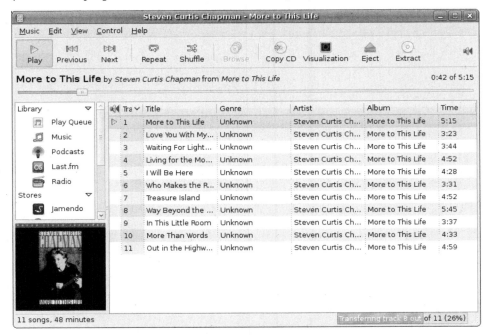

Figure 11-10: The Rhythmbox audio file extractor.

Brasero

The opposite of CD ripping is CD *burning*. Burning a CD is the process of taking audio files from your workstation and using them to create an audio CD. With burning you can mix and match songs from various CDs, or even downloaded songs, and place them on a single audio CD that you can play on any audio CD player.

Ubuntu uses the Brasero CD-burning software for creating audio CDs. Brasero is a full-featured CD-burning software package that can create both audio and data CDs.

caution | Be careful when you create your audio CD because you don't want to create a data CD of the audio files by mistake. Although some newer CD players can recognize and play data CDs, most older CD players, such as boom boxes and some car CD players, won't.

Just follow these steps to burn an audio CD from your audio files:

1. Start Brasero by selecting Applications ➪ Sound & Video ➪ Brasero Disc Burning from the Panel menu.
2. Click the Audio Project button. The Brasero package is a full-featured package that can create data CDs as well as create backups of CDs and CD image files. (Make sure that you select the Audio Project button to create an audio CD.) Figure 11-11 shows the main Brasero window.

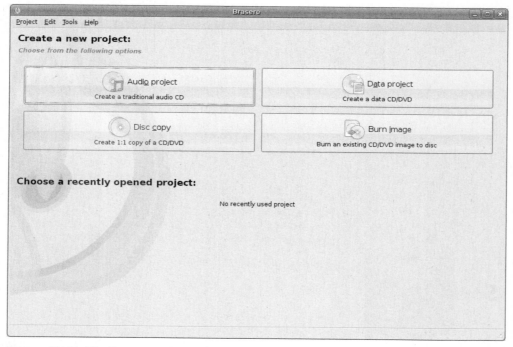

Figure 11-11: The Brasero main window.

3. Select the audio files to burn onto the CD. The left side of the window contains a browsing area where you can find and select the audio files to burn. Double-click a file to transfer it to the CD list in the main window. The bar at the bottom of the window provides a graphical indication of how much space is available on the CD after you add each audio file, as shown in Figure 11-12.

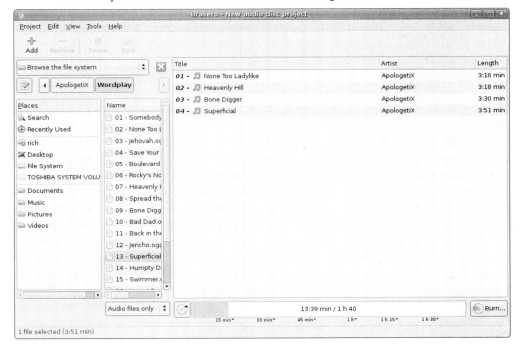

Figure 11-12: The Brasero New Audio Disc Project window.

4. Click the Burn button. The CD-burning process may take some time, depending on how many audio files you're burning and how fast your CD burner is.

5. Remove the CD from the tray and test it on another CD player.

You should be careful about what's running on your workstation while Brasero burns your audio files onto the CD. Brasero uses a buffering technique to ensure that a steady stream of data is provided while burning the CD, but if anything interrupts the stream of data, the CD will be ruined. It's usually best to close all other desktop applications while burning a new CD.

Sound Recorder

Ubuntu also provides software for you to record audio files from your workstation. The Sound Recorder package can record from either a built-in microphone or an external microphone. To start Sound Recorder, select Applications ➪ Sound & Video ➪ Sound Recorder. The main Sound Recorder window is shown in Figure 11-13.

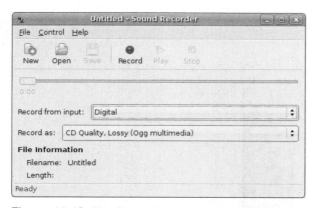

Figure 11-13: The Sound Recorder application window.

Select the input device from the drop-down menu, then, from the other drop-down menu, select the output audio file format you want to use. Sound Recorder will start recording when you press the Record button in the toolbar.

Sound Recorder can capture sound via any of the recording devices Ubuntu detects on your system and can store the recorded sounds in any audio file format supported by the installed codecs.

Secret

Sound Recorder won't start if it doesn't detect an audio input device on your Ubuntu system. If you receive an error message like the one shown in Figure 11-14, then Ubuntu didn't find an audio input device on your system.

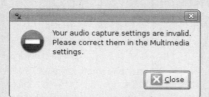

Figure 11-14: The Sound Recorder multimedia error message.

If you receive that error message, start the Sound Preferences configuration window (see the "Sound Preferences" section earlier in this chapter) and look at the Sound Capture setting under the Audio Conferencing section. Ensure that it's set to a sound management package.

Playing Audio Files from Nautilus

While browsing through your folders in Nautilus, no doubt you'll run across various audio files you have stored on your workstation, either from downloading files from the Internet or ripping songs from audio CDs. Nautilus allows you to quickly play an audio file by double-clicking the audio file. Nautilus will automatically launch an application to play the file.

The default application that Nautilus uses to play sound, though, may seem odd: It uses the Totem movie player (see Chapter 12, "Using Video"). The main Totem window is shown in Figure 11-15.

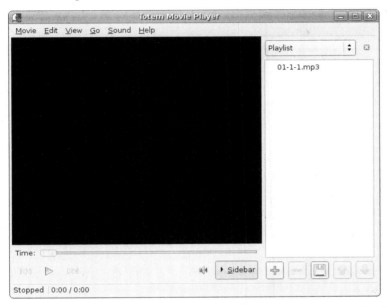

Figure 11-15: The Totem movie player playing an audio file from Nautilus.

You can change the application Nautilus uses to launch an audio file by right-clicking on the file. A menu appears, as shown in Figure 11-16, allowing you to select either the Rhythmbox application or another application from the system.

Figure 11-16: Selecting another audio application to open a file in Nautilus.

Once you select an alternative application to open a specific audio file format, Nautilus remembers that selection and provides it at the top of the menu the next time you right-click on an audio file of the same type.

Summary

In this chapter we explored the various audio features that Ubuntu provides. Ubuntu offers two systems for configuring the audio environment on your workstation. The Sound Preferences utility allows you to select which sound management software package to use for playing specific types of audio, whether those files are audio CDs or audio files stored on your workstation. Ubuntu also provides the Sound applet, which provides quick access to control volume levels for the master volume and for individual audio applications, such as playing audio files and CDs.

Next we discussed using the Rhythmbox application for playing audio CDs. If your workstation is connected to the Internet, Rhythmbox automatically retrieves information for the CD title, song track names, and cover art from an Internet CD information repository. From Rhythmbox you can play the songs on the CD or rip them to audio files to store in your music library. Rhythmbox also provides access to Internet radio stations and podcasts that stream music, news, and entertainment directly to your workstation via the Internet.

Ubuntu also uses the RhythmBox application to simplify the process of ripping songs from a CD. Just start RhythmBox, select the songs you want to rip, and start the process. RhythmBox automatically creates audio files from the selected songs and organizes them in your music library based on artist and album names.

After that we walked through the process of burning audio files to create an audio CD that you can play in any audio device. The Brasero program allows you to easily drag and drop audio files into a playlist that it then burns onto an audio CD.

The Sound Recorder application provides a way for you to record your own audio files, either from a built-in microphone on your computer or from an external microphone or sound device. Ubuntu can detect most recording devices installed on your system, and it allows the Sound Recorder to capture audio from them.

Finally, we discussed how to play music files directly from the Nautilus file manager. In Nautilus you can browse to a specific audio file in your library and double-click to play it. By default Nautilus uses the Totem movie player to play audio files, which works just fine. You can also change the application by right-clicking on the file and selecting another application.

In the next chapter we'll turn our attention to the video world. As you would expect, Ubuntu provides several ways to work with video files, DVDs, and Internet streaming video. As with audio though, there are several pitfalls in the Ubuntu video world that you'll need to watch out for.

Using Video

Chapter
12

◆ ◆

Secrets in This Chapter

◆ ◆

There's no question that video is one area where Linux systems have been playing catch-up. The original Linux systems didn't even support a Windows-style desktop! In the early days of Linux it was nearly impossible to display any type of video, let alone play movies or computer games. Things are a little better now. Ubuntu provides some of the basics for handling certain types of video, although there are still a few problems. This chapter helps you understand the Ubuntu video world, discussing how to view most types of video files and explaining why it's not possible to view some files.

Video Formats

With the popularity of digital video recorders, video clips are all the rage on the Internet. These days it's not uncommon to receive a video clip of your niece's ballet recital in an email message or see it posted on one of the many video file-sharing sites. Video files are stored in a variety of video formats:

- **AVI:** audio-visual interleave format, a standard video format supported by most video software packages
- **DIVX:** a proprietary AVI video compression format that must be licensed to work in Linux
- **MPG:** Moving Pictures Experts Group (MPEG) standard format, which includes both MPEG and MPG formats
- **OGG:** an open-source video format
- **VOB:** the DVD-video media format, used for storing MPG videos on DVDs
- **WMV:** Windows Media Video format, a proprietary Microsoft format
- **RM:** the RealNetworks proprietary video format, which requires the RealOne video player
- **MOV (and QT):** the proprietary Apple QuickTime video formats

Viewing video files in Ubuntu requires two separate pieces of software:

- A video-playing software package
- A video-decoding software package

The video-decoding software package tells the video-playing package how to read and interpret the video file. The decoding software is commonly called a *codec*. Usually, each codec decodes a single type of video file. Ubuntu contains only the codec package for decoding OGG video files. Viewing any other type of video file requires downloading a different codec package. This is where things get messy.

The MPG video file format is by far the most common video format in use, both on the Internet and in many digital movie cameras. It provides good-quality video with relatively small file sizes by using patented compression algorithms. Unfortunately, because of the patented algorithms, MPG is a licensed product, which is a bad thing in the open-source world. Reverse-engineered codec packages are available that can decode MPG video files in Linux systems. However, these packages are not legal for use in some countries.

Secret

The Microsoft Media Video, RealNetworks, and Apple QuickTime formats are also licensed products that are not available by default on the Ubuntu workstation. However, RealNetworks provides RealPlayer, a fully licensed, free, downloadable player for all of these video formats for Linux. You can download the Linux version of RealPlayer from the RealNetworks web site, www.realplayer.com. Follow the instructions on the web site to install the player on your Ubuntu workstation.

The Totem Movie Player

The default video-file viewer in Ubuntu is *Totem*. You can start Totem by double-clicking a saved video file, or you can launch it from the Panel menu by choosing Applications ➪ Sound & Video ➪ Movie Player.

Secret

You can also start the Totem movie player from the command line in a Terminal session (see Chapter 19, "The Ubuntu Command Line"). Just use the command `totem`.

Licensing restrictions limit the types of files that the default Totem installation can play. If you select a video file in a format that Ubuntu doesn't contain the codec for, Ubuntu will display a message, shown in Figure 12-1.

If your workstation is connected to the Internet, Ubuntu will attempt to locate the proper codec in a repository. It displays all codecs that it finds that can process the selected video file format.

Figure 12-1: The Ubuntu unrecognized multimedia format message.

When you start Totem, the main viewing window appears, shown in Figure 12-2.

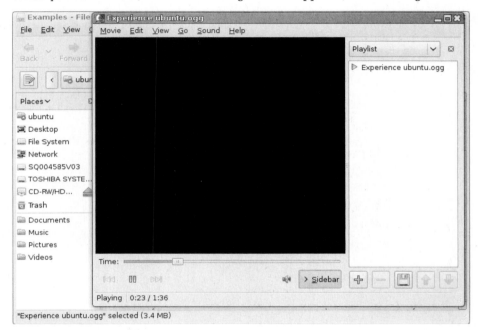

Figure 12-2: The main Totem viewing window.

The following sections describe the Totem movie player interface and how to set preferences for it.

The Totem Interface

The Totem window consists of a menu bar, the main viewing area, a sidebar, and a toolbar at the bottom.

The Menu Bar

The menu bar provides several options for viewing your videos. The Movie menu item provides options for loading movies into the Totem viewer:

- **Open:** Allows you to navigate to a stored video file on your computer and load it into the playlist.

- **Open Location:** Allows you to add a video file to the playlist from a network location specified in URL format.
- **Properties:** Displays the properties of the video file, such as the format, and any embedded information, such as the title, artist, and duration.
- **Eject:** Ejects a DVD that is playing.
- **Play/Pause:** Allows you to start a selected file in the playlist.
- **Quit:** Exits the Totem application.

The Edit menu item controls how the movie is played:

- **Take Screenshot:** Allows you to take a snapshot of a scene in the video file.
- **Repeat Mode:** Repeats the video file until you stop it.
- **Shuffle Mode:** Plays video files in the playlist in random order.
- **Clear Playlist:** Removes all files from the playlist.
- **Plug-ins:** Allows you to manage extra features in Totem.
- **Preferences:** Allows you to set basic video and audio settings, such as color balance and audio output format.

The Plug-ins option provides an interface to control extra features that are available in Totem, shown in Figure 12-3.

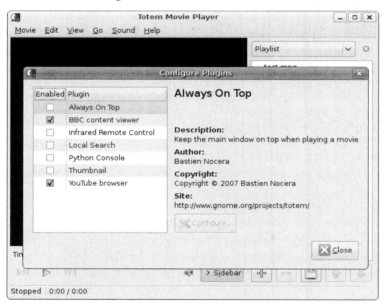

Figure 12-3: The Totem Plug-ins window.

The default Totem installation in Ubuntu contains the plug-ins shown in Table 12-1. Enable plug-ins by placing a check mark in the check box next to the plug-in name.

Table 12-1: The Default Totem Plug-ins

Plug-in	Description
Always on Top	Keeps the Totem movie player as the active window on the desktop
BBC Content Viewer	Plays video and audio made available by the British Broadcasting Corporation (BBC)
Infrared Remote Control	Interacts with the infrared input device on laptops to support a remote infrared remote control device
Local Search	Searches the hard drive for videos
Python Console	Provides an interactive Python programming language console for scripting
Thumbnail	Sets the window icon to a thumbnail of the video
YouTube browser	Browses the YouTube web site for videos

The View menu item controls how the video is displayed on the screen:

♦ **Full-Screen:** Displays the video file using the entire computer screen.

♦ **Fit Window to Movie:** Automatically alters the Totem viewing window to fit the default size of the video file. You can also select to view the movie at 50 percent (1:2) of the default size.

♦ **Aspect Ratio:** Allows you to set the viewing mode to standard 4:3 or 16:9 for widescreen videos.

♦ **Switch Angles:** If multiple camera angles are provided in the video content, lets you display another camera angle.

♦ **Show Controls:** Displays the Play, Skip, and Location controls at the bottom of the viewing window.

♦ **Subtitles:** Displays subtitles, if included in the video.

♦ **Sidebar:** Includes the playlist sidebar window in the viewing window.

The Go menu item controls which part of the video file is being played. For video files, it provides links to specific menus within the video, such as title menus, chapter menus, audio menus, and camera-angle menus. It also uses these generic options:

♦ **Skip To:** Locates a specific point in the video file.

♦ **Skip Forward:** Goes quickly forward in the video file.

♦ **Skip Backward:** Goes quickly backward in the video file.

The Sound menu item controls how the audio is handled:

♦ **Languages:** Plays alternative language audio tracks, if available in the video file.

♦ **Volume Up:** Increases the volume level of the audio track.

♦ **Volume Down:** Decreases the volume level of the audio track.

The Help menu item displays the Totem manual and information about the version.

The Sidebar

The right sidebar of the Totem movie player is used for the playlist. The playlist allows you to select multiple video files for playing. Click the plus-sign button to add videos to the playlist or to select a video already in the playlist; click the minus-sign button to remove it. You can reorder movies in the playlist by selecting a movie and clicking the up or down arrow to move the movie up or down in the playlist. When you have your playlist just the way you want it, click the Disk button to save the playlist for future use.

The Toolbar

The toolbar, located under the viewing window, contains the standard buttons you'd expect to find on a DVD player. The Previous Chapter and Next Chapter buttons (the double arrows) skip the player to the previous or next chapter in the DVD. The Play button changes to a Pause button while the movie is playing. The Speaker button allows you to adjust the volume of or mute the output.

The Totem Preferences Settings

Clicking the Edit ⇨ Preferences menu item produces the Totem Preferences window, shown in Figure 12-4.

Figure 12-4: The Totem Preferences window.

The Preferences window is divided into three tabbed sections:

   ◆ **General:** settings for the input and output features:
     • **Networking:** Sets the network connection speed for determining file buffering while playing video files as they download.

- **TV-out:** Sets the formatting used, if an external television connection is used to display the video.
  - **Text Subtitles:** Specifies whether subtitles are displayed and, if so, which font to use to display them.
- ◆ **Display:** settings for controlling the video output on the monitor:
  - **Display:** Specifies whether the video window automatically resizes to accommodate the default size of the video file and whether the screensaver is disabled when playing audio files.
  - **Visual Effects:** Enables display of screensaver-type video while playing an audio file.
  - **Color Balance:** Adjusts the video brightness, contrast, saturation, and hue components for the monitor.
- ◆ **Audio:** settings for the audio output for stereo, four-channel surround sound, or five-channel surround sound systems

Once you set the preferences for Totem they'll remain in effect for any video you play.

Secret

Ubuntu launches Totem by default when you insert a DVD into your workstation's CD/DVD tray. However, by default, Totem doesn't contain the proper codecs to play DVDs. When you first play a DVD, Ubuntu will ask whether you want to search for the proper codec. If you choose to search, Ubuntu will offer the available codec programs in the repositories for playing DVDs.

However, you may not be able to view your DVD even after installing the proper codec. Watching a DVD in Linux is a bit of a legal quagmire if you live in the United States. The Digital Millennium Copyright Act (DMCA) and other issues make it tricky for any open-source program to navigate the licensing maze when it comes to movies that are encoded or otherwise protected against pirating.

Not all DVDs have these features enabled, so you might be able to watch some DVDs on your Ubuntu workstation. If you burn your own DVDs from movie camera footage, they should work just fine.

Watching Web Clips

The Internet has become a clearinghouse for just about any type of video content you can imagine (and even some you couldn't imagine if you tried). From Google Video to YouTube, there are lots of sites to keep you entertained.

Your Ubuntu workstation has the ability through the Firefox web browser (see Chapter 8, "Network Applications") to display many types of web clips, but, unfortunately, not all of them are viewable by default.

This section walks through the process of working with Firefox to view different types of video clips.

Checking Your Plug-ins

The key to displaying web video content in Firefox is using *plug-ins*. As discussed in Chapter 8, plug-ins provide additional functionality to the Firefox browser.

You can easily check to see what plug-ins you already have installed in your Firefox setup by following these steps:

1. Open Firefox by choosing Applications ⇨ Internet ⇨ Firefox Web Browser. You can also start Firefox by clicking the Firefox globe icon on the top panel.

2. In the URL box, enter about:plugins and hit Enter. The about:plugins page displays information about the current plug-ins installed, as shown in Figure 12-5.

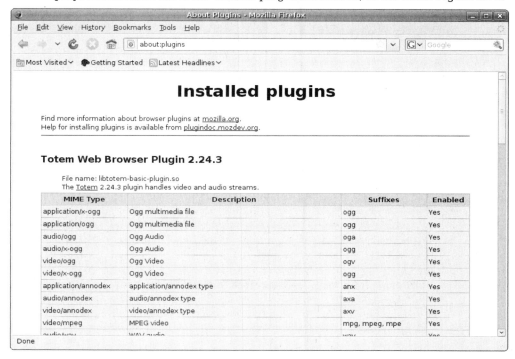

Figure 12-5: The Firefox about:plugins page in Ubuntu.

By default the Ubuntu Firefox installation includes the following plug-ins:

♦ **Default Plug-in:** for multimedia extensions that are not covered by other plug-ins, displays a generic message that the plug-in is not available

♦ **Demo Print Plug-in:** for printing from the web page

♦ **Totem Web Browser Plug-in:** a full-featured video and audio player that can display AVI, ASF, WMV, OGG, and MPG video formats, as well as play WAV and MP3 audio formats

♦ **Windows Media Player:** part of the Totem plug-in package

♦ **DivX Web Player:** for playing DivX-encoded AVI videos

♦ **QuickTime:** for playing Apple QuickTime MOV- and QT-formatted videos

Although it may seem that you've got most of your web video bases covered, you may be disappointed with your actual results. For example, although Totem is listed as supporting the popular WMV and MOV video formats, there's more to it than just that.

If you remember from the "Video Formats" section earlier in this chapter, it takes two pieces of software to play a video file. Firefox contains plug-ins to play the various video types, but those packages must also include the appropriate codec programs to play the specific video formats.

As you probably guessed, Ubuntu doesn't include the codecs for playing proprietary and licensed video files. That means Ubuntu doesn't support many of the popular Internet video file formats.

Adding Plug-ins

A plethora of free video-related plug-ins are available for the Firefox browser. The clearinghouse for Firefox plug-ins is `http://plugindoc.mozdev.org` (the Firefox web browser is based on the Mozilla open-source browser). Stop by that site and take a look at all of the video plug-ins available.

Many of the plug-ins listed on the Mozilla plug-in web site are available as software packages in the Ubuntu repositories. You can use the techniques shown in Chapter 13, "Software Installs and Upgrades," to install new plug-ins.

While looking at your plugs-ins list, you might notice that one popular video format is missing: Macromedia Flash (also called Shockwave Flash). This video format is popular with video-streaming sites, such as YouTube and Metacafe. If you want to use these sites, you'll need to install Flash in Firefox. Here are the steps to install it using the Ubuntu Synaptic Package Manager:

1. Open the Synaptic Package Manager by selecting System ➪ Administration ➪ Synaptic Package Manager from the top panel. For details on how to use the Synaptic Package Manager, see Chapter 13.

2. Click the Search button in the toolbar, enter the term `mozilla plugin` in the textbox, and click the Search button. The search results appear in the software list window on the right side of the Package Manager, as shown in Figure 12-6.

3. Scan the package list and find the entry for *flashplugin-nonfree*. Click in the package check box and select the Mark for Installation option from the popup menu. The *nonfree* part of the package name doesn't mean that you have to pay for it. It just means that it's not an open-source product. Adobe maintains the rights to the Flash plug-in but provides it for use without charge.

4. Click the Apply button from the top toolbar. The Package Manager displays a dialog box confirming your decision to install the new software package.

5. The Package Manager downloads and installs the plug-in file, then produces a dialog box indicating that the installation is complete. Click the Close button to exit the installation.

When you access the `about:plugins` URL from Firefox, you should see that you have the Shockwave Flash plug-in available, as shown in Figure 12-7.

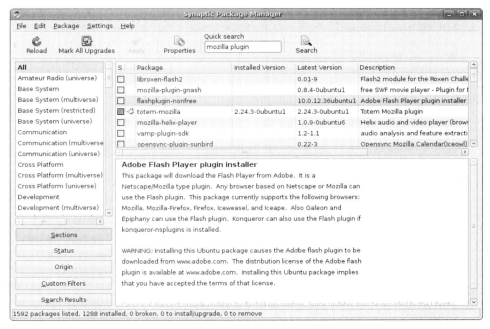

Figure 12-6: The Package Manager package list.

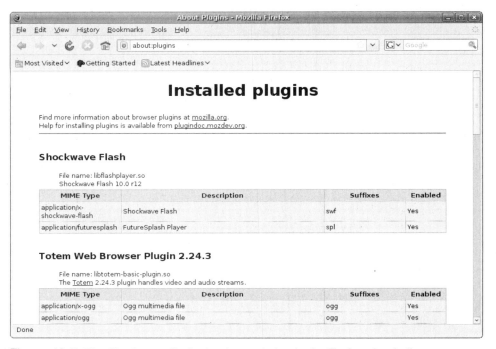

Figure 12-7: The Shockwave Flash plug-in appearing in the Firefox plug-in list.

You should now be able to view all of your favorite Flash-format videos from within the Firefox web browser.

More Video Support

If you remember from Chapter 8, Firefox also supports a feature called *extensions*. Extensions are small applications that provide additional features to your Firefox browser. If you're looking for more video support, or just some fancy video features, there are plenty of extensions available to help out. The official Mozilla sites for extensions is `https://addons.update.mozilla.org` (note that this is an https site).

One of my favorite extensions is Fast Video Download, which allows you to download embedded streaming video content on a web site, such as YouTube or MySpace, to a video file on your computer. Here's what you need to do to load and install it:

1. Open Firefox by choosing Applications ➪ Internet ➪ Firefox Web Browser. You can also start Firefox by clicking the Firefox globe icon on the top panel.

2. Go to the `https://addons.update.mozilla.org` web site, and search for Fast Video Download in all add-on pages. Currently it's located at `https://addons.update.mozilla.org/en-US/firefox/addon/3590`.

3. Click the Add to Firefox link on the Fast Video Download web page. Because the Fast Video Download extension is not signed, a dialog box will appear asking whether you want to install it, as shown in Figure 12-8.

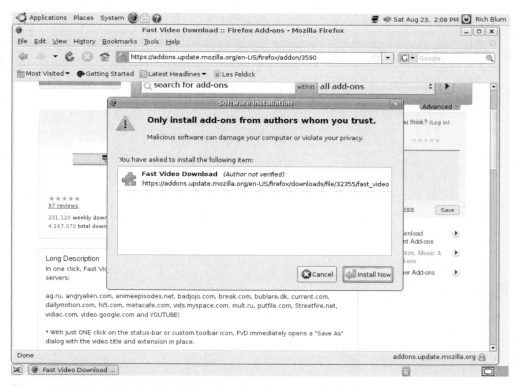

Figure 12-8: Installing the Fast Video Download extension in Firefox.

Click the Install Now button to install the Fast Video Download extension. When complete, the Add-ons dialog box appears, showing that the installation was successful.

4. Click the Restart Firefox button for the new extension to work.

When Firefox starts, you should notice a new icon on the right side of the bottom status bar. The Add-ons dialog box also appears, showing that the Fast Video Download extension has been installed properly, as shown in Figure 12-9.

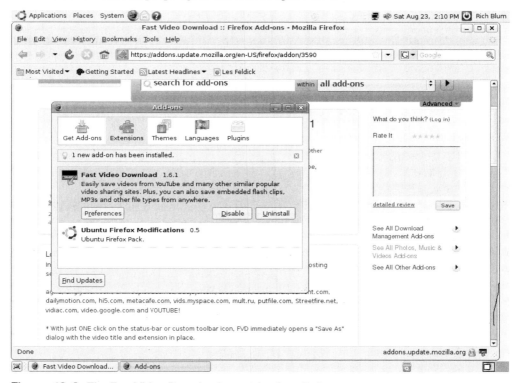

Figure 12-9: The Fast Video Download extension installed.

To use Fast Video Download, navigate to a web page that contains an embedded streaming video, then click the New icon in the status bar. Fast Video Download scans the web page looking for the video links, then displays a dialog box asking you where to save the file.

Editing Videos

Along with the popularity of digital cameras that can record video comes the popularity of video-editing software packages. Unfortunately, Ubuntu doesn't install a video-editing package by default. However, if your workstation is connected to the Internet, it's a snap to install a basic editing package.

The *Kino* video-editing package is the most popular video editor for the Linux platform. It uses a subtractive method of video editing, meaning that you add video clips to a library then remove the pieces that you don't want to use in your final video. This is a little more basic than what some advanced video editors allow you to do, but it should work just fine for most home-video enthusiasts.

This section describes how to install and use the Kino video-editing software in Ubuntu.

Installing Kino

Although Ubuntu doesn't install Kino by default, it does provide an easy installation package. You can install Kino from the Synaptic Package Manager (see Chapter 13). Just follow these steps to install Kino on your workstation:

1. Open the Synaptic Package Manager by selecting System ⇨ Administration ⇨ Synaptic Package Manager from the top panel. For details on how to use the Synaptic Package Manager, see Chapter 13.

2. In the Quick Search text box, enter the term `kino`. The search results appear in the software list window on the right side of the Package Manager, as shown in Figure 12-10.

3. Click the Kino package and select the Mark for Installation option from the popup menu.

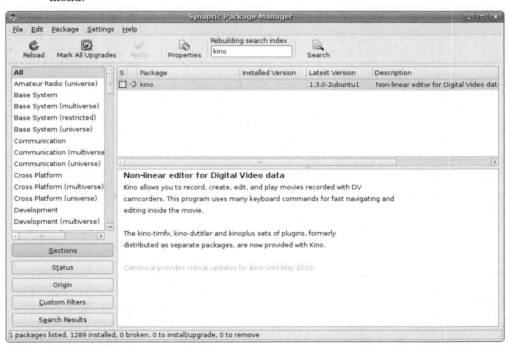

Figure 12-10: Finding Kino in the Package Manager package list.

4. Click the Apply button from the top toolbar. The Package Manager will display a dialog box confirming your decision to install the new software package.

5. The Package Manager downloads and installs Kino, then produces a dialog box indicating that the installation is complete. Click the Close button to exit the installation.

Once you've installed Kino it'll appear in the top panel, under Applications ➪ Sound & Video ➪ Kino. Select that entry to start Kino. The main Kino window, shown in Figure 12-11, appears on the desktop.

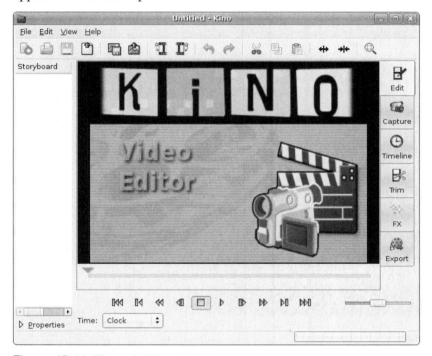

Figure 12-11: The main Kino window.

Now you're ready to start your video editing!

The Kino Interface

The Kino window consists of several elements:

- ◆ **The menu bar:** Provides access to all of the modes and editing features.
- ◆ **The toolbar:** Provides buttons for quick access to common editing features.
- ◆ **The storyboard:** Displays individual clips from a video for selecting and removing from the video file.
- ◆ **The mode pages:** Provides options for the specific editing mode used.
- ◆ **The scrub bar:** Allows you to seek within the movie by dragging the arrow pointer.
- ◆ **The transport controls:** Controls playback and fast seeking through the video file.

The mode pages are the key to Kino. Each mode page provides a different editing interface for interacting with the individual video clips in the video file. Six mode pages are available and are described in Table 12-2.

Table 12-2: The Kino Mode Pages

Mode Page	Description
Edit	Displays the video clip segment. You can use Edit mode to move clips around in order and remove clips from the storyboard. Once you rearrange the clips you can view the result in the Edit mode window.
Capture	Selects an external device from which to capture video. You can record the video captured from the external device to make new clips in the storyboard.
Timeline	Displays the video clips along with timestamp information, showing the relative times for each clip in the storyboard and how they contribute to the overall time of the video.
Trim	Provides basic cut-and-paste features within the video clips. You can use Trim mode to insert and remove clips from the video.
FX	Adds basic special effects to the video, such as blur, pixilation, flips, and changing colors.
Export	Allows you to output the current video to another format or device.

As you can see from its modes, Kino has a long way to go before it becomes a professional-quality video-editing tool, but it does provide a basic video-editing environment for working on simple video files.

The Kino Preferences Settings

You can reach the Kino Preferences window by clicking Edit ⇨ Preferences from the menu bar. The Preferences window is shown in Figure 12-12.

The Preferences window uses seven tabs to organize the various settings you can make:

- **Defaults:** for controlling the video and audio defaults:
  - **Normalisation:** Select NTSC or PAL video modes.
  - **Audio:** Select the default audio sampling rate.
  - **Aspect Ratio:** Select 4:3 full-screen or 16:9 widescreen formats.
- **Capture:** for controlling the settings for saving captured video:
  - **File:** Specify the default filename to store captured video.
  - **File Type:** Select AVI type 1, AVI type 2, or OpenDML AVI video format for storing the video.
  - **Other File Options:** Select file details such as how often to write frames to the file, whether to use the timestamp in the filename, and how to split the capture into multiple files.
- **IEEE 1394:** for specifying which IEEE 1394 (FireWire) device to capture from.

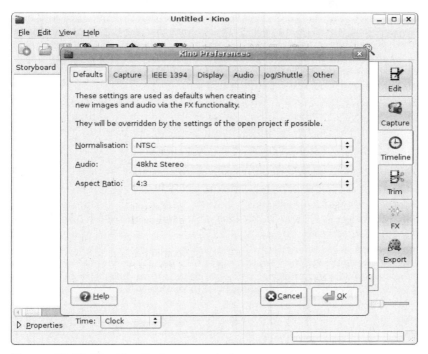

Figure 12-12: The Kino Preferences window.

- ◆ **Display:** for controlling how to display the video:
  - • **Display Method:** Select the system used to display video and how much data to use (such as dropping frames or enabling preview mode).
  - • **DV Decoder:** Select the quality of the video display. The higher the quality, the slower the performance.
- ◆ **Audio:** for specifying whether audio is enabled and, if so, which audio device to use
- ◆ **Jog/Shuttle:** for controlling button actions available on an external USB editing device
- ◆ **Other:** for controlling miscellaneous features such as key repeat, saving files with relative filepaths, storyboard features, and the default project directory.

The Kino Preferences settings remain in effect for each Kino session. The preferences are stored in each user's home folder so that each user can set his or her own preferences for editing.

Summary

This chapter examined video support on the Ubuntu workstation. The Ubuntu workstation includes some basic video support by default, but handling videos can be frustrating in the Ubuntu world. The chapter first discussed the different video file formats that are commonly used, both for video files and on the Internet for streaming video.

After that we discussed the Totem movie player. The Totem movie player can play video files, but only if it contains the proper codec program for the selected video file format. By default Ubuntu includes the codec for the OGG open video format. If you select another video file format Ubuntu will ask whether you want to search for the proper codec. If your workstation is connected to the Internet (and it's legal in your area to install it) you can select the appropriate codec file to install.

Besides allowing you to view video files, Ubuntu provides support for viewing files on the Internet. The Firefox web browser provides some basic support for viewing video files by utilizing plug-ins. Again, there are restrictions on which plug-ins Ubuntu supports by default. You can install additional plug-ins via the Synaptic Package Manager or directly from the Mozilla plug-in repository web site. Mozilla also provides Firefox extensions, which add features to Firefox, including the ability to capture video from web sites.

Finally, the chapter discussed the Kino video-editing tool. Although not included in the default Ubuntu installation, Kino can easily be added if your workstation is connected to the Internet. Kino allows you to combine video clips and edit out pieces of video clips to create a single video.

This chapter ends our tour through the application packages in Ubuntu. The next section of the book examines how to manage your workstation. The following chapter takes a closer look at how to manage the software installed on your Ubuntu system. Ubuntu provides some automated ways to update your existing software and some easy ways to install new software.

PART 3

Managing Your Workstation

Software Installs and Updates

♦ ♦

Secrets in This Chapter

Setting Repositories

Installing Updates

Managing Applications

Managing Packages

Managing Packages from the Command Line

♦ ♦

In the fast-paced world of Linux, it doesn't take long for an Ubuntu installation to become out of date. Security updates and bug fixes for open-source software packages are released almost daily. If your Ubuntu workstation or server is connected to the Internet, you can take advantage of software security and bug updates as they are released. Ubuntu includes both a manual and an automated method of updating the core software installation. This chapter looks at both of these methods of updating your Ubuntu system. This chapter also examines how to install additional software features onto your Ubuntu server or workstation from the Internet.

Software Management in Ubuntu

The Ubuntu operating system contains lots of software. Trying to keep track of which applications are installed, which ones can be installed, and which ones you can remove can be a full-time job. Fortunately Ubuntu offers some features that help make software management a little easier. This section walks through the basics of how Ubuntu handles software and shows how to access software for Ubuntu once you've installed the basic distribution.

Software Packages

Chapter 1, "What Is Ubuntu?" discussed the origins of the Ubuntu Linux distribution. The Ubuntu distribution consists of many different open-source software *packages.* A package is a self-contained application or a set of related applications that installs as a single component.

Examples of self-contained applications are common programs such as the Firefox web browser, the Evolution email client, and the GIMP image editor. Each of these applications loads as a self-contained package in Ubuntu. You can easily install or remove these applications individually without affecting the operation of your Ubuntu system.

Examples of an application set are the OpenOffice.org office automation suite of applications and the GNOME games package. These packages contain several individual applications that are installed in one package.

Ubuntu packages aren't limited to applications. Ubuntu also bundles the different operating system elements (see Chapter 1) into packages. The default Ubuntu installation includes packages for the Linux kernel, the GNU utilities used on the command line, and even the command-line shell itself.

As you can see, packages are the core of Ubuntu software management. The ability to add new packages to the system and remove old or unused packages makes Ubuntu an extremely versatile operating system. The key is knowing where to find those packages.

Software Repositories

When you install Ubuntu from either the LiveCD or the alternate CD, you're installing all of the individual packages that make up the system. The installation process copies each package bundled on the LiveCD or alternate CD to the hard drive and installs it in the proper location.

Unfortunately, there's a limited amount of space on the LiveCD and alternative CD, so Ubuntu can't include every software package in the default installation. However, if your workstation is connected to the Internet (see Chapter 14, "Networking"), you can easily retrieve additional software packages from Ubuntu servers for installation.

Ubuntu maintains multiple servers that contain software packages for downloading. These servers are called *software repositories*. Ubuntu maintains different repositories for different applications. You must configure your Ubuntu system to interact with the software repositories you want to use.

Secret If your Ubuntu system doesn't have Internet connectivity, you can get Ubuntu software package collections on DVDs. You can install software packages and updates directly from the DVDs instead of from a software repository. Check the Ubuntu web site for details on software repository DVDs you can download or purchase.

Configuring Software Repositories

The main Ubuntu installation includes a graphical utility that allows you to easily configure your Ubuntu system to access different software repositories. You can start the Software Sources tool by selecting System ➪ Administration ➪ Software Sources from the Panel menu. Figure 13-1 shows the main Software Sources window.

Figure 13-1: The Software Sources window.

The Software Sources window contains five tabbed sections:

◆ **Ubuntu Software:** Configure the types of software packages to download and from where to download them.

◆ **Third-Party Software:** Identify non-Ubuntu software repositories from which to retrieve software packages.

◆ **Updates:** Define the types of updates to download and how often to check for new updates.

◆ **Authentication:** Store public keys for verifying the authenticity of software repositories.

◆ **Statistics:** Allow your Ubuntu workstation to share information on the packages you install with an online statistical tracker.

Ubuntu classifies software packages into five categories of software, shown in Table 13-1.

Table 13-1: Ubuntu Software Repositories

Type	Description
Canonical-supported, open-source software	Large, open-source projects supported by formal organizations, such as OpenOffice.org and Firefox
Community-maintained, open-source software	Smaller, open-source projects, such as GIMP and Rhythmbox, supported by groups of individuals
Proprietary drivers for devices	Drivers supported by a commercial company for its own products only and not released to the open-source community (for example, packages such as video- and sound-card drivers)
Software restricted by copyright or legal issues	Software that may be illegal to use in some countries due to patent or copyright violations
Source code	The application source code for open-source packages

Just select the categories of software you're interested in keeping up with. By default Ubuntu will retrieve software from all of these repositories. You can remove the check mark next to any of the repositories if you prefer not to use that particular software category.

The Updates tab section allows you to customize how your Ubuntu workstation receives software *updates*. Updates provide a quick and easy way to update an installed software package with new patches that fix coding bugs and security problems. You can control several facets of software updates:

◆ **Ubuntu Updates:** Select which types of updates to look for in the repositories:

• **Security Updates:** updates that fix security-related bugs in installed software packages

• **Recommended Updates:** updates that fix nonsecurity-related code bugs in installed software packages

• **Pre-Released Updates:** updates that haven't been officially released by Ubuntu but may fix reported bugs in software

• **Unsupported Updates:** updates to installed software packages that aren't supported by the Ubuntu community

♦ **Automatic Updates:** Indicate whether the workstation should automatically check for available updates, how often to check, and whether to install security-related updates automatically without notification or user intervention.

♦ **Release Upgrade:** Opt to be notified when a new major Ubuntu distribution upgrade has been released.

The updates tab is where you configure Ubuntu to automatically check for updates available in the repositories for the software currently installed on your system. If you have the Update Manager Applet installed (discussed in the "Installing Updates" section later in this chapter), an icon appears in the top panel of your desktop notifying you of available updates to download and install. This makes managing software updates a breeze!

As you can see from this list, not only can you update the individual software packages installed on your workstation, you can also perform a complete upgrade from one version of Ubuntu to another via the package download process. This feature is a great time-saver if you have a high-speed Internet connection, because you don't have to mess with downloading and burning an installation CD. You can upgrade your Ubuntu workstation directly from the Internet.

Secret

The software updates allow you to keep an Ubuntu installation active and up to date when the next release becomes available, so there's no reason to rush out and install a new version when it comes out. However, Ubuntu eventually will cease to release updates for a particular version.

For most distribution versions, Ubuntu provides security and code updates for up to 18 months after the initial release date. The long-term support (LTS) Ubuntu distributions provide security updates for up to 3 years for workstations and 5 years for servers after the distribution release date. When Ubuntu no longer releases security updates for a distribution you can still run the system, but it's recommended to upgrade to a newer version of Ubuntu to avoid any future security problems.

Installing Updates

Once you have the software management settings configured, you're ready to start working with the actual software updates. This section walks through how to use the graphical Update Manager tool to check on, retrieve, and install updates on your Ubuntu workstation.

The Update Manager

The Update Manager provides a quick interface for downloading and installing all updates for your Ubuntu workstation. You can start the Update Manager by selecting System ➪ Administration ➪ Update Manager from the Panel menu. The main Update Manager window, shown in Figure 13-2, appears.

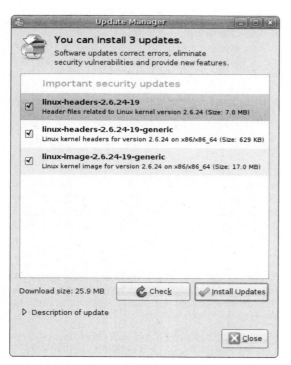

Figure 13-2: The Update Manager main window.

If you configured the Software Source settings to automatically check for updates, the Update Manager may already have a current list of the updates available for your installed software packages, depending on when it last checked for updates. You can manually force Update Manager to check the configured repositories by clicking the Check button.

The Update Manager connects to all of the remote repositories you configure in the Software Sources and checks for updates to all software packages installed on your specific Ubuntu distribution. If updates are available, they appear in the Update Manager main window.

From the main window you can view the title and summary for each update available for installation. Click on an individual update to highlight it, then click the Description of Update link at the bottom of the window to view a more detailed explanation of the update.

By default, all available updates are selected for download and installation. If there are any updates you don't want to apply, just remove the check mark from the check box.

To begin the update process, click the Install Updates button. The Update Manager produces a progress dialog box, shown in Figure 13-3, that indicates the download progress.

After the Update Manager downloads all of the updates, it processes each package update individually, applying the update to the installed software package.

Figure 13-3: The Update Download Progress dialog box.

Secret Sometimes, certain updates are required to be installed before other updates can process. Therefore, after you run an update you should manually check again for additional updates. If additional updates are still available, install them, then manually check again for more updates. Repeat this process until there are no more updates available to install.

Using the Update Manager Applet

By default, Ubuntu installs the Update Manager Applet (see Chapter 4, "Exploring the Desktop") in the top panel. If you've configured the Update Manager to retrieve updates automatically, the Update Manager Applet monitors the status of the Update Manager as it works in the background on your workstation.

The Update Manager Applet icon displays a quick status of the Update Manager:

- ◆ **Gray sun:** Update Manager is checking for updates.
- ◆ **Orange sun:** Software updates are available to download and install.
- ◆ **Gray down arrow:** Update Manager is checking for security updates.

◆ **Red down arrow:** Security patches are available to download and install.

◆ **Circling blue arrows:** A reboot is necessary after an update installation.

If the orange sun or red down arrow icon appears, Update Manager has determined that updates are available for your installation. Clicking the Update Manager Applet icon in the top panel starts the Update Manager window and displays the updates available to install. As with the manual method, click the Install Updates button to begin downloading and installing the selected updates.

Installing New Applications

Besides updating the existing software on your Ubuntu system, Ubuntu allows you to easily install new applications directly from the repositories. This section walks through the Add/Remove Applications tool.

The Add/Remove Applications Window

You can start the Add/Remove Applications tool by selecting Applications ⇨ Add/Remove from the Panel menu. The main Add/Remove Applications window, shown in Figure 13-4, appears.

If it's been a while since your Ubuntu workstation has contacted the software repositories, you may see a notice message telling you the list may be out of date and asking whether you want to update it. Click the Reload button to update the list of available applications.

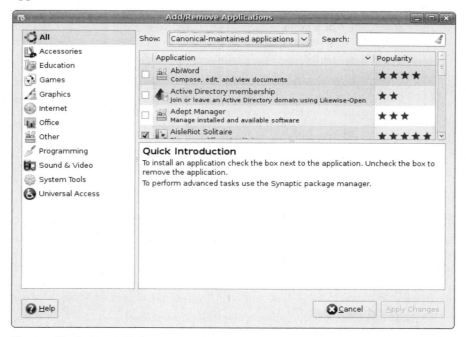

Figure 13-4: The Add/Remove Applications window.

The Add/Remove Applications window consists of four sections:

- ◆ The software catalog
- ◆ The Applications panel
- ◆ The Filter drop-down menu and Search text box
- ◆ The Application Description window

The application software catalog appears on the left side of the Add/Remove Applications window. It breaks down the applications into categories to help you find applications. There are eleven categories of applications you can browse through:

- ◆ **Accessories:** small utilities that can enhance your desktop experience, such as an advanced calculator, an alarm, a virtual keyboard, and a dictionary
- ◆ **Education:** programs for supporting educational purposes, such as a test and exam editor, educational games, and language translators
- ◆ **Games:** programs to help entertain and amuse you
- ◆ **Graphics:** programs for handling photos and images and for drawing pictures
- ◆ **Internet:** programs for accessing Internet features such as email, web browsing, and news reading
- ◆ **Office:** alternative office productivity tools such as basic word processors, calendars, and finance programs
- ◆ **Other:** the junk drawer of utilities and small programs, including programs for setting monitor features and setting laptop touchpad features, and packages restricted by patents or copyrights
- ◆ **Programming:** Programming tools such as integrated development environments (IDEs) and editors, as well as compilers and debuggers
- ◆ **Sound & Video:** a collection of multimedia applications for advanced audio and video capturing, editing, and CD burning
- ◆ **System Tools:** utilities that interact with the Ubuntu system, such as a battery monitor, all-in-one configuration editor, alternative file managers, and file backup managers
- ◆ **Universal Access:** applications that provide assistive technologies for workstations

Selecting a catalog from the list automatically filters the Application panel to display only the applications in that catalog.

The Filter drop-down menu and Search text box allow you to fine-tune the applications listed in the panel. The drop-down menu allows you to select the type of applications listed in the panel:

- ◆ **All Available Applications:** all applications available within the configured Ubuntu software repositories
- ◆ **All Open-Source Applications:** only applications that are part of the open-source community
- ◆ **Canonical-Maintained Applications:** only applications that are supported by Ubuntu and Canonical, Ltd.
- ◆ **Third-Party Applications:** applications that are not part of the Ubuntu software
- ◆ **Installed Applications Only:** only applications that are currently installed on the workstation

Selecting one of these options immediately changes the application list window to display only the applications that meet the filter specification.

The Search box allows you to search the application names and descriptions for keywords. Only applications that meet the search keywords appear in the application list window.

Adding a New Application

The Add/Remove Applications tool makes it simple to install new applications on your Ubuntu workstation. Here are the steps to install a new application:

1. Select the check box next to the application name in the panel. If the application is not an Ubuntu-supported application, a message will appear, as shown in Figure 13-5.

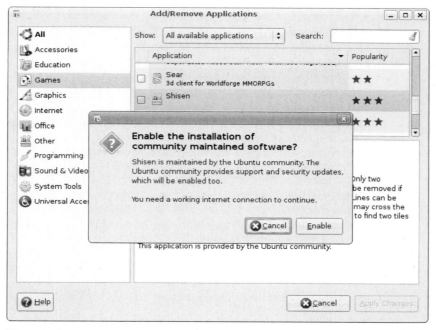

Figure 13-5: The Add/Remove Applications community software dialog box.

Click the Enable button to allow Ubuntu to use the community-supported software repository to install applications.

2. Select other applications you want to install at the same time. You can install as many applications as you want in the same Add/Remove session.

3. Click the Apply Changes button at the bottom of the Add/Remove Applications window. A dialog box, shown in Figure 13-6, confirms your selections.

4. Confirm the installation of the listed applications. After confirming the installation, the Update Manager prompts you for your password to ensure you have the proper privileges to add new applications to the system. It then retrieves the appropriate packages to install the application. When the installation is complete, a message appears, shown in Figure 13-7.

5. Click Continue to add or remove more applications, or click the Close button to close the Add/Remove Applications tool.

Figure 13-6: The Software Installation Confirmation dialog box.

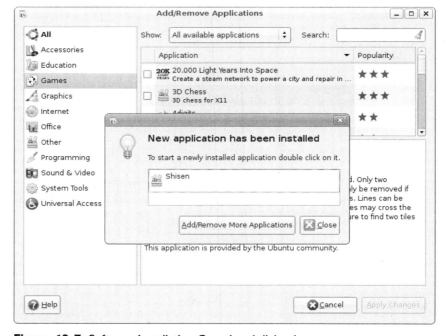

Figure 13-7: Software Installation Completed dialog box.

The newly installed applications should appear in the Panel menu under the appropriate menu.

Secret

The Add/Remove Applications tool adds the newly installed software packages to the Update Manager list, and any updates will automatically be retrieved during the next update connection. This feature offers a great advantage over installing applications yourself, because now you can get updates automatically, without having to manually watch for and install them.

Removing an Application

Removing an unwanted installed application is easy using the Add/Remove Applications tool. Just follow these steps:

1. Start the Add/Remove Applications tool from the Applications ⇨ Add/Remove menu.
2. Find the installed application you want to remove. You can use the Installed Packages filter from the drop-down menu to help locate the application to remove.
3. Remove the check mark from the check box next to the application name.
4. Click the Apply Changes button. A confirmation dialog box appears, shown in Figure 13-8, listing the application(s) to remove.

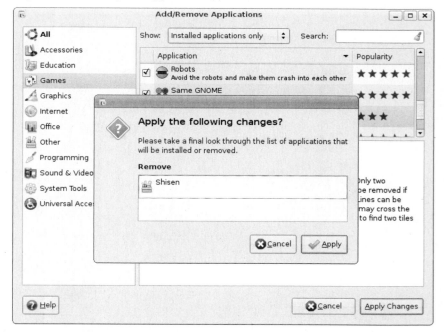

Figure 13-8: The Application Removal dialog box.

5. Click the Apply button to start the removal. The Update Manager prompts you for your password to ensure you have privileges to remove the application, then it removes the application and any other files that support the application. When the application removal is complete, a dialog box, shown in Figure 13-9, appears.

Figure 13-9: The Application Removal Completed dialog box.

6. Click Continue to add or remove more applications, or click the Close button to close the Add/Remove Applications dialog box.

All components from the installed application, including the menu entry, should now be removed from your system.

The Add/Remove Applications tool is a great way to painlessly test out new applications. If you decide you don't like the application, you can easily remove it without any hassle!

Installing New Packages

The Add/Remove Applications tool is a great feature in Ubuntu, but it has its limitations. It adds and removes only workstation application software packages. The Ubuntu distribution includes many more packages for server programs, utilities, drivers, and code libraries that cannot be managed by the Add/Remove Applications tool. Fortunately, Ubuntu also includes a program for handling the details of package management—the Synaptic Package Manager.

This section describes how to use the Synaptic Package Manager to install and remove individual packages on your Ubuntu workstation.

The Synaptic Layout

Start the Synaptic Package Manager by selecting System ⮕ Administration ⮕ Synaptic Package Manager. After you enter your password, the main Synaptic Package Manager window appears, as shown in Figure 13-10.

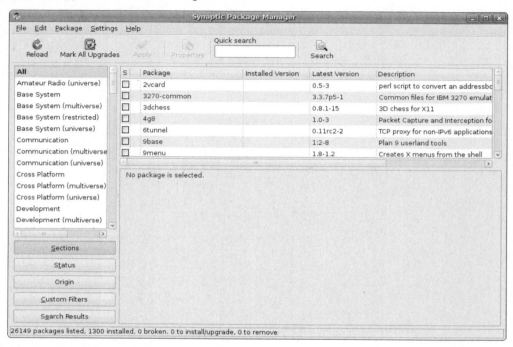

Figure 13-10: The Synaptic Package Manager window.

The main window is divided into six sections:

- The menu bar
- The toolbar
- The category selector
- The package list
- The description field
- The status bar

Each of these sections provides features for managing the packages on the system, as described in the following sections.

The Menu Bar

The menu bar provides access to all of the features in Synaptic, separated into standard menu categories:

- **File:** Provides features for saving selected package settings and restoring them from a file, generating a script to perform the selected package installations at a later time, adding downloaded packages, and displaying the history of package operations.

♦ **Edit:** Lets you undo a change, unmark all selections to start over, search for a specific package, reload package information from repositories, add a local CD to the repository list, mark all packages that have available upgrades, and fix broken packages.

♦ **Package:** Controls package management, such as marking packages for installation, reinstallation, upgrade, or removal; locking a package version; forcing a specific version of a package; and configuring a package.

♦ **Settings:** Allows you to configure repositories (the Software Sources window), preferences, and filters used for determining which packages are available.

♦ **Help:** Provides quick access to the Synaptic Package Manager manual, as well as access to online help, if available.

The Settings ⇨ Preferences option produces the Preferences window, shown in Figure 13-11.

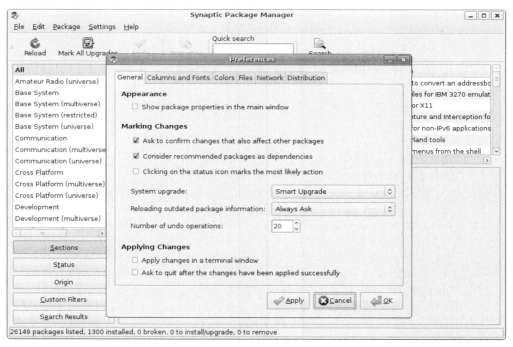

Figure 13-11: The Synaptic Preferences window.

In the Preferences window you can specify how Synaptic handles package changes, displays package information, and connects to the remote software repositories (if a network proxy server is required). You can also specify whether to load only the package versions that match the current distribution release.

Secret

By default, Ubuntu allows you to install the highest-available version of a software package. Sometimes, though, this can cause problems when working with other packages in the distribution. If you need to synchronize all of the packages in your distribution to the same release levels, click the Distribution tab in the Preferences window and select the Always Prefer the Installed Version option.

The Toolbar

The toolbar provides quick access to common functions in Synaptic:

- **Reload:** Refresh the package list from the configured repositories
- **Mark All Upgrades:** Mark all installed packages that have an upgrade available.
- **Apply:** Perform the operations as marked in the package list.
- **Properties:** Display the properties for the selected package.
- **Quick Search**: Enter text in the text box to perform a real-time search of the package based on package names and descriptions.
- **Search:** Search for packages using other attributes, such as version numbers, dependencies, and the maintainer.

Although there aren't many buttons in the Synaptic toolbar, the ones supplied should cover most of the features you need for normal operations.

The Category List

The category list helps filter the packages that appear in the package list. There are five categories of filters you can select from:

- **Sections:** Contains individual section filters based on the package application type.
- **Status:** Displays the status of the package—installed or not installed.
- **Origin:** Filters packages based on which repository they were loaded from.
- **Custom Filters:** Lets you create your own definitions for filtering packages.
- **Search Results:** Filters the results based on the Search tool.

The Sections filter divides packages into sections based on the primary category they belong to. There are 32 different categories of packages, such as base packages loaded at installation time, GNOME packages, KDE packages, networking packages, and library packages.

Within each category there may be multiple entries, depending on the type of applications:

- **Main:** open-source packages supported by Ubuntu
- **Multiverse:** packages that may be covered by copyright or patent licensing but are not supported by Ubuntu and are not provided with automatic updates
- **Restricted:** packages that are supported by Ubuntu but are not open-source programs, such as proprietary hardware drivers
- **Universe:** packages that are open-source and supported by the open-source community but are not supported directly by Ubuntu (Ubuntu doesn't guarantee updates for these packages but may provide them if they are available)

Packages not marked as one of these four types are part of the Ubuntu main repository and are fully supported by Ubuntu.

The Package List

The package list displays the packages available on the system, depending on the filters set in the category list. The package list provides five pieces of information about the packages:

- ◆ The package status (installed, not installed, marked for upgrade, marked for installation, or marked for removal)
- ◆ The package name
- ◆ The installed version of the package
- ◆ The version currently available in the repository
- ◆ A brief description of the package

When you select a package, the lower section of the package list provides a more detailed description of the package.

Installing Packages

Installing software packages using Synaptic is a breeze. Just follow these steps to install a new package:

1. Open Synaptic by selecting System ➪ Administration ➪ Synaptic Package Manager from the Panel menu.

2. Enter your password in the Password dialog box prompt. The Synaptic Package Manager requires administrative permissions to install and remove software packages. If your user account doesn't have administrative permissions, you won't be able to use the program.

3. Enter the package name in the Quick Search box. The Search tool searches all of the configured repositories, looking for packages that contain the search word in the name and description, then displays packages that match in the package list, shown in Figure 13-12.

Figure 13-12 displays the results of a search for the SuperTux game. If you require a more detailed search, use the Search button on the toolbar and select different search criteria.

4. Click the SuperTux package and select the Mark for Installation option from the menu. Synaptic automatically locates any dependent packages required by the selected packages and asks whether you want to mark those for installation as well, as shown in Figure 13-13.

Packages marked for installation appear with an error in the status box and are highlighted in green if all of the dependency packages are available.

5. Click the Apply button in the toolbar. The Synaptic installation process begins, downloading and installing the selected packages.

6. Synaptic asks whether you want to install more packages. If you're done, select No.

Secret

Once the packages are installed you may or may not see them in the Ubuntu menu system, depending on what type of packages they are. Some packages require opening a Terminal session and starting them from the command line. You can manually create a menu entry for these packages (see Chapter 4, "Exploring the Desktop").

44

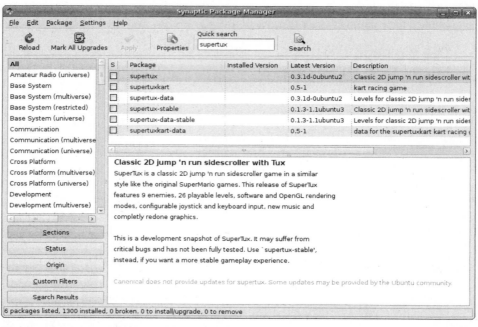

Figure 13-12: Displaying package search results.

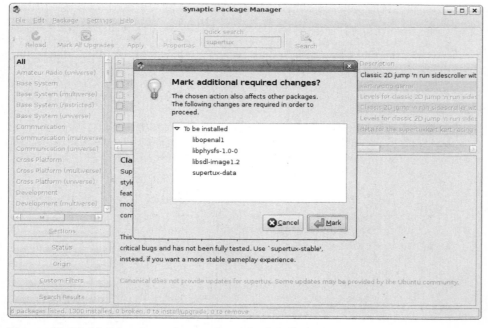

Figure 13-13: Marking dependent packages for installation.

Removing Packages

When you view the package list in Synaptic, installed packages have a green status box, indicating that all of the components for that package are installed. Right-clicking on the package produces a menu that gives you three options for managing the installed package:

- ◆ **Mark for Reinstallation:** Reinstall the package from the current version in the repository.
- ◆ **Mark for Removal:** Remove only the files installed by the package.
- ◆ **Mark for Complete Removal:** Remove the package files plus any additional configuration or data files associated with the application.

If you want to reinstall the package but have customized configuration files you'd like to use with the reinstallation, select Mark for Removal rather than Mark for Complete Removal. A complete removal will delete any custom configuration you've done to the package.

Secret
If you request to remove a package that installed dependencies, Synaptic will ask whether you want to remove those packages as well. Ubuntu attempts to determine whether any installed packages use the dependent packages, but sometimes things get missed, especially if you have installed universe packages that aren't closely monitored by Ubuntu. Pay attention to the list of packages that Synaptic asks to remove. Be especially careful when removing library packages.

Command-Line Package Management

If you're working on the Ubuntu server command line or just want to get to the command-line level on your workstation, you can't use the Synaptic graphical package management tools. Instead, you must use the command-line tool, *apt-get*. This section walks through how to use the apt-get tool to update and install software on your Ubuntu system.

Setting Repositories

Just as with the graphical package installers, you must configure the repositories the apt-get program contacts to update and install software packages. The list of repositories is stored in the /etc/apt/sources.list file.

The sources.list file contains multiple lines, one for each repository. The format of each line is

```
deb [address] [dist name] [package type list]
```

The [address] parameter specifies the web address of the repository. If Ubuntu detected your network connection during installation, it automatically provides the default Ubuntu repositories for your distribution version. If not, you'll need to go to the Ubuntu web site and find the current repository web addresses for your distribution.

The [dist name] parameter defines the name of the Ubuntu distribution version from which to retrieve package updates for installation (such as Gutsy, Hardy, or Intrepid).

This parameter helps maintain a consistent environment for the Ubuntu distribution and prevents the loading of packages released for other Ubuntu versions.

The [package type list] parameter lists the package types that the repository supports, such as main, multiverse, universe, and restricted.

To edit the file from the command line, you can use the vim editor (see Chapter 6, "Working with Text"):

```
$ sudo vim /etc/apt/sources.list
```

Only user accounts with administrative permissions can access and modify the sources. list file. The sudo command is required to gain administrative permissions on the system (see Chapter 19, "The Ubuntu Command Line").

Apt-get Commands

Once you configure the repository locations, you're ready to use apt-get to update installed software packages and install new packages. The command-line format of the apt-get command is

```
sudo apt-get command
```

The *command* parameter specifies the action the apt-get program takes. The actions available for you to use are listed in Table 13-2.

Table 13-2: The apt-get Commands

Command	Description
update	Retrieve package updates for the currently installed packages
upgrade	Install the newest versions available of the currently installed packages
dselect-upgrade	Alter the status field of the specified packages to the specified state
dist-upgrade	Upgrade to the newest Ubuntu distribution
install	Install one or more packages specified on the command line
remove	Remove one or more packages specified on the command line
purge	Remove packages and related files
source	Install source-code files for the packages specified on the command line
build-dep	Install or remove packages to satisfy the dependencies for a specific package
check	Update package cache and check for broken package dependencies
clean	Clear the local cache copies of all installed package files
autoclean	Automatically clear the local cache copies of package files that are no longer supported in the repositories
autoremove	Remove packages that were installed as dependencies and no longer needed

To install a new application, such as the SuperTux game, from the Ubuntu command line, use this format:

```
sudo apt-get install supertux
```

This command attempts to install the game from the configured repositories. If any dependencies are required, apt-get lists them and asks whether you want to install them as well. Be careful that you don't have the graphical Synaptic Package Manager running at the same time you try to use apt-get. Both packages will attempt to access the package database at the same time, which will generate errors.

Secret

When you manually install and update packages using apt-get, it downloads the package to a local cache area. Over time this cache area can become quite large. It's a good idea to manually clear out the cache area using the clean command.

Also, if you remove packages over time, the package dependencies become out of sync. Use the autoremove command to remove any packages that were installed as dependencies but are no longer needed. This helps make it easier to track what's installed on your system.

To see the status of the files currently stored in the cache area, you can use the apt-cache command with the stats option:

```
rich@testbox:/etc/apt$ apt-cache stats
Total package names : 32389 (1296k)
  Normal packages: 24730
  Pure virtual packages: 546
  Single virtual packages: 1838
  Mixed virtual packages: 234
  Missing: 5041
Total distinct versions: 27166 (1413k)
Total Distinct Descriptions: 27166 (652k)
Total dependencies: 186121 (5211k)
Total ver/file relations: 28776 (460k)
Total Desc/File relations: 27166 (435k)
Total Provides mappings: 5171 (103k)
Total globbed strings: 118 (1537)
Total dependency version space: 943k
Total slack space: 89.2k
Total space accounted for: 8574k
rich@testbox:/etc/apt$
```

Figure 13-14: The output from the apt-cache stats command.

The output shows the amount of disk space used by files in the cache area (shown in the line labeled "total space accounted for"). This amount is how much disk space you can recover by clearing out the cache. If you've installed a lot of large packages, this amount of space can be sizeable.

Summary

This chapter discussed how the Ubuntu distribution allows you to keep your system up to date and explained how to install new applications. Ubuntu uses repositories on the Internet to host software updates and packages. If you have a network connection you can configure your Ubuntu system to access these repositories.

The Software Update Manager provides a simple interface for downloading and installing updates to your installed packages. By default, Ubuntu installs the Update Manager Applet, which provides a visual tool on the desktop panel that indicates when new updates are available for download.

The Add/Remove Applications tool in Ubuntu provides a simple interface for installing and removing basic application packages on your Ubuntu system. Just find the application you want and select it for installation or removal.

For more detailed control over the software installed on your Ubuntu system, the Synaptic Package Manager provides access to individual packages. You can control which packages and versions are installed and which packages can be removed.

For the Ubuntu command-line environments, Ubuntu provides the apt-get program. It uses the same features as Synaptic, only from the command line. You can install, update, and remove any package on your Ubuntu system using the apt-get program.

Successfully keeping your Ubuntu system up to date requires a network connection. In the next chapter we'll take a look at how to manage network connections using the tools provided in Ubuntu.

Networking

Chapter
14

♦ ♦

Secrets in This Chapter

Connecting to the Internet

Configuring Your Workstation

Using Networking Tools

Firewalls

♦ ♦

Accessing the Internet from Ubuntu can sometimes be tricky. If you have a home network that's connected to the Internet, it's possible that Ubuntu detected your network hardware and configured everything for you during installation. If so, that's great! If not, you'll have to do some tweaking to get things going. This chapter walks through the various configuration settings required for different types of network connectivity methods. After helping you get your network connection working, the chapter discusses a few network tools that Ubuntu provides. Finally, the chapter takes a look at a feature that no networked workstation should be without, a firewall.

Networking Basics

Before you try to get your Ubuntu workstation or server running on the Internet, it's a good idea to take a few minutes and familiarize yourself with the various ways you can connect to the Internet. This section walks through the basic things you'll need to know to get your system up and running on a network.

Internet Connection Types

These days there are several popular methods for getting onto the Internet, which include

♦ Dial-up connection with a modem
♦ Broadband connection using a digital subscriber line (DSL) modem
♦ Broadband connection using a cable modem
♦ Broadband connection using a wireless modem

The method you need to use depends on the Internet service provider (ISP) you contract with to provide your access to the Internet. Let's take a closer look at each of these methods and see how they work.

Dial-up Modem

The oldest method available to access the Internet is the dial-up modem. This method is still in use in areas that don't have access to broadband technologies and by people who prefer a low-cost method of connecting to the Internet.

The dial-up modem uses standard telephone lines by converting the digital signal from the workstation to an analog signal, then sending the analog signal across the telephone lines to the ISP. The ISP converts the analog signal it receives back to a digital signal for processing on the server, which then forwards it to the Internet.

The dial-up modem uses the telephone line the same way a telephone does, so when you're using your dial-up modem to connect to the Internet, your phone line is busy and can't accept incoming calls. It's also not a good idea to pick up another telephone on the same line while the dial-up modem is operating.

Two basic types of dial-up modems are available:

♦ External modems
♦ Internal modems

External modems are separate from the workstation and connect to it with a USB cable or a *serial cable.* Serial cables are bulky, multi-pin cables that plug into the serial ports on the workstation, usually labeled COM1 or COM2. This is an old technology, and many newer workstations don't provide COM1 or COM2 ports. Therefore, it's difficult these days to find external modems that use serial port connections. USB external modems plug into the standard USB port on the workstation and communicate as a normal USB device.

Ubuntu can usually automatically detect an externally connected modem, whether it's a serial or USB connection. If Ubuntu doesn't automatically detect your external modem, first check to make sure the modem turned on when you boot your system. If it did, then check to make sure the cable is secured to the proper port on the workstation.

Internal modems are built inside the workstation. Some workstation motherboards contain modems built into them, while others use cards you can plug directly into the motherboard. Ubuntu has somewhat of a checkered past in dealing with internal modems. If Ubuntu automatically detects your internal modem, you're in good shape. If it doesn't, you may have to invest in an external modem instead.

Secret

There's a special type of internal modem, called *Winmodem,* that may cause problems for you. Winmodems perform some of the functionality of a modem in software that (as the name suggests) runs on the Windows platform. You must be careful about Winmodems because not all of them can be used by Linux.

The best resource for working with Winmodems in Linux is the linmodems.org web site: http://linmodems.org. This site provides detailed advice on which Winmodems are directly supported in Linux and how to obtain drivers for those that aren't.

The download speed of dial-up modems is limited to 56 kilobits per second (kbps). Unfortunately, this speed rate is not often achieved because the actual transmission speed of a connection depends on the clarity of the analog signal, which for many telephone lines isn't all that great. What may be annoying static on your phone line when you talk is death to a modem connection!

DSL Modem

The DSL modem uses normal telephone lines to communicate to the ISP. However, instead of converting the digital signal to analog, the DSL modem sends a digital signal directly across the telephone line. The telephone line carries both the analog voice signal and the digital signal on the same wires to the telephone provider, which in turn must separate the two signals, connecting the digital signal to its servers and the analog signal to the appropriate telephone exchange equipment.

Your telephone provider must have the proper equipment installed to be able to provide DSL service to your location. Not all areas are converted to support DSL connectivity. Check with your telephone provider to determine whether they support DSL modems in your area.

Three basic types of digital modems can be used on a digital telephone line:

◆ **Integrated services digital network (ISDN):** The ISDN modem is the oldest technology and is the most sensitive to distance. It offers up to 128 kbps of connectivity speed (more than double the speed of a dial-up modem), provided that the end connection is within 3.4 miles of the telephone exchange equipment. Performance degrades the farther away you are from the telephone exchange, which is one reason why ISDN didn't catch on all that well.

◆ **Symmetric digital subscriber line (SDSL):** SDSL provides a constant upload and download speed using the entire bandwidth provided on the telephone line, so it's not able to share the same line with an analog signal. SDSL lines can provide up to 2,320 kbps of upload and download speeds.

◆ **Asymmetric digital subscriber line (ADSL):** ADSL provides a constant upload and download speed but can share the same telephone line with an analog signal, allowing an ADSL modem and a telephone to operate at the same time on the single telephone line. ADSL splits the upload and download speeds, so they don't have to be the same. This method allows much faster download speeds but at the expense of the upload speeds. ADSL lines can provide download speeds up to 24 megabits per second (Mbps) but usually limit upload speeds to no more than 3.5 Mbps. A typical home ADSL installation provides 8 Mbps of download speed and 1 Mbps of upload speed. For the average home user who downloads videos, music, and Linux distribution ISO files, ADSL is a perfect solution.

The second and third categories of digital modem Internet access is referred to as *xDSL*. Most xDSL providers distribute a simple DSL modem, which you install by simply plugging it into your normal telephone jack to connect to the telephone company. The DSL modem is usually set to communicate automatically with the telephone system's ISP.

The DSL modem uses *Ethernet* to communicate with the workstation. The Ethernet protocol has been a communications standard for decades and is supported by various types of media. The two most popular methods for communicating via Ethernet today are

◆ Wired Ethernet network cards
◆ Wireless Ethernet cards

More about using these types of cards in Ubuntu is found in the "Ethernet Connections" section later in this chapter.

Cable Modem

Most cable television companies provide bandwidth on the cable to accommodate digital modem signals. The company provides a special cable modem, which plugs directly into the cable system, along with an Ethernet jack. You must have an Ethernet card in your workstation to connect to the cable modem.

Once you are connected, the cable television company provides Internet service to your workstation at a predetermined speed. Similar to ADSL, cable modems allocate more bandwidth to download speed than upload speed, providing a faster download experience for home users. Most cable television companies offer a variety of service options based on the download and upload speeds allowed.

Wireless Modem

With the popularity of wireless telephone (cell phone) networks, many ISPs now support Internet connectivity via wireless modem. Don't confuse this option with the home networking wireless solution (discussed later in the "Ethernet Connections" section).

Wireless modems are devices that plug into your workstation as a modem but use wireless cell phone signals to communicate directly back to the ISP. Wireless modems are great if you have a laptop and require Internet connectivity on the road. You can connect to the Internet anywhere a cell phone signal is available!

Secret

Much like cell phone connectivity, wireless modem connectivity depends on how many "bars" you have in your signal strength indicator. Check the different providers in your area to determine the best coverage pattern for your usage, especially if you plan to use this technology in a laptop that you'll be using at various locations.

Ethernet Connections

With the popularity of broadband Internet connections, home Ethernet networks are becoming popular. Both cable and DSL broadband networks require an Ethernet interface from the Ubuntu system to the cable or DSL modem. As mentioned earlier in the "DSL Modem" section, a workstation supports two types of Ethernet connectivity:

- ◆ Wired network card
- ◆ Wireless network card

This section digs deeper into each type of Ethernet interface and explains how they interact with the Ubuntu operating system.

Wired Ethernet Cards

Wired Ethernet cards use a standard eight-pin, RJ-45 jack. This plug looks like a standard phone cord plug, only larger. Many modern PCs have wired Ethernet cards built into the motherboard, so there's no need to purchase a separate Ethernet card.

If you're using your Ubuntu workstation directly with a cable or DSL modem, you'll need an Ethernet network cable to connect the two devices. Often the cable or DSL modem comes with a short Ethernet network cable for this purpose. The cable looks like an overgrown telephone cable, with eight-pin, RJ-45 plugs at both ends.

One of the advantages of Ethernet is that it allows multiple devices to communicate over the same communications channel. To do that you need a *network hub,* switch, or router. The network hub connects multiple Ethernet devices into one network, allowing them to communicate with each other. A network switch is similar, but it helps partition the network traffic between switch ports by isolating each port on the network. Depending on your network traffic patterns, a switch may help control some congestion in the network.

The network router helps you connect your home network to the cable or DSL network to access the Internet. The router often provides additional features, such as automatically assigning IP addresses to your network devices and a firewall service for blocking unwanted access to your network. With all of these methods you can often configure multiple workstations to share a single cable or DSL modem connection to the Internet.

Wireless Ethernet Cards

These days it seems that everything is going wireless, from ordinary household appliances to gadgets you hook to your cell phone. The computer world is no different. Wireless network connections are becoming more popular as home users search for an easier way to connect multiple computers to a broadband Internet connection.

There are three current standards and one proposed standard in the wireless network card world:

- ♦ **802.11a:** Provides up to 54 Mbps of data connectivity but has only a 35-meter range.
- ♦ **802.11b:** Provides only up to 11 Mbps but has a larger range than the 802.11a specification.
- ♦ **802.11g:** Provides up to 54 Mbps and has a larger range than the 802.11b specification.
- ♦ **802.11n (proposed):** Provides up to 248 Mbps, with a range of up to 70 meters.

The benefits of the new 802.11n wireless have made it a commercial success, even before its formal adoption as a network standard.

The downside to wireless network cards is that many of them don't provide drivers for Linux. Ubuntu can detect and use many wireless network cards, but not all of them.

Secret

The NDISWrapper project is an open-source project for configuring wireless network cards in Linux. The NDISWrapper software acts as a bridge between the Linux kernel and the Windows drivers provided for a wireless network card. NDISWrapper allows you to use any wireless network card that has drivers for Windows, which is just about every wireless network card available.

To use NDISWrapper, you must follow these steps:

1. Install the ndisgtk package (see Chapter 13, "Software Installs and Updates").
2. Copy the Windows drivers provided for your wireless network card onto your Ubuntu system.
3. Start a Terminal session window, then change to the folder that contains the wireless network card drivers using the cd command (see Chapter 19, "The Ubuntu Command Line").
4. On the command line, use the ndiswrapper command to install the Windows driver using the .inf file provided:

   ```
   sudo ndiswrapper -i file.inf
   ```

   where file.inf is the name of the .inf file for your Windows driver.

5. Load the NDISWrapper into the kernel using the command

   ```
   sudo modprobe ndiswrapper
   ```

6. Create an alias device for the new network interface:

   ```
   sudo ndiswrapper -m
   ```

7. Exit Terminal and reboot your system.

If all went well, the next time you log into Ubuntu the Network Manager applet should show a list of the wireless access points available.

Besides the network type, you also must worry about whether the wireless network is protected by a security system. Wireless networks offer several types of encryption schemes to protect them from unwanted visitors. The most popular encryption schemes used are

♦ **WEP:** The wired equivalent privacy protocol is the oldest and least secure encryption scheme. It uses RC4 encryption with either a 64- or 128-bit key. The key is usually entered as a series of hexadecimal digits, often as text characters, to create a password.

♦ **WPA:** The Wi-Fi protected access protocol uses the RC4 encryption scheme with a 128-bit key but dynamically changes the key as the system is used. It can be used with a server that provides separate keys to each device on the network or, for less secure environments, it can provide a pre-shared key (PSK) mode in which multiple computers on the network can share the same key.

♦ **WPA2:** The second version of the Wi-Fi protected access protocol uses a more secure advanced encryption standard (AES)-based scheme that for now is considered fully secure and not breakable.

You must know the encryption type as well as the password to connect to a wireless network that uses a security scheme. If you happen to find a network that's not encrypted, Network Manager will automatically connect you.

Connecting to the Network

Ubuntu provides the tools to make configuring your workstation on the network a snap. The *GNOME PPP* application helps you if you use a dial-up modem for Internet connectivity. For all other types of network connections, the *Network Manager* application detects the type of network card you have installed in your workstation and attempts to connect to networks automatically.

This section walks through using the GNOME PPP and Network Manager applications for the different types of hardware you might use for connecting to a network.

GNOME PPP

If you use a dial-up modem to access the Internet, you'll have to do some manual configuration to tell Ubuntu how to contact your ISP. This is done using the GNOME PPP application. You'll first have to manually install the GNOME PPP application using the Synaptic Package Manager before you can use it to connect to your ISP.

Just start Synaptic (discussed in Chapter 13, "Software Installs and Updates"), search for the GNOME PPP package, mark it for installation, then apply the changes. After installing the GNOME PPP package, follow these steps to configure a PPP session to connect to your ISP:

1. Start the GNOME PPP dialog box by selecting Applications ➪ Internet ➪ GNOME PPP from the Panel menu. The main GNOME PPP dialog box, shown in Figure 14-1, appears.

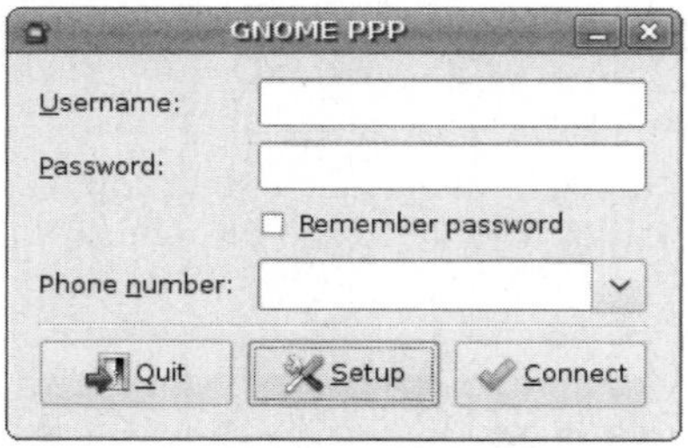

Figure 14-1: The GNOME PPP dialog box.

2. Click the Setup button at the bottom of the dialog box. This opens the Setup dialog box, shown in Figure 14-2, where you can configure you modem settings.

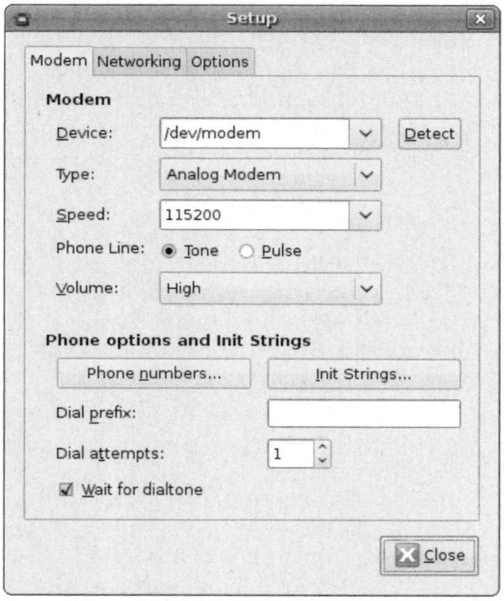

Figure 14-2: The GNOME PPP Setup dialog box.

3. Configure your modem settings in the Modem tab. You must select which port your modem uses to communicate. If Ubuntu automatically detects your modem, it assigns it to the special port /dev/modem. If that doesn't work, Ubuntu uses /dev/ttyS0 for COM1, /dev/ttyS1 for COM2, and so on.

4. Click the Networking tab to set your IP address information. If your ISP dynamically assigns an IP address to your workstation, select the Dynamic IP Address radio button. If you must specify a static IP address, select the Static IP Address radio button and enter your IP address information in the text boxes. If your ISP uses a static address, you'll also need to configure the DNS server to use for the network.

5. Click the Options tab to set additional features for the modem connection. You can set the Modem Connection icon to minimize when the connection is established or dock itself on the panel. You can also choose advanced connection features from this page, such as having the modem reconnect if the connection drops.

6. Click the OK button to save the settings.

7. Back in the main GNOME PPP dialog box, enter the information needed to contact your ISP account. You must provide the phone number, plus any special prefixes (such as a 9 to get an outside line). Enter the userID and password provided by your ISP and select the check box if you want GNOME PPP to remember your password.

8. Click the Connect button to initiate the connection to the ISP.

Once you've activated your dial-up modem, Ubuntu will attempt to use it to access the Internet via your ISP whenever a network request is made.

Network Manager

The GNOME Network Manager application provides one-stop shopping for all of your network configuration needs. You can start the Network Manager in one of two ways:

◆ If Ubuntu detected your network card, the Network Manager icon should appear in the top panel. Right-click the icon and select Edit Connections.

◆ If Ubuntu didn't detect your network card, start the Network Manager from the Panel menu by selecting System ➪ Preferences ➪ Network Configuration.

With either method, the Network Manager dialog box, shown in Figure 14-3, appears.

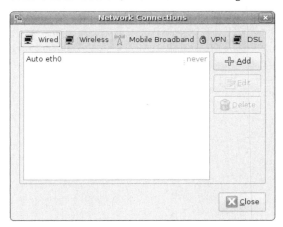

Figure 14-3: The GNOME Network Manager dialog box.

From this interface you can configure

◆ Wired Ethernet card connections

◆ Wireless Ethernet card connections

◆ Wireless broadband (modem) connections

◆ Virtual private network (VPN) connections

◆ DSL connections

The following sections walk through the basics of working on each of these types of networks.

Wired Network Cards

If you use a wired network card to access a broadband connection, most likely Ubuntu automatically detected and configured it for you during the installation process. You can tell by looking for the Network Manager applet icon on the top panel of your desktop.

 **Secret**

Ubuntu provides drivers to automatically detect and install many types of wired network cards. If Ubuntu doesn't detect your network card, you'll have quite a bit of work ahead of you. The easy solution is to find a network card that Ubuntu supports. Otherwise, you'll need to find the Linux driver for your network card, install it in Ubuntu, then use the `modprobe` command to insert the network card drivers into the Linux kernel. After all that's done, Ubuntu should recognize your network card.

If for some reason Ubuntu didn't detect your network settings correctly (or if you have to manually set a static IP address), you can do that using the Network Manager interface. Just right-click on the Network Manager icon in the top panel and select Edit Connections. The Network Manager dialog box, previously shown in Figure 14-3, appears.

From here, follow these steps to configure your wired network connection:

1. Click on the wired network card in the list, then click the Edit button. If there is more than one wired network card in the workstation, Ubuntu will name them starting at eth0 for the first card, eth1 for the second card, and so on. After you click the desired network card, the Editing dialog box, shown in Figure 14-4, appears.

Figure 14-4: The Network Manager Editing dialog box.

2. Configure the wired network card settings. The Editing dialog box contains three tabs of information for the network card:

- **Wired:** Sets the media access control (MAC) address for the card (which Ubuntu automatically detects) and the media transfer unit (MTU) size, with a default of automatic.

- **802.1x Security:** Sets login details for connecting to a protected wired network. This feature is used by some network switches to restrict access to a wired network. If your network uses 802.1x security, consult with your network administrator for the proper settings to use.

- **IPv4 Settings:** Determines how the IP address for the network card is set. This can be either dynamically from a DHCP server, using the Zeroconf protocol to negotiate an address with other devices on the network or statically, using a configured IP address.

3. Click the OK button to save the new settings.

To enable the network connection, right-click on the Network Manager applet icon on the top panel and ensure that the Enable Networking entry is checked. Once you've enabled networking, Ubuntu will automatically attempt to connect to the network.

Wireless Cards

If Ubuntu detected and installed your wireless network card, you'll see the Network Manager applet icon in your top panel, and it will appear as a signal strength indicator (a series of four bars of increasing height) instead of the dual monitor icon. The signal strength indicator provides real-time information on the strength of the wireless signal received.

To connect to a wireless network, follow these steps:

1. Left-click on the Network Manager applet icon to display a list of wireless access points detected, as shown in Figure 14-5.

   The signal strength of each network is depicted by the orange bar. Networks that are protected by a security password are indicated by an additional icon located next to the signal strength bar. Select the network you want to connect to.

Figure 14-5: The Wireless Networks list.

2. If you don't see the name of the network you want to connect to (for example, if the network uses a hidden SSID), select the Connect to Hidden Wireless Network menu item. This option produces the Existing Wireless Network dialog box, shown in Figure 14-6.

Figure 14-6: Specifying a hidden wireless network.

Enter the name of the wireless network, the security scheme (if any) that it uses, and the password.

3. Click the Connect button to connect to the wireless access point.

The Network Manager applet will display an animated icon indicating that it's trying to connect to the wireless network. If the connection is successful, you'll see the signal strength indicator icon.

Secret

Working with wireless network cards and wireless networks can be tricky. If you're in an area with intermittent signal strength, you may have to reboot your workstation a few times before Network Manager can detect any wireless access points. Also, make sure that your specific wireless access point is configured properly and isn't set to restrict devices connecting to it. If it is, make sure that the media access control (MAC) address of your workstation's wireless network card is added to the access list.

Wireless Broadband

A relatively new feature in Network Manager is the ability to manage wireless broadband modem cards. These cards allow you to connect to wireless Internet providers, much like a cell phone connects to a provider. You can have Internet access anywhere you can get a cell phone signal.

Most wireless broadband cards plug into the USB port on your workstation. Ubuntu will detect the card and start the Network Manager. The Network Manager uses a wizard to guide you through the steps in configuring your wireless broadband card.

VPN

A popular trend in networking is to connect two endpoints using an encrypted session. Two devices connected across a public network using an encrypted session is called a *virtual private network* (VPN).

The Network Manager application allows you to configure a VPN between your Ubuntu workstation and a remote network device. The VPN tab produces a list of configured VPN connections on the Ubuntu workstation. Click the Add button to add a new VPN connection.

DSL

The DSL tab in the Network Manager application allows you to configure a DSL modem card installed in your workstation. Figure 14-7 shows the Editing DSL Connection window that appears if you add a new DSL connection or edit an existing connection.

Figure 14-7: The Editing DSL connection window.

You must set the username, service name, and password to connect to the DSL provider. There's also a PPP tab, which allows you to configure any authentication settings required by the DSL provider, such as for an encrypted authentication.

Network Tools

Not everything is always perfect in the network world. Plenty of things can go wrong when trying to communicate with systems half a world (or more) away. Therefore, Ubuntu provides a handy set of network troubleshooting tools.

To start the network tools, select System ➪ Administration ➪ Network Tools from the Panel menu. The Network Tools window, shown in Figure 14-8, appears.

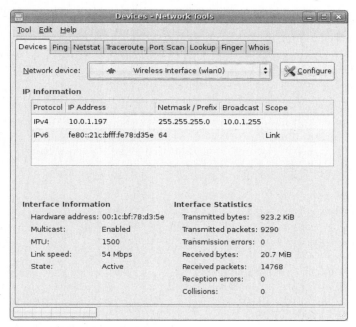

Figure 14-8: The Network Tools window.

There are eight different popular network tools provided in this one interface. The following sections walk through each of these tools.

Devices

The Devices tab provides access to all your network interface information. You can view information and statistics for all of the configured network interfaces on your workstation.

Clicking the Network Device drop-down box allows you to see information about a particular network interface.

The localhost network interface is a special device that's internal to the Ubuntu operating system. It allows programs running on the server to communicate with each other using TCP/IP without having to traverse the network card. This functionality greatly increases the performance of applications that use this feature.

The information presented on the page is separated into three categories:

♦ **IP Information**: Lists all the IP addresses assigned to the network interface. This information includes the traditional IPv4 network address, as well as the newer IPv6 network address.

♦ **Interface Information**: Provides the unique media access control (MAC) address of the network interface, along with information on the connection speed and the state of the interface.

♦ **Interface Statistics**: Provides data on the bytes and packets sent and received on the interface, as well as any errors detected on the interface.

This simple page can be invaluable when trying to troubleshoot network problems. It allows you to peek inside the network interface and see what's going on. By examining the status of the interface, and the bytes sent and received, you can determine whether the interface is working properly on the network.

Ping

The Ping tab provides access to one of the most basic troubleshooting tools in the network world. The Ping program uses the Internet control message protocol (ICMP) to send a packet to a remote device, then it listens for the device to respond. The Ping tab window is shown in Figure 14-9.

Enter the IP address or hostname of the remote host you want to ping, then set the number of ping requests you want to send (or select the Unlimited Requests radio button to send requests continually until you click the Stop button). After you've made your selection, click the Ping button to start the test.

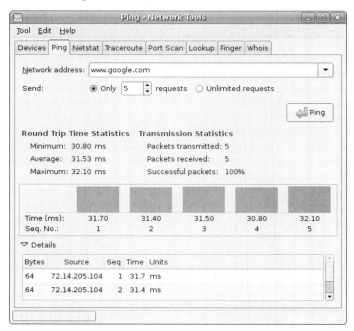

Figure 14-9: The Ping tab window.

The Ping program sends the ICMP requests to the remote host and determines the amount of time it takes for the request to return from the remote host. It creates a graphical histogram of each request time and provides statistics on the minimum, maximum, and average times. Clicking the Details arrow produces a list of the individual test results.

The Ping program is useful in troubleshooting *network latency.* Network latency is how much delay occurs when sending packets across the network to a specific host. Often you can troubleshoot network routing problems using the Ping program.

Secret Many system administrators now consider the Ping program a network vulnerability and block ping requests on their servers. Don't be too surprised if you try to ping a server and don't get a response.

Netstat

The Netstat tab provides information on three sets of network data available on the workstation:

- ◆ The routing table
- ◆ The active network services
- ◆ The multicast network information

Ubuntu maintains an internal routing table to keep track of how to forward network packets to remote networks. Selecting the Routing Table radio button then clicking the Netstat button produces a list similar to the one shown in Figure 14-10.

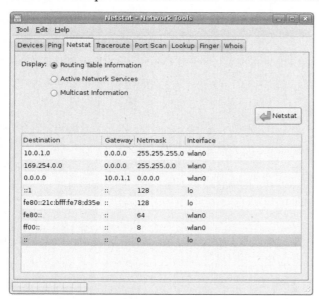

Figure 14-10: The Netstat routing table output.

The routing table matches network destinations with a gateway that can send the packets to the remote network. The routing table always includes at least two entries. One entry is the default route, 0.0.0.0. This route defines the gateway to use by default for sending packets to any network on the Internet. Usually this gateway is the IP address of your broadband modem connection.

The other route defines the local network your Ubuntu workstation is connected to. In the example in Figure 14-10, the workstation is connected to the 10.0.1.0 public network address and uses the default gateway to send packets to this network.

The active network services selection displays a list of what network ports are currently in use on the workstation. Different software packages use different network ports to listen for incoming connections. Many network servers are assigned standard network ports, such as TCP port 80 for web servers and TCP port 25 for email servers.

The network port list includes the current state of the port. TCP uses 11 states to define what mode the network port is in. These states are shown in Table 14-1.

Table 14-1: TCP Network Port States

State	Description
LISTEN	Waiting for a connection request from a remote client
SYN-SENT	Sent a connection acknowledgment and waiting for one in return
SYN-RECEIVED	Received a connection acknowledgment from remote client
ESTABLISHED	Port is ready to send and receive data with the remote client
FIN-WAIT-1	Sent a connection disconnect request to the remote client
FIN-WAIT-2	Received a connection disconnect from the remote client in response to a connection disconnect request sent by the port
CLOSE-WAIT	Remote client initiated a connection disconnect
CLOSING	Waiting for a response from a sent connection disconnect request
LAST-ACK	Waiting for remote client to acknowledge a connection disconnect request
TIME-WAIT	The port is on hold for a preset amount of time after the connection disconnects
CLOSED	The connection is officially closed

The TCP states are invaluable for troubleshooting network programs. By checking the network port states, you often can determine whether a remote device is closing a connection early or is keeping a connection open too long.

The final feature of the Netstat tab is the multicast network information. This protocol allows devices to subscribe to special multicast IP addresses on network routers. Network routers handle multicast packets only when they have a device on the network that requests them. This list displays whether the Ubuntu workstation has registered to receive any multicast packets on the network.

Traceroute

Traceroute provides a peek into the path your network packets take to get to a remote host. It does this by sending a series of ping packets to the destination, but it uses a trick within the packets. The ICMP packet used for the ping includes a time-to-live value. The time-to-live value is decreased by every router that handles the packet along the path. When the time-to-live value reaches zero, the packet is discarded by the network, and the router returns an error packet to the source.

Traceroute uses this process to slowly increase the time-to-live value in the ICMP ping packet. As each router along the path returns the error packet, Traceroute documents the router, then sends another ICMP ping packet with the time-to-live value increased by one.

This process provides a trail of each router the packet traverses to get to the final destination, as shown in Figure 14-11.

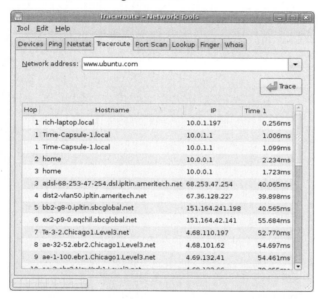

Figure 14-11: The Traceroute window with an active trace.

The first five entries in the list are for my internal home network. Once the packet leaves my DSL modem, it starts to traverse routers inside my ISP, then goes out to the Internet world until it reaches the final destination. Traceroute times each trip and displays the total amount of time each packet takes. This is great for determining whether you have a slow router in your network path.

Secret

Because the Traceroute program uses ping packets, it's also susceptible to hosts and routers that ignore ping packets due to security concerns. Don't be surprised if your traceroute dies before getting to its final destination.

Port Scan

In these days of Internet security you can't be too careful about attackers on the Internet. The Port Scan tool provides a quick way to determine which network ports are accepting connections on a network device.

Enter the IP address or hostname of the device you want to scan, then click the Scan button. The network port scan may take a while to complete. If you need to stop the port scan, just click the Stop button at any time during the scan.

As the scanner detects open ports, it displays them in a list. Figure 14-12 shows the results of a network port scan in progress.

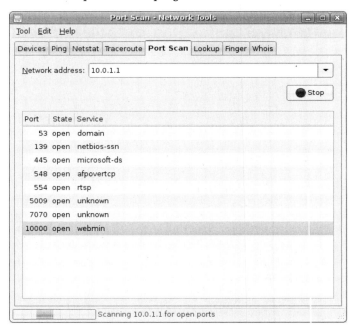

Figure 14-12: A port scan in progress.

The scan shows the numerical port number, the state of the port, and whether the port number is assigned to a well-known program.

Lookup

Lookup is a great tool for determining the network information for a network host or domain. It contacts the domain name server (DNS) assigned to the workstation and requests registered DNS information for the host or domain. The output from a Lookup request is shown in Figure 14-13.

In the example shown in Figure 14-13, I searched for the mail server responsible for the ubuntu.com domain. Lookup returned the address mx.canonical.com, the mail host for the Canonical corporation domain, which sponsors the Ubuntu web site.

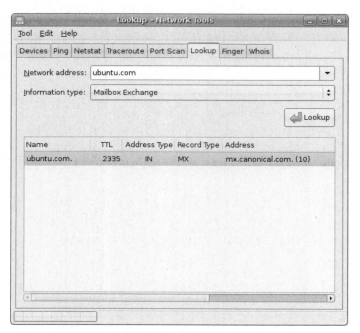

Figure 14-13: The results of a Lookup request.

You can extract several types of data from a Lookup request, as shown in Table 14-2.

Table 14-2: The Lookup Request Types

Request Type	Description
Default Information	Displays the network IP address associated with the hostname or the hostname associated with an IP address
Internet Address	Displays the IP addresses associated with the hostname
Canonical Name	Displays the full real name of a host if the hostname queried is an alias name (such as starting with "www")
CPU/OS Type	Displays the CPU or operating system of the server if that information is configured into the DNS database
Mailbox Exchange	Displays the mail server responsible for accepting mail for the host or domain
Mailbox Information	Displays information about the mail server program used on the host, if configured in the DNS database
Name Server	Displays the DNS name server(s) responsible for supporting the host or domain name

Table 14-2: *(continued)*

Request Type	Description
Hostname for Address	Displays the hostname associated with the specified numeric IP address
Start of Authority	Contains the authoritative information about a domain zone, including the primary name server and a point of contact for the domain administrator
Text Information	Displays any descriptive text information about the host or domain configured into the DNS database
Well-Known Services	Displays any advertised services, such as a web or database server, if configured in the DNS database
Any/All Information	Attempts to display as much DNS information as available on the primary name server for the host or domain

Although the DNS database was originally intended to share as much information about a host or domain as possible, it's become yet another controversial issue these days. Many domain administrators don't put descriptive information in the DNS database for fear it could be used to support network attacks. These days you'll be able to find hostname addresses and email server addresses in the DNS database, but that's probably about all.

Finger

From the Finger tab you can use the Finger protocol to look up a specific user on a server. The Finger protocol was popular back in the early days of the Internet and is still used in some internal network servers, but overall it's been discontinued due to security concerns.

If you have a server that supports the Finger protocol on your internal network, you can use this tool to retrieve basic information about a user account. This capability is helpful if you're trying to look up information about a particular email address on a server.

The Finger protocol returns information configured in the host server's user account (see Chapter 17, "Users and Groups"), such as the full name of the user.

Whois

The Whois tab provides information on registered hostnames. When companies and individuals register their servers for hostnames, Internet registration companies maintain databases with this information. The Whois protocol provides a way to query the registration database and extract the publicly available parts of that information.

Each registered Internet server must have a publicly available server administrator listed. This information provides a point of contact if you detect a problem with the server or suspicious activity coming from the server.

Figure 14-14 shows an example of running a Whois query on the ubuntu.com domain.

Figure 14-14: The Whois result for the ubuntu.com domain.

The Whois query returns all of the domain registration information for a domain, including the company used to register the domain, the name servers that support the domain, and, if you scroll down farther, the point of contact for the domain administrator.

Firewalls

Not all is fun and games on the Internet. Unfortunately, there are plenty of people out there who'd like nothing better than to break into your Ubuntu system and make your life miserable. Fortunately, Ubuntu provides a tool to help block these attacks.

Ubuntu doesn't install firewall software by default in the workstation environment, mainly because there isn't much running on the workstation to break into. However, that doesn't mean that you should ignore the possibility that someone may perform a port scan on your workstation and detect a way into it.

The most popular firewall application for the GNOME desktop is the Firestarter program. This section walks through installing, configuring, and using the Firestarter program on your Ubuntu workstation.

Installing Firestarter

You can install Firestarter from the Add/Remove Applications link in the Panel menu (see Chapter 13, "Software Installs and Updates"). Just follow these steps:

1. Start the Add/Remove Programs by selecting Applications ➪ Add/Remove Programs from the menu. The Firestarter application isn't part of the standard supported applications in Ubuntu, so you'll have to do some looking to find it.

2. Select the All category, then select the All Open-Source Applications filter, then enter *firewall* in the search text box. This displays a list of the available firewall applications in the Ubuntu repository, as shown in Figure 14-15.

Figure 14-15: Finding the Firestarter application in Add/Remove Applications.

3. Select the Firestarter program check box. A dialog box may appear asking whether you want to enable adding and supporting community-supported applications in your Ubuntu setup. Select the Enable button to do so.

4. Click the Apply Changes button to start the installation. The Add/Remove Applications wizard will query you for your password, then download and install the Firestarter program.

If all went well, you've just installed the Firestarter firewall program. You can check to see whether it's installed by selecting the System ➪ Administration Panel menu option. You should see Firestarter in the list of administration programs.

Starting Firestarter

The Firestarter program doesn't run automatically after you install it. You must run it once to set up the firewall parameters before it can start. After that, the Firestarter firewall will start automatically on your system.

Here are the steps for running Firestarter the first time:

1. Start Firestarter by selecting either System ⇨ Administration ⇨ Firestarter, or Applications ⇨ Internet ⇨ Firestarter.

2. The Firestarter Wizard starts, shown in Figure 14-16.

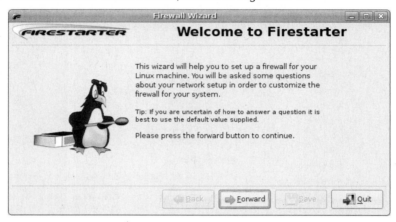

Figure 14-16: The Firestarter Wizard main window.

Click the Forward button to proceed with the wizard.

3. Select the network device that you want to protect from intruders. Firestarter automatically detects all of the network interfaces configured on your workstation. Select the one that connects you to the Internet. If you use a dial-up modem, check the check box to start the firewall only on dial-out. If you receive an IP address from a DHCP server (for example, if you're in roaming mode on your network device), check that box.

4. Select whether you want to share your Internet connection with other devices on your network. The Firestarter program is not only a firewall; it can also act as a router to share your Internet connection with other devices on your network. This feature is handy if you use a dial-up modem and want to share the dial-up Internet connection with other devices on your home network.

5. Click the Save button to save the configuration and start the firewall.

The Firestarter control window starts as soon as you finish the wizard. Use this interface to view network traffic that Firestarter blocks and as an interface to customize the Firestarter program to suit your network needs.

Using Firestarter

By default, Firestarter allows all outbound network connectivity and blocks all inbound network connection attempts. This functionality provides a fully secure environment from outside intruders, while still allowing you to send email messages, browse the Internet, and connect to remote devices such as FTP and Windows servers.

You can customize how Firestarter operates by setting *policies* (rules) that either lock down or open up specific TCP and UDP ports on your workstation. After starting Firestarter program from either the Applications or System menu, you'll see the main Firestarter control window, shown in Figure 14-17.

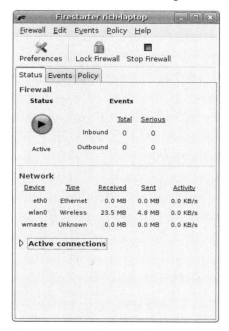

Figure 14-17: The main Firestarter control window.

The main window shows the current status of the firewall (either active or disabled), the number of connection attempts (called *events*) that the firewall blocked, and the general network activity of the network interface Firestarter is protecting.

You control the Firestarter firewall using the three tabbed windows in the control window and the three buttons in the toolbar. The following sections describe these features in more detail.

Tabbed Windows

The Firestarter control window uses three tabbed windows to control the operation of the firewall:

- ◆ **Status**: Provides a summary of the firewall operation.
- ◆ **Events**: Displays a detailed list of blocked connection attempts.
- ◆ **Policy**: Allows you to set additional rules to block or allow specific network traffic.

The Events tab displays a list of all the connection attempts Firestarter blocked on your workstation, as shown in Figure 14-18.

Figure 14-18: The Firestarter Events display.

The individual columns provide information about the event, such as the remote host that attempted to connect, the port number it attempted to connect to, and the name of the service that normally uses that port. You can add or remove columns to this display in the Preferences dialog box, as discussed in the next section.

The Policy tab allows you to define additional rules to the default rules. The Policy tab has a drop-down box that allows you to select which rules you're modifying:

- Inbound traffic policy
- Outbound traffic policy

When you select the outbound traffic policy, you'll notice that the default setting is to be permissive by default, allowing all outbound network connections. Right-click in the list box to add a rule to block specific network activity from the workstation, as shown in Figure 14-19.

The top list box allows you to block all network connectivity to all ports on a specific host, while the bottom list box allows you to block all network activity to all hosts on a specific port.

Alternatively, you can change the default behavior to be restrictive, blocking all outbound network connections by default. In this case, any hosts or ports you add to the list box are allowed instead of blocked.

Figure 14-19: Blocking specific outbound network traffic in Firestarter.

The Toolbar

The Firestarter toolbar is pretty basic, but it provides crucial control over the firewall. The toolbar changes depending on which tabbed window you're viewing:

- ◆ **Status**: Displays the Preferences, Lock Firewall, and Start/Stop Firewall buttons.
- ◆ **Events**: Displays the Save List, Clear, and Reload buttons.
- ◆ **Policy**: Displays the Add Rule, Remove Rule, Edit Rule, and Apply Policy buttons.

In the Status window, Start/Stop Firewall buttons provide an easy way to activate and disable the firewall. The Lock button locks down the firewall so you (or anyone else on the system) can't accidentally change the current status.

The Preferences button in the Status window provides a dialog box for setting various configuration features on the firewall, shown in Figure 14-20.

Firestarter divides the configuration settings into eight categories:

- ◆ **Interface:** Enable or disable the Firestarter panel icon applet.
- ◆ **Events:** Configure the behavior of the Events window by listing hosts and ports to not report events for and setting Firestarter to skip duplicate event entries in the log.
- ◆ **Policy:** Set policy rules to apply immediately after defining them.

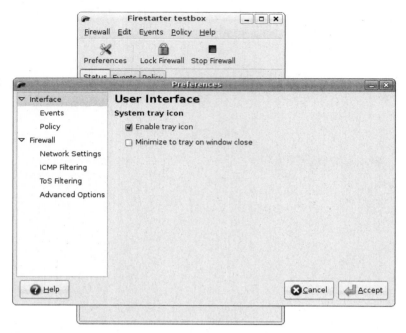

Figure 14-20: The Firestarter Preferences dialog box.

♦ **Firewall:** Configure Firestarter to start the firewall when you start the program, when the modem network interface dials out, or when a new IP address is assigned to a network interface that uses DHCP.

♦ **Network Settings:** Select the network interface to apply the firewall to and, if your workstation has multiple network interfaces, enable or disable Internet connection sharing along with a DHCP server.

♦ **ICMP Filtering:** Configure Firestarter to reject specific types of ICMP packets.

♦ **ToS Filtering:** Set Firestarter to prioritize inbound and outbound network traffic based on the application type.

♦ **Advanced Options:** Configure various Firestarter settings, such as whether to return an error message to the remote host when it blocks a connection attempt, the types of broadcast traffic to block, and whether to block packets from public network interfaces.

The Preferences dialog box allows you to further customize how Firestarter interacts with the network and your workstation.

Summary

This chapter discussed using your Ubuntu workstation on a network. The most common network connectivity for Ubuntu is to access the Internet. There are a few different ways to connect your Ubuntu workstation to the Internet. The chapter discussed how to configure and use a dial-up modem to access the Internet via the Network Manager applet interface. It also showed how to configure and use both wired and wireless Ethernet network cards. These cards are popular and are used with broadband Internet connections, such as cable and DSL modems.

After showing how to get your Ubuntu workstation on the network, the chapter focused on the Network Tools program provided in Ubuntu. The Network Tools program provides several common network tools for troubleshooting network issues. It includes the Ping, Netstat, Traceroute, Port Scan, Lookup, Finger, and Whois utilities all in one easy graphical interface. You can troubleshoot almost any network issue using these tools.

The next chapter focuses on using other devices with your Ubuntu workstation. In a real environment, most likely you'll want to connect devices to your workstation, such as printers, scanners, digital cameras, and portable music players. The next chapter walks through the steps required to get these devices working on your Ubuntu workstation and shows how to use them once they're connected.

External Devices

Chapter

15

♦ ♦

Secrets in This Chapter

Setting Up Printers

Scanning Documents

Playing with Pictures

Listening to Your iPod

♦ ♦

An Ubuntu workstation isn't an island. It must interact with other devices to achieve the most benefits. This chapter examines how to connect popular external devices and use them on your Ubuntu workstation. First, we'll take a look at how to get your printer working with Ubuntu. Whether it's an old parallel printer or a modern shared network printer, Ubuntu can most likely interface with it. After discussing printers, the chapter looks at another popular device, the scanner. Ubuntu uses the XSane application to provide a high-quality way to easily scan, edit, and save documents. These days, digital cameras are becoming the norm. You've already seen that Ubuntu provides the F-Spot Photo Manager software for handling digital images. We'll take a look at how to use that package with your digital camera. Finally, the chapter looks at how to interface your portable music device with your Ubuntu workstation so you can manage your music portfolio.

Printers

Even though technology gurus keep predicting a paperless society, for now we're stuck having to print some things out. In the past, printing was one of the dark areas in Linux. Trying to get modern printers working with Linux was a challenge. However, recently there've been some amazing advances that make Linux more printer friendly.

Possibly the biggest advance in this area has been the common UNIX printing system (CUPS). CUPS provides a common interface between UNIX (and Linux) systems and printers. It runs in the background as a service, connecting to any defined printers and waiting for applications to send print jobs. Because it runs in the background, CUPS can communicate with remote printers and accept print jobs from them.

Ubuntu provides a simple tool to access and set up the CUPS server running on your workstation. The Printer Configuration tool provides a graphical interface to add, configure, and remove printers on your Ubuntu workstation. This section describes how to use the Printer Configuration tool to manage your workstation printers.

The Printer Configuration Tool

The Printer Configuration tool provides an easy way to configure the CUPS server running on the system and any printers you've defined. Selecting System ➪ Administration ➪ Printing from the desktop menu starts the Ubuntu Printer Configuration tool. The main Printer Configuration window is shown in Figure 15-1.

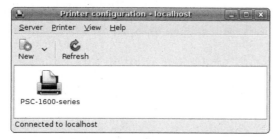

Figure 15-1: The Ubuntu Printer Configuration window.

There are two things you can configure from the Printer Configuration window:

♦ **Server settings:** Allows you to set features controlling how the CUPS server manages system printing features.

♦ **Local and network printers:** Displays icons for all of the printers defined on the system and allows you to change individual printer properties on them.

The following sections describe how to use the Printer Configuration window to set the CUPS and printer properties for your system.

Printer Server Settings

Selecting Server ⇨ Settings from the menu bar in the Printer Configuration window produces the Basic Server Settings window, as seen in Figure 15-2.

Figure 15-2: The Basic Server Settings window.

There are a few different settings you can play with here to help out with printer administration:

♦ **Show printers shared by other systems:** Displays printers found by browsing the network.

♦ **Share published printers connected to this system:** Allows local network clients to connect to any of the local printers marked as shared.

♦ **Allow printing from the Internet:** Allows remote network clients to connect to any of the local printers marked as shared.

♦ **Allow remote administration:** Enables remote clients to connect to the CUPS server running on this system.

♦ **Allow users to cancel any job (not just their own):** By default, users can cancel only their own print jobs. Enabling this feature allows any user to cancel any other user's print job. Although this is a handy feature, it can be dangerous in a multi-user environment (especially if your users like to play tricks on one another).

♦ **Save debugging information for troubleshooting:** By default, the CUPS server generates a moderate amount of logging information to monitor printer use or problems. If you're having trouble with a specific printer configuration, you can enable this feature to produce more (lots more) information in the log files.

After determining the settings appropriate for your CUPS server environment, you can add and set up individual local printers.

Adding a New Printer

One amazing feature of Ubuntu is its ability to automatically detect printers connected via USB cables, parallel cables, and even serial cables. If you have one of these printers, you most likely don't need to add it to the system. You should already see an icon appear under the Printers window. Just move on to the next section to configure it.

If you are not fortunate enough to have your printer automatically detected, you'll have to manually add it. Here are the steps for doing that:

1. Click the New button on the toolbar. The New Printer wizard appears and lists your printer options, as shown in Figure 15-3.

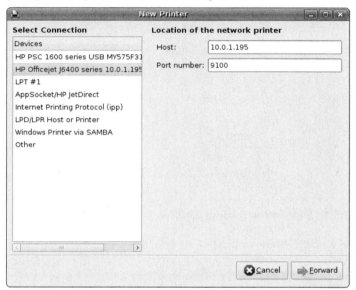

Figure 15-3: The New Printer wizard in the Printer Configuration tool.

Before the New Printer wizard appears, the Printer Configuration tool scans your workstation and the local network for any accessible printers. If it detects any, they're added to the top of the connection list.

2. Select the connection type of the new printer. Although the printer is defined as a local printer on your workstation, this utility also allows you to configure six types of printer connections (besides the currently connected printers) to make a printer available to the system. These printer connection types are listed in Table 15-1.

As you select each connection type in the left side of the window, a different Properties area appears in the right side. For example, if you select Windows Printer via Samba, text boxes appear where you can enter the printer name, a userID, and a password to access the network printer. Click the Browse button to browse your local network to locate shared printers.

After you've selected the connection type and changed any Properties settings, click Forward to continue with the wizard.

Table 15-1: Ubuntu Printer Connection Types

Connection Type	Description
LPT#1	A printer connected via the 25-pin LPT port on the local computer (if the workstation has an LPT port)
Serial Port #1	A printer connected via the 9-pin COM port on the local computer (if the workstation has a COM port); if more than one COM port is present, all of them will be listed
AppSocket/HP JetDirect	A printer directly connected to the network using a network card and Internet software
Internet Printing Protocol (IPP)	A remote CUPS system advertising local printers that can be used remotely
LPD/LPR Host or Printer	An older UNIX standard for remotely sharing local printers
Windows Printer via Samba	A Microsoft Windows workstation or server that advertises shared local printers
Other	A specific uniform resource identifier (URI) used to map to a network printer

3. Select the printer manufacturer or the location of the PPD file. Ubuntu uses PostScript printer description (PPD) files to format files for printing. PPD files are based on the same concept as the standard printer drivers you've probably used in Microsoft Windows. Each printer must have a PPD installed for CUPS to know how to format text and graphics sent to the printer.

This wizard window allows you to select the PPD file to use for the new printer. You have two options:

• Select the printer manufacturer from the list of installed drivers.

• Install your own PPD file for the printer.

If you're lucky enough to have the PPD file for your printer, copy it to a location on your workstation and select the Provide PPD File option. Browse to the location of the file and select it, then click Forward.

If you don't have the PPD file for your printer, you'll have to hope that Ubuntu has your specific printer make and model defined in its library. If you find the printer manufacturer listed, select it and click Forward.

4. If you selected a printer manufacturer, the next wizard window provides a list of specific printer models and PPD files. Select the printer model and (optionally) the proper PPD file. This wizard window asks you to select the specific model for your printer. Hopefully, your printer model will be listed. If not, you must go back a step and find your own PPD file to install.

If your specific model is listed, select it, and a list of available PPD files is shown. Some models may have only one PPD file, but others may have two or more files to choose from. In that case, one is usually marked as recommended. Try that PPD file first. If it doesn't work, select a different PPD file. Clicking the Forward button takes you to the final wizard window (some printer drivers also have an optional window, which appears before the final wizard window, for setting individual options).

5. Define a printer name for the printer, and add the optional description and location if you want to include more information about the printer.

6. Click Apply in the Summary window to finish adding the new printer.

The new printer is added as an icon in the Printer Configuration window (even if you mapped to a remote printer). You should now see the new printer when printing from applications on your system. However, before getting too carried away with printing, it's a good idea to check how the printer is configured.

Modifying Printer Properties

You can modify the properties of any printer on the system, whether Ubuntu automatically created it or you manually created it. If you double-click the icon for the printer you want to configure, the Printer Properties window appears, as seen in Figure 15-4.

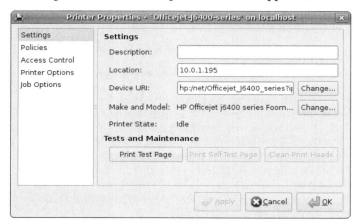

Figure 15-4: Modifying printer properties in the Printer Configuration tool.

The window on the left contains five main properties groups that contain printer information you can modify. The main groups are

◆ Settings
◆ Policies
◆ Access Control
◆ Printer Options
◆ Job Options

Some printers contain a sixth group for setting specific options for the printer. In the next sections, we take a closer look at each of the main groups.

Settings

The Settings group provides some basic settings you can change for the printer. From here, you can change the description and location tags for the printer, the URI of the printer, and the PPD file used for the printer.

There are also three other buttons that you can use:

- ◆ **Print Test Page:** Provides an easy way for you to test whether the printer and PPD file are working properly.
- ◆ **Print Self-Test Page:** Some printers support an internal self-test page. If your printer supports that feature, this button will be enabled.
- ◆ **Clean Print Heads:** Some printers support an external command to clean the print heads. If your printer supports that feature, this button will be enabled.

That covers the general settings for the printer. The other groups provide more advanced settings.

Policies

The Policies group contains three separate sections. The State section allows you to control the state of the printer:

- ◆ **Enabled:** Lets you take the printer offline if there's a problem.
- ◆ **Accepting Jobs:** Allows you to temporarily suspend processing print jobs.
- ◆ **Shared:** Allows you to set whether the printer is a shared resource on the network.

There are four policies (or rules) that control printer behavior. Two of the policies control banner pages for print jobs; the other two control how the printer operates.

There are two operation policies that you can set:

- ◆ **Error Policy:** Determines how the printer reacts to an error in the printing process. The choices are Abort-Job (giving up on printing the job), Retry-Job (trying again after manual intervention), or Stop-Printer (preventing all other print jobs from printing). The default value is to retry the job because the problem most likely can be resolved with an easy fix, such as turning the printer on or setting it as online.
- ◆ **Operation Policy:** Determines the mode the printer runs in. At this time, the only setting is default.

Banner pages allow you to print a special page describing the print job. The Starting Banner page prints out before the print job. This option allows you to print a cover sheet for the print job. Theoretically, it's supposed to provide some privacy, blocking people from seeing the first print page on the printer, but, really, who wouldn't just look under the banner page? There are several banner pages you can choose from.

The Ending Banner page allows you to print a page that signifies the end of the print job. If you're in a high-volume printing environment, using a starting or ending banner helps keep everyone's print jobs separate. In a workstation environment, it's pretty much a waste of paper. The default is to not print either of the banner pages.

Access Control

The Access Control group provides a method for you to restrict access to the printer. There are two ways to do this.

First, you can list every user account that the server will prevent from using the printer. This option means that any user *not* on the list can print and that any user *on* the list can't print.

The second method is to list the user accounts that are allowed to use the printer. This option means that only the users on the list can print. Obviously, which method you choose depends on whether you have more people you want to allow to print or to restrict from printing.

Be careful when setting this feature. Notice how the two radio buttons are labeled:

◆ Allow printing for everyone except these users.

◆ Deny printing for everyone except these users.

If you click the Allow Printing radio button, the user accounts you list will be denied access to the printer—and vice versa for the Deny Printing radio button. That's just a bit backward, if you ask me!

Printer Options

The Printer Options group allows you to set some physical properties for the printer. The properties available for you to modify are based on information provided by the individual printer's PPD file and depend on the physical characteristics of the printer.

These properties are divided into separate categories, depending on the printer's capabilities. The options available for my test printer are shown in Figure 15-5.

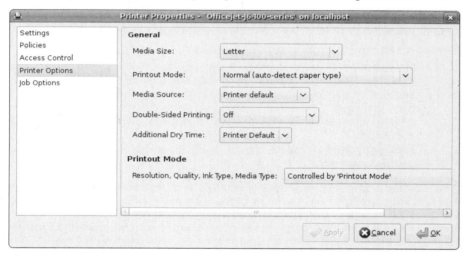

Figure 15-5: The Printer Options group of the Printer Configuration tool.

The General settings handle properties such as types of paper the printer can handle, print qualities it can produce, and number and types of input trays. You can force the printer server to request a specific paper size for all print jobs or to request which paper tray to take paper from.

The Printout Mode settings control the default print quality used by the printer. Again, these settings depend on the capabilities of the particular printer, but usually there's a range of dots per inch (dpi) and color settings to choose from.

Job Options

Finally, the Job Options tab allows you to set the default properties for print jobs sent to the printer. When you request an application to send something to the printer, a standard GNOME Print dialog box appears, as shown in Figure 15-6.

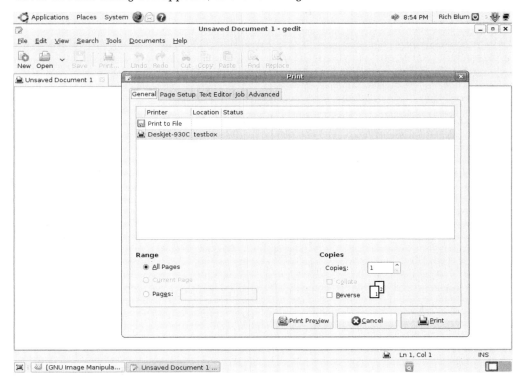

Figure 15-6: The standard GNOME Print dialog box.

You can select several printing properties for the specific print job, such as whether to print in landscape mode, how many copies of the document to print, the paper size to use, and so on. If you prefer to use any of these settings by default, you can set them in the Job Options tab.

Many more print job options can be specified. The job options are divided into four sections:

♦ **Common Options**: Sets common printer options, such as number of copies, page orientation, and number of printed sides (for duplex printing).

♦ **Image Options**: Sets imaging options such as scaling and hue adjustment.

♦ **Text Options**: Sets features that affect the printed text, such as characters per inch, lines per inch, and margins.

♦ **Advanced Options**: Allows you to set options available for a specific printer.

The complete list of options appears within the Printer Configuration Properties window, as shown in Figure 15-7.

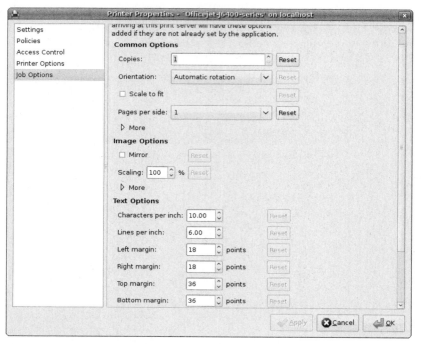

Figure 15-7: The Job Options Properties group in the Printer Configuration tool.

If you decide to revert to the default setting for an option, click the Reset button, and the option will return to the default value.

Scanners

In the digital world it seems like we're always having to convert paper documents into a digital format. Whether it's scanning old pictures to save as digital images or scanning important documents to save in PDF format, a scanner has almost become a necessity for any home workstation.

Ubuntu provides the XSane application to interface with most of the scanners available. This section walks through the things you'll need to know to get the most out of your scanner and Ubuntu.

Detecting the Scanner

Before you can start using your scanner you need to ensure that XSane can work with it. Here are the steps to do that:

1. Connect your scanner to your Ubuntu workstation, then turn on the scanner.
2. After starting Ubuntu and logging in to your desktop, start XSane by selecting Applications ⇨ Graphics ⇨ XSane Image Scanner. The XSane splash screen appears, allowing you to select the scanner, as shown in Figure 15-8.

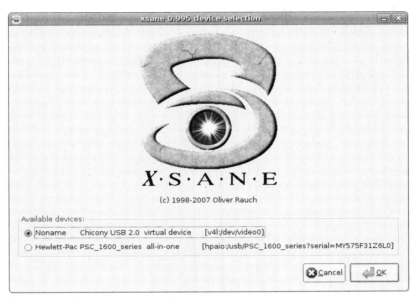

Figure 15-8: The XSane starting window.

The opening splash screen displays a list of the scanners XSane detects that are connected to the system, along with a default scanner.

2. Select your scanner, if it has been automatically detected.

3. The XSane workspace opens, with four separate windows, shown in Figure 15-9.

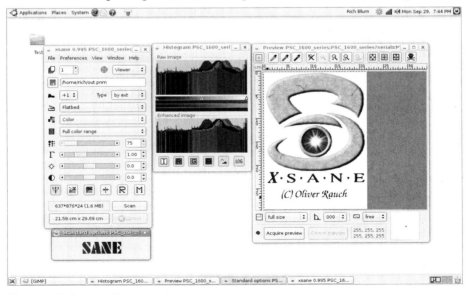

Figure 15-9: The XSane workspace.

We'll talk more about each of the windows in the XSane workspace a little later.

4. Click the Acquire Preview button in the Preview window. Your scanner should automatically start up and begin scanning the document. When the scanner finishes scanning, the document should appear in the Preview window display area.

If you can see the scanned document in the Preview window display area, you're ready to start using XSane.

Secret

Detecting the scanner is often the hardest part of using XSane. The XSane program is a graphical front end for the SANE (Scanner Access Now Easy) command-line utility, which detects and interacts with scanners based on a standard interface protocol. Many scanners have interfaces written to interact with SANE, but there are still those that won't work.

Although there are many types of scanners available, they break down into five basic categories, based on how they connect to the workstation:

● **Parallel port scanners:** Parallel port scanners connect to the LPT1 printer port on a workstation. These scanners are notoriously slow and often use low-resolution scans.

● **SCSI scanners:** The small computer system interface (SCSI) is a popular interface for older scanners. Some scanners come with their own SCSI card that you must install in the workstation to connect the scanner. The key to using SCSI scanners is that Ubuntu must detect the installed SCSI card. For the more-popular SCSI cards this isn't a problem, but SCSI cards that often come with older scanners can be an issue.

● **IDE scanners:** Some older scanners require an integrated device electronics (IDE) connection on the workstation. This is the same type of connection that most hard drives and CD drives use. If your scanner connects directly to the IDE port on your workstation, you may have to purchase a separate IDE card to support it.

● **USB scanners:** Most modern scanners connect to the workstation using a standard universal serial bus (USB) port. Ubuntu automatically attempts to detect USB devices connected to the workstation, and it often configures the scanner as a USB device before SANE even starts.

● **Network scanners:** Network scanners use proprietary software on Windows workstations to detect and connect to a scanner across the network. The Windows software used for this connection usually doesn't have a Linux counterpart. SANE has its own network protocol for sharing a scanner connected to a workstation on the network with other workstations, but it can't connect to network scanners that use a proprietary protocol.

The best source for SANE scanner information is the SANE Project web site at http://www.sane-project.org. Select the Supported Devices link to search for supported scanners.

Scanning a Document

Now that you have XSane set up to use your scanner, you're ready to start scanning documents and saving them on your workstation. Here are the basic steps to scan and save a document:

1. Start XSane from the Panel menu (Applications ➪ Graphics ➪ XSane Image Scanner).

2. Place the document you want to scan in your scanner. Some scanners use an auto-feeder, while others (known as flatbed scanners) have you place the document on the glass scanning surface and close the cover.

3. Click the Acquire Preview button in the Preview window of the work area. The preview function performs a low-resolution, quick scan so you can determine the basics of how the scanned image will look.

4. Select a mode for the scan in the Main window. XSane allows you to scan a document to a file, to a printer, to a fax program, or to an email message.

5. Make any necessary adjustments to the color settings in the Main window and, if you don't want to scan the entire document, select the area to scan in the Preview window. The XSane application provides many settings for customizing the scanning process, as discussed later in the "The Work Area" section of this chapter.

6. Click Scan in the Main window of the work area. The Scan button performs the scan as determined by the settings in the Main and Preview windows. When the scan completes, the scanned image appears in a new Viewer window, as shown in Figure 15-10.

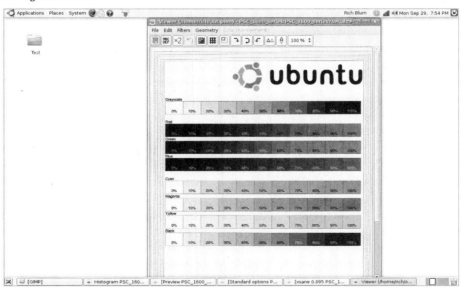

Figure 15-10: The XSane Viewer window with a scanned image.

7. In the Viewer window, click either File ➪ Save Image from the menu bar, or the green Disk icon at the upper-right corner of the window. Select the file type to use when saving the file. XSane supports JPG, PDF, PNG, PNM, PostScript, TXT, and TIFF file types.

8. Repeat the process to scan a new document, or close XSane by selecting File ➪ Quit from the Main window menu bar.

Now that we've walked through scanning a document, let's take a closer look at the various windows and features available in the XSane work area.

The Work Area

The XSane work area consists of four separate windows:

- ◆ **Main window:** Contains selections to set the scanning mode and features used in the scanning process.
- ◆ **Histogram window:** Shows the color-density spectrum of the image.
- ◆ **Preview window:** Displays a low-resolution scan of the image and allows you to alter the scan area.
- ◆ **Viewer window:** Displays the final scanned image and provides some rudimentary image functions.

Each window provides access to specific functions of the scanning process, as detailed in the following sections.

The Main Window

XSane's Main window interface depends on the mode you are working in. There are six different modes that the XSane interface uses. These modes are set with the drop-down box in the upper-right corner of the page (next to the sight icon).

Table 15-2 shows the six modes available in XSane.

Table 15-2: The XSane Operation Modes

Mode	Description
Viewer	Sends the scanned image to the Viewer window. You can set the default filename, file type, and a counter increment for storing multiple files.
Save	Saves the scanned image to a file using the filename and type specified.
Copy	Sends the scanned image directly to the specified printer.
Multipage	Collects multiple scans to combine into a single project that can be saved in PostScript, PDF, or TIFF format.
Fax	Sends the scanned image directly to faxing software, if installed.
Email	Sends the scanned image directly to an email software package.

The Main window also allows you to change settings for the scan, using a series of drop-down boxes, sliders, and buttons:

- **Scanner Hardware Type:** flatbed or autofeeder
- **Scanning Color Mode:** color, grayscale, or black and white
- **Image Adjustments:** brightness, contrast, and color
- **RGB Default:** red, green, and blue value enhancements
- **Negative:** invert black/white images, used for scanning negatives
- **Auto-enhancement:** automatically determine the best values for colors
- **Enhancement Default:** resets image adjustments to the default values
- **Restore Enhancement:** retrieves stored enhancement settings
- **Memory:** stores the set enhancement values in memory

Each of the modes allows you to set the color features of the scanning process so that you can fine-tune the results of the scan. The Histogram window also helps you out here.

The Histogram Window

The Histogram window (as seen back in Figure 15-9) displays a color spectrum of the color densities contained in the image. There are two histograms in this window. The top histogram displays the color densities of the raw image directly from the scanner. The bottom histogram displays the color densities after the color enhancements set in the Main window have been applied.

The Histogram window provides simple controls for viewing the histograms. The four sliders in the middle between the histograms allow you to define the black, white, and gray points in the histogram.

The buttons under the histograms allow you to single out a single color component (or the intensity for the I button). The fifth button in the row defines whether the histograms are drawn with pixels or lines, and the LOG button defines whether the densities are displayed as linear or logarithmic values.

The Preview Window

The Preview window (on the right side in Figure 15-9) allows you to adjust the scanning settings before making the final scan. It consists of a viewing area to preview the scanned document as a low-resolution scan, a toolbar at the top of the window with buttons for various features, and some selection buttons at the bottom of the window to customize the scanning settings.

To perform a preliminary scan, click the Acquire Preview button at the bottom of the Preview window. XSane performs a low-resolution scan of the document and displays it in the Preview window viewing area.

The buttons in the toolbar, from left to right, are

- **Batch scan add area:** Add the selected area on the preview image to a list of areas to scan.
- **White pipette:** After clicking this button, use the mouse pointer and left-click on an area in the preview image that is considered white. This value is used to adjust the automatic color settings.
- **Gray pipette:** After clicking this button, use the mouse pointer and left-click on an area in the preview image that is considered medium gray. This value is used to adjust the automatic color settings.

♦ **Black pipette:** After clicking this button, use the mouse pointer and left-click on an area in the preview image that is considered black. This value is used to adjust the automatic color settings.

♦ **Unzoom:** Return the preview area to the original scan area.

♦ **Zoom out:** Increase the preview area by 20 percent.

♦ **Zoom in:** Decrease the preview area by 20 percent.

♦ **Select zoom area:** Use the mouse to select an area to zoom.

♦ **Undo zoom:** Remove the previously set zoom area.

♦ **Autoselect:** Select the part of the image to edit.

♦ **Autoraise:** Click an image to raise it to the forefront.

♦ **Select visible area:** Select the visible area in the preview for scanning.

♦ **Delete preview image cache:** Preview images are cached to allow the undo function. Click this button to remove any previously previewed images.

Besides the toolbar buttons there are several buttons at the bottom of the Preview window that affect the operation of the scan:

♦ **Preset area:** Select an area of the preview image to be used as the maximum scanning area. This value is relative to the size of the scanner bed.

♦ **Rotation:** Select a rotation angle and axis to use to rotate the scanned image.

♦ **Aspect ratio:** Define a width:height aspect ratio to set for the scanned image. This option limits the selection frame size because the specified ratio is maintained.

♦ **Acquire preview:** Perform a low-resolution preview scan using the Preview window settings.

♦ **Cancel preview:** Stop the preview scan.

♦ **RGB settings:** Adjust the red, green, and blue values of the pixel pointed to with the mouse pointer.

♦ **Magnifier:** Magnify the area directly around the mouse pointer to allow more precise selection of scan and edit areas.

XSane allows you to perform quite a bit of customizing in the Preview window before you make the final scan of the image. This capability helps you avoid having to rescan an image until you get it right.

The Viewer

The Viewer window displays the final scanned image when you select the Scan button and allows you to perform some rudimentary operations on the image before saving it. The Viewer window contains a toolbar above the scanned image that provides access to the necessary functions. The toolbar buttons available are

♦ **Save image:** Save the image to disk, specifying the file type and name.

♦ **OCR:** Attempt to read any text on the image and save in a text file.

♦ **Clone image:** Open another Viewer window with a copy of the scanned image.

♦ **Flip:** Reverse the image in the Viewer window.

♦ **Despeckle image:** Remove spots from the scanned image.

♦ **Blur image:** Apply a blurring feature to the scanned image.

♦ **Scale image:** Change the size of the image.

♦ **Rotate image:** Three buttons that allow you to rotate the image 90, 180, and 270 degrees.
♦ **Mirror image:** Two buttons that mirror the image using the horizontal or vertical axis.
♦ **Zoom:** Zoom in to or out from the image in the Viewer window.

If you set the filename and extension of the file in the Main window, the Viewer automatically saves the image using that file type and name. If not, the Viewer provides a Save As dialog box that allows you to set these values. XSane supports saving images using the file types shown in Table 15-3.

Table 15-3: XSane Image File Types

File Type	Description
JPEG	A standard compressed image format defined by the Joint Photographic Experts Group
PNM	Portable anymap image format
PNG	Portable network graphics format, a standard open-source compressed image format
TIFF	Tagged image file format, an uncompressed image format controlled by Adobe
PostScript	A standard programming language that uses text commands to draw an image; popular in the UNIX world
PDF	Portable document format, a standard image format created and controlled by Adobe
TXT	Standard text file format, used only when operating XSane in optical character recognition (OCR) mode for saving text found in the scanned image

XSane provides a wide selection of standard file formats for storing your image file. Images saved as PDF files are compatible with Adobe Acrobat Reader applications on the Microsoft Windows platform, which is a great feature of XSane.

Digital Cameras

Chapter 10, "Image Manipulation," discussed the F-Spot Photo Manager software package. F-Spot is the default application Ubuntu uses when you connect a digital camera to your Ubuntu workstation.

When Ubuntu detects that you've connected a digital camera to your workstation, it starts the F-Spot Photo Manager, which queries you for the device to connect to, as shown in Figure 15-11.

You may have to experiment with which option to select. For example, when I selected the Olympus entry (which is the make of my digital camera) I received an error that F-Spot couldn't communicate with my camera. When I selected the Mass Storage Camera entry, it worked just fine.

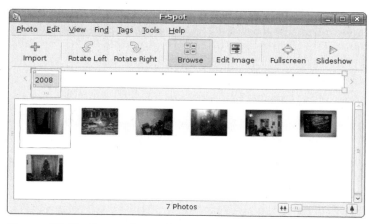

Figure 15-11: Connecting a digital camera to the Ubuntu workstation.

If images are stored on the camera, F-Spot Photo Manager will ask whether you want to download them to your library. If you choose to download the images, F-Spot will catalog the images it finds, then produce a dialog box allowing you to select which images to copy, shown in Figure 15-12.

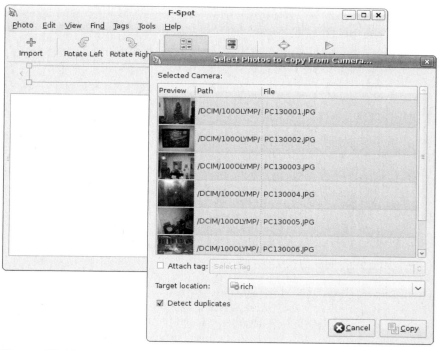

Figure 15-12: Retrieving images from the camera.

If you have lots of images stored on your camera, this process can take quite a bit of time. Once you've imported the images into your photo library, you can use the standard F-Spot image manipulation features discussed in Chapter 10 to edit and save your images.

Portable Music Players

Chapter 11, "Using Audio," discussed the Rhythmbox software package, which is the default application Ubuntu uses when you connect a portable music player to your Ubuntu workstation.

When you connect a portable music player, such as an Apple iPod, to the USB port on your workstation, Ubuntu detects it as both a storage device and a music player, as shown in Figure 15-13.

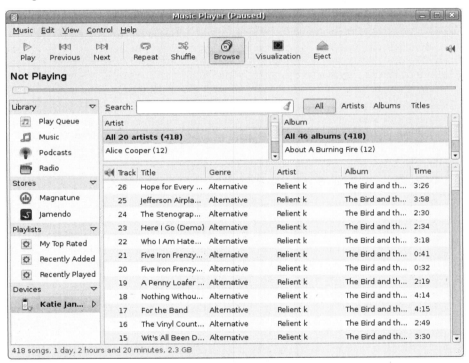

Figure 15-13: Connecting an iPod to the Ubuntu workstation.

Ubuntu creates a desktop icon for the device and starts Rhythmbox, using the device as the default location. The Rhythmbox window displays the music files available on the music player and attempts to retrieve any additional information from the Internet if your workstation is connected.

Secret

The Ubuntu workstation software doesn't include the ability to play MP3 or AAC (used on the Apple iPod) music files by default. If you attempt to play such a file, Ubuntu will produce an error message indicating that it doesn't have the proper codec.

If your workstation is connected to the Internet, you can click the Search button and Ubuntu will attempt to locate an appropriate codec in the repositories for the audio type you're trying to play. If it finds one or more codec packages that can handle that audio file format, it displays them in a selection box. Just select a codec to install, and Rhythmbox will be able to play that audio file type.s

Summary

This chapter discussed how to interface your Ubuntu workstation with a few types of external devices. Ubuntu provides excellent support for most printers. Often Ubuntu can automatically detect a connected printer and load the required software driver. You can also use the Printer Configuration wizard to manually install a printer, especially a network printer. Once a printer is installed you can use it from any application installed in Ubuntu.

Ubuntu uses the XSane application to detect and use scanners on your workstation. The XSane application provides a full work area that includes a Preview window for viewing a low-resolution version of the scanned image, along with a separate Viewer window that displays the final scanned image. You can set color features and scanning properties as well, all from the XSane work area.

Finally, the chapter discussed how to use digital cameras and portable music players with Ubuntu. Ubuntu does a good job of detecting both types of devices when you plug them into the USB port on your workstation. When you connect a digital camera, Ubuntu launches the F-Spot Photo Manager application, which allows you to import image files from the camera to your workstation photo library and edit or print them. When you connect a portable music player, Ubuntu launches the Rhythmbox music player application. Ubuntu scans the player and displays all of the music files in a user-friendly interface to allow you to play the music files on your workstation.

In the next chapter we'll continue our tour through the Ubuntu workstation by taking an in-depth look at how Ubuntu handles the video environment. There are lots of features you can customize in your video display, and Ubuntu provides an easy interface to set most of them.

The Display

Chapter
16

◆ ◆

Secrets in This Chapter

The X Windows System

Configuring the Ubuntu Display

Using 3-D Cards

◆ ◆

The video display is one of those areas in Ubuntu where things are still evolving. If you're fortunate, Ubuntu detected your monitor and video card setup during the installation process without any problems, and you can use your desktop without issue. However, this isn't always the case. If you have any exotic video hardware, such as dual monitors or an advanced 3-D video card, or you want to add a new video card or monitor after you've already installed Ubuntu, Ubuntu will often have trouble detecting the video setup. This chapter helps guide you through the Ubuntu video system. It starts out by walking through the *X Windows* system, the underlying video system Ubuntu uses to control the video environment on your workstation. After that we'll discuss how to modify your video setup by using the utilities Ubuntu provides by default, plus some utilities you can add from the repositories. Finally, the chapter walks through the sticky topic of using advanced 3-D video cards in your Ubuntu workstation.

The X Windows System

Before we dive into the details of working with the video display in Ubuntu, it helps to get a little background on how Linux generally handles video. If you run the Ubuntu server, or if you run your Ubuntu workstation in text mode, there's not much involved for Ubuntu to interact with the video card and monitor. By default Ubuntu can use just about any video card and monitor in text mode to display 25 lines of 80-column text. This feature is built into the Ubuntu Linux software so that it can directly send text to the monitor at all times.

However, when you use the graphical mode on your workstation, things are a bit different. Instead of directly sending text to the monitor, Ubuntu must be able to draw lines, shade colors, and manipulate images. To do that, Ubuntu makes use of a special type of software called X Windows to interface with the video card and monitor. This section walks through how Ubuntu deals with the special X Windows software to create your fancy desktop environment.

What Is X Windows?

Two basic elements control the video environment on your workstation:

- ◆ The PC video card
- ◆ The monitor

The Ubuntu operating system must interact with the video card in your PC to produce the graphical images for your desktop to appear and to run graphical applications. The video card controls how to draw the images on the monitor display, what colors are available to use, what size of display area you can use, and at what speed the system can draw the images.

The video card must be able to interact with the monitor to display the images sent by Ubuntu. There's wide choice of monitors available these days, with a wide variety of features, from standard old-style, picture-tube monitors to modern flat-screen plasma monitors. The combination of the video card features and monitor features determines the graphics capabilities of your workstation. Ubuntu needs to know how to use and exploit these features to produce the best possible graphics for the desktop and applications.

Given the wide variety of video cards and monitors available, it would be difficult for the GNOME desktop developers to have to code the features found in GNOME for every possible video card and monitor environment available. Instead, the X Windows software helps do that.

The X Windows software operates as an intermediary between the Ubuntu system and the input and output devices connected to the workstation. It's responsible for controlling the graphical environment so that GNOME doesn't have to support different types of video cards and monitors. Instead, the X Windows software handles all of that, and the GNOME software has to interact with just the X Windows software to display images on any type of video card and monitor combination.

Besides dealing with the video card and monitor, X Windows also handles any input devices attached to the workstation, such as the keyboard and mouse. It's the main clearinghouse for all interaction for the desktop environment. Figure 16-1 shows a typical X Windows system.

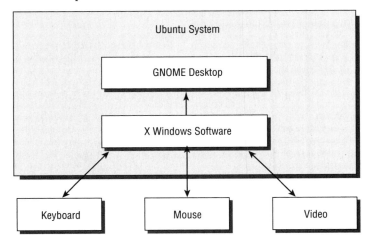

Figure 16-1: The X Windows system layout.

Because the X Windows software handles all of the input and output functions for the Ubuntu workstation, it's important to ensure that the X Windows software is working properly. It must know the type of input and output devices it's communicating with so that you can interact with your desktop.

The X Windows software is actually a specification of how to interact in a client/server methodology, serving the input and output devices to Ubuntu applications. Two popular X Windows implementations are currently available in the Linux world. The next section discusses them.

Linux X Windows Software

Over the years, two X Windows software packages have emerged in the Linux world:

◆ XFree86
◆ X.Org

Let's take a quick look at both of these packages.

XFree86

For a long time, the *XFree86* software package was the only X Windows package available for Linux. As its name implies, it's a free, open-source version of the X Windows software intended for the x86 computer platform.

Unfortunately, XFree86 is notorious for being extremely hard to configure and get working properly. It uses a cryptic configuration file to define the input and output device settings on the system, which is often confusing to follow. Having the wrong values set for a device could render your workstation useless! However, because XFree86 was once the only way to produce graphical windows on Linux PCs, it was necessary to learn how to use it.

As time progressed, several attempts to automate the XFree86 configuration were made. Many Linux distributions used a user-interactive method of automatically generating the XFree86 configuration file. Several dialog boxes would appear during installation, prompting the installer to select the video card and monitor setup from a list. The responses were then used to generate a configuration file.

There were also attempts at trying to automatically detect video card, monitor, keyboard, and mouse settings. Some of these attempts were better than others. These efforts, though, did eventually lead to another X Windows software package.

X.Org

More recently, a package called *X.Org* has come onto the Linux scene. It too provides an open-source software implementation of the X Windows system, but in a much more user-friendly way. It uses a combination of scripts and utilities to attempt to automatically detect the core input and output devices on a workstation, then creates the configuration file based on its findings.

X.Org is becoming increasingly popular, and many Linux distributions are starting to use it instead of the older XFree86 system. Ubuntu uses the X.Org package to produce the graphical X Windows you see for your desktop.

When you install Ubuntu, it goes through a series of steps to detect the input and output devices on your workstation (see Chapter 3, "Installing Ubuntu"). During the installation you may notice a time when it scans your video card and monitor for supported video modes. Sometimes this causes your monitor to go blank for a few seconds. Because there are many types of video cards and monitors out there, this process can take a little while to complete.

Unfortunately, sometimes Ubuntu can't autodetect what video settings to use, especially with some of the newer, more complicated video cards. If this happens, Ubuntu reverts to a default, safe X.Org configuration. The safe configuration assumes a generic video card and monitor and usually will produce a graphical desktop, although not at the highest resolution possible on your system.

If this happens in your installation, don't worry. Usually you can use the Screen Resolution utility (discussed in "The Screen Resolution Utility" section later in this chapter) to set the proper video mode for your setup. If all else fails, you can manually enter the settings in the X.Org configuration file.

The X.Org Configuration

The core of the X.Org configuration is the `xorg.conf` configuration file, located in the `/etc/X11` folder. This configuration file contains all of the settings detected by X.Org when you installed Ubuntu.

The `xorg.conf` configuration file contains several sections, each defining a different element of the input and output system. Each section itself may contain one or more subsections that further define the input or output device. The basic format of a section looks like this:

```
# Comment for a section
Section "Name"
EntryName EntryValue
...

...
Subsection "Subname"
EntryName EntryValue

...

...
EndSubsection
EndSection
```

The section and subsection areas consist of a name/value pair that defines a setting for the device, such as the type of mouse or the available viewing modes of a monitor.

Defining Sections

Nine predefined section names are used in the `xorg.conf` file:

- ◆ **Device:** Describes the characteristics of a video card.
- ◆ **DRI:** Includes information about the direct rendering infrastructure, which contains the hardware acceleration features found in many video cards.
- ◆ **Files:** Lists pathnames of font files along with the file containing the color database used for the display.
- ◆ **InputDevice:** Lists information about the keyboard and mouse or other pointing devices such as trackballs, touchpads, or tablets.
- ◆ **Module:** Defines X server extension modules and font modules to load.
- ◆ **Monitor:** Lists the monitor specifications.
- ◆ **ServerFlags:** Lists X server options for controlling features of the X Windows environment.
- ◆ **ServerLayout:** Combines one or more InputDevice and Screen sections to create a layout for an X Windows environment.
- ◆ **Screen:** Defines a video card and monitor combination used by the X server.

The sections appear on an as-needed basis. That is, you'll only see the sections defined in the X.Org configuration file that are actually used to describe devices on your workstation. Thus, if you don't have any special font or color files defined, you won't see a Files section in the configuration file on your Ubuntu workstation.

Example Configuration

To demonstrate the X.Org configuration file layout, let's take a look at an example configuration file from an Ubuntu workstation.

```
Section "InputDevice"
Identifier "Generic Keyboard"
Driver "kbd"
Option "XkbRules" "xorg"
```

```
Option "XkbModel" "pc105"
Option "XkbLayout" "us"
EndSection

Section "InputDevice"
Identifier "Configured Mouse"
Driver "mouse"
Option "CorePointer"
EndSection

Section "InputDevice"
Identifier "Synaptics Touchpad"
Driver "synaptics"
Option "SendCoreEvents" "true"
Option "Device" "/dev/psaux"
Option "Protocol" "auto-dev"
Option "HorizEdgeScroll" "0"
EndSection

Section "Device"
Identifier "Configured Video Device"
EndSection

Section "Monitor"
Identifier "Configured Monitor"
EndSection

Section "Screen"
Identifier "Default Screen"
Monitor "Configured Monitor"
Device "Configured Video Device"
EndSection

Section "ServerLayout"
Identifier "Default Layout"
Screen "Default Screen"
InputDevice "Synaptics Touchpad"
EndSection
```

This configuration file defines several sections for input and output devices. The first section defines an InputDevice—specifically, a standard U.S. 105-key keyboard as the input device. The section identifier for the device, Generic Keyboard, declares a name for the device. The driver that X.Org uses to manage the device is defined using the Driver entry. After that, the section includes a few options that define specific characteristics for the keyboard device.

The second section also defines an InputDevice, but in this instance it defines a standard mouse, using a standard mouse driver and no additional options. In the next section, you see yet another definition for an InputDevice, but this one defines a touchpad mouse used on a laptop. The touchpad uses a generic Synaptics driver to interact with the touchpad and defines a few options to control how the touchpad operates.

After the three `InputDevice` sections, the next three sections define the video environment for the workstation:

```
Section "Device"
Identifier "Configured Video Device"
EndSection

Section "Monitor"
Identifier "Configured Monitor"
EndSection

Section "Screen"
Identifier "Default Screen"
Monitor "Configured Monitor"
Device "Configured Video Device"
EndSection
```

You may notice something odd about the device and monitor sections that are defined in
the configuration file. The configuration file doesn't contain any drivers or settings for
the video card device or the monitor.

This X.Org feature is relatively new. When a device appears in the configuration file
without any settings, it forces the X.Org software to automatically attempt to detect the
device each time you start a new X Windows session.

Ubuntu started using this method in version 8.04 to help facilitate adding new video card
and monitor features after installation. By automatically detecting the video environment
each time the system starts, Ubuntu can detect when you install new hardware. The time
necessary to autodetect the new hardware isn't very significant, so the performance penalty of redetecting hardware is small, relative to the benefit of automatically detecting
new hardware.

The `Screen` section in the configuration file ties the monitor and video card together into
a single device for X.Org. Using this configuration, X.Org knows which video card and
monitor are paired. Although this feature is somewhat trivial in a single monitor situation,
if you have dual monitors and dual video cards, it's a must.

Secret

If X.Org is unable to detect your video card and monitor (or incorrectly detects
them), you can manually enter the settings in the `xorg.conf` file. When X.Org
detects manual settings for a device, it doesn't attempt to automatically detect
the device; it uses the predefined values instead.

For video cards, you'll need to enter the name of the video card driver used to
control the video card, plus any additional required options to define the video
card settings. Here's an example of a manual video card entry in the `xorg.conf`
configuration file:

```
Section "Device"
Identifier "Videocard0"
Driver "nv"
VendorName "Videocard vendor"
BoardName "nVidia GeForce 2 Go"
EndSection
```

continues

continued

The same applies to monitors. You can manually define settings for a monitor in the xorg.conf **configuration file so that X.Org doesn't attempt to automatically detect it. Here's an example of settings used for a monitor:**

```
Section "Monitor"
Identifier "Monitor0"
Vendorname "Monitor Vendor"
ModelName "HP G72"
DisplaySize 320 240
HorizSync 30.0 - 85.0
VertRefresh 50.0 - 160.0
Option "dpms"
EndSection
```

If you're using a special video card or monitor, the manufacturer often will provide the necessary X Windows driver and configuration settings required for it.

Once you've defined the video card and monitor, you must define a Screen section to link the two devices, plus define features for the screen:

```
Section "Screen"
Identifier "Screen0"
Device "Videocard0"
Monitor "Monitor0"
DefaultDepth 24
Subsection "Display"
Viewport 0 0
Depth 16
Modes "1024x768" "800x600" "640x480"
EndSubSection
EndSection
```

Ubuntu Video Configuration

After you've installed Ubuntu, you can perform a few manual changes to the X Windows system using graphical tools available on the desktop. This section walks through these tools for customizing your video environment.

The Screen Resolution Utility

The X.Org environment in Ubuntu is rapidly developing and changing. Further advances and ideas are implemented in each new Ubuntu distribution. Currently, the core utility for configuring your video settings in the Ubuntu desktop is the Screen Resolution utility.

Start the Screen Resolution utility from the Panel menu by selecting System ⇨ Preferences ⇨ Screen Resolution. The main Screen Resolution utility dialog box, shown in Figure 16-2, appears.

Figure 16-2: The Screen Resolution dialog box.

The Screen Resolution dialog box is pretty basic. There are only a few things you can modify here:

+ **Resolution:** Select the screen resolution from a list of supported resolutions for your video card and monitor combination. X.Org automatically detects resolutions that are supported and displays only those resolutions.
+ **Refresh Rate:** Select the screen refresh rate for your monitor.
+ **Rotation:** Set the screen orientation for the monitor. The options are
  • **Normal:** Display the desktop at the normal orientation for the monitor.
  • **Left:** Display the desktop using the left side of the monitor as the top of the desktop.
  • **Right:** Display the desktop using the right side of the monitor as the top of the desktop.
  • **Upside Down:** Display the desktop using the bottom of the monitor as the top of the desktop.
+ **Mirror Screens:** Create identical desktops on dual monitor setups instead of expanding the desktop to both monitors.
+ **Detect Displays:** Re-scan the video cards and monitors for the workstation.

The Mirror Screens option determines how X.Org handles two or more monitors connected to the workstation. When you select the Mirror Screens check box, X.Org duplicates the desktop on both monitors. However, when you deselect the check box, X.Org separates the two monitors and distributes the desktop layout between them.

When you use this feature, more screen areas appear on the Screen Resolution window area, one box for each monitor connected to the workstation, as shown in Figure 16-3.

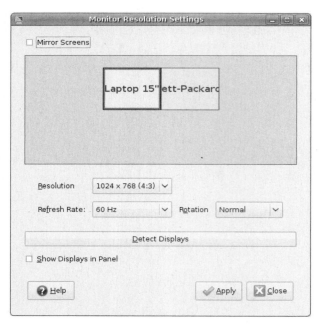

Figure 16-3: Using separate monitors in the Screen Resolution window.

You can drag and drop the different monitors in the window. The location of the moni-tor determines which part of the expanded desktop it displays. If you set the monitor images side by side, the desktop will expand sideways between the monitors. If you set the monitor images one on top of the other, the desktop will expand vertically between the monitors.

Each monitor image has its own group of settings. Click on a monitor image to view the settings for that monitor. By default, X.Org will set the display resolution of the two moni-tors to their highest common value.

Secret

If you plug a second monitor into a laptop to use as a cloned monitor, make sure that the additional video port on the laptop is enabled in the system BIOS settings. Some laptops disable external video ports when not being used.

Setting Compiz Fusion Features

If your workstation contains an advanced video card, besides the basic video settings avail-able in the Screen Resolution utility, you can enable advanced visual effects, depending on what your video card supports.

Ubuntu uses the *Compiz Fusion* software to provide advanced video features for the desktop. The Compiz Fusion software package is an open-source product that combines 3-D desktop features with advanced window management features using plug-ins. Ubuntu includes a generous sampling of plug-ins to provide lots of fancy graphical features for the desktop environment.

Ubuntu provides two interfaces you can use to control the Compiz Fusion features enabled on the desktop.

Basic Visual Effects

The Appearance Preferences window provides the Visual Effects tab for enabling or disabling the level of animated effects used on the desktop. To get there, select the System ⇨ Preferences ⇨ Appearance entry from the Panel menu, then select the Visual Effects tab. The resulting window is shown in Figure 16-4.

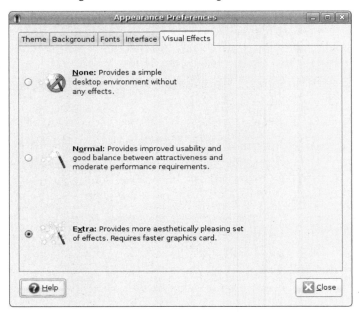

Figure 16-4: The Visual Effects tab in the Appearance Preferences window.

This window provides three generic settings for feature levels:

♦ **None:** No Compiz Fusion elements are enabled for the video card.

♦ **Normal:** Enables a few basic video elements, such as fading windows, to enhance the desktop look and feel.

♦ **Extra:** Enables advanced video features such as wobbly windows when you move a window, animations for windows operations, and extra window decorations to liven up your Ubuntu desktop.

The default setting depends on the capabilities of your video card. For basic video cards with no advanced features, Ubuntu sets this option to None by default. Unless you have a really old video card, you should be able to set this value to the Normal level. If you have an advanced video card in your workstation, try the Extra setting and see the extra effects in action!

Advanced Visual Effects

The Visual Effects settings provide a generic way to enable effects on your workstation. If your Ubuntu workstation is connected to the Internet, you can customize the Compiz Fusion visual effects settings by installing the *CompizConfig Settings Manager*. This tool allows you to enable and disable individual visual effects to liven up your desktop (if you have an advanced video card).

To install the CompizConfig Settings Manager, follow these steps:

1. Start the Add/Remove Applications program by selecting Applications ➪ Add/ Remove from the Panel menu.
2. Select the All section on the left side list and ensure that All Open Source applications is set for the Show drop-down box.
3. Type *compiz* in the search dialog box, then hit the Enter key.

   The search results will appear in the top application list, with the descriptions appearing below the list, as shown in Figure 16-5.

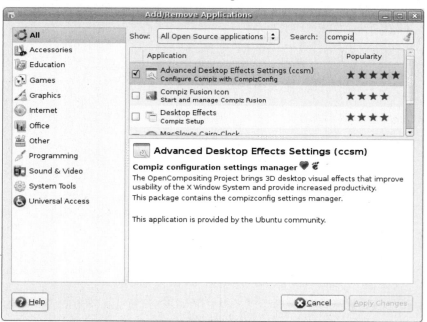

Figure 16-5: Searching for the Compiz applications.

4. Check the box for Advanced Desktop Effects Settings (ccsm).
5. Click the Apply Changes button to begin the installation. The Add/Remove Applications program will ask you to confirm your selection, then ask for your password to start the installation.
6. Close the Add/Remove Applications window.

Once you've installed the CompizConfig Settings Manager, you can access it by selecting System ⇨ Preferences ⇨ CompizConfig Settings Manager from the Panel menu. The default CompizConfig Settings Manager window is shown in Figure 16-6.

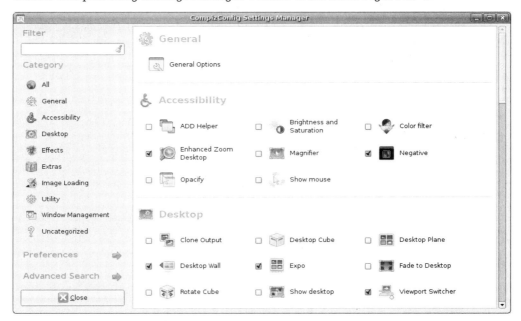

Figure 16-6: The main CompizConfig Settings Manager window.

The visual effects are divided into eight sections, shown in Table 16-1.

Table 16-1: CompizConfig Settings Manager Sections

Section	Description
Accessibility	Special video features to help the sight-impaired, such as desktop magnifiers, mouse pointer magnifiers, and color filters
Desktop	Effects for switching desktops, such as desktop cube (each desktop is displayed on the side of a 3-D cube) and desktop wall (flips the desktops from side to side or top to bottom)
Effects	Special effects when handling windows, such as wobbly or blurred windows when moving, and window reflections when stationary
Extras	Extra features such as advanced screen savers and using window previews from the taskbar
Image Loading	Plug-ins for loading different image types (and text) for windows
Utility	Plug-ins for adding functionality to other plug-ins, such as mouse handling and font scaling
Window Management	Plug-ins for handling windows on the desktop, such as resizing windows, moving windows, and switching applications
Uncategorized	Plug-ins to move a window or zoom in to the desktop

Each section contains a set of related plug-ins you can enable on your desktop. Each Compiz Fusion plug-in provides a different visual effect feature. Besides enabling an individual visual effect, you can customize it. Select a plug-in from the list to view and change the settings for the plug-in, as shown in Figure 16-7.

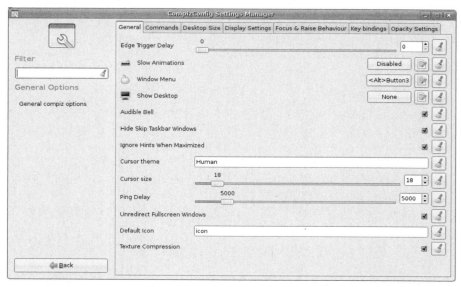

Figure 16-7: The General Options settings in CompizConfig.

Each plug-in has its own settings panel, which enables you to completely customize your desktop experience. Figure 16-8 demonstrates this feature using the Window Preview plug-in.

Figure 16-8: The Compiz Fusion Window Preview plug-in in action.

This plug-in displays a mini-sized version of the application window when you point to it in the bottom-edge taskbar. This allows you to quickly scan application windows when you have multiple applications running on your desktop, without having to switch between them.

Monitor and Video Cards

In the old days of Ubuntu (up to the 7.10 Gutsy Gibbon release), the Screens and Graphics utility was included so that you could manually change the video card and monitor settings for X.Org.

Because the Ubuntu developers are striving for automatic detection of the video environment using the Screen Resolution utility, the manual Screens and Graphics utility has been removed from the menu system. However, for the time being it's still included in the Ubuntu distribution, and you can use it to customize your video environment.

First, you need to add the Screens and Graphics utility to your menu. Follow these steps:

1. Select System ➪ Preferences ➪ Main Menu from the top panel. The Main Menu editor appears, as shown in Figure 16-9.

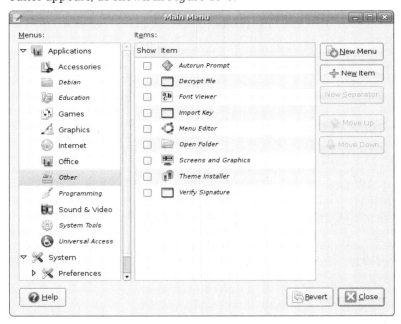

Figure 16-9: The Main Menu Editor window.

2. Click the Applications section drop-down arrow, then select the Other section heading. The list of other applications available appears on the right side of the window.

3. Select the check box next to the Screens and Graphics entry, then click the Close button.

This process adds the Other section to the Applications menu area and places the Screens and Graphics menu item in that section. To start it, just select Applications ⇨ Other ⇨ Screens and Graphics from the Panel menu. You'll see the main Screen and Graphics Preferences window, as shown in Figure 16-10.

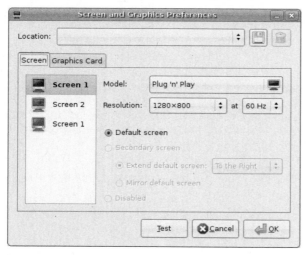

Figure 16-10: The Screens and Graphics Preferences window.

Now you're ready to manually configure your video card and monitor. The Screen tab shows the monitors detected on the system. You can manually set the features for each monitor, including its model and resolution capabilities. If you have multiple monitors, you can designate the default monitor and the secondary monitor. You can also indicate whether they should be cloned or, if you extend the desktop, which part of the desktop each one handles.

The Graphics Card tab, shown in Figure 16-11, lists the graphics cards detected on the system.

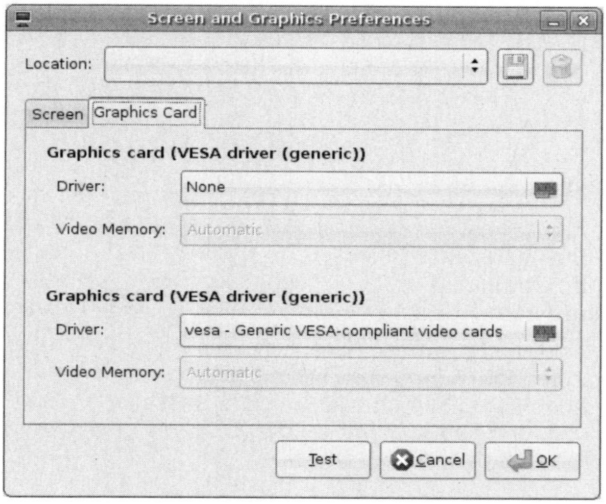

Figure 16-11: The Graphics Card tab.

This tab allows you to select the specific driver X.Org uses for the video card. You can select the driver by name used in the X.Org configuration file Driver entry, or you can select it from a list of video card manufacturers and models.

Once you've selected the video card and monitor settings, you can test your selection by clicking the Test button. X.Org will temporarily switch the desktop into the mode defined by the settings. In the new mode, a dialog box appears, asking whether you want to keep the new settings or revert to the original settings. Don't worry if your desktop is inoperable with the new settings. If you don't respond to the dialog box within 20 seconds, X.Org automatically reverts to the original settings.

Secret

Try to configure your desktop video settings using the Screen Resolution utility, if at all possible. Using the Screens and Graphics utility may (and usually does) break the default xorg.conf configuration file generated by Ubuntu. However, if X.Org can't automatically detect your video card or monitor, you have no choice but to resort to the Screens and Graphics utility.

Using 3-D Cards

In the past, one of the weaknesses of the Linux environment was its support for advanced video games. Many games popular in the Microsoft Windows world use advanced graphics that require specialized 3-D video cards, which Linux systems couldn't support.

In the past, specialized 3-D video cards were notorious for not working in the Linux environment because video card vendors never took the fledgling Linux market seriously. However, things are slowly starting to change. Two major 3-D video card vendors, ATI and NVIDIA, have released Linux drivers for their advanced products, allowing game developers to enter the Linux world.

There's a catch, though. Both ATI and NVIDIA released Linux binary drivers but not the source code for their 3-D video cards. A true open-source project must include source code for the binary drivers. This has caused a dilemma for Linux distributions.

A Linux distribution that includes ATI or NVIDIA binary drivers violates the true spirit of open-source software. However, if a Linux distribution doesn't provide these drivers, it risks falling behind in the Linux distribution wars and losing market share.

Ubuntu 3-D Support

Ubuntu has decided to solve this problem by splitting the difference. Ubuntu can detect ATI and NVIDIA video cards during the installation process and can install the proprietary binary drivers to support them. Ubuntu calls these *restricted hardware drivers*. Although Ubuntu supplies restricted hardware drivers, it doesn't support them in any way.

When you first log into the desktop after installation, Ubuntu displays a warning dialog telling you that restricted drivers have been installed. After the installation, an icon appears on the top panel, indicating that a restricted hardware driver has been installed and offering the option of removing the restricted drivers and replacing them with lesser-quality open-source drivers.

Secret

As with all things in the open-source programming world, there are current efforts to create open-source versions of many restricted hardware drivers. The Nouveau project is attempting to create a high-quality, open-source driver for operating NVIDIA cards in 3-D mode. At the time of this writing they've completed drivers for operating NVIDIA video cards in 2-D mode but haven't finished the 3-D features.

As Ubuntu progresses through new versions, it's possible that a video card that once required a restricted driver will have an open-source driver in a newer distribution.

Viewing Restricted Hardware Drivers

You can view which restricted hardware drivers Ubuntu installed by using the Restricted Hardware Driver Manager. Start the Restricted Driver Manager by selecting System ➪ Administration ➪ Hardware Drivers from the Panel menu. The Hardware Drivers window, shown in Figure 16-12, appears.

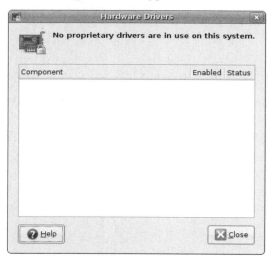

Figure 16-12: The Hardware Drivers window.

If restricted drivers for any hardware device have been loaded, they appear in this list. You can disable the restricted driver by removing the check mark from the box in the Enable column. You can also view the state of the installed driver.

Summary

This chapter discussed the software Ubuntu uses to control the display on your workstation. The Ubuntu video experience can be either a pleasure (if Ubuntu correctly detects your video card and monitor) or a nightmare (if Ubuntu can't correctly detect your video card or monitor). The chapter started out by walking through the basics of the X Windows software, which is the software that interfaces between the video card and the Ubuntu GNOME desktop. Ubuntu uses the X.Org open-source implementation of X Windows software. The X.Org software attempts to automatically detect the video card and monitor each time you start Ubuntu so that any new hardware you add to the system can be automatically detected.

Ubuntu provides a few basic tools for managing the display on the workstation. The chapter showed how to use the Screen Resolution utility to set the resolution, refresh rate, and orientation of the video on the monitor. Ubuntu also provides for configuring a dual display environment, by providing a graphical interface for managing which display covers which portion of the extended desktop (or to indicate whether the displays are clones of each other).

If you have an advanced video card installed in your workstation, Ubuntu lets you add some fancy visual effects to your desktop. The Visual Effects tab of the Appearances window allows you to enable advanced graphical features on your desktop, such as fading windows. For more control over the enhanced video, you can install the CompizConfig Settings Manager package. The chapter showed how to install that package and use it to manage the visual effects available on your desktop.

The chapter closed out by providing a brief word about restricted hardware drivers. Ubuntu provides restricted hardware drivers to support advanced hardware that doesn't have open-source drivers. Ubuntu uses the Restricted Hardware Driver Manager window to inform you when it has installed a restricted driver, and it offers you the opportunity to disable the restricted hardware driver and install an open-source one, if available.

The next chapter takes a look at access control on Ubuntu. Ubuntu employs the concept of users and groups to control access to files and folders. The chapter walks through using the graphical Users and Groups application to create, modify, and remove users and groups from your Ubuntu system, then demonstrates how to implement access control on your workstation.

Users and Groups

Chapter 17

◆ ◆

Secrets in This Chapter

The User Administration Tool

Command-Line User Administration

File Permissions

◆ ◆

U buntu controls all access to files and folders with user accounts. If you're the only person using your Ubuntu workstation or server, then you won't have much need for this chapter. However, if you're in an environment where you have to control access for several users on a system, it's imperative that you know how Ubuntu handles privileges and how to create and manage user and group accounts. This chapter discusses the Ubuntu User Administration tool, the graphical tool for managing your system users and groups. It also discusses how to handle user and group management from the command-line prompt, in case you need to do that without the GUI tool. The chapter closes out by discussing how to manage user and group accounts to restrict access to files and folders and how you can use them to provide an access control environment for your Ubuntu system.

The User Administration Tool

The User Administration tool is a graphical utility to help you easily manage users and groups on your Ubuntu workstation. Open the User Administration tool in the Panel menu by selecting System ➪ Administration ➪ Users and Groups. When you start it, the main window, shown in Figure 17-1, appears.

Figure 17-1: The Users Settings window.

When you first open the User Administration tool, you'll see a list of the full names of all the user accounts currently on the workstation. At this point, all you can do is view the properties of your own user account by clicking the Properties button.

If your user account has administrator privileges for the system (more on that in the "Adding Users" section, below), you can click the Unlock button and log in with your password to unlock the rest of the User Administration tool interface. After you enter your password, all of the user accounts in the list are available to edit, plus you can add new users or remove existing users. From the User Administration tool main window, you can perform just about every user and group management function required on your system. The following sections walk through the different functions you can perform.

Adding Users

When you first installed Ubuntu, it asked you for information to create your user account. That account has full administrative privileges on the Ubuntu system for adding and removing software packages, altering the running services, and, of course, adding and removing user and group accounts.

If you plan on sharing access to your Ubuntu workstation with others, you'll want to create a separate user account for each user. Having separate user accounts allows you to easily track in the system log files what each person does on the workstation (see Chapter 18, "Basic Administration"). Ubuntu also allows you to create a separate home folder for each user account, which lets all users store personal documents and any customized settings they make to the Ubuntu desktop.

To add a new user to the Ubuntu workstation, just follow these steps:

1. Click the Add User button. The New User Account window appears, shown in Figure 17-2 (remember to unlock the interface before trying to add a new user).

Figure 17-2: The New User Account window.

2. Type a username for the user in the Username text box. The username must start with a lowercase letter and must contain only numbers and lowercase letters.

3. For documentation purposes, type the full name of the user in the Real name text box. The full name makes it easier to identify a username. It's what Ubuntu displays on the top panel of the desktop, as well as in the User Administration list.

4. Select a default profile for the user from the Profile drop-down box. The profile sets up default files required for specific types of users. For example, if you select the Desktop user profile, Ubuntu automatically creates the default files required for the GNOME desktop in the user's home folder.

5. Enter contact information for the user in the Contact Information area. If you're working in a multi-user environment where you might not know everyone on the system, this can be a time saver. For example, as a system administrator you might come across a user trying to do something you need to stop. Knowing how to contact all your users can be crucial.

6. Select a password by either typing one in manually or allowing Ubuntu to automatically generate a secure password. Ubuntu won't let you select a password with fewer than six characters. Secure passwords are important. Don't allow users to select passwords that are simple to guess. The random password generator creates a nondictionary password that is difficult to guess (of course, it's also difficult to remember).

7. Select the User Privileges tab to assign system privileges to the user account. Ubuntu controls access to workstation features based on the access list. Figure 17-3 shows the Privileges check list, where you assign privileges to the new user account.

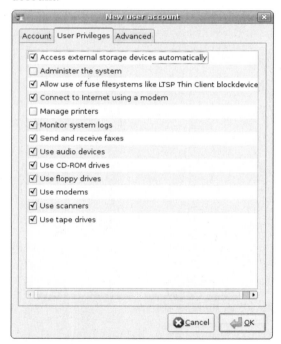

Figure 17-3: The User Privileges tab.

Select the privileges that you want the new user to have on the workstation.

8. Select the Advanced tab to modify the default settings for the new user account. The Advanced tab, shown in Figure 17-4, contains settings that control how Ubuntu creates the user account.

9. Create a home folder for the user. By default, Ubuntu creates a folder under the home folder with the same name as the username. This is where the user can store personal documents and settings. You can change this value if you want.

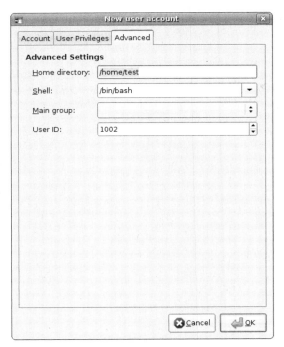

Figure 17-4: The Advanced tab.

10. Specify a login shell for the new user account. By default Ubuntu uses the bash shell (see Chapter 25, "Shell Scripts") for the user account. If you've installed additional Linux shells, they'll appear in this drop-down box, and you can select a different default shell for the user.

11. Select the main group that the user account belongs to. By default, Ubuntu creates a new group using the same name as the username, and assigns it as the main group for the user. If you want the user account to belong to another group as the main group, click the drop-down box and select the group from the list of existing groups.

12. Specify the user ID number. Ubuntu tracks users by a unique user ID number, so one must be assigned to the new user account. Ubuntu suggests the next available user ID number by default. You can change this value if you want to use your own numbering system, but if you do, be careful that you don't duplicate numbers.

13. Click the OK button to create the new user.

Once you've created the new user account, its full name appears in the user list in the main window.

When assigning privileges to a new user account, pay attention to the default privileges assigned by Ubuntu. By default Ubuntu allows users to do everything except administer the system and manage printers. You can customize the privileges to restrict what a user can do on the system, such as access the CD drive, view the system logs, or access external storage devices automatically.

If you want to allow a new user to be able to add new programs, or even install updates, you must select the Administer the System check box for that user.

Modifying Users

If you decide you need to update a user's information or change the privileges assigned, you can do so from the Properties window. Here are the steps for doing that:

1. Either double-click the user account in the list or select the user account and click the Properties button. The Account Properties window appears, as shown in Figure 17-5.

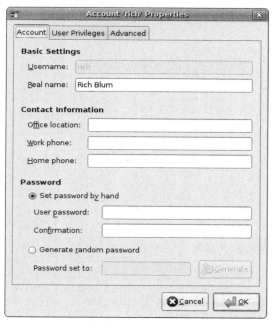

Figure 17-5: The Account Properties window.

Notice that the Account Properties window is the same as the New User Account window, except that existing data are already entered in the form fields.

2. Change any data for the user in the Account tab. The Account tab allows you to change information specified for the user, including his or her password.

Users can also change their own information and passwords using this interface.

Secret   Unfortunately, Ubuntu doesn't allow you to recover an existing password if a user forgets it. All you can do is change the password to a new value. Once you assign a new password, the user can log into the desktop, then use the User Administration tool to change the password to something else.

3. Click the User Privileges tab to modify the privileges set for the user account. Users can't change their own privileges unless they have the Administer the System privilege.

Be careful not to remove your own ability to administer the system! Ubuntu will happily allow you to remove the administer privilege from any account, including your own. If no user accounts have the ability to administer the system, no one will be able to add programs or updates or alter privileges for users.

If this happens to you, one way to fix the problem is to boot your workstation from the Ubuntu LiveCD, mount the root partition of the workstation, and manually change the group memberships of your user account in the /etc/group file (discussed later in the "User and Group Files" section).

4. Click the Advanced tab to modify the user account settings. From here you can change the location of the user's home folder and assign a new default shell if one is available. You can also reassign the user to a new main group on the system.

You'll notice that the Account Properties window doesn't allow you to change the user ID assigned to a user account. Changing this value would cause all sorts of file and folder privilege problems and is not recommended.

5. Click the OK button to save the changes and exit the Account Properties window.

Any informational changes you make to the user account take effect immediately (including changing the password). If you change the user's group, any new privileges assigned to that group may not take effect if the user is currently logged into the system. The user will have to log out and then back in for any group membership changes to take effect.

Deleting Users

Removing an existing user from the system is a snap. Just select the user account from the user list and click on the Delete button. A message dialog box appears, as shown in Figure 17-6, confirming that you want to remove the user account from the system.

Pay attention to the text of the warning in the Delete User dialog box. When you remove a user account, Ubuntu deletes the account but keeps the home folder and files for the user. If you also want to delete the user's files, you'll need to manually delete (from the home folder area) the folder with the user's username on it.

Figure 17-6: Delete User dialog box.

Ubuntu Groups

Individual user accounts are great for keeping documents and folders private on the Ubuntu workstation, but they are not at all useful for sharing documents and folders. Sharing documents is a common practice in many work environments.

The Ubuntu system provides another privilege level that facilitates sharing documents and folders. *Groups* are a collection of user accounts that have a privilege requirement in common. For example, you can create a group called "sales" that has read and write privileges to a folder specifically used for the sales team. Any user account that's a member of the sales group will have full access to any document in that folder.

Individual users can be members of more than one group, although only one group is considered the *main group* for the user account. The main group is what Ubuntu uses to assign group privileges on any files or folders a particular user creates. By default, Ubuntu creates a separate group for each user account to use as the main group. To keep things simple, Ubuntu names the user's group the same as the user account username.

The Ubuntu workstation comes with lots of groups already configured in the system. If you look at the groups, some of them should look similar to the options available in the User Privileges tab when you add a new user (see the "Adding Users" section earlier in this chapter).

Ubuntu creates special groups to control access to features on the system, such as administering the system and using specific hardware devices. To allow a user access to these features, Ubuntu assigns the user account to the appropriate group.

Besides these groups, Ubuntu also creates groups to be used by specific applications and services running on the system. Table 17-1 describes these groups.

All of the special groups have group ID values lower than 1,000, allowing Ubuntu to easily separate the special groups from the user groups. You can manage any of the groups on the system, but it's a good idea not to mess with the special groups unless you know what you're doing. Otherwise, the related services may break!

Table 17-1: The Default Ubuntu Groups

Group	Description
root	Assigned to the root administrator account
users	Used in some Linux distributions to contain all of the users on the system, but not used in Ubuntu
libuuid	Allows members to use external filesystems
syslog	Allows members to access the system logs
klog	Allows members to access the kernel log
scanner	Allows members to access an attached scanning device
nvram	Allows members to add modules to the kernel
fuse	Allows members to use the FUSE filesystem to mount removable media in their home folder without administrative privileges
ssl-cert	Special group used to control encryption certificates used for the server
lpadmin	Allows members to administer printers on the system
crontab	Allows members to schedule jobs for execution
mlocate	Allows members to use the mlocate database to locate files and folders on the system
ssh	Allows members to use an encrypted connection to communicate with a remote device
avahi-autopid	Special group used to control the automated IP detection software, which can determine an IP address on a network
gdm	Special group used for controlling the GNOME desktop services
admin	Allows members to control administrative functions on the system, such as adding programs and new user accounts
pulse	Allows members to use the audio configuration utilities
pulse-access	Special group used to control the audio detection services
pulse-rt	Special group used to control the audio real-time service features
saned	Special group used to run the software that controls network access to your local scanners
messagebus	Special group used to control internal application communications on the system
avahi	Allows members to use the automatic network device detection feature to detect devices on the network
netdev	Special group used by internal communications services
polkituser	Special group used by Ubuntu policy services
haldaemon	Special group used by the Linux hardware detection services

To manage groups on the workstation, click the Manage Groups button on the main User Administration tool window. The Groups Settings window, shown in Figure 17-7, appears.

Figure 17-7: The Groups Settings window.

All of the existing groups on the Ubuntu system are displayed in the group list. From here you can edit or delete existing groups or add new groups.

The following sections walk through the different ways you can manage groups using the User Administration tool.

Adding Groups

If you need to add a new group to your Ubuntu workstation, follow these steps:

1. Click the Add Group button from the Groups Settings window. The New Group dialog box, shown in Figure 17-8, appears.

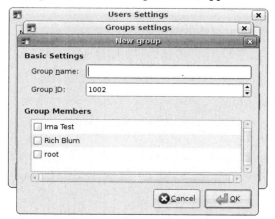

Figure 17-8: The New Group dialog box.

2. Enter a name for the new group. Group names must start with a letter and can contain only numbers and lowercase letters.

3. Select a group ID for the new group. Just like with user accounts, Ubuntu tracks groups based on a unique numerical ID value. The New Group dialog box suggests the next available group ID value on the system as a default. You can change this number if you desire, but be careful that each group you create uses a unique group ID value.

4. Select the members that belong to the new group from the user list. The user list displays the full names of each user account created on the system. Check the box next to each of the users you want to belong to the new group. The group will be added to that user's list of groups.

5. Select the OK button to save the new group definition and members.

The new group now appears in the list of existing groups on the main Groups Settings window.

Modifying Groups

Once you create a group, you can easily modify the properties of the group using the Groups Settings dialog box. Just double-click on the group you want to modify, or single-click to select the group and click the Properties button. The Group Properties dialog box, shown in Figure 17-9, appears.

Figure 17-9: The Group Properties dialog box.

In the Group Properties dialog box, you can select which users are in the group, and you can change the group ID value assigned to the group.

Secret

Be careful when changing the group ID value assigned to an existing group. Any files assigned to that group will keep the original group ID value, which means that group name won't have access to those files after you change the group ID value.

The easy way to change a group name is to reassign the existing group name to another group ID number, then create a new group using the original group ID number.

Deleting Groups

If you need to remove an existing group, just select it in the Group Settings dialog box and click the Delete button. Ubuntu will produce the warning message seen in Figure 17-10.

Figure 17-10: Deleting a group.

When you delete a group, any files that are assigned to the group retain the group ID value. That just means the group ID isn't assigned a group name. When you list the files, they'll appear with the group ID number instead of a group name.

User and Group Files

Ordinarily, it's a good idea to let the Ubuntu graphical utilities do all the hard work on the workstation, but user and group management is one of those areas where it helps to know what's happening under the hood. You may run into situations where you have only the command line available, and it helps to know how to manually add or modify a user account or group.

This section walks through the basics of the user and group system on the Ubuntu workstation.

The Users File

Ubuntu uses a system called *shadow passwords* to keep the encrypted passwords for each user in a secure location. This system requires using two separate files to track user account information.

The /etc/passwd File

The primary user account file is the /etc/passwd file. Despite what it says, that's not where user account passwords are stored. This file is set to be readable by every account on the system, because applications often need to know the users on the system.

A sample entry in the /etc/passwd file is

```
rblum:x:506:506:Rich Blum:/home/rich:/bin/bash
```

The entry contains seven data fields, each separated by a colon:

- The username
- A placeholder for the password
- The user ID number
- The group ID number
- The full name of user
- The home folder of the user
- The default shell

In the original days of Linux, the /etc/passwd file contained the actual encrypted version of the user's password. However, the /etc/passwd file must be readable to all users on the system so that the system can validate them. This requirement left the user passwords vulnerable to brute-force attacks using password-cracking software.

The solution to the problem was to hide the actual passwords in a separate file that's not readable by any user.

The /etc/shadow File

The /etc/shadow file is a secure file where Ubuntu stores the actual user account password, along with some other information about the account. Just like the /etc/passwd file, the /etc/shadow file contains a separate line for each user account.

A sample line from the /etc/shadow file looks like this:

```
rblum:Ep6sgekrHLChF.:10063:0:99999:7:::
```

The shadow password file contains eight data fields, each separated by a colon:

- The username
- The encrypted password
- The number of days since the password was last changed
- The number of days before the password may be changed
- The number of days after which the password must be changed
- The number of days to warn the user of an upcoming password change
- The number of days since January 1, 1970, that the account has been disabled
- Reserved data field that's not used

The Groups File

Ubuntu keeps track of all the group information in the /etc/group file. This file has each group on a separate line, using the format:

```
admin:x:115:rich
```

The group file contains four data fields, each separated by a colon:

- The group name
- A password, if assigned to the group
- The group ID value
- A comma-separated list of user accounts that belong to the group

Secret

Because Ubuntu doesn't use a specific root user account to administer the system, keeping at least one user account in the admin group is a must. If you accidentally remove all of the users from the admin group, no one will be able to add software patches or updates, add new users, or even move users to other groups.

If this happens to you, don't worry, there's a solution. Just follow these steps to get things back to normal:

1. Boot your workstation using the Ubuntu LiveCD.
2. Mount the workstation hard drive on the LiveCD's virtual file system.
3. Open a Terminal session on the LiveCD.
4. Use the command-line navigation commands (discussed in Chapter 19, "The Ubuntu Command Line") to navigate to the mount point of the workstation hard drive, then to the /etc folder on the hard drive.
5. Use a text editor to open the group file.
6. Find the admin group and add a username from your system onto the line. To append a value to a line in the vi editor, use the A command.
7. Exit and save the file.
8. Reboot the workstation and let the normal Ubuntu installation on the hard drive boot.

Once you've added the username to the admin group, it should have administrator privileges on the workstation.

Using the Command Line

Although it can be done, it's usually not a good idea to directly edit the /etc/passwd or /etc/group files. Bad things can happen, and you wouldn't want them to happen while you're in the middle of editing one of those two files!

Instead, the safer way to manage user and group accounts from the command line is to use the two commands explained in this section.

The User Commands

When working on the command line, you should use the adduser command to create a new user or add a user to an existing group. To add a user with the adduser command, use this format:

```
sudo adduser --home /home/rich rich
```

This command creates the new user account, rich, and creates a home folder at /home/rich for the account.

You can also use the adduser command to add an existing user account to a group:

```
sudo adduser rich users
```

This command adds the username rich to the users group.

The deluser command deletes a user account from the system:

```
sudo deluser rich
```

By default, the `deluser` command doesn't remove the home folder of the user. To do that, you need to add the `--remove-home` parameter:

```
sudo deluser --remove-home rich
```

Similar to the `adduser` command, you can use the `deluser` command to remove a username from a group:

```
sudo deluser rich users
```

These two commands give you complete control over user accounts from the command line, but there are more commands for controlling groups, discussed next.

The Group Commands

As you might have guessed by now, you can use the `addgroup` command to add a new group to the Ubuntu system:

```
sudo addgroup sales
```

This command creates the new group, `sales`, and automatically assigns the next available group ID value to it. To add users to the group, use the `adduser` command, shown in the previous section.

Finally, to remove a group, there's the `delgroup` command:

```
sudo delgroup sales
```

This command removes the group from the system, but any files or folders that you assign group privileges to will retain the group ID value.

Secret
If a group is set as the primary group for an existing user account, Ubuntu will prevent you from deleting it. If you want to ensure that you delete empty groups only, you can add the `--only-if-empty` parameter to the `delgroup` command. If any users belong to the group, Ubuntu will prevent you from deleting the group.

Understanding File Permissions

Once you set up specific groups that your user account belongs to, you can easily alter the privilege settings for files and folders using Nautilus. This allows you to share files and folders with other members of your group.

This section walks through how Ubuntu handles file and folder permissions and shows you how to modify them on your system.

File Properties

Ubuntu uses three classes of access control for files and folders on the system:

- The file or folder owner
- The default group
- Everyone else on the system

Each file and folder on the Ubuntu system has an *owner*. The owner of the file or folder is by default the username of the person who created the file or folder. Ubuntu tracks this value so that it can control the permissions of the file or folder, and it gives special permissions to the owner of the file. By default, the owner of a file or folder has full permissions to access, modify, and delete the file or folder.

Next, Ubuntu provides access permissions to a default group defined for the file or folder. By default, the group assigned to a file or folder is the main group of the user who creates the file or folder. You can change the default group for files and folders to allow sharing among different users in the group.

Finally, Ubuntu provides access permissions to all other users who aren't in the group defined for the file or folder. These access permissions can be set to none, preventing anyone else from accessing the file or folder.

Changing File Permissions

To see the permissions set for a file or folder, right-click on the object in Nautilus and select Properties from the menu. In the Properties window, select the Permissions tab. Figure 17-11 shows the Permissions tab settings for a folder.

The Permissions window shows the three separate groups of permissions that you can assign to the folder:

- Owner
- Group
- Others

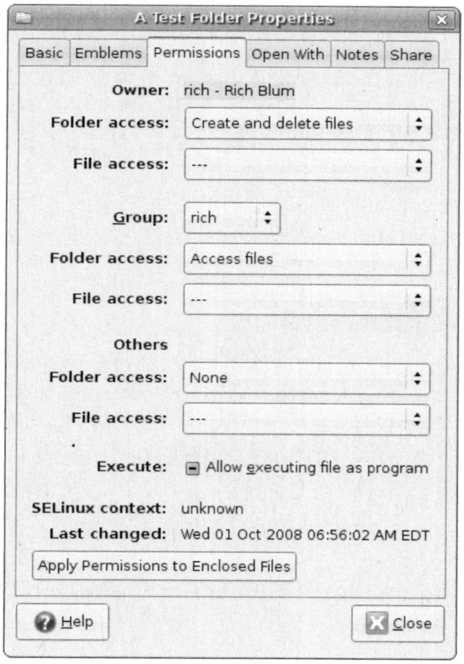

Figure 17-11: The Permissions tab in the Properties window.

These permissions correspond to the three classes of permissions for the file or folder. You set specific access rules for each group of permissions using the drop-down boxes provided. The permissions available depend on whether the object is a file or folder. The permissions for folders are shown in Table 17-2.

Table 17-2: Ubuntu Folder Permissions

Permission	Description
List files only	Be able to see the files in the folder but not be able to read or write to the individual files
Access files	Read and write to existing files in the folder
Create and delete files	Full access to all files in the folder, including creating new ones
None	No access to view or use the files in the folder

You can use these permissions to restrict access to a folder or allow access for other users to a folder if you want to share files on your system.

The permissions for an individual file are shown in Table 17.3.

Table 17-3: Ubuntu File Permissions

Permission	Description
None	No access to the file
Read-only	Only able to view the contents of the file
Read and write	Able to view and modify the contents of the file

Read-only permission allows you to permit others to view a file but not change its contents. This restriction can come in handy when posting information that you want to control on your system.

Summary

This chapter walked through the Ubuntu system of controlling user access. Ubuntu uses a system of user and group accounts to limit access to specific files, folders, and features of the Ubuntu workstation and server. The User Administration tool provides a graphical environment where you can create, modify, and delete user and group accounts. The chapter demonstrated how to manage user and group accounts using this tool.

The chapter also discussed how to perform user and group management using the command line programs `adduser`, `deluser`, `addgroup`, and `delgroup`. These programs provide all the access you need to manage user and group accounts from the command line.

Finally, the chapter showed how to use the Nautilus file manager to control permissions on files and folders. You can use Nautilus to assign specific permissions to users and groups to restrict access to files and folders or to share them.

The next chapter takes a brief walk into the world of Ubuntu system administration. Whether you're running an Ubuntu workstsation or server, it helps to know how to look under the hood and see what's happening on the system. The next chapter discusses some simple utilities you can use on your workstation to monitor the programs running on the system, as well as the overall health of the system.

Basic Administration

Chapter
18

◆ ◆

Secrets in This Chapter

Monitoring the System

Viewing Log Files

Managing Services and Programs

Monitoring Disk Usage

◆ ◆

N ot everything is fun and games on your Ubuntu workstation. There are a few things you should do to help ensure that your system is running properly. There are also times when things go wrong. When that happens, it helps to know how to look at various parts of your system and see what's going on. This chapter walks through some of the basics of managing your Ubuntu workstation. It discusses how to use the simple utilities Ubuntu provides for interacting with your system and determining how it's doing.

First we'll take a look at the System Monitor, which can provide some excellent information about what programs are running and how much of the system resources they're using. We'll then take a look at how Ubuntu uses log files to document when things go wrong on the system. Next, we'll look at a couple of utilities that Ubuntu provides for configuring which system services and applications run, both when your system starts and when you log into your desktop. Finally, we'll discuss the Disk Usage Analyzer tool, which allows you see where your disk space is going.

Monitoring the System

The best tool for administering your Ubuntu workstation is the System Monitor. Start the System Monitor by selecting System ⇨ Administration ⇨ System Monitor from the Panel menu. The System Monitor tool provides information about how the system hardware and software are working.

There are four window tabs of information in the System Monitor:

♦ **System:** Displays general information about the Ubuntu workstation.

♦ **Processes:** Shows real-time information about programs currently running on the system.

♦ **Resources:** Shows real-time information about CPU and memory usage.

♦ **File Systems:** Shows information about the hard drives that are mounted on the system.

Of course, just having a bunch of information thrown at you doesn't help at all. For that information to be useful, you need to know what it means. The following sections help you interpret the various pieces of information contained in the System Monitor.

System

The System tab provides an easy, one-stop-shopping location to find basic information about the system. There are three sections in the System tab:

♦ **Ubuntu:** Provides information on the version of Ubuntu installed, the Linux kernel version, and the GNOME desktop version.

♦ **Hardware:** Displays the processor type and the amount of physical memory installed in the system.

♦ **System Status:** Displays the amount of disk space available on the system.

Although not a major source of information, the System tab does provide some of the basic things you might be curious to know about your Ubuntu system, or might need to know if you stumble across another Ubuntu system and need to know what it's running.

Processes

In the Linux world, *processes* are the programs running on the system. It often helps to know what processes are running on the Ubuntu system, especially because many of them run in *background mode*. Processes running in background mode don't appear on your desktop, so you have no way of knowing they're running. These programs perform most of the behind-the-scenes work, such as monitoring the battery level in your laptop and scheduling programs to run at specific times.

Clicking the Processes tab provides an overview of the programs currently running on the system, as shown in Figure 18-1.

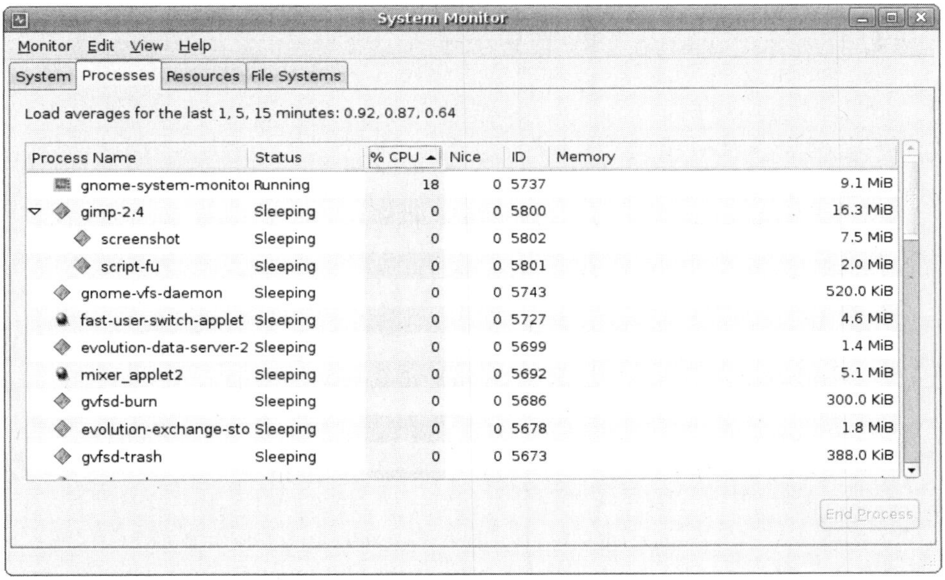

Figure 18-1: The Processes tab in the System Monitor tool.

Processes appear in a table format in the window display. The default view shows all processes currently being run by your user account. Alternatively, you can watch all of the processes running on the system, or just the ones that are actively working, by clicking the View menu item from the menu bar and selecting which option you want to view.

Selecting the Dependencies entry in the View menu reorders the process list to show which processes started which other processes. This option produces a drop-down tree, with parent processes at the top level and, below that, any child processes that the parent started. You can roll up the children processes and display only the parent processes by clicking the arrow icon next to the parent process.

You can sort the process rows in the list based on any of the table columns. For example, to see what processes are using the largest percentage of CPU time, click the % CPU column heading. The System Monitor automatically sorts the rows based on percentage of CPU usage. Clicking the column heading a second time reverses the order of the list.

You can customize the table by adding or removing data columns for the processes. Click Edit ⇨ Preferences with the Processes tab selected to see the options available for the Processes tab. Table 18-1 lists the data available to display in the Processes tab table.

Table 18-1: System Monitor Process Table Columns

Column	Description
Process Name	The program name of the running process
User	The owner of the process
Status	The status (either sleeping or running) of the process
Virtual Memory	The amount of virtual system memory allocated for the process
Resident Memory	The amount of physical memory allocated for the process
Writable Memory	The amount of memory allocated to the process currently loaded into physical memory (active)
Shared Memory	The amount of memory shared between this process and other processes
X-Server Memory	The amount of memory the process shares with the X Windows (GUI) server
% CPU	The percentage of total CPU time the process is using
CPU Time	The actual CPU time the process is using
Started	The time the process started running
Nice	The system priority of the process (higher nice numbers have lower priority on the system)
ID	The unique process ID (PID) the system assigned to the process
Security Context	The security classification assigned by the SELinux security system
Command Line	The name of the command and any command-line arguments used to start it
Memory	The amount of system memory the process is using

There are also a few other options you can set while you're in the Properties dialog box of the Processes tab:

◆ **Update Interval in Seconds:** Specifies how frequently the System Monitor refreshes the process table data.

◆ **Enable Smooth Refresh:** Gathers new process information before refreshing the process table data, rather than refreshing table data as it gathers process information.

◆ **Alert Before Ending or Killing Processes:** Produces a warning that you are about to terminate a running process.

◆ **Solaris Mode:** Calculates the percentage of CPU utilization based on the number of active CPU cores. Thus, if two separate processes are maxing out two separate CPU cores, they would both show 50 percent CPU utilization instead of both showing 100 percent.

You can also control processes that you own from the Processes tab. Right-clicking a process produces a menu that allows you to stop, end, or kill a process, along with entries that allow you to change the priority of the process.

The System Monitor allows you to stop only the processes that you own. These are processes that your desktop started when you logged in and any programs or applets that you run from your desktop environment. Unfortunately, it doesn't tell you that. It'll allow you to select a process that you don't own and click the End Process button. However, the attempt to end a process you don't own will fail.

To stop system processes you must have administrative privileges (see Chapter 17, "Users and Groups").

Resources

Clicking the Resources tab provides a quick graphical overview of the hardware status of the system, as shown in Figure 18-2.

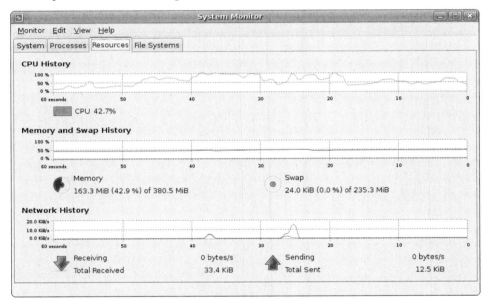

Figure 18-2: The Resources tab in the System Monitor tool.

There are three graphs displayed:

♦ **CPU History:** Displays the running real-time CPU percentage utilization. If the system contains more than one processor, each processor is shown as a separate history line.

♦ **Memory and Swap History:** Displays two running real-time graphs, one for the amount of memory used by the user and one for the amount of swap space used by the user.
♦ **Network History:** Displays the amount of data sent and received from the network interfaces.

Each graph displays the values for the last minute of operation, starting with the current time on the right side of the graph. The Resources tab can give you a quick overall picture of how your system is doing. If you see that the CPU or memory usage is running high, you can flip over to the Processes tab and sort the list based on that parameter.

Besides the graphical view, the Resources tab displays the current real-time information for each value, under the graph. The CPU History displays the current CPU load as a percentage of the CPU capacity. The Memory and Swap History displays the physical and swap memory areas used, as a pie chart icon. The more memory or swap space used, the more of the icon is filled. The Network History displays both the sent and received data on the network interfaces. It displays graphs of the current KB/s data flow on the network interfaces, as well as a numerical value of the total data sent and received since the system was started.

File Systems

Clicking the File Systems tab gives you a quick look at the amount of disk space used on each mounted filesystem, shown in Figure 18-3.

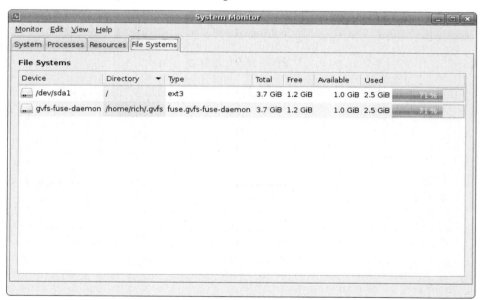

Figure 18-3: The File Systems tab in the System Monitor tool.

All hard drives and partitions mounted on the Ubuntu system are shown, along with their total disk space, free disk space, and used disk space. This tab gives you a quick indication of how much free space you have left on your hard drive.

Secret

You'll notice that there's a phantom entry in the File Systems devices, called *gvfs-fuse-daemon*. This is the GNOME Virtual File System (GVFS). The GVFS acts as a proxy to the real filesystem, translating read and write requests from a real mounted device and the GVFS object. The main purpose of GVFS is to allow normal system users to mount filesystems, especially removable filesystems such as USB Memory Sticks and CD-ROMs.

The GVFS simulates the root filesystem in the user's home folder so that any attempts to mount a media device can be made in the user's home folder area with the user's privileges instead of requiring root privileges. This crucial feature of the GNOME desktop allows normal system users to use removable media.

Log Files

An important part of Ubuntu system administration is knowing what's happening on the system. Because there's so much activity happening behind the scenes, it's often hard to keep tabs on your workstation. Fortunately, Ubuntu provides a relatively easy way for you to look at what's happening on the system. This section walks through the use of *log files* and explains how to easily view them all from one location.

Ubuntu Log Files

Ubuntu provides several levels of log files for the system. Log files are used by processes to track errors, warnings, and general items of information that may be important. It's usually a good idea to take a peek at the log files on a regular basis to see what's happening on the system.

The process that controls logging on the Ubuntu system is *syslogd*. The syslogd process runs in the background and directs log messages from applications and the Linux kernel to different log files. Because there's so much activity going on, Ubuntu uses several different log files to track different features of the system. All of the log files are stored in the /var/log directory on the Ubuntu system. Table 18-2 describes the different log files in that folder.

Table 18-2: The Ubuntu Log Files

Log File	Description
auth.log	System authentication events, such as login attempts
daemon.log	Background process events
kern.log	Linux kernel events
messages	Standard system and application events
syslog	System errors
user.log	User events
Xorg.0.log	X Window system events

Fortunately, you don't have to hunt for each of these log files individually. Ubuntu provides a handy utility that helps manage all of the log files from a single graphical interface.

Secret

The log files used by the `syslogd` process are defined in the `/etc/syslog.conf` file. This file defines what type of log entries are stored in which log files.

Log entries are classified by a tiered system, from lowest to highest priority:

- debug: application debugging messages
- info: informational messages
- notice: event notices from applications
- warning: minor error messages
- err: an error condition in an application
- crit: a critical system error
- alert: a system error that requires immediate action
- emerg: an error that prevents the system from running

Some Linux distributions provide a single log file for handling critical and alert messages, but Ubuntu doesn't use this technique. Instead, it separates log messages by source and importance.

For example, you'll find four log files for logging mail activity on the Ubuntu system: `mail.error`, `mail.info`, `mail.log`, and `mail.warn`. Each log file contains messages for the specified log level for the mail system.

The System Log Viewer

The System Log Viewer is a utility in the Administration menu (select System ⇨ Administration ⇨ System Log from the Panel menu). It allows you to quickly view all of the configured log files from a single location. Figure 18-4 shows the main System Log Viewer window.

The System Log Viewer window has three sections:

◆ **The log file list:** Lists the log files available to view. Log files with data that have been added since the System Log Viewer was started appear in bold.

◆ **The calendar:** Allows you to select a day from the log files to view. Ubuntu creates a new version of each log file each day. You can view any of the available daily log files by selecting the date in the calendar. Days with available log files appear in bold.

◆ **The log viewer:** Displays the contents of the selected log file.

The System Log Viewer uses *monitored mode* to watch the log files in real-time. This mode notifies you of new log file entries by displaying the log filename in bold in the log file list and making the new entries appear in bold in the log viewer. If your system is experiencing a problem that is quickly filling up the log file, you can disable monitored mode by selecting View ⇨ Monitor from the menu bar.

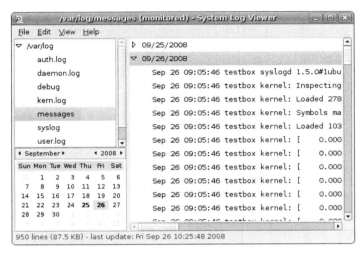

Figure 18-4: The main System Log Viewer window.

Starting Services

If you have administrative privileges, the Services Settings dialog box allows you to set which system programs start when you boot the Ubuntu workstation. This feature provides an easy interface for controlling system programs on your Ubuntu system without having to go to the command line.

This section discusses how you can control system services from the Services Settings dialog box.

Starting and Stopping Services

To start the Services Settings dialog box, select System ➪ Administration ➪ Services from the Panel menu. Figure 18-5 shows the main Services Settings dialog box.

Figure 18-5: The Services Settings dialog box.

As you can see from Figure 18-5, there's not much to the Services Settings dialog box. It lists the services you can control, with a check box for each service. The services that are already set to start when the system boots have a check mark in the box. You can set the service to not start at boot time by unchecking the box.

Similarly, you can select a new service to start at boot time by checking its box. The Ubuntu system adds the service to the list to start when the system boots. If it was successful, the check mark remains in the box. If it wasn't successful in setting the service, the check mark disappears. If that happens, you'll need to look at the messages log file using the System Log Viewer (discussed earlier, in the "Log Files" section of this chapter) to find any error messages indicating why the service couldn't start.

Table 18-3 shows the services you can control from the Services Settings dialog box.

Table 18-3: The Services Settings Dialog Box Services

Service	Name	Description
anacron	Actions scheduler	Schedules background processes for future days
atd	Actions scheduler	Schedules background processes for a later time in the same day
alsa-utils	Audio settings manager	Provides a common software interface for audio hardware
apport	Automated crash reports support	Debugging tool for producing reports when the system crashes
bluetooth	Bluetooth device manager	Interfaces with Bluetooth devices
britty	Braille display manager	Interfaces with Braille reading devices
klogd	Kernel event logger	Logs events from the Linux kernel
syslogd	Application activity logger	Logs events from processes running on the system
powernowd	CPU frequency manager	Controls the speed of the processor to conserve power on laptops
gdm	Graphical login manager	Provides the graphical login screen
hotkey-setup	Hotkeys manager	Detects type of keyboard in use and configures special keys
avahi-daemon	Multicast DNS service discovery	Detects devices on the network
acpid	Power management	Uses the Advanced Configuration and Power Interface to query and control battery life
apmd	Power management	Uses the Advanced Power Management system to query and control battery life
dbus	System communication bus	Provides a communications channel for applications to send and receive messages

The Ubuntu boot process is somewhat complicated because not all services start at the same time when you boot. You can define when specific services start, using the Properties feature of the Services Settings dialog box, discussed next.

Service Properties

Right-clicking on a service name in the Services Settings dialog box and selecting Properties displays the startup options for the service, as shown in Figure 18-6.

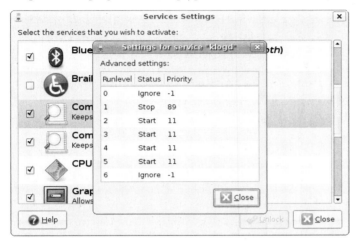

Figure 18-6: The Service Properties dialog box.

The Service Properties dialog box contains three columns of information:

◆ **Runlevel:** the operating mode level of the system
◆ **Status:** what state the service should be at
◆ **Priority:** the priority level the system should assign the service

The *runlevel* defines a mode of operation in a Linux system. Ubuntu is configured to start different types of applications when it enters different runlevels. Table 18-4 displays the runlevels available in Ubuntu.

Table 18-4: The Ubuntu Runlevels

Runlevel	Description
0	Halt the system
1	Start all system services but allow only a single user to log in
2-5	Start all system services, plus the graphical desktop environment
6	Reboot the system

The Ubuntu workstation usually runs at runlevel 5, which starts all of the system services and the graphical desktop. You'll notice that the properties for each service are the same for runlevels 2 through 5. Ubuntu doesn't differentiate among these runlevels.

The *status* defines what state the service should be in:

◆ **Ignore:** Don't worry about the service at this runlevel.

+ **Start:** Attempt to start the service at this runlevel.
+ **Stop:** Attempt to stop the service at this runlevel.

If you look at the status values in Figure 18-6, you'll notice that when the system is at runlevel 0 or 6, Ubuntu ignores the services. At runlevel 1, most of the services are stopped to allow the single user (the administrator) to log in and maintain the system. All of the services are started at runlevels 2 through 5.

The *priority* determines the order in which the system should start or stop services when the system enters the runlevel. This value is a number from 1 to 100, with 100 meaning that a service is a high priority and 1 meaning the service is a low priority. A value of –1 indicates that the service priority doesn't matter—the system can handle the service whenever possible.

Sessions

Although the Services Settings dialog box handles system services, it doesn't help out with the normal system processes that need to run. The Sessions Preferences dialog box helps you there.

Selecting System ⇨ Preferences ⇨ Sessions from the Panel menu starts the Sessions Preferences dialog box, shown in Figure 18-7. This interface allows you to control what programs run in your specific session.

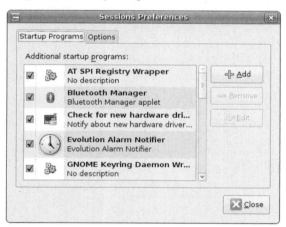

Figure 18-7: The Sessions Preferences dialog box.

There are two tabbed windows in the dialog box:

+ **Startup Programs:** Displays applets and programs that you've configured to start up when you log into the system.
+ **Options:** Allows you to set your session to automatically start any applications that are running when you log out and back in.

This section walks through how to control your session preferences using this utility.

Startup Programs

The Startup Programs list displays all of the applets and programs that you've configured in your desktop session to run automatically. This display includes any applets that you've added to your panel (see Chapter 4, "Exploring the Desktop"), such as the Network Manager applet, the Update Notifier, and the Volume Manager.

From this interface you can temporarily disable an applet or program from starting simply by removing the check mark from the Enabled check box. This action keeps the applet or program available to start later if you want—it just prevents it from starting the next time you log into the system.

You can completely remove an applet or program from the startup list by selecting the entry in the list and clicking the Remove button. Also, you can edit the settings an applet or program starts with by clicking the Edit button. The Edit Startup Program dialog box allows you to set command-line parameters used when starting the application, as shown in Figure 18-8.

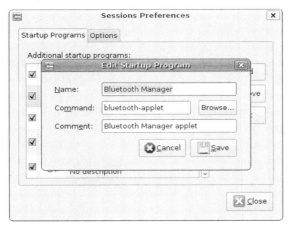

Figure 18-8: The Edit Startup Program dialog box.

Once you remove a startup applet or program from the session, it won't start for any subsequent sessions.

Options

The Options tab provides a way for you to save your existing sessions. The check box titled Automatically Remember Running Applications When Logging Out pretty much does what it says. It saves the currently running applications in the session manager when you log out and automatically starts them the next time you log in.

If you prefer to have specific applications automatically start, you can start the applications, then click the Remember Currently Running Applications **button**. This option saves all of the applets and programs currently running on the desktop in the session manager and attempts to start them every time you log into the system.

Disk Usage Analyzer

Disk space usage is one of the hardest things to manage on an Ubuntu system. With applications getting larger and digital multimedia becoming more popular, there never seems to be enough disk space available to do everything you want.

The problem with running out of disk space is that often you don't have a clue as to what caused the problem. With just the Nautilus file-browsing tool, you can't easily tell where all of the disk space is being used. Fortunately, Ubuntu provides a graphical tool to help you determine where all your disk space is going.

The Disk Usage Analyzer tool provides a quick and easy way to examine the layout of your Ubuntu filesystem and identify areas where disk usage is great. To start the Disk Usage Analyzer tool, click Applications ⇨ Accessories ⇨ Disk Usage Analyzer. The main window, shown in Figure 18-9, appears.

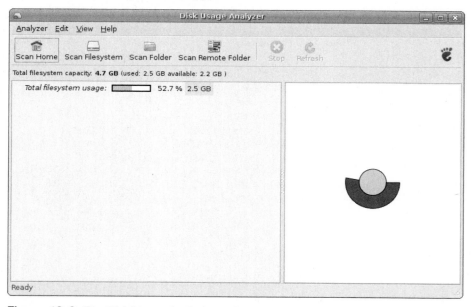

Figure 18-9: The Disk Usage Analyzer tool.

The main window displays the current state of the Ubuntu filesystem. The window displays the filesystem summary information at the top (the total amount of disk space in the complete filesystem, the amount used, and the amount available). If the filesystem contains multiple partitions, this window summarizes the totals of all of the partitions used in the filesystem.

The left side of the main window displays a graphical bar indicating the percentage of the filesystem disk space used, along with the numeric total. The right side of the main window displays a *treemap* of the results. A treemap graphically displays the hierarchy of each folder in the system. The default treemap shows the filesystem as a whole.

To perform a detailed analysis of your system, select one of the four scanning buttons in the toolbar:

◆ **Scan Home:** to analyze the folders contained in your home folder
◆ **Scan Filesystem:** to analyze the entire filesystem
◆ **Scan Folder:** to single out a folder to analyze
◆ **Scan Remote Folder:** to scan a remote filesystem

Be careful when selecting to scan the entire filesystem or a remote filesystem. Analyzing the disk space requires reading the entire disk area. This process can take some time, depending on the size of the disk and, in the case of a remote scan, network connectivity speeds.

The result of a complete scan is shown in Figure 18-10.

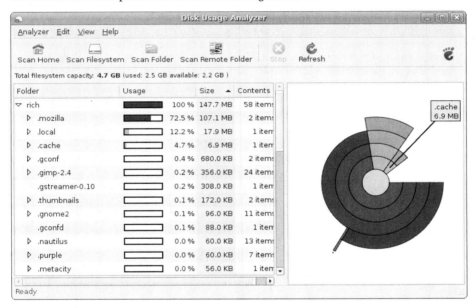

Figure 18-10: A complete disk scan analysis.

The treemap view can seem confusing at first, but once you get the hang of it you'll see that you can glean quite a bit of information from the treemap.

The treemap works from the core of the diagram outward. The core represents the top level of the tree. In my example, because I performed a home scan, the core is my home folder, /home/rich. If you hover the mouse pointer over the core, it shows the name of the folder and the amount of disk space used by that folder.

The next layer of rings depicts the next level of folders. In my home folder I have three subfolders. Each subfolder is a section of the first-layer ring, and its size is relative to the amount of used disk space in that subfolder.

The second layer of rings relate to the first layer. If there are subfolders beneath a subfolder, they appear in the second layer of rings, above their parent folder. Again, each folder in the second layer has a size relative to the amount of disk space it uses.

This process continues for however many subfolders are contained in the filesystem being analyzed. You can quickly spot areas that use the most disk space by looking at the relative size of the ring sections (you can compare ring section sizes only on the same layer). This tool provides a great way to see at a glance where all of your disk space is going!

Summary

This chapter discussed some of the system administration utilities provided in the Ubuntu workstation. The System Monitor allows you to monitor and control processes running on the system, as well as view the current CPU, memory, network, and disk utilization on that system.

The System Log Viewer provides an easy way to view all of the log files available in the Ubuntu workstation from a single window. You can view those log files, plus look at the daily log files from separate days that are stored on the system.

The Services Settings window allows you to view and change which system services are started when the system boots. You can select which services start, what system runlevel they start in, and the priority (order) in the runlevel that they start.

Separate from the Services Settings window, the Sessions Preferences window allows you to configure the individual applets and programs that automatically start when you log into your desktop. The Sessions Preferences window provides options for selecting which applets and programs start, for viewing which applets and programs are currently running in your session, and for saving your session settings so that the same applets and programs start the next time you log in.

The last section of this chapter discussed how to use the Disk Usage Analyzer tool. This tool helps you identify the areas in a filesystem that use the most amount of disk space. The Disk Usage Analyzer scans a disk area (or the entire disk) and provides a graphical treemap of the results. Each ring on the treemap represents a folder level in the filesystem hierarchy. Folders at the same level in the same ring are depicted with sizes relative to the amount of disk space they use.

In the next chapter we'll take a look at the Ubuntu command line. The command-line interface can come in handy when trying to administer your system because it's often quicker to enter commands than to interact with a graphical tool.

The Ubuntu Command Line

Chapter 19

Although Ubuntu is known for its fancy, user-friendly graphical desktop interface, there may be times when you have to interface directly with the underlying Ubuntu operating system at a more primitive level. The core of the Ubuntu operating system is Linux, and the main mechanism for interfacing with Linux is the command line. The command line provides direct control over what's running on the system. Knowing how to use the command line is a great benefit to anyone but is a necessity for server system administrators. This chapter discusses how to use the Terminal program, which is an easy way to get to the Ubuntu command line from the graphical desktop, then walks through how to perform some basic filesystem functions from the command line.

The GNOME Terminal Program

Ubuntu uses the GNOME Terminal software package to provide a graphical interface to the command line. To start the GNOME Terminal, select Applications ⟹ Accessories ⟹ Terminal from the Panel menu. The main GNOME Terminal window, shown in Figure 19-1, appears.

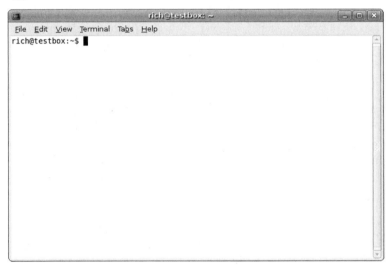

Figure 19-1: The main GNOME Terminal window.

Although the Terminal program provides basic access to the Ubuntu command line, it has several features that can come in handy. This section walks through the various parts of configuring and using the GNOME Terminal.

Session Tabs

The GNOME Terminal calls each session a *tab* because it uses tabs to keep track of multiple sessions running within the window. Figure 19-2 shows a GNOME Terminal window with three session tabs active.

Figure 19-2: The GNOME Terminal with three active sessions.

You can right-click in the tab window to see the tab menu. This quick menu lets you do a few things in the tab session:

- ◆ **Open Terminal:** Open a new GNOME Terminal window with a default tab session.
- ◆ **Open Tab:** Open a new session tab in the existing GNOME Terminal window.
- ◆ **Close Tab:** Close the current session tab.
- ◆ **Copy:** Copy highlighted text in the current session tab to the clipboard.
- ◆ **Paste:** Paste data from the clipboard to the current session tab at the cursor location.
- ◆ **Change Profile:** Change the profile for the current session tab.
- ◆ **Edit Current Profile:** Edit the profile for the current session tab.
- ◆ **Show Menu Bar:** Toggle whether the menu bar is hidden or visible.
- ◆ **Input Methods:** Set the types of inputs (including special language keys) allowed in the Terminal window.

The quick menu provides easy access to commonly used actions that are available from the standard menu bar in the Terminal window.

The Menu Bar

The main operation of GNOME Terminal occurs in the menu bar. The menu bar contains all of the configuration and customization options you'll need to set up your GNOME Terminal just the way you want it. The following sections describe the different items in the menu bar.

File

The File menu contains items to create and manage the Terminal tabs.

- ◆ **Open Terminal:** Starts a new shell session in a new GNOME Terminal window.
- ◆ **Open Tab:** Starts a new shell session in a new tab in the existing GNOME Terminal window.
- ◆ **New Profile...:** Allows you to customize the tab session and save it as a profile that you can recall for use later.
- ◆ **Close Tab:** Closes the current tab in the window.
- ◆ **Close Window:** Closes the current GNOME Terminal session, including all active tabs.

Most of the items in the File menu are also available by right-clicking in the session tab area.

The New Profile entry allows you to customize your session tab settings and save them for future use. The New Profile first requests that you provide a name for the new profile, then produces the Editing Profile dialog box, shown in Figure 19-3.

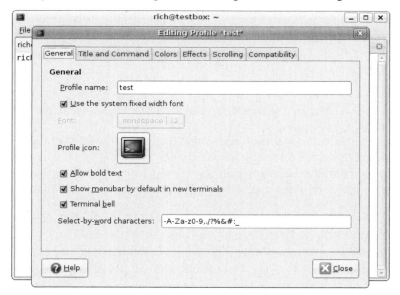

Figure 19-3: The GNOME Terminal Editing Profile dialog box.

In this dialog box you can set the Terminal emulation features for the session. It consists of six areas:

- ◆ **General:** Provides general settings such as font, the bell, and the menu bar (which beeps when you've reached the end of a line of text).
- ◆ **Title and Command:** Allows you to set the title for the session tab (displayed on the tab) and determine whether the session starts with a special command rather than a shell.
- ◆ **Colors:** Sets the foreground and background colors used in the session tab.
- ◆ **Effects:** Allows you to set a background image for the session tab or make it transparent so you can see the desktop through the session tab.

- ◆ **Scrolling:** Controls whether a scroll region is created, and how large.
- ◆ **Compatibility:** Allows you to set what control codes the Backspace and Delete keys send to the system.

Once you configure a profile, you can specify it when opening new session tabs, and those features are automatically set by Terminal for the tab session.

Edit

The Edit menu contains items for handling text within the tabs. You can use your mouse to copy and paste text anywhere within the tab window. This feature allows you to easily copy text from the command-line output to a clipboard and import it into an editor. You can also paste text from another GNOME application into the tab session.

- ◆ **Copy:** Copy selected text to the GNOME clipboard.
- ◆ **Paste:** Paste text from the GNOME clipboard into the tab session.
- ◆ **Profiles...:** Add, delete, or modify profiles in the GNOME Terminal.
- ◆ **Keyboard Shortcuts...:** Create key combinations to quickly access GNOME Terminal features.
- ◆ **Current Profile...:** Provides a quick way to edit the profile used for the current session tab.

The profile editing feature is an extremely powerful tool for customizing several profiles, then changing profiles as you change sessions.

View

The View menu contains items for controlling how the session tab windows appear.

- ◆ **Show Menubar:** Either shows or hides the menu bar.
- ◆ **Full Screen:** Enlarges the GNOME Terminal window to the entire desktop.
- ◆ **Zoom In:** Makes the font in the session windows larger.
- ◆ **Zoom Out:** Makes the font in the session windows smaller.
- ◆ **Normal Size:** Returns the session font to the default size.

If you hide the menu bar, you can easily get it back by right-clicking in any session tab and toggling the Show Menubar item.

Terminal

The Terminal menu contains items for controlling the terminal emulation features of the tab session.

- ◆ **Change Profile:** Allows you to switch to another configured profile in the session tab.
- ◆ **Set Title...:** Sets the title on the session tab to easily identify it.
- ◆ **Set Character Encoding:** Selects the character set used to send and display characters.
- ◆ **Reset:** Sends the reset control code to the Linux system.
- ◆ **Reset and Clear:** Sends the reset control code to the Linux system and clears any text currently showing in the tab area.

The character encoding offers a large list of character sets to choose from. This feature is especially handy if you must work in a language other than English.

Tabs

The Tabs menu provides items for controlling the location of the tabs and selecting which tab is active.

◆ **Previous Tab:** Makes the previous tab in the list active.

◆ **Next Tab:** Makes the next tab in the list active.

◆ **Move Tab to the Left:** Shuffles the current tab in front of the previous tab.

◆ **Move Tab to the Right:** Shuffles the current tab in front of the next tab.

◆ **Detach Tab:** Removes the tab and starts a new GNOME Terminal window using this tab session.

◆ **The Tab List:** Lists the currently running session tabs in the Terminal window. Select a tab to quickly jump to that session.

This section allows you to manage your tabs, which can come in handy if you have several tabs open at once.

Help

The Help menu provides the full GNOME Terminal manual so that you can research individual items and features used in GNOME Terminal.

The Command-Line Parameters

You can also start the GNOME Terminal application from a command line using the command:

```
gnome-terminal
```

The GNOME Terminal application provides a wealth of command-line parameters that allow you to control its behavior when starting it. Table 19-1 lists the parameters available.

Table 19-1: The GNOME Terminal Command-Line Parameters

Parameter	Description
-e command	Execute the specified command inside a default Terminal window
-x	Execute the entire contents of the command line after this parameter inside a default Terminal window
--window	Open a new window with a default Terminal window (you may add multiple --window parameters to start multiple windows)
--window-with-profile=	Open a new window with a specified profile (you may also add this parameter multiple times to the command line)
--tab	Open a new tabbed Terminal window inside the last opened Terminal window
--tab-with-profile=	Open a new tabbed Terminal window inside the last opened Terminal window, using the specified profile
--role=	Set the role for the last specified window

Table 19-1: *(continued)*

Parameter	*Description*
--show-menubar	Enable the menu bar at the top of the Terminal window
--hide-menubar	Disable the menu bar at the top of the Terminal window
--full-screen	Display the Terminal window fully maximized
--geometry=	Specify the X Window geometry parameter
--disable-factory	Don't register with the activation nameserver
--use-factory	Register with the activation nameserver
--startup-id=	Set the ID for the Linux startup notification protocol
-t, --title=	Set the window title for the Terminal window
--working-directory=	Set the default working directory for the Terminal window
--zoom=	Set the Terminal window's zoom factor
--active	Set the last specified Terminal tab as the active tab

The GNOME Terminal command-line parameters allow you to set a number of features automatically as the GNOME Terminal starts. However, you can also set most of these features from within the GNOME Terminal window after it starts.

Command-Line Basics

Once you've started the Terminal program, you have the command-line prompt at your disposal. Now you'll need to know what you can do from here to interact directly with the Ubuntu system. This section goes over the basics of moving around the Ubuntu filesystem and manipulating the files that are there.

Setting the command prompt

The Ubuntu workstation uses the popular *bash shell* as the command-line interface. The bash shell provides an interactive environment for you to start programs, view running programs, and manage files on the system.

Once you start the Terminal package you get access to the shell command-line interface (CLI) prompt. The prompt is your gateway to the shell. This is the place where you enter shell commands.

The default prompt symbol for the bash shell is the dollar sign ($). This symbol indicates that the shell is waiting for you to enter text. However, you can change the format of the prompt used by your shell. In fact, Ubuntu sets a specific default format for the prompt. The default Ubuntu bash shell prompt looks like this:

```
rich@testbox:~$
```

You can configure the prompt to provide basic information about your environment. The Ubuntu default shows three pieces of information in the prompt:

◆ The username that started the shell

◆ The hostname of the workstation

◆ The current directory (the tilde symbol is shorthand for the home directory)

Two *environment variables* control the format of the command-line prompt:

◆ **PS1:** Controls the format of the default command-line prompt.

◆ **PS2:** Controls the format of the second-tier command-line prompt.

Environment variables are values that are set in the bash shell to store information. The shell itself sets several environment variables when you boot the Ubuntu system. You can access these variables to determine information about the shell environment.

The shell uses the default PS1 prompt for initial data entry into the shell. If you enter a command that requires additional information, the shell displays the second-tier prompt specified by the PS2 environment variable.

To display the current settings for your prompts, use the echo command:

```
rich@testbox:~$ echo $PS1
${debian_chroot:+($debian_chroot)}\u@\l[\W]\$
rich@testbox:~$ echo $PS2
>
rich@testbox:~$
```

The format of the prompt environment variables can look odd. The shell uses special characters to signify elements within the command-line prompt. Table 19-2 shows the special characters that you can use in the prompt string.

Table 19-2: bash Shell Prompt Characters

Character	Description
\a	Bell character
\d	Date, in the format "day month date"
\e	ASCII escape character
\h	Local hostname
\H	Fully qualified domain hostname
\j	Number of jobs currently managed by the shell
\l	Basename of the shell's terminal device name
\n	ASCII new-line character
\r	ASCII carriage return
\s	Name of the shell
\t	Current time in 24-hour HH:MM:SS format
\T	Current time in 12-hour HH:MM:SS format

Table 19-2: *(continued)*

Character	Description
\@	Current time in 12-hour a.m./p.m. format
\u	Username of the current user
\v	Version of the bash shell
\V	Release level of the bash shell
\w	Current working directory
\W	Basename of the current working directory
\!	bash shell history number of this command
\#	Command number of this command
\$	A dollar sign if a normal user, or a pound sign if the root user
\nnn	Character corresponding to the octal value *nnn*
\\	Backslash
\[	Begin a control code sequence
\]	End a control code sequence

Notice that all of the special prompt characters begin with a backslash (\). The backslash distinguishes a prompt character from normal text in the prompt. In the earlier example, the prompt contained prompt characters and a normal character (the @ sign and the square brackets). You can create any combination of prompt characters in your prompt. To create a new prompt, just assign a new string to the PS1 variable:

```
rich@testbox:~$ PS1="[\t][\u]\$ "
[14:40:32][rich]$
```

This new shell prompt now shows the current time, along with the username. The new PS1 definition lasts only for the duration of the shell session. When you start a new shell, the default shell prompt definition is reloaded.

Secret

When you change the bash shell environment variables, the changes apply only to the current shell. To make changes that apply each time the bash shell runs, you need to store them in a special file, called the *profile*.

The profile file is called .bashrc, and it's located in your home folder. The bash shell processes this file each time it starts. You can set any environment variable you want in this file using the export command:

```
export PS1="[\t][\u]\$ "
```

By adding this command to the bottom of the existing .bashrc file in your home folder, your command-line prompt will always show the current time and your user account.

The bash Manual

Ubuntu includes an online manual for looking up information on shell commands, as well as many other GNU utilities included in the distribution. It is a good idea to become familiar with the manual because it's invaluable for working with utilities, especially when trying to figure out various command-line parameters.

The man command provides access to the manual pages stored on the Linux system. Entering the man command followed by a specific utility name provides the manual entry for that utility. Figure 19-4 shows an example of looking up the manual pages (called *man pages*) for the date command.

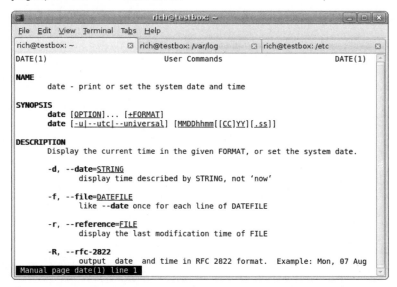

Figure 19-4: Displaying the manual pages for the Linux date command.

The manual page divides information about the command into separate sections, shown in Table 19-3.

Table 19-3: The Linux man Page Format

Section	Description
Name	Displays the command name and a short description
Synopsis	Shows the format of the command
Description	Describes each command option
Author	Provides information on the person who developed the command
Reporting Bugs	Provides information on where to report any bugs found
Copyright	Contains information on the copyright status of the command code
See Also	Refers you to any similar commands available

You can step through the man pages by pressing the spacebar or using the arrow keys to scroll forward and backward through the man page text (assuming your terminal emulation package supports the arrow key functions). To exit the man pages, just hit the Q key.

To see information about the bash shell, look at the man pages for it using the command:

```
$ man bash
```

This command allows you to step through the entire man pages for the bash shell. The information is extremely handy when working on the command line because you don't have to refer to books or Internet sites to look up specific formats for commands. The manual is always there for you in your session.

Traversing Directories

The change directory command (cd) is what you use to move your shell session to another directory in the Ubuntu filesystem. The format of the cd command is pretty simple:

```
cd destination
```

The cd command may take a single parameter, *destination*, which specifies the directory name you want to go to. If you don't specify a destination on the cd command, it will take you to your home directory.

The destination parameter can be expressed by two methods:

- ◆ An absolute filepath
- ◆ A relative filepath

The following sections describe the differences between these two methods.

Absolute Filepaths

You can reference a directory name within the Ubuntu virtual directory using an *absolute filepath*. The absolute filepath defines exactly where the directory is in the virtual directory structure, starting at the root of the virtual directory. Thus, to reference the X11 directory that's in the lib directory, which in turn is in the usr directory, you would use the absolute filepath:

```
/usr/lib/X11
```

With the absolute filepath there's no doubt as to where you want to go. To move to a specific location in the filesystem using the absolute filepath, just specify the full pathname in the cd command:

```
rich@testbox:~$cd /etc
rich@testbox:/etc$
```

The prompt shows that the new directory for the shell after the cd command is now /etc. You can move to any level within the entire Linux virtual directory structure using the absolute filepath:

```
rich@testbox:/etc$ cd /usr/lib/X11
rich@testbox:/usr/lib/X11$
```

However, if you're working within your own home directory structure, using absolute filepaths can often be tedious. For example, if you're already in the directory /home/rich, it seems cumbersome to have to type the command

```
cd /home/rich/Documents
```

just to get to your Documents directory. Fortunately, there's a simpler solution.

Relative Filepaths

Relative filepaths allow you to specify a destination filepath relative to your current location, without having to start at the root. A relative filepath doesn't start with a forward slash (the forward slash indicates the root directory).

Instead, a relative filepath starts with either a directory name (if you're traversing to a directory under your current directory) or a special character indicating a relative location to your current directory location. The two special characters used for this purpose are

- ◆ The single dot (.)represents the current directory.
- ◆ The double dot (..) represents the parent directory.

The double-dot character is extremely handy when trying to traverse through a directory hierarchy. For example, if you are in the Documents directory under your home directory and need to go to your Desktop directory, also under your home directory, you can do this:

```
rich@testbox:~/Documents$ cd ../Desktop
rich@testbox:~/Desktop$
```

The double-dot character takes you back up one level to your home directory, then the /Desktop portion of the command takes you back down into the Desktop directory. You can use as many double-dot characters as necessary to move around. For example, if you are in your home directory (/home/rich) and want to go to the /etc directory, you could type

```
rich@testbox:~$ cd ../../etc
rich@testbox:/etc$
```

Of course, in that example, you actually have to do more typing to use the relative filepath. It would be quicker to type the absolute filepath, /etc.

File and Directory Listing

The most basic feature of the shell is its ability to show you what files are available on the system. The list command (ls) is the tool that helps do that. This section describes the ls command and all of its options for format the file information.

Basic Listing

The ls command at its most basic form displays the files and directories in your current directory:

```
$ ls
4rich Desktop Download Music Pictures store store.zip test
backup Documents Drivers myprog Public store.2 Templates Videos
$
```

Notice that the ls command produces the list in alphabetical order (in columns rather than rows). If you're using a profile in a Terminal session that supports color, the ls command will also show different types of entries in different colors. The LS_COLORS environment variable controls this feature.

The basic list isn't all that exciting. Fortunately, you can modify the way the ls command displays data. You can use *parameters* with a command to modify the default behavior of the program. Command-line parameters are preceded by a dash to distinguish them from data.

For example, if you don't use color to distinguish the different types of entries, use the -F parameter with the ls command to add symbols to the file and directory names to easily distinguish files from directories. Using the -F parameter produces the following output:

```
$ ls -F
4rich/ Documents/ Music/ Public/ store.zip Videos/
backup.zip Download/ myprog* store/ Templates/
Desktop/ Drivers/ Pictures/ store.2 test
$
```

The -F parameter now flags the directories with a forward slash to help identify them in the list. Similarly, it flags executable files (like the myprog file in the example) with an asterisk to help you easily identify the files that can be run on the system.

The output of the basic ls command can be misleading. It shows the files and directories contained in the current directory, but not necessarily all of them. Linux often uses hidden files to store configuration information. In Linux, hidden files have filenames that start with a period. These files don't appear in the default ls list (thus, they are called *hidden*).

To display hidden files along with normal files and directories, use the -a parameter. Figure 19-5 shows an example of using the -a parameter with the ls command.

Figure 19-5: Using the -a parameter with the ls command.

In a home directory for a user who has logged into the Ubuntu workstation using the graphical desktop, you'll see lots of hidden configuration files. Also notice that there are three files that begin with `.bash`. These files are hidden files used by the bash shell environment.

The `-R` parameter is another commonly used `ls` parameter. It shows files that are contained within any subdirectories in the current directory. If you have many directories, this list can be long. Here's a simple example of what the `-R` parameter produces:

```
rich@testbox:~$ ls -F -R
.:
file1 test1/ test2/

./test1:
myprog1* myprog2*

./test2:
rich@testbox:~$
```

Notice that first the `-R` parameter shows the contents of the current directory, which is a file (`file1`) and two directories (`test1` and `test2`). Following that, it traverses each of the two directories, showing whether any files are contained within each directory. The `test1` directory shows two files (`myprog1` and `myprog2`), while the `test2` directory doesn't contain any files. If there had been further subdirectories within the `test1` or `test2` directories, the `-R` parameter would continue to traverse those as well. As you can see, for large directory structures, the output of this parameter can be large.

Modifying the Information Presented

As you can see in the basic file lists, the `ls` command doesn't produce a whole lot of information about each file. For additional information, a useful parameter is `-l`:

```
rich@testbox:~$ ls -l
total 2064
drwxrwxr-x 2 rich rich    4096 2008-08-24 22:04 4rich
-rw-r--r-- 1 rich rich 1766205 2008-08-24 15:34 backup.zip
drwxr-xr-x 3 rich rich    4096 2008-08-31 22:24 Desktop
drwxr-xr-x 2 rich rich    4096 2001-11-01 04:06 Documents
drwxr-xr-x 2 rich rich    4096 2001-11-01 04:06 Download
drwxrwxr-x 2 rich rich    4096 2008-07-26 18:25 Drivers
drwxr-xr-x 2 rich rich    4096 2001-11-01 04:06 Music
-rwxr--r-- 1 rich rich      30 2008-08-23 21:42 myprog
drwxr-xr-x 2 rich rich    4096 2001-11-01 04:06 Pictures
drwxr-xr-x 2 rich rich    4096 2001-11-01 04:06 Public
drwxrwxr-x 5 rich rich    4096 2008-08-24 22:04 store
-rw-rw-r-- 1 rich rich   98772 2008-08-24 15:30 store.sql
-rw-r--r-- 1 rich rich  107507 2008-08-13 15:45 store.zip
drwxr-xr-x 2 rich rich    4096 2001-11-01 04:06 Templates
drwxr-xr-x 2 rich rich    4096 2001-11-01 04:06 Videos
rich@testbox:~$
```

The long list format displays each file and directory in the specified directory on a single line. Besides the filename, it shows additional useful information. The first line in the output shows the total number of blocks contained within the directory. Following that, each line contains the following information about each file (or directory):

♦ The file type, such as directory (d), file (-), character device (c), or block device (b)
♦ The permissions for the file (see Chapter 17, "Users and Groups")
♦ The number of hard links to the file (see the "Linking Files" section in this chapter)
♦ The username of the owner of the file
♦ The name of the group the file belongs to
♦ The size of the file in bytes
♦ The time the file was modified last
♦ The file or directory name

The -l parameter is a powerful tool. It gives you just about any information you'd need for any file or directory in the system.

The Complete Parameter List

The ls command has many parameters that can come in handy for file management. If you use the man command for ls, you'll see several pages of parameters to modify the output of the ls command.

The ls command uses two types of command-line parameters:

♦ Single-letter parameters
♦ Full-word (long) parameters

The single-letter parameters are always preceded by a single dash. Full-word parameters are more descriptive and are preceded by a double dash. Many parameters have both a single-letter and full-word version, while some have only one type. Table 19-4 lists some of the more popular parameters that'll help you out with using the bash ls command.

Table 19-4: Some Popular ls Command Parameters

Single Letter	Full Word	Description
-a	--all	Don't ignore entries starting with a period
-A	--almost-all	Don't list the . and .. files
	--author	Print author name for each file
-b	--escape	Print octal values for nonprintable characters
	--block-size=size	Calculate block sizes using size-byte blocks
-B	--ignore-backups	Don't list entries with the tilde (~) symbol (used to denote backup copies)
-c		Sort by time of last modification
-C		List entries by columns
	--color=when	Specify when to use colors (always, never, or auto)

continues

Table 19-4: *(continued)*

Single Letter	Full Word	Description
-d	--directory	List directory entries instead of contents, and don't de-reference symbolic links
-F	--classify	Append file-type indicator to entries
	--file-type	Append file-type indicators to specific file types only (not executable files)
	--format=word	Format output (across, commas, horizontal, long, single-column, verbose, or vertical)
-g		List full file information except for the file owner
	--group-directories-first	List all directories before files
-G	--no-group	Don't display group names in long list format
-h	--human-readable	Print sizes using K for kilobytes, M for megabytes, and G for gigabytes
	--si	Same as -h, but use powers of 1000 instead of 1024
-i	--inode	Display the index number (inode) of each file
-l		Display the long list format
-L	--dereference	Show information for the original file for a linked file
-n	--numeric-uid-gid	Show numeric userID and groupID instead of names
-o		In long list, don't display owner names
-r	--reverse	Reverse the sorting order when displaying files and directories
-R	--recursive	List subdirectory contents recursively
-s	--size	Print the block size of each file
-S	--sort=size	Sort the output by file size
-t	--sort=time	Sort the output by file modification time
-u		Display last access time instead of last modification time for files
-U	--sort=none	Don't sort the output list
-v	--sort=version	Sort the output by file version
-x		List entries by lines instead of columns
-X	--sort=extension	Sort the output by file extension

You can use more than one parameter at a time. The double dash parameters must be listed separately, but the single-dash parameters can be combined into a string behind the dash.

A common combination to use is the `-a` parameter to list all files, the `-i` parameter to list the inode for each file, the `-l` parameter to produce a long list, and the `-s` parameter to list the block sizes of the files. (The inode of a file or directory is a unique identification number the kernel assigns to each object in the filesystem.) Combining all of these parameters creates the easy-to-remember `-sail` parameter:

```
rich@testbox:~$ ls -sail
total 2360
301860 8 drwx------ 36 rich rich 4096 2007-09-03 15:12 .
65473 8 drwxr-xr-x 6 root root 4096 2007-07-29 14:20 ..
360621 8 drwxrwxr-x 2 rich rich 4096 2007-08-24 22:04 4rich
301862 8 -rw-r--r-- 1 rich rich 124 2007-02-12 10:18 .bashrc
361443 8 drwxrwxr-x 4 rich rich 4096 2007-07-26 20:31 .ccache
301879 8 drwxr-xr-x 3 rich rich 4096 2007-07-26 18:25 .config
301871 8 drwxr-xr-x 3 rich rich 4096 2007-08-31 22:24 Desktop
301870 8 -rw------- 1 rich rich 26 2001-11-01 04:06 .dmrc
301872 8 drwxr-xr-x 2 rich rich 4096 2001-11-01 04:06 Download
360207 8 drwxrwxr-x 2 rich rich 4096 2007-07-26 18:25 Drivers
301882 8 drwx------ 5 rich rich 4096 2007-09-02 23:40 .gconf
301883 8 drwx------ 2 rich rich 4096 2007-09-02 23:43 .gconfd
360338 8 drwx------ 3 rich rich 4096 2007-08-06 23:06 .gftp
```

Besides the normal `-l` parameter output information, you'll see two additional numbers, plus a third entry with some strange letters on each line. The first number is the file or directory inode number. The second number is the block size of the file. The third entry is a diagram of the type of file, along with the file's permissions.

Following that, the next number is the number of hard links to the file (discussed later in the "Linking File" section of this chapter), the owner of the file, the group the file belongs to, the size of the file (in bytes), a time stamp showing the last modification time by default, and, finally, the actual filename.

Filtering the List Output

As you've seen in the examples, by default the `ls` command lists all of the nonhidden files in a directory. Sometimes this can be overkill, especially when you're just looking for information on a single file.

Fortunately, the `ls` command also provides a way to define a filter on the command line. It uses the filter to determine which files or directories it should display in the output.

The filter works as a simple text-matching string. Include the filter after any command-line parameters you want to use:

```
rich@testbos:~$ ls -l myprog
-rwxr--r-- 1 rich rich 30 2008-08-23 21:42 myprog
rich@testbox:~$
```

When you specify the name of specific file as the filter, the `ls` command shows only the information for that file. Sometimes, though, you might not know the exact name of the file you're looking for. The `ls` command also recognizes standard wildcard characters to match patterns within the filter:

- ◆ A question mark to represent one character
- ◆ An asterisk to represent zero or more characters

The question mark can be used to replace exactly one character anywhere in the filter string. For example,

```
rich@testbox:~$ ls -l mypro?
-rw-rw-r-- 1 rich rich 0 2008-09-03 16:38 myprob
-rwxr--r-- 1 rich rich 30 2008-08-23 21:42 myprog
rich@testbox:~$
```

The filter `mypro?` matched two files in the directory. Similarly, the asterisk can be used to match zero or more characters:

```
rich@testbox:~$ ls -l myprob*
-rw-rw-r-- 1 rich rich 0 2008-09-03 16:38 myprob
-rw-rw-r-- 1 rich rich 0 2008-09-03 16:40 myproblem
rich@testbox:~$
```

The asterisk matches zero characters in the `myprob` file, but it matches three characters in the `myproblem` file.

This is a powerful feature to use when searching for files when you're not quite sure of the filenames.

File Handling

The bash shell provides lots of commands for manipulating files on the Linux filesystem. This section walks through the basic commands you will need to work with files from the command-line interface.

Creating Files

Every once in a while you run into a situation where you need to create an empty file. Sometimes applications expect a log file to be present before they can write to it. In these situations, you can use the `touch` command to easily create an empty file:

```
rich@testbox:~$ touch test1
rich@testbox:~$ ls -il test1
1954793 -rw-r--r-- 1 rich rich 0 Sep 1 09:35 test1
rich@testbox:~$
```

The `touch` command creates the new file you specify and assigns your username as the file owner. Because I used the `-il` parameters for the `ls` command, the first entry in the list shows the inode number assigned to the file. Every file on the Linux system has a unique inode number.

Notice that the file size is zero because the `touch` command just created an empty file. The `touch` command can also be used to change the access and modification times on an existing file without changing the file contents:

```
rich@testbox:~$ touch test1
rich@testbox:~$ ls -l test1
-rw-r--r-- 1 rich rich 0 Sep 1 09:37 test1
rich@testbox:~$
```

The modification time of `test1` is now updated from the original time. If you want to change only the access time, use the `-a` parameter. To change only the modification time, use the `-m` parameter. By default, `touch` uses the current time. You can specify the time by using the `-t` parameter with a specific time stamp:

```
rich@testbox:~$ touch -t 200812251200 test1
rich@testbox:~$ ls -l test1
-rw-r--r-- 1 rich rich 0 Dec 25 2008 test1
rich@testbox:~$
```

Now the modification time for the file is set to a date significantly in the future.

Copying Files

Copying files and directories from one location in the filesystem to another is a common practice for system administrators. The `cp` command provides this feature.

In its most basic form, the `cp` command uses two parameters—the source object and the destination object:

```
cp source destination
```

When both the source and destination parameters are filenames, the `cp` command copies the source file to a new file with the filename specified as the destination. The new file acts like a brand new file, with updated file-creation and last-modified times:

```
rich@testbox:~$ cp test1 test2
rich@testbox:~$ ls -l
total 0
1954793 -rw-r--r-- 1 rich rich 0 Dec 25 2008 test1
1954794 -rw-r--r-- 1 rich rich 0 Sep 1 09:39 test2
rich@testbox:~$
```

The new file, `test2`, shows a different inode number, indicating that it's a completely new file. You'll also notice that the modification time for the `test2` file shows the time it was created. If the destination file already exists, by default the `cp` command will overwrite the old file with the new file. Using the `-i` parameter provides a prompt that asks whether you want to overwrite the file:

```
rich@testbox:~$ cp -i test1 test2
cp: overwrite 'test2'? y
rich@testbox:~$
```

If you don't answer `y`, the file copy will not proceed.

You can also copy a file to an existing directory:

```
rich@testbox:~$ cp test1 dir1
rich@testbox:~$ ls -il dir1
total 0
1954887 -rw-r--r-- 1 rich rich 0 Sep 6 09:42 test1
rich@testbox:~$
```

The new file is now under the `dir1` directory, with the same filename as the original.

These examples all use relative pathnames, but you can just as easily use the absolute pathname for both the source and destination objects.

To copy a file to the directory you're currently in, use the period:

```
rich@testbox:~$ cp /home/rich/dir1/test1 .
cp: overwrite './test1'?
```

As with most commands, cp has a few command-line parameters to help us out. These parameters are shown in Table 19-5.

Table 19-5: The cp Command Parameters

Parameter	Description
-a	Archive files by preserving their attributes
-b	Create a backup of each existing destination file instead of overwriting
-d	Preserve linked data files
-f	Force overwriting of existing destination files without prompting
-i	Prompt before overwriting destination files
-l	Create a file link instead of copying the files
-p	Preserve file attributes, if possible
-r	Copy directories recursively
-R	Copy directories recursively (same as -r)
-s	Create a symbolic link instead of copying the file
-S	Override the backup feature
-u	Copy the source file only if it has a newer date and time than the destination (update)
-v	Verbose mode, explaining what's happening
-x	Restrict the copy to the current filesystem

Use the -p parameter to preserve the file access or modification times of the original file in the copied file.

```
rich@testbox:~$ cp -p test1 test3
rich@testbox:~$ ls -il
total 4
1954886 drwxr-xr-x 2 rich rich 4096 Sep 1 09:42 dir1/
1954793 -rw-r--r-- 1 rich rich 0 Dec 25 2008 test1
1954794 -rw-r--r-- 1 rich rich 0 Sep 1 09:39 test2
1954888 -rw-r--r-- 1 rich rich 0 Dec 25 2008 test3
rich@testbox:~$
```

Now, even though the test3 file is a completely new file, it has the same time stamp as the original test1 file.

The -R parameter is extremely powerful. It allows you to recursively copy the contents of an entire directory in one command:

```
rich@testbox:~$ cp -R dir1 dir2
rich@testbox:~$ ls -l
total 8
drwxr-xr-x 2 rich rich 4096 Sep 6 09:42 dir1/
```

```
drwxr-xr-x 2 rich rich 4096 Sep 6 09:45 dir2/
-rw-r--r-- 1 rich rich 0 Dec 25 2008 test1
-rw-r--r-- 1 rich rich 0 Sep 6 09:39 test2
-rw-r--r-- 1 rich rich 0 Dec 25 2008 test3
rich@testbox:~$
```

Now dir2 is a complete copy of dir1. You can also use wildcard characters in your cp commands:

```
rich@testbox:~$ cp -f test* dir2
rich@testbox:~$ ls -al dir2
total 12
drwxr-xr-x 2 rich rich 4096 Sep 6 10:55 ./
drwxr-xr-x 4 rich rich 4096 Sep 6 10:46 ../
-rw-r--r-- 1 rich rich 0 Dec 25 2008 test1
-rw-r--r-- 1 rich rich 0 Sep 6 10:55 test2
-rw-r--r-- 1 rich rich 0 Dec 25 2008 test3
rich@testbox:~$
```

This command copied all of the files that started with test to dir2. I included the -f parameter to overwrite the test1 file that was already in the directory without asking.

Linking Files

You may have noticed that the explanations for a couple of the parameters for the cp command referred to *linking files*. This is a pretty cool option available in the Linux filesystems. If you need to maintain two (or more) copies of the same file on the system, instead of having separate physical copies, you can use one physical copy and multiple virtual copies, called *links*. A link is a placeholder in a directory that points to the real location of the file. There are two different types of file links in Linux:

- ◆ A symbolic, or soft, link
- ◆ A hard link

A hard link creates a separate file that contains information about the original file and where to find it. When you reference the hard link file, it's as if you're referencing the original file:

```
rich@testbox:~$ cp -l test1 test4
rich@testbox:~$ ls -il
total 16
1954886 drwxr-xr-x 2 rich rich 4096 Sep 1 09:42 dir1/
1954889 drwxr-xr-x 2 rich rich 4096 Sep 1 09:45 dir2/
1954793 -rw-r--r-- 2 rich rich 0 Sep 1 09:51 test1
1954794 -rw-r--r-- 1 rich rich 0 Sep 1 09:39 test2
1954888 -rw-r--r-- 1 rich rich 0 Dec 25 2008 test3
1954793 -rw-r--r-- 2 rich rich 0 Sep 1 09:51 test4
rich@testbox:~$
```

The -l parameter created a hard link for the test1 file called test4. In the file list you can see that the inode number of the test1 and test4 files is the same, indicating that, in reality, they are the same file. Also notice that the link count (the third item in the list) now shows that both files have two links.

Secret

You can create a hard link only between files on the same physical media. You can't create a hard link between files under separate mount points. In that case, you'll have to use a soft link.

On the other hand, the -s parameter creates a symbolic, or soft, link:

```
rich@testbox:~$ cp -s test1 test5
rich@testbox:~$ ls -il test*
total 16
1954793 -rw-r--r-- 2 rich rich 6 Sep 1 09:51 test1
1954794 -rw-r--r-- 1 rich rich 0 Sep 1 09:39 test2
1954888 -rw-r--r-- 1 rich rich 0 Dec 25 2008 test3
1954793 -rw-r--r-- 2 rich rich 6 Sep 1 09:51 test4
1954891 lrwxrwxrwx 1 rich rich 5 Sep 1 09:56 test5 -> test1
rich@testbox:~$
```

You'll notice a couple of things in the file list. First, the new test5 file has a different inode number than the test1 file, indicating that Ubuntu treats it as a separate file. Second, the file size is different. A linked file needs to store information about the source file only, not about the actual data in the file. The filename area of the list shows the relationship between the two files.

Secret

You can use the ln command instead of the cp command to link files. By default, the ln command creates hard links. If you want to create a soft link, you'll still need to use the -s parameter.

Be careful when copying linked files. If you use the cp command to copy a file that's linked to another source file, all you're doing is making another copy of the source file. This can quickly get confusing. Instead of copying the linked file, you can create another link to the original file. You can have many links to the same file, with no problems. However, you don't want to create soft links to other soft linked files. Doing so creates a chain of links that can not only be confusing but easily broken, causing all sorts of problems.

Renaming Files

In the Ubuntu world, renaming files is called *moving*. You simply move a file from one name to another. The mv command can move both files and directories to another location:

```
rich@testbox:~$ mv test2 test6
rich@testbox:~$ ls -il test*
1954793 -rw-r--r-- 2 rich rich 6 Sep 1 09:51 test1
1954888 -rw-r--r-- 1 rich rich 0 Dec 25 2008 test3
```

```
1954793 -rw-r--r-- 2 rich rich 6 Sep 1 09:51 test4
1954891 lrwxrwxrwx 1 rich rich 5 Sep 1 09:56 test5 -> test1
1954794 -rw-r--r-- 1 rich rich 0 Sep 1 09:39 test6
rich@testbox:~$
```

Notice that moving the file changed the filename but kept the same inode number and the time stamp value. Moving a file with soft links is a problem:

```
rich@testbox:~$ mv test1 test8
rich@testbox:~$ ls -il test*
total 16
1954888 -rw-r--r-- 1 rich rich 0 Dec 25 2008 test3
1954793 -rw-r--r-- 2 rich rich 6 Sep 1 09:51 test4
1954891 lrwxrwxrwx 1 rich rich 5 Sep 1 09:56 test5 -> test1
1954794 -rw-r--r-- 1 rich rich 0 Sep 1 09:39 test6
1954793 -rw-r--r-- 2 rich rich 6 Sep 1 09:51 test8
rich@testbox:~$ mv test8 test1
```

The test4 file that uses a hard link still uses the same inode number, which is perfectly fine. However, the test5 file now points to an invalid file and is no longer a valid link.

You can also use the mv command to move directories:

```
mv dir2 dir4
```

The entire contents of the directory are unchanged. The only thing that changes is the name of the directory.

Deleting Files

At some point, you'll want to be able to delete existing files. Whether it's to clean up a file-system or to remove a software package, there are always opportunities to delete files.

In the Ubuntu world, deleting is called *removing*. The command to remove files in the bash shell is rm. The basic form of the rm command is pretty simple:

```
rich@testbox:~$ rm test2
rich@testbox:~$ ls -l
total 16
drwxr-xr-x 2 rich rich 4096 Sep 1 09:42 dir1/
drwxr-xr-x 2 rich rich 4096 Sep 1 09:45 dir2/
-rw-r--r-- 2 rich rich 6 Sep 1 09:51 test1
-rw-r--r-- 1 rich rich 0 Dec 25 2008 test3
-rw-r--r-- 2 rich rich 6 Sep 1 09:51 test4
lrwxrwxrwx 1 rich rich 5 Sep 1 09:56 test5 -> test1
rich@testbox:~$
```

Notice that by default, the command doesn't prompt you to make sure you're serious about removing the file. You can use the -i parameter to force the rm command to prompt you to remove the file. There's no trash can in the bash shell. Once you remove a file it's gone forever, so you better be sure about what you're doing!

Now, here's an interesting tidbit about deleting a file that has links to it:

```
rich@testbox:~$ rm -i test1
rm: remove 'test1'? y
rich@testbox:~$ ls -l
```

```
total 12
drwxr-xr-x 2 rich rich 4096 Sep 1 09:42 dir1/
drwxr-xr-x 2 rich rich 4096 Sep 1 09:45 dir2/
-rw-r--r-- 1 rich rich 0 Dec 25 2008 test3
-rw-r--r-- 1 rich rich 6 Sep 1 09:51 test4
lrwxrwxrwx 1 rich rich 5 Sep 1 09:56 test5 -> test1
rich@testbox:~$ cat test4
hello
rich@testbox:~$ cat test5
cat: test5: No such file or directory
rich@testbox:~$
```

I removed the test1 file, which had a hard link to the test4 file and a soft link to the test5 file. Noticed what happened. Both of the linked files still appear, even though the test1 file is now gone (although on my color Terminal window the test5 filename now appears in red). When I look at the contents of the test4 file, which was a hard link, it still shows the contents of the file. When I look at the contents of the test5 file, which was a soft link, bash indicates that it no longer exists.

Remember that the hard link file uses the same inode number as the original file. The hard link file maintains that inode number until you remove the last linked file, preserving the data. All the soft link file knows is that the underlying file is now gone, so it has nothing to point to. This is an important feature to remember when working with linked files.

If you're removing lots of files and don't want to be bothered with the confirmation prompt, use the -f parameter to force the removal. Just be careful!

Secret As with copying files, you can use wildcard characters with the rm command. Again, use caution when doing this, because anything your remove, even by accident, is gone forever!

Directory Handling

In Ubuntu there are a few commands that work for both files and directories (such as the cp command) and some that work only for directories. To create a new directory, you'll need to use a specific command, which we'll discuss in this section. Removing directories can get interesting, so we'll look at that as well.

Creating Directories

There's not much to creating a new directory in Ubuntu. Just use the mkdir command:

```
rich@testbox:~$ mkdir dir3
rich@testbox:~$ ls -il
total 16
```

```
1954886 drwxr-xr-x 2 rich rich 4096 Sep 1 09:42 dir1/
1954889 drwxr-xr-x 2 rich rich 4096 Sep 1 10:55 dir2/
1954893 drwxr-xr-x 2 rich rich 4096 Sep 1 11:01 dir3/
1954888 -rw-r--r-- 1 rich rich 0 Dec 25 2008 test3
1954793 -rw-r--r-- 1 rich rich 6 Sep 1 09:51 test4
rich@testbox:~$
```

The system creates a new directory (in this example, dir3) and assigns it a new inode
number.

Deleting Directories

Removing directories can be tricky, but there's a reason for that. Things can easily go
wrong when you start deleting directories, but the bash shell tries to protect you from
accidental catastrophes as much as possible. The basic command for removing a directory is rmdir:

```
rich@testbox:~$ rmdir dir3
rich@testbox:~$ rmdir dir1
rmdir: failed to remove 'dir1': Directory not empty
rich@testbox:~$
```

By default, the rmdir command works only for removing empty directories. Because there
is a file in the dir1 directory, the rmdir command refuses to remove it. You can remove
non-empty directories using the --ignore-fail-on-non-empty parameter.

Our friend the rm command can also help in handling directories. If you try using it without
parameters, as with files, you'll be disappointed:

```
rich@testbox:~$ rm dir1
rm: cannot remove 'dir1': Is a directory
rich@testbox:~$
```

However, if you really want to remove a directory, you can use the -r parameter to recursively remove the files in the directory, then remove the directory itself:

```
rich@testbox:~$ rm -r -i dir2
rm: descend into directory 'dir2'? y
rm: remove 'dir2/test1'? y
rm: remove 'dir2/test3'? y
rm: remove 'dir2/test4'? y
rm: remove directory 'dir2'? y
rich@testbox:~$
```

Although this command works, it's somewhat awkward. The ultimate solution for throwing
caution to the wind and removing an entire directory, contents and all, is the rm command
with both the -r and -f parameters:

```
rich@testbox:~$ rm -r -f dir2
rich@testbox:~$
```

That's it. No warnings, no fanfare—just another shell prompt. This, of course, is an
extremely dangerous tool to have, especially if you're logged in as the root user account.
Use it sparingly, and only after triple checking to make sure you're doing exactly what
you want to do.

Summary

This chapter took you into the world of the Ubuntu command line. The primary interface to the command line is the Terminal program. The Terminal program provides access to the command line from a graphical window. You can customize the Terminal program to display features in colors, display multiple command-line prompts in tabbed windows, and save settings.

The chapter also walked through some commands to interact with the Ubuntu filesystem. It showed how to use the `ls` command to list the files and directories on the system. There are plenty of command-line parameters that modify the output of the `ls` command to customize how you view the directories and files.

After showing you how to list directories and files, the chapter walked through how to create new files using the `touch` command, copy files using the `cp` command, delete files using the `rm` command, and rename files using the `mv` command. The chapter finished by showing how to handle directories using the `mkdir` and `rmdir` commands.

This chapter ends our discussion on managing your Ubuntu workstation. In the next section we'll turn our attention to the Ubuntu server distribution. Plenty of server programs are available in that distribution. In the next chapter we'll see how to create our own domain name server (DNS) for a network.

PART 4

Using the Ubuntu Server

DNS Server

Chapter
20

◆ ◆

Secrets in This Chapter

◆ ◆

W hat's in a name? Plenty, if you're a Montague or are using the Internet. How would you react if your favorite product was advertised on television stating, "Just visit our web site at 198.182.196.56 for more information"? Unfortunately, humans do not process numbers as well as computers do. To compensate for that, systems administrators use names to identify their computer systems. The domain name system (DNS) was developed to help humans easily locate computer names on the Internet. If you choose to let your ISP handle your domain name and email, you may not need to know the details about DNS configurations, but it might not be a bad idea to know how DNS works in general (just in case of any problems). This chapter discusses where DNS came from, why it is so vital to email and web operations, and how you can configure your Ubuntu server to utilize it either as a client or as a DNS server.

History of Computer Names

Back in the old days when the Internet was small (just a few hundred computers) it was not too complicated to locate another computer. Each Internet computer had a database of hostnames and IP addresses. Internet hostnames could be anything the administrator desired—Fred, Barney, Acct1, anything. There was a central clearinghouse for keeping track of new computer names and addresses. Once a week or so, a systems administrator would download a new copy of the current database from the clearinghouse.

Of course, this system did have its drawbacks. When someone brought a new computer online they needed to search the database to make sure nobody had already used the clever new hostname they wanted to use. It didn't take systems administrators long to figure out that this method was on a collision course with progress.

As the Internet grew, so did the database. As the database grew, so did the time it took to download and search it. It was also starting to get difficult coming up with a unique hostname for new systems. Something had to change, and it did.

Domain Names

The method agreed on was the *domain name system* (DNS). DNS uses a hierarchical, distributed database to break up the hostnames database. That's a catchy way of saying that no single computer has to maintain the entire database of Internet devices. The database is distributed among multiple computers, called DNS servers, on the Internet. For client computers to locate another computer on the Internet, they need only find the nearest DNS server and query for the IP address of a hostname.

To implement this system, developers invented a new protocol to pass the DNS information from the DNS server to the client, as well as develop software for DNS servers to implement the new database system.

This section describes in detail the DNS server that Ubuntu uses.

DNS Structure

The structure of a hierarchical database is similar to an organization chart, with nodes connected in a tree-like manner (the hierarchical part). The top node is called the *root*.

The root node does not explicitly show up in addresses, so it's called the *nameless node*. Multiple categories were created under the root level to divide the database into pieces called *domains*.

Each domain contains DNS servers that are responsible for maintaining the database of computer names for that area of the database (the distributed part). The first level of distribution is divided into domains based on country codes. Additional first-level domains for specific U.S. organizations were created to prevent the .us domain from getting overcrowded.

The domain name is appended to the end of the computer hostname to form the unique Internet hostname for that computer. This is the popular hostname format that we are now familiar with. Table 20-1 shows how the first-level DNS domains are laid out.

Table 20-1: DNS First-Level Domain Names

Name	Description
.com	U.S. commercial organizations
.edu	U.S. educational institutions
.gov	U.S. government organizations
.mil	U.S. military sites
.net	U.S. Internet providers
.org	U.S. nonprofit organizations
.us	Other U.S. organizations
.ca	Canadian organizations
.de	German organizations
(other country codes)	Other countries' organizations

As the Internet grows, each first-level domain is divided into subdomains, or *zones*. Each zone is an independent domain in itself, but it relies on its parent domain for connectivity to the database. A parent zone must grant permission for a child zone to exist and is responsible for the child zone's behavior.

Each zone has at least two DNS servers that maintain the DNS database for the zone. For fault-tolerance purposes, the original specifications stipulated that the DNS servers for a single zone must have separate connections to the Internet and be housed in separate locations. Because of this stipulation, many organizations rely on other organizations to host their secondary and tertiary DNS servers.

Hosts within a zone add their domain name to their hostname to form their unique Internet name. Thus, computer fred in the smallorg.org domain would be called fred.smallorg.org.

Because a domain can contain hosts as well as zones, the domain naming protocol can become confusing. For example, the smallorg.org domain can contain host fred.smallorg.org, as well as grant authority for zone acctg.smallorg.org to be a subdomain, which in turn can contain the host barney.acctg.smallorg.org. Although this protocol simplifies the database system, it makes finding hosts on the Internet more complicated.

Finding Domains

The main purpose of the DNS server is to provide an easy method for computers to locate one another by name. The three scenarios for finding an IP address using the DNS server are as follows:

◆ A computer that wants to communicate with another computer in the same zone queries the local DNS server in the zone to find the address of the remote computer. The local DNS server, which should have the address of the remote computer in its local database, returns that IP address directly to the computer.

◆ A computer that wants to communicate with a computer in another zone queries the local DNS server in its zone. The local DNS server realizes that the requested computer is in a different zone and queries a root-level DNS server for the answer. The root DNS server then walks the tree of DNS servers to find the correct local zone DNS server and obtain the IP address for the remote computer. It then passes the address to the local DNS server, which in turn passes the information it receives to the requesting computer. Part of the information returned with the IP address of the remote computer is a time-to-live (TTL) value. The TTL value is the length of time that the local DNS server can keep the IP address information of the remote computer in a local name cache. This will speed up any subsequent name requests for the same remote computer.

◆ A computer that wants to communicate with the same remote computer in another zone queries the local DNS server in its zone. The local DNS server checks its name cache, and, if the TTL value has not expired, sends the IP address of the remote computer to the requesting client computer. This is considered a *nonauthoritative response* because the local DNS server is assuming that the remote computer's IP address has not changed since it was last checked.

In all three instances, the local computer needs to know only the IP address of its own local DNS server to find the IP address of any computer on the Internet. It's the job of the local DNS server to find the proper IP address for the given hostname. The local computer's life is now much simpler. Figure 20-1 shows a sample tree structure for the current DNS hierarchy.

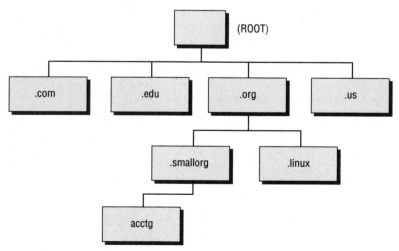

Figure 20-1: Diagram of the Internet domain name system.

As the tree grows, new requirements are made on DNS servers. As mentioned, parent DNS servers are required to know the IP addresses of their child-zone DNS servers to properly pass DNS queries on to them for resolution. The tricky part comes into play with the lower level-zone DNS servers. To properly process DNS queries, those servers have to be able to start their name searches somewhere in the DNS tree.

When the Internet was in its infancy, most of the name searches were for local hostnames. The bulk of the DNS traffic was able to stay local to the zone DNS server or, at worst, its parent. However, with the increased popularity of the Internet and web browsing, more DNS requests are being made for remote hostnames. When a DNS server does not have the hostname in its local database, it needs to query a remote DNS server.

The most likely candidate is a root-level DNS server that has the knowledge to work its way down the tree until it finds the responsible zone DNS server for the remote host and returns the result to the local DNS server. Unfortunately, this puts a great deal of stress on the root servers. Fortunately, there are quite a few of them and they do a good job of distributing the load.

DNS is a two-way street. Not only is it useful for finding the IP address of a computer based on its hostname, it is also useful for finding the hostname of a computer based on its IP address. Many Internet web and FTP sites restrict access based on a client computer's domain. When the connection request is made from a client, the host server passes the IP address of the client to the DNS server as a reverse DNS query. If the client's DNS zone database is configured correctly, the client's hostname should be returned to the server, which in turn can decide whether to grant access to the client.

DNS Database Records

Each DNS server is responsible for keeping track of the hostnames in its zone. To accomplish this task, the DNS server must have a method for storing host information in a database that can be queried by remote machines. The DNS database is a text file that consists of resource records (RRs) that describe computers and functions in the zone. The DNS software on the server can read and process this database information.

The DNS server's database first has to declare the zone that it is responsible for. Then, it must declare each host computer in its zone. Finally, the database can declare special information for the zone, such as email and nameservers. RR formats were created to track all of the information required for the DNS server. Table 20.2 shows some of the basic RRs that a DNS database could contain.

DNS database design has become a hot topic lately with researchers who want to add more information to the database, as well as increase the security of the information that is there. New record types are constantly being added to the DNS database. The record types in Table 20-2 represent the core records needed to establish a zone in the DNS database.

Table 20-2: DNS Database Resource Record Types

Record Type	Description
SOA	Start of authority
A	Internet address
NS	Nameserver

continues

Table 20-2: *(continued)*

Record Type	Description
CNAME	Canonical name (nickname)
HINFO	Host information
MX	Mail server
PTR	Pointer

The following sections describe the various RR types in detail.

The SOA Record

Each database starts with an SOA (start of authority) record that defines the zone the database is in. The format for the SOA record is

```
domain name [TTL] [class] SOA origin person (
serial number
refresh
retry
expire
minimum)
```

The parameters used in the SOA record are

- ◆ **domain name:** The name of the zone that is being defined (the @ sign can be used as a placeholder to signify the computer's default domain).
- ◆ **TTL:** The time (in seconds) that a requesting computer will keep any DNS information from this zone in its local name cache. This parameter is optional.
- ◆ **class:** The protocol that is being used (which, in our case, will always be class IN, for Internet). This parameter is optional.
- ◆ **origin:** The name of the computer where the master zone database is located. Be sure to include a trailing period (.) after the hostname; otherwise, your local domain name will be appended to the hostname (unless, of course, you want to use that feature).
- ◆ **person:** An email address of a person responsible for the zone. The format of this parameter is a little different than usual because the @ sign is already used to signify the default domain name, so it can't be used in the email address. Instead, use a period in place of the @ sign. For example, instead of using sysadm@smallorg.org you would use sysadm.smallorg.org. If there are any periods in the name, they must be preceded by a backslash (\), such as rich\.blum.smallorg.org
- ◆ **serial number:** A unique number that identifies the version of the zone database file. The date created plus a version count is often used (such as 0905051).
- ◆ **refresh:** The time (in seconds) that a secondary DNS server should query a primary DNS server to check the SOA serial number. A common value is one hour (3600 seconds).
- ◆ **retry:** The time (in seconds) that a secondary DNS server should retry after a failed refresh attempt.

◆ `expire:` The time (in seconds) that a secondary DNS server can use the data retrieved from the primary DNS server without being refreshed. This value should usually be large, such as 3600000 (42 days).

◆ `minimum:` The time (in seconds) that should be used as the TTL in all RRs in this zone. A good value is 86400 (1 day).

The `SOA` record defines the amount of time a local DNS server can cache information about the zone. If the DNS server hosts a zone that doesn't change often, these values can be large, which reduces traffic to the local zone DNS server. However, if you're hosting a zone where servers come and go quite frequently, you'll need to set the `expire` parameter to a shorter value.

The A Record

Each host in the zone defined by the database should have a valid A record to define its hostname to the Internet. The format for the A record is

```
host [TTL] [class] A address
```

The parameters used in the A record are:

◆ `host:` The fully qualified hostname for the computer (including the domain name).

◆ `TTL:` The time (in seconds) that a requesting computer will keep any DNS information from this zone in its local name cache. This parameter is optional.

◆ `class:` The protocol that is being used (which, in our case, will always be class `IN`, for Internet). This parameter is optional.

◆ `address:` The IP address of the computer.

The *TTL* and *class* parameters can be added to override the values set in the `SOA` record. This feature allows you to customize your settings for individual hosts in your zone.

The CNAME Record

Besides a normal hostname, many computers have nicknames, which is useful if you wish to identify particular services without having to rename computers in your domain, such as **www.smallorg.org**. The `CNAME` record links nicknames with the real hostname.

The format of the `CNAME` record is

```
nickname [TTL] [class] CNAME hostname
```

The *nickname* parameter refers to a *hostname* already defined in an A record. This feature allows you to create common names for hosts, such as www for web servers or ftp for FTP servers, then point those names to the appropriate real server name that hosts that service.

The NS Record

Each zone should have at least two DNS servers. `NS` records are used to identify these servers to other DNS servers trying to resolve hostnames within the zone. The format of an `NS` record is

```
domain [TTL] [class] NS server
```

The *domain* parameter is the domain name of the zone that the DNS server is responsible for. If it is blank, then the `NS` record refers to the zone defined in the `SOA` record. The *server* parameter is the hostname of the DNS server. There should also be an associated A record to identify the IP address of the DNS server.

The HINFO Record

Additional information about a computer can be made available to DNS servers by using the HINFO record. The format of the HINFO record is

```
host [TTL] [class] HINFO hardware software
```

The parameters for this record are:

- ◆ host: The hostname of the computer the information applies to.
- ◆ hardware: The type of hardware the computer is using.
- ◆ software: The OS type and version of the computer.

The HINFO record is optional and, because of security concerns, isn't used very often any more.

The PTR Record

In addition to an A record, each computer in the zone should have a PTR record. This record allows the DNS server to perform reverse queries from the IP address of the computer. Without this information, remote servers could not determine the domain name where your computer is located. The format of a PTR record is

```
IN-ADDRname [TTL] [class] PTR name
```

The parameters used in this record are

- ◆ IN-ADDRname: The reverse DNS name of the IP address. If that sounds confusing, it is. This name allows the DNS server to work its way backward from the IP address of the computer. The IN-ADDRname of a computer with IP address 192.168.0.1 would be 1.0.168.192.IN-ADDR.ARPA.
- ◆ name: The hostname of the computer, as found in the A record.

Secret

> The PTR record is crucial for allowing reverse lookups of a host IP address. Without it, devices such as firewalls can't determine the hostname or domain of your host based on its IP address.

The MX Record

With the popularity of email, it's no surprise that the DNS system makes a special accommodation for defining email servers. This is done using the MX records. The MX records instruct remote mail servers where to forward mail for your zone. The format of the MX record is

```
name [TTL] [class] MX preference host
```

The special parameters for this record are

- name: The zone name (or the SOA zone if the zone name is blank). This parameter can also be a hostname if you want to redirect mail for a particular host in your network.
- preference: An integer signifying the order in which remote servers should try connecting if multiple mail servers are specified, with 0 being the highest preference (the preference decreases as the number increases). This parameter is used to create primary and secondary mail servers for a zone. When a remote mail server queries the DNS server for a mail server responsible for the zone, the entire list of servers and preferences is sent. The remote mail server should attempt to connect to the highest-priority mail server listed and, if that fails, continue down the list by preference.
- host: The hostname of the mail server. There should also be an associated A record to identify the IP address of the mail server.

Most larger domains have more than one mail server that can accept mail for the domain. It's common to see multiple mail servers with the same preference value. When that happens, the sending mail server can send to any mail server in the list with the same preference value.

Sample DNS Configuration

If you allow your ISP to host your domain name and email, they will have records in their DNS database identifying your domain to the Internet. The SOA record will identify your domain name but point to the ISP's host as the authoritative host. The NS records for your domain will point to your ISP's DNS servers, and your MX records will point to your ISP's mail servers.

As far as the rest of the Internet is concerned, these computers are part of your network, even though they do not really exist on *your* network. Here's an example of how an ISP might define zone definitions in its DNS database:

```
smallorg.org IN SOA master.isp.net. postmaster.master.isp.net (
1999080501 ;unique serial number
8H ; refresh rate
2H ;retry period
1W ; expiration period
1D) ; minimum

NS ns1.isp.net. ;defines primary name server
NS ns2.isp.net. ; defines secondary name server

MX 10 mail1.isp.net. ; defines primary mail server
MX 20 mail2.isp.net. ; defines secondary mail server

www CNAME host1.isp.net ;defines your www server address
ftp CNAME host1.isp.net ; defines your FTP server address

host1.isp.net A 10.0.0.1
1.0.0.10.IN-ADDR.ARPA PTR host1.isp.net ; pointer address
```

The first six lines show the SOA record for your new domain. The ISP points your domain name smallorg.org to the ISP server master.isp.net.

The two NS records define the primary and secondary DNS servers that will be used to resolve your hostnames (again, belonging to the ISP), and the two MX records define the primary (mail1.isp.net) and secondary (mail2.isp.net) mail servers that will receive and spool mail for your domain.

This configuration contains two CNAME records, which define nicknames for services in your domain. The hostname www.smallorg.org is a nickname that points to the ISP server that hosts your web pages. The address ftp.smallorg.org is also a nickname, and it points to the same ISP server that hosts your FTP site.

This is a service that most ISPs provide to customers who cannot afford to have a dedicated connection to the Internet but want to provide web and FTP services to their customers. The last two lines provide the Internet IP address information so that remote clients can connect to this server.

Once a DNS server has a valid database installed, it must be able to communicate with other DNS servers to resolve hostname requests from clients and respond to other DNS servers' queries about hosts in its zone. The DNS protocol was invented to accomplish that.

DNS Protocol

The DNS protocol serves two functions. It allows client computers to query a DNS server for an IP address or a hostname, and it allows DNS servers to communicate with each other and pass DNS database information back and forth.

It uses a standard request/response format, where the client submits a request packet, and the server returns a response packet with either the information from the database or an error message stating the reason the query could not be processed.

The DNS protocol uses either TCP or UDP well-known ports 53 to communicate. UDP has become the preferred method of transportation across the Internet because of its low packet overhead (UDP doesn't need to establish the connection to verify packets like TCP does).

The DNS packet contains five main sections:

- ◆ **Header:** Contains information identifying the packet and its purpose.
- ◆ **Question:** Contains the DNS queries the client wants answers for.
- ◆ **Answer:** Contains the DNS server response to the client questions.
- ◆ **Authority:** Contains information about which local DNS server is the authority for the zone of the requested questions.
- ◆ **Additional Information:** Contains information about the caching length and other features of the returned information.

Both the DNS client and server use the same DNS protocol packets, just with different information in them.

Ubuntu as a DNS Client

If you do not have a dedicated connection to the Internet, you should not use your Ubuntu server as a DNS server for your domain. If someone tried sending email to you at 3 a.m., and your Ubuntu server was not up and connected to the Internet, they might not be able to resolve your domain name and send your message. Most ISPs provide a DNS server for their clients. You can use the DNS server that your ISP provides to resolve hostnames using your Ubuntu server as a client.

Configuring DNS Client Files

Three files are needed to use your Ubuntu server as a DNS client. All three files are normally located in the /etc directory. They are resolv.conf, hosts, and host.conf. The following sections describe these files in more detail.

The /etc/resolv.conf File

The /etc/resolv.conf file tells Ubuntu which DNS server you want to send your DNS queries. You can list up to three DNS servers in this file. The second and third entries will be used as backup if no response is received from the first (primary) server.

If you have a local DNS server in your network, you should use that as your primary, although you do not have to. If you access other computers in your local network by name, it would improve performance to specify the local DNS server, because it would quickly resolve the name. If you use DNS only to access remote computers, then there probably won't be much performance improvement.

You can also specify a default domain name to use when looking up domain names. If your domain is smallorg.org, you can specify that as the default domain to search in. That way, if you need the IP address for hostname fred.smallorg.org, you can just specify fred as the default domain name, and Ubuntu will automatically append the smallorg.org to it.

Unfortunately, that can work against you. The DNS software will automatically append smallorg.org to everything that it tries to resolve. If you try connecting to www.linux .org, it will first attempt to find www.linux.org.smallorg.org. When that fails, it will try www.linux.org.

Here's a sample /etc/resolv.conf file used in an Ubuntu system:

```
domain smallorg.org
search smallorg.org
nameserver 10.0.0.1
nameserver 10.0.0.2
nameserver 10.0.0.3
```

The first line shows the search statement that defines the default domain to use in all DNS queries. Remember, this will slow down queries for hosts not in your domain, because the search text is appended to all queries. The next three lines show the primary, secondary, and tertiary DNS servers that service this Ubuntu system. Most often they are the DNS servers assigned to you by your ISP, although you are free to try other DNS servers if you want to (unless, of course, your ISP filters out DNS requests).

Secret

The Ubuntu server installation process will attempt to create the /etc/resolv. conf file for you automatically. If your server uses DHCP to acquire a network address, the installer will enter the nameserver specified by the DHCP server. If you manually configure a static IP address during installation, you must manually specify the nameserver value to use.

The /etc/hosts File

Another method of resolving hostnames is to use a local host database, much like what was previously done on the Internet. The /etc/hosts file contains a list of hostnames and related IP addresses.

Here's an example of an /etc/hosts file created on an Ubuntu server:

```
127.0.0.1 localhost
192.168.0.1 shadrach.smallorg.org
10.0.0.1 mail1.isp.net
10.0.0.2 mail2.isp.net
10.1.2.3 fred.otherplace.com
```

At a minimum, this file should contain your local hostname and IP address, as well as the common loopback address 127.0.0.1 for internal communications on the Ubuntu server. If there are remote hosts that you regularly access, you could find their IP addresses and manually enter them into the /etc/hosts file. Then every time you accessed those hostnames, Ubuntu would have the addresses on hand and not have to perform a DNS lookup. This greatly improves the connection time.

Secret

Besides the normal IP address section, the default Ubuntu /etc/hosts file contains a section for the newer IPv6 addresses. The IPv6 protocol is an expanded version of the IP address scheme, providing a larger address base for more hosts. The IPv6 section of the /etc/hosts file looks like this:

```
# The following lines are desirable for IPv6 capable hosts
::1 localhost ip6-localhost ip6-loopback
fe00::0 ip6-localhost
ff00::0 ip6-mcastprefix
ff02::1 ip6-allnodes
ff02::2 ip6-allrouters
ff02::3 ip6-allhosts
```

The IPv6 addresses list the IPv6 address version of the localhost address, as well as IPv6 common network addresses.

The /etc/host.conf File

The /etc/host.conf file specifies the methods and order that Ubuntu can attempt to resolve hostnames. Here's an example of a sample /etc/host.conf file:

```
order hosts,bind
multi on
```

The first line lists the order in which hostnames should be resolved. This example shows that Ubuntu will first look up the hostname in its /etc/hosts file, then attempt to use DNS (the bind option) if the hostname isn't found in the hosts file.

Ubuntu Client DNS Programs

Numerous programs have been written for Linux that help system administrators find DNS information for remote hosts and networks. The Internet Software Consortium created the Berkeley Internet Name Domain (BIND) package for UNIX systems, which includes three of my favorite and often used programs: host, nslookup, and dig.

The following sections describe these three programs and show how to use them on your Ubuntu server

The Host Program

The host program does basic DNS name resolution. The format of the host command is as follows:

```
host [-aCdlnrsTwv] [-c class] [-N ndots] [-R retries] [-t querytype] [-W wait]
[-m flag] [-4] [-6] host [server]
```

There are lots of parameters to customize the output of the host command. By default, host will attempt to resolve the hostname *host* by using the default DNS server specified in the /etc/resolv.conf file:

```
$ host www.ubuntu.com
www.ubuntu.com has address 91.189.94.249
$
```

If *server* is added, host will attempt to use that instead of the default DNS server for the system. This feature is particularly useful if you suspect your local DNS server is caching the host IP address and you want to go directly to the local DNS server for the remote host.

By adding parameters to the command line, you can modify the output and behavior of host. These parameters are shown in Table 20-3.

Table 20-3: The Host Command Parameters

Parameter	Description
-a	Request all domain info
-C	Display SOA records from all nameservers for the domain
-c *class*	Request domain information for the specified class (the default class is IN)
-d	Enable verbose output for debugging
-l	List the complete domain info
-I	Use the IP6.INT domain for reverse IPv6 lookups
-m *flag*	Set memory usage flags for debugging
-N *ndots*	Set the number of dots that have to be in the domain name for it to be absolute
-R *retries*	Specify the number of retries to attempt to contact the DNS server
-r	Enable recursion
-s	Don't send the query to the next DNS server
-T	Use a TCP connection instead of a UDP connection with the DNS server

continues

Table 20-3: *(continued)*

Parameter	Description
-t *querytype*	Specify query type
-W *wait*	Wait for *wait* seconds for a response from the DNS server
w	Wait indefinitely for a response from the DNS server
-4	Use only an IPv4 transport
-6	Use only an IPv6 transport

You can use the -l option to find information about all of the hosts listed in a domain. The -l option is often used with the -t option to filter particular types of information (such as -t MX, which returns all of the MX records for a domain). Unfortunately, in this day of security awareness it is often difficult to use the -l option because many DNS servers refuse attempts to access all of the host information contained in the database.

If you are trying to get information from a slow DNS server (or a slow link to the network) you may want to try the -w parameter. This parameter tells the host program to wait forever for a response to the query. By default, it will time out after about 1 minute.

One particularly useful parameter is -r, which tells the DNS server to return only information that it has in its own local DNS database regarding the query. The DNS server will not attempt to contact a remote DNS server to find the information.

The -r parameter is useful in determining whether your DNS server is properly caching DNS answers. First, try resolving a hostname using the -r parameter. If no one else has tried to resolve the hostname of this location, you should not get an answer back from your local DNS server.

Then try it without the -r parameter. You should get the normal DNS information back because the local DNS server was allowed to contact a remote DNS server to retrieve the information.

Next, try the host command again with the -r parameter. You should now get the same information that you received from the previous attempt. This means that the DNS server did indeed cache the results from the previous DNS query in its local name cache.

If you did not receive any information back, then your local DNS server did not cache the previous response. You should have noticed a significant decrease in the time it took to respond with an answer from cache compared to the response time after performing the DNS query on the network.

By default, the host command attempts to produce its output in human-readable format. Here's an example of a typical output:

```
$ host ubuntu.org
ubuntu.com has address 91.189.94.250
ubuntu.com mail is handled by 10 mx.canonical.com
```

If you specify a domain name, the host command automatically attempts to find the MX records associated with the domain.

The nslookup Program

The `nslookup` program is an extremely versatile tool that can be used in a variety of troubleshooting situations. There are two modes that `nslookup` can be run under.

In *non-interactive mode* it behaves very much like the `host` command previously discussed. Just enter the host or domain name you're interested in on the command line, and `nslookup` displays basic information about it. The basic format of the `nslookup` command is

```
nslookup [-option…] [host | - ] [server]
```

If you enter the *host* parameter on the command line, `nslookup` operates in non-interactive mode and returns the result of the query, similar to the `host` command.

If no arguments are given, or if the first argument is a hyphen (-), `nslookup` enters *interactive mode*. In interactive mode, the `nslookup` program provides its own command line where you can enter commands.

If you want to use a different DNS server, you can specify it using the *server* parameter, where *server* is the IP address of the DNS server to use. Otherwise, `nslookup` will use the default DNS server as listed in the /etc/resolv.conf file.

There are three ways to change option settings in the `nslookup` program:

- List them as options in the command line.
- Specify them on the interactive command line by using the `set` command.
- Create a file in your $HOME directory called .nslookuprc and enter the options, one per line.

A list of options available is shown in Table 20-4.

Table 20-4: The nslookup Options

Option	Description
all	Print current values of options
class	Set the DNS class value (default = IN).
[no]debug	Turn debugging mode on (or off) (default = nodebug)
[no]d2	Turn exhaustive debugging mode on (or off) (default = nod2)
domain=*name*	Set the default domain name to *name*
srchlist=*name1/name2*	Change default domain name to *name1* and the search list to *name1,name2*, etc.
[no]defname	Append default domain name to a single component lookup request
[no]search	Append domain names in search list to the hostname (default = search)
port=*value*	Change TCP/UDP port to *value* (default = 53)
querytype=*value*	Change type of information requested to type *value* (default = A)

continues

Table 20-4: *(continued)*

Option	Description
type=*value*	Same as querytype
[no]recurse	Tell nameserver to query other servers to obtain an answer (default = recurse)
retry=*number*	Set number of retries to *number* (default = 4)
root=*host*	Change name of root server to *host* (default = ns.internic.net)
timeout=*number*	Change initial timeout interval to wait for a reply to *number* (default = 5 seconds)
[no]vc	Always use a virtual circuit (default = novc)
[no]ignoretc	Ignore packet truncation errors (default = noignoretc)

Let's take a look at a sample nslookup session used to get information for host www.ubuntu.com:

```
$ nslookup
> www.ubuntu.com
Server: 10.0.1.1
Address: 10.0.1.1#53

Non-authoritative answer:
Name: www.ubuntu.com
Address: 91.189.94.249
>
```

When you enter nslookup on the command line, it produces its own command-line prompt, the greater-than sign (>). At this point, you can enter a command or the hostname you want to find information for.

The following example shows retrieving the basic IP address information on a typical hostname. You can also set the output for a specific type of DNS record to retrieve that information:

```
> set type=MX
> ubuntu.com
Server: 10.0.1.1
Address: 10.0.1.1#53

Non-authoritative answer:
ubuntu.com mail exchanger = 10 mx.canonical.com

Authoritative answers can be found from:
>exit
$
```

In this example, I set the record type to MX to return the mail servers for the domain.

The dig Program

The dig program uses a simple command-line format to query DNS servers to return all information for a domain. It provides one-stop shopping for all the DNS information you could possibly need for a site. The format for the dig command is a follows:

```
dig [@server] [options] domain [query-type] [query-class] [query-options]
```

There are several types of parameters that modify the DNS information the dig command retrieves and displays:

- ◆ **@server:** An optional DNS server to use instead of the default system setting.
- ◆ **query-type:** The RR-type information that you are requesting, such as the A, SOA, NS, and MX records. Use a query type of any to return all information available about a domain.
- ◆ **query-class:** The network class of information that you are requesting. The default is Internet (IN).
- ◆ **query-options:** Used to change an option value in the DNS packet or to change the format of the dig output. These options mirror the options available in the nslookup program.

Besides these parameters, the dig command also has its own set of parameters to specify other options that affect the operation of dig. Table 20-5 shows some of the other options available to fine-tune the dig command and its output.

Table 20-5: The dig Command Options

Option	Description
-b *address*	Specify the source address of the query
-c *class*	Specify the query class (default is IN)
-f *filename*	Read a file for batch mode processing
-k *filename*	Specify a file to read the encryption key used to sign the DNS query
-p	Specify a port number to use
-q *name*	Specify the query name
-t *type*	Specify type of query
-x *addr*	Specify a reverse lookup of the address specified
-y	Specify an encryption key to digitally sign the DNS query

The dig program produces the same information as host and nslookup, but it provides more detail about how and where the answers came from:

```
$ dig ubuntu.com MX

; <<>> DiG 9.5.0-P2 <<>> ubuntu.com MX
;; global options: printcmd
;; Got answer:
;; ->>HEADER<<- opcode: QUERY, status: NOERROR, id: 6464
```

```
;; flags: qr rd ra; QUERY: 1, ANSWER: 1, AUTHORITY: 0, ADDITIONAL: 0

;; QUESTION SECTION:
;ubuntu.com. IN MX

;; ANSWER SECTION:
ubuntu.com. 3583 IN MX 10 mx.canonical.com.

;; Query time: 4 msec
;; SERVER: 10.0.1.1#53(10.0.1.1)
;; WHEN: Tue Oct 14 19:01:32 2008
;; MSG SIZE rcvd: 57
$
```

The output shows the DNS records as they appear in the nameserver for the domain, which is much more detail than you'd get using the host or nslookup programs.

Ubuntu as a DNS Server

If you have a direct, full-time connection to the Internet, you may want to host your own DNS server for your domain. You can easily do this with your Ubuntu server and the BIND software package.

The DNS server software program in BIND is called *named*. When you select the DNS server option in the Ubuntu server installation, Ubuntu installs the named package automatically. All you need to do is configure it for your specific network requirements.

The named software is completely configurable, allowing you to create several different types of DNS server environments. There are two common configuration setups for DNS servers:

♦ **Local cache server:** The Ubuntu server acts as an intermediary between the local network and a remote DNS server. The named software receives DNS requests from local clients and hosts and forwards them to a remote DNS server, but it keeps the responses in a local cache. The next time a client or host on your local network requests the IP address for the same hostname, the named software returns the answer from the local cache without having to contact the remote DNS server.

♦ **A zone DNS server:** The Ubuntu server is responsible for maintaining the IP address and hostname information for all hosts on a local network. It must respond to DNS requests from the root-level DNS servers requesting name lookup for hosts on your local network.

The named package contains several configuration files that you must set to tell it how to operate. The tricky part of configuring the named package is getting the correct DNS settings in the correct configuration file.

The followings sections describe the layout of the named environment in Ubuntu and demonstrate how to implement both of these DNS server methods for using the DNS named program on an Ubuntu server.

The named Files

The Ubuntu server places all of the configuration files needed for the named program in the /etc/bind folder. Table 20-6 shows these files and their purpose on the server.

Table 20-6: The Ubuntu named Files

File	Description
db.0	Zone file containing reverse lookup data for the network address
db.127	Zone file containing reverse lookup data for the localhost address
db.255	Zone file containing reverse lookup data for the broadcast address
db.empty	Blank zone file
db.local	Zone file for the local loopback address
db.root	Zone file containing information on root zone DNS servers
named.conf	The named master zone configuration file
named.conf.local	Zone configuration file for adding local zones
named.conf.options	Zone configuration file for adding named options
rndc.key	Encryption key file for communicating with remote DNS servers
zones.rfc1918	Zone file containing reverse lookup data for private network addresses

The named.conf configuration file is the master file that defines the zones recognized by the named service. It contains references to the other zone files, along with options files, so that the named program can incorporate all of the information into the configuration.

You may notice a trend to the DNS zone file-naming convention used by Ubuntu:

- ◆ named. files contain the zone hostname information.
- ◆ db. files contain reverse lookup data information.

The zones.rfc1918 file is a zone file that contains standard reverse lookup data for the special private network addresses defined in Request for Comments (RFC) 1918. If your local network uses a private network addressing scheme (such as 10.x.x.x or 192.168.x.x) you should include this file in your named.conf configuration.

Secret

DNS server configurations can get pretty messy, especially for large networks. Using separate files to contain different zone information is a great way to help organize information. The filename extension on the db. files is used by named to identify the first octet value in the IP address for the reverse lookup area. For example, the db.127 file contains the lines:

```
;
; BIND reverse data file for local loopback interface
;
$TTL 604800
@    IN SOA localhost. root.localhost. (
1 ; Serial
604800 ; Refresh
86400 ; Retry
```

continues

continued

```
2419200 ; Expire
604800 ) ; Negative Cache TTL
;
@ IN NS localhost.
1.0.0 IN PTR localhost.
```

This information defines a single PTR **record for the 127.0.0.1 address (remember, the IP octets are listed in reverse order in the** PTR **record). This defines the reverse lookup for the special localhost IP address.**

Using named as a Local Cache Server

The easiest way to use the named program on your server is to cache DNS responses on the Ubuntu server for future DNS requests. This configuration points all DNS requests received by the Ubuntu server (either from the server itself or from other network devices pointing to the Ubuntu server) to the named program running on the local server. The named program configuration redirects all requests to a common remote DNS server, usually provided by an ISP.

The benefit to this method is that the named program will cache all the DNS requests it handles. Thus, it can immediately answer any future requests for the same hostname without having to contact the remote DNS server. This capability can significantly speed up interactions on the Internet for your local network.

There are two things you'll need to do to get this method set up on your Ubuntu server:

  ◆ Set the nameserver entry in the resolv.conf file to point to the localhost.
  ◆ Set the named configuration to point to a common remote DNS server.

Here are the steps required to change the nameserver entry in the resolv.conf file:

1. Open the /etc/resolv.conf file in a text editor. If you're working on the Ubuntu server, you'll need to use a command-line editor such as the vim editor. To edit this file you must have administrative privileges (see Chapter 17, "Users and Groups"). Enter the command:

```
sudo vim /etc/resolv.conf
```

2. Copy the current value set in the nameserver line. The default Ubuntu configuration should have detected the network nameserver via DHCP unless you manually entered that value to set a static IP address for your server at installation time. The nameserver line should look like this:

```
nameserver 10.0.1.1
```

Copy that IP address. You'll need it for a later step.

3. Change the IP address on the line to 127.0.0.1. This redirects all DNS requests to the named program running on the server.

4. Save the file and exit the editor. The vim command to save the file and exit the editor is ZZ.

Next you'll need to configure the named program to forward all DNS requests to the remote DNS server that was originally listed in the resolv.conf file. Follow these steps:

1. Open the /etc/bind/named.conf.options file in a text editor. Again, if you're working on the Ubuntu server, you'll need to use a command-line editor such as vim to edit the file. To edit this file you must have administrative privileges (see Chapter 17, "Users and Groups"). To edit the file, enter this command:

```
sudo vim /etc/bind/named.conf.options
```

2. Look for the forwarders section in the named.conf.options file, and change it to look like this:

```
forwarders {
10.0.1.1;
};
```

You'll have to remove the comments (double forward slashes) in front of these lines to make them active. The IP address you use should be the one you copied from the original resolv.conf file.

3. Save the file, and edit the editor. The vim command to save the file and exit the editor is ZZ.

The named program is now ready to go. You'll need to restart the named program, either by rebooting the Ubuntu server or entering the command:

```
sudo /etc/init.d/bind9 restart
```

This command restarts the named program, which will read the new configuration and run as a local cache server.

Using named as a Master DNS Server

If you want your Ubuntu server to be the main DNS server for your network, you'll need to do a bit more work. The DNS server responsible for a network is called a *master DNS server*. A master DNS server contains records that define all of the hosts on the network, both for internal communications and for communications outside of your network. If any server on the Internet needs to know the IP address for a hostname of your network, your Ubuntu server must be available to answer the request.

This configuration uses the same named configuration files as in the local cache server example, but it adds the network zone information to the configuration files. The configuration files need both the hostname and IP address information for the hosts you want to make available to the Internet.

You'll need to configure three additional files to add your local network zone:

◆ /etc/bind/named.conf.local: This file stores the zone names and file locations.

◆ /etc/bind/db.smallorg.org: A zone configuration file based on your domain name, it stores the zone hostname information for your hosts.

◆ /etc/bind/db.10: A reverse lookup configuration file based on the first octet of your IP network address, it stores the reverse IP address information for your hosts.

The first file already exists in the /etc/bind folder. All you need to do is add two definitions to point to your zone and reverse lookup files. Here are the steps required to configure the named.conf.local file for your network:

1. Open the /etc/bind/named.conf.local file in a text editor. If you're working on the Ubuntu server, you'll need to use a command-line editor to do this. The vim editor is installed by default in Ubuntu server and should work fine:

   ```
   sudo vim /etc/bind/named.conf.local
   ```

2. Add a zone definition pointing to the zone configuration file. The zone definition defines the domain name, along with the type of DNS server (master) and the filename of the zone configuration file:

   ```
   zone "smallorg.org {
   type master;
   file "/etc/bind/db.smallorg.org";
   };
   ```

   The semicolons at the end of the lines are important—they signify the end of a line.

3. Add a zone definition pointing to the reverse lookup configuration file. The reverse lookup configuration uses the backward IP address format to define the network:

   ```
   zone "0.0.10.in-addr.arpa" {
   type "master";
   file "/etc/bind/db.10";
   };
   ```

   Again, each line in the zone file must end with a semicolon.

4. Save the named.conf.local file and exit the text editor. The vim command to save the file and exit the editor is ZZ.

Once you've updated the named.conf.local file, you're ready to create your zone configuration and reverse lookup configuration files. First, here are the steps for creating the zone configuration file:

1. Create a new file called /etc/bind/db.smallorg.org using a text editor. If you specify the filename in the vim command line, the vim editor will automatically create it for you:

   ```
   sudo vim /etc/bind/db.smallorg.org
   ```

2. Add an SOA record for your zone. The SOA record needs to name your DNS server, along with the email address of an administrator account (remember to place a dot in place of the @ sign in the email address, and also remember to place a dot at the end of your DNS server name). A sample looks like this:

   ```
   @ IN SOA testbox.smallorg.org. postmaster.smallorg.org. (
   2008810151 ; serial, todays date + todays serial #
   3600 ; refresh, seconds
   1800 ; retry, seconds
   604800 ; expire, seconds
   3600) ; minimum, seconds
   ```

3. Add an NS record to define the nameserver for the domain. The NS record points to the name of the Ubuntu server that's running DNS:

```
NS testbox ; name server
```

4. Add any MX records to point to mail servers on your network. The mail servers can be advertised with either the same priority (to perform load balancing) or with differing priorities (to define a primary and secondary mail server). The mail server doesn't have to be on your network.

```
MX 10 mail.smallorg.org. ; Primary mail server
MX 20 mail.isp.net. ; Secondary mail server at ISP
```

5. Add A records to define hosts on the local network that you want to advertise to the Internet, along with any CNAME records to define alias names. This area needs to list all of the hosts on your network:

```
www CNAME fred.smallorg.org ; defines the Web host alias
localhost A 127.0.0.1
testbox A 10.0.0.1 ; defines the DNS server
fred A 10.0.0.2 ; defines Web server
mail A 10.0.0.3 ; defines the mail host
```

6. Save the file and exit the editor. The vim command to save the file and exit the editor is ZZ.

Now you're halfway to hosting your domain! Next you must create the DNS database file for your reverse domain address as listed in the named.conf.local file. Here are the steps for doing that:

1. Create the /etc/bind/db.10 file using a text editor. The number in the filename must match the first octet of your network IP address. Again, you can use the vim editor to create the file:

```
sudo vim /etc/bind/db.10
```

2. Add an SOA record to define your network. You can use the same SOA record you used in the zone configuration file:

```
@ IN SOA testbox.smallorg.org. postmaster.smallorg.org. (
2008810151 ; serial, todays date + serial #
3600 ; refresh, seconds
1800 ; retry, seconds
604800 ; expire, seconds
3600) ; minimum, seconds
```

3. Add an NS record to define the nameserver for the domain. The NS record points to the name of the Ubuntu server that's running DNS:

```
NS testbox ; name server
```

4. Add PTR records for each host defined in the zone configuration file. Each host that may require a reverse lookup should be added to this list, along with the host portion of their IP address on your network:

```
1 PTR testbox.smallorg.org.
2 PTR fred.smallorg.org.
3 PTR mail.smallorg.org.
```

5. Save the file and exit the editor. The vim command to save and exit is ZZ.

These configuration files allow your `named` program to respond to DNS queries for your domain. Of course, this assumes that you have properly registered your domain with the Internet Network Information Center (NIC) and that the root DNS servers for the proper first-level domain (.org in this example) have pointers to the IP address of the Ubuntu server that is acting as your DNS server.

One final word of caution: The examples in this chapter use fictitious IP addresses. To host your own domain you must have a valid IP address on the Internet, as assigned by the NIC, and use a valid IP address for your DNS server so that other Internet computers can connect to it. If you choose to let your ISP host your domain, you can use the public IP address network of 192.168.0.0 to assign IP addresses to hosts on your network.

Secret

The `PTR` records in the DNS database can be the most confusing part of the configuration. IP addresses are split into two portions: a network portion and a host portion. The split is determined by the value of the network subnet mask.

For an IP address of 10.0.0.1 using a subnet mask of 255.255.255.0, the 10.0.0 part is considered the network portion of the IP address. This identifies the subnetwork the host resides in. The .1 part is considered the host portion, which uniquely identifies a host within the subnetwork. The zone definition for the reverse lookup filename uses only the network portion of the address in its definition:

```
zone "0.0.10.in-addr.arpa" {
```

and the reverse lookup file uses only the host portion of the address:

```
1 PTR testbox.smallorg.org.
```

The host portion is added to this information to create the full reverse lookup IP address: 1.0.0.10.in-addr.arpa.

Summary

This chapter discussed the domain name system (DNS) and explained how it relates to your network. Each server connected to the Internet has a unique hostname and a unique IP address. The DNS database system matches the hostnames and IP addresses. The database is distributed among many different servers on the Internet so that no one server has to maintain the list of all computers. You can find a remote computer's IP address by its hostname by sending a DNS query to a DNS server. That server has the capability of walking the DNS tree to find the database record that relates the hostname to the IP address, or vice versa.

Many domains use their domain name as a generic email address. The Ubuntu server distribution provides the BIND package to help you run a DNS server for your network. You can run your DNS server as either a local cache that stores DNS requests to help speed up future requests, or as a full-blown zone DNS server that manages the hostnames on your network for other networks to use.

In the next chapter we'll take a look at the web server features the Ubuntu server distribution has to offer. The Ubuntu server distribution can pre-install the two most popular web server platforms on the Internet, making it a snap to get your web applications up and running!

Web Server

Chapter
21

In today's world, where practically everything revolves around the Internet, making your applications network accessible is almost a necessity. Fortunately, there's plenty of help available in the Ubuntu server distribution. The Ubuntu server distribution is created specifically for running server applications, as opposed to desktop applications. It provides two popular web server packages for you to install, the Linux–Apache–MySQL–PHP (LAMP) platform, as well as the Tomcat Java application server. Mostly due to its simplicity and robustness, the LAMP platform has quickly become one of the hottest web application platforms on the Internet. The Tomcat Java application server provides an environment for creating JavaServer Pages (JSP) applications as well as Java servlet applications, both extremely popular in the Java programming world. This chapter describes the Ubuntu server web platform as installed from the Ubuntu server distribution and walks you through setting up and using both the LAMP and Tomcat servers.

Ubuntu Web Servers

With literally millions of web pages on the Internet, and more springing up every day, it's getting harder to attract and impress online visitors. Having outdated information on your web page will not only frustrate your visitors, but it might even damage your company or organization. To avoid this problem, web pages must be *dynamic.*

Dynamic web pages allow you to change your content in real time, without having to touch any of the code used to create the page. With dynamic web pages you can keep the content fresh so that what visitors see there now may be updated or replaced the next time they visit, whether that's a week from now, tomorrow, or the next hour. The core layout of the web page can remain the same (such as corporate logos, links, and headings), but the data presented on the page constantly change.

The key to doing this without keeping a full-time staff of web site designers busy is to use *web scripting languages.* Web scripting languages allow you to incorporate programming code within your web pages that can access external data and display them just as if the data had been coded into your web page.

The following section walks through how web scripting languages work, then it discusses the three types of web scripting languages installed on the Ubuntu server.

Web Scripting Languages

The client browser displays only what the web server sends it. For a dynamic web page to change what it sends to visitors in real time, the HTML coding must be able to automatically change. To accomplish this, developers embed programming code using a scripting language within the HTML code. As the embedded program runs, it automatically changes the content (or layout) of the web page without any intervention from the web designer. Figure 21-1 demonstrates this process.

The embedded program code generates standard HTML code that the client browser interprets. Because programming code is embedded in the dynamic web page, something somewhere must run the code to produce the HTML for the new content.

The embedded programming code can run in two places:

- ◆ **Client side:** on the client's workstation after it downloads the web page
- ◆ **Server side:** on the web server before the web page is sent

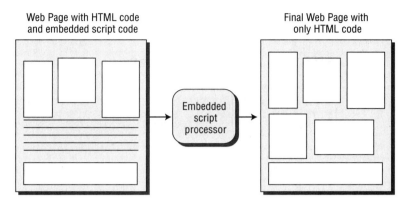

Figure 21-1: Program code embedded in a web page.

The most popular client-side scripting language is JavaScript. JavaScript is code that's embedded in an HTML web page and runs within the client browser. It can utilize features of the browser, or even of the PC itself, that are not normally accessible from standard HTML code.

A common use for JavaScript code is to produce pop-up messages and dialog boxes that interact with the viewer. These are elements that HTML code can't generate. Figure 21-2 demonstrates how a web page embeds JavaScript and sends it to the client.

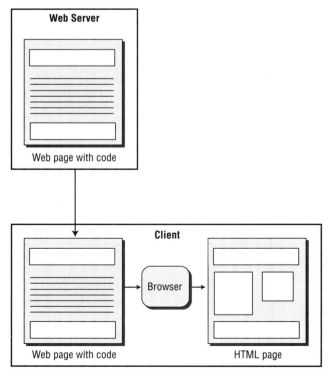

Figure 21-2: Running client-side scripting programs.

The downside of client-side scripting languages is that you're at the mercy of the client's web browser. Although the HTML language is standard, web scripting languages aren't. It's not uncommon to run across a client-side web page that works just fine in one type of browser but not at all in another type.

Server-side scripting languages solve this problem. In server-side scripting, the web server interprets the embedded programming code before sending the web page to the client's browser. The server then takes the HTML that the programming code generates and inserts it directly into the web page being sent. The server does all of the work running the scripting code, so you are guaranteed that every web page will run properly. Figure 21-3 illustrates this process.

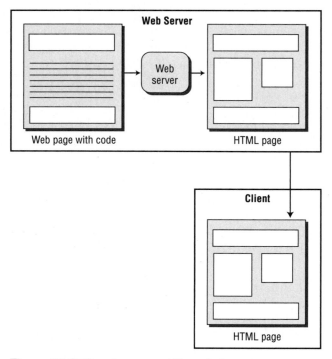

Figure 21-3: Running server-side scripting programs.

Many server-side scripting languages are available. The Microsoft server platform offers the proprietary ASP and ASP.NET languages. UNIX and Linux platforms (including Ubuntu) support various scripting languages, such as Perl, Python, PHP, and Java. You can use any of these to incorporate dynamic content on a web page. This section focuses on the three scripting languages the Ubuntu server installs by default:

- ◆ PHP
- ◆ JavaServer Pages
- ◆ Java servlets

The following sections describe these three server-side scripting environments in more detail.

PHP

The PHP: Hypertext Preprocessor (PHP) scripting language was created in 1995 by Rasmus Lerdorf and, although not officially open-source software, it's considered free software by the Free Software Foundation. The PHP scripting language now includes a command-line interface to allow you to write standalone PHP scripts without a web interface.

By far, the most popular use of PHP is to generate dynamic web pages. The output of the PHP program appears to the client browser as normal HTML text within the web page. The host web server (usually the Apache web server) detects PHP code using an opening and closing tag combination:

```
<html>
<body>
<h2>This is a PHP example</h2>
<?php
echo "This is PHP code!";
?>
</body>
</html>
```

PHP prides itself on simplicity, which allows most web developers to learn the basics and use it with minimal effort (see Chapter 30, "PHP"). That simplicity, along with the popularity of the LAMP platform, has made knowing PHP a necessity for the dynamic web programmer.

JavaServer Pages

JavaServer Pages (JSP) are part of the Java group of programming languages developed and released by Sun Microsystems. The JSP language works similar to PHP in that you embed JSP code directly into an HTML web page to provide dynamic content:

```
<html>
<body>
<h2>This is a JSP example</h2>
<% out.println("This is JSP code!"); %>
</body>
</html>
```

The JSP language uses Java statements to generate code, as well as special tags that invoke built-in JSP functions in the script.

Java Servlets

The downside to scripting languages is that the web server must process them in real time as a client browser requests the page. The web server routes the requested web page to either the PHP or JSP preprocessor to interpret the code. The preprocessor must run though the program code line by line and execute each script statement.

This process can take quite a bit of time, relatively speaking. For large, complicated web pages, the delay between the web page request and the returned data can be significant.

Java servlets attempt to solve this problem by compiling JSP scripts into byte code, similar to how you compile a normal Java application. The byte code that's generated handles most of the script processing ahead of time and creates a streamlined application contained in byte code. The preprocessor can then run the Java servlet byte code significantly faster than the original JSP script code.

The LAMP Platform

The open-source community embraced the PHP programming language for dynamic web page development and created an environment specifically suited for hosting PHP web pages, called *AMP*.

AMP is an acronym that stands for the three software elements used to create the server:

 ◆ The **A**pache web server
 ◆ The **M**ySQL database server
 ◆ The **P**HP programming language

The Apache web server is the most popular web server platform in use on the Internet. It provides plug-in modules to support lots of features, including PHP embedded scripting. It can run on virtually any operating system platform, including Linux workstations and servers.

The MySQL database server is an extremely popular open-source database platform. Although it lacks some of the more advanced features of commercial database products, it makes up for it in ease of use and quickness. Many commercial Internet sites use MySQL as the back-end database to support functions such as online shopping and content management.

The PHP programming language is a package that plugs into many different web servers to process PHP code. Usually there's some configuration required for the web server so that it knows how to detect a PHP code file and where to route the file for processing. The PHP Project has created plug-in modules for both the Apache web server and the Microsoft Internet Information Server (IIS), the two main web servers available on the Internet.

In the early days of AMP, you had to install and configure each of these elements yourself. But now you can find prebuilt AMP packages for many different operating systems. For the Microsoft Windows environment, the complete package is called *WAMP* (the *W* stands for Windows). Because you're reading this book, I assume that you're interested in using the open-source Linux operating system. That package is called *LAMP* (you guessed it: *L* for Linux).

The Ubuntu server LAMP installation automatically installs and preconfigures the Apache web server, MySQL database server, and the PHP programming language processor module for you to use. All you'll need to do is start writing web programs!

The Tomcat Platform

For JSP and Java servlet applications to work, you must have a Java environment, along with a web server. The Apache Project created a separate software package just for handling the Java web environment.

Tomcat is a combination Java code processor and web server that can handle both JSP and Java servlet applications as a single package. It bundles three separate packages into one application:

 ◆ **Catalina:** a Java servlet container for managing Java servlet applications
 ◆ **Coyote:** a web server component to accept and process incoming web connections using HTTP

◆ **Jasper:** a JSP engine that processes the Java code contained in JSP files; it compiles JSP files into Java code at runtime and passes the Java code to Catalina for processing as a servlet application

Tomcat installs all three components as a single, standalone package. It is usually used separately from any existing web server packages, such as the Apache web server.

Because it's separate from the standard Apache web server, Tomcat must use a different TCP port to communicate with clients. The default, TCP port used by Apache web servers is 80. By default the Tomcat web server uses TCP port 8080. This is important to know when working in a Tomcat development environment.

Usually after an application is developed and moved into production, the production Tomcat server is changed to run on TCP port 80 so that clients can connect to the application using a normal-style URL instead of having to include the TCP port. Therefore, if there's an Apache web server on the same host server, it must be moved to another TCP port.

The Apache Web Server

The core of the Ubuntu web server is the Apache web server software. The Apache web server software can serve standard HTML web pages and also support the dynamic PHP web pages used in the LAMP environment.

This section discusses the Ubuntu server distribution's Apache web server installation and shows how to customize it for your environment.

You can also install the Apache web server in an Ubuntu workstation environment, but it isn't recommended for a production environment. A web server shouldn't have the performance overhead of managing a graphical desktop environment while trying to serve clients.

If you do decide to install the Apache web server on an Ubuntu workstation, be careful. The version of the Apache web server available from the Synaptic Package Manager repositories is not the same as what's available for the Ubuntu server installation. If you're planning on running a real web server, your best solution is to use the web server in the Ubuntu server distribution.

Instead of installing the Apache web server from the Synaptic Package Manager, install it using the `tasksel` utility. From a Terminal command prompt, enter the command:

```
sudo tasksel
```

A menu similar to the installation menu in the Ubuntu server install appears, showing several packages to install. Select the LAMP package from this list, but be careful not to deselect any previously selected options. Doing so will install the Apache web server, MySQL database server, and PHP programming language files, just as in the Ubuntu server distribution.

Apache Configuration Files

The Apache web server requires a few configuration files to operate. When you select to install the LAMP server from the Ubuntu server installation menu, the installation process installs the Apache web server package, including preconfigured Apache files, to create a basic web server environment.

All of the Apache web server configuration files are located in the /etc/apache2 folder. They include the following files and folders:

- ◆ **apache2.conf:** the main Apache web server configuration file that the Apache web server reads
- ◆ **conf.d:** a folder containing files that have specific configuration features included in the Apache configuration (by default, Ubuntu creates configurations to define the character set of the server and set the security level of the server)
- ◆ **envvars:** a configuration file to set specific environment variables for the Apache web server
- ◆ **httpd.conf:** a configuration file for adding local configuration customizations
- ◆ **mods-available:** a folder that contains the configuration settings for modules available for the server
- ◆ **mods-enabled:** a folder containing links to the enabled configuration settings stored in the mods-available folder.
- ◆ **ports.conf:** a configuration file that specifies which TCP ports the Apache web server should listen on
- ◆ **sites-available:** a folder containing available site definitions for virtual hosts
- ◆ **sites-enabled:** a folder containing links to the active site definition files in the sites-available folder

The /etc/apache2/apache2.conf file is the main configuration file that the Apache web server processes. This file references the individual configuration files for specific configuration features, such as the TCP ports used and the virtual hosts to create.

Apache Modules

The core Apache2 program supports only basic web page hosting features. Any other functionality needed for the web server (including sending PHP files to the PHP preprocessor) requires a plug-in *module*. Modules provide a host of various additional features to the Apache web server, including the capability to process PHP files.

Ubuntu stores modules in the /etc/apache2/mods-available folder. You can look in that folder to see what modules are installed by default in the Ubuntu server.

However, there's a subtle difference in what the Ubuntu server does when handling Apache modules. Although modules are stored in the /etc/apache2/mods-available folder, those modules aren't necessarily active in the Apache web server configuration.

For a module to become active, Ubuntu creates a file link in the /etc/apache2/mods-enabled folder that points to the module files in the mods-available folder. The Ubuntu server enables a few modules by default, providing for a robust web server environment. The modules enabled by default in the Ubuntu server are shown in Table 21-1.

Table 21-1: Apache Modules Loaded in Ubuntu Server

Module	Description
alias	Maps directory paths on the server to the web server document tree
auth_basic	Provides basic user authentication by looking up user accounts in a specific provider
authn_file	Restricts access based on a user account defined in a text file
authz_default	Rejects user access if no authentication is used (default module)
authz_groupfile	Restricts access based on groups defined in a text file
authz_host	Restricts access based on hostnames or IP addresses
authz_user	Restricts access to specific pages using user accounts
autoindex	Creates automatic directory listings
cgi	Executes common gateway interface (CGI) scripts from web pages
dir	Handles basic filesystem directories
env	Passes system environment variables to CGI scripts
mime	Determines file types using file extensions for handling files
negotiation	Selects a document type that matches the client's capabilities
php5	The PHP version 5 preprocessor
setenvif	Sets environment variables based on client information
status	Displays the server status using a specially formatted web page

Use the apt-get program (see Chapter 13, "Software Installs and Updates") from the command line to install additional modules directly from the Ubuntu server software repositories. To download a new module, use this command:

```
sudo apt-get install modname
```

This command downloads the module from the Ubuntu server repository into a special folder located at /etc/apache2/mods-available. To enable the module, you need to perform one more command:

```
a2enmod modname
```

This command makes the module active in the Apache web server.

Secret

To remove an active module from the configuration, don't delete the configuration files. Instead, use this command:

```
a2dismod modname
```

This command removes the module from the configuration files but keeps it in the mods-available folder for future use, if required.

Creating Virtual Hosts

By default, the Ubuntu server creates a single web server interface for the local server. The Apache web server has the ability to support *virtual hosts.* A virtual host is a method of allowing the Apache web server to accept HTTP requests from clients for servers other than itself.

Each virtual host has its own set of configuration parameters that define what TCP port the host listens on, what folder the server retrieves files from, and what security features it should utilize to allow or restrict clients.

Apache handles the virtual host features using a separate configuration file for each defined virtual host. These files are located in the /etc/apache2/sites-available and /etc/apache2/sites-enabled folders. As you can probably guess from the discussion on modules, the sites-available folder contains virtual host definitions, while the sites-enabled folder contains links to the virtual hosts that are enabled. This feature allows you to create a virtual host file ahead of time but not enable it until you're ready.

The default Ubuntu server configuration defines two virtual hosts:

- ◆ default:the default web host for the server using TCP port 80
- ◆ default-ssl: the default web host to use if secure sockets layer (SSL) encryption is enabled on the server, using TCP port 443

Only the default virtual host is activated. The default virtual host predefines several features of the web server so that you can get a simple web server up and running on the default installation. Table 21-2 shows the default virtual host configuration settings for the Ubuntu server web server.

Table 21-2: Default Ubuntu Web Server Settings

Setting	Value	Description
ServerAdmin	webmaster@localhost	The email address defined for the server administrator
DocumentRoot	/var/www/	The folder pathname to serve documents from
<Directory foldername>		Options and security settings for folder foldername
ScriptAlias	/cgi-bin/ /usr/lib/ cgi-bin/	The location of CGI scripts available for the server
ErrorLog	/var/log/apache2/ error.log	The location of the Apache error log file
LogLevel	warn	The default level to log Apache system messages
CustomLog	/var/log/apache2/access .log combined	The location and type of logging to log connections
Alias	/doc/ "/usr/share/doc"	Defines a default alias for the server, pointing to the shared documents folder

The default web server configuration uses the folder /var/www as the DocumentRoot location. This is where you place the files you want to offer to your customers on your web site.

Testing the Apache Server

To test the Ubuntu web server installation, you'll need to use a client that has a graphical desktop to view the web page. From a remote client on your network, open a browser and go to the IP address of your Ubuntu server:

```
http://10.0.0.1/
```

By default, the Apache web server will attempt to serve the file named index.html from the /var/www folder, as shown in Figure 21-4.

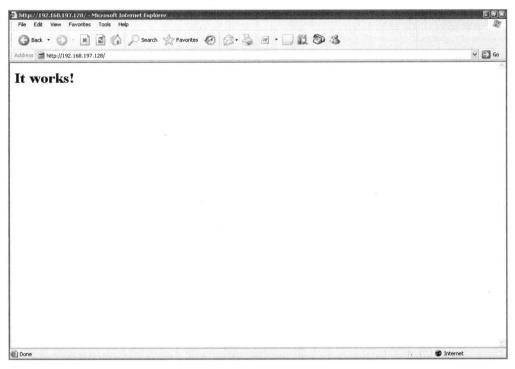

Figure 21-4: The default Ubuntu server web page.

If you want to view the status of your Ubuntu server, you can access the special server status web page provided by the status module. However, you need to change the default configuration for the module first. The status module configuration information is in the file /etc/apache2/mods-enabled/status.conf. It contains a <Location> section that defines what sites are allowed to connect to the server status web page:

```
<Location /server-status>
SetHandler server-status
Order deny,allow
```

```
Deny from all
Allow from localhost ip6-localhost
# Allow from .example.com
</Location>
```

The Allow directive defines locations that are allowed to access this web page. Add an Allow line that defines the hostname, IP address, or domain name you want to allow:

```
Allow from 192.168.197.1
```

Once you've added that line, restart the Apache web server using the command:

```
sudo /etc/init.d/apache2 restart
```

You can then access the server status page using the URL:

```
http://10.0.0.1/server-status
```

This command displays a status page showing the current operating status of the Apache web server, as shown in Figure 21-5.

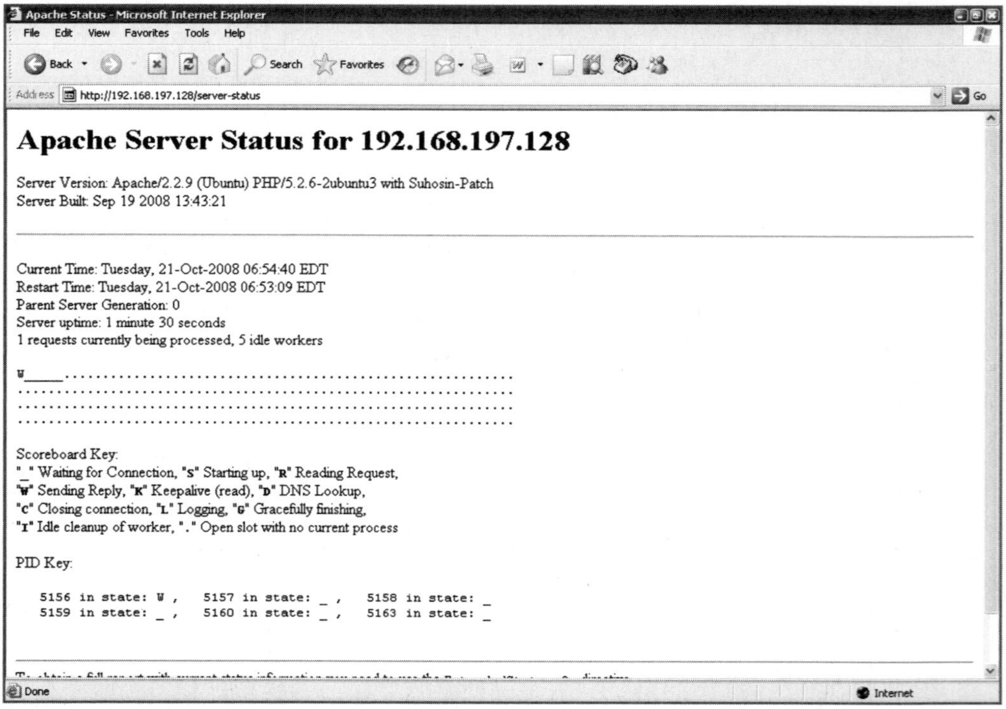

Figure 21-5: The Apache server status page.

Now that the Apache web server is running, you can turn your attention to the next component in the LAMP system, MySQL database server. That's covered in the next section.

Secret

By default, Ubuntu doesn't activate the Apache SSL module that allows you to use encryption when transmitting web pages. The SSL module requires that you have a valid certificate to use for encryption.

You can purchase a certificate from an authorized certificate authority (CA) or you can create your own self-signed certificate using the OpenSSL package if you selected to install SSL during the Ubuntu server installation process.

To create a self-signed certificate, follow these steps:

1. Generate a key for the certificate using the command:

   ```
   openssl genrsa -des3 -out server.key 1024
   ```

   Enter a passphrase to protect the key from unauthorized modification.

2. Generate a certificate signing request (CSR), which is used to identify you and your server for the certificate. Do this using the command:

   ```
   openssl req -new -key server.key -out server.csr
   ```

   The `server.key` file you created in step 1 must be in the folder where you run this command from. This command will ask questions about your name, organization, and server information. This information will be used in your certificate to identify you to your customers.

3. Create the self-signed certificate using the command:

   ```
   openssl x509 -req -days 365 -in server.csr -signkey server
   .key -out server.crt
   ```

   The `server.key` and `server.csr` files you previously generated must be in the same folder where you run this command from.

4. Copy the key and certificate to the server `/etc/ssl` folder locations:

   ```
   sudo cp server.key /etc/ssl/private
   sudo cp server.crt /etc/ssl/certs
   ```

5. Specify the file locations in the `default-ssl` virtual host configuration lines for the web host:

   ```
   SSLCertificateFile /etc/ssl/certs/server.crt
   SSLCertificateKeyFile /etc/ssl/private/server.key
   ```

6. Enable the SSL module in Apache:

   ```
   sudo a2enmod ssl
   ```

7. Add the `default-ssl` virtual host to the enabled sites using the command:

   ```
   sudo a2ensite default-ssl
   ```

Now you should be able to connect using the HTTPS protocol to your web site. When you use a self-signed certificate, most web browsers will produce a warning message indicating that there's a security risk involved with accepting a self-signed certificate from a web server. Self-signed certificates shouldn't be used in a production environment, as it forces your customers to accept you as the signing authority.

The MySQL Software

A main component of a successful dynamic web page environment is a database for storing and accessing data. The most popular database platform used in the open-source world is the MySQL database server.

Much of the popularity of MySQL comes from it being the original default database used in the PHP programming language (however, PHP can now interface with many different database packages), as well as the speed of the MySQL database server.

The original MySQL database server was well known for being fast but not overly robust. It lacked many of the advanced features commonly found in commercial databases, such as transactions, foreign keys, and row-level record locking.

To solve this problem, the developers at MySQL redesigned MySQL to work with multiple *storage engines.* A storage engine is the core of the database server. It handles the database interface—storing, managing, and deleting data for the server.

MySQL now supports several different types of storage engines, each one with a different specialty. Table 21-3 lists the different storage engines available in MySQL.

Table 21-3: The MySQL Storage Engines

Engine	Description
MyISAM	The original storage engine; speedy, but lacking many advanced database features
InnoDB	The newest, full-featured storage engine; although it supports many commercial-quality features, it's significantly slower than the MyISAM storage engine
Memory	Provides tables in memory
Merge	Combines multiple MyISAM tables into a single table
CSV	Stores data as comma-separated values in text files

Many high-volume web application sites still use the original MyISAM storage engine for its speed qualities, forsaking advanced features for performance.

The following sections describe how to use the MySQL database server installed on the Ubuntu server.

Accessing the Server

On the Ubuntu server you access the MySQL server via a command-line interface tool. The mysql program allows you to connect to the MySQL server, execute SQL commands, and view the results.

To connect to the default MySQL database using the root user account, type

```
mysql -u root -p
```

After entering the password, you should be at the MySQL prompt:

```
$ mysql -u root -p
Enter password:
Welcome to the MySQL monitor. Commands end with ; or \g.
```

```
Your MySQL connection id is 250 to server version: 3.23.36

Type 'help;' or '\h' for help. Type '\c' to clear the buffer

mysql>
```

Now you're ready to start entering SQL commands to build your database. Chapter 24, "Database Server," provides detailed information on creating databases and tables in the MySQL server environment.

Changing the Root Password

If you want to change the password for the root user account in MySQL, use the mysqladmin command:

```
sudo mysqladmin -p password 'newpassword'
```

The -p parameter causes the mysqladmin program to prompt you for the root user's password. After you type the current password, the mysqladmin program changes the password of the root user account to *newpassword*.

One of the most frustrating things that can happen to you as the administrator of a LAMP server is forgetting the MySQL root user's password. The root user account in MySQL controls all aspects of the database server. Not being able to log into the MySQL server as the root user means that you can't create new databases or user accounts, or modify existing ones.

Fortunately, there's a trick to recreate the root user account's password if you've forgotten it. Just follow these steps to get things back to normal:

1. Stop the MySQL server process. This requires using the mysql script in the /etc/init.d folder:

```
sudo /etc/init.d/mysql stop
```

2. Start the MySQL server without using the user tables. MySQL maintains its own set of internal user account tables. You can tell MySQL to start without reading those tables using the command:

```
sudo -u mysql mysqld_safe --skip-grant-tables &
```

You must start the MySQL server script as the special mysql system user account, and you must use the ampersand symbol (&) at the end to ensure that the MySQL server runs as a background process rather than tying up your command-line session.

3. Connect to the MySQL server as the root user without a password. Now that MySQL isn't using the default user tables, you can connect to the server without using a password:

```
mysql -u root
```

4. Define a new root password for the root user account. This requires a few lines of SQL code entered at the command-line interface:

```
mysql> use mysql;
mysql> UPDATE user SET password=PASSWORD('newpassword') WHERE
user = 'root';
mysql> flush privileges;
mysql> exit;
```

Note that each SQL statement ends with a semi-colon.

5. Stop, then restart, the MySQL server. For the new password to take effect, you must stop the current MySQL server, then start the server again—this time with the normal start parameters:

```
$ sudo /etc/init.d/mysql stop
$ sudo /etc/init.d/mysql start
```

Because you're starting the MySQL server with the normal start parameters, you can use the standard start script.

6. Log into the MySQL server as the root account with the new password. Use the `mysql` command-line program with the option to ask for a password:

```
$ mysql -u root -p
Enter password:
Welcome to the MySQL monitor. Commands end with ; or \g.
Your MySQL connection id is 250 to server version: 3.23.36

Type 'help;' or '\h' for help. Type '\c' to clear the buffer

mysql>
```

Congratulations! You've successfully recovered from a potential tragedy.

The phpMyAdmin Tool

An extremely handy tool for managing the MySQL database server via a graphical web interface is the *phpMyAdmin tool*. The phpMyAdmin tool isn't installed by default in the Ubuntu server installation process, but it is easy to install if your Ubuntu server is connected to the Internet:

1. Start a command-line interface prompt on your system.

2. Use the `apt-get` software to retrieve and install phpMyAdmin:

```
sudo apt-get install phpmyadmin
```

The command retrieves the phpMyAdmin package, along with any dependencies required to install it on your Ubuntu server. During the installation, `apt-get` provides a dialog box asking which web server to install phpMyAdmin for. Select the apache2 web server option.

3. Close the command-line interface.

4. Open a browser and navigate to the phpMyAdmin tool. Ubuntu installs the phpMyAdmin tool outside of the document root area of the Apache web server, but it creates an alias pointing to the location. This enables you to connect to the phpMyAdmin tool using the URL:

```
http://10.0.0.1/phpmyadmin
```

Be sure to use the IP address of your Ubuntu server in the URL.

The first phpMyAdmin tool web page prompts you for a MySQL userID and password to log into the server, as shown in Figure 21-6.

Log in with the root user account, using the password you assigned to it during the Ubuntu server installation. The main phpMyAdmin tool web page showing the databases and the various options available in the tool appear, as shown in Figure 21-7.

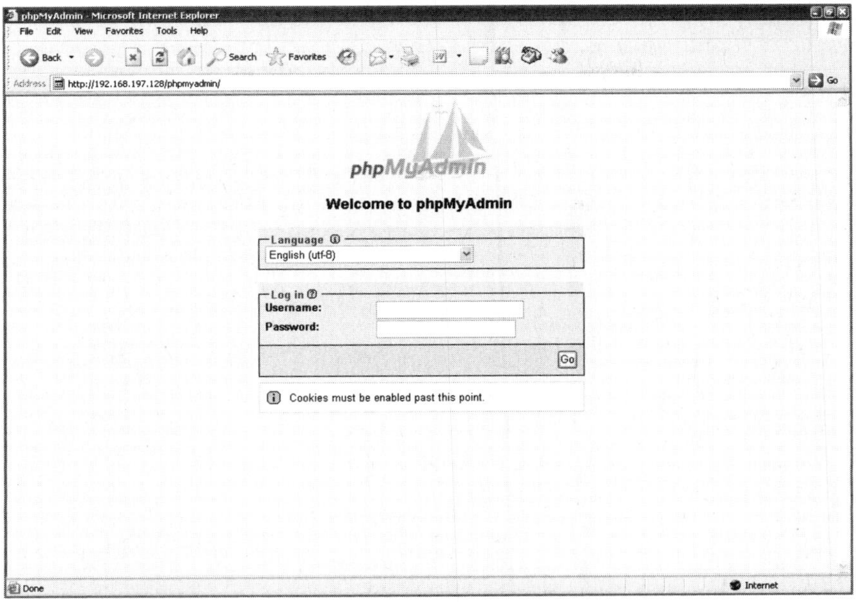

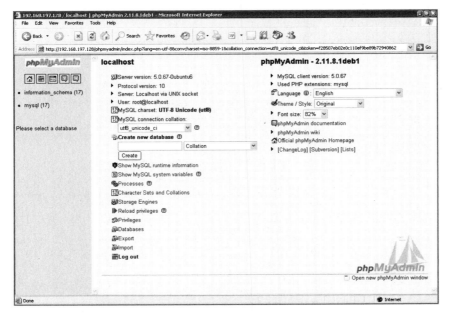

Figure 21-6: The phpMyAdmin tool login page.

Figure 21-7: The phpMyAdmin main page.

From here you can select an existing database, create a new database, export or import databases, and manage MySQL user accounts.

The PHP Software

When you select to install the LAMP server from the Ubuntu server installation, Ubuntu creates the PHP environment automatically. PHP is tightly coupled with the Apache web server environment. The following sections walk through the PHP configuration in Ubuntu server.

The PHP Configuration Files

Ubuntu places the PHP configuration files in the /etc/php5 folder. That folder contains two additional folders: apache2 and conf.d.

The apache2 folder contains two files:

◆ A link to the conf.d folder
◆ The php.ini configuration file

The php.ini configuration file is where the main configuration settings for PHP are. These settings control how the PHP preprocessor handles PHP code. Table 21-4 shows some of the more important settings and how they're set in the Ubuntu server.

Table 21-4: The PHP php.ini Configuration File Settings

Setting	Value	Description
short_open_tag	On	Allows PHP to recognize <? tags as well as <?php tags in HTML code
asp_tags	Off	Allows PHP to recognize ASP-style <% %> tags
output_buffering	Off	Buffers output from PHP code before sending to the client browser
expose_php	On	Adds PHP signature to the web server header to indicate PHP is installed
max_execution_time	30	Specifies the number of seconds a PHP program is allowed to run before being stopped, which helps prevent infinite loops from locking up the server
memory_limit	16M	Sets the maximum amount of memory a program is allowed to use
error_reporting	E_ALL & ~E_NOTICE	Displays all PHP errors except notices
display_errors	On	Enables displaying PHP errors on the web page
log_errors	Off	Logs PHP errors in a log file
post_max_size	8M	Specifies the amount of data an HTML page can post to the server

Table 21-4: *(continued)*

Setting	Value	Description
magic_quotes_gpc	On	Automatically adds backslashes to single and double quotation marks in data retrieved from a web page
file_uploads	On	Allows HTTP file uploading
upload_max_filesize	2M	Specifies the amount of data that can be uploaded
allow_url_include	Off	Allows the PHP include() function to reference files on remote servers
extension		Defines one or more PHP extensions to load at runtime

Secret

The magic_quotes_gpc **setting is somewhat controversial in the PHP world. This feature was designed to solve a specific problem: When a web site visitor submits data that contain a single or double quotation mark, you must "escape" it using a backslash character before using the data in a database query. Because retrieving data from HTML forms and using them in a database query is a common use for PHP, the PHP developers provided a setting to automatically add the backslash character to all data submitted on the web page.**

The problem with this method is that if you don't use the data in a database query, you're stuck with a backslash in front of your quotation marks. This causes all sorts of problems when trying to handle data in your web applications because you have to check whether the magic_quotes_gpc **setting is enabled before you can determine how you must handle the form data.**

The recommended way of handling this potential problem is to turn the magic_ quotes_gpc **setting off and manually add backslashes using the** addslashes() **PHP function, if necessary. Future versions of PHP are rumored to be removing this setting completely to avoid the confusion.**

The conf.d folder contains additional configuration settings required by any PHP extensions. The next section discusses PHP extensions.

PHP Extensions

Just like Apache, PHP uses a modular approach to the software package. There's a core set of functions that are compiled directly into the PHP executable program, but you can add functions using *extensions.*

Extensions provide a simple way to add features to the PHP processor without having to overload it with features you won't use. There are two ways to include extensions in PHP:

◆ Load them at compile time.
◆ Load them dynamically at run time.

The Ubuntu server creates a PHP executable program that contains four extensions compiled into the executable program:

- php_mysl
- php_mysqli
- php_pdo
- php_pdo_mysql

These extensions provide basic and advanced functions for accessing the MySQL server from your PHP programs—exactly what you need for a LAMP server!

You can also add PHP extensions for other features. Table 21-5 shows some of the more popular PHP extensions available in the Ubuntu repositories.

Table 21-5: Ubuntu PHP Extension Packages

Extension	Description
php_apc	Alternative PHP cache code for caching output
php_apd	Advanced PHP debugger; provides debugging capabilities in PHP code
php_bz2	For reading and writing compressed .bz2 files
php_crack	For testing the strength of a password using the crack library
php_curl	The cURL library; for connecting to remote sites using HTTP, FTP, and Telnet
php_dbase	For accessing dBase .dbf files
php_exif	For reading metadata in JPG and TIFF files
php_gd2	For reading, converting, and writing JPG, GIF, TIFF, and PNG image files
php_ibm_db2	For accessing IBM DB2 and Cloudscape databases
php_id3	For reading and manipulating ID3 tags in MP3 files
php_imap	For connecting to an IMAP mailbox and reading mail
php_ingres	For accessing an Ingres database
php_java	For creating and invoking methods on Java objects from PHP
php_ldap	For reading and writing directory information in an LDAP server
php_mailparse	For creating and manipulating MIME mail messages
php_mssql	For accessing an MS SQL server database
php_mysql	For accessing a MySQL database
php_mysqli	Advanced functions for accessing a MySQL database
php_openssl	For using digital signatures and encrypting data
php_oracle	For accessing an Oracle database
php_pdf	For creating a PDF document

Table 21-5: *(continued)*

Extension	Description
php_pgsql	For accessing a PostgreSQL database
php_pop3	For connecting to a POP3 mailbox and reading mail
php_smtp	For connecting to an SMTP server to send mail
php_ssh2	Secure socket functions for sending and receiving encrypted data
php_zip	For reading and writing compressed .zip files

You can use the apt-get command from the command line (see Chapter 13, "Software Installs and Updates") to install the PHP extensions you need in your Ubuntu server. The extension packages are prebuilt so that they're automatically enabled when you install them.

Using PHP

The PHP preprocessor uses the same DocumentRoot location that the Apache web server uses (the /var/www folder). Place your PHP code files in that folder for them to be accessible from the web server.

To test your installation, follow these steps:

1. Open a new vim session as the root user to create a file called test.php in the /var/www folder:

```
sudo vim /var/www/test.php
```

2. In the file, enter this code:

```
<?php
phpinfo();
?>
```

To enter data in the vim editor, you must be in Insert mode. To enter Insert mode, press i, then type your data. To exit Insert mode, press the Esc key.

3. Save the file using the ZZ command in vim.

4. Open your browser and go to the URL:

```
http://10.0.0.1/test.php
```

You'll need to use the IP address of your Ubuntu server for the hostname in the URL.

You should see the output of the phpinfo() function, shown in Figure 21-8.

The phpinfo() command produces a web page that displays all of the configuration and extension settings for the Apache web server and the PHP preprocessor.

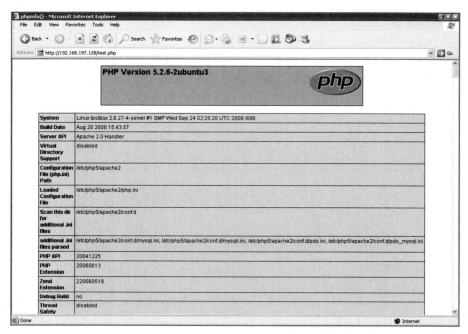

Figure 21-8: The phpinfo() function output.

Tomcat

If you chose to install Tomcat from the Ubuntu server installation menu, it installed Tomcat 6, the latest release of the Tomcat server. The Tomcat 6 server is called a *servlet container*. A servlet container has the ability to load Java servlets and process JavaServer Pages from a web interface.

The following sections describe the Tomcat environment on the Ubuntu server and show how to use Tomcat to serve JavaServer Pages and servlets.

Secret

Just as with the Apache web server installation, you can also install the Tomcat server in the Ubuntu workstation distribution; however, Tomcat isn't recommended for a production web server.

If you do decide to install the Tomcat server in an Ubuntu workstation installation, don't install it using the Synaptic Package Manager. The Tomcat packages available in the workstation software repositories aren't the same as the ones in the server repositories.

Instead, use the `tasksel` utility from a Terminal command prompt:

```
sudo tasksel
```

Select the Tomcat entry from the menu, being careful not to deselect any already-selected entries.

Tomcat Configuration

The Tomcat installation in Ubuntu is somewhat complex. It involves several configuration files and folders. Tomcat uses the XHTML markup language (XML) format in all of its configuration files. This format defines one or more settings related to a specific configuration variable and the values associated with them:

```
<variable setting1="value" setting2="value" />
```

There are two main Tomcat folders you should become familiar with on the Ubuntu server:

- **/etc/tomcat6:** Contains the Tomcat configuration files.
- **/var/lib/tomcat6:** Contains the JSP and servlet application files.

The /var/lib/tomcat6 folder is actually the main folder that Tomcat uses for storing all of the required files. However, the Ubuntu installation creates additional file links to help divide up the files for easier access. It creates links in the /etc/tomcat6 folder for the Tomcat configuration files, the /var/log/tomcat6 folder for the Tomcat log files, and the /var/cache/tomcat6 folder for a working folder.

In the /etc/tomcat6 folder you'll find all of the configuration files required to define the Tomcat server parameters. Ubuntu creates generic defaults so that the server can operate. Table 21-6 describes the files and folders you'll find here.

Table 21-6: The Tomcat Configuration Files and Folders

File or Folder	Description
Catalina	The folder for the Catalina servlet container files
catlina.properties	Defines settings for the Catalina servlet container
content.xml	Defines properties for servlet applications supported by the server
logging.properties	Defines settings for logging activities on the Tomcat server
policy.d	Defines security policies for Tomcat
server.xml	The main Tomcat feature configuration file
tomcat-users.xml	Defines users and roles that applications can use for access control
web.xml	Defines settings and properties for servlet applications

The Tomcat configuration files shouldn't be modified while the Tomcat server is running. It's always a good idea to stop the server, modify the configuration, then restart the server for the new settings to take effect.

Testing Tomcat

To see whether the Tomcat server is running properly on your Ubuntu server, you can run this quick test. Just open a browser on another device on your network and connect to TCP port 8080 on your Ubuntu server (using the IP address of your Ubuntu server):

```
http://10.0.0.1:8080/
```

You should see the default test Tomcat web page, shown in Figure 21-9.

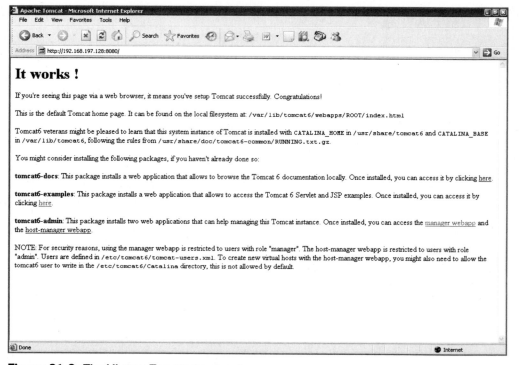

Figure 21-9: The Ubuntu Tomcat 6 test web page.

The default page contains two links to applications you can use to manage your Tomcat applications and server. Unfortunately, you can't connect to these applications using the default Tomcat configuration because it would be a security risk.

To test the actual JavaServer Pages feature in Tomcat, let's create a test JSP page. Just follow these steps:

1. Use the vim editor to create a file called `test.jsp` in the `ROOT` folder in the `webapps` folder:

```
sudo vim /var/lib/tomcat6/webapps/ROOT/test.jsp
```

2. Add the following code to the file:

```
<html>
<body>
<%
out.println("<h2>Tomcat Server JSP Test</h2>");
java.util.Date datenow = new java.util.Date();
%>
The current date and time are:
<%
```

```
out.println(String.valueOf(datenow));
%>
<h2>This is the end of the test</h2>
</body>
</html>
```

To insert the code into the file, you must be in Insert mode in the vim editor. To enter Insert mode, press the i key. After typing the code, you must exit Insert mode. To exit Insert mode, press the Esc key.

3. Press ZZ to save the file and exit the editor.

4. Open a browser and go to your new application using the URL:

```
http://10.0.0.1:8080/test.jsp
```

Again, use the IP address of your Ubuntu server for the hostname in the URL

You should see the output of your test JSP application, as shown in Figure 21-10.

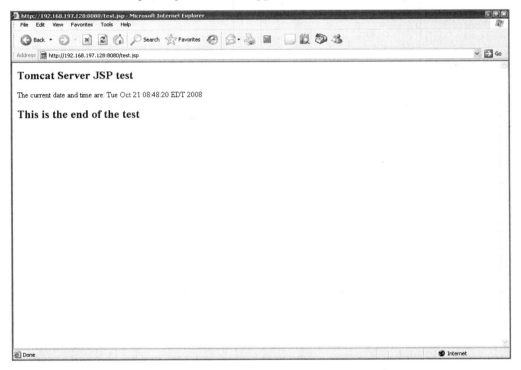

Figure 21-10: The test.jsp program output.

Congratulations! You've written a JSP application and ran it from your Ubuntu server.

Managing Tomcat

The Tomcat servlet container provides a web interface for managing the applications and the Tomcat server itself. These functions require a user account login, which must be set in the configuration files.

1. Stop the Tomcat server using the command:

```
sudo /etc/init.d/tomcat6 stop
```

2. Open the `/etc/tomcat6/tomcat-users.xml` file using the vim editor:

```
sudo vim /etc/tomcat6/tomcat-users.xml
```

3. Create a manager and an admin role entry, then create a user entry for your username:

```
<role rolename="admin"/>
<role rolename="manager"/>
<user username="rich" password="myword" roles="admin,manager"/>
```

Be careful when adding the new lines. Scroll down below the `<tomcat-users>` tag to add new lines, but you must add them before the `<!--` comment tag line. If you place the lines after the `<!--` comment tag, Tomcat will assume they're commented out.

4. Save the file and exit. Use the `ZZ` command to save the text and exit the vim editor.

5. Restart Tomcat using the command:

```
sudo /etc/init.d/tomcat6 start
```

6. Open a browser program on a client PC and access the manager page:

```
http://10.0.0.1:8080/manager/html
```

7. Access the host admin page from the browser:

```
http://10.0.0.1:8080/host-manager/html
```

The Manager web page, shown in Figure 21-11, allows you to manage existing Java servlet applications, as well as deploy new applications.

The Host Manager web page, shown in Figure 21-12, allows you to manage the virtual hosts created on the Tomcat 6 server (similar to the virtual hosts in the Apache web server).

For Java servlet applications, deploying a new application is a little more complicated than just copying a file, as you did with the JSP test application. Java servlet applications are deployed using a web archive (WAR) file. The WAR file contains compiled Java code files from the application. The manager web page allows you to upload a completed application WAR file to the server, then it places the WAR file in a new folder structure. Tomcat expands the WAR file automatically and modifies the configuration files to create the new application.

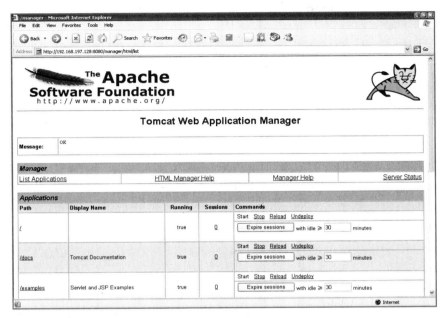

Figure 21-11: The Tomcat 6 Manager web page.

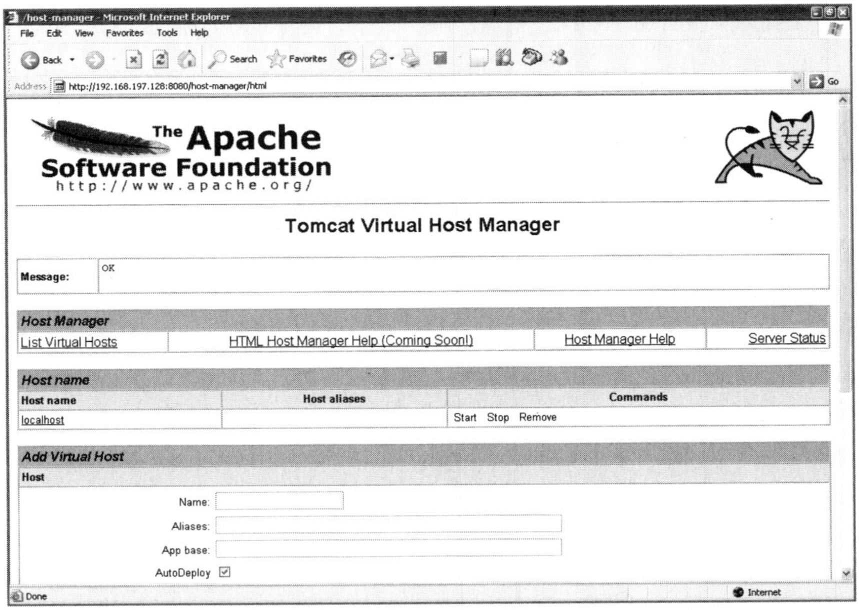

Figure 21-12: The Tomcat 6 Virtual Host Manager web page.

Summary

This chapter discussed the two types of web servers you can install by default on your Ubuntu server. The Linux–Apache–MySQL–PHP (LAMP) server supports web pages that contain the PHP scripting language. LAMP includes the popular Apache web server and MySQL database server to provide an excellent platform for creating dynamic web applications. The other web server platform that you can install is Tomcat. Tomcat provides support for JavaServer Pages (JSP) and Java servlets. The Tomcat server is a self-contained server that doesn't require any external software, not even an additional web server. The chapter showed the configuration files for each server environment and how to utilize code for each one.

The next chapter discusses how to implement Samba software on your Ubuntu server. The Samba software package allows your Ubuntu server to interact on a Windows network, acting as both a client and a server to serve files and printers for the Windows PCs on your network.

Samba and Print Server

Chapter
22

Even though the Linux movement is gaining popularity, there's no denying that the Microsoft Windows platform is still the major player in most computing environments. This doesn't mean that you have to give up on your Ubuntu server if all of your workstations use Microsoft Windows. Your Ubuntu server is perfectly capable of playing nicely in your Windows environment, thanks to the Samba software package. This chapter discusses how to use Samba to allow the Microsoft Windows clients on your network to connect to shared folders and printers on your Ubuntu server. The chapter describes how Samba works in Ubuntu and demonstrates some simple configuration guides for creating shared folders and printers. The chapter also discusses the common UNIX printing system (CUPS), which allows you to share your Ubuntu system printers with other types of devices on your network.

What Is Samba?

The Samba software was created in 1992 by Andrew Tridgell to allow Linux systems to share resources with Microsoft Windows systems on a Windows network. The name *Samba* is somewhat of a play on the main protocol used in Microsoft networks, the server message block (SMB) protocol. Andrew fed the term SMB into a dictionary program to produce words that include those three letters. He decided on the name Samba.

Samba is now maintained by a team of volunteer developers, and it allows Linux systems to fully interact with all levels of the Microsoft Windows platform, both servers and workstations. Your Ubuntu server running Samba can interact with everything from Windows workstations using the old Windows 3.11 operating system to Windows 2008 servers. Samba also supports Microsoft's common Internet file system (CIFS), which is Microsoft's newer standard for PC network communication, based on the SMB protocol. This allows your Ubuntu server to access a shared folder on a Windows system as if it were mounted on the local Ubuntu server.

Samba implements the four basic CIFS services provided on a Windows network:

♦ File and print sharing
♦ Authentication and authorization
♦ Name resolution
♦ Service announcement (browsing)

By setting up the Samba software, you can use your Ubuntu server to share folders and printers from your Ubuntu server with any Windows client on the network, as well as with other Ubuntu servers and workstations running Samba. The Samba software also allows the Ubuntu workstation or server to connect to remote shared Windows folders and printers.

Besides managing shared folders and printers, Windows networking also manages hostnames. Windows networks use their own hostnames and their own hostname protocol, the NetBIOS name service (NBNS). The NBNS protocol allows clients and servers to connect to Windows servers using the name of the server rather than a network address. Windows networks use the Windows Internet name service (WINS) protocol to manage client and server names on the network.

Since the release of the Microsoft Windows NT server version, Microsoft networks also can contain specialized servers called *domain controllers*. A domain controller centralizes user account and share information for an entire Microsoft network. Once a server or client logs into a domain, its access is managed by the domain controller. This provides a centralized way of managing multiple servers and shares.

The Samba server allows you to make your Ubuntu server into one of three different types of domain controllers:

- ◆ **Primary domain controller (PDC):** the central domain controller in a Windows network domain, maintaining all of the domain information
- ◆ **Backup domain controller (BDC):** Two or more secondary domain controllers in a Windows network that duplicate information contained in the PDC
- ◆ **Domain member server (DMS):** a server whose share access is controlled by the domain but doesn't contain the domain controller information

Domain controllers allow you to run an entire Microsoft Windows domain from your Ubuntu server or just add it to an existing domain.

Secret

Starting in version 3.0.20, the Samba software can connect to an existing Microsoft Active Directory (AD) network. To join your Ubuntu Samba server to an existing AD network you must have the Kerberos encryption package installed as part of the Samba package, and you must have administrative privileges on the AD network to join the Ubuntu server as a domain member server.

Once the Samba server is joined to the AD network as a DMS, any authenticated client or server can access the shares advertised by the Samba software. Many network administrators, however, still prefer to use Samba as a standalone domain server, allowing selected users to connect via the Samba password file.

The Ubuntu Samba Environment

When you select to install the Samba software from the main Ubuntu server installation window, Ubuntu pre-installs several components to support the Samba environment. This section describes each of these components.

Secret

If you didn't select the Samba server option during the Ubuntu server installation, you can install it using the `tasksel` command

```
sudo tasksel
```

You can also install the Samba server and client software in an Ubuntu workstation environment using the Synaptic Package Manager. Just search for the Samba package.

Samba Programs

The Samba software package includes several programs and files to implement Windows networking on your Ubuntu server. The three most important files are

- ◆ `smbd`: Provides access to the shared folders and printers on the Ubuntu server.

♦ nmbd: Provides access to the WINS protocol to advertise the Ubuntu server and recognize other Windows servers on the network.

♦ winbindd: Resolves server names for servers on remote networks.

These files run in background on the Ubuntu server to support Samba. Besides these three programs, several utilities are available to support Samba, shown in Table 22-1.

Table 22-1: Samba Utility Programs

Program	Description
nmblookup	Look up Windows NetBIOS names on the network
smbcacls	Set or get access control lists (ACLs) on a file or directory
smbclient	Connect to a remote Windows share or printer
smbcontrol	Send control messages that the Samba processes
smbcquotas	Set or get quotas on Windows NTFS shares
smbget	Download a file from a remote Windows share
smbmount	Mount a remote Windows share on the local virtual filesystem
smbpasswd	Set or change Samba user account passwords
smbspool	Send a file to a Windows network printer
smbstatus	Display the status of the Samba system
smbtar	Back up a Windows share to an archive device or file
smbtree	A text-based Windows network browser for the command line
smbumount	Unmount a remote Windows share mounted on the local virtual filesystem
testparm	Test the Samba configuration file for errors

The Samba software also uses configuration files to define the Samba environment on the Ubuntu server. The next section describes the Samba configuration files you'll need to set up your Samba server.

Samba Configuration Files

The Ubuntu installation of Samba places all of the Samba configuration files in the /etc/samba folder. You'll see two configuration files in this folder:

♦ dhcp.conf: Sets the location of the WINS server for the local network.

♦ smb.conf: Contains the Samba settings for the server.

You should use the dhcp.conf configuration file when you need to contact a Windows server on a remote network using the WINS protocol. By default, Samba can connect only to remote servers that it sees on the network via the nmbd program. The Windows network can use *WINS proxy servers* to advertise remote Windows servers on local networks. The WINS proxy server rebroadcasts information about remote Windows servers on the local network. However, you must know the network IP address of the WINS proxy server to be able to connect to the remote Windows server. The dhcp.conf configuration file sets the IP address of the local WINS proxy server, if there is one on your network.

The bulk of the Samba configuration is done in the smb.conf configuration file. The smb.conf configuration file is a text file that looks suspiciously like an ordinary Windows .ini file, complete with section headings in square brackets. There is a reason for that. One of the goals of the Samba developers was to make Samba as easy as possible for a typical Windows network administrator to configure.

Changing the Samba server configuration is as simple as editing the smb.conf text file with your favorite text editor and restarting the Samba server programs. All lines in the configuration file that start with either a pound sign (#) or a semicolon (;) are considered comments and are not processed by the server.

The smb.conf file contains separate sections defining the characteristics of each individual file area or printer shared, as well as three special sections:

- The **global** section defines parameters that affect the operation of the whole server.
- The **homes** section defines parameters for individual users' home shares.
- The **printers** section defines parameters for any printers shared by the server.

Let's take a walk through the default smb.conf file in Ubuntu to see what each of these sections contains.

The Global Section

The global section is where the system parameters are set to control how the server appears on the network and how clients can access it. The settings in this section can be separated into six parts, as described in the following sections.

Browsing

The first part of the global section defines the browsing settings. The browsing settings determine how the Samba server interacts on the Windows network:

```
[global]
workgroup = MYGROUP
server string = %h server (Samba, Ubuntu)
# wins support = no
; wins server = w.x.y.z
dns proxy = no
name resolve order = lmhosts host wins bcast
```

The workgroup parameter determines the network workgroup or domain that the server will try to join. If workgroup is set to a domain name, the server tries to locate a domain controller for the domain and join the domain as a client. If MYGROUP is not a domain, the server will attempt to locate and join the workgroup named MYGROUP using standard CIFS methods.

The server string parameter sets the description of the server that is broadcast to other nodes in the workgroup. The %h parameter takes the server network name used on the network from the Ubuntu server hostname. If your Ubuntu server is called testbox, Samba broadcasts the string

```
testbox server (Samba, Ubuntu)
```

This is what will appear in the Network Neighborhood browser window on Windows servers and workstations. If your Ubuntu Samba server is participating on a network with WINS support, you can remove the comments in the two `wins` lines and enter the appropriate settings for your WINS network.

WINS networks can also utilize the standard domain name system (DNS) to advertise Windows server names and IP addresses. If your network utilizes this service you can set the `dns proxy` parameter to `yes`.

The `name resolve order` parameter defines what order the Samba software uses to attempt to resolve a hostname into an IP address on the network. The `lmhosts` file is the Windows version of the Linux `host` file, but it relates Windows hostnames to IP addresses.

Networking

The networking part of the global section defines settings for interfacing the Samba server on the network.

```
interfaces = 127.0.0.1/8 eth0
; bind interfaces only = yes
```

The `interfaces` parameter defines which network interfaces the Samba software will use to listen for connection attempts. By default, this value is set to only the 127.0.0.1 localhost address for the server. To allow remote clients and servers to connect to your Ubuntu Samba server, you'll need to add either the interface name of your network interface (such as eth0, as shown in this example) or the IP address of the interface.

If you don't have a firewall between your Ubuntu server and the network you can enable the `bind interfaces only` parameter. This parameter restricts connections to only those destined to the server's IP address. Broadcast messages aren't accepted.

Debugging/Accounting

The debugging part of the global section defines some features that provide logs allowing you to monitor the Samba server activity for problems.

```
log file = /var/log/samba/log.%m
max log size = 1000
# syslog only = no
syslog = 0
panic action = /usr/share/samba/panic-action %d
```

By default, Samba places the log file in the directory specified when it was compiled. You can override this location by using the log file parameter. The variable %m expands to the hostname of the device connecting to Samba. This configuration will produce a separate log file for each device that connects to the server. You can also limit the size of the log file using the `max log size` parameter. By default, Samba will start a new log file when the file reaches 1 MB (the parameter units are in kilobytes).

Instead of keeping a separate log file for Samba you can instruct Samba to use the standard `syslog` facility on the Ubuntu server. This incorporates Samba messages into the normal system logging in the `/var/log/messages` log file. By default, Samba will send important messages to the `syslog` facility. The level of the messages is defined in the `syslog` parameter. The higher the value, the lower the priority of messages that are sent to the `syslog`. The `syslog only` parameter allows you to disable the Samba logging and only use the system `syslog`.

The `panic-action` setting allows Samba to run a script when it crashes. The `panic-action` script is a canned script that sends information to the system administrator account of the Ubuntu server, providing basic information about the system crash.

Authentication

The authentication section determines how user accounts are validated for access to the Samba server:

```
# security = user
encrypt passwords = true
passdb backend = tdbsam
obey pam restrictions = yes
unix password sync = yes
passwd program = /usr/bin/passwd &u
passwd chat = *Enter\snew\spassword:* %n\n *Retype\snew\spassword:* %n\n
*password\supdated\ssuccessfully*
pam password change = yes
map to guest = bad user
```

These are very important parameters. They control how the Samba server authenticates users who request access to the server. User authentication can be done in three different ways:

- User
- Share
- Domain

With the `security` parameter set to `user` (the default value since Samba 2.0), the Samba server will try to validate the requesting user by an existing Ubuntu system userID. If it's found, the user then has access to shares as determined by the standard Ubuntu file permissions for that userID (unless specifically restricted by the share section).

With the `security` parameter set to `share`, the Samba server attempts to authenticate users based on individual shared resources on the server. This setting is commonly used on Windows workstations that share folders by setting a password. Samba uses the standard Ubuntu system userID/password combination just as it does with the user security method.

By setting the security parameter to `domain`, Samba will try to find a domain controller to validate the userID and password. If the domain controller authenticates the userID and password, Samba grants access to the user connection.

In the past, Microsoft clients would transmit their passwords across the network in plain text format. Now, with security such a large concern, things have changed. In all Windows workstations and servers the default logon method is to use encrypted passwords. This complicates things considerably.

For Samba to be able to authenticate a password that has been encrypted it must have access to the encrypted version of the password. There are two ways to accomplish this.

The easiest method (from Samba's point of view) is to set the security parameter to `domain` and let another server validate the password. For this to work you must also set the `encrypt passwords` parameter to `true` and make sure the `password server` parameter is set to the name of a domain server that can validate the user passwords. Samba will then forward the encrypted password to the password server and receive a response indicating whether the user is validated.

If you are not fortunate enough to have a separate password server handy, Samba must maintain an encrypted password database itself. For Samba to maintain its own encrypted password file, extra administration work is required.

First, in the smb.conf file, the security parameter should be set to user and the encrypt passwords parameter set to true. Then a separate Samba password file must be created to manage user passwords encrypted by Windows encryption method.

Each user who needs to access the Samba server must have an Ubuntu system account and an entry in the Samba password file. The smbpasswd utility is used to add users to the Samba password file and set their Windows passwords.

You must use the -a option to add new userIDs to the file. Make sure that the smbpasswd userIDs match valid Ubuntu system userIDs. Otherwise, smbpasswd will not add them to the password file. Here's an example of creating a new Samba user account:

```
$ sudo smbpasswd -a rich
New SMB password:
Retype new SMB password:
$
```

After you do this, clients that use encrypted passwords can connect to the Samba server and have access to shares as defined in the configuration file.

Domains

The domains part of the global section defines settings to use if your Samba server is a PDC or BDC in a Windows domain.

```
;  domain logons = yes
;  domain master = no
;  logon path = \\%N\Profiles\%U
;  logon drive = H:
;  logon home = \\%N\%U
;  logon script = logon.cmd
```

These parameters control how Samba behaves if it is participating in a Windows domain. If the Samba server is emulating a Windows domain controller, the logon parameters allow Samba to service Windows client logons. Windows domain client logons require a network folder that can run automated scripts.

The logon script parameter allows Samba to download a logon script to clients when they authenticate. The locations of the scripts are relative to the share named [netlogon]. The script files must be Windows-style ASCII text files (using cr/lf line endings) so that the workstations can execute them. The logon path parameter is used to set the directory where roaming profiles for Windows clients are stored. This is customized by using the device name (%N) and the username (%U) of the logged-in user.

Printers

Although there's an entire section specific to setting up individual printer shares, Samba allows you to bypass that with a couple of global settings.

```
#  load printers = yes
;  printing = bsd
;  printcap name = /etc/printcap
;  printing = cups
;  printcap name = cups
```

The `load printers` parameter allows you to automatically share any locally defined Ubuntu printers in the Windows network. If you use the common UNIX printing system (CUPS) to configure your Ubuntu server printers (see "The CUPS Print Server" section later in this chapter) you can enable all of the printers defined in CUPS by enabling the second pair of parameter lines. This allows you to manage your printers using the CUPS administration tool, plus share them on your Windows network as Windows shared printers.

The Share Definitions Section

The share definitions section defines any shared folders or printers you define on your server. Each separate section starts with a tag in the format

```
[sharename]
```

The *sharename* parameter defines the name of the share on the network. The [homes] sharename is a special name that allows you to configure default shares for all of your users in one place. By default, each userID share will be mapped to the home directory of the userID on the Ubuntu server, with the sharename being set to the userID. As expected, there are some parameters that can fine-tune the behavior of the [homes] section.

```
[homes]
comment = Home Directories
browseable = no
; read only = yes
; create mask = 0700
; directory mask = 0700
; valid users = %S
```

The `comment` parameter further identifies the service to other devices on the network. If you want to advertise the home shares on the network, you can set the `browseable` parameter to `yes`. Enabling the `valid users` parameter sets security so that users can access only their own home folder. By default, any user can access the home folder of any other user, but access is limited by the Ubuntu system permissions for the folder.

By default, the home shares are read-only, so no new data can be written to the share folder. You can change this by setting the `read only` parameter to `no`.

Secret

If you set the `browseable` parameter to `yes`, be careful, because all of the home folders on the Ubuntu server will appear in the Network Neighborhood list on Windows clients. This can be a security risk, depending on who's on your network.

The [printers] sharename is another special share that allows you to fine-tune printers that are being shared by Samba on the network. Settings in this section apply to all printers shared by Samba.

```
[printers]
comment = All Printers
```

```
browseable = no
path = /var/spool/samba
printable = yes
guest ok = no
read only = yes
create mask = 0700
```

As with the homes folders, the `browseable` parameter determines whether other devices on the network can see the printers. The `path` parameter points to the directory where Samba will create the print spool files. The Ubuntu permissions for this directory should be writable for everyone, and the sticky bit should be set.

Setting the `read only` parameter to `yes` prevents unauthorized use of this directory. However, you must ensure that the `printable` parameter is set to `yes`. It allows users to submit spool files to the directory specified without having write access to the directory. If clients don't have permission to write to the spool directory, they will not be able to submit print jobs.

If you prefer to allow anyone to print to your shared printers, set the `browseable` parameter to `yes`. If the `guest ok` parameter is also set to yes, clients can map to the printer without having to supply a userID and password.

Creating New Shares

Each individual share that is available on the Samba server must have a separate share section in the `smb.conf` file. The sharename is used as the heading name, and any parameters that are needed for the share apart from the global parameters should be included in the share section. An example share configuration would look like this:

```
[katiedir]
comment = Katie's shared disk area
path = /data/katie
valid users = katie jessica haley riley
public = no
read only = no
```

This example demonstrates how to set up a share that can be accessed by more than one user. The location of the share is determined by the `path` parameter. The `valid users` parameter sets the users who will be allowed access to the share. Multiple users are listed with a space between the userIDs. If the `valid users` parameter is not set, all Ubuntu system userIDs will have access to the share.

All users who will access the share should have read and write permissions to the share directory by Ubuntu (i.e., be members of a group that has write privileges). As shown by the `read only` parameter, all of the listed users will have write access to the share. If the `read only` parameter is set to `yes`, users (including the owner of the share) will have read-only access to the share, even if the Ubuntu permissions would allow them write access.

Printer shares can be customized in the same way that disk shares are, by using a share section for the individual printer.

```
[franksprn]
comment = Frank's shared printer on the server
valid users = frank melanie nick
path = /home/frank/spool
printer = franks_printer
```

```
public = no
read only = yes
printable = yes
```

This section defines a printer share that only the userIDs `frank`, `melanie`, and `nick` can access from the network. Because the `printable` parameter is enabled, they don't need to have write permission to the `/home/frank/spool` directory for them to be able to print from the shared printer.

Creating a Samba Server

Now that you've seen the different parts of the `smb.conf` configuration file, let's try to get a working server going on the network. There are three things you need to do to get your Samba server ready for the network:

- ♦ Edit the `smb.conf` configuration file.
- ♦ Add Samba user passwords to the system.
- ♦ Restart the Samba software.

The following sections walk through each of these processes.

Editing the smb.conf File

You'll first need to configure your Samba server for your network. Follow these steps to start your server:

1. Open the `smb.conf` file in a text editor. If you're using the Ubuntu server installation from the console, you'll need to use a command-line editor such as vim. You can open the file using the vim editor using the command

```
sudo vim /etc/samba/smb.conf
```

2. Set the workgroup to an existing workgroup or to a new workgroup. The workgroup line defines what Windows network workgroup to belong to:

```
workgroup = WORKGROUP
```

If you're using your Ubuntu server on an existing Windows network, entering the workgroup name here allows your server to appear in the Network Neighborhood browse list so that clients can connect to it without having to know its name.

3. Remove the comment from the `interfaces` line to enable connectivity from other network devices. The default setting should be

```
interfaces 127.0.0.1/8 eth0
```

Use the `ifconfig` command at the command line to ensure that the Ethernet port defined (`eth0`) is also active on your server.

4. Remove the comment from the `security` line to enable user-level security. This allows you to run your Samba server as a standalone server on the network and manage your own user accounts on the Ubuntu server.

5. Remove the comments from the `[homes]` section. There are three lines used in the `[homes]` section:

```
[homes]
comment = Home Directories
browseable = no
```

If you want to allow users to browse to their home folder, change the `browseable` setting to `yes`.

6. Remove the comment from the `read only` line, and change the setting to `no`. This allows your users to write files to their home folder:

```
read only = no
```

7. Remove the comment from the `valid users` line. This setting restricts users to connecting only to their own home folder:

```
valid users = %S
```

8. Remove the comments from the `printing` and `printcap` name lines for the CUPS server entry. This enables your Samba server to share any printers defined in the CUPS server:

```
printing = cups
printcap name = cups
```

9. Save the new `smb.conf` file and exit the editor.

Now you have the Samba server configuration set for your network environment. The next step is to create the Samba account passwords for your users.

Defining Samba Passwords

The default Samba configuration in Ubuntu uses the Ubuntu user account system to track users in the Samba configuration. However, there's one problem with this setup. When a user attempts to connect to the Samba server with his or her userID, Windows servers and clients pass the password using an encryption scheme. Samba must know what the encrypted password is to be able to authenticate the user login request.

To do that, the Samba software maintains a separate password file that contains the user passwords encrypted by the Windows encryption algorithm. You must set the Samba user passwords separate from the Ubuntu passwords for this to work.

The tool used to encrypt Samba passwords is called `smbpasswd`. You must use the `smbpasswd` program to define each Ubuntu user account that's going to access the Samba server. To define a user account password for the first time, you must use the `-a` parameter:

```
rich@testbox:~$ sudo smbpasswd -a test
New SMB password:
Retype new SMB password:
Added user test.
rich@testbox:~$
```

This creates a Samba password for the new user account. If you need to change the password for the account, you don't need the `-a` parameter:

```
rich@testbox:~$ sudo smbpasswd test
New SMB password:
Retype new SMB password:
rich@testbox:~$
```

You'll need to do this for all Ubuntu users who want to connect to their home folder as a Windows shared drive via the network.

Managing Samba

After making changes to the Samba configuration, you'll need to restart the Samba programs. The easiest way to do this to utilize the Ubuntu startup script in the /etc/init.d folder:

- ♦ /etc/init.d/samba start: Starts the Samba server.
- ♦ /etc/init.d/samba stop: Stops the Samba server.
- ♦ /etc/init.d/samba restart: Stops then starts the Samba server.

When you restart the Samba server, it reads the current smb.conf configuration file and processes the configuration settings.

Secret

If poring over a text configuration file isn't your idea of a good time, try the Samba web administration tool (called SWAT). It provides a web-based way to create shares and change settings in your Samba configuration file. To run SWAT you must install the swat package using apt-get:

```
sudo apt-get install swat
```

Once you've installed the package, you need to start the inetd program, which runs in background and listens for connections on the SWAT port:

```
sudo /usr/sbin/inetd
```

The Samba Client

After you work out the Samba server configuration for your environment, you'll want to test it out. You can do that from your Ubuntu server using the smbclient program.

The smbclient program provides a command-line interface to interact with a Windows share on the network, whether it's a Samba share or a shared folder from a Windows server or workstation. The command-line interface is a little clunky, but it accomplishes the task of allowing you to store and retrieve files between a remote Windows share and your Ubuntu server.

The smbclient Program

You can control the behavior of the smbclient program using several command-line parameters. The format of the smbclient program is

```
smbclient servicename [password] [options]
```

The *servicename* parameter defines the Windows share to connect to. Windows shares are specified using the format

```
//server/share
```

where *server* is the Windows hostname of the server, and *share* is the sharename of the shared folder.

By default, smbclient attempts to connect to the share using the user account that's running the command. You can specify the account password on the command line or, if you prefer, you can leave it off and smbclient will prompt for you it.

Here's an example of connecting to the home folder for the current user account:

```
test@testbox:~$ smbclient //localhost/test
Enter test's password:
Domain=[TESTBOX] OS=[Unix] Server=[Samba 3.2.3]
smb: \>
```

After you enter the password, the smbclient program connects to the share and produces the smb> prompt.

If you want to connect as a different user account, use the -U parameter:

```
test@testbox:~$ smbclient //localhost/rich -U rich
Enter rich's password:
Domain=[TESTBOX] OS=[Unix] Server=[Samba 3.2.3]
smb: \>
```

The smbclient program connects to Windows shares as easily as to other Samba shares:

```
rich@testbox:~$ smbclient //elijah/testshare
Enter rich's password:
Domain=[ELIJAH] OS=[Windows 5.1] Server=[Windows 2000 LAN Manager]
smb: \>
```

In this example, the server Elijah is a Windows XP Home Edition workstation. The smbclient connection information shows as a Windows 5.1 operating system.

Once you connect to the share, you're greeted by the smb> prompt. The next section discusses how to interact with the remote server from the prompt.

Secret   Another handy parameter is the -I parameter. It allows you to specify the IP address of the remote server so that Samba doesn't have to try to resolve the server name. This parameter is especially useful if the server is on a remote network and you don't have a WINS server that services that network.

Interacting with a Windows Share

Once you connect to the remote share with the smbclient program, you'll want to be able to interact with the remote share. The smbclient program provides many commands for performing various functions on the remote share.

The smb> prompt works like the command-line prompt in Ubuntu. Type the commands and press Enter to send them for processing. Table 22-2 lists some of the more commonly used commands.

Table 22-2: Commonly Used smbclient Commands

Command	Description
cd	Change the remote directory
chmod	Change the mode of a remote file using the Linux permissions
chown	Change the owner of a remote file
close	Close an open file with the specified file ID
del	Delete the specified file(s)
dir	List the contents of the remote directory
exit	Exit from the connection
get	Retrieve the specified remote file, saving it as either the same filename or as a second specified filename
help	List the smbclient commands
l	List the contents of the remote directory
lcd	Change the local directory
ls	List the contents of the remote directory
md	Create a new directory under the current remote directory
mget	Get multiple files from the remote directory based on a specified wildcard template
mkdir	Create a new directory under the current remote directory
more	View a file in the remote directory using the Linux more command
mput	Send multiple files from the local directory to the current remote directory based on a specified wildcard template
open	Open a file in the remote directory
put	Send a specified file from the local directory to the current remote directory
pwd	Display the current remote directory pathname
q	Log off from the server share
rd	Remove a directory under the current remote directory
reget	Get a file from the remote directory, restarting at the end of an existing local file location
rename	Rename a file on the current remote directory
reput	Send a file starting from the end of an existing remote file location
rm	Delete the specified files from the current remote directory
rmdir	Delete the specified directory under the current remote directory
showconnect	Display information about the current server connection
wdel	Delete a group of remote files using a wildcard template
quit	Log off from the server share

Here's an example of using commands in an smbclient session:

```
rich@testbox:~$ smbclient //localhost/test -U test
Enter test's password:
Domain=[TESTBOX] OS=[Unix] Server=[Samba 3.2.3]
smb: \> dir
. D 0 Sat Nov 8 18:35:30 2008
. . D 0 Sat Nov 8 18:35:30 2008
.profile H 675 Sat Nov 8 18:35:30 2008
.bash_logout H 220 Sat Nov 8 18:35:30 2008
.bashrc H 3115 Sat Nov 8 18:35:30 2008

61335 blocks of size 131072. 47710 blocks available
smb: \> put test.txt
putting file test.txt as \test.txt (3.6 kb/s) (average 3.6 kb/s)
smb: \> dir test.*
test.txt A 44 Sat Nov 8 19:36:37 2008

61335 blocks of size 131072. 47710 blocks available
smb: \>
```

After connecting with the share on the Samba server, I used the dir command to list the files in the share. I then used the put command to send the file test.txt from the local folder to the shared folder and used the dir command again to make sure it really got there.

After sending the file to the share, you can also see the file in the folder from the Ubuntu command line:

```
rich@testbox:~$ ls -al /home/test
total 24
drwxr-xr-x 2 test test 4096 2008-11-08 19:36 .
drwxr-xr-x 4 root root 4096 2008-11-08 18:35 . .
-rw-r--r-- 1 test test 220 2008-11-08 18:35 .bash_logout
-rw-r--r-- 1 test test 3115 2008-11-08 18:35 .bashrc
-rw-r--r-- 1 test test 675 2008-11-08 18:35 .profile
-rwxr--r-- 1 test test 44 2008-11-08 19:36 test.txt
rich@testbox:~$
```

As expected, the new file is indeed in the folder.

Secret

Be careful with text files if you share your Ubuntu folders using Samba with Windows clients. Ubuntu and Windows use slightly different text file formats. Ubuntu uses a single newline character at the end of each line, while Windows uses a carriage control character along with the newline character. If you save a Windows text file in a Samba share and try to look at it in Ubuntu, you may be disappointed.

Ubuntu provides a set of utilities for converting Windows text files to Linux format, and vice versa. Just use the apt-get program to install the tofrodos package.

Connecting from Windows

You're not limited to connecting to your Samba server using the `smbclient` program. The Samba server is a complete Windows network server. You can connect to your shares from any Windows device on the network—either a Windows server or a Windows workstation.

Here are the steps for mapping a Windows XP workstation to the remote share:

1. Open the My Computer window. You can get to the My Computer window by double-clicking the My Computer icon on the desktop or selecting Start ⇨ My Computer.

2. Select Tools ⇨ Map Network Drive from the My Computer menu bar. This displays the Map Network Drive dialog box, shown in Figure 22-1.

Figure 22-1: The Windows XP My Computer dialog box.

3. Enter the hostname and share name of your Samba share in the Folder textbox. You can use the hostname of your Ubuntu server or the IP address of the server.

4. Click the Connect button using a different user name link in the dialog box. The Connect As dialog box appears, as shown in Figure 22-2. Enter your Ubuntu user account and the password assigned using the `smbpasswd` tool, then click the OK button.

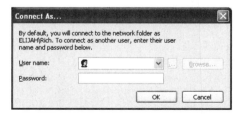

Figure 22-2: The Windows XP Connect As dialog box.

5. Select the Reconnect at Logon check box if you want the drive to map automatically each time you boot.

6. Click the Finish button at the bottom of the Map Network Drive window.

If the connection is successful the shared folder will open in a new Windows Explorer window, as shown in Figure 22-3.

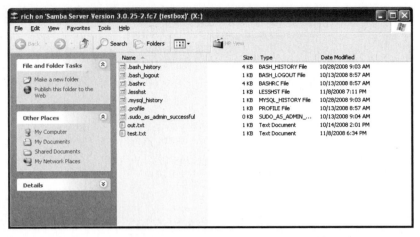

Figure 22-3: The Samba shared folder open in Windows XP.

You can now use the shared folder as you would any other folder in your Windows XP system: copying files, cutting files, opening files, and even starting program files stored in the shared folder.

The process for mapping to a shared network drive in Windows Vista workstations is almost the same as in Windows XP. The only difference is that you select the Map Network Drive entry from the top toolbar, as shown in Figure 22-4.

Figure 22-4: The Windows Vista My Computer window.

After you select the Map Network Drive option, the rest of the dialog boxes are exactly the same.

The CUPS Print Server

The Samba server software also allows you to share any system printers you have configured on the Ubuntu server on your Windows network. As discussed earlier in the "Creating a Samba Server" section, it's easier to utilize the common UNIX printing system (CUPS) software on your Ubuntu server to interface between your system printers and Samba.

This section walks through the CUPS software and demonstrates how to use CUPS to define the printers on your system for Samba.

Printing in Linux

One of the reasons printing in the Linux world is complicated is that, like everything else in Linux, there is more than one way of doing it. But before tackling how to use CUPS, let's first look at how printing works in Ubuntu.

Direct Printing

The most basic type of printing involves an application sending information directly to a printer that's connected to the PC. This is called *direct printing*. With direct printing, printer data are sent from an application to a printer handler then directly to the printer. No data formatting or manipulation is performed by the Ubuntu system. In Ubuntu there are two printer applications you can use for direct printing: *System V* and *Berkeley LPD*.

Both of these systems have their roots in the old UNIX days, so you know they are complicated. In the past, you had to know exactly which print system your particular Linux distribution used and had to manually edit configuration files to get a printer to work. That was a painful process to go through to get a printer to work.

First, you had to know what port on the PC your printer was connected to. Second, you had to know what data format your printer used to accept data for printing.

In the Windows world you usually don't have to know these things, because the operating system usually figures them out automatically for you. But with direct printing in Linux we are not so lucky.

There are several ways to connect printers to a PC, such as through the standard printer ports LPT1 and LPT2 and through standard USB ports. Also, to make life more interesting, in Linux, parallel printers are called lp0, lp1, and so forth (note that the first printer starts at 0, not 1, as in Windows). When a Linux application uses direct printing, it needs to know exactly where the printer is connected. Of course, if you move the printer, you must also configure the application accordingly.

With the thousands of different types of printers available, it's hard to know the data format a specific one uses. In fact, most use proprietary languages to format print data. Therefore, each application on your PC needs to know what format to use when sending data to a specific printer. Fortunately, Linux geeks developed a solution to this problem.

Filtered Printing

The geeks' solution to direct printing problems in Linux was to create an intermediary between printers and applications. It's called a *filter*. The job of the filter is to convert raw data sent from an application into data that a printer can use.

Each type of printer requires a unique filter configuration. So, in order to work, filter configurations have to contain information about the connected printer. Linux systems often include many different filter configurations for various types of printers.

The input of the filter requires a standardized, generic printing language. Linux uses one called *PostScript*. Business-class printers typically can print PostScript data without any data conversion, making the job of the filter quite easy. Unfortunately, most home printers don't utilize the PostScript language, so Linux had to incorporate a more advanced filter system for them.

GhostScript

The most popular filter program used in Linux is *GhostScript*, an open-source application that converts raw data into the PostScript printer language. It uses individual printer drivers to convert the raw data into the proper format for each printer. GhostScript drivers are available for various types of home printers.

This makes the job of using multiple printers much easier, both for you and for application developers.

The Scheduler

What happens if you are in the middle of printing a 10-page document and want to print something else, such as a copy of an email message? With direct printing, you'll get an error message because the printer is busy.

To solve this problem, there needs to be another front end to the filter that allows multiple applications to send data to the printer, hold the data as they come in, and pass them off to the filter when it's time to print. This front end is called the *scheduler.*

The scheduler uses a concept called *spooling.* Spooling provides a queue for printer data to accumulate on their way to the printer. Multiple applications can send data to the scheduler at the same time with no problem.

Each time an application sends data to the scheduler, it's called a *print job.* The scheduler handles each print job separately and can remove individual print jobs from the print queue, if necessary.

Confused yet? Figure 22-5 demonstrates how these pieces fit together into a printing system.

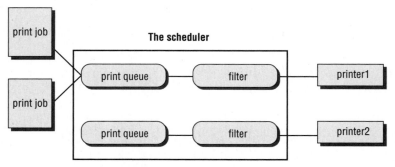

Figure 22-5: Printing flowchart on a Linux system.

With all of these pieces required to implement printing in Linux, it's no wonder that printing was often considered the most difficult part of Linux. Fortunately, CUPS was developed to solve all of this complexity.

The CUPS Software

CUPS is open-source software that was created in an attempt to tie all of the steps required for UNIX printing together in one package. The CUPS Software uses the standard Internet printing protocol (IPP) to provide a standard method for interfacing with printers, whether they are on a local PC or on another system on a network.

The CUPS Software includes

◆ A scheduler that runs continuously in the background on a PC
◆ Print queues for each printer
◆ A customized version of GhostScript to work as the filter

The CUPS filter contains numerous printer drivers to support the many business and home printers currently on the market. CUPS also contains various utility programs that allow you to configure printers, easily submit print jobs, and monitor jobs waiting to print. It even offers a great web interface application so that you can manage all of your system printers remotely!

The Ubuntu server uses CUPS as the default printer control package when you select the Printer Server option at installation time. It automatically starts the CUPS scheduler when you boot the system. It also contains configuration files that create the default CUPS environment to support some common printing functions.

CUPS Configuration

The Ubuntu installation of CUPS creates the /etc/cups folder for storing all of the configuration files required for operating the CUPS server. The main file to concentrate on is the cupsd.conf file.

This file contains the main settings for running the CUPS server. Once you get this file configured for your server you can use the web interface to control everything else.

Here are the steps required to reconfigure the cupsd.conf file to allow you to access the CUPS server configuration via the web interface:

1. Open the cupsd.conf file with a text editor. If you're using the Ubuntu server installation from the console you'll need to use a command-line editor such as vim. You can open the file in the vim editor using the command

```
sudo vim /etc/cups/cupsd.conf
```

2. Modify the Listen line to listen on the network interface. By default, the Listen line is set to accept connections only from the localhost. Change the Listen parameter to

```
Listen 631
```

3. Allow remote devices to connect to the CUPS server. By default, no devices are allowed to connect to the CUPS server. To allow a network device to access the CUPS server you must add an Allow line to the existing <Location /> section in the configuration:

```
<Location />
Order allow,deny
Allow all
</Location>
```

This allows every device on your network to connect to the CUPS server and access a printer. If you have non-Windows devices (such as Ubuntu workstations) on your network, they can access your printers directly via the CUPS server instead of having to go through the Samba server (although they can do that, as well).

4. Allow your workstation to connect to the CUPS server admin pages. By default, no devices are allowed to connect to the CUPS server admin pages. You probably don't want all of the devices on your network to access the admin pages to control the CUPS server, but you'll want to allow your workstation's IP address to access them. Just add an Allow line to the existing <Location /admin> section in the configuration. The Allow line should contain a comma-separated list of IP addresses allowed to control the server:

```
<Location /admin>
Encryption required
Order allow,deny
Allow 10.0.1.196
</Location>
```

The Encryption line requires that the remote browser use HTTPS to connect to the CUPS server web interface.

5. Allow access to the configuration files for your remote host. Similar to the admin pages, the CUPS configuration file restricts access to the configuration pages. If you want to be able to add or remove printers from a remote location, you'll need to list the IP addresses of the remote workstations in the <Location /admin/conf> section:

```
<Location /admin/conf>
Auth default
Require user @SYSTEM
Order allow,deny
Allow 10.0.1.196
</Location>
```

This allows you to add, modify, and remove printers from the comfort of your own workstation, instead of having to muddle through the CUPS configuration files.

6. Save the new configuration file and exit the editor.

To make the new configuration settings take effect, you must restart the CUPS server:

```
$ sudo /etc/init.d/cups restart
```

You're now ready to connect to the CUPS web interface and start working with your printers.

Managing CUPS Printers

The CUPS software contains its own web interface to help you manage the printers in CUPS. The CUPS web interface listens for connections on TCP port 631. It uses HTTP and HTTPS, but if you've required encryption in your configuration setup (as we did in the previous steps), you'll need to connect using HTTPS.

Just open the browser on your workstation and connect to the IP address of your Ubuntu server using the URL https://192.168.197.128:631.

If everything worked well, you'll be greeted by the CUPS main admin page, shown in Figure 22-6.

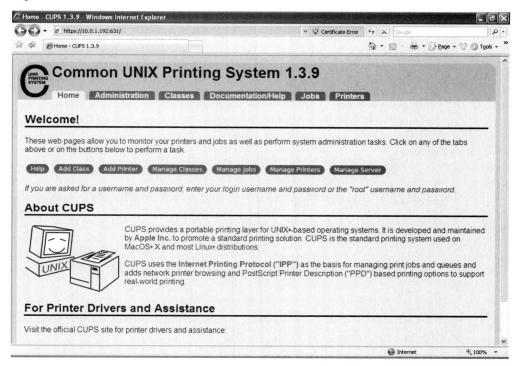

Figure 22-6: The main CUPS administration web page.

Secret
The CUPS server uses a self-signed encryption certificate for HTTPS traffic. Most modern browsers will produce a warning about accessing a site using a self-signed certificate. Because you know that this is your own server, it's perfectly okay to ignore the warnings and continue accessing the CUPS server web interface.

From the main CUPS admin page, select the Add Printer button to add a new printer for your system. The Add Printer window, shown in Figure 22-7, appears next.

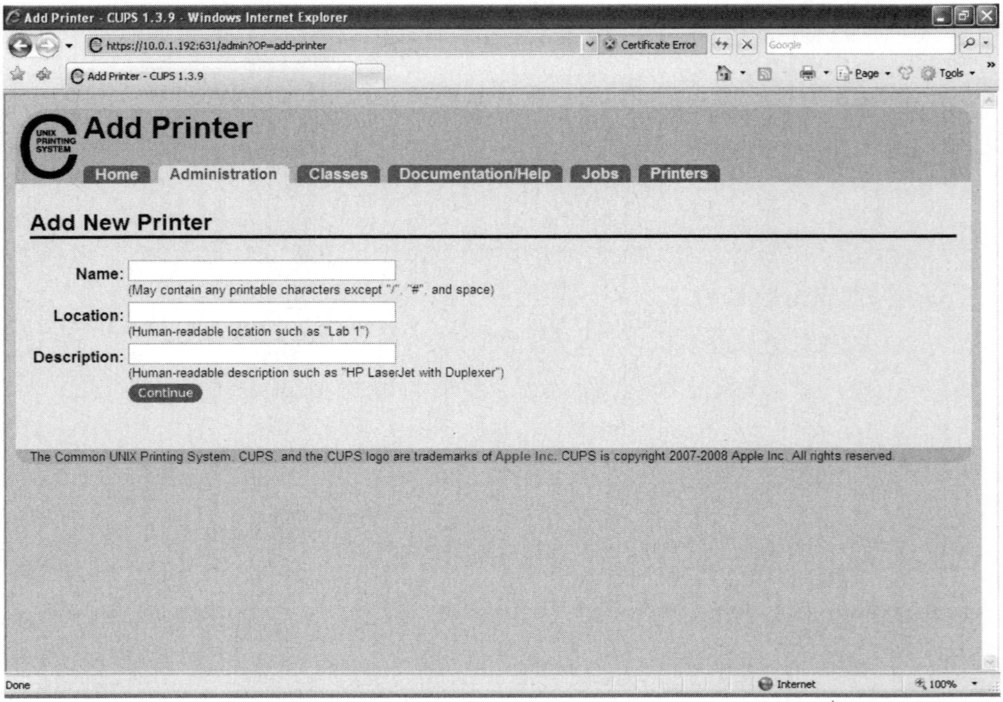

Figure 22-7: The CUPS Add Printer window.

The Add Printer option produces a wizard to help you define your system printer. Follow these steps to add your new printer.

1. Enter a name for the new printer, along with a location and description. These values will appear in the information provided when the printer is shared on the network. Click the Continue button when finished.

2. Enter the method by which the printer is connected to the server. The next window asks how the printer is connected to the Ubuntu server. There are several options to choose from. Select the option that describes how your printer is connected and click the Continue button.

3. Select the manufacturer of the printer. The drop-down box contains printer manufacturers for the printer drivers installed in the Ubuntu server. Select your printer's manufacturer and click the Continue button. You can also install your own printer driver file using the Browse button, then click the Add Printer button.

4. Select the model of the printer. If you selected a manufacturer from the previous window, the next window allows you to select the model of your printer. If your exact model number doesn't appear, try selecting a similar model number. Click the Add Printer button when you've selected the model.

5. To modify the configuration file you must be authenticated as an Ubuntu user with administrative privileges. Enter the userID and password for an administrative account on the Ubuntu server. A login dialog box appears (shown in Figure 22-8) to allow you to log in with your Ubuntu administrative user account.

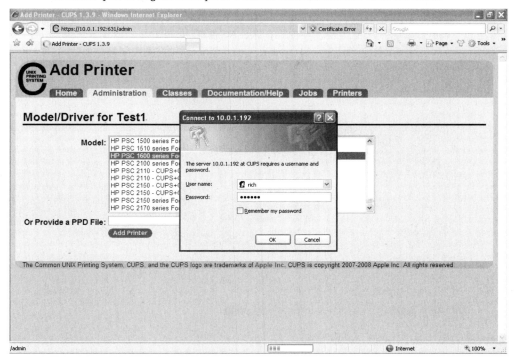

Figure 22-8: The CUPS admin login dialog box.

6. The CUPS window confirms the new printer has been added.

After you've added the new printer, you can view the printer status and manage the printer by selecting the Printers tab at the top of the CUPS main page. Each printer configured on the CUPS server appears with a series of buttons that allow you to control the printer operation, as shown in Figure 22-9.

From this interface you can print a test page, stop the printer, remove jobs from the print queue, and delete the printer.

After you've added the new printer via the CUPS web interface, it'll automatically become available on the Samba server. If you set the `browseable` setting for printers to `yes` in your Samba `smb.conf` configuration file, you can browse to connect to the printer from your Windows workstations.

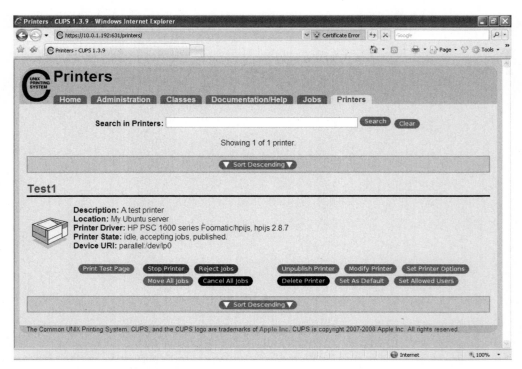

Figure 22-9: The CUPS printer admin page.

Summary

This chapter walked through how to set up your Ubuntu server to share folders and printers on a Microsoft Windows network. The Samba software package allows you to add your Ubuntu server to a Windows network as a member server or as a domain controller server. You can also have your Ubuntu server act as a standalone server in a Windows workgroup if you're just operating on a small home network.

The chapter discussed how to modify the smb.conf configuration file to create a standalone server using the Ubuntu system user accounts to authenticate users and control permissions on the shared folders. The Ubuntu server can also work as a print server on networks using both Samba and the CUPS server software. The CUPS server provides a simple interface for controlling printers on the system. Its web interface allows you to control your printers from a graphical environment.

The next chapter continues our discussion of the Ubuntu server by examining the Postfix email server. You can create a full-featured email server for your network simply by changing a few configuration parameters!

Email Server

Chapter
23

◆ ◆

Secrets in This Chapter

How Does Email Work?

Email in Ubuntu

The Postfix Package

The procmail Package

◆ ◆

Over the years, email has become the "killer app" of the Internet. These days, just about everyone has an email address, and many people have more than one! The Ubuntu server provides a great platform for creating your own email server, whether it's for you or for a small business or organization. It uses the popular Postfix email server to process messages from internal users on the server and from external mail sources. This chapter first describes how email works in the Ubuntu environment and how Ubuntu uses Postfix to handle email as a server. It then looks at how to configure Postfix and procmail (a popular mail delivery tool) to work in your specific email environment.

How Email Works

When you send an email message to your Aunt Betty, it passes through several programs along the way before she gets to view it in her email client program. Different types of operating systems handle email differently. The Linux operating system breaks the function of Internet email into separate processes that are each handled by separate programs. Figure 23-1 shows how most Linux email software (including Ubuntu) modularizes email functions.

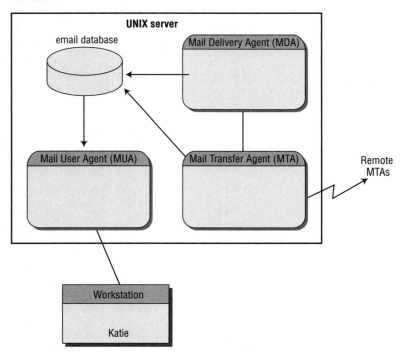

Figure 23-1: Linux modular email environment.

As you can see in Figure 23-1, a Linux email server is normally broken into three separate functions:

- ◆ The mail transfer agent (MTA)
- ◆ The mail delivery agent (MDA)
- ◆ The mail user agent (MUA)

The job of the MTA is to deliver mail messages between different mail servers on the Internet—most likely you and Aunt Betty use different Internet service providers (ISPs), each with its own email server. The job of the MDA is to move mail received by the MTA to the appropriate user's local mailbox. Finally, the job of the MUA is to allow individual users access to their own mailboxes to read and send messages.

The lines between these three functions can sometimes be fuzzy. Some email packages combine functionality for the MDA and MTA functions, while others combine the MDA and MUA functions. The following sections describe these basic email agents and show how they are implemented in Linux systems (and specifically in Ubuntu) in more detail.

Mail Transfer Agent

The MTA software is responsible for handling both incoming and outgoing mail messages on a mail server. For each outgoing mail message, the MTA determines the destination of the recipient addresses. If the destination host is the local machine itself, the MTA can either deliver the message directly to the recipient's local mailbox or pass the message off to the local MDA program for delivery.

However, if the destination host is a remote mail server, the MTA must establish a communication link with the remote host to transfer the message. Similarly, for incoming messages, the MTA must be able to accept connection requests from remote mail servers and receive messages destined for local users.

Many types of protocols can be used to transfer messages between two remote MTAs. The most common protocol used for Internet mail transfer is the simple mail transfer protocol (SMTP). This protocol is used only for passing messages to mail servers. It's not normally used for retrieving messages from an individual mailbox.

There are three popular MTA packages you'll often find on Linux servers:

- ◆ sendmail
- ◆ qmail
- ◆ Postfix

Each of these MTA packages provides the same basic functions of using SMTP to send and receive mail messages. However, there are a few differences among them. The following sections describe these three MTA programs.

sendmail

The sendmail MTA program is one of the most popular Linux MTA programs available. The program was originally written and supported by Eric Allman, but the Sendmail Consortium (http://www.sendmail.org) currently maintains the source code for sendmail. Eric has moved on to Sendmail, Inc., which provides commercial versions of the sendmail program.

The sendmail program is popular mainly because of its versatility. Many of the standard features of sendmail have become synonymous with email systems. Features such as virtual domains, message forwarding, user aliases, mail lists, and masquerading all got their start in the sendmail system.

Its versatility enables you to use sendmail for many types of email configurations. It can support large corporate Internet email servers, small corporate servers that dial into ISPs, and even standalone workstations that forward mail through a mail hub. Simply changing a few lines in sendmail's configuration file can change its characteristics and behavior.

The sendmail program also has the ability to parse and handle mail messages according to predefined rule sets. If you are a mail administrator, you know that it's often desirable to filter messages depending on particular mail requirements. To do this, all that's needed are new rules added to the sendmail configuration file.

Unfortunately, with versatility comes complexity. The sendmail program's large configuration file often becomes overwhelming for novice mail administrators to handle. Entire books have been written to assist the mail administrator in determining the proper configuration file settings for a particular email server application!

Secret

Over the years, the sendmail program has gotten a bad rap for being full of security holes. Although it's true that sendmail was first developed in the early days of the Internet when security issues weren't as prevalent, the sendmail program has been rewritten several times over to implement advanced security features. Don't discount using sendmail based on its history.

qmail

The qmail package is a complete MTA program written and maintained by Dan Bernstein (http://www.qmail.org). It supports all of the MTA functionality of the sendmail program but from a different perspective.

The qmail package takes the idea of modular email software in Linux one more step. Unlike sendmail, which performs all of the MTA functions in one program, qmail is a set of modular programs, each of which performs a specific task in the overall MTA function.

Not only are there several programs running to support qmail, each program runs under a different user account on the Linux system. If an intruder compromises one module program, it most likely won't affect the other modules. The security features of qmail are often touted as the best feature of qmail and the most advanced of any open-source server package.

Still another feature of qmail is its reliability. As each message enters the qmail system, it's placed in a mail queue. The qmail package uses a system of mail subdirectories and message states to ensure that no message stored in the message queue is lost.

As an added feature, qmail can use *maildir-style mailboxes*. These mailboxes separate user mail into folders, which reduces the chance of messages being corrupted or lost, as can sometimes happen in the single-message mailbox file system.

The qmail package also uses multiple configuration files, one for each feature of qmail. Although this avoids the problem of one large configuration file, it can be a distraction. Novice administrators often get confused about which qmail feature is defined in which configuration file.

Postfix

Postfix is the default MTA package installed on the Ubuntu server. Wietse Venema wrote the Postfix program to be a complete MTA package replacement for sendmail. Like qmail, Postfix is a modular program that uses several programs to implement the MTA functionality.

Unlike qmail, which uses a separate userID for each module, Postfix runs each module under one userID. Although it uses only one userID, if an intruder compromises a Postfix module, he or she most likely will still not be able to control the Ubuntu server.

One of the nicest features of Postfix is its simplicity. Instead of one large, complex configuration file like sendmail has, or multiple small configuration files like qmail, Postfix uses just two files that use plain-text parameters and value names to define functionality. Postfix even includes a simple command-line program for changing settings within the configuration files so that no file editing is required. This makes the Postfix server both flexible and easy to use.

However, in the Ubuntu server configuration, you might not even need to worry about manually setting the Postfix configuration files. The Ubuntu server installation process provides a great interface for you to easily set your desired email server features without having to write any configuration lines!

Mail Delivery Agent

Although each of the popular Linux MTA packages has the ability to deliver messages directly to users' mailboxes, Linux email implementations often rely on separate, stand-alone MDA programs to deliver messages to local users. Because these MDA programs concentrate only on delivering mail to local users, they offer additional bells and whistles that aren't available on MTA programs that include MDA functionality.

Some of these bells and whistles include

- Automatic mail filtering
- Automatic mail replying
- Automatic program initialization

Possibly the best and most used feature of MDA programs is the ability to filter incoming mail messages. For users who get lots of email, this can be a lifesaver. Messages can be automatically sorted into separate folders based on a subject header value, or even on just one word within a subject header. Figure 23-2 demonstrates this process.

The MDA program utilizes a configuration file that allows the user to specify regular expressions to search for in the various fields in the incoming message header. As expressions are matched, the message is saved in a predetermined folder in the user's mail area. A similar feature is the ability to filter messages and throw away unwanted messages. This feature can be used to help reduce spam.

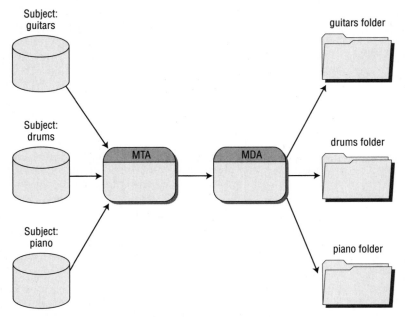

Figure 23-2: Sorting incoming email messages to separate folders.

MDA programs also provide the ability to run separate programs when email is received, without the user having to do anything. If you have used commercial email packages in a work environment, no doubt you are aware of the ability to leave out-of-office messages. This feature requires that the MDA automatically reply to any emails you receive. It can also be used to run external anti-virus and spam detection software on each message that is received.

Several open-source MDA programs are available for the mail administrator to incorporate with the email system. Three of the most popular programs are mailx, mail.local, and procmail. This section describes these programs.

mailx

The mailx program is the most popular MDA program used on Linux systems (and is the default MDA used in Ubuntu). You may not recognize it by its official name, but you most likely have used it by its system name, `mail`.

Messages are passed from the MTA program to the mailx program, which delivers the messages to the standard mailbox directory. Each user on the system has a separate file in the mailbox system that contains only their messages (new messages are appended to the end of the file as they are received).

The mailx program also allows you to create a `.forward` file in your home directory. The `.forward` file can contain an email address where you wish to temporarily forward your incoming mail messages. This is an extremely handy way to allow individual users to forward their mail to external email accounts while they are out of the office.

mail.local

Although not found in Linux systems, the mail.local program is used for local mail delivery by systems based on the Berkeley Software Distribution (BSD) UNIX model (such as FreeBSD and NetBSD). Similar to the mailx program, messages are passed from the MTA program to the mail.local program, which then determines how to deliver them.

The mail.local program also operates similar to the mailx program in that it uses the same standard format of mailboxes as mailx, although most BSD systems use /var/mail as the mailbox directory.

procmail

One of the most popular and versatile MDA programs in use is the procmail program written by Stephen R. van den Berg. It has become so popular that many Linux implementations (including Ubuntu) now install it by default, and many MTA programs utilize it in default configurations.

The popularity of the procmail program comes from its ability to process user-configured *recipes*. Recipes are short scripts that users write to control how their own mail is processed. Similar to the mailx .forward file, procmail allows users to create a .procmailrc file in their home directories to redirect messages based on the recipe scripts.

The procmail recipes utilize complex regular expressions to filter incoming mail messages to separate mailbox files, alternative email addresses, or even to the /dev/null file to automatically trash unwanted mail. The procmail MDA is an excellent tool to help keep your mailbox in order.

Mail User Agent

The next step in the process is for individual users to be able to read messages in their mailboxes. The Linux email model uses a local mailbox for each user to hold messages for that user. MUA programs provide a method for users to interface with the mailbox to read messages stored there.

MUAs do not receive messages; they only display messages that have already been placed in the user's mailbox by either the MTA or MDA program.

Because the basic feature of all MUA programs is the same (that is, to read messages from a mailbox), each MUA program must use different features to distinguish itself from other MUA programs. Two of the primary characteristics that differentiate MUA packages are:

- ♦ The location in which the MUA program stores read mail
- ♦ The method by which messages are displayed

Over the brief history of Internet mail, two different philosophies regarding where user mail messages should be stored have developed. Both philosophies have proponents and opponents. In reality, both philosophies can be beneficial, given a particular email environment.

One philosophy of message location is to download messages directly to the user's workstation, thus freeing up disk space on the mail server. Although this method makes the job of the mail administrator easier, it often leads to confusion for users who check their mail from multiple workstations (having your mailbox split between several computers is not fun).

The other philosophy for message location solves the problem of multiple workstations by keeping all of the messages on a central mail server. As users read their mailboxes, a copy of the message is sent to the workstation for display purposes. The actual messages remain in a file or directory on the mail server. No matter which workstations the users use to check their mail, the same messages will be available for viewing. This makes life much simpler for users, but it complicates the mail administrator's life. With all of the mail messages stored on the mail server, disk space becomes a crucial factor.

The second distinguishing feature in MUA packages is how messages are displayed. With the advent of fancy GUI devices, MUA programs have become more sophisticated in how they can display messages.

The original Linux MUA programs used text mode from a console screen to display email messages. Of course, this limited what could be sent in an email message (no fancy fonts or backgrounds). However, with the popularity of Linux graphical desktop systems such as KDE and GNOME, many Linux MUA programs now have the ability to display rich text and HTML-formatted emails.

To accommodate these additional features, many email messages use the multipurpose Internet mail extensions (MIME) format. MIME allows the message to contain multiple versions of the same message; each is formatted using a different display method. It's the job of the MUA to determine which method to use to display the message. Thus, text-based terminals can display the message in text mode, while graphical terminals can display the message in HTML mode.

The open-source movement has created several very good MUA programs for Linux operating systems. Chapter 9, "Evolution," discussed the popular Evolution graphical MUA package. It's great for interactively accessing your mailbox from a graphical desktop environment.

However, that's not the only time you may need to access your mail. Often the Ubuntu email server requires access to mailboxes so that you can read mail from the command-line interface or so that the server can process remote requests for mailbox access. This section describes three popular Linux MUA packages that come in handy in the Ubuntu email server environment:

- ◆ **mailx** for text terminal mail access
- ◆ **Dovecot** for remote client mail access
- ◆ **fetchmail** for system-to-system remote access

The following sections describe each of these packages.

mailx

Although the mailx program was discussed as an MDA program, it does double duty as an MUA program as well. The `mailx` program allows users to access their mailboxes to read stored messages and send messages to other email users. Here's an example of sending a message to a user using the mailx program:

```
rich@testing:~> mail rich
Subject: Test message
This is a test message.
.
Cc:
rich@testing:~>
```

The first line shows the mailx program being executed with a single command-line option, the email address of the mail recipient. If you're sending messages to other users on the same mail server, you can omit the hostname part of the email address; otherwise, be sure to use the full email address.

When the program starts, the mailx program automatically enters compose mode, querying you for a subject line and then the body of the message. To exit compose mode, type a single period on a line by itself. This generates a prompt to allow you to enter addresses for the carbon copy recipients. If there aren't any addresses to add, just hit the Enter key; mailx returns you to the command line, then sends the message to the MTA for processing.

To read mail messages in your mailbox, just type `mail` on the command line by itself:

```
rich@testbox:~$ mail
Mail version 8.1.2 01/15/2001. Type ? for help.
"/var/mail/rich": 1 message 1 new
>N 1 rich@testbox.loca Mon Oct 27 06:46 14/494 Test message
&
Message 1:
From rich@testbox.localdomain Mon Oct 27 06:46:26 2008
X-Original-To: rich
To: rich@testbox.localdomain
Subject: Test message
Date: Mon, 27 Oct 2008 06:46:26 -0400 (EDT)
From: rich@testbox.localdomain (Rich Blum)

This is a test message.


&
```

After you enter the `mail` command, a summary of all of the messages in your mailbox is displayed. Individual messages can be displayed, copied, or deleted using simple, single-letter commands within the mail prompt.

Dovecot

The *Dovecot* server provides a way for remote users to access their mailboxes on the Ubuntu server. Most likely you won't want your users to telnet into the Ubuntu server and have to use the mailx program to read their messages. Instead, you'll want them to use the fancy graphical email client programs on their desktop, such as Evolution, to remotely access your Ubuntu email server to read their mail.

Accessing a mailbox remotely requires using a special network protocol. Most common email client programs use either the post office protocol, version 3 (POP3) or the interactive mail access protocol (IMAP) to access a remote mail server and process mail stored in a user's mailbox.

To support this feature, the Ubuntu email server package includes the Dovecot server software. Once connected to the Dovecot server, users can read mail messages, as well as store them within subfolders under their Dovecot mailbox folder on the server. This feature allows users to connect from any remote client to view mail messages.

Here's an example of using a POP3 connection to retrieve a mail message:

```
rich@testbox:~$ telnet localhost 110
Trying 127.0.0.1…
Connected to localhost.
Escape character is '^].'
+OK Dovecot ready.
USER rich
+OK
PASS test
+OK Logged in.
LIST
+OK 1 messages:
1 449
.
RETR 1
+OK 449 octets
Return-Path: <rich@testbox.localdomain>
X-Original-To: rich
Delivered-To: rich@testbox.localdomain
Received: by testbox.localdomain (Postfix, from userid 1000)
id 641A2180E1; Mon, 27 Oct 2008 06:51:26 -0400 (EDT)
To: rich@testbox.localdomain
Subject: Test message
Message-Id: <20081027145126.641A2180E1@testbox.localdomain>
Date: Mon, 27 Oct 2008 06:51:26 -0400 (EDT)
From: rich@testbox.localdomain (Rich Blum)

This is a test message.
.
DELE 1
+OK Marked to be deleted.
QUIT
+OK Logging out, messages deleted.
Connection closed by foreign host.
rich@testbox:~$
```

The POP3 connection uses simple text commands that allow you to interact with the Dovecot server and manage and read messages stored in the Ubuntu server mailbox. Most common email packages, such as the Evolution graphical email package in the Ubuntu workstation distribution (see Chapter 9, "Evolution") can use either POP3 or IMAP to connect to the Dovecot server running on your Ubuntu server.

fetchmail

The fetchmail program is a slightly different type of MUA program. Instead of being a user's MUA interface, it runs behind the scenes, allowing one mail server to contact another remote mail server to download user mail from a mailbox.

Smaller organizations often can't afford (or for security reasons, don't want) to install a dedicated Internet connection. This means that they can't run an Ubuntu email server dedicated to receiving mail from the Internet. As an alternative, they can purchase email services from a remote ISP, which stores their corporate messages within a single mailbox on the ISP server.

The fetchmail program allows an Ubuntu server with limited network capability (such as a dial-up connection) to contact the remote ISP server using either POP3 or IMAP as a normal email client and download any messages stored on the ISP server to the local system.

This means that instead of having multiple individuals connect to the ISP to download their messages, a small organization can run an Ubuntu server and configure fetchmail to download all of their messages at once and place them in local mailboxes on the server. The fetchmail software can redistribute individual messages for employees to the appropriate mailboxes on the Ubuntu server. Once the messages are on the local mailboxes, employees can connect to the Ubuntu server using their desktop email client package and retrieve their messages. For companies that don't have a full-time Internet connection, fetchmail can be a cost-effective solution.

Secret

The Ubuntu server's email server installation doesn't include the fetchmail program by default, but it's easy to install. Just use the `apt-get` program to install fetchmail:

```
sudo apt-get install fetchmail
```

For more information about configuring and using the fetchmail program, check out the main fetchmail web site at `http://fetchmail.berlios.de.`

Postfix Setup

The Postfix system consists of several mail queue directories and executable programs, all interacting with each other to provide mail service. Figure 23-3 shows a block diagram of the core Postfix parts.

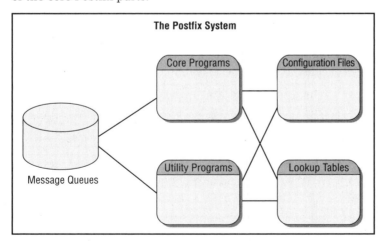

Figure 23-3: Block diagram of Postfix.

Each piece of the Postfix block diagram provides a different function for the whole email process. The following sections describe the different pieces of the Postfix block diagram in more detail.

Postfix Core Programs

The Postfix package utilizes a master program that runs as a background process at all times. The master program allows Postfix to spawn programs that scan the mail queues for new messages and send them to the proper destinations.

Postfix allows you to configure the core programs so that they can remain running for a set period of time after they are opened. This allows for the master program to reutilize a running helper program, if necessary, which saves processing time. After a set time limit, the helper program quietly stops itself. You can see the default Postfix programs running on the server by listing the processes:

```
$ ps ax
4479 ? Ss 0:00 /usr/lib/postfix/master
4485 ? S 0:00 pickup -l -t fifo -u -c
4486 ? S 0:00 qmgr -l -t fifo -u
$
```

These three programs run continuously in the background to control mail delivery on the Postfix system. The master program controls the overall operation of Postfix. It's responsible for starting other Postfix processes as needed. The qmgr and pickup programs are configured to remain as background processes longer than other core programs. The pickup program determines when messages are available to be routed by the Postfix system. The qmgr program is responsible for the central message routing system for Postfix.

Table 23-1 lists other core programs that Postfix uses in addition to qmgr and pickup to transfer mail messages.

Table 23-1: Core Postfix Mail-Processing Programs

Program	Description
bounce	Posts a log in the bounce message queue for bounced messages and returns the bounced message to the sender
cleanup	Processes incoming mail headers and places messages in the incoming queue
error	Processes message delivery requests from qmgr, forcing messages to bounce
flush	Processes messages waiting to be retrieved by a remote mail server
local	Delivers messages destined for local users
pickup	Waits for messages in the maildrop queue and sends them to the cleanup program to begin processing
pipe	Forwards messages from the queue manager program to external programs
postdrop	Moves an incoming message to the maildrop queue when that queue is not writable by normal users

Table 23-1: *(continued)*

Program	Description
qmgr	Processes messages in the incoming queue, determining where and how they should be delivered and spawning programs to deliver them
sendmail	Provides a sendmail-compatible interface for programs to send messages to the maildrop queue
showq	Reports Postfix mail queue status
smtp	Forwards messages to external mail hosts using the SMTP
smtpd	Receives messages from external mail hosts using the SMTP
trivial-rewrite	Receives messages from the cleanup program to ensure header addresses are in a standard format for the qmgr program; also used by the qmgr program to resolve remote host addresses

Depending on what the Postfix email server is processing, you may see any of these programs running at any given time. Each program runs only when it's needed by the overall Postfix mail process.

Postfix Message Queues

Unlike some other MTA packages, Postfix uses several message queues for managing email messages as they are processed. Each message queue contains messages in a different message state in the Postfix system. Table 23-2 lists the message queues that are used by Postfix.

Table 23-2: Postfix Message Queues

Queue	Description
maildrop	New messages waiting to be processed, received from local users
incoming	New messages waiting to be processed, received from remote hosts, as well as processed messages from local users
active	Messages that are ready to be delivered by Postfix
deferred	Messages that have failed on an initial delivery attempt and are waiting for another attempt
flush	Messages that are destined for remote hosts that will connect to the mail server to retrieve them
mail	Delivered messages stored for local users to read

If the Postfix system should be shut down at any time, messages remain in the last queue where they were placed. When Postfix is restarted, it will automatically begin processing messages from the queues.

Message queues are often an item of contention for busy mail servers. As new messages are received, they are placed in separate files in the message queues. As more files are stored in the message queues, file-handling performance decreases.

It is a well-known fact that accessing files on UNIX systems in a directory with lots of files is slower than accessing fewer files in multiple subdirectories. Using this information, Postfix was created so that the message queue directories can be divided into separate subdirectories.

Each of these message queues divides the main queue directory into two levels of subdirectories. Each message is placed into a subdirectory based on the first two characters of its filename. Figure 23-4 demonstrates this layout.

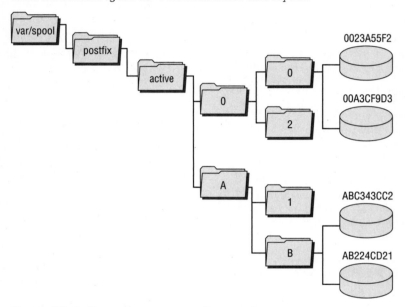

Figure 23-4: New message queue directory format.

As new messages are received in the message queues, the new subdirectories are created. As files are retrieved from the directories, the created subdirectories remain behind to be used by other messages. Although this structure appears more complicated, it has been determined that this directory structure outperforms the old structure in retrieving messages from the message queue.

Postfix Utility Programs

Besides the Postfix core programs, there are several utilities that are used by Postfix processes and local Postfix users to help manipulate and transfer messages. Table 23-3 shows the different Postfix utilities available on a Postfix system.

Table 23-3: Postfix Utility Programs

Program	Description
mailq	Checks the Postfix mail queues for messages and displays the results
postfix	Controls starting, stopping, and reloading the Postfix system
postalias	Creates, updates, or queries the Postfix alias database
postcat	Displays the contents of Postfix queue files
postconf	Displays and modifies parameter entries in the `main.cf` configuration file
postkick	Sends command requests to running Postfix services
postlock	Locks specified Postfix files and executes a specified command
postlog	Logs a message to the system-logging facility using Postfix-style log messages
postmap	Creates or queries a Postfix lookup table
postsuper	Performs maintenance on specified Postfix queue directories

Each Postfix utility program plays a different role in either processing mail messages or querying the Postfix system for status information. Some of the utilities are utilized by Postfix core programs to process mail, while others can be used by the Postfix administrator to manipulate messages and obtain statistics about the running system.

Postfix Configuration Files

The next block in the diagram (Figure 23-3) is the Postfix configuration files. The configuration files contain information that the Postfix programs use when processing messages. Unlike some other MTA programs, it is possible to change configuration information while the Postfix server is running and issue a command to have Postfix load the new information without completely downing the mail server.

Postfix separates the main configuration elements into two separate configuration files:

- ◆ `main.cf`: Contains parameters used by the Postfix programs when processing messages.
- ◆ `master.cf`: Contains parameters used by the Postfix master program when running core programs.

The operation of the core Postfix programs can be controlled using the `master.cf` configuration file. Each program is listed in a separate line along with the parameters to control its operation. Here are a few examples from the `main.cf` configuration file:

```
# svc type private unpriv chroot wakeup maxproc command+args
# (yes) (yes) (yes) (never) (50)
#
=====================================================================
```

```
smtp inet n - - - - smtpd
pickup fifo n - - 60 1 pickup
cleanup unix n - - - 0 cleanup
qmgr fifo n - - 300 1 qmgr
tlsmgr unix - - - 1000? 1 tlsmgr
rewrite unix - - - - - trivial-rewrite
bounce unix - - - - 0 bounce
defer unix - - - - 0 bounce
trace unix - - - - 0 bounce
verify unix - - - - 0 verify
flush unix - - - 1000? 1 flush
local unix - n - - - local
```

The Postfix operational parameters are set in the main.cf configuration file. Postfix parameters have a default value that is implied within the Postfix system. If a parameter value is not present in the main.cf file, its value will be preset by Postfix. If a parameter value is present in the main.cf file, its contents override the default value.

Each Postfix parameter is listed on a separate line in the configuration file along with its value, in the form

```
parameter = value
```

Both *parameter* and *value* are plain ASCII text strings that can be easily read by the mail administrator. The Postfix master program reads the parameter values in the main.cf file when Postfix is first started and again whenever a Postfix reload command is issued.

Here are a few examples from the main.cf configuration file:

```
myhostname = testbox.localdomain
alias_maps = hash:/etc/aliases
alias_database = hash:/etc/aliases
myorigin = /etc/mailname
mydestination = testbox.localdomain, localhost.localdomain,
localhost
relayhost =
mynetworks = 127.0.0.0/8 [::ffff:127.0.0.0]/104 [::1]/128
mailbox_command = procmail -a "$EXTENSION"
mailbox_size_limit = 0
recipient_delimiter = +
inet_interfaces = all
inet_protocols = ipv4
default_transport = smtp
relay_transport = smtp
```

Most of the parameters defined here are automatically set when you walk through the steps of the Postfix wizard during the Ubuntu server installation process.

Postfix Lookup Tables

Postfix also uses several lookup tables to control the behavior of the email server. Each lookup table defines parameters that control the delivery of mail within the Postfix system. Table 23-4 shows the different lookup tables that can be created for Postfix.

Table 23-4: Postfix Lookup Tables

Table	Description
access	Maps remote SMTP hosts to an accept/deny table for security
aliases	Maps alternative recipients to local mailboxes
canonical	Maps alternative mailbox names to real mailboxes for message headers
relocated	Maps an old user mailbox name to a new mailbox name
transport	Maps domain names to delivery methods for remote host connectivity and delivery
virtual	Maps recipients and domains to local mailboxes for delivery

Each lookup table is created as a plain ASCII text file, but it must be converted to a binary file for Postfix to use. Once you've created the text file version , use the `postmap` command to create the binary database file version of the file. Postfix uses the binary database file when searching the lookup tables. This helps speed up the lookup process for Postfix.

Installing Postfix

When you select the email server option in the Ubuntu server installation process, a special setup wizard appears. This wizard prompts you to select the type of email server you want to install. This window provides five options to choose from:

- No configuration
- Internet site
- Internet with SmartHost
- Satellite system
- Local only

The type of email server you select determines the default configuration settings for Postfix. The first option, no configuration, allows you to pass through the wizard without changing your Postfix configurations. The rest of the options require that you know the email environment you're trying to create for your Ubuntu server. The following sections explain the other server options and help you set up your email server environment.

Internet Site

When you select the Internet site option, Ubuntu configures Postfix to send email messages directly to remote email servers, as well as receive messages directly from other Internet servers, as shown in Figure 23-5.

This configuration means that your Ubuntu server must have a full-time Internet connection and must be turned on at all times. The Ubuntu server must also use the domain name system (DNS) so that it can resolve the destination email host responsible for accepting mail for a specified email address (see Chapter 20, "DNS Server"). The Postfix software will contact the remote email server, then deliver the email message.

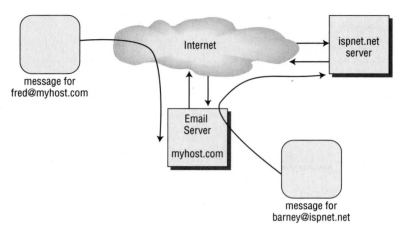

Figure 23-5: Email Internet site configuration.

With this configuration the Ubuntu server must also be able to accept email messages from remote email servers. The server can accept email messages for just users on the local server or for users on an entire domain, such as a corporate network.

To accept mail messages from remote servers, the Ubuntu server must be listed as a mail provider server in the DNS records using the MX record (again, see Chapter 20). The MX record determines whether mail for just the server or for the entire domain is forwarded to the Ubuntu server's address. Remote email servers use this information to decide when to send messages to your Ubuntu server.

Internet with SmartHost

When you select the Internet with SmartHost option, the Ubuntu installation automatically configures Postfix to handle inbound and outbound mail as two separate functions:

- ◆ Inbound mail is retrieved either directly from the Internet or from a remote ISP using fetchmail.
- ◆ Outbound mail is forwarded to a remote host for processing.

Instead of worrying about your Ubuntu server being able to resolve and contact remote email servers, all that work is pushed off to a single remote host. This allows your Ubuntu server to have to contact only a single host for all outbound messages.

This option is popular for Ubuntu server installations that don't have a continuous Internet connection, such as a dial-up environment. Postfix can wait until a dial-up Internet connection is established, then forward all outbound email messages to the remote host at the same time that the fetchmail program retrieves all inbound messages. This is demonstrated in Figure 23-6.

The remote SmartHost is defined in the DNS MX records as being the actual email server for your domain. Remote email servers forward all messages for your users to the remote SmartHost, which should be connected to the Internet 24/7. Your Ubuntu server can then contact the remote SmartHost on a scheduled basis or on an as-needed basis.

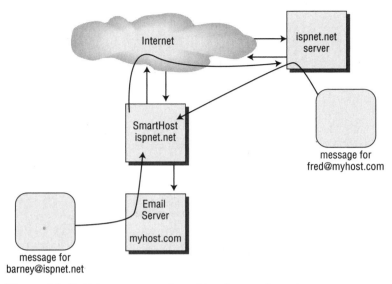

Figure 23-6: Using a remote SmartHost for email services.

Satellite System

The satellite system option available in the email server configuration assumes that all mail functions are handled by a remote email server, including mail for local users of the server. The remote email server operates similar to the SmartHost option but is used for internal as well as external email.

This means that even if you send an email message to another user on the Ubuntu server, the message is sent to the remote SmartHost. All of the users on the Ubuntu server must contact the remote email server for their email. This is demonstrated in Figure 23-7.

In this setup, no mail is stored on the Ubuntu mail server, so the local mailboxes aren't used.

Be careful when setting up a satellite system. Even system mail messages intended for the root user are forwarded to the remote SmartHost. This could be a problem if the system is experiencing network issues and the mail can't be sent. You won't have access to crucial system error messages that may be mailed to the root user!

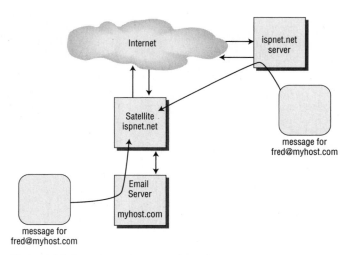

Figure 23-7: Using the satellite system email setup.

Local Only

The local-only option for the Postfix configuration allows sending mail only to other user accounts on the Ubuntu server. The Ubuntu server can't forward email to external email addresses, nor does it accept or retrieve any mail from external hosts.

This is a safe setting to use if you want to support internal email on your server without using it as a public email server. It's usually a good idea to support local email, because many programs use email to contact the system administrator if something goes wrong.

Secret   When setting up the local-only email option, make sure that you redirect mail destined for the root user account to the normal user account of the administrator. This setting allows you to view any critical system error messages that are generated by applications or by the Ubuntu system itself.

Configuring Postfix

Once you've decided what type of email server to use, you must answer a series of wizard questions to determine your email environment. This section walks through the email wizard configuration and shows how to respond based on your specific email environment.

If you didn't set up your Postfix email environment during the installation wizard, don't worry. You can restart the installation wizard by using the command:

```
sudo dpkg-reconfigure postfix
```

This command reruns the same wizard that appears during the installation process, and it reconfigures the Postfix configuration files based on your replies to the wizard questions.

Wizard Windows

Possibly one of the most confusing aspects of setting up an Ubuntu email server is working your way through the series of wizard windows that appear. Each window requests specific information about your email setup. Ubuntu uses the information you provide to automatically configure Postfix for handling email.

This section walks through the individual wizard windows, describing the information that's being requested and showing how to enter that information based on your email environment.

System Mail Name

The first wizard window that appears is the System Mail Name window, shown in Figure 23-8.

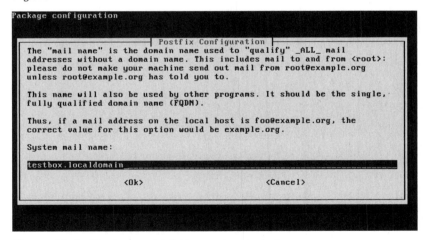

Figure 23-8: The System Mail Name wizard window.

This window appears in all of the configuration options and asks what default domain name to use for all email addresses processed by Postfix that don't already use a domain name. For example, when I use the mailx program from the command line and want to send a message to myself, I use the command:

```
mail rich
```

Postfix will automatically append the domain name you enter here to the email address rich. There are basically two choices for this entry:

- ◆ If your Ubuntu server is processing mail for an entire domain, such as for a small business or home office, enter your domain name in this section, such as mydomain.org.

- ◆ If your Ubuntu server is processing mail only for the local system users, enter your full host and domain name here, such as myhost.mydomain.org.

It's imperative that you enter the name that the Postfix server accepts mail for; otherwise, Postfix won't be able to process mail that you send to local users on the system. Most email clients use either the From or Reply-To headers in the email message to determine how to reply to an email message. Postfix (and most other email programs such as Evolution) automatically adds the system name you specify here to your userID for your From and Reply-To headers.

Relay Host

If you select the Internet with SmartHost or satellite site options, the next window that appears in the wizard process is the Relay Host window, shown in Figure 23-9.

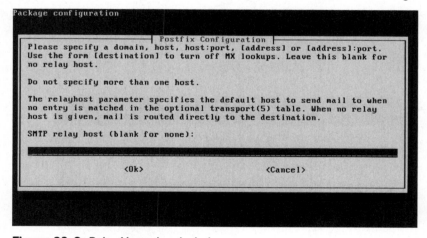

Figure 23-9: Relay Host wizard window.

The relay host entry is the SmartHost server used to forward all outbound email messages to remote hosts. If Postfix can't resolve the destination address as a local user, it forwards the message to the relay host.

You can enter the relay host information using five different formats:

- ◆ A domain name that uses an MX record to identify the email server
- ◆ A hostname of the remote email server
- ◆ A hostname:port format to specify an alternative TCP port used to receive mail
- ◆ An [*IPaddress*] (including the square brackets) to specify the IP address of the remote email server
- ◆ An [*IPaddress*]:port (including the square brackets) to specify the IP address and alternative TCP port used to receive mail

Leaving this field blank results in no relay host being defined, and Postfix will attempt to directly deliver all email destined for remote hosts.

System Mail Redirection

The Ubuntu system often sends email messages to the root user account to notify you of system errors or potential errors. Unfortunately, Ubuntu doesn't use the root user account as a normal login account. Instead, Ubuntu provides the admin group to specify normal user accounts that have administrative privileges (see Chapter 17, "Users and Groups").

To account for this problem, the wizard allows you to redirect any email messages destined for the root user or the special postmaster mail accounts to a normal user account on the system, see Figure 23-10.

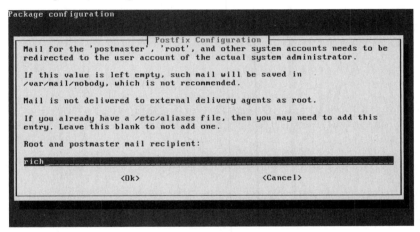

Figure 23-10: The System Mail Redirection wizard window.

Select a user account that should receive all email messages destined for the root and postmaster accounts. Make sure that someone logs in using that user account on a regular basis to watch for important system messages!

Final Destination Domains

The Postfix email server is an extremely versatile email system. Not only can it accept email destined for your local host, it can accept email destined for one or more domains. The Final Destination Domain wizard window allows you to list all of the domains that Postfix should accept messages for.

By default Postfix will accept email messages for three locations:

- ◆ The local *hostname.domain* address
- ◆ The *localhost.domain* address
- ◆ The special *localhost* address

If your Ubuntu server is acting as the email server for an entire domain, you must add that domain to the list here. Any domains not listed are considered remote by Postfix, which forwards email messages it receives destined for those addresses to the remote address (either directly or via the remote SmartHost).

Synchronous Updates

One of the main features of Postfix is its reliability. The developer of Postfix boasts that, unlike some other email servers, once Postfix receives an email message it's an almost certainty that the message will get delivered to the destination on the server.

Postfix accomplishes this feat by using a system of checks and balances when processing incoming messages. This system involves using several layers of message queues to manage messages as they are processed. Each queue contains messages in a different state in the Postfix system.

If the Postfix system should be shut down at any time, messages remain in the last queue where they were placed. When Postfix is restarted, it will automatically begin processing messages from the queues.

However, there's still a hidden vulnerability in this process. By default, Ubuntu uses a system of buffering data before writing them to the disk. Although buffering increases performance of the system, it creates a period of time when email messages are vulnerable to a system crash. Any messages stored in the buffer but not yet written to the disk are lost when the system crashes.

To increase the reliability of your data, you can disable the write buffer by forcing *synchronous updates,* as shown in Figure 23-11.

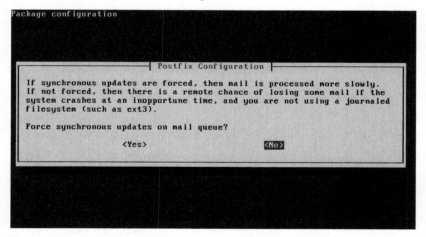

Figure 23-11: Enabling synchronous updates from the wizard.

Synchronous updates use the Linux sync filesystem option, which allows Ubuntu to write data directly to the hard disk instead of buffering the data. This option reduces the amount of time that data are vulnerable to a system crash. As you can imagine, however, synchronous updates slow down performance because programs must wait for Ubuntu to write the files to the disk before continuing. However, this feature greatly increases the reliability of email messages surviving a system crash.

Secret

Ubuntu can use several types of filesystems for storing data (see Chapter 1, "What Is Ubuntu?"). Not all of the filesystem types support synchronous updates, and not all require synchronous updates. Filesystems such as ext3 and reiserfs use journaling, which keeps logs of data written to the disks. These filesystems are designed to automatically recover from a system crash, so synchronous updates aren't necessary.

If you selected to use the default ext3 filesystem for your Ubuntu server, you can disable the synchronous updates feature for Postfix without worrying about losing email messages during a system crash.

Networks Allowed to Relay

The network relay wizard window allows you to decide what clients your Ubuntu server will relay messages for.

Most email client programs can't send email directly to users on remote email servers. Instead, they point to a relay email server that can forward the message to the intended recipient. You can use your Ubuntu server to forward outbound email messages from your network clients.

There are three categories of addresses you can add to the network relay list:

♦ The localhost IP address
♦ The network IP address for local network users
♦ Multiple network IP address for customers using your server as a SmartHost

The default configuration suggested in the wizard is to specify the localhost IP address, using both IPv4 and IPv6 formats. This setting allows your internal email users to send outbound email messages through the Postfix server.

If your Ubuntu server is providing email services for a small business or home office that has other client workstations, you'll want to add your local network IP address to the list. This setting allows clients on your local network to relay outbound email messages through your Ubuntu server.

If you're creating an email server to support more than one network (such as being a SmartHost for other networks), you must list the networks you support. Only clients coming from listed networks will be allowed to relay email messages through your server.

Postfix uses the classless inter-domain routing (CIDR) format to list a network IP address:

networkaddress/subnetbits

The *networkaddress* portion reflects the common network address used for the local network. The *subnetbits* portion defines how many bits are used to reference the network portion of the IP address. For example, the entry 192.168.0.0/24 allows up to 255 hosts on the 192.168.0.x network to relay messages through the Ubuntu server.

In the old days of the Internet, it was common for a mail server to automatically redirect any email messages it received to the proper destination. This allowed clients on the local network to relay an email message through a remote email server to the final destination email server.

Unfortunately, as the Internet grew in popularity, spammers realized they could exploit relay email servers. Spammers could use a fictitious From address to hide their identities and relay their spam through an *open relay server*. An open relay server allows any remote server or workstation to relay email messages through it.

These days, email servers shouldn't be open relay servers (in fact, several services scan the Internet looking for open relay email servers and blacklisting them). Please take the time to make sure that your Ubuntu server isn't an open relay on the Internet by entering only the appropriate local networks in the Network Relay wizard window.

procmail

The next wizard window asks whether you want to use the popular procmail MDA package in your email system. As discussed in the Mail Delivery Agent section in this chapter, procmail allows your local users to customize how their mail is delivered. It provides some great features that allow your customers to implement fancy features such as using out-of-office messages, filtering messages to separate mailboxes, and archiving messages.

The procmail section later in this chapter demonstrates how to create procmail recipes to control mail delivery.

Mailbox Size Limit

The next wizard window allows you to set the maximum size that Ubuntu allows for your user mailboxes. The size you set for a mailbox limit depends on the philosophy you take on where mail should be stored.

If you're implementing a setup where clients store their email messages to their local PC, you can set the mailbox limit to a relatively low number. However, if you allow your clients to store email messages on the server and access them from multiple locations, you'll need to increase the mailbox size limit.

Local Address Extension

The local address extension is a neat feature provided by Postfix to allow users to create separate mail addresses on their own. By default, the Postfix system accepts mail messages destined only for valid user accounts defined in the Ubuntu system, and rejects any email messages destined for any other address.

However, by enabling the local address extension feature, you can allow your email users to expand their user account address on the system, creating additional virtual accounts. The virtual accounts are created by adding additional text after the normal user account name, after a separator.

For example, if you use the default local address extension of the plus sign (+), Postfix will accept mail destined for addresses such as `rich+guitars`, `rich+computers`, or `rich+work`. Postfix knows to deliver the email messages to the user account that's identified before the local address extension character.

After Postfix delivers the email message to the user account, the user can tell what category the message belongs in by looking at the destination address. Alternatively, users can use the procmail program (see the procmail section later in this chapter) to redirect messages to separate mail folders, based on the extension text that appears in the destination address. This is a great way to create additional mail accounts for special occasions.

IPv4 and IPv6

The final wizard window in the Postfix configuration allows you to select which Internet protocols are activated in the Postfix configuration. The choices are

+ **all:** Support both IPv4 and IPv6 addresses.
+ **ipv6:** Support only IPv6 addresses.
+ **ipv4:** Support only IPv4 addresses.

Both the Ubuntu server and the Postfix software support using the IP version 4 (IPv4) format and the newer IP version 6 (IPv6) format. This option allows you to limit Postfix to using one format or the other, or allow both formats in the configuration.

IPv6 addresses use a 128-bit value to represent the network and host addresses. Usually, this address is represented as a series of eight groups of four hexadecimal values:

```
XXXX:XXXX:XXXX:XXXX:XXXX:XXXX:XXXX:XXXX
```

Each group is separated by a colon. However, trying to use this format can get cumbersome, so some shortcuts are allowed when specifying IPv6 addresses:

+ Leading zeroes within a group of four digits are omitted:
  ```
  2030:0:0:0:30:4c45:0:100
  ```
+ Groups containing all zeroes are replaced with double colons:
  ```
  2030::30:4c45:0:100
  ```

This setting depends on how you have to reference network and host addresses on your network. If your network supports only IPv4 style addresses, you can set this to `ipv4`. However, it doesn't hurt to set this to `all` in case you'll need to support IPv6 addresses in the near future.

Modifying Configuration Settings

Although the Ubuntu installation wizard walks through your email server environment and automatically configures Postfix, you may want to customize a few things on your server. You can use the `postconf` program to do this without having to touch the `main.cf` configuration file.

The format of the `postconf` program is

```
postconf [options] parameter = value
```

To view the existing value of a parameter, just enter the parameter name without setting a value:

```
rich@testbox:/etc$ postconf myorigin
myorigin = /etc/mailname
rich@testbox:/etc$ cat /etc/mailname
testbox.localdomain
rich@testbox:/etc$
```

This shows that the myorigin parameter is set to the contents of the /etc/mailname file. This allows you to define the origin address used for outbound email messages outside of the main.cf configuration file. You can use the cat command to display the contents of the /etc/mailname file, which shows the hostname used for the server.

procmail

The procmail program acts as an intermediary, filtering each user's mail as it comes from the server, but before it is written to the mailbox. The procmail program is extremely versatile. You can configure the Postfix MTA to directly send all incoming messages to procmail for local delivery or allow individual mail users to customize their mail environment to use procmail.

Once you decide to send all messages to procmail, individual users can take advantage of the power of procmail by creating a .procmailrc file in their home folder to instruct procmail on how to process incoming mail messages.

The .procmailrc File

The .procmailrc file defines how procmail delivers mail based on *recipes* defined in the file. Each procmail recipe defines a matching expression value and an action for procmail to take when a message matches the expression. The format of a procmail recipe is

```
recipe header line
condition line(s)
action line
```

The recipe header line defines the basic action of the recipe. All recipe lines start with the heading

```
:0 [flags] [: locallockfile]
```

The *flags* identify the basic function that the recipe will perform. Table 23-5 lists the flags that are available.

Table 23-5: procmail Recipe Flags

Flag	Description
A	Do not execute the recipe unless the conditions of the all the preceding recipes are met
a	Do not execute the recipe unless the conditions of the immediately preceding recipe are met
B	egrep the body of the message
b	Feed the body of the message to the destination (default)
c	Generate a carbon copy of this message
D	Distinguish between uppercase and lowercase (the default is to ignore case)
E	Do not execute the recipe unless the conditions of the all the preceding recipes were not met
e	Do not execute the recipe unless the immediately preceding recipe failed

Table 23-5: *(continued)*

Flag	Description
f	Consider the pipe as a filter to extract messages
H	`egrep` the message header (default)
h	Feed the header of the message to the destination (default)
i	Ignore any write errors on the recipe
r	Do not ensure that messages end with an empty line (raw mode)
W	Wait for the filter or program to finish and check the exit code; suppresses any "program failure" messages
w	Wait for the filter or program to finish and check the exit code; does not suppress any error messages

The flags are listed in the recipe header line after the :0 header. More than one flag can be entered on the recipe header line.

After the flags, if a lock file is required, the mail administrator can specify either a specific lock file by name or omit the lock file name to allow procmail to use a default lock file. For example, the recipe header line

```
:0:
```

specifies that procmail uses the default flags (Hhb) and utilizes the default lock file when processing the message. Alternatively, the mail administrator can specify a lock file to use:

```
:0 Whc: msgid.lock
```

After the header line, one or more recipe condition lines must be defined. Each condition line must start with an asterisk (*). After the asterisk, a normal regular expression is used as the matching condition. Besides normal regular expressions, procmail defines seven special conditions. Table 23-6 lists these special conditions.

Table 23-6: procmail Special Conditions

Condition	Description
!	Invert the condition
$	Evaluate the condition according to shell substitution rules inside double quotation marks
?	Use the exit code of the specified program
<	Check whether the total message length is less than the specified number of bytes (in decimal)
>	Check whether the total message length is greater than the specified number of bytes (in decimal)
variable ??	Match the remainder of the condition against the environment variable specified
\	Quote any of the special characters to use as normal characters

The easiest way to learn to write condition lines is to see a few examples. This condition line checks whether the message's Subject header field contains the word guitars:

```
* ^Subject:.*guitars
```

The condition uses the caret (^) regular expression character to match any message header lines that start with the word "Subject:". Next, it checks to see whether the word "guitars" is anywhere in that line.

You can also check on multiple words in a line. The next condition line checks whether the message's Subject header field contains the words "guitars" and "bass":

```
* ^Subject:.*guitars.*bass
```

Received messages with both the words "guitars" and "bass" in the Subject header field would match this condition line.

Finally, this condition line checks the entire message for the word "meeting":

```
* meeting
```

Any received message with the word "meeting" anywhere in it would match this condition line.

After the condition lines are defined, the procmail action line must be defined. The action line defines the action that procmail will take if the condition line is matched with a message.

Much like the condition line, the action line can start with a special character that describes the basic action that will be taken. Table 23-7 describes the action line special characters.

Table 23-7: procmail Action Line Special Characters

Character	Description
!	Forward message to the specified addresses
|	Start the specified program
{	Start a block of recipes checked if the condition is matched
}	End a block of recipes checked if the condition is matched
mailbox	Forward message to the mailbox defined by mailbox

Each recipe has only one action line. The action line defines what procmail will do with any messages that match the condition lines. Again, the easiest way to explain this is to show some examples.

Using procmail

Once you've activated procmail in your Postfix setup, any user on the local system can use the .procmailrc file to control how his or her email is handled. The best way to discuss this process is to walk through a sample .procmailrc file. Here's an example of a simple .procmailrc file for a sample user on the mail server:

```
MAILDIR=$HOME/folders

:0 c
archive

:0
* ^From.*guitar-list
{
:0 c
! rich@ispnet3.net

:0
guitars
}

:0 hc
* !^FROM_DAEMON
* !^X-Loop: rich@ispnet1.net
| (formail -r -I"Precedence: junk" \
-A"X-Loop: rich@ispnet1.net" ; \
echo "Thanks for your message, but I will be out of the office until 1/4") \
| $SENDMAIL -t

:0
* ^Subject.*pills
/dev/null
```

The first line in the sample .procmailrc file tells procmail where you want to keep your mail folders. Each folder will be created as a separate file under the MAILDIR directory specified. Make sure that the folder exists on your system:

```
rich@testbox:~> mkdir folders
```

Once procmail starts forwarding messages to the mailboxes defined in your recipes, you'll see the new mailbox files appear under the folder:

```
rich@testbox:~/folders> ls
archive guitars
rich@testbox:~/folders>
```

To read messages in folders using mailx, you can use the -f command-line option:

```
$ mail -f /home/rich/folders/guitars
```

The sample .procmailrc file shown here contains four separate recipes that are processed by procmail. Each procmail recipe is separated by a blank line. The first recipe simply places a copy of all received messages in the mail folder archive.

The second recipe demonstrates the use of recipes within a recipe. The main recipe first checks whether the received message is from a user called guitar-list. If it is, both of the internal recipes are checked. First a copy of all of the messages is forwarded to the email address rich@ispnet3.net. Next, a copy of all the messages is placed in the mail folder `guitar`. Because these are only copies, the original message will still be placed in the normal user account's mail folder on the Ubuntu server.

The third recipe demonstrates redirecting messages to an external program. All messages that are not sent from either a daemon (system) process or from the original user are forwarded to the `formail` program. This program is included with the procmail distribution. It's used to help filter header information from messages. Two header fields are added to the message header by formail: a Precedence line and an X-Loop line. These lines are used by `formail` to help prevent message loops. After that, a simple shell command is used to generate a message and redirect it to the local MTA process, which is defined by the `$SENDMAIL` environment variable.

The last recipe demonstrates filtering messages based on a Subject header line. Any message with a subject containing the word "`pills`" is placed in the mail folder `/dev/null`. The `/dev/null` file maintains a 0-byte file size. Any information copied there is lost forever. Thus, this recipe deletes any messages with the word "`pill`" in the Subject line. Although this technique can be used for blocking known spam messages from your email server, it is extremely dangerous. If any valid emails get caught by this recipe, they are deleted without your knowing it. It is much safer to redirect suspected spam to a separate folder and manually sift through the messages in that folder.

Each message delivered by procmail is processed against each recipe. Any recipes whose condition line matches the message are processed. However, recipes that match a message but that are not specifically set to copy the message redirect the message from the normal user mailbox file on the server. For example, the second recipe redirects messages from the `guitar-list` to the `guitar` folder. These messages will not appear in the normal mail file.

The third example shown, creating auto-reply messages, is a great feature to use when you know you will be away from your mail server for an extended period of time. Any message sent to your email account will generate an automatic reply message to the sender with any text that you specify.

Summary

This chapter examined how to use your Ubuntu server as an email server. It first discussed how the Linux environment handles email, then it showed how to configure the Postfix email software installed in Ubuntu server to satisfy your email server requirements. Postfix can be used in many different email environments, such as a standalone server, an Internet email server, or as an email server that requires a remote SmartHost to process mail messages. Besides the Ubuntu installation wizard, you can use the Postfix `postconf` program to change the Postfix configuration file parameters for your environment. The chapter closed by examining the procmail mail delivery agent program. The versatile procmail program allows individual mail users to customize their mail delivery options.

The next chapter completes the server section. It discusses how to implement a database server on Ubuntu. The Ubuntu server installation provides two popular database platforms. The next chapter shows you how to use both of them.

Database Server

Chapter 24

The world runs on data. Just about every application you use needs to store data in some form or another. The Ubuntu server provides two popular open-source database servers for your data storage applications. This chapter first looks at the MySQL database server. The MySQL database server is quite possibly the most popular open-source database server available. It's the database engine behind many popular web sites, and it is used by hobbyists and corporations around the world. The second database server we'll look at is PostgreSQL. Although not as popular as MySQL, PostgreSQL has gained following in the open-source database world, mostly because of its commercial-quality features. Both of these database servers can be invaluable in your data storage applications.

The MySQL Server

Chapter 21, "Web Server," described the MySQL database server and showed the basics of how to use it as part of the Linux-Apache-MySQL-PHP (LAMP) environment. This section digs deeper into the operation of the MySQL database server, showing the files that the MySQL server needs to operate and walking through the `mysql` command-line interface, which provides a simple environment for interacting with your MySQL database server.

Secret

If you didn't install the LAMP server on your Ubuntu server, or if you want to install MySQL on your Ubuntu workstation, you can do so using either the `apt-get` program or the Synaptic Package Manager (see Chapter 13, "Software Installs and Updates").

The MySQL server package comes as two main packages, with a number of dependent packages. The `mysql-client` package installs the application necessary to connect to a MySQL server, while the `mysql-server` package installs the MySQL server itself. The easiest way to install a complete MySQL environment on your Ubuntu system is to install the `mysql` package. It includes all of the client and server packages as dependencies.

The MySQL Server Files

The Ubuntu server installs the MySQL database server package by default when you install the LAMP server. Four components to the MySQL database server software package are installed:

+ The MySQL server program
+ Configuration files for setting features that control the operation of the server
+ Database files used to store the data elements (databases, tables, data fields, and user accounts) managed by MySQL
+ Scripts and executable programs used to interact with the database server

The following sections walk through the various files that the Ubuntu server installation process provides to run and manage the MySQL database server.

Managing the Server

The main MySQL server program is called `mysqld`, and it is located in the `/usr/sbin` folder. It normally starts automatically as a background process when you start the Ubuntu server.

MySQL uses a special script, called `mysqld_safe`, to start the MySQL server. This script executes the `mysqld` program, defining several command-line options, such as the location of the database files and the user account that starts the server. It uses the special `mysql` user account created in Ubuntu to run the MySQL server. This helps prevent problems should the MySQL server become compromised, because the `mysql` user account has privileges only to the MySQL database areas on the server.

You should never have to worry about actually running the `mysqld_safe` script in Ubuntu. You can control the MySQL server using the `mysql` `init.d` script installed in Ubuntu. If you need to shut down or restart the MySQL server by itself, just use one of these formats:

- `/etc/init.d/mysql` **stop:** Stops the server.
- `/etc/init.d/mysql` **restart:** Stops then starts the server.
- `/etc/init.d/mysql` **start:** Starts the server.

Secret

The `mysql` `init.d` **script uses the standard command-line features of the** `mysqld` **program to start MySQL. If you need to start the MySQL server without the standard features, such as using an alternative database file, you can use the** `mysqld_safe` **script directly. Chapter 21 demonstrates this process by using the** `mysqld_safe` **script to start the MySQL server without the grant tables so that you can change the root password for the MySQL server if you forget it.**

MySQL stores data in the `/var/lib/mysql` folder. As discussed in Chapter 21, MySQL has several methods for storing data. Because each method utilizes a different file scheme, you may see several types of files in this folder:

- `ibdata1` **file:** the main data storage file for the InnoDB storage engine
- `ib_logfile0` **file:** stores (logs) SQL statements that process data in the database for the InnoDB storage engine in case of a system crash
- `ib_logfile1` **file:** secondary log for SQL statements
- `mysql` **folder:** contains folders and files for the `mysql` system database, created using the MyISAM storage engine

As discussed in Chapter 21, the InnoDB storage engine in MySQL provides an advanced method for handling database data. The MySQL InnoDB storage engine stores all data in a single file, called the *tablespace*. The `ibdata1` file contains the tablespace. MySQL creates a tablespace file as a large block so that it can add and remove data within the file without having to interact with the operating system to request more space. This feature helps speed up insertion and removal of data from the database. Don't be surprised if you add a lot of new data to a table but don't see the `ibdata1` file size grow.

Secret

Don't attempt to manually manipulate these files and folders, because MySQL controls the tablespace data internally. Altering any of the files could corrupt your MySQL database.

The default Ubuntu MySQL configuration automatically extends the `ibdata1` tablespace file by 10 MB when it reaches capacity. You can create additional tablespace files by defining them in the `my.cnf` configuration file described in the next section.

If you want to back up the tablespace data files to an alternative location, make sure that the MySQL server is not running when you copy the files. If you attempt to copy the files while database operations are in progress, you might corrupt the data.

Configuring the Server

Ubuntu stores the MySQL configuration files in the `/etc/mysql` folder. There are four items in this folder from the default Ubuntu installation:

- ◆ `conf.d:` folder for local-specific configuration items
- ◆ `debian.cnf:` configuration file special system user account
- ◆ `debian-start:` script to run at system boot time to check and repair tables
- ◆ `my.cnf:` master MySQL configuration file

The main MySQL configuration file, `my.cnf`, is where Ubuntu specifies most of the MySQL server settings. There are several system settings that you can modify to alter the default behavior of the MySQL server. Table 24-1 shows some of the settings that you may want to know about.

Table 24-1: MySQL Server Configuration Settings

Setting	Default Value	Description
port	3306	The default TCP port to listen for connections
socket	/var/run/mysqld/mysqld.sock	The default socket file to listen for connections
user	mysql	The system user that runs the MySQL server program
datadir	/var/lib/mysql	The location of the MySQL database files
bind-address	127.0.0.1	The network interface to listen for connections
max_connections	100	The maximum number of concurrent connections
log	/var/log/mysql/mysql.log	The server log file for displaying errors
skip-innodb	commented out	If present, prevents MySQL from using the InnoDB storage engine

By default, Ubuntu sets the MySQL server to use the InnoDB storage engine (see Chapter 21, "Web Server"), which provides advanced database features but at a slower performance than the original MyISAM storage engine. If you prefer to use the MyISAM storage engine, you can remove the comment from the `skip-innodb` setting line in the configuration file so that MySQL uses only the MyISAM storage engine for all tables.

Secret

The default Ubuntu installation of MySQL uses the `bind-address` setting to allow only applications on the local server to connect to the MySQL server. If you want to allow applications on remote servers to have access to the MySQL server, you'll need to change the `bind-address` setting in the configuration file to the address of your network interface card:

```
bind-address = 10.0.0.192
```

This setting allows MySQL to listen for incoming connections on the local network. Be careful with this feature; if it is enabled, remote clients can access your MySQL server. The MySQL privileges allow you to specify separate privilege levels for the same user based on where the user logs in from. This setting allows you to assign more-limited privileges to users when they're on remote hosts.

The `conf.d` folder contains files that are automatically included into the MySQL configuration file. The only file placed there by default is the `old_passwords.cnf` file, which contains a single setting:

```
old_passwords = false
```

This setting disables using the MySQL `OLDPASSWORD()` function, which uses an older, less-secure encryption algorithm to generate passwords.

The `debian.cnf` configuration file contains a user account configuration for a special MySQL user account called `debian-sys-maint`. The `debian-sys-maint` user account is used by Debian systems to automatically clean and repair MySQL tables at boot time. The script that performs that function is the `debian-start` script.

Interacting with the Server

MySQL offers many scripts and programs that provide different ways for you to interact with the MySQL server from the Ubuntu server command line. Table 24-2 shows what's available on the Ubuntu server.

Table 24-2: MySQL Programs

Program	Description
mysql	Provides an interactive interface to the MySQL server
mysqlaccess	Tests access privileges for a username, hostname, and database combination
mysqladmin	Interface to perform administrative functions on the MySQL server
mysqlbinlog	Displays the contents of the MySQL data log files

continues

Table 24-2: (continued)

Program	Description
mysqlbug	Generates a bug report to send to MySQL developers to report a problem
mysqlcheck	Analyzes, repairs, and optimizes MySQL tables
mysql_client_test	Performs tests on the MySQL client API set
mysql_client_test_embedded	Performs tests on the MySQL client API set on an embedded MySQL server
mysql_convert_table_format	Converts an existing table to a different storage engine
mysqld_multi	Manages multiple MySQL servers running on the same host
mysqld_safe	MySQL server startup script
mysqldump	Exports database definitions and data into a text file for backup or migrating to another MySQL server
mysqldumpslow	Parses the MySQL slow query log
mysql_explain_log	Uses the EXPLAIN statement on SQL statements in the query log to define how queries operate on tables in the database
mysql_find_rows	Extracts SQL statements from a file based on a regular expression definition
mysql_fix_extensions	Repairs MyISAM table files
mysql_fix_privilege_tables	Updates the MySQL system tables to add new features when upgrading from a previous version of MySQL
mysqlhotcopy	Script to back up tables built using the MyISAM storage engine while the MySQL server is still running
mysqlimport	Imports data from a data file into a MySQL table.
mysql_install_db	Initializes a new set of MySQL data files
mysqlreport	Creates a report of common MySQL system status values
mysql_secure_installation	Script used to harden a MySQL server installation by removing common security threats, such as allowing the root user account to log in from a remote host
mysql_setpermission	Script to set user privileges on databases and tables
mysqlshow	Displays database, table, and data field information
mysql_tableinfo	Displays information about specific tables
mysqltest	Runs canned tests against a MySQL server and compares the results to an expected results file

continues

Table 24-2: *(continued)*

Program	Description
mysqltest_embedded	Runs canned tests against an embedded MySQL server and compares the results to an expected results file
mysqltestmanager	A background program that can manage multiple MySQL server installations
mysqltestmanagerc	A command-line client to interface with the `mysqltestmanager` program
mysqltestmanager-pwgen	Generates a password file to use with the `mysqltest` program
mysql_tzinfo_to_sql	Loads the system time-zone tables into MySQL
mysql_upgrade	Checks all tables for incompatibilities with the current version of MySQL
mysql_upgrade_shell	Utility to run the `mysql_upgrade` program on non-UNIX systems
mysql_waitpid	Sends a KILL signal to the process with the specified `pid` and waits for it to exit
mysql_zap	Sends a KILL signal to any process that matches a specified pattern

As you can see, quite a few utilities come with the MySQL installation on the Ubuntu server. Most likely you'll never use most of them, but it's good to know they're there (and what they do) in case you need them.

For most normal interactions with the MySQL server you'll use the `mysql` command-line program, which is discussed in the next section.

The mysql Command

The `mysql` command provides an interactive interface to the MySQL server. When you start the command, you'll get an interactive prompt:

```
$ mysql
Welcome to the MySQL monitor. Commands end with ; or \g.
Your MySQL connection id is 28
Server version: 5.0.67-0ubuntu6 (Ubuntu)

Type 'help;' or '\h' for help. Type '\c' to clear the buffer.

mysql>
```

From the `mysql>` prompt you can submit SQL statements and special commands directly to the MySQL server. The `mysql` command provides a handful of command-line parameters that allow you to customize what it does when you start it. Table 24-3 shows these command-line parameters.

Table 24-3: The mysql Command Parameters

Parameter	Description
`--auto-rehash`	Enable database, table, and data field name completion
`--batch`	Display results using the tab character as a field separator, with each row on a separate line
`--character-sets-dir=path`	Define the location where character sets are installed
`--column-names`	Display data field names in results
`--comments`	Preserve comments sent to the server (the default is to suppress comments)
`--compress`	Compress all information sent between the client and the server
`--database=dbname`	Specify the default database to connect to on the server
`--debug=[options]`	Enable debugging, and specify optional debugging settings
`--debug-info`	Display debugging information when `mysql` exits
`--default-character-set=name`	Define the default character set
`--delimiter=char`	Define the SQL statement delimiter (default is a semicolon)
`--disable-named-commands`	Disable using long-format MySQL commands from the command line
`--execute=statement`	Send the specified SQL statement to the MySQL server and exit
`--force`	Continue if an SQL error occurs
`--host=hostname`	Connect to the specified host
`--html`	Display all output in HTML format
`--ignore-spaces`	Ignore spaces placed after function names
`--line-numbers`	Display line numbers with errors
`--local-infile[={0|1}]`	Enable or disable the local feature of the `LOAD DATA INFILE` statement
`--named-commands`	Enable long-format MySQL commands
`--no-beep`	Don't produce an audible signal when an error occurs
`--no-tee`	Don't copy output to a file
`--one-database`	Allow SQL statements only for the database specified on the command line
`--pager=command`	Use the specified command to page output (usually the `less`, `more`, or `cat` commands)
`--password[=passwd]`	Specify the user password to connect to the MySQL server (if the password isn't specified, `mysql` prompts for the password before connecting)

continues

Table 24-3: *(continued)*

Parameter	Description
`--port=`*num*	Specify the TCP port of the remote MySQL server (default is 3306)
`--prompt=`*str*	Specify the command-line prompt to use
`--protocol=`*value*	Specify how to connect to the MySQL server, either *TCP, SOCKET, PIPE,* or *MEMORY*
`--quick`	Don't cache the result from each query
`--raw`	Don't display text boxes around the query results
`--reconnect`	Automatically attempt to reconnect if the connection to the MySQL server is lost
`--safe-updates`	Only allow `UPDATE` and `DELETE` statements that use a `WHERE` clause to specify rows to update or delete (doesn't allow updating or deleting all of the rows at once)
`--secure-auth`	Don't send passwords to servers using the older format
`--show-warnings`	Display any warnings from the server after each SQL statement
`--sigint-ignore`	Ignore attempts to interrupt the program
`--silent`	Display less output, such as the starting version information
`--skip-column-names`	Don't display the data field names in result sets
`--skip-line-numbers`	Don't display line numbers for errors
`--socket=`*path*	Specify a local socket file to connect to the MySQL server
`--ssl*`	Series of parameters to specify a secure connection to the MySQL server, if supported
`--table`	Display output in table format (the default in interactive mode but not in batch mode)
`--tee=`*file*	Copy all output to the specified file
`--unbuffered`	Flush the command buffer after each query
`--user=`*userid*	Specify a MySQL user account with which to connect to the server
`--verbose`	Display more output than normal
`--version`	Display the version of the `mysql` program
`--vertical`	Display data field names and values vertically, one data field per line
`--wait`	Retry the connection to the server if it fails
`--xml`	Display all output in XML format

That's a lot of control you can have over the `mysql` command line! By default, `mysql` attempts to connect to the MySQL server running on the same system. Most likely the only parameters you'll need to worry about are `--user` and `--password`. These parameters allow you to specify your user ID and password when you connect to the server:

```
$ mysql --user=rich --password
Enter password:
ERROR 1045 (28000): Access denied for user 'rich'@'localhost' (using
password: YES)
$
```

When you use the `--password` parameter by itself (without a specified value), the `mysql` command prompts you to enter your password as a hidden entry. The error message indicates that I entered the wrong password for my user account, so I wasn't allow to connect to the MySQL server.

The next section describes what to do once you are logged into the MySQL server.

Using mysql

The MySQL server uses a special administrative account, called `root`. When you install LAMP from the Ubuntu server installation program, the installation script queries you for the password to use for the MySQL `root` user account. You can log into the MySQL server from the `mysql` command using the `root` user and the password you specified during installation:

```
$ mysql --user=root --password --silent
Enter password:
mysql>
```

Once you get to the `mysql>` interactive prompt, you have complete access to the MySQL server. The `mysql` command interface allows you to submit normal SQL statements to the MySQL server for processing, then it returns the results to the command line:

```
mysql> SELECT id,data FROM test;
+----+-------------+
| id | data |
+----+-------------+
| 1 | test data 1 |
| 2 | test data 2 |
+----+-------------+
2 rows in set (0.01 sec)
mysql>
```

When entering SQL statements from the command line you must terminate them with a semicolon to indicate the end of the SQL statement. This also allows you to break up long SQL statements onto several lines. The `mysql` interface doesn't submit the statement to the MySQL server until it sees the semicolon:

```
mysql> select id,data
-> from test
-> where id = 1;
+----+-------------+
| id | data |
+----+-------------+
| 1 | test data 1 |
```

```
+----+-------------+
1 row in set (0.00 sec)

mysql>
```

The mysql command line provides an alternate prompt to let you know you're in the middle of a pending SQL statement. The output from the query shows the data field names at the top, with the data field values listed below them.

Besides SQL statements, the mysql command also supports a few special commands of its own. Each command has a full name and a shortcut. The shortcut is preceded by a backward slash character. These commands are shown in Table 24-4.

Table 24-4: The mysql Commands

Command	Shortcut	Description
connect	\r	Reconnect to the server with a specified database
delimiter	\d	Set the delimiter used between SQL statements (default is semicolon)
edit	\e	Edit the command with the default editor
ego	\G	Send command to MySQL server and display results
exit	\q	Exit the mysql command line
go	\g	Send the command to the MySQL server
help	\h	Display available commands
nopager	\n	Disable the pager and send output to the standard output
notee	\t	Don't redirect output to an output file
pager	\P	Define a program to use to page output (such as less or more)
print	\p	Print the current command
prompt	\R	Change the mysql command-line prompt
quit	\q	Quit the mysql command line
rehash	\#	Rebuild the command completion hash
source	\.	Execute the specified SQL script file
status	\s	Retrieve status information from the MySQL server
tee	\T	Redirect output to specified output file as well as the display
use	\u	Use another database as the default database
charset	\C	Switch to another character set for the output
warnings	\W	Display MySQL warnings after each command
nowarning	\w	Don't display MySQL warnings after each command

After you enter a command, the `mysql` program processes it and displays the results within the command-prompt environment. Figure 24-1 demonstrates the output from using the `status` command.

```
--------------
mysql  Ver 14.12 Distrib 5.0.67, for debian-linux-gnu (i486) using readline 5.2

Connection id:         36
Current database:      test
Current user:          root@localhost
SSL:                   Not in use
Current pager:         more
Using outfile:         ''
Using delimiter:       ;
Server version:        5.0.67-0ubuntu6 (Ubuntu)
Protocol version:      10
Connection:            Localhost via UNIX socket
Server characterset:   latin1
Db     characterset:   latin1
Client characterset:   latin1
Conn.  characterset:   latin1
UNIX socket:           /var/run/mysqld/mysqld.sock
Uptime:                1 hour 6 min 23 sec

Threads: 1  Questions: 155  Slow queries: 0  Opens: 25  Flush tables: 1  Open ta
bles: 18  Queries per second avg: 0.039
--------------

mysql> _
```

Figure 24-1: The status command output.

To exit the `mysql` command-prompt environment, just type `exit`.

The "Working with Databases" section later in this chapter describes how to create and work with databases using the `mysql` command-line interface.

The PostgreSQL Server

PostgreSQL is yet another open-source database package that has gained popularity in the Linux world. The claim to fame for PostgreSQL is that it implements many of the advanced database features that the commercial products do, such as views, stored procedures, triggers, and hot backups. Unfortunately, PostgreSQL offers those advanced features at the expense of data access speed. This is one reason why MySQL has beat out PostgreSQL in the web server wars.

However, if you are looking for advanced database features in a free software package, PostgreSQL is definitely the way to go. This section describes how to configure and use the PostgreSQL server on your Ubuntu server.

Secret

When you install the Ubuntu server software, select the Database Server option to automatically install PostgreSQL. If you didn't do so during installation, you can install PostgreSQL from the PostgreSQL installation package in the Ubuntu repository using `apt-get` or the Synaptic Package Manager (see Chapter 13, "Software Installs and Updates").

The PostgreSQL package installs as a single package called `postgresql`. Just select that package, and Ubuntu will install the dependencies necessary to get your PostgreSQL environment up and running.

The PostgreSQL Files

Much like the MySQL server, the PostgreSQL server consists of a main program file, a few configuration files, a handful of utility and script files, and a set of files for storing data in the database.

PostgreSQL handles the database application functions a little differently from how MySQL does. PostgreSQL uses two separate programs to handle the database server operations. The main PostgreSQL application program file is called `postmaster`. This program connects to a single set of database files, called a *cluster*. You can have multiple `postmaster` programs running on your server, each connecting to a different cluster of database files.

Each `postmaster` program spawns one or more copies of the `postgres` program. The `postgres` program is responsible for processing database queries. The number of `postgres` programs spawned depends on the configuration settings.

Besides the main `postmaster` and `postgres` files, there are a host of other files required to manage the PostgreSQL database server. The Ubuntu installation of PostgreSQL involves quite a few folders and files. The files are placed in the following folders:

- `/etc/postgresql/8.3/main`: configuration files
- `/usr/share/postgresql/8.3`: sample configuration files
- `/usr/share/postgresql-common`: scripts to create the default database
- `/usr/lib/postgresql/8.3/bin`: PostgreSQL scripts and utilities
- `/usr/lib/postgresql/8.3/lib`: PostgreSQL library files
- `/var/lib/postgresql/8.3/main`: PostgreSQL database files

As you can see from the list, PostgreSQL installs files in more places than the MySQL setup does. This can sometimes get confusing.

Notice that part of the pathname is the version of the PostgreSQL installation. If you're using a newer version of Ubuntu server, it's likely that it contains a newer version of PostgreSQL, so your folder pathnames may differ.

Managing the Server

The PostgreSQL server program uses the `init.d-functions` script, located in the `/usr/share/postgresql-common` folder, to start, stop, and restart the database server. Similar to the MySQL server, though, the best way to manage the PostgreSQL server is through the Ubuntu `init.d` scripts:

- `/etc/init.d/postgresql-8.3`: Stop.
- `/etc/init.d/postgresql-8.3`: Restart.
- `/etc/init.d/postgresql-8.3`: Start.

The PostgreSQL database files are located in the `/var/lib/postgresql/8.3/main` folder. This folder contains additional subfolders for maintaining the PostgreSQL database cluster. These subfolders are shown in Table 24-5.

Table 24-5: PostgreSQL Database Cluster Folders

Folder	Description
base	Contains one folder for each created database
global	System tables for PostgreSQL
pg_clog	Status files on transaction commits
pg_multixact	Multi-transaction status information used for table locking
pg_subtrans	Subtransaction status information
pg_tblspc	Links to database tables
pg_twophase	Phase files for the two-phase transaction commit process
pg_xlog	Transaction log files

Ubuntu places the PostgreSQL system log file in the /var/log/postgresql folder. That file logs all connections to the database, as well as any system errors that occur while the database is running. It's always a good idea to peruse the log file at regular intervals to check for problems.

Configuring the Server

Unlike MySQL, PostgreSQL uses several configuration files to control different aspects of the PostgreSQL server behavior. All of the PostgreSQL configuration files are located in the /etc/postgresql/8.3/main folder. The configuration files are shown in Table 24-6.

Table 24-6: PostgreSQL Configuration Files

File	Description
pg_hba.conf	Defines which hosts are allowed to connect to the server and what authentication method users on that host should use
pg_ident.conf	Maps PostgreSQL users to system user accounts
postgresql.conf	Contains the PostgreSQL server settings
start.conf	Defines how PostgreSQL starts the database at startup: manual, auto, or disabled

The postgresql.conf configuration file controls how each of the features of PostgreSQL behaves on your system. The configuration file consists of records that define each PostgreSQL feature. The format of a feature record is

```
featurename = value
```

Although this is the default format of the feature record, the equal sign is optional. The first section in this file defines where the other configuration files are located:

```
data_directory = '/var/lib/postgresql/8.3/main'
hba_file = '/etc/postgresql/8.3/main/pg_hba.conf'
ident_file = '/etc/postgresql/8.3/main/pg_ident.conf'
exernal_pid_file = '/var/run/postgresql/8.3-main.pid'
```

You can restrict how clients connect to the PostgreSQL server by editing the `pg_hba.conf` configuration file. This file defines four features of the PostgreSQL connection:

- ◆ Which network hosts are allowed to connect to the server
- ◆ Which PostgreSQL user accounts can be used to connect from that host
- ◆ What authentication method users must use to log into the server from that host
- ◆ Which PostgreSQL databases an authenticated client from the host can connect to

This is a pretty complicated access control system, but it provides great flexibility in controlling your database users. Not only can you restrict users, but you can also restrict their access based on what remote host they connect from.

The format of each record in the `pb_hba.conf` file is

```
connection-type database user network-address login-method options
```

The default `pb_hba.conf` file in Ubuntu defines four records:

```
local all postgres ident sameuser
local all all ident sameuser
host all all 127.0.0.1/32 md5
host all all ::1/128 md5
```

By default, PostgreSQL allows the special administrator account `postgres` and all other users to connect from the local system using the Ubuntu system authentication system. The `sameuser` option tells PostgreSQL to map the PostgreSQL user account to the Ubuntu login account connecting to the server. The two host connection types allow all users on the local network to connect using the MD5 encryption algorithm.

The `pg_ident.conf` file allows you to map remote user accounts to PostgreSQL user accounts. By default Ubuntu maps all local user accounts to the PostgreSQL user accounts. If you want to allow users from remote systems to connect as themselves, you can add their information to this configuration file.

Secret

The default Ubuntu configuration binds the PostgreSQL server to the local-host address, permitting only applications on the Ubuntu server to connect. To allow remote users to connect to the PostgreSQL server, you must modify the `postgresql.conf` **file setting:**

```
listen_addresses = 'localhost'
```

Just use the IP address of the network interface on your Ubuntu server to allow remote users to connect. The `pg_hba.conf` configuration file must be set to allow hosts from the network to access the PostgreSQL server. Do this by adding a host entry in the file:

```
host all all 192.168.0.0/24 md5
```

This allows users from hosts on the 192.168.0 local subnetwork to use password authentication to connect to the PostgreSQL server.

Interacting with the Server

The PostgreSQL package provides a few files and scripts of its own for working with the PostgreSQL server. Table 24-7 shows the files that may come in handy when working in the PostgreSQL server environment.

Table 24-7: The PostgreSQL Programs

Program	Description
pg_createcluster	Create a new PostgreSQL server database instance
pg_ctlcluster	Start, stop, restart, or reload a PostgreSQL server
pg_dropcluster	Remove a PostgreSQL server instance
pg_dump	Export data in a PostgreSQL database to a text file
pg_dumpall	Export all databases in a PostgreSQL server to a text file
pg_lsclusters	Display the PostgreSQL servers and information
pg_restore	Restore a PostgreSQL database from an export file
pg_upgradecluster	Upgrade an existing PostgreSQL server to a new version
psql	The PostgreSQL command-line interface

The `pg_lsclusters` command is a great way to easily list all of the PostgreSQL servers running on the Ubuntu server:

```
$ pg_lsclusters
Version Cluster Port Status Owner Data Directory Log file
8.3 Main 5432 online postgres /var/lib/postgresql/8.3/main
/var/log/postgresql/postgresql-8.3-main.log
$
```

The output from the `pg_lsclusters` command shows the running PostgreSQL server, where the data files are stored, and where the log files are stored. This is great command to use if you're looking at a server and trying to figure out how the PostgreSQL server software is installed to operate.

The psql Command

Just like the `mysql` command, the `psql` command uses command-line parameters to define its behavior. Table 24-8 shows the available `psql` command-line parameters.

Table 24-8: The psql Command parameters

Long parameter	Short parameter	Description
--echo-all	-a	Display all input lines as they are read
--no-align	-A	Enable unaligned output mode
--command	-c	Execute the specified command and exit
--dbname	-d	Connect to the specified database
--echo-queries	-e	Display all SQL statements sent to the server

continues

Table 24-8: *(continued)*

Long parameter	Short parameter	Description
--echo-hidden	-E	Echo queries created by psql commands
--file	-f	Run the SQL statements in the specified file and exit
--field-separator	-F	Use the specified character as the data field separator in output
--host	-h	Connect to the specified host
--html	-H	Enable HTML output format
--list	-l	List the available databases and exit
--log-file	-L	Send all query output to the specified log file as well as display it
--output	-o	Send all query output to only the specified output file
--post	-p	Connect to the specified TCP port
--pset	-P	Set the specified printing options
--quiet	-q	Don't display heading information at start
--record-separator	-R	Use the specified character as the record separator in the output
--single-step	-s	Prompt before each step in a command
--single-line	-S	Terminate the SQL statement at each newline character
--tuples-only	-t	Display query data with no data field headers
--username	-U	Specify a user account with which to connect to the server
--variable	-v	Set a variable value
--version	-V	Display the psql version and exit
--password	-W	Specify a user password with which to connect to the server
--expanded	-x	Enable expanded table-formatting features
--nopsqlrc	-X	Don't process the psql startup file
--single-transaction	-1	Execute an SQL statement script as a single transaction

The `--username` and `--password` parameters allow you to connect to the PostgreSQL server with any username. By default, the `psql` command uses the Ubuntu system user account as the default login username:

```
rich@testbox:~$ psql
psql: FATAL: Ident authentication failed for user "rich"
rich@testbox:~$
```

This example shows that the Ubuntu user `rich` doesn't have a PostgreSQL account. The default master administrator user account in PostgreSQL is called `postgres`. This account has full access to the entire server. The easiest way to log into PostgreSQL with the `postgres` account is to use the `sudo` command at the command prompt:

```
$ sudo -u postgres psql
[sudo] password for rich:
Welcome to psql 8.3.3, the PostgreSQL interactive terminal.

Type: \copyright for distribution terms
\h for help with SQL commands
\? for help with psql commands
\g or terminate with a semicolon to execute query
\q to quit

postgres=#
```

The `-u` option specifies to change the active user to the `postgres` user account. When you run the `psql` program as the `postgres` system user, PostgreSQL logs you in as the `postgres` admin user account. Now the `postgres` user account can interact with the PostgreSQL server, creating users, databases, and tables.

Secret

By default, the `postgres` administrative account doesn't have a password assigned to it. This isn't a problem if you keep your PostgreSQL access restricted to the localhost, but if you open your PostgreSQL server to the network you'll want to assign a password to that account to prevent any problems.

To do that, just follow these steps:

1. Connect to the PostgreSQL server using the `postgres` user account and the default `template1` database in PostgreSQL:

   `sudo -u postgres psql template1`

2. Use the SQL `ALTER` statement to change the `postgres` user's password:

   `ALTER USER postgres WITH encrypted password 'newpassword';`

3. Edit the `/etc/postgresql/8.3/main/pg_hba.conf` file to change the `postgres` user line to use passwords instead of the system authentication:

   `local all postgres md5 sameuser`

4. Restart the PostgreSQL server:

   `sudo /etc/init.d/postgresql-8.3 restart`

Now you'll have to use the password you set to log in as the `postgres` user account on your PostgreSQL server.

Using psql

Once you get into the `psql` command-line interface, you can enter standard SQL statements to interact with the PostgreSQL server:

```
test=# SELECT * FROM test;
id | data
---+----------------
1 | this is data 1
2 | this is data 2
(2 rows)

test=#
```

Besides standard SQL, the `psql` command recognizes its own set of commands, shown in Table 24-9.

Table 24-9: The psql Commands

Command	Description
\c	Connect to the specified database
\cd	Change to the specified working directory
\copyright	Display the PostgreSQL use and distribution terms
\encoding	Display or set the client encoding
\h	Display help on the specified SQL command
\prompt	Prompt the user to set the specified variable
\q	Exit psql
\set	Set the specified variable to the specified value
\timing	Toggle timing commands on or off
\unset	Remove the specified variable
\!	Execute the specified command in the system shell
\e	Edit the query buffer or specified file with the default text editor
\g	Send the query buffer to the server and, if a file is specified, send the results to the file
\p	Display the contents of the query buffer
\r	Clear the query buffer
\s	Display the command history, or save it to the specified file
\w	Write the query buffer to the specified file
\echo	Display the specified string on standard output
\i	Execute the commands in the specified file

continues

Table 24-9: *(continued)*

Command	Description
\o	Send all query output to the specified file
\qecho	Display the specified string in the query output stream
\d	Display information on the specified table, index, sequence, or view
\dt	Display tables in the database
\di	Display indexes in the database
\ds	Display sequences in the database
\dv	Display views in the database
\da	Display aggregate functions in the database
\db	Display tablespaces in the database
\dc	Display character set conversions in the database
\dC	Display casts in the database
\dD	Display domains in the database
\df	Display functions in the database
\dF	Display text-search configurations in the database
\dg	Display groups in the database
\dn	Display schemas in the database
\do	Display operators in the database
\dl	Display large objects in the database
\dp	Display access privileges in the database
\dT	Display data types in the database
\du	Display all users
\l	Display all databases
\z	Display access privileges for specified table, view, or sequence
\a	Toggle between aligned and unaligned output
\C	Set the table title
\f	Show or set the field separator for unaligned output
\H	Toggle HTML output mode (default is off)
\pset	Set table output options
\t	Display only data rows in the output

continues

Table 24-9: *(continued)*

Command	Description
\T	Set HTML table tag attributes
\x	Toggle expanded output (default is off)
\copy	Perform an SQL COPY command
\lo_	Commands to export, import, list, and unlink PostgreSQL large object data types

You can enter any of the psql commands from the command prompt, as shown in Figure 24-2. This figure demonstrates using the \l command to list the databases available in the current database, then using the CREATE DATABASE statement to create a new database.

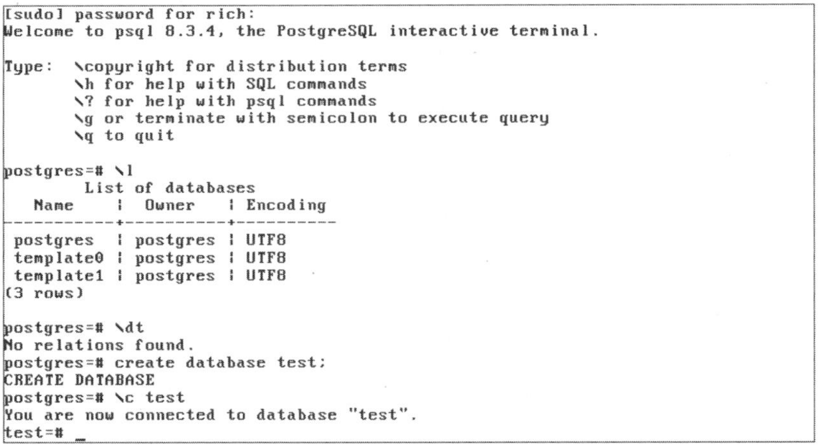

```
[sudo] password for rich:
Welcome to psql 8.3.4, the PostgreSQL interactive terminal.

Type:  \copyright for distribution terms
       \h for help with SQL commands
       \? for help with psql commands
       \g or terminate with semicolon to execute query
       \q to quit

postgres=# \l
        List of databases
   Name    |  Owner   | Encoding
-----------+----------+----------
 postgres  | postgres | UTF8
 template0 | postgres | UTF8
 template1 | postgres | UTF8
(3 rows)

postgres=# \dt
No relations found.
postgres=# create database test;
CREATE DATABASE
postgres=# \c test
You are now connected to database "test".
test=# _
```

Figure 24-2: Using psql commands for the PostgreSQL server.

Working with Databases

Now that you have either (or both) MySQL and PostgreSQL installed, you'll want to start using them for your data management needs. This section walks through the basics of creating a database, users, and tables to manage your data in both the MySQL and PostgreSQL environments.

Creating a Database

The core of your data management is the database. Both MySQL and PostgreSQL control data based on databases. You can use the SQL CREATE DATABASE statement on both servers to create a new database:

```
$ mysql -u root -p
Enter password:
```

```
mysql> create database test;
Query OK, 1 row affected (0.01 sec)

mysql> use test;
Database changed
mysql>
```

The new database is created on the server. In MySQL and PostgreSQL you can connect to only one database at a time. You can specify the default database either on the command line or by using the `connect` command at the prompt:

```
$ sudo -u postgres psql test
test=#\c test;
You are now connected to database "test."
test=#

$mysql test -u root -p
Enter password:
mysql>connect test;
Connection id: 32
Current database: test
mysql>
```

The MySQL server also allows you to use the SQL `USE` statement to change to another database.

Secret

The PostgreSQL server also supports a feature called *schemas*. Each database has a default schema, called *public*, where you can store tables. However, you can also create additional schemas to control data layout and access within the database level.

Managing Users

Once you create a database, you'll probably want to create one or more user accounts that can have access to the database. Unfortunately, creating user accounts is one place where MySQL and PostgreSQL differ. This section demonstrates how to create user accounts in both server environments.

Creating User Accounts in MySQL

In MySQL you create user accounts using one of two methods. MySQL maintains user accounts in the special `user` table contained in the `mysql` database. You can look at the existing user accounts by performing a `SELECT` statement to query the table:

```
mysql> select user,host from user;
+-------------------+-----------+
| user | host |
```

```
+-------------------+-----------+
| root | 127.0.0.1 |
| | localhost |
| debian-sys-maint | localhost |
| root | localhost |
| | testbox |
| root | testbox |
+-------------------+-----------+
6 rows in set (0.00 sec)

mysql>
```

MySQL controls access based on both a user account and the location from where the user connects to the server. Adding a new user account in MySQL is as simple as using the SQL INSERT statement:

```
mysql> insert into user (user,host,password) values ('rich,' 'localhost,'
'');
Query OK, 1 row affected (0.00 sec)
mysql> insert into user (user,host,password) values ('rich,'
-> 'testbox.localdomain,' '');
Query OK, 1 row affected (0.00 sec)
mysql>
```

Because we don't want to add data for all of the fields in the user table, we must specify the fields we are populating. After the INSERT commands are executed, the new user account exists, but there is no password assigned, which prevents the account from logging in. The next step is to assign a new password for the user account.

This is done using the SQL UPDATE statement, along with the special MySQL PASSWORD() function, which encrypts the password using the MySQL encryption method:

```
mysql> update user set password = PASSWORD('testing')
-> where user = 'rich';
Query OK, 2 rows affected (0.00 sec)
mysql>
```

You can use the SELECT command to query the user table and verify that the new user entries have been entered correctly. Once a normal user account is created, you are ready to start creating some database objects for your application.

Secret

Since MySQL version 5, you can also use the CREATE USER command to add a new user account and assign a password in one step:

```
mysql> create user 'mytest'@'localhost' identified by 'test';
Query OK, 0 rows affected (0.00 sec)
mysql>
```

This creates a new user account called mytest that can log in from the localhost, with a password of test.

After you create the user account, use the SQL GRANT statement to grant privileges for a user to a database:

```
mysql> grant select,insert,update on test.* to rich;
Query OK , 0 rows affected (0.00 sec)
mysql>
```

In the GRANT statement you define all of the tables you want the user account to have access to [using the wildcard character (*) means all of the tables in the database], along with the specific privileges to grant.

The new user account rich can now log into the MySQL server and access the test database:

```
$ mysql test -u rich -p -s
Enter password:
mysql>
```

Because I didn't grant the CREATE privilege for the rich user account, I can't create a new table in the database. I can work with existing tables only.

Creating Users in PostgreSQL

In PostgreSQL, user accounts are called *login roles*. The postgres administrator user can create new login roles and grant user permissions to database objects to those roles. Remember though, the Ubuntu installation of PostgreSQL uses the Ubuntu system password files to authenticate login roles, so your PostgreSQL login roles must match an existing Ubuntu system user account:

```
postgres=# create role rich login password 'test';
CREATE ROLE
postgres=# grant all on database test to rich;
GRANT
postgres=#
```

Now the user account rich has full privileges in the test database:

```
rich@testbox:~$ psql test -q
test=>
```

The rich user can now create a new table in the test database.

Building Tables

In a database, tables are what store the actual data. Tables contain *data fields*, which define the individual data elements to store. In a data field, you must define the data type of the data, because the database server must know the amount of storage space required for each data field. Common data types used in both MySQL and PostgreSQL are

- ◆ char: a fixed-length text string; if the data do not fill the fixed length, spaces are added to the stored data
- ◆ varchar: a variable-length text string; the database server creates only enough storage for the specified text
- ◆ integer: whole numbers with no decimal places
- ◆ floating point: a decimal number with varying decimal places
- ◆ text: a data storage type for large quantities of text
- ◆ binary large object (BLOB): a binary data storage type that allows you to store binary files such as images, video and audio clips, and PDF files

Both MySQL and PostgreSQL use the CREATE TABLE statement to create a new table in the database you're currently connected to. The CREATE TABLE statement defines the data field names and the data type for the data, along with any special features required for the data:

```
test=> create table test1(
test(> employeeid int primary key,
test(> lastname varchar(20),
test(> firstname varchar(20),
test(> datehired date);
NOTICE: CREATE TABLE / PRIMARY KEY will create implicit index
"test1_pkey" for table "test1"
CREATE TABLE
test=> \dt
List of relations
Schema | Name | Type | Owner
--------+-------+-------+-------
public | test1 | table | rich
(1 row)1
test=>
```

PostgreSQL automatically creates an index file for the primary key data field. The \dt command displays the new table in the database.

Adding and Viewing Data

Once you've created a table in the database, you can use it to store your data. Use the SQL INSERT statement to specify the data set for each individual data record:

```
test=> insert into test1 values ('1234,' 'Blum,' 'Rich,' '01/01/09');
INSERT 0 1
test=> insert into test1 values ('1234,' 'Blum,' 'Barbara,' '01/15/09');
ERROR: duplicate key value violates unique constraint "test1_pkey"
test=> insert into test1 values ('1235,' 'Blum,' 'Barbara,' '01/15/09');
INSERT 0 1
test=>
```

Notice that PostgreSQL wouldn't allow me to add another data record that used the same primary key value.

After your data are entered, you'll want to be able to extract the information from the tables. The SQL SELECT statement provides the interface for doing that:

```
test=> select employeeid from test1 where firstname = 'Rich';
employeeid
------------
1234
(1 row)

test=>
```

The WHERE clause defines a filter expression to test against each data record in the table. The SELECT statement returns only the data records that match the filter.

Summary

This chapter discussed how to implement a database server using your Ubuntu server distribution. Ubuntu provides default installations for both the popular MySQL and PostgreSQL database server packages. The MySQL database server is installed as part of the LAMP server installation, while the PostgreSQL database server is installed when you select the Database Server option during the server installation process. The chapter walked through the file layout and commands used in both database servers. It's important to know where the data files are and how to access the log files that display any error messages that may occur while running the database servers. The chapter closed out with a brief overview of using the command-line interfaces for MySQL and PostgreSQL to create databases, users, and tables, as well as to store and retrieve data on the servers.

This chapter concludes the server section. The next section dives into the programming environment that Ubuntu provides for developing your own applications. The next chapter discusses using shell scripts to make your life as a system administrator easier, or to just help automate common tasks you might perform on your Ubuntu workstation or server.

Part 5

Programming in Ubuntu

Shell Scripts

Chapter
25

◆ ◆

Secrets in This Chapter

What are Shell Scripts?

Shell Script Basics

Creating Your Own Scripts

◆ ◆

This chapter examines the world of Ubuntu shell scripts. Shell scripts allow you to write programs to automate tasks instead of having to manually process them. The chapter starts out by showing how shell scripts work, then it walks you through how to create your own shell scripts to help automate your daily Ubuntu tasks.

Using Multiple Commands

In Chapter 19, "The Ubuntu Command Line," you saw how to use the command-line interface (CLI) prompt of the shell to enter commands and view the command results. The key to shell scripts is the ability to enter multiple commands and process the results from each command, possibly even passing the results of one command to another. The shell allows you to chain commands together into a single step.

If you want to run two commands together, you can enter them on the same prompt line, separated with a semicolon:

```
$ date ; who
Mon Nov 03 19:44:35 EST 2008
rich :0 2008-11-03 18:23 (console)
rich pts/1 2008-11-03 18:24
rich pts/0 2008-11-03 18:42
barbara pts/2 2008-11-03 19:30
katie pts/3 2008-11-03 19:39
$
```

Congratulations, you just wrote a shell script! This simple script uses just two shell commands. The date command runs first, displaying the current date and time, followed by the output of the who command, showing who is currently logged on to the system. Using this technique you can string together as many commands as you wish, up to the maximum command-line character count of 255 characters.

Though using this technique is fine for small scripts, it has a major drawback: you have to enter the entire command on the command prompt every time you want to run it. Instead of having to manually enter the commands onto a command line, you can combine the commands into a simple text file. When you need to run the commands, just simply run the text file.

Creating a Script File

To place shell commands in a text file, first you'll need to use a text editor (see Chapter 6, "Working With Text") to create a file, then enter the commands into the file.

When creating a shell script file, you must specify the shell you are using in the first line of the file. The format for this is:

```
#!/bin/bash
```

In a normal shell script line, the pound sign (#) is used as a comment line. A comment line in a shell script isn't processed by the shell. The first line of a shell script file, however, is a special case, and the pound sign followed by the exclamation point tells the shell what shell to run the script under (you can be using a bash shell and run your script using another shell).

After indicating the shell, commands are entered onto each line of the file, followed by a carriage return. As mentioned, comments can be added by using the pound sign. An example looks like this:

```
#!/bin/bash
# This script displays the date and who's logged on
date
who
```

That's all there is to it. You can use the semicolon and put both commands on the same line if you want to, but in a shell script you can also list commands on separate lines. The shell will process commands in the order they appear in the file.

Also notice that I added another line that starts with the pound symbol—this adds a comment. Lines that start with the pound symbol (other than the first #! line) aren't interpreted by the shell. This is a great way to leave comments for yourself about what is happening in the script, so when you come back to it two years later you can easily remember what you did.

Save this script in a file called test1, and you are almost ready. There are, however, still a couple of things to do before you can run your new shell script file.

If you try running the file now, you'll be somewhat disappointed:

```
$ test1
bash: test1: command not found
$
```

The first hurdle is getting the bash shell to find your script file. The shell uses an environment variable called PATH to find commands. These environment variables are used to define features and settings for the shell. Looking at the PATH environment variable explains my problem:

```
$ echo $PATH
/usr/local/bin:/bin:/usr/bin:/usr/X11R6/bin:/usr/X11R6/bin
$
```

The PATH environment variable is set to only look for commands in a handful of directories. To get the shell to find my test1 script, I need to do one of two things:

- ◆ Add the directory where my shell script file is located to the PATH environment variable.
- ◆ Use an absolute filepath to reference my shell script file in the prompt.

Secret

Some Linux distributions add the $HOME/bin directory to the PATH environment variable. This creates a place in every user's HOME directory to place files where the shell can find them to execute.

For this example, I'll use the second method to tell the shell exactly where my script file is located. Remember, to reference a file in the current directory, you can use the single dot operator in the shell:

```
$ ./test1
bash: ./test1: Permission denied
$
```

Now the shell found the shell script file, but there's another problem: The shell indicated that I don't have permission to execute the file. A quick look at the file permissions should show what's going on here:

```
$ ls -l test1
-rw-r--r-- 1 rich rich 73 2008-11-03 17:56 test1
$
```

When I created the new test1 file, the default settings for my user account determined the default permission settings for the new file. The system created the file with only read/write permissions for me.

The next step is to give myself permission to execute the file using the chmod command:

```
$ chmod u+x test1
$ ./test1
Mon Nov 3 19:58:35 EST 2008
rich :0 2008-11-03 18:23 (console)
rich pts/1 2008-11-03 18:24
rich pts/0 2008-11-03 18:42
barbara pts/2 2008-11-03 19:30
katie pts/3 2008-11-03 19:39
$
```

Success! Now all of the pieces are in the right place to execute the new shell script file.

Displaying Output

Most shell commands produce their own output, which is displayed on the console monitor where the script is running. Many times when you're writing a script you'll want to add your own text messages to help the script user know what is happening within the script. This is done using the echo command. The echo command can display a simple text string by adding the string following the command:

```
$ echo This is a test
This is a test
$
```

Notice that by default you don't need to use quotes to delineate the string you're displaying. Sometimes, however, this can get tricky if you are using quotes within your string:

```
$ echo Let's see if this'll work
Lets see if thisll work
$
```

The echo command uses either double or single quotes to delineate text strings. If you use them within your string, you need to use one type of quote within the text, and the other type to delineate the string:

```
$ echo "This is a test to see if you're paying attention"
This is a test to see if you're paying attention
$ echo 'Rich says "scripting is easy."'
Rich says "scripting is easy."
$
```

Now all of the quotes appear properly in the output.

You can add echo statements anywhere in your shell scripts where you need to display additional information:

```
#!/bin/bash
# This script displays the date and who's logged on
echo The time and date are:
date
echo "Let's see who's logged into the system:"
who
```

When you run this script, it produces the output:

```
$ ./test1
The time and date are:
Mon Nov 3 20:09:35 EST 2008
Let's see who's logged into the system:
rich :0 2007-11-03 18:23 (console)
rich pts/1 2007-11-03 18:24
rich pts/0 2007-11-03 18:42
barbara pts/2 2007-11-03 19:30
katie pts/3 2007-11-03 19:39
$
```

That's nice; but what if you want to echo a text string on the same line as a command output? You can use the -n parameter for the echo statement to do that. Just change the echo statement line to:

```
echo -n "The time and date are: "
```

You'll need to use quotes around the string to ensure there's a space at the end of the echoed string. The command output begins exactly where the string output stops. The output will now look like this:

```
$ ./test1
The time and date are: Mon Nov 3 20:11:35 EST 2008
Let's see who's logged into the system:
rich :0 2007-09-24 18:23 (console)
rich pts/1 2007-09-24 18:24
rich pts/0 2007-09-24 18:42
barbara pts/2 2007-09-24 19:30
katie pts/3 2007-09-24 19:39
$
```

Perfect! The echo command is a crucial piece of shell scripts that interacts with users. You'll find yourself using it in many situations, especially when you want to display the values of script variables. Let's look at that next.

Using Variables

Just running individual commands from the shell script is useful, but it has its limitations. Often you'll want to incorporate other data in your shell commands to process information. You can do this using variables. Variables allow you to temporarily store information within the shell script for use with other commands in the script. This section shows how to use variables in your shell scripts.

Environment Variables

You've already seen this type of Linux variable in action. In the "Creating a Script File" section (seen earlier in this chapter) we needed to use the PATH environment variables to define where Ubuntu could find our script file. There are plenty of other environment variables available for you to use as well.

The shell maintains environment variables that track specific system information, such as the name of the system, the name of the user logged into the system, the user's system id (called UID), the default home directory of the user, and the search path used by the shell to find programs. You can display a complete list of active environment variables available by using the set command:

```
$ set
BASH=/bin/bash
BASH_ARGC=()
BASH_ARGV=()
BASH_COMPLETION=/etc/bash_completion
BASH_COMPLETION_DIR=/etc/bash_completion.d
BASH_LINENO=()
BASH_SOURCE=()
BASH_VERSINFO=([0]="3" [1]="2" [2]="39" [3]="1" [4]="release" [5]="i486-pc-
linux
-gnu")
BASH_VERSION='3.2.39(1)-release'
COLUMNS=80
DIRSTACK=()
EUID=1000
GROUPS=()
HISTCONTROL=ignoreboth
HISTFILE=/home/rich/.bash_history
HISTFILESIZE=500
HISTSIZE=500
HOME=/home/rich
HOSTNAME=testbox
HOSTTYPE=i486
IFS=$' \t\n'
LANG=en_US.UTF-8
...
```

You can tap into these environment variables from within your scripts by using the environment variable name preceded by a dollar sign. This is demonstrated in the following script:

```
#!/bin/bash
# display user information from the system.
echo "User info for userid: $USER"
echo UID: $UID
echo HOME: $HOME
```

The $USER, $UID, and $HOME environment variables are used to display the pertinent information about the logged-in user. The output should look something like this:

```
$ ./test2
User info for userid: rich
UID: 501
HOME: /home/rich
$
```

Notice that the environment variables in the echo commands are replaced by their current value when the script runs. Also notice that we were able to place the $USER system variable within the double quotes in the first string, and the shell script was still able to figure out what we meant. There is a drawback to using this method though. Look at what happens in this example:

```
$ echo "The cost of the item is $15"
The cost of the item is 5
```

That is obviously not what I intended. Whenever the script sees a dollar sign within quotes, it assumes you're referencing a variable. In this example, the script attempted to display the variable $1 (which was not defined), then the number 5. To display an actual dollar sign, you must precede it with a backslash character:

```
$ echo "The cost of the item is \$15"
The cost of the item is $15
```

That's better. The backslash allowed the shell script to interpret the dollar sign as an actual dollar sign, not a variable. The next section shows how to create your own variables in your scripts.

User Variables

Besides the environment variables, a shell script allows you to set and use your own variables within the script. Setting variables allows you to temporarily store data and use it throughout the script, making the shell script more like a real computer program.

User variables can be any text string of up to 20 letters, digits, or an underscore character. Also, user variables are case sensitive, so the variable Var1 is different from the variable var1. This little rule often gets novice script programmers in trouble.

Values are assigned to user variables using an equal sign. No spaces can appear between the variable, the equal sign, and the value (another trouble spot for novices). Here are a few examples of how to assign values to user variables:

```
var1=10
var2=-57
var3=testing
var4="still more testing"
```

The shell script automatically determines the data type used for the variable value. Variables defined within the shell script maintain their values throughout the life of the shell script, but are deleted when the shell script completes.

Just like system variables, user variables can be referenced using the dollar sign:

```
$cat test3
#!/bin/bash
# testing variables
days=10
guest="Katie"
echo "$guest checked in $days days ago"
days=5
guest="Jessica"
echo "$guest checked in $days days ago"
Running the script produces the output:
$ ./test3
Katie checked in 10 days ago
Jessica checked in 5 days ago
$
```

Each time the variable is referenced, it produces the value currently assigned to it. It's important to remember that when referencing a variable value, you use the dollar sign, but when referencing the variable to assign a value to it, you do not use the dollar sign. Here's an example of what I mean:

```
#!/bin/bash
# assigning a variable value to another variable

value1=10
value2=$value1
echo The resulting value is $value2
```

When you use the value of the value1 variable in the assignment statement, you must still use the dollar sign. This code produces the output:

```
$ ./test4
The resulting value is 10
$
```

If you forget the dollar sign, and make the value2 assignment line look like:

```
value2=value1
```

you get the following output:

```
$ ./test4
The resulting value is value1
$
```

Without the dollar sign the shell interprets the variable name as a normal text string, which is probably not what you wanted.

The Backtick

One of the most useful features of shell scripts is the lowly back quote character (`), usually called the backtick in the Linux world. Be careful, this is not the normal single quote character you are used to using for strings. Because it is not used very often outside of shell scripts, you may not even know where to find it on your keyboard. You should become familiar with it, because it's a crucial component of many shell scripts (hint: on PCs it is usually on the same key as the tilde symbol).

The backtick allows you to assign the output of a shell command to a variable. Though this doesn't seem like much, it is a major building block in script programming.

You must surround the entire command-line command using the backtick character:

```
testing=`date`
```

The shell runs the command within the backticks, and assigns the output to the variable testing. Here's an example of creating a variable using the output from a normal shell command:

```
#!/bin/bash
# using the backtick character
testing=`date`
echo "The date and time are: " $testing
```

The variable testing receives the output from the date command, and it is used in the echo statement to display it. Running the shell script produces the following output:

```
$ ./test5
The date and time are: Mon Nov 3 20:23:25 EDT 2008
$
```

That's not all that exciting in this example (you could just as easily put the command in the echo statement), but once you capture the command output into a variable, you can do anything with it.

Here's a popular example of how the backtick is used to capture the current date, and use it to create a unique filename in a script:

```
#!/bin/bash
# copy the /usr/bin directory listing to a log file
today=`date +%y%m%d`
ls /usr/bin -al > log.$today
```

The today variable is assigned the output of a formatted date command. This is a common technique used to extract date information for log file names. The +%y%m%d format instructs the date command to display the date as a two digit year, month, and day:

```
$ date +%y%m%d
081103
$
```

The script assigns the value to a variable, which is then used as part of a filename. The file itself contains the redirected output (discussed later in the "Redirecting Output" section) of a directory listing. After running the script, you should see a new file in your directory:

```
-rw-r--r-- 1 rich rich 769 2008-11-03 19:15 log.081103
```

The log file appears in the directory using the value of the $today variable as part of the file name. The contents of the log file are the directory listing from the /usr/bin directory. If the script is run the next day, the log filename will be log.081104, thus creating a new file for the new day.

Redirecting Input and Output

There are times when you'd like to save the output from a command instead of just having it display on the monitor. The bash shell provides a few different operators for allowing you to redirect the output of a command to an alterative location (such as a file). Redirection can also be used to input and output, redirecting a file to a command for input. This section describes what you need in order to use redirection in your shell scripts.

Output Redirection

The most basic type of redirection is sending output from a command to a file. The bash shell uses the greater-than symbol for this:

```
command > outputfile
```

Anything that would appear on the monitor from the command is stored in the output file specified instead:

```
$ date > test6
$ ls -l test6
-rw-r--r-- 1 rich rich 29 2008-11-04 17:56 test6
$ cat test6
Tue Nov 4 17:56:58 EDT 2008
$
```

The redirect operator created the file test6 and redirected the output from the date command to the test6 file. If the output file already exists, the redirect operator overwrites the existing file with the new file data:

```
$ who > test6
$ cat test6
rich pts/0 Nov 4 17:55
$
```

Now the contents of the test6 file contain the output from the who command.

Sometimes, instead of overwriting the file contents you may need to append output from a command to an existing file—for instance, if you're creating a log file to document an action on the system. For this situation, you can use the double greater-than symbol (>>) to append data:

```
$ date >> test6
$ cat test6
rich pts/0 Nov 4 17:55
Tue Nov 4 18:02:14 EDT 2008
$
```

The test6 file still contains the original data from the who command processed earlier, and now it contains the new output from the date command.

Secret

Output redirection is commonly used with the cat command to concatenate files. Just redirect the output from the cat command with a single greater-than symbol for the first file, and with the double greater-than symbol for any additional files you want to add:

```
cat file1 > outfile
cat file2 >> outfile
cat file3 >> outfile
```

The contents of the outfile file now contain the contents of the three files concatenated.

Input Redirection

Input redirection is the opposite of output redirection. Instead of taking the output of a command and redirecting it to a file, input redirection takes the contents of a file and redirects it to a command.

The input redirection symbol is the less-than symbol (<):

```
command < inputfile
```

The easy way to remember this is to recall that the command is always listed first in the command line, and the redirection symbol "points" to the way the data is flowing. The less-than symbol indicates the data is flowing from the input file to the command.

Here's an example of using input redirection with the wc command:

```
$ wc < test6
2 11 60
$
```

The wc command provides a count of text in the data. By default it produces three values:

* The number of lines in the text
* The number of words in the text
* The number of bytes in the text

By redirecting a text file to the wc command, you can get a quick count of the lines, words, and bytes in the file. The example shows that there are two lines, 11 words, and 60 bytes in the test6 file.

There's another method of input redirection, called inline input redirection. This method allows you to specify the data for input redirection on the command line instead of in a file. This may seem somewhat odd at first, but there are a few applications for this process (such as shown in the "Performing Math" section later).

The inline input redirection symbol is the double less-than symbol (<<). Besides this symbol, you must specify a text marker that delineates the beginning and end of the data used for input. You can use any string value for the text marker, but it must be the same at the beginning of the data and at the end of the data:

```
command << marker
data
marker
```

When using inline input redirection on the command line, the shell will prompt for data using the secondary prompt, defined in the PS2 environment variable. Here's how this looks when you use it:

```
$ wc << EOF
> test string 1
> test string 2
> test string 3
> EOF
3 9 42
$
```

The secondary prompt continues to prompt for more data until you enter the text marker. The wc command performs the line, word, and byte count of the data supplied by the inline input redirection.

Pipes

There are times when you need to send the output of one command to the input of another command. This is possible using redirection, but somewhat clunky:

```
$ ls /etc > etc.list
$ more < etc.list
adduser.conf
adjtime
aliases
aliases.db
alternatives
apache2
apm
apparmor
apparmor.d
apt
at.deny
avahi
bash.bashrc
bash_completion
bash_completion.d
belocs
bind
bindresvport.blacklist
blkid.tab
blkid.tab.old
ca-certificates
ca-certificates.conf
calendar
chatscripts
ConsoleKit
--More--
```

The ls lists the contents of the /etc folder, and using the standard output redirection, I was able to redirect the output from the ls command to a file, called etc.list. After the command finished, the etc.list file contained a list of all the files in the /etc folder on my system.

Next, I used input redirection to send the contents of the etc.list file to the more command so I could view the file list on the monitor.

That was useful, but again, a somewhat clunky way of producing the information. Instead of redirecting the output of a command to a file, you can also redirect the output directly to another command. This process is called piping. The pipe symbol is the bar operator (|):

```
command1 | command2
```

Piping provides a way to link commands together to provide more detailed output.

Secret Don't think of piping as running two commands back-to-back though. The Linux system actually runs both commands at the same time, linking them together internally in the system. As the first command produces output, it's sent immediately to the second command. No intermediate files or buffer areas are used to transfer the data.

Now, using piping you can easily pipe the output of the rpm command directly to the sort command to produce your results:

```
$ ls /etc | more
adduser.conf
adjtime
aliases
aliases.db
alternatives
apache2
apm
apparmor
apparmor.d
apt
at.deny
avahi
bash.bashrc
bash_completion
bash_completion.d
belocs
bind
bindresvport.blacklist
blkid.tab
blkid.tab.old
ca-certificates
ca-certificates.conf
calendar
chatscripts
ConsoleKit
--More--
```

Now that's much better! There's no limit to the number of pipes you can use in a command (up to the 255 character limit on the line length), and you can continue piping the output of commands to other commands to refine your operation.

To get even fancier, you can use redirection along with piping, to save your output to a file:

```
$ ls /etc | sort -r > etc.list
$more etc.list
zsh_command_not_found
xml
X11
wpa_supplicant
wgetrc
w3m
vim
update-motd.d
update-manager
updatedb.conf
ufw
udev
ucf.conf
tomcat6
...
```

The `-r` parameter of the `sort` command reverses the order of the data. As expected, the data in the etc.list file is now sorted in reverse order!

Secret

By far one of the most popular uses of piping is piping the output of commands that produce long output to the `more` command.

The `ls -l` command produces a long listing of all the files in the directory. For directories with lots of files, this can be quite a listing. By piping the output to the more command, you force the output to stop at the end of every screen of data.

Performing Math

Another crucial feature to any programming language is the ability to manipulate numbers. Unfortunately, for shell scripts this process is a bit awkward. There are two different ways to perform mathematical operations in your shell scripts.

The expr Command

Originally, the Bourne shell provided a special command that was used for processing mathematical equations. The `expr` command allowed for processing equations from the command line, but is extremely clunky:

```
$ expr 1 + 5
6
```

The `expr` command recognizes a few different mathematical and string operators, shown in Table 25-1.

Table 25-1: The expr Command Operators

Operator	Description
ARG1 | ARG2	Return *ARG1* if neither argument is null or zero, otherwise return *ARG2*
ARG1 & ARG2	Return *ARG1* if neither argument is null or zero, otherwise return 0
ARG1 < ARG2	Return 1 if *ARG1* is less than *ARG2*, otherwise return 0
ARG1 <= ARG2	Return 1 if *ARG1* is less than or equal to *ARG2*, otherwise return 0
ARG1 = ARG2	Return 1 if *ARG1* is equal to *ARG2*, otherwise return 0
ARG1 != ARG2	Return 1 if *ARG1* is not equal to *ARG2*, otherwise return 0
ARG1 >= ARG2	Return 1 if *ARG1* is greater than or equal to *ARG2*, otherwise return 0
ARG1 > ARG2	Return 1 if *ARG1* is greater than *ARG2*, otherwise return 0
ARG1 + ARG2	Return the arithmetic sum of *ARG1* and *ARG2*
ARG1 - ARG2	Return the arithmetic difference of *ARG1* and *ARG2*
ARG1 * ARG2	Return the arithmetic product of *ARG1* and *ARG2*
ARG1 / ARG2	Return the arithmetic quotient of *ARG1* divided by *ARG2*
ARG1 % ARG2	Return the arithmetic remainder of *ARG1* divided by *ARG2*
STRING : REGEXP	Return the pattern match if *REGEXP* matches a pattern in *STRING*
match STRING REGEXP	Return the pattern match if *REGEXP* matches a pattern in *STRING*
substr STRING POS LENGTH	Return the substring *LENGTH* characters in length starting at position *POS* (starting at 1)
index STRING CHARS	Return position in *STRING* where *CHARS* is found, otherwise return 0
length STRING	Return the numeric length of the string *STRING*
+ TOKEN	interpret *TOKEN* as a string, even if it's a keyword
(EXPRESSION)	Return the value of *EXPRESSION*

While the standard operators work fine in the `expr` command, the problem comes in actually using them from a script or the command line. Many of the `expr` command operators (such as the asterisk) have other meanings in the shell. Using them in the expr command produces odd results:

```
$ expr 5 * 2
expr: syntax error
$
```

To solve this problem, you need to use the shell escape character (the backslash) to identify any characters that may get misinterpreted by the shell before being passed to the expr command:

```
$ expr 5 \* 2
10
$
```

That's really starting to get ugly! Using the expr command in a shell script is equally cumbersome:

```
#!/bin/bash
# An example of using the expr command
var1=10
var2=20
var3='expr $var2 / $var1'
echo The result is $var3
```

To assign the result of a mathematical equation to a variable, you have to use the backtick character to extract the output from the expr command:

```
$ ./test7
The result is 2
$
```

Fortunately, the bash shell has an improvement for processing mathematical operators.

Using Brackets

The bash shell includes the expr command to stay compatible with the Bourne shell; however, it also provides a much easier way of performing mathematical equations. In bash, when assigning a mathematical value to a variable, you can enclose the mathematical equation using a dollar sign and square brackets ($[*operation*]):

```
$ var1=$[1 + 5]
$ echo $var1
6
$ var2 = $[$var1 * 2]
$ echo $var2
12
$
```

Using brackets makes shell math much easier than the expr command. This same technique also works in shell scripts:

```
#!/bin/bash
var1=100
var2=50
var3=45
var4=$[$var1 * ($var2 - $var3)]
echo The final result is $var4
```

Running this script produces the output:

```
$ ./test8
The final result is 500
$
```

Also notice that when using the square brackets method for calculating equations you don't need to worry about the multiplication symbol, or any other characters getting misinterpreted by the shell. The shell knows that it's not a wildcard character since it is within the square brackets.

There's one major limitation to performing math in the bash shell script. Take a look at this example:

```
#!/bin/bash
var1=100
var2=45
var3=$[$var1 / $var2]
echo The final result is $var3
```

Now run it and see what happens:

```
$ ./test9
The final result is 2
$
```

The bash shell mathematical operators only support integer arithmetic. This is a huge limitation if you're trying to do any sort of real-world mathematical calculations.

Secret The z shell (zsh) provides full floating-point arithmetic operations. If you require floating point calculations in your shell scripts, you might consider checking out the z shell, which you can easily install using the Synaptic installer in Ubuntu.

A Floating-Point Solution

There have been several solutions for overcoming the bash integer limitation. The most popular solution uses the built-in bash calculator (called bc).

The Basics of bc

The bash calculator is actually a programming language that allows you to enter floating point expressions at a command line, interpret the expressions, calculate them, and return the result. The bash calculator recognizes:

- Numbers (both integer and floating-point)
- Variables (both simple variables and arrays)
- Comments (lines starting with a pound sign, or the C language /* */ pair
- Expressions

- ◆ Programming statements (such as if-then statements)
- ◆ Functions

You can access the bash calculator from the shell prompt using the `bc` command:

```
$ bc
bc 1.06
Copyright 1991-1994, 1997, 1998, 2000 Free Software Foundation, Inc.
This is free software with ABSOLUTELY NO WARRANTY.
For details type 'warranty.'
12 * 5.4
64.8
3.156 * (3 + 5)
25.248
quit
$
```

The example starts out by entering the expression 12 * 5.4. The bash calculator returns the answer. Each subsequent expression entered into the calculator is evaluated and the results are displayed. To exit the bash calculator, you must enter `quit`.

The floating point arithmetic is controlled by a built-in variable called `scale`. You must set this value to the desired number of decimal places you want in your answers, or you won't get what you were looking for:

```
$ bc -q
3.44 / 5
0
scale=4
3.44 / 5
.6880
quit
$
```

The default value for the `scale` variable is zero. Before the scale value is set, the bash calculator provides the answer to zero decimal places. After setting the `scale` variable value to four, the bash calculator displays the answer to four decimal places. The `-q` command-line parameter suppresses the lengthy welcome banner from the bash calculator.

Besides normal numbers, the bash calculator also understands variables:

```
$ bc -q
var1=10
var1 * 4
40
var2 = var1 / 5
print var2
2
quit
$
```

Once a variable value is defined, you can use the variable throughout the bash calculator session. The print statement allows you to print variables and numbers.

Using bc In Scripts

At this point, you may be wondering how the bash calculator is going to help us with floating point arithmetic in your shell scripts. Do you remember our friend the backtick character? You can use the backtick to run a bc command, and assign the output to a variable. The basic format to use is:

```
variable='echo "options; expression" | bc'
```

The first portion, options, allows us to set variables. If you need to set more than one variable, separate them using the semicolon. The expression parameter defines the mathematical expression to evaluate using bc. Though this looks pretty odd, trust me, it works great. Here's a quick example of doing this in a script:

```
#!/bin/bash
var1='echo " scale=4; 3.44 / 5" | bc'
echo The answer is $var1
```

This example sets the scale variable to 4 decimal places, then indicates a specific calculation for the expression. Running this script produces the following output:

```
$ ./test10
The answer is .6880
$
```

Now that's fancy! You aren't limited to just using numbers for the expression value. You can also use variables defined in the shell script:

```
#!/bin/bash
var1=100
var2=45
var3='echo "scale=4; $var1 / $var2" | bc'
echo The answer for this is $var3
```

The script defines two variables that are used within the expression sent to the bc command. Remember to use the dollar sign to signify the value for the variables, and not the variables themselves. The output of this script is:

```
$ ./test11
The answer for this is 2.2222
$
```

Of course, once a value is assigned to a variable, that variable can be used in yet another calculation:

```
#!/bin/bash
var1=20
var2=3.14159
var3='echo "scale=4; $var1 * $var1" | bc'
var4='echo "scale=4; $var3 * $var2" | bc'
echo The final result is $var4
```

This method works fine for short calculations, but sometimes you need to get more involved with your numbers. If you have more than just a couple of calculations, it's confusing to try to list multiple expressions on the same command line.

There's a simple solution to this problem. The bc command recognizes input redirection, allowing you to redirect a file to the bc command for processing. This can just as easily become confusing, however, as you'd need to store your expressions in a file.

Instead of using a file for redirection, you can use the inline input redirection method, which allows for redirecting data directly from the command line. In the shell script, you can assign the output to a variable. This looks like this:

```
variable='bc << EOF
options
statements
expressions
EOF
'
```

The EOF text string indicates the beginning and end of the inline redirection data. Remember that the backtick characters are still needed to assign the output of the bc command to the variable.

Now you can place all of the individual bash calculator elements on separate lines in the script file. Here's an example of using this technique in a script:

```
#!/bin/bash
var1=10.46
var2=43.67
var3=33.2
var4=71

var5='bc << EOF
scale = 4
a1 = ( $var1 * $var2)
b1 = ($var3 * $var4)
a1 + b1
EOF
'

echo The final answer for this mess is $var5
```

Using this you can place each option and expression on a separate line in your script, making things cleaner and easier to follow. The EOF string indicates the beginning and end of the data to redirect to the bc command. Of course, you need to use the backtick characters to indicate the command to assign to the variable.

You'll also notice in this example that you can assign variables within the bash calculator. It's important to remember that any variables created within the bash calculator are only valid within the bash calculator, and can't be used in the shell script.

Exiting the Script

So far, in our example, scripts terminated things pretty abruptly. When we were done with our last command, we just ended the script. There's a more elegant way of completing things available to us.

Every command that runs in the shell uses an exit status to indicate to the shell that it's done processing. The exit status is an integer value between 0 and 255 that's passed by the command to the shell when the command finishes running. You can capture this value and use it in your scripts.

Checking the Exit Status

Linux provides the $? special variable that holds the existing status value from the last command that executed. You must view or use the $? variable immediately after the command you want to test, as it changes values to the exit status of the last command:

```
$ date
Sat Nov 01 10:01:30 EDT 2008
$ echo $?
0
$
```

By convention, the exit status of a command that successfully completes is zero. If a command completes with an error, then a positive integer value is placed in the exit status:

```
$ asdfg
-bash: asdfg: command not found
$ echo $?
127
$
```

The invalid command returns an exit status of 127. There's not much of a standard convention to Linux error exit status codes. Nevertheless, there are a few guidelines you can use, as shown in Table 25-2.

Table 25-2: Linux Exit Status Codes

Code	Description
0	Successful completion of the command
1	General unknown error
2	Misuse of shell command
126	The command can't execute
127	Command not found
128	Invalid exit argument
128+x	Fatal error with Linux signal x
130	Command terminated with Ctl-C
255	Exit status out of range

An exit status value of 126 indicates that the user didn't have the proper permissions set to execute the command:

```
$ ./myprog.c
-bash: ./myprog.c: Permission denied
$ echo $?
126
$
```

Another common error you'll encounter occurs if you supply an invalid parameter to a command:

```
$ date %t
date: invalid date '%t'
$ echo $?
1
$
```

This generates the general exit status code of one.

The exit Command

By default, your shell script will exit with the exit status of the last command in your script:

```
$ ./test12
The result is 2
$ echo $?
0
$
```

You can change that to return your own exit status code. The exit command allows you to specify an exit status when your script ends:

```
#!/bin/bash
# testing the exit status
var1=10
var2=30
var3=$[ $var1 + var2 ]
echo The answer is $var3
exit 5
```

When you check the exit status of the script, you'll get the value used as the parameter of the exit command:

```
$ ./test13
The answer is 40
$ echo $?
5
$
```

You can also use variables in the exit command parameter:

```
#!/bin/bash
# testing the exit status
var1=10
var2=30
var3=$[ $var1 + var2 ]
exit $var3
```

When you run this command, it produces the following exit status:

```
$ ./test14
$ echo $?
40
$
```

You should be careful with this feature though, as the exit status codes can only go up to 255. Watch what happens in this example:

```
#!/bin/bash
# testing the exit status
var1=10
var2=30
var3=$[ $var1 * var2 ]
echo The value is $var3
exit $var3
```

Now when you run it, you get the following:

```
$ ./test14
The value is 300
$ echo $?
44
$
```

The exit status code is reduced to fit in the 0 to 255 range. The shell does this by using modulo arithmetic. The modulo of a value is the remainder after a division. The resulting number is the remainder of the specified number divided by 256. In the case of 300 (the result value), the remainder is 44, which is what appears as the exit status code.

Structured Commands

Many programs require some sort of logic flow control between the commands in the script. This means that the shell executes certain commands given one set of circumstances, but has the ability to execute other commands given a different set of circumstances. There is a whole class of commands that allows the script to skip over or loop through commands based on conditions of variable values, or the result of other commands. These commands are generally referred to as structured commands.

The structured commands allow you to alter the flow of operation of the program, executing some commands under some conditions, and skipping others under other conditions. There are quite a few structured commands available in the bash shell, so we'll look at them individually. In this section, we'll look at a couple of popular structured commands you can use in your shell scripts.

The if-then-else Statement

The most basic type of structured command is the if-then-else statement. The format for the if-then-else statement is:

```
if command
then
commands
else
commands
fi
```

If you're used to using if-then-else statements in other programming languages, this format may be somewhat confusing. In other programming languages, the object after the i f statement is an equation that is evaluated for a TRUE or FALSE value. That's not how the bash shell i f statement works.

If the *command* in the i f statement line returns with an exit status code of zero, the *commands* listed in the then section are executed. If the *command* in the i f statement line returns a non-zero exit status code, the bash shell executes the *commands* in the el se section.

Let's take a look at an example of using the if-then-else statement:

```
$ cat test15
#!/bin/bash
# testing the else section
testuser=badtest
if grep $testuser /etc/passwd
then
echo The files for user $testuser are:
ls -a /home/$testuser/.b*
else
echo "The user name $testuser doesn't exist on this system"
fi
$ ./test15
The user name badtest doesn't exist on this system
$
```

The grep command checks to see if the text string listed as the first parameter is contained in the file listed as the second parameter. If it is, the grep command returns a TRUE value, and the i f statement executes the code in the then code block, listing the files in the user's home folder. However, if the text string isn't in the passwd file, the grep command returns a FALSE value, and the i f statement executes the code in the else code block. The if statement delineates the end of the el se section.

Secret

You can also nest if-then statements to check for several situations in your script code. Instead of having to write separate if-then statements, you can use an alternative version of the else section, called elif:

```
if command1
then
commands
elif command2
then
more commands
fi
```

The el i f statement line provides another command to evaluate, similar to the original if statement line. If the exit status code from the elif command is zero, bash executes the commands in the section with the second then statement.

You can continue to string elif statements together, creating one huge if-then-elif conglomeration:

```
if command1
then
```

continues

continued

```
command set 1
elif command2
then
command set 2
elif command3
then
command set 3
elif command4
then
command set 4
fi
```

Each block of commands is executed depending on which command returns the zero exit status code. Remember, the bash shell will execute the if statements in order, and only the first one that returns a zero exit status will result in the then section being executed.

The test Command

So far all you've seen in the if statement line are normal shell commands. You might be wondering if the bash if-then statement has the ability to evaluate any condition other than the exit status code of a command.

The answer is no, it can't. There's a neat utility available in the bash shell, however, that helps us evaluate other things using the if-then statement.

The test command provides a way to test different conditions in an if-then statement. If the condition listed in the test command evaluates to TRUE, the test command exits with a zero exit status code, making the if-then statement behave much like the if-then statements in other programming languages. If the condition is FALSE, the test command exits with a one, which causes the if-then statement to fail.

The format of the test command is pretty simple:

```
test condition
```

The condition is a series of parameters and values that the test command evaluates. When used in an if-then statement, the test command looks like this:

```
if test condition
then
commands
fi
```

The bash shell provides an alternative way of declaring the test command in an if-then statement:

```
if [ condition ]
then
commands
fi
```

The square brackets define the condition that's used in the test command. Be careful, you must have a space after the first bracket, and a space before the last bracket or you'll get an error message.

There are three classes of conditions the test command can evaluate:

- ◆ Numeric comparisons
- ◆ String comparisons
- ◆ File comparisons

The next sections describe how to use each of these classes of tests in your if-then statements.

Numeric Comparisons

The most common method for using the test command is to perform a comparison of two numeric values. Table 25-3 shows the list of condition parameters used for testing two values.

Table 25-3: The test Numeric Comparisons

Comparison	Description
$n1$ -eq $n2$	Check if $n1$ is equal to $n2$
$n1$ -ge $n2$	Check if $n1$ is greater than or equal to $n2$
$n1$ -gt $n2$	Check if $n1$ is greater than $n2$
$n1$ -le $n2$	Check if $n1$ is less than or equal to $n2$
$n1$ -lt $n2$	Check if $n1$ is less than $n2$
$n1$ -ne $n2$	Check if $n1$ is not equal to $n2$

The numeric test conditions can be used to evaluate both numbers and variables. Here's an example of doing that:

```
$ cat test16
#!/bin/bash
# using numeric test comparisons
val1=10
val2=11

if [ $val1 -gt 5 ]
then
echo "The test value $val1 is greater than 5"
fi

if [ $val1 -eq $val2 ]
then
echo "The values are equal"
else
echo "The values are different"
fi
```

The first test condition tests if the value of the variable val1 is greater than 5:

```
if [ $val1 -gt 5 ]
```

The second test condition tests if the value of the variable val1 is equal to the value of the variable val2:

```
if [ $val1 -eq $val2 ]
```

Run the script and observe the results:

```
$ ./test16
The test value 10 is greater than 5
The values are different
$
```

Both of the numeric test conditions evaluated as expected.

String Comparisons

The test command also allows you to perform comparisons on string values. Performing comparisons on strings can get tricky, as you'll see. Table 25-4 shows the comparison functions you can use to evaluate two string values.

Table 25-4: The test Command String Comparisons

Compaison	Description
str1 = str2	Check if str1 is the same as string str2
str1 != str2	Check if str1 is not the same as str2
str1 < str2	Check if str1 is less than str2
str1 > str2	Check if str1 is greater than str2
-n str1	Check if str1 has a length greater than zero
-z str1	Check if str1 has a length of zero

The equal and not equal conditions are fairly self-explanatory with strings. It's pretty easy to know whether or not two string values are the same:

```
$cat test17
#!/bin/bash
# testing string equality
testuser=rich

if [ $USER = $testuser ]
then
echo "Welcome $testuser"
fi
$ ./test17
Welcome rich
$
```

Similarly, using the not equals string comparison:

```
$ cat test18
#!/bin/bash
# testing string equality
testuser=baduser

if [ $USER != $testuser ]
then
echo "This isn't $testuser"
else
echo "Welcome $testuser"
fi
$ ./test18
This isn't baduser
$
```

The test comparison takes all punctuation and capitalization into account when comparing strings for equality.

Secret

Testing for string inequality is where things get tricky. There are two problems that often plague shell programmers when trying to use the greater than or less than features of the test command:

- The greater-than and less-than symbols must be avoided, or the shell will use them as redirection symbols, with the string values as filenames.
- The greater-than and less-than order is not the same as that used with the sort command.

If you forget to place a backslash character in front of the greater-than and less-than symbols, the shell interprets them as redirection symbols. Capitalized letters appear less than lowercase letters in the test command; however, when you put the same strings in a file and use the sort command, the lowercase letters appear first.

Also, notice that the test command uses the standard mathematical comparison symbols for string comparisons, and text codes for numerical comparisons. This is a subtle feature that many programmers manage to reverse.

File Comparisons

The last category of test comparisons is quite possibly the most powerful and most used comparisons in shell scripting. The test command allows you to test the status of files and directories on the Ubuntu filesystem. Table 25-5 lists these comparisons.

Table 25-5: The test Command File Comparisons

Comparison	Description
-d file	Check if file exists and is a directory
-e file	Checks if file exists

continues

Table 25-5: *(continued)*

Comparison	Description
`-f` *file*	Checks if *file* exists and is a file
`-r` *file*	Checks if *file* exists and is readable
`-s` *file*	Checks if *file* exists and is not empty
`-w` *file*	Checks if *file* exists and is writeable
`-x` *file*	Checks if *file* exists and is executable
`-O` *file*	Checks if *file* exists and is owned by the current user
`-G` *file*	Checks if *file* exists and the default group is the same as the current user
file1 `-nt` *file2*	Checks if *file1* is newer than *file2*
file1 `-ot` *file2*	Checks if *file1* is older than *file2*

These conditions give you the ability to check files in your filesystem within your shell scripts, and are often used in scripts that access files. The `-e` comparison allows you to check if a file or directory object exists before you attempt to use it in your script:

```
$ cat test19
#!/bin/bash
# checking if a directory exists
if [ -e $HOME ]
then
echo "OK on the directory, now let's check the file"
# checking if a file exists
if [ -e $HOME/testing ]
then
# the file exists, append data to it
echo "Appending date to existing file"
date >> $HOME/testing
else
# the file doesn't exist, create a new file
echo "Creating new file"
date > $HOME/testing
fi
else
echo "Sorry, you don't have a HOME directory"
fi
$ ./test19
OK on the directory, now let's check the file
Creating new file
$ ./test19
OK on the directory, now let's check the file
Appending date to existing file
$
```

The first check uses the -e comparison to determine if the user has a HOME directory. If so, the next -e comparison checks to determine if the testing file exists in the HOME directory. If the file doesn't exist, the shell script uses the single greater-than redirect symbol, creating a new file with the output from the date command. The second time you run the shell script, it uses the double greater-than symbol, so it just appends the date output to the existing file.

Summary

In this chapter we discussed how to use the bash shell scripting environment to create and run shell script programs. A shell script allows us to string several shell commands together and run them simultaneously. It also allows us to store values in variables and manipulate the output of commands to assist us in normal system tasks, such as listing files, viewing logged in users, and handling running processes.

The next chapter looks at some more advanced scripting environments available in Ubuntu. The Perl and Python scripting languages are similar to shell scripts, but provide many more features that allow us to customize our data handling.

Perl and Python

Chapter
26

♦ ♦

Secrets in This Chapter

What is Perl?

Using Perl

What is Python?

Using Python

♦ ♦

Chapter 25, "Shell Scripts," showed a basic way of using automated programs in Ubuntu using scripts containing command-line commands. Unfortunately, writing shell script programs to manipulate large amounts of data using shell commands can be somewhat tedious. The Ubuntu environment provides two other popular scripting languages that are better suited for working with data. This chapter looks at both the Perl and Python languages available in Ubuntu, and demonstrates how to use them to help manage data.

What Is Perl?

Larry Wall wrote the Practical Extraction and Report Language (Perl) is an *interpreted scripting language* to augment standard shell languages. An interpreted scripting language is a set of commands that are interpreted by a program rather than directly by the operating system. As you can probably guess from its name, the basic intent for Perl was to help manipulate data to produce reports in a way that was simpler and more elegant than what's available in shell scripts.

Perl was modeled after several different programming languages, combining features from shell scripting, the C programming language, and even the Basic programming language to create a versatile programming language that's useful for UNIX system administrators. A motto commonly found in Perl circles is "there is more than one way to do it" (abbreviated TIMTOWTDI, and often called tim toady). Perl has so many features that it's common to be able to solve data-manipulation problems in several different ways. Of course, whenever there's more than one way to do something, that leads to interesting debates in the programming world, and Perl certainly has its share of debates!

Due to the popularity of Perl, many system scripts that manipulate data are written in Perl. Because of that, most Linux distributions (including Ubuntu) install Perl by default. For the few that don't install Perl by default, it's easy to download and install the Perl interpreter package to run the programs. This provides a great programming platform to write your own scripting code with.

Working with Perl

Because Perl is an interpreted language, Ubuntu can't run a Perl program by itself. Instead, there must be an external program for you to run to interpret the Perl commands and execute them. The program used to interpret and execute Perl commands is called perl, and is usually found in the /usr/bin folder on Linux systems (including Ubuntu).

There are two methods to invoke the Perl interpreter to run your programs:

◆ On the command line, specifying a Perl file as a parameter to the perl program
◆ Defining the perl program within the Perl script itself

The following sections demonstrate how to run Perl programs using both of these methods.

Command-Line Interpreter

You can manually run the `perl` interpreter program directly from the command line to process a Perl script. To demonstrate this, let's first create a simple Perl script to run. Here's an example of a simple script to use:

```
$ cat test1.pl
# This is a test Perl script
print "This is a test.\n";
$
```

This two-line script incorporates a comment line (the line starting with a pound sign), which is ignored by Perl, and a single line of Perl code. The `print` command sends a string to the default standard output, which is the console when running interactively, such as from the Terminal program in Ubuntu (see Chapter 19, "The Ubuntu Command Line").

Secret   The \n character at the end of the string represents a carriage-control character, allowing the cursor to move to the next line on the display. In shell scripts, the `echo` command (see Chapter 25) automatically adds the carriage-control character when displaying text. The Perl print command requires that you manually add the carriage-control character, which is a subtle difference that many programmers forget!

After saving the `test1.pl` file, you can run it from the command-line interface using the `perl` interpreter:

```
$ perl test.pl
This is a test script.
$
```

When using the `perl` interpreter, you can also invoke several command-line options to control the behavior of the interpreter. The most popular options are `-w`, which produces warnings about any errant syntax in your Perl code, and `-d`, which runs the script within the Perl debugger:

```
rich@testing:~> perl -d test1.pl

Loading DB routines from perl5db.pl version 1.3
Editor support available.

Enter h or 'h h' for help, or 'man perldebug' for more help.

main::(test.pl:1): print "This is a test script\n";
DB<1>
```

The debugger allows you to interactively step through the Perl script line by line, examining the results as each statement is executed. This is extremely handy when trying to find a bug in a large script.

Creating a Perl Program

The automatic method of running Perl scripts is accomplished by directly defining the Perl interpreter within the script itself. This uses the same technique we used in creating shell scripts to define the shell (see Chapter 25).

The first line in a Perl script must tell the shell what program to run to process the commands. For Perl, just as in the command-line method, this is the Perl interpreter program, which is located in the /usr/bin folder. After you define the Perl program in the script, you can enter the Perl commands for the program code.

Here's an example of writing a Perl script that runs on its own in the shell:

```
$ cat test2.pl
#!/usr/bin/perl
# This is another simple test Perl script
print "This is the second test script.\n";
$
```

Before you can run this Perl program, though, you must ensure that the Perl script file is set with execute permissions:

```
$ chmod +x test2.pl
$ ./test2
This is the second test script.
$
```

The chmod command changes the permissions for the owner of the file to run it from the shell. Now the Perl script can be run directly from the command-line prompt, or even from within shell scripts.

Secret

Depending on how your PATH environment variable is set, you'll most likely need to use the ./ symbol before the script file name to tell the shell that the script file is located in the current folder. If you plan on running lots of Perl scripts from your current folder, you can add the dot symbol to the PATH environment variable in your shell session using the command:

```
$ PATH=$PATH:. ; export PATH
```

After running this command, you don't need to include the ./ portion when running your Perl scripts.

Perl Programming

Just like any other programming language, Perl has specific rules for handling data, along with predefined operators and functions for acting on the data. This section describes the basic format of the Perl programming language. This should get you started in your Perl programming journey.

Using Variables in Perl

Just like in shell scripts, Perl uses variables to store data within the script. Once you store a value in a variable, Perl retains that value so you can use it later in the script. There are three types of variables available in Perl:

- ◆ Scalar
- ◆ Array
- ◆ Hash (also called associative array)

The following sections describe each of these types of variables, and show how to use them.

Scalar Variables

Scalar variables hold a single data value. Unlike in shell scripts, scalar variables are always preceded by a dollar sign. To place a value in a variable requires an *assignment statement:*

```
$variable = value;
```

Some assignment statement examples using scalar variables are:

```
$x = 10;
$pi = 3.14159;
$value1 = $value2;
$pet = "cat";
```

Scalar variables can hold text strings, integer numbers, or floating-point numbers, and can change from one type to the other, depending on the operator. If an operator expects a number, Perl will use the value as a number, and if an operator expects a string, Perl will use the value as a string. Unlike some more formal programming languages that require you to define a data type for a variable ahead of time, then only use that type of data for that variable, Perl lets you use any type of data type in a variable at any time in your code.

Whenever you reference the scalar variable in the Perl script, Perl uses the value stored in the variable. Here's a demonstration of that:

```
$ cat test3.pl
#!/usr/bin/perl
# testing Perl scalar variables
$test = "Jessica";
$pi = 3.14159;
$radius = 5;
$area = $pi * $radius ** 2;
print "$test says the area should be $area\n";
$ chmod +x test3.pl
$ ./test3.pl
Jessica says the area should be 78.53975
$
```

The Perl script calculated the formula (including using the floating-point values) and used the `print` statement to display the output. If you've done any programming in higher-level programming languages such as Java or C, you'll notice how nice it is in Perl to be able to use a variable that contains a numerical value in a `print` statement without having to reformat the value to a string. Perl automatically uses the numerical value as a string for us.

Array Variables

Arrays are indexed lists of scalar data. Each index is an integer value, starting at 0 and incrementing through however many elements are stored in the array. You identify an array variable by using the @ sign in front of the variable name instead of a dollar sign. An example of creating an array variable and assigning values to it is:

```
@days = ("Monday," "Tuesday," "Wednesday," "Thursday," "Friday");
```

Notice that the array definition is enclosed in parentheses, and a comma separates each value. The tricky part about arrays is trying to reference a single data value from within the array. To retrieve an individual value, you must use the dollar sign in front of the array variable name, plus add the index that references the value you want to retrieve within square brackets, like this:

```
$array[index]
```

For example, if you need to retrieve the second value stored in the @days array, you'd use the format:

```
print "Today is $days[1]\n";
```

Because the array index starts at zero, the 1 value references the second data value (Tuesday in this example) in the array. Here's a short script that demonstrates using array variables in a Perl script:

```
$ cat test4.pl
#!/usr/bin/perl
# testing arrays in Perl
@days = ("Monday," "Tuesday," "Wednesday," "Thursday," "Friday");

print "I always have practice on $days[2]\n";
print "I'm not sure what we're doing on $days[4]\n";
$ chmod +x test4.pl
$ ./test4.pl
I always have practice on Wednesday
I'm not sure what we're doing on Friday
$
```

The script replaced the array variable with the appropriate element value stored in the array.

Hash Variables

Hashes (also known as associative arrays) are collections of scalar values arranged in key/value pairs, similar to an array. The difference is that in hashes, the key is a text string instead of a numerical index. This allows you to relate one word with another. You retrieve the data value stored in the hash based on the key value.

Hashes are identified with a percent sign instead of a dollar sign. An example of a creating a hash is:

```
%favorites = ("fruit" => "banana," "vegetable" => "carrot");
```

The data value in hashes follows the same format as scalar data values. You can store text string, integer, or floating point values in the hash data. Similar to the array, you can refer to an individual data value in a hash using the key. The format is slightly different from the method used for arrays, though:

```
$hash{key}
```

The *key* is a text string representing the specific element in the hash, and is enclosed in braces. Also unlike arrays that have incremental numerical indexes, the hash keys don't have any set values. You can use any type of string value as a key:

```
$ cat test5.pl
#!/usr/bin/perl
# testing hash variables
%favorites = ("fruit" => "banana," "vegetable" => "carrot");
print "My favorite fruit is $favorites{'fruit'}\n";
$ chmod +x test5.pl
$ ./test5.pl
My favorite fruit is banana
$
```

This works just fine when you're looking for a specific key value, but it can make trying to iterate through a hash variable that contains unknown keys somewhat tricky.

Fortunately, Perl provides two handy functions to help determine what's inside a hash variable:

- **keys:** returns an array containing the key values in the hash
- **values:** returns an array containing the values in the hash

The keys function allows us to retrieve the individual key values so we can iterate through them, even though we might not know what they are. The best way to process keys in an array is with the foreach statement.

The foreach statement iterates through a set of statements for each element in the defined array. Here's a sample program that uses the foreach statement to iterate through the keys in a hash variable:

```
$ cat test6.pl
#!/usr/bin/perl
# more testing of hash variables
%favorites = ("fruit" => "banana," "vegetable" => "carrot");

foreach $key (keys %favorites)
{
print "My favorite $key is $favorites{$key}\n";
}
$ chmod +x test6.pl
./test6.pl
My favorite fruit is banana
My favorite vegetable is carrot
$
```

In each iteration, the foreach statement assigns the next key in the %favorites hash to the $key variable. When there aren't any more keys, the foreach statement stops. Notice that when I reference the hash variable for the `keys` function, I used the `%favorites` form of the hash variable name. When you reference the hash as a hash, you must include the percent symbol.

Secret

The `=>` identifier used to associate the key with a value is called a *fat comma* because it behaves much like a comma in other contexts. In fact, you can also use commas in place of the fat commas to define the hash:

```
%favorites = ("fruit," "banana," "vegetable," "carrot");
```

I'll let you decide which method is easier to follow. A perfect example of the TIMTOWTDI principle in Perl!

Structured Commands

As with shell scripts, Perl provides lots of statements to help alter the logic flow of the script based on data values. You've already seen how the `foreach` statement is used to loop through a block of code. There are several other popular statements used to alter the program flow.

If-then-else Statements

The basic format for the if-then-else statement in Perl is:

```
if (condition1)
{
code block1
} elsif (condition2)
{
code block2
} else (condition3)
{
code block3
}
```

Each code block can contain one or more Perl statements that are executed depending on the outcome of each condition. Only one code block is executed in the if-then-else statement. Here's a quick example of this:

```
$ cat test7.pl
#!/usr/bin/perl
# demonsrating the if-then-else statement
$test = 6;

if ($test > 50)
{
print "The number is high\n";
} elsif ($test > 25)
{
print "The number is medium\n";
} else
```

```
{
print "The number is low\n";
}
$ ./test7.pl
The number is low
$
```

Each condition tests the value of the $test variable. The else condition is blank, so if the code falls through to this condition, the else code block is always executed.

While Loops

The while loop allows you to iterate through a block of code multiple times until a defined condition is met. The format of the while loop is:

```
while (condition)
{
code block
}
```

For each iteration of the while loop, Perl evaluates the defined condition. If it evaluates to a TRUE Boolean value, Perl executes the code in the code block section. When the condition evaluates to a FALSE Boolean value, the while loop exits.

Here's an example of using the while loop to process a calculation that requires iteration:

```
$ cat test8.pl
#!/usr/bin/perl
# using the while loop
$count = 1;
$factorial = 1;
$number = 5;
while ($count <= $number)
{
$factorial = $factorial * $count;
$count++;
}
print "The factorial of $number is $factorial\n";
$ ./test8.pl
The factorial of 5 is 120
$
```

This example defines the variables required for the calculation, then uses the while loop to iterate through the numbers until the $count variable value is greater than the $number variable value.

For Loops

The for loop is similar to the while loop, but provides some added features to make things easier. The for loop checks a condition to determine if it continues to loop through the defined code block or not, but it also allows you to define all of your variables inside the statement. The format of the for loop is:

```
for ( initial expressions; condition; loop expressions)
{
code block
}
```

The *initial expressions* section allows you to define one or more variable values before the loop starts processing. If there are multiple statements, they must be separated by a comma. The *loop expressions* section allows you to alter variable values at the end of each iteration.

The `for` loop iterates through the code block, checking the *condition* at the start of each iteration. If the condition evaluates to a `FALSE` Boolean value, the for loop exits.

Here's a Perl script example that uses the `for` loop to perform the same factorial calculation as before:

```
$ cat test9.pl
#!/usr/bin/perl
# using the for statement
$number = 5;
for( $count = 1, $factorial = 1; $count <= $number; $count++)
{
$factorial = $factorial * $count;
}
print "The factorial of $number is $factorial\n";
$ ./test9.pl
The factorial of 5 is 120
$
```

The `for` loop allows you to define all of the variables used in the loop within the statement. Just like the `while` loop, it continues looping until the `$count` variable value is greater than the dollar number variable that we're trying to find the factorial of.

Perl Operators

Perl provides all the standard types of data operators you'd expect from a programming language to manipulate data, plus a few special tricks of its own. There are three main categories of operators in Perl:

- comparison operators
- logical operators
- arithmetic operators

The following sections explore operators and demonstrate how to use them in Perl scripts.

Comparison Operators

Comparison operators compare the value of one variable or statement with that of another to see if the overall statement resolves to either a Boolean `TRUE` or `FALSE` value.

Table 26-1 lists the comparison operators offered by Perl, both for numeric and string values.

These operators can be used in any Perl statement that evaluates a condition. The <=> operator is especially handy. Because of how it looks, it's often called the *spaceship operator*. It saves lots of time in sorting routines by being able to determine if two values are less than, greater than, or equal in a single operation.

Table 26-1: Perl Comparison Operators

Operation	Numeric Operator	String Operator
Equal to	==	eq
Less than	<	lt
Greater than	>	gt
Less than or equal to	<=	le
Greater than or equal to	>=	ge
Not equal to	!=	ne
Return -1 if less than, 0 if equal, and 1 if greater than	<=>	cmp
Range between first and second operands	. .	_
Matched by regular expression		=~
Not matched by regular expression		!~

Secret

Be careful with comparison operators when programming in both shell scripts and Perl. You may notice that Perl uses the mathematical symbols with numbers, and the text symbols with strings—the complete opposite of how the bash shell scripts do it. This is a huge source of coding errors for beginners.

Logical Operators

Logical operators implement Boolean logic between values to produce a Boolean value. They can be combined with other operator types into more complex forms of results. The logical operators are listed in Table 26-2.

Table 26-2: Perl Logical Operators

Operation	Operator
Logical AND	&&
Logical OR	; ;
Logical NOT	!
Group logical operators	( )

When working with multiple compound operators you must be careful of the operator order. You can group them together using parentheses to establish the proper operations. An example of this is:

```
if ($test == 0 || ($test == 1 && $test2 == 0))
```

The condition evaluates to a TRUE value if the $test variable value is either 0, or the value of $test is 1 and the value of $test2 is 0.

Arithmetic Operators

Arithmetic operators can be used to perform the standard mathematical operations on variables. The available operators are listed in Table 26-3.

Table 26-3: Perl Arithmetic Operators

Operation	Operator
Raise x to the y power	$x**y$
Calculate the remainder of x/y	$x\%y$
Add x to y	$x+y$
Subtract y from x	$x-y$
Multiply x times y	$x*y$
Divide x by y	x/y
Negate y	$-y$
Increment y by 1 and uses value	$++y$
Use value of y and then increments by 1	$y++$
Decrement y by 1 then uses value	$--y$
Use value of y and then decrements by 1	$y++$
Assign value of y to x	$x=y$

These operators are mostly used in assignment statements when performing mathematical calculations:

```
$area = $pi * $radius ** 2;
```

The standard order of operators applies when using multiple operators in a statement. You can use parentheses to alter the order of the operators.

Regular Expressions

Regular expressions are templates that you use to help simplify searching for data. The regular expression template is compared against a pool of data. Any data that matches the template passes the test, while any data not matching the template is rejected. This is a great way to quickly sort through various types of data.

While a great feature to have, regular expression templates are quite possibly the most complicated part of Perl programming. They use cryptic symbols and expressions to define the matching criteria. Statements with regular expressions use several of the same symbols that wildcards and operators use, but for slightly different reasons, which complicates things all the more.

It's often said that Perl regular expressions even represent a small programming language of their own. Entire books have been dedicated to just writing regular expressions.

Regular expressions are tested using the =~ and !~ symbols. The =~ symbol compares the regular expression for equality, while you use the !~ symbol to compare for an inequality. For example, to find the word *test* in "This is a test," use this line in a Perl script:

```
if ("This is a test" =~ /test/)
{
print "It's there\n";
}
```

This script tells Perl to find the expression test in the "This is a test" string and then print a statement if it is found. However, if you wanted to check if the word *test* isn't in the phrase, you'd write:

```
if ("This is a check" !~ /test/)
{
print "It's not there\n";
}
```

Any scalar value can be matched against a regular expression in a script. This offers a wealth of possibilities to locate and manipulate data. The trick is learning the template formats involved in getting it. This is because regular expression patterns are made up of metacharacters that some people find cryptic and difficult to decipher.

Table 26-4 shows just some of the primary metacharacters and their uses in Perl.

Table 26–4: Some Perl Metacharacters

Description	Metacharacter
Match any single character (except a newline).	.
Match the preceding character(s), any number of times.	*
Match the preceding character(s), one or more times.	+
The preceding character(s) may not be in the string, but it will still match if the other requirements are present.	?
Boolean OR statement.	|
Text matches if a tab character is present.	\t
Pattern matches if it is at the beginning of a line.	^
Pattern matches if it is at the end of a line.	$
Match a letter, number, or underscore.	\w
Match a number.	\d
Match any whitespace character such as a space, tab, or newline	\s
Escape any metacharacter into an ordinary character.	\

These days one of the most popular things regular expressions are used for is validating input data. Often if you have a script that requires user interaction, it's crucial that you ensure the users are inputting the correct data. One such function is validating e-mail addresses. There is a whole host of regular expression templates used to validate e-mail addresses. A simple one looks like this:

```
$email = "rich@myhost.com";
if ($email =~ \[A-Za-z0-9._%-]+@[A-Za-z0-9._%-]+\.[A-Za-z]{2,4}\ )
{
print "The e-mail address is valid\n";
}
```

This is just a short example of how to use regular expressions in Perl. As I mentioned, entire books have been written on just how to use regular expressions. They are powerful tools to add to your programming tool belt.

Perl Command-Line Arguments

As with shell scripts, Perl allows you to retrieve arguments entered on the command line when the script is run. Perl places any supplied arguments into the special array ARGV. You can reference each individual argument using the appropriate array element, just as you would any other array element.

Here's an example of a using an argument in a Perl script:

```
$cat test10.pl
#!/usr/bin/perl
# determine if a specified year is a leap year
if ($ARGV[0])
{
$year = $ARGV[0];
if (( $year % 4 == 0) xor ( $year % 100 == 0 ) xor ( $year % 400 == 0 ) )
{
print "$year is a leap year\n";
} else
{
print "$year is not a leap year\n";
}
} else
{
print "Sorry, you did not provide a year.\n";
}
$ ./test10.pl 2009
2009 is not a leap year.
$
```

This script accepts a year value as a single argument on the command line and then determines if the year is a leap year. The argument is retrieved from the array as $ARGV[0], and assigned to the scalar variable $year. That's not absolutely necessary, but often it's easier to work with a real variable name within the program rather than carry the ugly argument names around.

The first if statement checks to make sure that an argument was included on the command line. If not, a warning message is displayed and the script exits.

The standard tests for a leap year are then performed within another if statement. First, the year is checked if it is divisible by 4. Years that are divisible by 4, but also by either 100 or 400, are not leap years. The Boolean xor function is used to ensure that the year can only be divisible by 4.

The answer is displayed using the standard print command. Notice that the $year variable is included in the output within the string.

Perl Modules and CPAN

The UNIX (and Linux) philosophy of creating and using small programs that do one thing well, often in conjunction with other similar programs, has led to the largely modular design of Perl. Although the core Perl interpreter program provides lots of features for your scripting needs, Perl also includes lots of other specialized functions through modules that plug in to the core Perl environment. Ubuntu installs many Perl modules along with the basic Perl installation, but dozens more are optionally installable through Synaptic (see Chapter 13, "Software Installs and Updates").

One important component included in the base Perl installation is the *CPAN.pm module*, which makes it easy to download and install other modules from the Comprehensive Perl Archive Network (CPAN). CPAN is a large repository of Perl modules, reusable code, and documentation where you can find more Perl functions than you can imagine.

CPAN is also accessible directly from the Web at http://www.cpan.org. You can search and download modules with your browser from that site, but for ease of installation, the Perl CPAN module is the preferred way of installing modules.

To start CPAN, you'll need to run Perl as the administrative account using the command:

```
$ sudo perl -MCPAN -e shell
```

The first time you run CPAN, you'll go through a configuration dialog. If you select to try automatic configuration, the CPAN module attempts to select the settings it can detect from your environment. When it finishes, you'll get the cpan> prompt, as shown in Figure 26-1.

```
variable.

 <show_unparsable_versions>
Show all individual modules that have no $VERSION? [no]


During the 'r' command CPAN.pm finds modules with a version number of
zero. When the command finishes, it prints a report about this. If you
want this report to be very verbose, say yes to the following
variable.

 <show_zero_versions>
Show all individual modules that have a $VERSION of zero? [no]


Autoconfigured everything but 'urllist'.
Please call 'o conf init urllist' to configure your CPAN server(s) now!

commit: wrote '/etc/perl/CPAN/Config.pm'
Terminal does not support AddHistory.

cpan shell -- CPAN exploration and modules installation (v1.9205)
ReadLine support available (maybe install Bundle::CPAN or Bundle::CPANxx1?)

cpan[1]> _
```

Figure 26-1: The Perl CPAN Prompt

After you see the cpan> prompt you're ready to start using CPAN. You can now search CPAN for something useful.

Type h at the command prompt to see a list of available commands. Reading the help screen, you'll see that regular expressions can be used to search for a specific module. To search for a specific package with the regular expression, type

```
m /package/
```

Secret On each visit to the CPAN mirror, run the command reload index to ensure that you can access the latest modules to hit the mirror.

The CPAN module searches the database for modules that fit the search criteria, then lists the matching modules. To download and install a module, type

```
install modulename
```

CPAN will download the module, configure it for your system, and install all at once. If you prefer to download now and install later, use the get command instead of install. The h or ? command is always available to help you decide what to do next.

Secret The CPAN module offers a command history if ReadLine support is enabled. If it is, you can use your up and down arrows to repeat or edit a recent command.

When you have found and installed all the modules you want, type q at the cpan> prompt to quit the module and return to the shell command-line prompt.

What Is Python?

The Python scripting language was created by Guido van Rossum, and first released to the public in 1991. It's actually not named after the reptile, but oddly, after the popular British comedy TV show *Monty Python's Flying Circus*. The naming of the project might give you a clue as to light-heartedness found in the Python programming culture. Yet for all the silliness, the language is responsible for some very hard-working tools.

Quality assurance teams for both computer hardware and software use Python scripts to get their products ready for release. Search engines (including Google) use Python to perform their tasks. Web designers and bloggers use Python-based tools Zope and Plone to generate their content. Top-flight scientists in geophysics, electromagnetics, and fluid dynamics use the SciPy library in their research.

Python programmers are very productive because the language is easy to grasp, and it doesn't take much to get going. It puts an emphasis on creating human-readable code and being explicit about what is going on in the code. The language handles many housekeeping activities, such as I/O, memory management, data typing, and variable binding with ease.

The next section tells you a little bit about programming in Python and the tools available to you in the Ubuntu environment.

Working with Python

Like Perl, Python is also an interpreted scripting language, and requires an interpreter to execute Python scripts. Unlike Perl, though, the Python interpreter also includes an interactive mode. Typing the command python on the command line invokes the interpreter in interactive mode:

```
$ python
Python 2.5.2 (r252:60911, Sep 14 2008, 10:31:08)
[GCC 4.3.2] on linux2
Type "help," "copyright," "credits" or "license" for more information.
>>>
```

The interactive prompt is now waiting for you to type Python commands:

```
>>> print "This is a test"
This is a test
>>> 2 + 2
4
>>>
```

There is no exit command in the Python interactive environment. To exit from the interactive interpreter, press Ctl+D, which returns you to the normal command-line prompt.

Entering Python commands directly into the interpreter is not an easy way to program. Alternatively, you can store your Python commands in a text file and then include the filename on the command line:

```
$ cat test11.py
# this is a sample Python script
print "This is a test Python script"
$ python test.py
This is a test Python script
$
```

Similar to shell and Perl scripting, you can also invoke the Python interpreter from within your scripts:

```
$ cat test12.py
#!/usr/bin/python
# Running a Python script
print "This is another script test"
$
```

As with other scripts, you must make the script file executable before you can run it on the system:

```
$ chmod +x test12.py
$ ./test2.py
This is another script test
$
```

The script runs as expected from the command line.

Programming in Python

While Python acts like a typical scripting language, it was designed to be much more. The Python language provides many features found in higher-level languages such as high-level data types, structures, and built-in error checking. The following sections describe some of the programming features found in Python.

Python Variables and Data Structures

Python has four variable types to work with:

- ◆ scalars
- ◆ lists
- ◆ tuples
- ◆ dictionaries

Let's take a closer look at each of these.

Scalar Variables

Scalar variables are those that hold a single value, much the same as in Perl. Unlike Perl, though, numeric and string types are segregated and no extra symbols are prefixed to variables in Python. Examples of numeric and string scalar variable assignments are

```
x = 5
pi = 3.14159
animal = "dog"
```

Using variables in Python scripts is also a little different:

```
$ cat test13.py
test = "Jessica"
pi = 3.14159
radius = 5
area = pi * radius ** 2
print test, "says the area should be," area
$ chmod +x test13.pl
$ ./test13.pl
Jessica says the area should be 78.53975
$
```

Again, notice that Python doesn't use any symbols around the variable names. Because of that, when you want to display a variable value in the print statement, it must be outside of the string text defined.

List Variables

Lists are numerically indexed lists of objects (similar to arrays in Perl). They can be made up of any combination of things you choose, such as scalar data, dictionaries, tuples, and even other lists. An example of a list assignment is

```
days = ["Monday," "Tuesday," "Wednesday," "Thursday," "Friday"]
```

The beauty of lists in Python is that there are several great built-in functions that can operate directly on the values in the list. These are shown in Table 26-5.

Table 26-5: Python List Functions

Function	Description
append(*x*)	Add an item to the end of an existing list.
count(*x*)	Return the number of times the specified item appears in the list.
extend(*L*)	Extends a list by appending all of the items in the specified list.
index(*x*)	Return the index value of the specified item in the list.
insert(*i*, *x*)	Insert an item into the list at a specified location.
pop(*i*)	Remove an item from the specified index in the list. If no index is specified, removes the last item in the list.
remove(*x*)	Remove an item from an existing list.
reverse()	Reverses the items in the list.
sort()	Sorts the items in the list.

Here's a simple example of working with a list in Python:

```
$ cat test14.py
#!/usr/bin/python
# testing lists in Python
days = ["Monday," "Tuesday," "Wednesday," "Thursday," "Friday"]
print "Before:," days
print "I have practice on," days[2]
days.sort()
print "After:," days
$ ./test14.py
Before: ['Monday,' 'Tuesday,' 'Wednesday,' 'Thursday,' 'Friday']
I have practice on Wednesday
After: ['Friday,' 'Monday,' 'Thursday,' 'Tuesday,' 'Wednesday']
$
```

The sort() function sorts the data inside the list variable. Also, notice that you can quickly display the list contents just by using the print statement!

Tuples Variables

Tuples are almost identical to lists, except they are immutable. That means unlike a list, which you can change and modify any way you like, you cannot change a tuple. To create a tuple, just list the values separated by commas:

```
days = "Monday," "Tuesday," "Wednesday," "Thursday," "Friday"
```

Because tuples don't allow you change any of the values assigned to the tuple, there aren't any functions for altering the data contained in the tuple.

Dictionary Variables

Dictionaries are associative arrays, similar to hashes in Perl. They are a collection of objects or values arranged in key/value pairs. An example of a dictionary assignment is

```
favorites = {"fruit" : "banana," "vegetable" : "carrot" }
```

The dictionary elements can be referenced directly using the format:

```
favorites['fruit']
```

Secret

You can also use the special dict() function to assign a key/value tuple to a dictionary variable:

```
dict([('fruit,' 'banana'), ('vegetable,' 'carrot')])
```

This allows you to build separate tuples of key/value pairs and enter them into the dictionary variable as necessary.

Indentation in Structured Commands

Just like Perl, Python supports the standard structured commands you'd expect to use in your scripts, such as the if-then-else statement, while loop, and for loop. However, there's one little quirk about Python that may trip you up.

Every programming language has a way of organizing code so that it appears in readable chunks. Examples of these separators include whitespace, braces, and explicit line terminations (such as the semicolon in C). Python uses indents as a formal part of the language, and lines end with a hard return.

The rules on indentation are simple. Be consistent in how you indent. Use the same number of spaces to indent a block of code. If you need a statement that spans more than one line, use the backslash (\) to continue the line. Here's an example of Python's indentation rule at work:

```
$ cat test16.py
#!/usr/bin/python
# using structured commands
count = 1
factorial = 1
number = 5
while count <= number:
factorial = factorial * count
count = count + 1
print "The factorial of," number, "is," factorial
$ ./test16.py
The factorial of 5 is 120
$
```

Notice that the while loop doesn't use braces to define the code block. Instead, Python assumes the indented code is within the code block. Python's indentation rules may take a little getting used to if you're coming from another programming language such as Perl, but they will make your code more readable and thus easier to maintain.

Object-Oriented Programming

In Python, everything is an object. Each object has an identity, type, and a value, but also inherent properties and methods. You already saw this when using the sort ( ) method for the list variable. Instead of using a sort() function and having to assign the output to another variable, we use the sort() method by adding it to the end of the days list variable:

```
days.sort()
```

This feature is a fundamental cornerstone in *object-oriented programming*. Almost every object has some methods that it inherits that you can use.

You can also create your own objects with the class statement. User-defined classes can have class variables and class methods, which govern all instances of the class. Each instance of a class can, in turn, have its own instance variables that don't apply to other instances.

Python Command-Line Arguments

Passing command-line arguments to a Python program is slightly different from Perl. Because Python in a modularized language, it uses modules for everything, including how it interacts with the command line.

The sys module is required to interact with the system. It contains the argv array, which passes command-line arguments to the script. To use the sys module, you must import it into your code:

```
import sys
```

This is yet another feature of object-oriented programming, the ability to import additional features into your code.

Here's an example of using the argv array to process command-line arguments:

```
$ cat test17.py
#!/usr/bin/python
# determine if a specified year is a leap year
import operator, string, sys
if (len(sys.argv) == 2):
year = string.atoi(sys.argv[1], 10)
by4 = year % 4
by100 = year % 100
by400 = year % 400
if (operator.xor(by4 , operator.xor(by100, by400))):
print sys.argv[1] + " is not a leap year"
else:
print sys.argv[1] + " is a leap year"
else:
print "Sorry, you did not provide a year."
$ ./test17.py 2009
```

```
2009 is not a leap year
$ ./test17.py 2008
2008 is a leap year
$
```

As you can see from this example, Python is a little more complicated than Perl when using command-line arguments. The command-line argument is placed in the sys.argv array as element 1 (not 0 as in Perl). You might also notice that unlike Perl, Python is very specific about data types. The command-line arguments are all captured as string values.

Because the program needs to use the command-line argument as an integer value, it must be converted. The string module provides the atoi function, which converts ASCII strings to integer values. After assigning the new integer value to a variable, the calculations can begin.

However, in Python, special mathematical operators (such as the Boolean XOR) are also functions, and must be used as functions instead of operators. This requires importing the operators module and rewriting the if statements to use the xor() function.

Python Modules

All object-oriented programming languages include libraries that contain pre-built classes that are useful to programmers. The Python programming language is no different.

In Python, class libraries are called *modules.* A module contains classes and functions that can be called from within a Python script. The standard Python installation includes a library of standard modules that are built into the interpreter. To reference classes and functions from the module, you must define the module name within the script using the import command, as was demonstrated in the previous section.

Here is an example of using the SMTP module to easily send a mail message from your Python script:

```
$ cat test18.py
#!/usr/bin/python
# using the SMTP module to send mail
import smtplib, time

From = "rich"
To = "rich"
Subject = "Test mail from Python"
Date = time.ctime(time.time())
Header = ('From: %s\nTo: %s\nDate: %s\nSubject: %s\n\n'
% (From, To, Date, Subject))
Text = "This is a test message from my Python script"
server = smtplib.SMTP('localhost')
result = server.sendmail(From, To, Header + Text)
server.quit()
if result:
print "problem sending message"
else:
print "message successfully sent"
$ ./test18.py
```

```
message successfully sent
$ mail
Mail version 8.1.2 01/15/2001. Type ? for help.
"/var/mail/rich": 1 message 1 new
>N 1 rich@testbox.loca Fri Nov 7 06:56 15/553 Test mail from Python
&
Message 1:
From rich@testbox.localdomain Fri Nov 7 06:56:44 2008
X-Original-To: rich
From: rich@testbox.localdomain
To: rich@testbox.localdomain
Date: Fri Nov 7 06:56:43 2008
Subject: Test mail from Python

This is a test message from my Python script

&
```

This sample program imports two standard modules. The `smtplib` module provides SMTP functions, and the `time` module provides modules for getting the time from the system.

The script uses the SMTP Python module, which interfaces with the `mail` program on the local system to send the created message. If you do not have your mail system configured, this script won't work.

Besides the standard modules, there are a host of other modules available for just about any type of programming function. Scanning the Web for the term "Python modules" produces thousands of code modules freely available to incorporate into your own applications.

Summary

This chapter dove into the worlds of Perl and Python. The Perl scripting language has become a popular platform for system utilities, mostly because of its data-handling capabilities. Perl provides a simple way to scan data using regular expressions and easily manipulate the data however you need. The Ubuntu installation of Perl also uses the CPAN module, which allows Perl to connect with remote CPAN databases to update modules and load new modules to provide specific functionality to your system.

The Python scripting language provides an object-oriented programming approach to scripted languages. It references items as objects, and provides lots of methods to easily manipulate objects within the script. Similar to Perl, Python also uses modules to provide additional functionality to the core features.

The next chapter looks at a higher-level programming platform available in Ubuntu, the C programming language. The Linux platform has been built around the C programming language, and many Open Source programs and utilities require a C programming environment to install properly. We'll take a look at the C programming environment provided by Ubuntu, and see how to use the C programming language to build our own projects.

C Programming

Chapter 27

The Linux world revolves around the C programming language. Many programs and utilities (including the core of the operating system) are written using the C language and distributed as C source code programs under the open-source environment. Therefore, it's crucial for any Linux system to include a C programming environment, and Ubuntu is no different. This chapter first walks through the C programming environment provided by Ubuntu, showing you the steps required to compile open-source applications written in C. The last section in the chapter walks through the C programming language and shows how you can create your own applications to run on your Ubuntu system. If you already know how to compile C programs in Ubuntu, feel free to skip to the last section.

C Programming in Ubuntu

Unlike shell scripts, Perl scripts, or Python scripts, C programs must be *compiled* before you can run them on the Ubuntu system. The compiling process reads and processes the C program code and creates an *assembly language* program to run on the system. Assembly language is the low-level programming language that runs directly on the microprocessor chip installed in the workstation.

The GNU Compiler

The GNU Compiler Collection (gcc) is the most popular development system for UNIX systems. Not only is it the default compiler for Linux and most open-source BSD-based systems (such as FreeBSD and NetBSD), it is also popular on many commercial UNIX distributions as well.

gcc is capable of compiling many different high-level languages. At the time of this writing gcc could compile the following high-level languages:

- C
- C++
- Objective-C
- Fortran
- Java
- Ada

Not only does gcc provide a means for compiling C and C++ applications, it also provides the libraries necessary to run C and C++ applications on the system.

The GNU compiler can be invoked using several command-line formats, depending on the source code to compile and the underlying hardware of the operating system. The generic command-line format is

```
gcc [-c|-S|-E] [-std=standard]
[-g] [-pg] [-Olevel]
[-Wwarn…] [-pedantic]
[-Idir…] [-Ldir…]
[-Dmacro[=defn]…] [-Umacro]
[-foption…] [-mmachine-option…]
[-o outfile] [@file] infile…
```

The generic command-line parameters used in gcc are described in Table 27-1.

Table 27-1: The gcc Compiler Parameters

Parameter	Description
-c	Compile or assemble code, but do not link
-S	Stop after compiling, but do not assemble
-E	Stop after preprocessing, but do not compile
-o	Specify the output filename to use
-v	Display the commands used at each stage of compilation
-std	Specify the language standard to use
-g	Produce debugging information
-pg	Produce extra code used by gprof for profiling
-O	Optimize executable code
-W	Set compiler warning message level
-pedantic	Issue mandatory diagnostics listing in the C standard
-I	Specify directories for include files
-L	Specify directories for library files
-D	Predefine macros used in the source code
-U	Cancel any defined macros
-f	Specify options used to control the behavior of the compiler
-m	Specify hardware-dependant options

As you can see, there are lots of command-line parameters that you can use to control the behavior of gcc. In most cases, you'll need to use only a couple of parameters. To test the compiler on your Ubuntu system, let's create a simple C language program to compile. Just follow these steps:

1. Open a text editor to create the file ctest.c. You can use the gedit text editor on the Ubuntu workstation or the vim command-line editor on the Ubuntu server to create the file in your home folder. Don't use a word-processing program such as OpenOffice.org Writer to create the file. Word processors add extra, nontext data to the file, which will confuse the C compiler.

2. Enter the following code:
```
#include <stdio.h>
int main()
{
printf("My first C program!\n");
return(0);
}
```

3. Save the file. To compile the C program you'll need access to the command line—either a Terminal window in the graphical workstation environment or the command-line prompt in the server environment. Here's an example of compiling the program:

```
$ gcc -o ctest ctest.c
$ ls -al ctest
-rwxr-xr-x 1 rich rich 9041 2008-11-11 12:02 ctest
$ ./ctest
My first C program!
$
```

The gcc compiler creates an executable program file, called ctest, and assigns it the proper permissions to be executed. When you run the program, it produces the expected output on the console.

Secret

The -o parameter specifies the name of the output file created by the compiler. By default it creates a file called a.out, which isn't very descriptive.

One extremely useful command-line parameter in gcc is the -S parameter. This parameter generates the intermediate assembly language file created by the compiler, before the assembler assembles it. Here's a sample output using the -S parameter:

```
$ gcc -S ctest.c
$ cat ctest.s
.file "ctest.c"
.section .rodata
.LC0:
.string "My first C program!"
.text
.globl main
.type main, @function
main:
leal 4(%esp), %ecx
andl $-16, %esp
pushl -4(%ecx)
pushl %ebp
movl %esp, %ebp
pushl %ecx
subl $4, %esp
movl $.LC0, (%esp)
call puts
movl $0, %eax
addl $4, %esp
popl %ecx
popl %ebp
```

```
leal -4(%ecx), %esp
ret
.size main, .-main
.ident "GCC: (Ubuntu 4.3.2-1ubuntu11) 4.3.2"
.section .note.GNU-stack,"",@progbits
$
```

The ctest.s file shows how the compiler created the assembly language instructions to implement the C source code program. This is the actual low-level code that runs on the PC's microprocessor. Seeing this code is useful when trying to optimize C applications to determine how the compiler implements various C language functions in instruction code.

The GNU Assembler

When working with C language programs, you usually don't need to worry about the assembly language level of the code. However, if you get into any device driver work or try to optimize C programs, you may run into a situation where you need to use it.

The GNU assembler program (called gas) is the most popular assembler for the UNIX environment. Because an assembler program creates code intended to run directly on the system processor, each hardware platform requires its own version of gas. Currently, gas has the ability to assemble instruction codes from several hardware platforms, including

- ◆ VAX
- ◆ AMD 29K
- ◆ Hitachi H8/300
- ◆ Intel 80960
- ◆ M680x0
- ◆ SPARC
- ◆ Intel 80x86
- ◆ Z8000
- ◆ MIPS

The Ubuntu distribution bundles the correct gas package for the proper platform distribution.

The GNU assembler is a command line–oriented program. It should be run from a command-line prompt, with the appropriate command-line parameters. One oddity about the assembler is that, although it is called gas, the command-line executable program is called as.

The command-line parameters available for as vary, depending on the hardware platform used for the operating system. The command-line parameters common to all hardware platforms are

```
as [-a[cdhlns][=file]] [-D] [--defsym sym=val]
[-f] [--gstabs] [--gstabs+] [--gdwarf2] [--help]
[-I dir] [-J] [-K] [-L]
[--listing-lhs-width=NUM] [--listing-lhs-width2=NUM]
[--listing-rhs-width=NUM] [--listing-cont-lines=NUM]
[--keep-locals] [-o objfile] [-R] [--statistics] [-v]
[-version] [--version] [-W] [--warn] [--fatal-warnings]
[-w] [-x] [-Z] [--target-help] [target-options]
[--|files...]
```

These command-line parameters are explained in Table 27-2.

Table 27-2: The GNU Assembler Command-Line Parameters

Parameter	Description
-a	Specify which listings to include in the output
-D	Included for backward compatibility, but ignored
--defsym	Define symbol and value before assembling source code
-f	Fast assemble (skips comments and whitespace)
--gstabs	Include debugging information for each source code line
--gstabs+	Include special gdb debugging information
-I	Specify directories to search for include files
-J	Do not warn about signed overflows
-K	Included for backward compatibility, but ignored
-L	Keep local symbols in the symbol table
--listing-lhs-width	Set the maximum width of the output data column
--listing-lhs-width2	Set the maximum width of the output data column for continual lines
--listing-rhs-width	Set the maximum width of input source lines
--listing-cont-lines	Set maximum number of lines printed in a list for a single line of input
-o	Specify name of output object file
-R	Fold the data section into the text section
--statistics	Display the maximum space and total time used by assembly
-v	Display the version number of as
-W	Do not display warning messages
--	Use standard input for source files

The assembler creates an *object file.* The object file contains the operation codes (called OP codes) for the program but isn't yet in a format to run on the system. The object file must first be linked to any required system libraries (discussed next in the "The GNU Linker" section).

Let's walk through an example of assembling an assembly language program. First, you'll need to create a test assembly language program:

```
#cpuid.s Sample program to extract the processor Vendor ID
.section .data
output:
```

```
.ascii "The processor Vendor ID is 'xxxxxxxxxxxx'\n"
.section .text
.globl _start
_start:
movl $0, %eax
cpuid
movl $output, %edi
movl %ebx, 28(%edi)
movl %edx, 32(%edi)
movl %ecx, 36(%edi)
movl $4, %eax
movl $1, %ebx
movl $output, %ecx
movl $42, %edx
int $0x80
movl $1, %eax
movl $0, %ebx
int $0x80
```

Just create the file cpuid.s and save this code into it. Then assemble the code using the command:

```
$ as -o cpuid.o cpuid.s
$
```

That wasn't too exciting. That step simply creates an object file, ctest.o, containing the instruction codes for the assembly language program. If anything is wrong in the program, the assembler will let you know and identify the location of the problem in the source code:

```
$ as -o cpuid.o cpuid.s
cpuid.s: Assembler messages:
cpuid.s:16: Error: no such instruction: 'mpvl $output,%ecx'
$
```

The error message produced points out that the error was in line 16 and displays the text for that line.

Secret

One of the more confusing parts of the GNU assembler is the syntax it uses for representing assembly language code in the source code file. The original developers of gas chose to implement AT&T opcode syntax for the assembler.

The AT&T opcode syntax originated from AT&T Bell Labs, where the UNIX operating system was created. It was based on the opcode syntax of the popular processor chips used to implement UNIX operating systems at the time. Although many processor manufacturers used this format, Intel unfortunately chose to use a different opcode syntax.

Consequently, using gas to create assembly language programs for the Intel platform can be tricky. Most documentation for Intel assembly language programming uses the Intel syntax, while most documentation written for older UNIX systems uses AT&T syntax. This disparity can cause confusion and extra work for the gas programmer.

continues

continued

The differences between Intel and AT&T `syntax` **are as follows:**

- **AT&T immediate operands use a** `$` **to denote them, whereas Intel immediate operands are undelimited. Thus, to reference the decimal value 4 in AT&T syntax, you would use** `$4`**, but in Intel syntax you would use just** 4.
- **AT&T prefaces register names with a** `%`**, while Intel does not. Thus, to reference the EAX register in AT&T syntax, you would use** `%eax`.
- **AT&T syntax uses the opposite order for source and destination operands. To move the decimal value 4 to the EAX register, AT&T syntax would be** `mov $4, %eax`**, while for Intel it would be** `mov eax, 4`.
- **AT&T syntax uses a separate character at the end of mnemonics to reference the data size used in the operation. In Intel syntax the size is declared as a separate operand. The AT&T instruction** `movl $test, %eax` **is equivalent to** `mov eax, dword ptr test` **in Intel syntax.**
- **Long calls and jumps use a different syntax to define the segment and offset values. AT&T syntax uses** `ljmp $section, $offset`**, while Intel syntax uses** `jmp section:offset`.

These differences can make it difficult to switch between the two formats, but if you stick to one or the other you should be okay. If you learn assembly language coding using the AT&T syntax, you will be comfortable creating assembly language programs on almost any UNIX system available and on almost any hardware platform. If you plan to do cross-platform work between UNIX and Microsoft Windows systems, you may want to consider using Intel syntax for your applications.

The GNU assembler provides a method for using Intel syntax instead of AT&T syntax, but at the time of this writing it is clunky and mostly undocumented. The `.intel_syntax` **directive in an assembly language program tells** `as` **to assemble the instruction code mnemonics using Intel syntax instead of AT&T syntax. Unfortunately, there are still lots of limitations to this method. For example, even though the source and destination orders switch to Intel syntax, you must still prefix register names with the percent sign (as in AT&T syntax). Hopefully, some future version of** `as` **will support full Intel syntax assembly code.**

Once you've generated the object code file for the program, you can link it to create an executable file.

The GNU Linker

The GNU linker, `ld`, is used to link object code files into either executable program files or library files. The `ld` program is part of the GNU `binutils` package. If you already have the GNU assembler installed, the linker is most likely installed as well.

The format of the `ld` command is

```
ld [-o output] objfile…
[-Aarchitecture] [-b input-format] [-Bstatic]
[-Bdynamic] [-Bsymbolic] [-c commandfile] [--cref]
[-d|-dc|-dp]
```

```
[-defsym symbol=expression] [--demangle]
[--no-demangle] [-e entry] [-embedded-relocs] [-E]
[-export-dynamic] [-f name] [--auxiliary name]
[-F name] [--filter name] [-format input-format]
[-g] [-G size] [-h name] [-soname name] [--help]
[-i] [-lar] [-Lsearchdir] [-M] [-Map mapfile]
[-m emulation] [-n|-N] [-noinhibit-exec]
[-no-keep-memory] [-no-warn-mismatch] [-Olevel]
[-oformat output-format] [-R filename] [-relax]
[-r|-Ur] [-rpath directory] [-rpath-link directory]
[-S] [-s] [-shared] [-sort-common]
[-split-by-reloc count] [-split-by-file]
[-T commandfile]
[--section-start sectionname=sectionorg]
[-Ttext textorg] [-Tdata dataorg] [-Tbss bssorg]
[-t] [-u sym] [-V] [-v] [--verbose] [--version]
[-warn-common] [-warn-constructors]
[-warn-multiple-gp] [-warn-once]
[-warn-section-align] [--whole-archive]
[--no-whole-archive] [--wrap symbol] [-X] [-x]
```

Although that looks like a lot of command-line parameters, in reality you should not have to use very many of them at any one time. The example just shows that the GNU linker is an extremely versatile program and has many different capabilities. Table 27-3 describes the command-line parameters that are used for the Intel platform.

Table 27-3: The GNU Linker Command-Line Parameters

Parameter	Description
-b	Specify the format of the object code input files
-Bstatic	Use only static libraries
-Bdynamic	Use only dynamic libraries
-Bsymbolic	Bind references to global symbols in shared libraries
-c	Read commands from the specified command file
--cref	Create a cross-reference table
-d	Assign space to common symbols even if relocatable output is specified
-defsym	Create the specified global symbol in the output file
--demangle	Demangle symbol names in error messages
-e	Use the specified symbol as the beginning execution point of the program
-E	For ELF-format files, add all symbols to the dynamic symbol table
-f	For ELF-format shared objects, set the DT_AUXILIARY name

continues

Table 27-3: *(continued)*

Parameter	Description
-F	For ELF-format shared objects, set the DT_FILTER name
-format	Specify the format of the object code input files (same as -b)
-g	Ignored. Used for compatibility with other tools
-h	For-ELF format shared objects, set the DT_SONAME name
-i	Perform an incremental link
-l	Add the specified archive file to the list of files to link
-L	Add the specified path to the list of directories to search for libraries
-M	Display a link map for diagnostic purposes
-Map	Create the specified file to contain the link map
-m	Emulate the specified linker
-N	Specify read/write text and data sections
-n	Set the text section to be read-only
-noinhibit-exec	Produce an output file even if nonfatal link errors appear
-no-keep-memory	Optimize link for memory usage
-no-warn-mismatch	Allow linking mismatched object files
-O	Generate optimized output files
-o	Specify the name of the output file
-oformat	Specify the binary format of the output file
-R	Read symbol names and addresses from the specified filename
-r	Generate relocatable output (called partial linking)
-rpath	Add the specified directory to the runtime library search path
-rpath-link	Specify a directory to search for runtime shared libraries
-S	Omit debugger symbol information from the output file
-s	Omit all symbol information from the output file
-shared	Create a shared library
-sort-common	Do not sort symbols by size in output file
-split-by-reloc	Create extra sections in the output file based on the specified size
-split-by-file	Create extra sections in the output file for each object file
--section-start	Locate the specified section in the output file at the specified address

Table 27-3: *(continued)*

Parameter	Description
-T	Specify a command file (same as -c)
-Ttext	Use the specified address as the starting point for the text section
-Tdata	Use the specified address as the starting point for the data section
-Tbss	Use the specified address as the starting point for the bss section
-t	Display the names of the input files as they are being processed
-u	Force the specified symbol to be in the output file as an undefined symbol
-warn-common	Warn when a common symbol is combined with another common symbol
-warn-constructors	Warn if any global constructors are used
-warn-once	Warn only once for each undefined symbol
-warn-section-align	Warn if the output section address is changed due to alignment
--whole-archive	For the specified archive files, include all of the files in the archive
-X	Delete all local temporary symbols
-x	Delete all local symbols

For the simplest case, to create an executable file from an object file generated from the assembler you would use the command:

```
ld -o cpuid cpuid.o
```

This command creates the executable file cpuid from the object code file cpuid.o. The executable file is created with the proper permissions so that it can be run from the command line in a command-line prompt. Here's an example of the process:

```
$ld -o cpuid cpuid.o
$ ls -al cpuid
-rwxr-xr-x 1 rich rich 663 2008-11-13 19:53 cpuid
$ ./cpuid
The processor Vendor ID is 'GenuineIntel'
$
```

The linker automatically created the executable file, allowing anyone on the system to execute it but only the owner to modify it.

The GNU Debugger Program

Many professional programmers use the GNU debugger program (gdb) to debug and troubleshoot C and C++ applications. What you may not know is that it can also be used to debug assembly language programs as well. This section describes the gdb package and how to use it to troubleshoot your own C, C++, and assembly language programs.

The debugger is also used by the system to provide troubleshooting information for standard programs that crash while running on the system. You can use that information to determine where in the program the application crashed.

gdb can be run with several different parameters to modify its behavior. The command-line format for gdb is

```
gdb [-nx] [-q] [-batch] [-cd=dir] [-f] [-b bps] [-tty=dev]
[-s symfile] [-e prog] [-se prog] [-c core] [-x cmds] [-d dir]
[prog[core|procID]]
```

The command-line parameters are described in Table 27-3.

Table 27-3: The gdb Command-Line Parameters

Parameter	Description
-b	Set the line speed of serial interface for remote debugging
-batch	Run in batch mode
-c	Specify the core dump file to analyze
-cd	Specify the working directory
-d	Specify a directory to search for source files
-e	Specify the file to execute
-f	Output filename and line numbers in standard format when debugging
-nx	Do not execute commands from .gdbinit file
-q	Run in quiet mode (don't print introduction)
-s	Specify filename for symbols
-se	Specify filename for symbols and to execute
-tty	Set device for standard input and output
-x	Execute gdb commands from the specified file

To use the debugger, the executable file must have been compiled or assembled with the -gstabs option, which includes the necessary information in the executable file for the debugger to know where in the source code file the instruction codes relate. Once gdb starts, it uses a command-line interface to accept debugging commands:

```
$ gcc -gstabs -o ctest ctest.c
$ gdb ctest
GNU gdb 6.8-debian
Copyright (C) 2008 Free Software Foundation, Inc.
License GPLv3+: GNU GPL version 3 or later <http://gnu.org/licenses/gpl.html>
This is free software: you are free to change and redistribute it.
There is NO WARRANTY, to the extent permitted by law. Type "show copying"
```

and "show warranty" for details.
This GDB was configured as "i486-linux-gnu"…
(gdb)

At the (gdb) command prompt you can enter debugging commands. An extensive number of commands can be used. Some of the more useful ones are shown in Table 27-4.

Table 27-4: The gdb Commands

Command	Description
break	Set a breakpoint in the source code to stop execution
watch	Set a watchpoint to stop execution when a variable reaches a specific value
info	Observe system elements, such as registers, the stack, and memory
x	Examine memory location
print	Display variable values
run	Start execution of the program within the debugger
list	List specified functions or lines
next	Step to the next instruction in the program
until	Run the program until it reaches the specified source code line (or greater)

Here's a short example of a gdb session:

```
(gdb) list
1 #include <stdio.h>
2 int main()
3 {
4 printf("My first C program!\n");
5 return(0);
6 }
(gdb) break main
Breakpoint 1 at 0x80483d5: file ctest.c, line 4.
(gdb) run
Starting program: /home/rich/ctest

Breakpoint 1, main () at ctest.c:4
4 printf("My first C program!\n");
(gdb) next
My first C program!
5 return(0);
(gdb) next
6 }
(gdb) next
0xb7e22685 in __libc_start_main () from /lib/tls/i686/cmov/libc.so.6
(gdb) next
Single stepping until exit from function __libc_start_main,
```

```
which has no line number information.

Program exited normally.
(gdb) quit
$
```

First, the list command was used to show the source code line numbers. Next, a breakpoint is created at the main label using the break command, and the program is started with the run command.

Because the breakpoint was set to main, the program immediately stops running before the first source code statement after main. The next command is used to step to the next line of source code, which executes the printf statement in the C code. Another next command is used to execute the return statement in the C code, which terminates the application. Although the application terminated, you are still in the debugger and can run the program again.

The GNU objdump Program

The GNU objdump program is another utility found in the binutils package that can be of great use to programmers. Often it is necessary to view the instruction codes generated by the compiler in the object code files. The objdump program will display not only the assembly language code but the raw instruction codes generated as well.

This section describes the objdump program and how it is used to view the underlying instruction codes within a high-level language program.

Using objdump

The objdump command-line parameters specify functions the program will perform on the object code files and how it will display the information it retrieves. The command-line format of objdump is

```
objdump [-a|--archive-headers] [-b bfdname|--target=bfdname]
[-C|--demangle[=style] ] [-d|--disassemble]
[-D|--disassemble-all] [-z|--disassemble-zeroes]
[-EB|-EL|--endian={big | little }] [-f|--file-headers]
[--file-start-context] [-g|--debugging]
[-e|--debugging-tags] [-h|--section-headers|--headers]
[-i|--info] [-j section|--section=section]
[-l|--line-numbers] [-S|--source]
[-m machine|--architecture=machine]
[-M options|--disassembler-options=options]
[-p|--private-headers] [-r|--reloc]
[-R|--dynamic-reloc] [-s|--full-contents]
[-G|--stabs] [-t|--syms] [-T|--dynamic-syms]
[-x|--all-headers] [-w|--wide]
[--start-address=address] [--stop-address=address]
[--prefix-addresses] [--[no-]show-raw-insn]
[--adjust-vma=offset] [-V|--version] [-H|--help]
objfile…
```

The command-line parameters are described in Table 27-5.

Table 27-5: The objdump Parameters

Parameter	Description
-a	If any files are archives, display the archive header information
-b	Specify the object code format of the object code files
-C	Demangle low-level symbols into user-level names
-d	Disassemble the object code into instruction code
-D	Disassemble all sections into instruction code, including data
-EB	Specify big-endian object files
-EL	Specify little-endian object files
-f	Display summary information from the header of each file
-G	Display the contents of the debug sections
-h	Display summary information from the section headers of each file
-i	Display list showing all architectures and object formats
-j	Display information for the specified section only
-l	Label the output with source code line numbers
-m	Specify the architecture to use when disassembling
-p	Display information specific to the object file format
-r	Display the relocation entries in the file
-R	Display the dynamic relocation entries in the file
-s	Display the full contents of the specified sections
-S	Display source code intermixes with disassembled code
-t	Display the symbol table entries of the files
-T	Display the dynamic symbol table entries of the files
-x	Display all available header information of the files
--start-address	Start displaying data at the specified address
--stop-address	Stop displaying data at the specified address

The objdump program is an extremely versatile tool to have available. It can decode many different types of binary files besides object code files. For the C programmer, the -d parameter is the most useful because it displays the disassembled object code file.

An objdump Example

Using the sample C program, you can create an object file to dump by compiling the program with the -c option:

```
$ gcc -c ctest.c
```

This creates an *object file*. The object file contains the raw assembly language code that the program generates, before being linked into a system application file. At this point you can use the objdump program to peek at the raw assembly language code generated by the C program:

```
$ objdump -d ctest.o

ctest.o: file format elf32-i386


Disassembly of section .text:

00000000 <main>:
0: 8d 4c 24 04 lea 0x4(%esp),%ecx
4: 83 e4 f0 and $0xfffffff0,%esp
7: ff 71 fc pushl -0x4(%ecx)
a: 55 push %ebp
b: 89 e5 mov %esp,%ebp
d: 51 push %ecx
e: 83 ec 04 sub $0x4,%esp
11: c7 04 24 00 00 00 00 movl $0x0,(%esp)
18: e8 fc ff ff ff call 19 <main+0x19>
1d: b8 00 00 00 00 mov $0x0,%eax
22: 83 c4 04 add $0x4,%esp
25: 59 pop %ecx
26: 5d pop %ebp
27: 8d 61 fc lea -0x4(%ecx),%esp
2a: c3 ret
$
```

The disassembled object code file shows the assembly language mnemonics created by the compiler and the corresponding instruction codes. You may notice, however, that the memory addresses referenced in the program are zeroed out. These values will not be determined until the linker links the application and prepares it for execution on the system. In this step of the process, though, you can easily see the instructions used to perform the functions.

The GNU Profiler Program

The GNU profiler (gprof) is another program included in the binutils package. This program is used to analyze program execution and determine where "hot spots" are in the application.

Application hot spots are functions that require the most amount of processing time as the program runs. Often they are the most mathematically intensive functions, but that is not always the case. Functions that are I/O intensive can also increase processing time.

This section describes the GNU profiler and demonstrates how it is used in a C program to view how much time different functions consume in an application.

Using the Profiler

As with all the other tools, gprof is a command-line program that uses multiple parameters to control its behavior. The command-line format for gprof is

```
gprof [ -[abcDhilLsTvwxyz] ] [ -[ACeEfFJnNOpPqQZ][name] ]
[ -I dirs ] [ -d[num] ] [ -k from/to ]
[ -m min-count ] [ -t table-length ]
[ --[no-]annotated-source[=name] ]
[ --[no-]exec-counts[=name] ]
[ --[no-]flat-profile[=name] ] [ --[no-]graph[=name] ]
[ --[no-]time=name] [ --all-lines ] [ --brief ]
[ --debug[=level] ] [ --function-ordering ]
[ --file-ordering ] [ --directory-path=dirs ]
[ --display-unused-functions ] [ --file-format=name ]
[ --file-info ] [ --help ] [ --line ] [ --min-count=n ]
[ --no-static ] [ --print-path ] [ --separate-files ]
[ --static-call-graph ] [ --sum ] [ --table-length=len ]
[ --traditional ] [ --version ] [ --width=n ]
[ --ignore-non-functions ] [ --demangle[=STYLE] ]
[ --no-demangle ] [ image-file ] [ profile-file…]
```

This alphabet soup of parameters is split into three groups:

- Output format parameters
- Analysis parameters
- Miscellaneous parameters

The output format options allow you to modify the output produced by gprof. These options are shown in Table 27-6.

Table 27-6: The gprof Output Format Options

Parameter	Description
-A	Display source code for all functions or for only the functions specified
-b	Do not display verbose output explaining the analysis fields
-C	Display total tally of all functions or for only the functions specified
-i	Display summary information about the profile data file
-I	Specify list of search directories to find source files
-J	Do not display annotated source code
-L	Display full pathnames of source filenames
-p	Display flat profile for all functions or for only the functions specified
-P	Suppress printing of flat profile for all functions or for only the functions specified

continues

Table 27-6: *(continued)*

Parameter	Description
-q	Display the call graph analysis
-Q	Do not display the call graph analysis
-y	Generate annotated source code as separate output files
-Z	Do not display total tally of functions and number of times called
--function-reordering	Display suggested reordering of functions based on analysis
--file-ordering	Display suggested object file reordering based on analysis
-T	Display output in traditional BSD style
-w	Set width of output lines
-x	Display every line in annotated source code within a function
--demangle	Demangle C++ symbols when displaying output

The analysis parameters modify the way gprof analyzes the data contained in the analysis file. These parameters are shown in Table 27-7.

Table 27-7: The gprof Analysis Parameters

Parameter	Description
-a	Do not analyze information about statistically declared (private) functions
-c	Analyze information on child functions that were never called in the program
-D	Ignore symbols that are not known to be functions (only on Solaris and HP OSs)
-k	Do not analyze functions matching a beginning and ending symspec
-l	Analyze the program by line instead of function
-m	Analyze only those functions called more than a specified number of times
-n	Analyze only the times for specified functions
-N	Do not analyze times for specified functions
-z	Analyze all functions, even those that were never called

Finally, the miscellaneous parameters modify the behavior of gprof but don't fit into the output or analysis groups. The miscellaneous parameters are described in Table 27-8.

Table 27-8: The gprof Miscellaneous Parameters

Parameter	Description
-d	Put gprof in debug mode, specifying a numerical debug level
-0	Specify the format of the profile data file
-s	Force gprof to summarize only the data in the profile data file
-v	Print the version of gprof

To be able to use gprof on an application, you must ensure that the functions you want to monitor are compiled using the -pg parameter in the gcc program. This parameter compiles the source code, inserting a call to the mcount subroutine for each function in the program. When the application is run, the mcount subroutine creates a call graph profile file, called gmon.out, which contains timing information for each function in the application.

Secret

Be careful when running the application, because each run will overwrite the gmon.out file. If you want to take multiple samples, you must temporarily rename the gmon.out files but then change them back when you are ready to run gprof.

After the test program finishes, the gprof program is used to examine the call graph profile file to analyze the time spent in each function. The gprof output contains three reports:

- ◆ A flat profile report, which lists total execution times and call counts for all functions
- ◆ A list of functions sorted by the time spent in each function and its children
- ◆ A list of cycles, showing the members of the cycles and their call counts

By default the gprof output is directed to the standard output of the console. You must redirect it to a file if you want to save it.

A Profile Example

To use the gprof program, you must have a high-level language program that uses functions to perform actions. I created a simple demonstration program in C, called demo.c, to demonstrate the basics of gprof:

```
#include <stdio.h>

void function1()
{
int i, j;
for(i=0; i <100000; i++)
```

```
j += i;
}
void function2()
{
int i, j;
function1();
for(i=0; i < 200000; i++)
j = i;
}

int main()
{
int i, j;
for (i = 0; i <100; i++)
function1();

for(i = 0; i<50000; i++)
function2();
}
```

This is about as simple as it gets. The main program has two loops—one that calls `function1()` 100 times and one that calls `function2()` 50,000 times. Each of the functions performs only simple loops, although `function2()` also calls `function1()` every time it is called.

The next step is to compile the program using the `-pg` parameter for `gprof`. After that the program can be run:

```
$ gcc -o demo demo.c -pg
$ ./demo
$
```

When the program finishes, the `gmon.out` call graph profile file is created in the same directory. You can then run the `gprof` program against the `demo` program and save the output to a file:

```
$ ls -al gmon.out
-rw-r--r-- 1 rich rich 440 2008-11-11 12:39 gmon.out
$ gprof demo > gprof.txt
$
```

Notice that the name of the executable program was referenced in the command line, but the `gmon.out` file was not. The `gprof` program automatically uses the `gmon.out` file located in the same directory.

This example redirects the output from the `gprof` program to a file named `gprof.txt`. The resulting file contains the complete `gprof` report for the program. You can view that file in any text editor. Here's what the flat profile section looked like on my system:

```
% cumulative self self total
time seconds seconds calls us/call us/call name
67.02 22.78 22.78 50000 455.60 679.35 function2
32.98 33.99 11.21 50100 233.75 233.75 function1
```

This report shows the total processor time and times called for each individual function that was called by `main`. As expected, `function2` took the majority of the processing time.

The next report is the call *graph*, which shows the breakdown of time by individual functions and how the functions were called:

```
index % time self children called name
<spontaneous>
[1] 100.0 0.00 33.99 main [1]
22.78 11.19 50000/50000 function2 [2]
0.02 0.00 100/50100 function1 [3]
-------------------------------------------------
22.78 11.19 50000/50000 main [1]
[2] 99.9 22.78 11.19 50000 function2 [2]
11.19 0.00 50000/50100 function1 [3]
-------------------------------------------------
0.02 0.00 100/50100 main [1]
11.19 0.00 50000/50100 function2 [2]
[3] 33.0 11.21 0.00 50100 function1 [3]
-------------------------------------------------
```

Each section of the call graph shows the function analyzed (the one on the line with the index number), the functions that called it, and its child functions. This output is used to see the flow of time throughout the program.

Writing C Programs

With a full C programming environment pre-installed on your Ubuntu system, you're ready to start coding C programs. This section walks through the basics of programming in C.

C Program Format

Possibly one of the most confusing parts of C programming is the precise format used in creating C programs. The C language is picky about how it handles things. There are generally three sections in a C program:

♦ Headers section
♦ Declaration section
♦ Code section

The content of each of these sections is described in the following sections.

Header Section

In the headers section, variables and functions used in external libraries are declared in *header files*. The files are separate from the main program and must be declared so that the compiler knows where to get them. Standard library header files are specified in the format:

```
#include <library>
```

where library is the header file name (usually with a .h extension). If your code uses any of the standard input and output functions, you'll need to define the stdio.h header file in your C program:

```
#include <stdio.h>
```

Alternatively, if you create your own functions, they should have their own header files, which may be located in the same folder as the main program code. The format to declare that file is

```
#include "local.h"
```

where local.h is the name of the local function header file.

Declaration Section

The declaration section defines all of the variables and functions used in the program. In the C language, you must declare the data type of a variable, and the variable can hold only that type of data for the entire program. C supports many types of data. Table 27-9 lists the basic data types you can use in your programs.

Table 27-9: The C Language Basic Data Types

Parameter	Description
int	Integer value (32 bits)
float	Floating-point, single-precision value (32 bits)
double	Floating-point, double-precision value (64 bits)
char	A single character value (8 bits)
void	No data

Besides the data types there are also *modifiers*, which define the storage allocated for a specific data type. There isn't a set standard on the amount of storage used when modifiers are defined, but generally they're

- ◆ **Short:** Half of the normal size, so a short int value is 16 bits
- ◆ **Long:** Double the normal size, so a long int value is 64 bits
- ◆ **Signed:** Contains negative and positive values; a signed int value can have a value between −32,768 and +32,767
- ◆ **Unsigned:** Contains only positive values; a signed int value can have a value between 0 and 65,535

Secret

With the popularity of 64-bit computing platforms, the base size of data types is changing. While some data types double in size (such as int and float) others stay the same (such as char).

The declaration section declares a data type, a variable name, and an optional default variable value:

```
int counter;
float price = 0.00;
char data;
```

Each variable declaration remains in effect for the entire program. In the C language, once you declare the data type of a variable you can't store data from other data types in that variable.

Code Section

The C program itself is defined as a code block enclosed in braces. The code block must have a name and a declared data type. There can be any number of code blocks defined in a single C program file. Each code block must have a unique name assigned to it.

The starting code block in every C program is called *main*. That's how the compiler knows where to start the program. You must also declare a *return data type* for each code block. This is the type of data that's expected to be returned when the code block completes.

The main code block must return an integer data type to the operating system. The operating system will then pass the return value to the shell so that you can tell whether your program terminated properly.

The general format for the code block is

```
int main()
{
local variables

code
}
```

Inside the code block you can also declare additional variables. These are called *local variables*, and they are available for use only inside the code block. Any variables declared in the declaration section are considered *global variables* and can be used in any of the code blocks in the program.

Secret

Be careful when creating C programs on your Ubuntu system. The program file must be a plain text file, without any formatting code. Most word-processing programs (such as the OpenOffice.org Writer program) add binary formatting codes to the text file, which will confuse the C compiler. It's best to use the Ubuntu gedit text editor to create your C program files, and make sure that you save them with the .c file extension.

Sample Program

The easiest way to see the C programming language work is to create an example. Follow these steps to create and run a sample C program on your system:

1. Open a text editor and create the file factorial.c. You can use either the gedit program from the workstation graphical environment or the vim editor from the server command-line environment.

2. Enter the following code into the file:

```
#include <stdio.h>

int counter;
int factorial = 1;
int number;

int main(int argc, char** argv)
{
number = atoi(argv[1]);

for (counter = 1; counter <= number; counter++)
{
factorial = factorial * counter;
}
printf("The factorial of %d is %d\n," number, factorial);
return(0);
}
```

3. Save the file, and exit the editor.

4. Compile the new C program using the gcc command-line command:

```
$ gcc -o factorial factorial.c
```

The newly created program, factorial, should appear in your folder. This program uses a single command-line parameter to specify the number to calculate the factorial for. The main() function retrieves any command-line parameters and places them in the character array argv. The code then uses the atoi() function to convert the command-line parameter to an integer value, then uses a for-loop to iterate through the values, multiplying each value to obtain the factorial value.

The printf() function is the standard way to send output from a C program. It uses template format codes to define the data type of the variables displayed. Each variable is matched in order as the format codes appear in the template.

Running the program produces the factorial:

```
$ ./factorial 5
The factorial of 5 is 120
$ ./factorial 3
The factorial of 3 is 6
$ ./factorial 7
The factorial of 7 is 5040
$
```

The code calculates the factorials and displays the results on the command line.

Summary

This chapter walked through the C programming environment supported by Ubuntu. Because the C programming language is a crucial element in the Linux world, Ubuntu includes all of the utilities required to compile C programs by default. These utilities include the gcc compiler, the as assembly language assembler, and the ld linker. Besides these basic tools for creating C programs, Ubuntu also includes a few utilities that are useful in the C programming environment. The gdb debugger can help debug difficult programs. The gprof program is crucial for finding performance bottlenecks in C programs, and the objdump program is helpful in altering assembly language–level code to help improve performance.

The next chapter walks through the Java environment in Ubuntu. Although the C programming language is part of the default Ubuntu setup, the Java environment isn't. The chapter will walk you through getting a Java development environment set up in Ubuntu, as well as walk through the basics of the Java programming language.

Java

Chapter
28

◆ ◆

Secrets in This Chapter

The Ubuntu Java Environment

Running Java Programs

Using Java IDE Packages in Ubuntu

◆ ◆

This chapter takes a look at the Java environment in Ubuntu. Unfortunately, there is some controversy with Java in Ubuntu, mostly because of open-source problems and licensing restrictions. Consequently, there are multiple ways to implement a Java development environment in Ubuntu. This chapter walks you through the controversy and shows you how to implement an open-source solution for a complete graphical Java development environment on your Ubuntu workstation.

The Java Development Environment

The Java programming language has become a popular tool for developers who need to make applications work in environments that support multiple operating system platforms. Instead of having a different version of an application for each operating system platform, you can create Java programs on one platform (such as Ubuntu), then run them on a completely different platform (such as Microsoft Windows workstations), usually with no modifications or problems.

Because of its versatility, the Java programming language has been used in many types of programming environments, from standalone workstation applications to dynamic web programming. This section describes the different ways you can use the Java programming language and discusses the different development environments available for creating your Java programs.

Java Programs

Part of the confusion over Java is trying to define just what type of Java application you're talking about when you mention a Java development environment. There are four basic types of Java programs that you may run into on the Ubuntu environment:

- ◆ **Applications:** Standalone, text-based console or graphical windows applications that can run on any system
- ◆ **Applets:** Web-based applications that load via a web browser on a client workstation
- ◆ **Java ServerPages (JSP):** Web-based applications that run on a web server and produce output that's sent by the server to the client's browser, usually mixed with HTML code
- ◆ **Java servlets:** Compiled JSP applications that run more quickly on a web server and produce output that's sent by the server to the client's browser.

Java applications are portable, in that the same compiled Java application can run on any *Java virtual machine* (JVM) on any computer platform. Each computer platform utilizes a specialized JVM program that interprets the compiled Java code and converts the code into executable code for the specific host platform.

Java applets are stored on a host web server and downloaded as part of a web page by a client browser. Once downloaded, the applets are run inside a Java environment in the client browser. The client browser must contain a JVM plug-in to interpret and run the applet code. All of the popular web browsers include JVM support, including Firefox on the Ubuntu workstation (see Chapter 8, "Network Applications").

JSP programs are also stored on a host web server as part of a web application but are processed by the host web server instead of being downloaded to the client. This server-side processing allows you to create dynamic web pages directly on the server that can alter the appearance of the web page as the data change, without having to alter any

HTML code. This is a popular method of interacting with database servers to extract data from tables to produce in a web page.

Output from the JSP code is directed to the client browser, just like the HTML code. This allows you to output HTML code directly from your JSP programs.

Java servlets are JSP files that have been compiled and bundled together into an application so that they run faster on the host web server. Java servlets use a special Java library method to combine the servlets into a single distribution file for the server.

Secret Don't confuse the popular JavaScript client-side scripting language with real Java. JavaScript is a web-based scripting language used to interact with the web browser in a real-time environment, providing fancy features such as animated drop-down menus, clickable directory trees, and real-time error checking in form fields. The JavaScript language is not part of the Sun Microsystems Java specifications.

Platforms

Although Java technology is relatively new to the programming world, it has already matured into a full-blown programming environment. There are three types of Java programming platforms to choose from:

- **J2SE:** Java 2 Standard Edition, for developing workstation and server applications and applets
- **J2EE:** Java 2 Enterprise Edition, for developing server-side JSP and Java servlet web applications
- **J2ME:** Java 2 Micro Edition, for developing mobile device applications

The Java Runtime Edition (JRE) package is not a development platform, but it must be loaded on a system for Java applications to execute. It provides the JVM core libraries required for Java applications (both desktop and web based) to execute. There are different versions of the JRE for each operating system platform. Once you compile a Java application you can run it on any JVM on any operating system platform without having to recompile it for other operating systems.

You can't develop new applications with just the JRE, though. To develop Java applications you must have the J2SE, J2EE, or J2ME software packages installed. All three of these environments include the Java compiler for creating Java applications, along with the standard Java library files for their specific programming environments.

All of these development environments support interacting with databases using the Java Database Connectivity (JDBC) library for connecting to database servers running on your Ubuntu server (see Chapter 24, "Database Server").

JDBC is the Java layer that allows Java applications to connect and interact with any database. JDBC is a standard interface for all Java applications—you use the same database functions to interact with any type of database. Database vendors must supply a compatible JDBC library file so that Java applications can interface with their individual database products. Java programmers write code that interfaces with the JDBC to access the database server. This code can then be used to access any database that provides a JDBC driver. This is demonstrated in Figure 28-1.

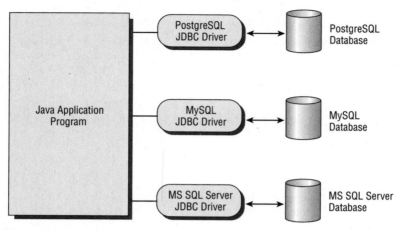

Figure 28-1: The Java JDBC environment.

After connecting to the database using JDBC, the Java application can access tables and data using standard JDBC methods and properties. These methods and properties remain consistent for all databases using the JDBC driver.

To develop Java applications in Ubuntu you must have the appropriate J2SE, J2EE, or J2ME development environment installed. This is discussed in the next section.

Ubuntu Java Environments

The Java programming language was created and is currently supported by Sun Microsystems, Inc. Sun provides free versions of all the Java development environments for use in just about any operating system you can imagine, including Linux. However, there's one sticking point.

In the past, Sun Microsystems, while allowing free download and use of the Java binary development software packages, has kept the source code for the Java programming language closed. This has prevented Java from being classified as an open-source language, even though it's free to use on any system.

Due to the licensing restrictions, open-source purists have objected to using the Sun Microsystems Java development packages in Linux distributions. Coders have worked on reverse engineering the Java specifications, and there are now alternatives for Linux that provide a Java development environment that don't use the official Sun Microsystems Java:

+ **GNU Classpath:** A basic Java J2SE compiler based on the GNU gcc C compiler
+ **OpenJDK:** An open-source J2SE and J2ME implementation of Java supported by Sun Microsystems
+ **IcedTea:** A specialized version of OpenJDK built for Red Hat systems, which also includes other development tools

♦ **Tomcat:** The Apache Foundation's J2EE application server platform, which also supports JSP and Java Servlets

♦ **Blackdown Java:** The original Linux reverse engineering port of Sun Microsystems' Java J2SE that's no longer maintained but still available for use

If you're doing any development work for the J2EE environment, the best way to install a development environment is to use the Ubuntu server's default Tomcat package installation (see Chapter 21, "Web Server"). This installs the complete Tomcat J2EE package, which allows you to develop Java applications and applets, as well as develop JavaServer Pages (JSP) and Java servlets.

If you're doing development work with just Java applications or applets, the most popular Java J2SE development environment for the Linux platform (including Ubuntu) is the OpenJDK implementation. The following section walks through installing OpenJDK and discusses the components of the package.

Secret

When downloading the Sun Java development packages, make sure that you download the Java Development Kit (JDK) packages, and not just the JRE package. Select the Linux platform, and choose the non-rpm packages. For example, the current J2SE JDK package for Linux is called `jdk-6u10-linux-i586.bin`.

The JDK installation file is a binary, self-extracting executable file. You'll first need to give yourself execute privileges to the file, then you can run it to extract the installation program:

```
$ chmod u+x jdk-6u10-linux-i586.bin
$ ./jdk-6u10-linux-i586.bin
```

Once you extract the contents of the JDK package, follow the included instructions for installing it on your Ubuntu system. Remember, though, once you install the Sun installation packages they will not be part of the Ubuntu Synaptic installed software database, so they won't be automatically upgraded by Ubuntu. It's up to you to install patches and upgrades to the Sun software packages.

Using OpenJDK

The OpenJDK project is an initiative by Sun Microsystems to provide an open-source version of the Java development platform. Although technically a separate project from the standard Sun Microsystems Java packages, OpenJDK's main contributor is Sun, which provides technical support and the source code for the OpenJDK development packages. For all practical purposes the OpenJDK packages are equivalent to the corresponding standard Sun Microsystems Java packages.

The Ubuntu software repositories contain the OpenJDK software packages for both the JRE and J2SE environments. You can install the JRE package if you need to run Java applications on your system without having to do any development work.

If you want to do Java development work in Ubuntu you'll need to install the OpenJDK J2SE package from the Ubuntu repository. The following sections explain the installation process and discuss the software available in the package.

Installing OpenJDK

You can install the OpenJDK J2SE development package directly from the Synaptic Package Manager program on your Ubuntu workstation or from the apt-get installer program on your Ubuntu server.

To install the complete OpenJDK package, follow these steps:

1. Open the Synaptic Package Manager application. On the Ubuntu workstation, select System ➪ Administration ➪ Synaptic Package Manager from the Panel menu.

2. Enter *openjdk* in the search textbox. This displays only the OpenJDK packages in the package list.

3. Mark the `openjdk-6-jdk` package for installation. Be careful, because Synaptic also includes the OpenJDK JRE package for running Java applications. That package doesn't install the development environment, just a JVM for running Java applications.

4. Click the Apply button at the top of the page.

5. Click the OK button to install any dependencies required for the `openjdk-6-jdk` package.

6. Close the Synaptic Package Manager.

Once you install the OpenJDK Java package it's available for use on your Ubuntu system. To test the installation, open a Terminal window from the workstation or use the command-line prompt from the server and enter the `java` and `javac` command-line programs with the `-version` parameter:

```
$ java -version
java version "1.6.0_0"
IcedTea6 1.3.1 (6b12-0ubuntu6) Runtime Environment (build 1.6.0_0-b12)
OpenJDK Client VM (build 1.6.0_0-b12, mixed mode, sharing)
$ javac -version
javac 1.6.0_0-internal
$
```

Both the `java` and `javac` command-line programs indicate that the OpenJDK 1.6.0 environment is installed. You're ready to start your Java development work! In the next section we'll take a look at what the OpenJDK package provides for a Java development environment.

OpenJDK Components

After you've installed OpenJDK plenty of Java programs and utilities are at your disposal. All of the programs are accessible from the command-line prompt, from any folder on your system. Table 28-1 lists the packages contained in OpenJDK that'll help you out with your Java development.

Table 28-1: OpenJDK Programs

Program	Description
appletviewer	View Java applets without a browser

Table 28-1: *(continued)*

Program	Description
apt	Java code annotation processor for documenting Java class methods
jar	Combine multiple Java classes into a single application file
jarsigner	Sign jar files
java	Run Java class files
javac	Compile Java code files into Java class files for execution
javadoc	Document Java code files by generating HTML-formatted pages on the Java functions used in the code file
javah	Produce C headers and source files from Java code
javap	Disassemble a Java class file into Java code
jconsole	Monitor and manage a running Java virtual machine instance
jdb	Java debugger
jhat	Heap analysis tool
jmap	Java memory mapper
jps	Java virtual machine process status tool
jstat	Display Java virtual machine statistics

These programs can be run directly from the command line, but there are several graphical Java integrated development environment (IDE) packages that provide a graphical front end to the OpenJDK programs (see the "Eclipse" and "NetBeans" sections later in this chapter). The next section shows how to use the OpenJDK development environment from both a text-based and a graphical environment.

Java Development Environments

Ubuntu offers several options to help you develop your Java applications. The most basic is the command-line javac Java compiler in OpenJDK that allows you to compile your Java applications and applets directly on the command line. Ubuntu also provides access to two popular Java graphical IDE environments that provide a graphical interface for compiling, testing, and debugging your Java programs:

- ◆ The Sun Microsystems NetBeans IDE package
- ◆ The open-source Eclipse IDE package

Each package provides a graphical, windows-based front end to the OpenJDK Java programs. This section walks through the basics of using the OpenJDK command-line programs as well as the two graphical IDE packages to create Java applications on your Ubuntu workstation.

Command-Line Tools

The core of the Java development environment is the command line. The OpenJDK package provides several command-line programs for working with Java programs directly from the command line. The best part of the command-line Java tools is that you can use them in just about any environment, even on the Ubuntu server, which offers only the command-line interface. This section walks through the basic tools you'll use to develop, run, and test your Java application in Ubuntu.

The javac Program

The command-line Java compiler program supplied by OpenJDK is javac. It compiles a Java source code file into a Java class file that runs in the JVM on any platform. You can create Java applications and applets using the javac compiler.

The format of the javac program is

```
javac [options] [sourcefiles] [@argfiles]
```

The *sourcefiles* parameter is a list of Java code files that are to be compiled by the javac program. (Java programs often comprise multiple files that need to be compiled into one class file.)

Secret

Java is very particular about source file name format. Each Java source file must end with a .java file extension, and the filename must match the Java class that it contains the code for.

To make matters even worse, Java is case sensitive, so the case of the filename must match the case of the Java class. For example, if the code file contains code for the MyTestClass Java class, the file must be named MyTestClass.java.

The *argfiles* section allows you to list one or more files that contain a list of options and source file names. Because you must name a source code file based on the Java class it contains, Java projects can often become complicated and have numerous code files for the different Java classes used in an application. Instead of listing all of the code files required to create a single application every time you compile the project, you can create a text file that lists the source file names along with any options required to compile the application. Then all you have to do to compile the project is include the argfile name in the javac compiler command line, using the @ symbol in front of the argfile name. The compiler automatically extracts the options and source file names from the argfile and processes them as if you had entered the information on the command line.

The *options* section for the javac program is optional. Various options are available for you to modify the behavior of the compiler. The options are divided into two groups:

◆ **Standard options:** Options that are common for the Java language and used in all JVM environments

◆ **Nonstandard options:** Options that are specific to a particular JVM environment that aren't standard in Java

Table 28-2 shows the standard Java compiler options supported by OpenJDK.

Table 28-2: Standard Java Compiler Options

Option	Description
-classpath	Specify the location to look for Java class library files
-d	Specify the destination directory for class files
-deprecation	Display a description for each deprecated class used in the code
-encoding	Set the file-encoding format
-g	Generate debugging information
-g:none	Don't generate debugging information
-g:{source,lines,vars}	Generate only specific debugging information for source files (source), line numbers (lines), or variables (vars)
-implicit:{class,none}	Control the generation of class files for implicitly loading source files
-nowarn	Disable compiler warning messages
-proc:{none,only}	Specify whether no annotation processing, or only annotation processing, is performed
-processor	Specify the annotation processors to run
-processorpath	Specify the location of the annotation processors
-s	Specify the location to place generated source files
-source	Specify the version of Java source code
-sourcepath	Specify the path to look for source code files
-target	Specify the Java version to create the class file for
-verbose	Produce additional information about the compile process
-X	Display nonstandard options available and exit

Simply add any options you need to the command line before listing the source files.

Let's walk through compiling a simple Java application program. The following steps show how to use the `javac` compiler from the command line to do that.

1. Start a Terminal session from the workstation, or enter the command line on the server.
2. Open an editor and create the file `MyTestClass.java`. Then enter the code:
   ```
   class MyTestClass {
   public static void main(String[] arg) {
   int number = (int)(Math.random() * 10);
   int factorial = 1;
   int counter;
   for (counter = 1; counter <= number; counter++)
   ```

```
    {
    factorial = factorial * counter;
    }
    System.out.println("The factorial of "
    + number
    + " is "
    + factorial);
    }
    }
```

   3. Save the file and exit the editor.

   4. Compile the Java code into a class file using the command:

```
    $ javac MyTestClass.java
```

If all goes well, this will create the MyTestClass.class file:

```
    $ ls -al My*
    -rw-r--r-- 1 rich rich 727 2008-11-18 06:33 MyTestClass.class
    -rw-r--r-- 1 rich rich 346 2008-11-18 06:31 MyTestClass.java
    $
```

If you have any typos in your code, the javac compiler will let you know by pointing out the error and the line in the program code where it found the error.

You're now ready to run your new Java program. The next section walks through how to use the OpenJDK JVM to run your Java applications from the command line.

Secret

Be careful when creating Java programs. The code file must be in plain text format. Most word-processing programs, such as OpenOffice.org Writer, add binary formatting data to the text file, which will confuse the Java compiler. The best solution is to use the standard gedit text editor, available from the Accessories menu, to create and save your Java programs.

Using the java Program

The java program provides a JVM for running Java applications from the command line on your Ubuntu system. The java program has two basic formats:

```
    java [options] class [ argument…]
    java [options] -j file.jar [ argument…]
```

The first format runs a standard Java class file. The JVM looks for a class method called main defined in the class file and starts executing the Java code at that point. If there is no main method defined, the JVM produces an error message and halts.

The second format runs a Java application contained in a Java *jar* (short for *Java archive*) file, which allows you to bundle several Java class files (along with other files, if necessary) into one package. One of the classes contained in the jar file must have a main class method defined, which is where the JVM will start executing the application.

You may also specify one or more command-line *arguments* for the Java application in the java program command line. Each argument is specified after the class or jar file name, and each argument is separated with a space. The command-line arguments are passed to the Java program, which can retrieve them and use them in the program code.

The options control the behavior of the java program. Just like the javac program, there are standard and nonstandard java program options. Table 28-3 shows the standard java program options.

Table 28-3: The Java JVM Standard Options

Option	Description
-client	Use the client JVM instead of a server JVM if both are available
-server	Use the server JVM instead of a client JVM if both are available
-classpath	Specify the location of a directory to look for class files
-D	Set a system property and value used in the class code
-enableassertions	Enable assertions only in the specified Java code files
-disableassertions	Disable assertions only in the specified Java code files
-enablesystemassertions	Enable assertions in all system classes
-disablesystemassertions	Disable assertions in all system classes
-jar	Execute the Java classes contained in the specified jar file
-javaagent	Load the specified Java programming language agent
-verbose	Display information about each class loaded
-verbose:gc	Display information on each garbage collection event
-verbose:jni	Display information on each native method use
-version	Display version information and exit
-X	Display nonstandard options available and exit

Once you have obtained your class file from compiling the Java source code, you can run it using the java program from the command line:

```
$ java MyTestClass
The factorial of 5 is 120
$
```

If the program uses the Java System.out class to display data, the output generated by the application appears directly on the console, as demonstrated in this example.

The jdb Program

If things go wrong in your code you'll want to troubleshoot your Java application. The jdb debugger program allows you to step through your Java code and examine what's going

on inside the program as the program runs. To properly debug a Java application, you
need to compile it using the -g option. You can then start the class file in the debugger:

```
$ javac -g MyTestClass.java
$ jdb MyTestClass
Initializing jdb…
>
```

The jdb debugger is now ready for action. There are several commands you can use to
control the operation of the debugger, shown in Table 28-4.

Table 28-4: The jdb Debugger Commands

Command	Description
connectors	List available connectors and transports in the JVM
run	Start execution of the main class
threads	List the threads
thread	Set the default thread
suspend	Suspend the specified thread ID
resume	Resume the specified thread ID
where	Dump the specified thread's stack
wherei	Dump the specified thread's stack with pc info
up	Move up a thread's stack
down	Move down a thread's stack
kill	Kill the specified thread
interrupt	Interrupt the specified thread
print	Display the value of the specified expression
dump	Display all object information
eval	Evaluate the specified expression
set	Assign a new value to a variable
locals	Display all local variables
classes	List currently known classes
class	Display details of the specified class
methods	Display the methods of the specified class
fields	Display the fields of the specified class
threadgroups	List the thread groups
threadgroup	Set the current thread group to the specified thread group
stop in	Set a breakpoint at the specified class method or line

Table 28-4: *(continued)*

Command	Description
stop at	Set a breakpoint at the specified line
clear	Remove the specified breakpoint
clear	List all breakpoints
catch	Break when the specified exception occurs
ignore	Remove the specified exception break
watch	Display access and modifications to the specified field
unwatch	Remove a set watch
trace	Trace method entries and exits
untrace	Stop a set trace
step	Execute the current line of the code
step up	Execute until the current code method returns to the caller
stepi	Execute the current instruction
next	Step one line of code (don't step into calls)
cont	Continue normal execution of code
list	Display the entire source code
use	Display or change the source path
exclude	Don't report step or method events for the specified class
classpath	Display the classpath information for the JVM
monitor	Execute the specified command each time the program stops
read	Read and execute the specified command file
lock	Display lock information for the specified object
threadlocks	Display lock information for the specified thread
pop	Execute the current stack, including the current frame
reenter	Re-enter the current frame in the stack
redefine	Redefine the code for the specified class
disablegc	Disable garbage collection for the specified object
enaglegc	Enable garbage collection for the specified object
!!	Repeat the last command
<n> command	Repeat the specified command n times
version	Display the version number and exit
exit	Stop the debugger and return to the command line

As you can see, there are many commands you can use to examine your running Java application. Here's a small example of starting the debugger with the sample Java code and setting a breakpoint to stop the program:

```
$ jdb MyTestClass
Initializing jdb…
> stop in MyTestClass.main
Deferring breakpoint MyTestClass.main.
It will be set after the class is loaded.
> run
run MyTestClass
Set uncaught java.lang.Throwable
Set deferred uncaught java.lang.Throwable

VM Started: > Set deferred breakpoint MyTestClass.main

Breakpoint hit: "thread=main," MyTestClass.main(), line=3 bci=0
3 int number = 5;

main[1]
```

After starting the debugger, I used the stop in command to set a breakpoint at the main method in the MyTestClass class. After setting the breakpoint, I used the run command to execute the program.

The debugger started the program, then stopped at the first line in the main method. At this point you can use the list command to display where in the code you are:

```
main[1] list
1 class MyTestClass {
2 public static void main(String[] arg) {
3 => int number = (int)(Math.random() * 10);
4 int factorial = 1;
5 int counter;
6 for(counter = 1; counter <= number; counter++) {
7 factorial = factorial * counter;
8 }
9 System.out.println("The factorial of "
10 + number
main[1]
```

The debugger knows the source code and indicates the line in the source code the program stopped. You can then step through the code one line at a time using the step command, then examine variable values using the print command:

```
main[1] step
>
Step completed: "thread=main," MyTestClass.main(), line=4 bci=2
4 int factorial = 1;

main[1] step
>
Step completed: "thread=main," MyTestClass.main(), line=6 bci=4
6 for(counter = 1; counter <= number; counter++) {
```

```
main[1] print number
number = 5
main[1]
```

You can step through the `for` loop and watch the `factorial` variable value change in each iteration. At the end of the `for` loop, the factorial value will contain the final value:

```
main[1] step
>
Step completed: "thread=main," MyTestClass.main(), line=9 bci=21
9 System.out.println("The factorial of "

main[1] print factorial
factorial = 120
main[1]
```

You can release the program to finish by using the `cont` command:

```
main[1] cont
The factorial of 5 is 120
>
The application exited
$
```

After the program completes, the debugger automatically exits and returns you to the command line prompt. The debugger is a great tool to have available to troubleshoot your Java programs.

Secret

Most graphical IDE packages provide a graphical debugging environment, which is what makes them easier to use than the command-line `jdb` debugger. If you have access to a graphical IDE package to develop your Java applications, you should use the debugger in that software rather than the `jdb` program. However, if you're in a command-line environment (such as the Ubuntu server) and need to debug a Java application, `jdb` can be a lifesaver!

The jar Program

One disadvantage to Java is that you often have multiple `.class` files as a result of compiling separate Java programs for a single application. Distributing an application that requires multiple class files can be a problem.

To solve this problem, Java uses the `jar` program. The `jar` program creates a single library file that contains all of the class files required for an application.

The format of the `jar` program changes, depending on the function you're trying to perform. To create a new `jar` file, you'd use the format:

```
$ jar cf myjar.jar MyTestClass.class
```

This command adds the class file `MyTestClass.class` into a `jar` file called `myjar.jar`. If you need to add multiple files to the `jar` file, just add them to the command line. You can also update an existing `jar` file using the `uf` parameter. For example, if you had another class file called `AnotherClass.class` that you want to add to your `jar` file, you'd use the format:

```
$ jar uf myjar.jar AnotherClass.class
```

After creating a `jar` file you can list the contents of the file using the format:

```
$ jar tf myjar.jar
META-INF/
META-INF/MANIFEST.MF
MyTestClass.class
AnotherClass.class
$
```

Notice that by default the `jar` process adds a file called `MANIFEST.MF`. This file is called the *manifest*, and it is used to track the features of the classes contained in the `jar` file. We'll experiment with that file in a little bit.

To extract the files contained in the `jar` file, you'd use the format:

```
$ jar xf myjar.jar
$ ls -al
total 20
drwxr-xr-x 3 rich rich 4096 2008-11-18 05:36 .
drwxr-xr-x 37 rich rich 4096 2008-11-18 06:23 . .
drwxr-xr-x 2 rich rich 4096 2008-11-18 06:18 META-INF
-rw-r--r-- 1 rich rich 928 2008-11-18 06:23 myjar.jar
-rw-r--r-- 1 rich rich 727 2008-11-18 06:33 MyTestClass.class
-rw-r--r-- 1 rich rich 727 2008-11-18 06:35 AnotherClass.class
$
```

The manifest file helps the JVM determine what files are in the `jar` file and the location class that contains the `main` method (called the application *entry point*). Take a look at the default manifest file that the `jar` process created:

```
$ cd META-INF
$ ls -al
total 12
drwxr-xr-x 2 rich rich 4096 2008-11-18 05:18 .
drwxr-xr-x 3 rich rich 4096 2008-11-18 06:36 . .
-rw-r--r-- 1 rich rich 70 2008-11-18 06:18 MANIFEST.MF
$ cat MANIFEST.MF
Manifest-Version: 1.0
Created-By: 1.6.0_0 (Sun Microsystems Inc.)
$
```

The default manifest shows generic information. You can use that file to give the JVM specific instructions about your application, such as the entry point of your Java application. To do that, you must create a manifest file to add to your `jar` file. The `jar` program will add the information from your manifest file to the standard manifest information.

To specify the class that contains the `main` method, create a manifest file called `Manifest.txt` and use the `Main-Class:` tag to define the class that contains the `main` class method. After adding the file, the contents of your `Manifest.txt` file should look like this:

```
$ cat Manifest.txt
Main-Class: MyTestClass
$
```

Next, use the `Manifest.txt` file when you create your `jar` file:

```
$ jar cfm myjar.jar Manifest.txt MyTestClass.class
$
```

Make sure that the new `Manifest.txt` file is in the same folder as your `MyTest.Class.class` file when you run this command. This rebuilds the `myjar.jar` file, including the information from the `Manifest.txt` file, which indicates where the `main` method is in the test code. With just one file in the `jar` file, doing this seems kind of silly, but think how confusing it would be if you had hundreds of class files in the `jar` file, which often happens for large applications.

Once you build the `jar` file with the manifest, you can distribute that as your application, and anyone can run your application directly from the `jar` file by simply using the command:

```
$ java -jar myjar.jar
The factorial of 4 is 24
$
```

There's no need to extract the class files from the `jar` file—the JVM can process them just fine within the `jar` file!

Secret

You can also use the `-classpath` option to run a class from a `jar` file if you know what the `main` class for the application is:

```
$ java -classpath myjar.jar MyTestClass
The factorial of 5 is 120
$
```

This allows you to build library files of classes and store them in `jar` files, then access the libraries using the `-classpath` option.

NetBeans

These days a simple command-line compiler just doesn't cut it. It's useful to have a graphical development environment available to help you create and debug your programs.

The Sun NetBeans IDE package is a freely available, non-open–source development package for Java. Because it's not open source, it's somewhat frowned on in the Linux community. Nonetheless, it's a great way to create and troubleshoot Java code.

You can download the NetBeans IDE package directly from the Sun Microsystems' Java web site (`http://java.sun.com`); however, it's also available in the Ubuntu software repositories to install via the Synaptic Package Manager. All you need to do is install the `netbeans` package, and everything you need for graphical Java development is installed on your Ubuntu workstation!

Once you install NetBeans, it appears in the Applications menu. Follow these steps to write a simple Java application using NetBeans:

1. Start the NetBeans application. Start NetBeans in Ubuntu by selecting Applications ➪ Programming ➪ NetBeans IDE from the Panel menu. The main NetBeans window, shown in Figure 28-2, appears.

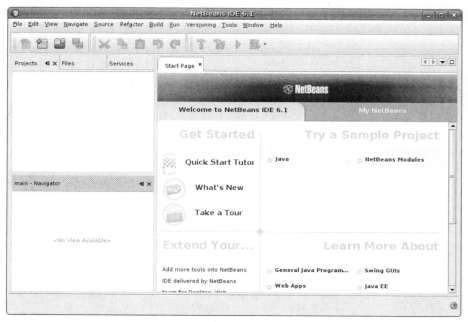

Figure 28-2: The main NetBeans window.

2. Select File ⇨ New Project to start a new project. The New Project window, shown in Figure 28-3, appears.

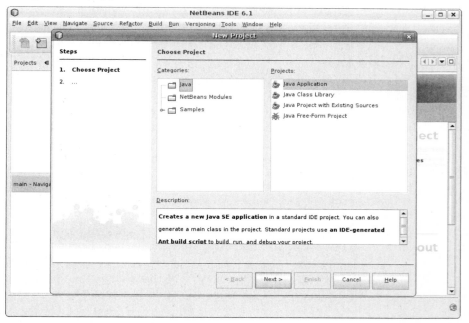

Figure 28-3: The New Project window.

3. Click the Next button to start a new application project. The New Project Application window, shown in Figure 28-4 appears. Enter the project name (shown as *Factorial* in the figure) and click the Finish button.

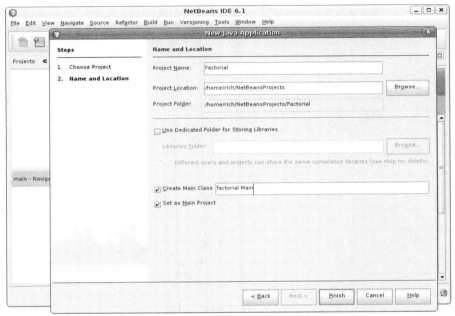

Figure 28-4: The New Project Application window.

The NetBeans interface automatically creates the main Java code file for the application and generates the class code required.

4. Enter your application code in the `main` method section. The code view window appears for the `Main.java` code file, which contains the `main` class method for the application. Scroll down to the `main` method, and enter the following code:

```
int number = (int)(Math.random() * 10);
int factorial = 1;
int counter;

for(counter = 1; counter <= number; counter++)
{
factorial = factorial * counter;
}
System.out.println("The factorial of "
+ number
+ " is "
+ factorial);
```

As you type the code, notice that NetBeans automatically color-codes the program text. Color coding helps you pick up any typos or coding goofs before compiling the program. Also, pause for a little bit as you type the period after the `Math` class. NetBeans automatically brings up a list of all the methods available in the `Math` class, allowing you to pick the one you need! The completed code should look like the code in Figure 28-5.

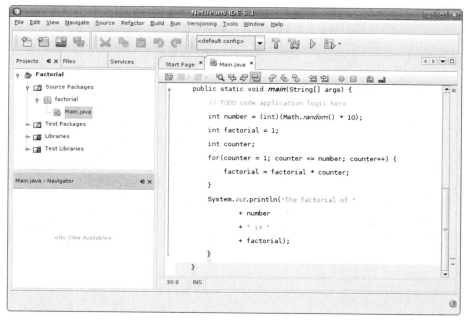

Figure 28-5: The Factorial class code.

5. Save the file, and build the new code by selecting the Build Main Project icon (the hammer) on the toolbar.

6. Run the code by selecting the Run Main Project icon (the green arrow) on the toolbar.

When the application runs, NetBeans opens a text output window at the bottom of the NetBeans window to display the program output.

NetBeans also provides a complete debugging feature, allowing you to set breakpoints in the code by simply clicking in the left margin next to the code line. To start the debugger, all you need to do is click the Debug Main Project icon (the list with the green arrow) on the toolbar.

Secret

Once you've completed your project, NetBeans creates a `jar` file containing all of the class files required for your application. To find the `jar` file, though, you'll need to do some digging. If you used the default locations for the project, the `Factorial` `jar` file will be located in the NetBeansProjects folder in your home folder, under the Factorial folder, in a folder called dist.

To run the `Factorial` class from this `jar` file, you can use the `-jar` option of the Java program:

```
rich@testbox:~/NetBeansProjects/Factorial/dist$ java -jar Factorial.jar
The factorial of 3 is 6
rich@testbox:~/NetBeansProjects/Factorial/dist$
```

Eclipse

The Eclipse IDE is an open-source graphical environment for creating and troubleshooting different types of program code, including Java code. Because of its versatility, installing Eclipse requires a couple of different software packages. Fortunately, the Synaptic Package Manager can take care of that for us.

Just start the Synaptic Package Manager (by selecting System ⇨ Administration ⇨ Synaptic Package Manager), then search for the `eclipse-jdt` package. Mark that package for installation, and Synaptic automatically installs everything that's required to develop Java applications (including the OpenJDK package, if it's not already installed).

Secret

The Eclipse package is not supported by Canonical, so it doesn't appear in the standard Ubuntu repositories. You must ensure you have the universe repository selected in your Synaptic Package Manager configuration to download the Eclipse package.

To do that, start the Synaptic Package Manager, then select Settings ⇨ Repositories from the menu. In the Ubuntu Software tab section, ensure that the community-maintained, open-source software (universe) check box is selected. Then click the Reload toolbar button on the main page to reload the repository library information.

Once you install the Eclipse package it appears in the Programming menu area as well. Follow these steps to create a Java application using the Eclipse IDE:

1. Start the Eclipse IDE package. Select Applications ⇨ Programming ⇨ Eclipse from the Panel menu. The Eclipse main window, shown in Figure 28-6 appears.

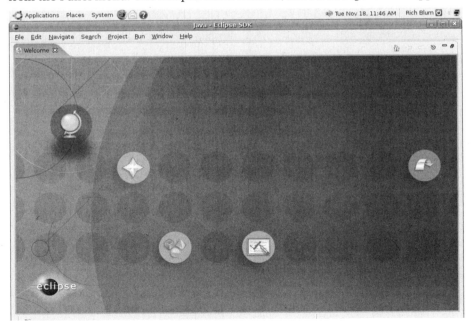

Figure 28-6: The Eclipse IDE main window.

Click the far right highlighted icon to start the workbench area.

2. Start a new project by selecting File ⇨ New ⇨ Project. The New Project wizard, shown in Figure 28-7, appears.

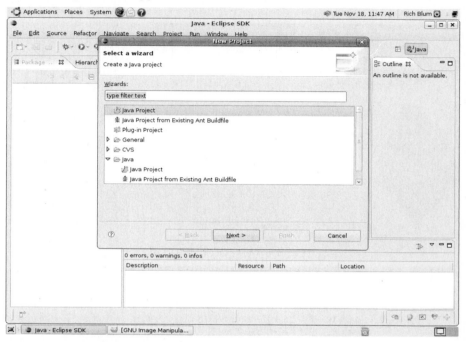

Figure 28-7: The Eclipse new project wizard.

Make sure the Java project entry is highlighted, then click the Next button to continue.

3. Enter a name for the project. The New Java Project window (shown in Figure 28-8) allows you to select the name for the project (shown as *Factorial* in the figure) and select which JVM to use to run your application inside Eclipse.

Click the Next button to proceed to the next wizard window.

4. Click the Finish button in the Java Settings window. This window allows you to add any Java libraries that are required for the application (such as JDBC libraries to access database servers).

Once you finish these steps you have a new Java project started but no actual application files. You'll need to add a new class to your project to start building code. Follow these steps to do that:

1. Create a new class by selecting File ⇨ New ⇨ Class. The New Java Class wizard window appears, as shown in Figure 28-9.

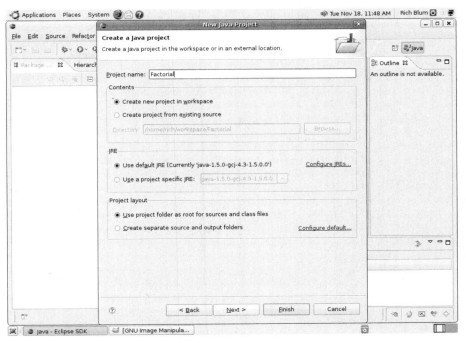

Figure 28-8: The New Java Project window in Eclipse.

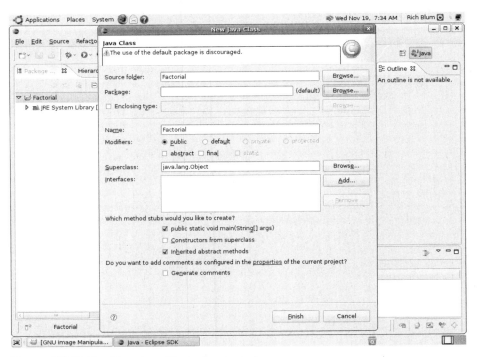

Figure 28-9: The New Java Class wizard window.

2. Enter the class name (shown as *Factorial* in the figure) and select the check box to create the `main` method stub for the class. When you create the `main` method stub, Eclipse will create the framework for the `main` method in the new class.

Click the Finish button when you are done entering the information.

3. In the newly opened `Factorial.java` code window, enter the following code:

```
int number = (int)(Math.random() * 10);
int factorial = 1;
int counter;
for(counter = 1; counter <= number; counter++) {
factorial = factorial * counter;
}
System.out.println("The factorial of "
+ number
+ " is "
+ factorial);
```

4. Save the code by clicking the Save icon (the disk) on the toolbar. The `Factorial.java` code should look as shown in Figure 28-10.

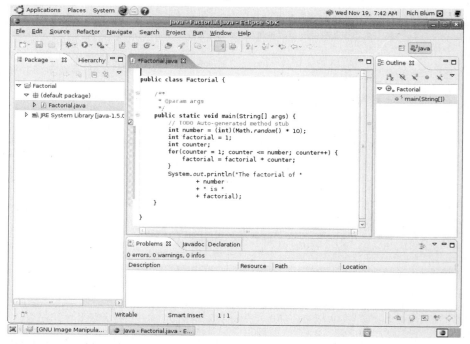

Figure 28-10: The Factorial.java code file in Eclipse.

5. Run the application by clicking the Run icon (the green circle with the right arrow) in the toolbar. The Run wizard appears (shown in Figure 28-11), allowing you to select the environment to run the application.

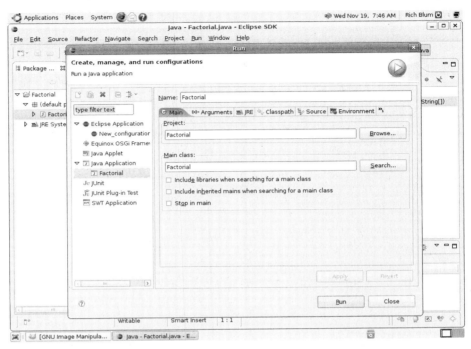

Figure 28-11: The Eclipse Run wizard.

6. Double-click Java Application, then select the Factorial project that appears under it. The Run wizard allows you to set the classpath, add command-line arguments, set the JVM used to run the application, and set environment variables.

7. After initializing the Run wizard, click the Run toolbar button again to run the application.

The Eclipse window produces a console window, which displays any output generated from the program for the console.

Summary

This chapter discussed how to create a Java development environment on your Ubuntu workstation or server. The Java environment can be complicated, in that there are several different options available. The J2SE development environment allows you to create Java programs for running as standalone applications on any computer platform, including Microsoft Windows workstations. It also allows you to create Java applets, which you can include in web pages to download and run on client browsers. The open-source OpenJDK package provides a simple Java J2SE development environment for both the Ubuntu workstation and server distributions.

The chapter also discussed using the popular NetBeans IDE package for a graphical development environment. This package isn't open source but is included in the Ubuntu repositories because it's provided as a free application by Sun Microsystems. The chapter walked through creating a simple Java application using the NetBeans interface. Another popular graphical Java IDE package is the open-source Eclipse package. This package has some features similar to NetBeans but in a completely open-source environment. The chapter walked through how to install and use the Eclipse package as well.

The next chapter dives into the Ruby programming world in Ubuntu. The Ruby programming language is another relatively new language that is gaining popularity due to its use as a dynamic web programming language. The Ruby on Rails project provides a simple way to create dynamic web pages. The chapter discusses how to set up a Ruby development environment on your Ubuntu system, then walks through how to develop a Ruby on Rails project.

Ruby

Chapter
29

♦ ♦

Secrets in This Chapter

What Is Ruby?

Installing Ruby in Ubuntu

The Ruby Language

Ruby on Rails

♦ ♦

Although a relative newcomer to the programming world, the Ruby programming language is starting to pick up steam, mostly due to the Ruby on Rails project, which provides an object-oriented framework environment for creating dynamic web pages. However, the core Ruby programming language provides a feature-rich scripting environment that Linux system administrators are growing to love. The Ubuntu system supports both the Ruby scripting environment and the Ruby on Rails web programming framework. This chapter shows you how to create a Ruby development environment on your Ubuntu workstation or server for generating everything from simple Ruby scripts to complex web applications.

What Is Ruby?

The Ruby programming language was created by Yukihiro Matsumoto in the mid-1990s as an improved scripting language for the Linux environment. It incorporates many features of the Perl scripting language (see Chapter 26, "Perl and Python"), but it provides a true object-oriented programming environment that is more advanced than the Python programming environment.

Secret

Much has been made over the origin of the name *Ruby*. Often it's assumed that Ruby was chosen because it's often considered superior to Perl (think rubies versus pearls). Another theory is based on the fact that the pearl is the birthstone for the month of June and the ruby is the birthstone for July, the next month in the progression. The "official" explanation from Yukihiro is that the ruby just happens to be the birthstone of a colleague of his, and he thought it would make for a good project name.

Ruby has caught on with many Linux system administrators due to its simplicity and its ability to perform complex tasks with a minimal amount of code. Many system administrators use Ruby scripts to perform both administrative and data manipulation functions in the Linux environment.

Ruby on the Web

Along with its use as a scripting language, Ruby has found another niche in the programming world. As dynamic web programming became popular, web programmers searched for robust programming languages to create *dynamic web pages*. Dynamic web pages allow programmers to dynamically alter the contents of a web page, incorporating real-time data from databases or files inside the web pages at the time clients request the page from the server.

The Ruby scripting language was adapted to work in the web programming world. The Embedded Ruby (ERb) language has become yet another programming platform for dynamic web page programmers. The ERb language utilizes Ruby code directly in standard HTML web pages to create dynamic content.

A Ruby interpreter must be installed on the web server to interpret the ERb code embedded in a web page when the page is requested by a client. The Ruby project includes a Ruby interpreter that can be used in the Apache web server used in Ubuntu and the Microsoft IIS web server used in Windows servers.

Creating a web site using HTML and Embedded Ruby can be a challenge. Fortunately, help has arrived for the Ruby world, in the form of *application frameworks.*

Ruby on Rails

When writing code for a dynamic web site, you'll notice that a lot of it is repetitive. Functions such as displaying data values, creating HTML forms, and storing information in the database use the same or similar code over and over. Application frameworks have become a popular feature in web programming because they provide prebuilt code that handles common features of a dynamic site. All you have to do to create a web page is plug in the correct framework pieces in the appropriate places in your HTML code. You need to write code only if you want to customize the appearance of the framework.

The Ruby world now includes an application framework. *Ruby on Rails* (often called RoR or Rails) creates prebuilt templates of Ruby and HTML code that interface with databases. Rails generates code layouts that guide you through creating a dynamic web site, much like rails guide a train on a track. All you need to do is follow the rails, and you'll get to where you want to go!

The framework code in Rails is called *scaffolding.* Scaffolding automatically produces basic features for your application that you can easily modify. Because most dynamic web sites rely heavily on stored data, Rails automatically provides code to create, read, update, and delete (abbreviated CRUD) data. All you need to do is create the HTML around the scaffolding, then add a little extra Ruby code of your own and you've produced a customized, professional-quality site.

Installing Ruby

Neither the Ubuntu server nor workstation installations include a Ruby programming environment by default, but software packages are included in the standard Ubuntu repositories. If you have an Internet connection, you can easily install a full Ruby programming environment. This section walks through setting up your Ruby environment so that you can start working with Ruby code.

Ruby Components

Several different programs and libraries are provided in the Ruby environment. Table 29-1 shows the main programs you'll want to install for Ruby.

Table 29-1: The Ruby Programs

Program	Description
ruby	Ruby script file processor
erb	Ruby interpreter for embedded Ruby
irb	Ruby interactive interpreter
gem	Ruby installer and updater
rake	Ruby program and utility builder
rails	Ruby on Rails framework file generator
WEBrick	A simple, Ruby-enabled web server
mongrel	A full-featured, Ruby-enabled web server

The Ruby script file processor (ruby) runs Ruby program scripts. It allows you to write Ruby scripts and run them from the Ubuntu command line or from batch programs on your system.

The Ruby embedded interpreter (erb) processes HTML files that contain embedded ERb code. The output generated by the erb program is exactly what would be sent to the client browser via the Mongrel or WEBrick web servers. The erb program is a great way to quickly test embedded Ruby code in your web pages without having to start a web server.

The Ruby interactive interpreter (irb) allows you to run Ruby code in an interactive environment, similar to what Python does. It produces its own command prompt where you enter Ruby code one line at a time and see the results instantly. This functionality comes in handy when you're trying to troubleshoot code or test coding ideas.

The Ruby Gems program (gem) is a fully automated installer and updater for Ruby. The gem program allows you to easily download new versions of any of the Ruby components on your system. Doing that can be confusing, though, because Ubuntu includes its own software installer and updater, Synaptic (see Chapter 13, "Software Installs and Updates"). It can be a challenge deciding when to use gem to update Ruby elements. We'll discuss that later, in the "Installing Ruby in Ubuntu" section of this chapter.

The rake program is responsible for building Ruby objects. If you've programmed in the C or C++ environments, you're probably familiar with the make utility (see Chapter 27, "C Programming"). Similar to make, rake allows you to build objects such as databases, tables, and code files from Rails-created templates.

To implement Rails on your Ubuntu system, you'll need a few more pieces. The rails program is the core of Rails. It generates the default framework code for your Rails application using a library of template files to create all of the scaffolding for a project based on the data elements you define.

The Rails system also can use two separate web servers for processing ERb code. The *WEBricks* server is a bare-bones web server that can process single client requests. It processes any ERb code found in a web page before returning the web page data to the client. Because it can process only single client requests, its use is limited to development web servers; it is not suitable for a production web site.

The *Mongrel* web server is a more advanced web server that can act as a standalone web server or be used as a *proxy* server for a larger package web server, such as Apache or IIS. A proxy web server receives client requests on behalf of the main web server. It allows you to utilize the advanced features of larger package servers, and you can add Ruby functionality with Mongrel running in the background.

Installing Ruby in Ubuntu

When you peruse the software packages in the Ubuntu repositories, you might be confused about which ones to install for Ruby. The Ubuntu distribution includes an installation package for each component for Ruby, plus several all-in-one installation packages. Which package you install depends primarily on what you're going to use Ruby for:

- ◆ **eruby:** to develop embedded Ruby programs in web pages without running them on the web server
- ◆ **ruby:** to install Ruby for creating command-line scripts only

- **ruby-full:** the full Ruby development environment, without Rails
- **ruby-x.y:** the latest development version of Ruby available, where x is the major release version and y is the minor release version
- **rails:** the full Ruby development environment plus the Ruby on Rails framework for web programming

To install the full Ruby on Rails environment, follow these steps:

1. Start the Synaptic Package Manager, Select System ⇨ Administration ⇨ Synaptic Package Manager from the Panel menu.

2. Find the `rails` package, then mark it for installation. The easiest way to find the rails package is to enter *rails* in the Quick Search text box, then scroll through the package list area until you see the entry for `rails`. Figure 29-1 shows what the package selection should look like.

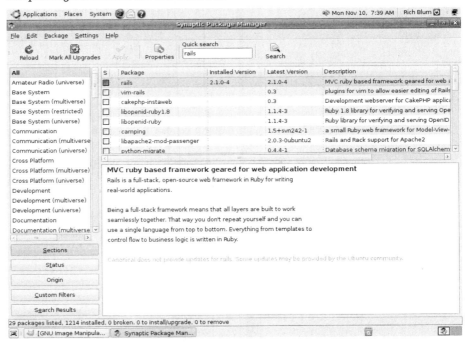

Figure 29-1: Installing the rails package from Synaptic.

Right-click on the `rails` package and select Mark for Installation. By default, the `rails` package installs only the WEBrick web server (as part of the `rails` package). If you want to install the Mongrel web server, mark it for installation as well. It should appear in the package list (as `mongrel`).

3. Click the Apply button to install the package. A dependencies list appears asking whether you want to install the packages that are required to support the `rails` package. Click the OK button to continue with the installation.

4. After the installation finishes, close the Synaptic Package Manager window.

You can test the Ruby on Rails installation by checking the versions installed. Open a Terminal session by selecting Applications ⇨ Accessories ⇨ Terminal from the Panel menu, then enter the command:

```
$ ruby -v
ruby 1.8.7 (2008-08-11 patchlevel 72) [i486-Linux]
$
```

This output shows that Ruby is installed and ready to go.

Secret

There is currently a disagreement between the Debian developers and the Ruby developers about the best way to install and update Ruby on Debian-based Linux systems (which is what Ubuntu is). The Ruby application comes with its own installer and updater program, called gems. Unfortunately, if you install or update Ruby programs using gems, those programs won't appear in the Debian software installation database, nor will they be automatically updated by the Synaptic updater. However, if you install Ruby via the Ubuntu Synaptic Package Manager, you're not guaranteed to get the latest version of Ruby available—only what's been added to the Ubuntu repositories.

The Ubuntu repositories have been doing a fairly decent job of keeping up with Ruby development, but the repositories don't always contain the latest release. If you're not concerned about working with the absolute latest version of Ruby, using the Synaptic Package Manager is a perfectly valid (and the easiest) way to install Ruby on your Ubuntu system. If you want to work with the latest version of Ruby, here's the recommended way:

1. Install only the ruby package from the Synaptic Package Manager.

2. Download the latest version of gems directly from the Ruby web site:

    http://rubyforge.org

3. Install the latest version of gems you downloaded:

    tar -zxvf rubygems-1.3.1.tgz
    cd rubygems-1.3.1
    sudo ruby setup.rb
    cd ..
    rm -r rubygems-1.3.1

4. Update Ruby and gems using gems:

    sudo gem update --system

5. Install Rails using gems:

    sudo gems install rails

This procedure installs the latest versions of Ruby and Rails available, directly from the Ruby software repository. Because the Ruby installation is no longer part of the Debian software database on your system, the Synaptic Package Manager will not be able to maintain it. You'll have to manually update Ruby and Rails using the gems update command from time to time.

Secret

If you're trying to install Ruby on your Ubuntu server, just use the apt-get program to install the rails package:

```
sudo apt-get install rails
```

It might be a good idea to perform an update command in apt-get first to ensure that you've updated the software repository list on your Ubuntu server.

Once you have your Ruby environment installed you're ready to start coding. The next section walks through the basics of the Ruby programming language.

Working with Ruby Code

The Ruby programming environment provides three basic programs for working with Ruby code:

- ◆ **irb:** the interactive Ruby environment
- ◆ **ruby:** the scripted Ruby environment
- ◆ **erb:** the embedded Ruby environment

The following sections demonstrate how to use each environment.

Interactive Ruby

You use the Ruby irb program to work out your Ruby code interactively. To start the irb program, just start a Terminal session on your Ubuntu workstation, then type the command:

```
$ irb
irb(main):001:0>
```

The irb interactive prompt appears, waiting for you to enter some Ruby code to process:

```
irb(main):001:0> test1 = 3
=> 3
irb(main):002:0> test2 = 45.36
=> 45.36
irb(main):003:0> test3 = test1 + test2
=> 48.36
irb(main):004:0>
```

The irb program displays the result of each statement as you type it on the line. It places the => symbol on the line to indicate that the result is an internal value that Ruby processes from the statement. It's not what you would see in the program output. In each of these three lines, Ruby indicates that it stored the values in the specified variables.

To display a variable value from Ruby, use the `puts` command. The `puts` command displays the result of an assignment or the value of a variable. Type this command in your `irb` session:

```
irb(main):004:0> puts test3
48.36
=> nil
irb(main):005:0>
```

The `irb` display first shows the output of the `puts` command, which is the current value stored in the `test3` variable. It then displays the result of the `puts` command, using the `=>` symbol.

The result of the `puts` command is a special value called *nil*. The nil value represents no value, which is different from a zero value (zero can be a numerical value).

Notice that the `test3` value retained the result from the mathematical operation (the `48.36` value). You can now use the `test3` variable anywhere else in Ruby to represent that value. To see this in action, enter this code at your `irb` prompt:

```
irb(main):005:0> result = test3 / 2
=> 24.18
irb(main):006:0> puts result
24.18
=> nil
irb(main):007:0>
```

Another important feature that you can see from this example is that variables retain the data type assigned to them. Because the value in the `test3` variable is a floating-point value, the output from the result variable is also a floating-point value.

To exit the `irb` prompt, just type *exit*.

Scripting with Ruby

Using the `irb` program to assign values to variables and see the results is fine, but it's not all that practical. The last thing you'll want to do is enter a 1,000-line program by hand every time you want to run it.

Instead, Ruby provides a method to store programs in files and then run them through the Ruby interpreter. The Ruby interpreter program is simply called *ruby*. It processes Ruby code files and displays any output on the command prompt.

Let's create a simple Ruby program in a file and run it through the Ruby interpreter. Just follow these steps:

1. Open a text editor and enter the following lines of code:
   ```
   test1 = 10.25
   test2 = 5.2
   result1 = test1 * test2
   puts result1
   ```

2. Save the file as `first.rb` in your home folder.

3. Open a Terminal session and enter the `ruby` command, along with the name of your Ruby code file.

The output from the `ruby` script should appear in your terminal output:

```
$ ruby first.rb
53.3
$
```

Congratulations—your first Ruby program! Not too exciting, but it did produce the expected output.

Programs usually aren't as simple as the one we just played with. Although I'm sure you're a perfect typist and an even better programmer, at some point you'll probably experience an error in your Ruby code. Fortunately, the Ruby interpreter can help us out.

If there's an error in your code, the Ruby interpreter will point it out and attempt to tell you just what the error is:

```
$ ruby first.rb
first.rb:4: undefined local variable or method 'result' for main:Object
(NameError)

$
```

The Ruby interpreter produced an error message telling me exactly what file and line the error was found in, and what the error is. This information can be invaluable in a 1,000-line application.

Embedded Ruby

The `erb` program processes Ruby code that's embedded in standard HTML web pages. It looks for tags that indicate where the Ruby code is. The tags used in embedded Ruby are

- ◆ **<% *code* %>:** Execute the Ruby code between the two tags.
- ◆ **<%= *variable* %>:** Display the Ruby variable between the two tags.

Any Ruby code between the opening <% tag and the closing %> tag is processed by `erb`. However, no output can be generated from these tag sections. Output from Ruby code is generated by the <%= and %> tag pair. Any output from this section is part of the HTML code that's sent to the client browser.

Let's create a simple, embedded Ruby page and run it through the `erb` program:

1. Open a text editor and enter the following lines of code:

```
<html>
<body>
<h2>This is a test of embedded Ruby</h2>
<% test1 = "This is a line of Ruby code" %>
<p>Here's the first test:</p>
<%= test1 %>
<p>Here's the second test:</p>
<% test2 = 10 * 3.14159 %>
The value of test2 is: <%= test2 %>
<h2>This is the end of the test</h2>
</body>
</html>
```

2. Save the file as `first.html.erb` in your home folder.

3. Open a Terminal session and run the page with the `erb` embedded Ruby processor.

Enter the `erb` command along with the name of your embedded Ruby page:

```
$ erb first.html.erb
<html>
<body>
<h2>This is a test of embedded Ruby</h2>

<p>Here's the first test:</p>

This is a line of Ruby code

<p>Here's the second test:</p>

The value of test2 is: 31.4159

<h2>This is the end of the test</h2>
</body>
</html>
$
```

The output generated from the `erb` program mimics what would be sent to the client browser via the web server after the embedded Ruby code was processed. Notice that only the HTML code and the output from the Ruby code appear in the web output.

The Ruby Language

The Ruby programming language uses many of the same features as other programming languages, so if you're familiar with another programming language you'll feel comfortable in Ruby. There are a few things that Ruby does differently though, which may throw some programmers. The following sections walk through the various parts of the Ruby programming language.

Variables

Ruby provides three types of variables to use in your applications.

- Scalar variables
- Array variables
- Hash variables

The following sections discuss each of these types of variables.

Scalar Variables

A scalar variable name in Ruby can be any combination of letters and numbers, but it must start with a lowercase letter. To place a value in a variable, you use what Ruby calls an *expression*. An expression assigns a result or a value to a variable. Here are some examples of simple Ruby expressions:

```
test1 = 3
test2 = 45.36
testString = "This is a test string"
result = test1 + test2
```

The first expression simply assigns the integer value 3 to the variable named test1. The second expression assigns a floating-point value to the variable test2. The third expression assigns a string value to the variable. The last expression performs a mathematical operation and assigns the result to the variable result.

Array Variables

Just like in other programming languages, an array in Ruby allows you to assign a collection of values to a single variable name. To create an array, enclose the values in square brackets when assigning them to the variable:

```
names = ["Rich," "Barbara," "Katie Jane," "Jessica"]
```

There are now four separate values assigned to the names array. I imagine you're now wondering how to retrieve those values! You can work with the array data as a whole simply by using the variable name, or you can handle each value individually by using an *index*.

Each value in an array has an index number, and the index numbers start at 0. So the first data value is always at index 0, the second data value is at index 1, and so on.

Here's an example of how to create a simple array in Ruby:

```
irb(main):001:0> names = ["Rich," "Barbara," "Katie Jane," "Jessica"]
=> ["Rich," "Barbara," "Katie Jane," "Jessica"]
irb(main):002:0>
```

The irb program displays the values of the elements created in the array. To reference the array as a whole, you just need to reference the array variable name:

```
irb(main):002:0> names
=> ["Rich," "Barbara," "Katie Jane," "Jessica"]
irb(main):003:0>
```

Ruby also provides some common functions for arrays. Here's an example of the sort function:

```
irb(main):003:0> names.sort
=> ["Barbara," "Jessica," "Katie Jane," "Rich"]
irb(main):004:0>
```

The sort function automatically returns the array elements in a sorted order. The array itself is still in the same order—only the output is sorted. This method allows you to easily sort data stored in an array, without having to use any messy formulas.

To reference the array values individually, you must specify the index value, using square brackets around the index value:

```
irb(main):005:0> names[0]
=> "Rich"
irb(main):006:0> names[3]
=> "Jessica"
irb(main):007:0>
```

Ruby provides a feature called *iterators* to help you work with arrays. An iterator steps through the array one index or key at a time to extract the stored values.

The format of the each iterator statement is

```
array.each do |variable|
statements to execute
end
```

This format may look odd if you're not used to object-oriented programming. The array in Ruby is an object, and each is a method that acts on the data stored in the object. Ruby uses the *variable* defined between the two pipe symbols to contain the value of the current data element in the array. You can place the variable anywhere within the code block. The end statement determines the end of the code to run for each iteration. Let's give this a try:

1. Open a text editor and enter the following code:

    ```
    family = ["Rich," "Barbara," "Katie Jane," "Jessica"]
    family.each do |member|
    puts member + " is a member of my family"
    end
    ```

2. Save the file as arraytest.rb in your home folder.

3. Open a Terminal session and run the code file from the command line using the Ruby interpreter.

The output from the Ruby interpreter should show each member of the hash.

```
$ ruby arraytest.rb
Rich is a member of my family
Barbara is a member of my family
Katie Jane is a member of my family
Jessica is a member of my family
$
```

As expected, the output from the script retrieved each element from the array, one by one, to use in the puts statement.

Secret

You can also add other functions to the each iterator. If you want to try something really fancy, change the iterator line to this:

```
family.sort.each do |member|
```

Then run the program. You'll notice that the sort method sorts the data in the array before the each iterator goes through it. This is an amazing feature of Ruby that often comes in handy.

Hash Variables

Hashes are a special type of array variable. A hash stores multiple values similar to the array, but uses strings instead of numbers as the index keys. This use allows you to reference a value by name instead of a number, sort of like a mini-database. Often it's easier to remember items by name rather than the order in which they appear in the array index. Each key must be unique in the hash so that you can use it to reference each value.

Creating a hash is a little tricky, as you must define both the key and value at the same time:

```
name = {"key1" => "value1," "key2" => "value2," "key3" => "value3"}
```

You must use the => symbol to assign the keys and values in the hash. Also, notice that the hash uses braces to delimit the values.

To access the values in a hash variable, you need to know the individual key values, and, like array index numbers, you must enclose them in square brackets:

```
irb(main):007:0> test = {"key1"=>"value1,""key2"=>value2,""key3"=>"value3"}
=> {"key3"=>"value3,""key1"=>value1,""key2"=>"value2"}
irb(main):008:0> name["key1"]
=> "value1"
irb(main):009:0>
```

But what if you don't know what keys are in a hash? Fortunately, there's a simple solution. When working with hashes, if you don't know the key name you can't write the code to access the value. Ruby provides an iterator for hashes to help solve this problem.

The *hash iterator* works the same as the array iterator but with a twist. You can extract the key as well as the value in each iteration. The hash iterator uses the format:

```
hash.each do |key, value|
statements to execute
end
```

Let's work on an example to demonstrate the procedure:

1. Open a text editor and enter the following code:

```
information = { "city" => "Chicago," "state" => "Illinois," "zip" =>
"60633" }
information.each do |key, value|
puts key + ": " + value
end
```

2. Save the file as hashtest.rb in your home folder.
3. Open a Terminal session and run the code using the Ruby interpreter.

When you see the output from this process, you might be surprised:

```
$ ruby hashtest.rb
city: Chicago
zip: 60633
state: Illinois
$
```

The keys aren't listed in the same order in which we created them! This is a drawback to using hashes. It's not guaranteed that the hash iterator will return the hash elements in the same order, so don't count on it in your program! If you require your data to appear in the same order, you need to write extra Ruby code to store the output of the iterator and display it appropriately.

Structured Commands

As with the other programming languages, Ruby supports a set of structured commands that allow you to alter the flow of the program based on a condition. This section discusses the two most popular structured commands used in Ruby.

The if-then Statements

The most common structured command you'll see in Ruby programming is the if-then statement. The if-then statement checks the result of a condition and then performs a block of code depending on the value of the result. This feature allows you to control the operation of the program based on real-time data values.

Here's the basic format of the if-then statement:

```
if condition
statements to execute
end
```

If the condition results in a true Boolean value, Ruby executes the statements that appear before the end keyword. If the condition results in a false value, Ruby skips the statements and continues with the code immediately after the end keyword. Here's an example:

```
if num > 5
puts "The value is larger than 5"
end
```

If we ran this code, we'd see that the string "The value is larger than 5" appears only if the variable num contains a value of 6 or greater. If the value is 5 or less, Ruby doesn't execute the puts statement.

Comparing Data Types

The condition is the core of the if-then statement. You can use conditions to compare just about any data type and value. However, Ruby does have specific rules for comparing data types.

Unlike some of the other scripting languages (like Perl), Ruby uses the same comparator symbols for both numerical and text values. These symbols are shown in Table 29-2.

Table 29-2: Ruby Comparator Symbols

Description	Symbol
Equals	==
Not equal	!=
Less than	<
Greater than	>
Less than or equal	<=
Greater than or equal	>=

Ruby can determine the data type used in the comparison and act accordingly. Even without running it, you can probably figure out the result you'd get from this code:

```
value1 = 50
value2 = 100
if value2 > value1
puts "The value is larger"
end
```

In the example, both values in the condition are numerical. Here's an example of code that uses a condition to compare text values:

```
value1 = "testing"
if value1 == "testing"
puts "This is only a test"
end
```

Secret

The string comparator operators allow you to easily compare string values in your programs. What gets tricky is when you use the greater-than and less-than comparators with strings. How do you know whether the word *banana* is less than or greater than the word *orange?* Ruby uses the alphabetical order of text characters to perform the comparison. An *a* character is 1, a *b* character is 2, and so on through the alphabet. So, for example, the word *banana* is less than the word *orange*.

The if-then-else Statement

You'll often need to execute one set of statements when a condition is true and another set of statements when it's false. The else keyword is used to provide an alternate set of statements for Ruby to execute, like this:

```
if condition
statements to execute if true
else
statements to execute if false
end
```

In this format, if the condition is true, Ruby executes only the code between the if statement and the else keyword. You can put more than one statement in each section of the if-then-else code.

```
if price > 100
price = price * .90
puts "The new price is " + price.to_s
else
price = price * .95
puts "The new price is " + price.to_s
end
```

This example demonstrates checking to see whether the price variable value is larger than 100. If the price value is larger than 100, the price is changed to discount it by 10 percent (by multiplying by .90), and the result is displayed on the monitor (you need to use the .to_s method to convert the integer value into a string value to display it). If the price isn't greater than 100, the else block of code implements a 5 percent discount, then displays the new price.

The elsif Keyword

You can expand on the functionality of the if-then statement by stringing if-then statements together using the elsif keyword:

```
value = rand(100)
if value > 50
puts "The value is big: " + value.to_s
elsif value > 25
```

```
puts "The value is medium: " + value.to_s
else
puts "The value is small: " + value.to_s
end
```

That's quite a string of options! Often it's hard to follow along in the `elsif` statement string. Let's create an example using this code and walk through it:

1. Open a text editor and enter the following code:

```
value = rand(100)
if value > 50
puts "The value is big: " + value.to_s
elsif value > 25
puts "The value is medium: " + value.to_s
else
puts "The value is small: " + value.to_s
end
```

2. Save the file as `iftest.rb` in your home folder.
3. Open a Terminal session and run the code file using the Ruby interpreter.

The `rand()` function picks a random number from 0 to 100 and assigns it to the variable called `value` in our code example. Ruby walks through the `if-then` conditions and displays the appropriate message based on the value of the random number.

```
$ ruby iftest.rb
The value is big: 93
$ ruby iftest.rb
The value is medium: 29
$
```

The `elsif` makes trying to check multiple conditions considerably easier.

The Loop Statements

Loops are another popular way to alter the flow of a program. Loops do what the name implies: They loop through a block of code for a predetermined number of times. This is a handy feature if you're trying to loop through an equation a set number of times, such as in a counter.

Times Loops

Ruby has a unique way of implementing simple loops, called the `times` method. The `times` method can be used on both variables and constant numerical values. Here's an example:

```
5.times do
statements to execute
end
```

If you're familiar with other programming languages, this may seem somewhat odd, but if you read the line of code, it makes perfectly good sense. The block of statements will repeat five times, just like the code says.

If you need to increment or decrement a variable value inside a loop, you have to manually create it and process it inside the loop. Try this example:

```
counter = 1
5.times do
```

```
puts "This is loop number " + counter.to_s
counter = counter + 1
end
puts "This is the end of the loop"
```

You should see the output showing the five lines created from inside the loop block of code. Notice that in each loop iteration the counter value is different.

You can also use variables for the times loop:

```
value = 10
counter = 1
value.times do
puts "This is loop number " + counter.to_s
counter = counter + 1
end
```

Now you can create dynamic loops and control them within your program code. This is an invaluable tool to have at your disposal!

While Loops

Times loops are perfect when you must repeat a block of code multiple times. Other times, you may not want to repeat the block of code at all, or there might be cases in which you won't know exactly how many times to repeat it.

For these situations, you'll need the while loop. The while loop allows you to specify a condition that controls the looping. Instead of using a preset numerical value, you define a condition that Ruby tests before each loop iteration. If the condition results in a true value, Ruby executes the code in the code block. When the condition results in a false value, Ruby stops the loop.

Here's the general format of the while loop:

```
while condition
statements to execute
end
```

The condition used in the while loop is exactly the same format as in the if-then statement. Let's look at an example of using the while loop:

Create a file called whiletest.rb, and enter this code:

```
counter = 1
while counter < 10
puts "The value is " + counter.to_s
counter = counter + 1
end
puts "The while loop is complete"
```

Then run it using the ruby command. The while loop continues looping as long as the counter variable value is less than 10. Once the value is equal to 10 the loop stops.

There will be times when you'd like to exit prematurely from a while loop, such as when a value gets too large in an equation to continue. Ruby provides the break statement to do this. It looks like this:

```
break if condition
```

The condition allows you to set an equation that, when `true`, causes Ruby to exit the `while` loop, even if the `while` condition hasn't been met. Here's what the `break` statement looks like in the code:

```
counter = 1
while counter < 10
puts "The value is " + counter.to_s
counter = counter + 1
break if counter == 5
end
puts "The while loops is complete"
```

Now, when the counter variable value reaches 5, the `break` statement kicks in and jumps out of the `while` loop.

Object-Oriented Programming

One of the best features of Ruby is that it's completely object oriented. In object-oriented programming (OOP), everything is related to objects. Objects are the data you use in your application, grouped together into a single entity.

If you're writing a program that uses cars, you can create a car object that contains information on the car's weight, size, engine, and number of doors. If you're writing a program that tracks people, you might create a people object that contains information on each person's name, height, weight, and gender. We'll use a restaurant review application that uses three objects: articles, comments, and news items.

Ruby uses *classes* to define objects. A class is the written definition in the program code that contains all of the characteristics of the object, using variables and functions. The benefit to OOP is that once you create a class for an object, you can use that same class any time in any other application. Just plug in the class definition code and put it to use.

An OOP class is made up of *members*. There are two types of members:

♦ Properties
♦ Methods

Class *properties* denote attributes for the object (such as the date, author, and text of a restaurant review article). A class can contain many properties, with each property describing a different feature of the object.

The other type of class member is *methods.* Methods are similar to the standard Ruby functions that we've already been using. A method performs an operation using the properties in a class. For instance, we could create class methods to retrieve a specific article from the database or add a comment to an existing article. Each method should be contained within a class and perform operations only in that class. The methods for one class shouldn't deal with properties in other classes.

Creating Classes

To create a class in Ruby, use the `class` keyword. Here's an example of a simple class definition in Ruby:

```
class Product
attr_accessor :description, :price, :quantity

end
```

The class definition begins with the class keyword and the class name, Product. Next come the definitions for the members of Product. The class definition stops with the end keyword. In this example, the class Product defines only three properties:

- description: a text value to describe the product
- price: a floating-point value for the price of the product
- quantity: an integer value for the number of items on hand

In addition to the properties, this class definition includes an attribute keyword, attr_accessor. This keyword determines how the class controls access to the property from other program code. There are three types of property attributes:

- attr_reader: provides read-only access to the property
- attr_writer: provides write-only access to the property
- attr_accessor: provides read/write access to the property

By using these attribute keywords, we can prevent outside code from modifying class properties or we can allow complete access to the properties, as we do in this example. We can also mix and match which properties are accessible and which aren't.

Using Objects

As you've just seen, Ruby code uses classes to define objects. *Instantiating* is the process of using the object in your program code. Once you instantiate an object, you can use it to reference the class and its properties and methods. To instantiate an object in Ruby code, use the following format:

```
prod1 = Product.new
```

This creates (instantiates) the object called prod1 using the Product class. Once you instantiate prod1, you can access the properties of the Product class from anywhere in your application:

```
prod1.description = "carrot"
prod1.price = 1.50
prod1.quantity = 10
```

This code sets values for the properties of this instance of the Product class. Notice that you must use a period to reference the individual properties of the object. The prod1 object now contains these values (carrot, 1.50, and 10), and you can use the properties anywhere within your application code to reference the values:

```
puts prod1.description
```

That code will give you the result: carrot.

You can instantiate a second instance of the Product object, and the values won't conflict with the first instance of the Product object:

```
prod2 = Product.new
prod2.description = "eggplant"
prod2.price = 2.25
prod2.quantity = 5
```

Now when you reference the prod2 object, you'll get the values related to eggplant, while the prod1 object still contains the values related to carrot.

Adding Methods

Besides defining properties, most classes also define methods that interact with the properties. Let's expand on the `Product` class a little more:

```
class Product
attr_accessor :description, :price, :quantity

def buyProduct(amount)
@quantity = @quantity - amount
end
end
```

This version of the class definition adds a method to the class. The `buyProduct()` method provides a function that allows program code to reduce the quantity value assigned for the object (for instance, when someone buys a product, your inventory is reduced).

Notice how the method references the `quantity` property in the class. It uses an odd format for the variable name, `@quantity`. The `@quantity` variable is called a *class variable*. It references the current value of the `quantity` property used in the class instance. If the `prod1.quantity` value is 10, the `@quantity` value for that instance is also 10.

The `buyProduct()` method requires a way to provide a value to the method. It does this using a method *parameter*. A parameter defines a value that the program that uses the method (called the *calling program*) passes to the method. The variable within the parentheses retrieves the value supplied by the calling program. You can then use this variable anywhere within the code for the method.

In the example above, the parameter is defined as the variable `amount`. The `amount` parameter is subtracted from the quantity value whenever you reference the `buyProduct()` method of the class.

To use the class method, just reference it from the class instance in your program, the same way you reference properties:

```
prod1.buyProduct(4)
```

This code runs the `buyProduct()` method, passing along the value 4 as the `amount` value. Because the `buyProduct()` method alters the `quantity` value in the `prod1` object, which was set at 10, the next time you reference the `prod1.quantity`, it will have the value 6.

Ruby on Rails

The Ruby on Rails framework generates the framework for an entire dynamic web application. The Rails framework utilizes a concept in web programming called *Model-View-Controller* (MVC).

The MVC concept divides a web application into three components:

 ◆ **Model:** the Ruby code required to interface with data stored in a database
 ◆ **View:** the HTML and ERb code required to display the application and data on a browser
 ◆ **Controller:** the Ruby code required to process data and business rules

The model code creates a Ruby class for each table used in the application. The model code implements each of the CRUD elements to create, read, update, and delete data in the table. All interaction with the database is performed using the Model code.

The controller code implements actions that the client takes within the application, called the *representational state* (shortened to REST) of the application. Each representational state of a web application indicates an action that's requested by a client regarding the data in the application, such as viewing, adding, or deleting data. Table 29-3 shows the REST actions implemented in Rails.

Table 29-3: The Rails REST Actions

Action	Description
create	Retrieve the data from an HTML form and create a new data record in the table
destroy	Remove an existing data record from the table
edit	Display an HTML form for an existing data record in the table
index	Display information about all of the records in the table
new	Display an HTML form to enter a new data record in the table
show	Display the values of a single data record in the table
update	Retrieve the data from the edit form and update the values of an existing data record in the table

The Rails controller code generates a single Ruby class file that contains methods for each REST action in the application.

The view code implements each of the controller code actions in a web page using both HTML and ERb code. It uses ERb code to retrieve the data elements calculated in the controller code and display them on the web page.

The best way to get a feel for Rails is to play with it. The following sections walk through creating and testing a simple Rails application on your Ubuntu system.

Creating a Project

To create a new Rails project you'll need to use the `rails` program. The `rails` program automatically generates the generic framework code for the project to get you started.

For this example we'll create an online address book for storing names, addresses, and phone numbers for friends. First, we'll need to generate the Rails project framework. From either a Terminal session on the workstation or the command line on the server, enter this command:

```
$ rails addressbook
```

The Rails software creates a new folder called `addressbook` under the current folder and creates quite a few files and folders inside of it.

Secret

Since Rails 2.0, Rails utilizes the SQLite3 database system by default to store data values. The SQLite3 database system uses a single file to store all tables in a database. Part of the Rails process is to create the database file used for the application.

If you prefer to use a MySQL server to store your Rails project database, you must ensure that MySQL is installed on your Ubuntu system, either by installing the LAMP server in Ubuntu server (see Chapter 21, "LAMP Server") or just the MySQL server package, if you don't want to install Apache and PHP as well.

After ensuring you have the MySQL server installed, you have to add the MySQL Rails library file, called `libmysql-ruby` from Synaptic or `apt-get`. This allows Rails to access the MySQL database server from the project code.

After your Rails and MySQL environments are installed, you can specify the MySQL database on your rails command line:

```
rails -D mysql addressbook
```

The rails application creates a file called `database.yml` in the `config` folder created for the Rails project. You'll need to edit this file to add the password for the MySQL root user account for your MySQL server.

After creating the Rails project environment, you're ready to create your application code. First, you'll need to be in the newly created application folder that was created by the `rails` command:

```
rich@testbox:~$ cd addressbook
rich@textbox:~/addressbook$
```

The Rails framework creates a series of Ruby scripts you use to interact with the Rails environment. The `generate` script creates the model, controller, and view code files automatically.

Rails also includes a special generate option called *scaffold.* The scaffold option creates the model and controller code files, along with all of the required view code files to implement a complete CRUD web application for a table you define in the command line.

You just define the controller name, along with the data fields and data types you want in the table. Here's how to do that: From the newly created `addressbook` folder (make sure you're in the `addressbook` folder or this procedure won't work), enter this command (on one line):

```
rich@testbox:~/addressbook$ ruby script/generate scaffold person lastname:string
firstname:string address:string city:string state:string zip:string phone:string
comments:text
```

This command is just one statement and should all be on one command line. It generates all of the MVC files required to implement the `person` controller and interface with a database table called `people` (Rails makes all table names plural from the model names).

The model code includes code to interact with the database table, as well as create the database table. Before you can use the new code, you need to use the `rake` command to build the actual database in the database server from the model code. Again, from the `addressbook` folder, enter these commands:

```
rich@testbox:~/addressbook$ rake db:migrate
(in /home/rich/addressbook)
== 20081111220445 CreatePeople: migrating =======================================
-- create_table(:people)
-> 0.0262s
== 20081111220445 CreatePeople: migrated (0.0295s) ===========================

rich@testbox:~/addressbook$
```

The `db:migrate` command builds the new table for the `person` model. You can use the `sqlite3` program installed in Ubuntu to take a peek at the database table created here.

The database file is located in the `db` folder under the `addressbook` folder:

```
rich@testbox:~/addressbook$ cd db
rich@testbox:~/addressbook/db$ ls -l
total 16
-rw-r--r-- 1 rich rich 5120 2008-12-21 16:13 development.sqlite3
drwxr-xr-x 2 rich rich 4096 2008-12-21 16:12 migrate
-rw-r--r-- 1 rich rich 1082 2008-12-21 16:13 schema.rb
rich@testbox:~/addressbook$
```

Rails creates separate databases for the development, test, and production environments. It creates the default database for the development environment and calls it `development.sqlite3`. You can use the `sqlite3` command to look at what's inside:

```
rich@testbox:~/addressbook/db$ sqlite3 development.sqlite3
SQLite version 3.5.9
Enter ".help" for instructions
sqlite> .tables
people schema_migrations
sqlite> .dump people
BEGIN TRANSACTION;
CREATE TABLE "people" ("id" INTEGER PRIMARY KEY AUTOINCREMENT NOT NULL,
"lastname" varchar(255) DEFAULT NULL NULL, "firstname" varchar(255) DEFAULT NULL
NULL, "address" varchar(255) DEFAULT NULL NULL, "city" varchar(255) DEFAULT NULL
NULL, "state" varchar(255) DEFAULT NULL NULL, "zip" varchar(255) DEFAULT NULL
NULL, "phone" varchar(255) DEFAULT NULL NULL, "comment" text DEFAULT NULL NULL,
"created_at" datetime DEFAULT NULL NULL, "updated_at" datetime DEFAULT NULL
NULL);
COMMIT;
sqlite> .exit
rich@testbox:~/addressbook/db$
```

The `rake` command created the `people` table in the database, using the data field names supplied, plus a few extra data fields to track information specifically for Rails.

Believe it or not, you're now ready to test out your Rails project!

Secret

One of the great features of Rails is that the code generated for a project doesn't depend on the underlying database server. You can use your same project code with any type of database server. All of the specific database server connection information is contained in the `database.yml` configuration file. Just modify this file to change the database server used for the application.

Testing the Project

The Rails project includes the WEBrick web server that can interpret the Ruby and ERb code generated by the Rails project and to output HTML code to send to the client browser.

Each Rails project contains its own WEBrick server in the script area that you can use for testing. To start the WEBrick server for your project, just type this command-line prompt in the `addressbook` folder:

```
rich@testbox:~/addressbook$ ruby script/server
=> Booting WEBrick…
=> Rails 2.1.0 application started on http://127.0.0.1:3000
=> Ctrl-C to shutdown server; call with --help for options
[2008-11-11 17:18:59] INFO WEBrick 1.3.1
[2008-11-11 17:18:59] INFO ruby 1.8.7 (2008-08-11) [i486-linux]
[2008-11-11 17:18:59] INFO WEBrick::HTTPServer#start: pid=4759 port=3000
```

Secret

By default, the WEBrick server listens for client connections only on the 127.0.0.1 local host address. If you're running your application from an Ubuntu workstation, you can use the Firefox browser on your desktop to connect to the WEBrick server. If you want to connect to your WEBrick server from a remote network client, you'll need to use the `-b` command-line parameter to specify the IP address of the network card you want WEBrick to listen on.

In the development environment, the WEBrick server listens for connections on TCP port 3000. You'll need to specify the TCP port in the URL, as well as the controller name used in the application to access the Rails project. Just open Firefox on your Ubuntu workstation and go to the URL:

```
http://127.0.0.1:3000/people/
```

The main application web page should appear, as seen in Figure 29-2.

The main page shows a listing of the current records in the table (which is now empty) and a link to create a new record. Click the New Person link, and a data entry form appears, shown in Figure 29-3.

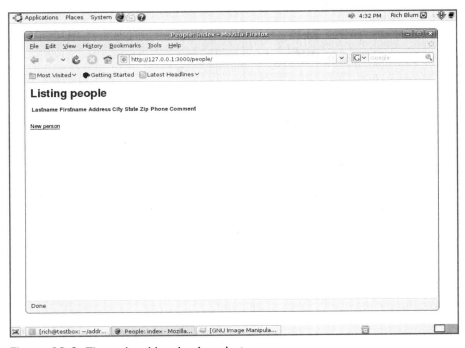

Figure 29-2: The main addressbook project page.

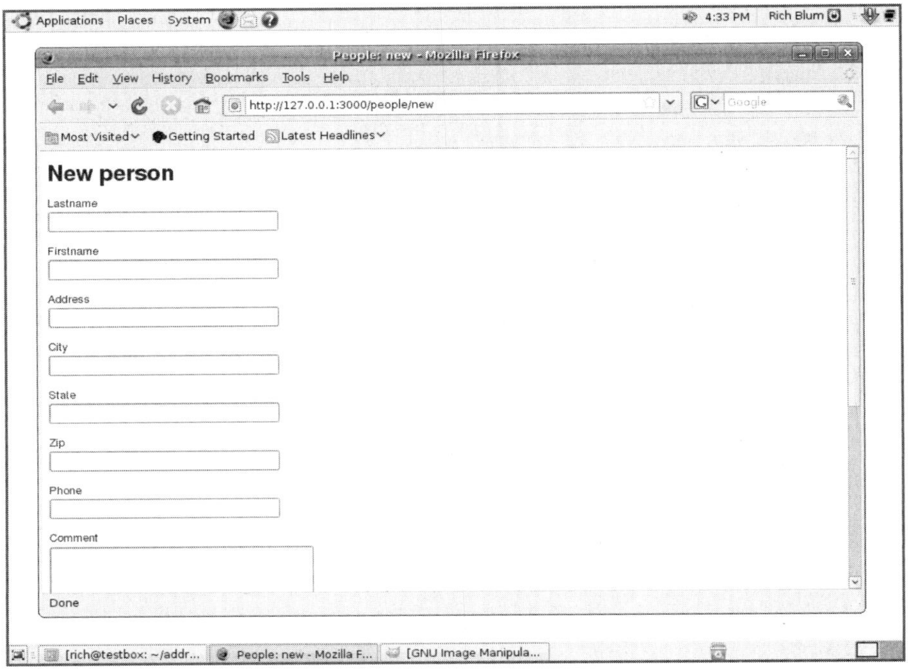

Figure 29-3: The new person data entry form web page.

There's nothing fancy here—just a text box for each string data field and a text area for the single text data field. Enter some test data into the form fields, then click the Create button. The Rails code automatically retrieves the data and enters it into the table. It also generates a new web page to confirm the new information entered, shown in Figure 29-4.

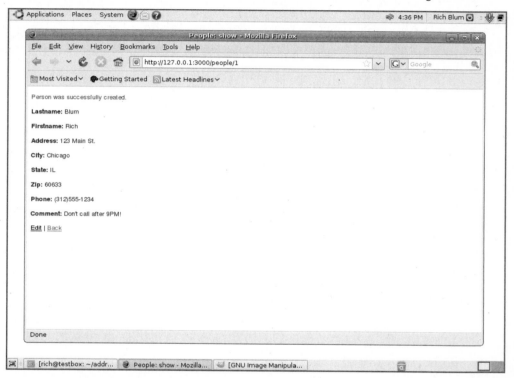

Figure 29-4: The new data confirmation page.

Click the Back link to return to the main index page for the controller. The main page uses the index REST action, which displays all of the data in the table, shown in Figure 29-5.

Although not fancy, you now have the framework for your dynamic web application—and without having to write a single line of code! All you need to do is add a little bit of styling to the project [for which the Rails project automatically generates a cascading style sheet (CSS) file], and you're ready to go live!

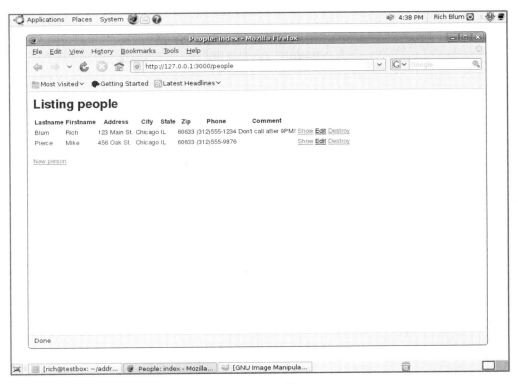

Figure 29-5: The main index page for the people table.

Summary

This chapter discussed the Ruby programming environment supported by Ubuntu. You can use Ruby to create shell scripts, embedded web pages, and full-featured dynamic web applications. The Ruby on Rails project automatically generates application framework code for handling standard operations on database tables. The chapter walked through the steps of installing Ruby (and Ruby on Rails) on your Ubuntu workstation or server, then discussed the various features of the Ruby scripting language. The chapter closed out by demonstrating the power of the Ruby on Rails framework by showing just how easy it is to get the core of a full-featured web application up and running, without having to write a single line of code.

The next chapter continues with the web programming theme by discussing another popular web-based programming language, PHP. The PHP programming language provides a simple interface to get you started in dynamic web programming and is relatively easy to install and get running in Ubuntu.

PHP

Chapter 30

With the popularity of the Internet, dynamic web programming has taken the world by storm, and the PHP programming language is at the forefront. PHP provides a relatively easy scripting language that you can add to your web pages to retrieve data from databases and display in your web pages. This chapter walks through the basic features of PHP and demonstrates how to use them in your dynamic web applications. The chapter concludes by discussing the object-oriented features of PHP and how to incorporate them to provide more advanced features in your web programs.

What Is PHP?

Chapter 21, "Web Server" described the popular Linux–Apache–MySQL–PHP (LAMP) web application environment in Ubuntu and showed how to use it to serve dynamic web pages to clients. The core of this technology is the PHP programming language.

PHP started out as a personal project by Rasmus Lerdorf in the mid 1990s, but it quickly rose to the top of the dynamic web programming world because it was specifically designed for web programming. Unlike Perl, Python, and Ruby, which were originally designed as command-line scripting languages, PHP was designed to be run within web pages in a web application.

Secret   The name PHP originally came from *Personal Home Page* because Rasmus intended for it to be used only on his own personal home page. Nonetheless, he released it into the open-source software world. Two developers (Zeev Suraski and Andi Gutmans) picked up the original code and rewrote it to form PHP version 3. The PHP initials were kept as part of the name, but the full name changed to PHP: Hypertext Preprocessor to more accurately identify the package. You'll notice that the term *PHP* appears in the definition itself. This practice is called *recursive initialism,* and it is common in the open-source world.

The PHP language is now maintained by the PHP Group and released under a special license. It is considered by the Free Software Foundation as free software. The Zend Corporation is a major contributor to the PHP Group and provides commercial support for the programming language.

The latest version of PHP (version 5) incorporates advanced object-oriented principles, as well as standard procedural programming principles. You can create PHP code using either technique, making PHP a robust language for beginning and advanced programmers alike.

Secret   As in the Ruby on Rails project (see Chapter 29, "Ruby Programming"), PHP incorporates a framework environment. The two most popular PHP framework packages are CakePHP and Zend Framework, both of which are available for the Ubuntu platform.

PHP in Ubuntu

The Ubuntu distribution allows you to install a LAMP server on the Ubuntu server as a part of the standard installation process. The LAMP server installation automatically incorporates the PHP preprocessor with the Apache web server and the MySQL database server installations. This is probably the easiest way to create a LAMP server. However, you can install the LAMP components separately if you either want to run them from an Ubuntu workstation or if you want to customize the installation on your Ubuntu server.

The following sections discuss how to install PHP in an Ubuntu environment.

Core Installation

There are two ways to install the core LAMP packages in your Ubuntu system:

♦ Use `tasksel` to install the LAMP application.
♦ Install the individual packages required to build a LAMP server.

This section walks through both methods, demonstrating how to use them.

Using tasksel

The Ubuntu `tasksel` utility allows you to easily install prebuilt packages from the Ubuntu software repositories. The prebuilt packages provide all of the software packages required to implement commonly used configurations in Ubuntu, such as the LAMP server package.

You can use `tasksel` to install the core LAMP server on your Ubuntu workstation (or server, if you didn't already select that at installation time).

To install LAMP using `tasksel`, follow these steps:

1. Open a Terminal session in your workstation, or log into the command line from your server.
2. Start the `tasksel` application.
   Enter the command:
   `sudo tasksel`

   The `tasksel` menu, shown in Figure 30-1, appears.
3. Select the LAMP server entry, then select OK. The `tasksel` utility goes to the Ubuntu repositories and downloads the appropriate packages required to install the LAMP components, then installs them.
4. Exit the `tasksel` utility.

And that's all there is to do! After `tasksel` finishes, the LAMP server is installed and running. To test it, just open a browser and go to the localhost address, shown in Figure 30-2.

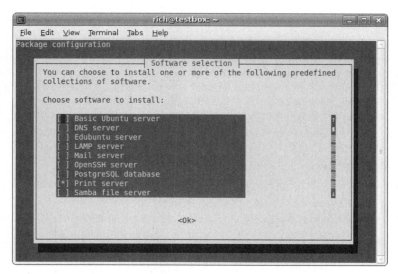

Figure 30-1: The tasksel menu.

Figure 30-2: Testing the Apache web server.

Secret

You can also use the `tasksel` packages from the `apt-get` command-line tool:

`sudo apt-get install lamp-server^`

The caret at the end is important, so don't forget it!

Be very careful when using the graphical `tasksel` utility. All of the `tasksel` packages appear in the menu. Installed packages (such as the Ubuntu server or Ubuntu workstation) are already selected with asterisks. Keep those asterisks in place! If you remove the asterisk from an installed package, `tasksel` will remove that package. Trust me; I speak from experience. Removing all the desktop packages is a bad thing—a very bad thing.

Installing Individual Packages

The obvious individual packages that you'll need to install for the LAMP server are:

- ◆ `apache2`: the latest version of the Apache web server
- ◆ `php5`: the latest version of the PHP preprocessor
- ◆ `mysql-server`: the latest version of the MySQL server

However, there are a couple of not-so-obvious packages that you'll need to install as well:

- ◆ `libapache2-mod-auth-mysql`: enables HTTP authentication against a MySQL database
- ◆ `php5-mysql`: the MySQL extension for PHP

If you start the Synaptic Package Manager application (see Chapter 13, "Software Installs and Upgrades") and search for each of the individual packages you'll be able to select and install them all.

If you're using the Ubuntu server, use the `apt-get` application from the command-line prompt to manually install each package (as shown in Chapter 13).

Secret

You may notice that several web programming platforms, such as Ruby and PHP, share many of the same components. If you've installed the Apache and MySQL server packages for one programming platform, they'll work just as well with the other. All you need to do is install the language-specific packages to support the other programming platform.

PHP Extensions

One feature of the PHP programming language is the use of *extensions*. Extensions provide additional functionality not compiled into the core PHP functions. There are PHP extensions for a host of different features, including access to various database servers, graphical manipulation tools, and additional mathematical processing functions.

Ubuntu includes different PHP extensions as separate software packages that you can install. Table 30-1 lists the different PHP extension packages available.

Table 30-1: The PHP Extension Packages

Package	Description
php5-adodb	Interfaces with the ADO database
php5-auth-pam	Allows PHP applications to access the Ubuntu PAM system to authenticate users
php5-curl	Provides functions to interact on the network, such as HTTP, FTP, and Telnet connectivity
php5-ffmpeg	Provides access to audio and video file formats
php5-gd	Supports advanced graphical rendering functions
php5-geoip	Determines the geographic location of an IP address
php5-gmp	Provides arbitrary precision mathematical operations
php5-gpib	Provides support for IEEE 488 hardware
php5-idn	Allows international characters in DNS addresses
php5-imagick	Provides an image processing library
php5-imap	Allows access to remote email servers via the Internet message access protocol (IMAP).
php5-interbase	Provides functions for accessing an Interbase/Firebird database server
php5-lasso	Provides functions for interacting with single sign-on protocols
php5-ldap	Provides lightweight directory access protocol (LDAP) functions.
php5-mapscript	Provides MapServer functions
php5-mcrypt	Provides encryption functions
php5-mhash	Provides encryption hashing functions
php5-ming	Provides functions to create and modify Flash-format movies
php5-mysql	Provides functions to interact with a MySQL database server
php5-odbc	Provides functions to interact with the ODBC database specification
php5-pgsql	Provides functions to interact with a PostgreSQL database server
php5-ps	Provides functions to create and modify PostScript files
php5-pspell	Provides functions for spell checking
php5-radius	Provides RADIUS authentication
php5-sasl	Provides simple authentication and security layer (SASL) authentication functions
php5-snmp	Provides simple network management protocol (SNMP) functions
php5-sqlite	Provides functions to interact with an SQLite database server
php5-sybase	Provides functions to interact with a Sybase database server
php5-syk	Provides functions to parse data in YAML-formatted files
php5-tidy	Cleans, repairs, and traverses HTML, XHTML, and XML documents
php5-xapian	Provides advanced indexing and searching functions

As you can see, there are plenty of PHP extension packages you can install to provide additional functionality to your LAMP server. Be careful, though, because you don't want to install packages that you don't need. Doing so will needlessly slow down your PHP preprocessor.

Working with PHP

Before getting into PHP programming it's a good idea to understand the fundamentals of working with PHP in your web programs. This section walks through the basics of incorporating PHP in your web applications.

Defining PHP Code

PHP was designed to work within the standard HTML framework in web pages. If you're familiar with HTML coding, no doubt you know about HTML tags. All HTML pages use tags to identify sections within the web page. Each HTML section uses an opening tag and a closing tag. For example, to form a basic web page, you would use this code:

```
<html>
<body>
<h1>This is a simple Web page.</h1>
This is the text portion.
</body>
</html>
```

The <html> and </html> tag combination marks the start and end of the web page. The <body> and </body> tag combination marks the start and end of the body of the web page. Text that requires special formatting is also enclosed in tags. The <h1> and </h1> tag combination marks the text as using the heading 1 HTML font style.

PHP code is no different. You can embed code blocks anywhere within the standard HTML code page, but they must be identified by start and end tags. There are a few different ways you can do this.

The most basic method is to use the <?php and ?> tag combination:

```
<html>
<body>
<?php
php scripting code
?>
</body>
</html>
```

The PHP tags are contained within the normal HTML web page. You can also have other HTML tags outside of the PHP code area, such as heading and paragraph tags. Notice that the PHP begin tag (<?php) is open ended. The web server interprets everything between the begin and the end tags. Everything you put between the <?php and the ?> tags is considered PHP code. You can't use normal HTML tags within this area, only PHP code.

Another, more formal, way of identifying PHP code uses the <script> HTML tag:

```
<html>
<body>
<script language="php">
```

```
php scripting code
</script>
</body>
</html>
```

This method is sometimes required by integrated development environment (IDE) packages that utilize PHP code.

Yet another tag format, called *short open tags*, allows you to utilize a tagging method that's commonly used in other web programming languages, such as Microsoft's ASP.NET:

```
<html>
<body>
<?
php scripting code
?>
</body>
</html>
```

The simplified <? and ?> tag pair doesn't specifically declare the programming language used, which sometimes causes confusion when trying to maintain program code.

Secret

The short open tag method is configured in the php.ini configuration file, and it is often not set by default. To check the setting, open the php.ini configuration file (see Chapter 13, "Software Installs and Updates") and look for this line:

```
short_open_tag = Off
```

If the value is set to Off, change it to On and restart the Apache web server to support short open tags.

You aren't limited to having just one PHP coding block in your HTML code. You can have as many PHP coding sections as are necessary. For example, your code could look like this:

```
<html>
<body>
<h2>This is the first PHP coding section</h2>
<?php
echo "This is <i>PHP code</i>\n";
?>
<h2>This is the second PHP coding section</h2>
<?php
echo "This is <b>more</b> PHP code\n";
?>
</body>
</html>
```

Each PHP code section has its own beginning and end tag combination. Anything outside of the PHP tags is considered normal HTML code and is treated as such by the web server. This example also demonstrates how PHP displays information in the final HTML page using the echo statement.

PHP Output

For a web page to be dynamic, the PHP code must create HTML code for the client to interpret. The example in the previous section used the PHP `echo` command to send text to the client web browser. The web browser interprets the text as if it were part of the normal HTML code page.

Let's do an exercise to see how this works. Follow these steps to create a dynamic web page:

1. Create a text document in the `/var/www` folder called `phptest.php`. You can use either the standard gedit program or the vim editor from the command prompt, but you must have administrative privileges to create the file. You can do that by running the command:

   ```
   sudo gedit /var/www/phptest.php
   ```

2. Copy the following sample code (which we looked at in the previous section) and paste it into your text file:

   ```
   <html>
   <body>
   <h2>This is the first PHP coding section</h2>
   <?php
   echo "This is <i>PHP code</i>\n";
   ?>
   <h2>This is the second PHP coding section</h2>
   <?php
   echo "This is <b>more</b> PHP code\n";
   ?>
   </body>
   </html>
   ```

   If you use the gedit editor, it'll automatically highlight your code for you. The code creates a web page and displays two text lines within the page using PHP code.

3. Save the file and exit the editor.

4. Test the code by opening your browser and using the URL `http://localhost/phptest.php`.

Any web page file that contains PHP code must use a `.php` file extension. This extension notifies the Apache web server that it must run the web page through the PHP preprocessor to execute the embedded PHP code. If you use the standard `.htm` or `.html` file extension, the web server won't process your PHP code, and your clients will see just the raw PHP code on their screens (ouch).

Figure 30-3 shows what you should see when you view the web page from a browser.

If you view the web page HTML code from your browser, you'll see the exact code that the server sent. In Microsoft Internet Explorer, you can do this by clicking View ⇨ Source, or in Firefox by selecting View ⇨ Page Source. Notice that the HTML code shown doesn't include the embedded PHP code, just the HTML code that the PHP `echo` commands generated, as shown in Figure 30-4.

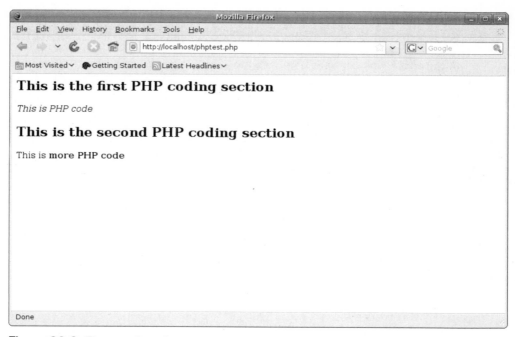

Figure 30-3: The sample web page.

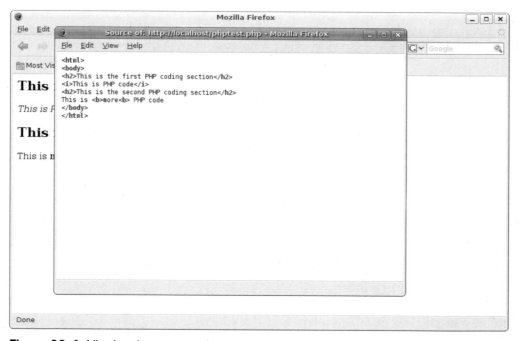

Figure 30-4: Viewing the output web page source code.

This demonstrates exactly how PHP works. The only thing the web browser sees within the PHP coding sections is any output from the PHP script, nothing else. The web server hides all of the PHP code from the client. Now that you've seen how to run PHP code, it's time to go through a few of the basics of PHP programming.

Secret

There's a known problem with the Debian php5 installation package that Ubuntu uses. It's possible that after installing your LAMP server you won't be able to view the .php files from your browser (your browser will ask you to save the file instead of displaying the file contents). If this happens, first try to reboot your Ubuntu server. If that doesn't solve the problem, reinstall the libapache2-mod-php5 package that's normally installed as part of the php5 package, using either the Synaptic Package Manager or apt-get, then restart the Apache web server (see Chapter 13, "Software Installs and Updates"). This should solve the problem.

The PHP Language

This section walks through some of the basics of the PHP programming language that'll come in handy as you create your web applications.

PHP Variables

Just like any other programming language, PHP allows you to use variables within your scripts. Variables are placeholders that you assign values to throughout the duration of the program. When the program references the variable, it represents the actual value that the program last assigned.

Variables are what make PHP an excellent choice for dynamic web pages. You can create web pages using variables whose values change based on data stored in a database. Each time the web server references a variable, the variable can contain a value from a different record in the database.

There are three types of variables you can use in PHP:

◆ Scalar variables
◆ Array variables
◆ Associative array variables

Each type of variable has different uses in your programs.

Scalar Variables

A PHP *scalar variable* is identified by a leading dollar sign ($) in front of a text variable name. You must start a variable name with a letter or an underscore character (_), and it can contain only letters, numbers, and underscores (a variable name can't contain spaces).

You set values to variables using assignment statements, like this:

```
$test = "This is a test string";
```

Notice that the PHP assignment statement (like the echo statement we saw earlier) ends with a semicolon. This is how PHP recognizes the end of a statement. I can't tell you how many PHP coding errors I've created by forgetting semicolons!

Variables can contain either string values (common text characters such as letters, numbers, and special characters) or numerical values. A single variable can hold either type at any time (in this way, PHP is unlike some programming languages that force you to declare a variable's type at the start of the program).

Here's a simple example demonstrating using different data types in a variable in PHP:

```
<html>
<body>
<?php
$name = "Rich";
echo "<h2>Hello, $name, how are you?</h2>\n";
$name = "Joe Bob";
echo "<h2>Oh, so now your name is $name, huh?</h2>\n";
$name = 4.2;
$name = $name * 2;
echo "<h2>That's tricky, now the variable is equal to $name!</h2>\n";
?>
</body>
</html>
```

Let's look at exactly what's going on here. First, the program assigns a string value of "Rich" to the variable $name:

```
$name = "Rich";
```

Notice that you must enclose the string in double quotation marks when you assign it (to mark the beginning and end of the assigned string value).

The next statement uses the variable value by echoing an HTML-encoded text string that includes the variable:

```
echo "<h2>Hello, $name, how are you?</h2>\n";
```

Unlike some other programming languages, PHP allows you to insert the variable within the echo statement. It'll automatically determine how to display the variable value, no matter what the data type.

The \n characters at the end of the echo statement are code to indicate a standard *newline character*. The newline character forces the cursor to start a new line on the display. Although not absolutely necessary, it helps separate the output line within the HTML code.

Next, the program changes the variable to a different string value, which includes a space:

```
$name = "Joe Bob";
```

When the program uses the variable in the echo statement, the client browser will display the entire variable string value exactly as it's stored, including the space (instead of removing the space, as it does when displaying HTML code).

Finally, the program assigns a numerical value to the variable, then it uses an arithmetic statement to calculate a new value for the variable:

```
$name = 4.2;
$name = $name * 2;
```

This is an example of PHP's ability to use any data type in any variable at any time. You can use variables in just about any type of arithmetic statement that uses standard arithmetic operators. Here, the result of the operation is stored in the $name variable, then the program uses an echo statement to display the variable's new value.

Array Variables

Arrays allow you to group similar values in a list using a single variable name. You can then either handle the values as a whole by referencing the variable name or handle each value individually within the array by referencing its place in the array list. When you access data from a MySQL database, you'll need to use arrays. So, it helps to get a handle on them early.

PHP groups database results into arrays based on the individual data records. When you query the database, PHP will push the returned data into an array. You'll then have to extract the individual data elements from the array so that you can display them in the proper location on the web page.

You define an array variable in a normal assign statement that uses the array() function. The array() function creates a list of values instead of a just a single value:

```
$family = array("Rich," "Barbara," "Katie," "Jessica");
```

This assign statement creates an array of string values. You must list each element in the array and separate them with a comma. Although this example uses string values for the elements within the array, you can also use numbers.

PHP references each element in an array using a positional number. The first element in the array is element 0, the second is element 1, and so on. So, for example, in the assign statement above, Rich = 0, Barbara = 1, Katie = 2, and Jessica = 3. (PHP arrays always start counting array elements with the number 0.)

To reference a single element in an array, you add the desired element number (enclosed in square brackets) to the variable name:

```
<html>
<body>
<?php
$family = array("Rich," "Barbara," "Katie," "Jessica");
echo "The first person is $family[0]<br>";
echo "The last person is $family[3]<br>";
?>
</body>
</html>
```

PHP provides the count() function to determine how many elements are in an array:

```
$count = count($family);
```

This lets you know how many times you need to iterate through the array to retrieve all of the data elements.

Associative Array Variables

PHP also supports *associative arrays* (sometimes known as hashes), which associate an array value with a text key. Take a look at this example:

```
$favorite = array("fruit" => "banana," "vegetable" => "carrot");
```

The array definition assigns a key value of fruit to the data value of banana, and a key value of vegetable to the data value of carrot. Now, if you reference the array with one of the key values, PHP automatically retrieves the data value. This code statement:

```
echo "My favorite fruit is a {$valarray ['fruit'] } ";
```

will produce the output:

```
My favorite fruit is a banana
```

Notice that when you use an associative array variable in the echo statement, you must enclose it with braces. This is different from numerical arrays, which don't need the braces.

Iterating Through Arrays

The tricky part of working with array and associative array variables is extracting all of the data they contain. If you use associative array variables, you may have no way of knowing what key values the array contains. Even if you use numeric array variables, there's no guarantee that the key numbers are sequential (you can assign a value to $myarray[6] without assigning a value to $myarray[3], $myarray[4], or $myarray[5]).

Fortunately for us, the thoughtful programmers who developed PHP came up with a simple solution. The foreach statement iterates through an array, extracting every key/value pair defined within the array, one at a time.

There are a couple of ways to use the foreach statement with an array. The first method extracts only the value stored in the array, without regard to the key:

```
$myarray = array("state"=>"Illinois," "city"=>"Chicago," "zip"=>"60633");
foreach ($myarray as $value)
{
echo "The value is $value<br>\n";
}
```

In this code snippet, the foreach statement loops through the $myarray array variable. Each value stored in the array is extracted as the variable $value and can be used anywhere within the foreach loop. Notice that the $value variable is a normal variable and can be used without the braces.

The second way to extract array values pulls the entire key/value pair:

```
$myarray = array("state"=>"Illinois," "city"=>"Chicago," "zip"=>"60633");
foreach($myarray as $key=>$value)
{
echo "The $key value is $value<br>\n";
}
```

Now you have access to both the key and the data value within the array. Again, the $key and $value variables are normal variables you can use anywhere within the foreach loop to represent the key and data value.

Structured Commands

The PHP programming language supports program flow control using structured commands. The most common methods are the if-then statements and various looping statements. This section discusses both of these structured command statements.

if-then Statements

A standard if-then statement executes one or more statements based on evaluating a condition. If the condition is true, the statements are executed. This feature allows you to execute PHP code based on the results of a comparison, such as adding tax to a price only if the item is a luxury item. The basic format of the if-then statement in PHP is

```
if (condition)
{
code block 1
} elsif
{
code block 2
} else
{
code block 3
}
```

The if-then statement contains the statements it controls within braces and the *condition* it evaluates within parentheses. The condition must be an expression that results in either a true or false Boolean value.

You can check for all sorts of conditions, such as whether a number is a specific value or within a range of values, or whether a string value is equal to specific text (for example, checking for database records that are marked as active).

Let's create a test file to demonstrate using the if-then statement. Follow these steps:

1. Open a text editor and enter this code:

```
<html>
<body>
<h1>Random number test</h1>
<?php
$value = rand(0, 100);
if ($value > 50)
{
echo "<h2>The value is big: $value</h2>\n";
} elseif ($value > 25)
{
echo "<h2>The value is medium: $value</h2>\n";
} else
{
echo "<h2>The value is small: $value</h2>\n";
}
?>
</body>
</html>
```

2. Save the file in the /var/www folder as a file called randomtest.php.

3. Open a browser window and go to the URL http://localhost/randomtest.php.

This script uses the rand() PHP function to generate a random integer value between 0 and 100, which it stores in the variable $value. The script then uses that variable in three separate if-then statements.

You can run the PHP script multiple times by clicking the reload button on your browser. Each time you reload the web page, the script generates a new random number, producing a different answer.

while Loops

while loops allow you to process a set of statements repeatedly until a specific condition is met:

```
while ( condition)
{
statements to repeat
}
```

Usually, within the repeated statements is a statement that alters the value of the variable in the condition. Here's a simple example of how this works:

```
$count = 0;
while ($count < 10)
{
echo "the value is $count";
$count = $count + 1;
}
```

The while loop will continue executing the two statements as long as the $count variable is less than the value 10.

Including External Files

One feature of PHP that many web developers love is the ability to create *include files*. You might also hear these referred to as *server side includes*. The include() statement allows you to include the contents of one web page within another web page simply by referencing a filename. This process is a lot like using a frame or an iframe in HTML, but it's easier, and you can be surer that web browsers will display everything the way you want.

The include() Statement

The PHP processor inserts all of the lines in the include file directly into the PHP code exactly where you place the include() statement. It's just as if you typed all of those lines of code yourself into the page that's displaying it. The server then processes the included lines as normal PHP code. Any variables within the include file are handled as if they were defined within the main script.

Developers use this feature to create standard header and footer include files, which they can then easily incorporate into all of their web pages. Imagine having a standard header and footer section on all of your web pages by just adding two lines of code!

You could create the navigation for your site once and then be guaranteed that it will display exactly the same way on every page. If you ever needed to change something in your navigation, you'd have to alter your only code one time, in one place. What could be better?

The format of the include() statement is simple:

```
include("filename");
```

You just replace *filename* with the actual name of the file. That's all there is to it. Let's try it out by following these steps:

1. Create a sample file called header.inc.php in the /var/www folder, containing the text:

```
<?php
echo "<h1 align=\"center\">This is a test header</h1>\n";
```

```
echo "<a href=main.php>Main</a>\n";
?>
```

Developers often give include files the .inc extension to indicate that they are not complete web pages on their own. You can also attach the .php file extension to indicate that the file contains PHP code. It's not necessary to do this because the server doesn't process the actual include file itself. Instead, it inserts it into the main PHP file.

2. Create another file in the same folder and call it main.php. Type the following code and text into it:

```
<html>
<body>
<?php include("header.inc.php"); ?>
<br><br>
<h2>This is the body of the main page</h2>
</body>
</html>
```

3. Open your browser and view the URL http://localhost/main.php.

You should see the header file information, followed by the main file information, as shown in Figure 30-.5.

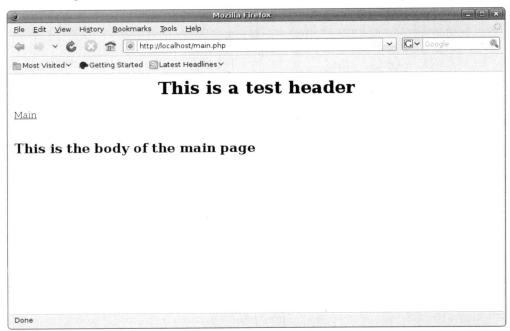

Figure 30-5: Using the include() function to include a PHP file.

Now if you want to use a common header for all of your application pages, all you need to do is use the `include()` function to include the same `header.inc.php` code file. When you need to change the contents of the header, all you have to do is change a single file, and the change applies to all of your pages!

Secret This little example also demonstrates another PHP tidbit to remember. Notice in step 1 that you must escape the double quotation marks in the h1 tag using the backslash character. Doing so prevents the `echo` statement from thinking that the quotation marks represent the end of the string.

Referencing include() Files

The simple example shown in the previous section referenced the include file only by its filename. There was no path information provided. You can get away with this as long as the include file is located in the same directory as the main file.

But some web programmers prefer to keep include files separate from the main files by placing them in a folder under the document root directory. To reference these include files, you must use a pathname along with the filename. However, this can be a tricky business that leads to interesting results.

You can use two pathname methods to reference the include file:

♦ Absolute pathnames
♦ Relative pathnames

Absolute pathnames reference the include file from the root folder on the system. If you're referencing the include file using an absolute pathname, the filename must begin with a slash:

```
include("/var/www/includes/header.inc.php");
```

In this example the `header.inc.php` file is located in the `includes` folder, which is under the `www` folder.

The relative pathname method references the include file based on the current location of the main program code using the `include()` function. For example, if you wanted to reference the `header.inc.php` include file from the `main.php` file located in the `www` folder, you'd use the relative pathname:

```
include("includes/header.inc.php");
```

This relative pathname assumes that the `includes` folder is under the current folder and that the `header.inc.php` include file is located there.

If the `include()` function can't find the file that you're trying to reference, it produces two errors on the web page:

```
Warning: include(header.inc.php) [function.include]: failed to open stream:
No such file or directory in /var/www/main.php on line 3

Warning: include() [function.include]: Failed opening 'header.inc.php' for
inclusion (include_path='.;/usr/lib/pear') in /var/www/main.php on line 3
```

However, even though the `include()` function failed, the rest of the PHP code continues processing. This may not be what you want to have happen.

The require() Statement

The last example demonstrated another limitation of the `include()` statement. When it failed, it produced an error on the web page, but the PHP program just kept on going.

Sometimes you don't want to continue if an error occurs in your web page. Instead of just plowing through the rest of the code, you want the server to stop immediately so that the error message is the only thing you see. PHP has a solution for this.

The `require()` statement works exactly like the `include()` statement except for one difference: It forces the web server to stop all processing if it fails.

Working with MySQL

The key to a dynamic web page is the ability to interact with the MySQL database to retrieve data to display on the web page. PHP provides a host of functions to interact with the MySQL server. Table 30-2 lists the main PHP functions you'll want to learn how to use.

Table 30-2: The Main PHP MySQL Functions

Function	Description
`mysq_connect(host, userid, password)`	Establish a connection with the MySQL server
`mysql_select_db(dbname, connection)`	Define a default database to interact with
`mysql_query(query)`	Submit an SQL statement to the MySQL server
`mysql_num_rows(result)`	Return the number of records present in a result set
`mysql_fetch_array(result, type)`	Retrieve the individual records from a query result set

The basic flow of interacting with the MySQL server is

1. Connect with the server.
2. Select a default database.
3. Submit an SQL query.
4. Retrieve the query result set one record at a time.

Here's an example of using the PHP MySQL functions to interact with a database and retrieve data:

```
<html>
<body>
<h2>Product Listing</h2>
<?php
$connection = mysql_connect("localhost," "test," "test");
mysql_select_db("store," $connection);
```

```
$query = "SELECT prodid, description, price FROM products";
$result = mysql_query($query);
while ($row = mysql_fetch_array($result, MYSQL_ASSOC))
{
$prodid = $row['prodid'];
$description = $row['description'];
$price = $row['price'];

echo "$prodid - $description<br>\n";
echo "Cost: $$$price<br><br>\n";
}
?>
</body>
</html>
```

This example submits a simple SELECT SQL statement to the MySQL server to retrieve three data fields from the products table.

Object-Oriented PHP

One of the neat features about PHP is that as well as using standard procedural programming, it fully supports object-oriented programming (OOP). You can ease your way into the object-oriented world by applying the skills you've used in PHP.

In OOP, everything is related to a *class*. A class defines the characteristics of an object that you're using in your application. Every application revolves around handling objects. For example, a store application revolves around handling three objects: products, customers, and orders.

OOP classes define the objects that your application uses. Each class contains both the data and functions (called *methods* in OOP) required to interact with the object. Once you define the objects, all your application code needs to do is use the data and methods defined for the objects to process and manipulate them.

The benefit to OOP is that once you create a class for an object, you can use that same object any time in any other application, because you already have the code for using that object. Just plug in the class definition code, and you can use it in your application.

An OOP class consists of *members*. There are two types of members:

- ◆ **Properties:** Properties define attributes for the object (such as the description, price, and quantity in stock of a product). A class can contain many different property members, with each property describing a different feature of the object.
- ◆ **Methods:** A class method performs an operation using the properties defined in the class.

You create class methods to perform specific functions on the class data, such as a method to buy a product (where you subtract a value from the quantity property) or change the price of the product (where you add or subtract a value to the price property). Each class should be self-contained. The methods in a class should operate only on properties within the class and shouldn't deal with properties in other classes.

Creating a Class in PHP

The class definition in PHP declares all the members that comprise the class, both properties and methods. Here's an example of a simple class definition in PHP:

```
class Product {
public $description;
public $price;
public $quantity;
public $onsale;

public function buyProduct($amount) {
$this->quantity -= $amount;
}
}
```

This class defines four property members and one method member. Each member is defined using one of three visibility classifications. The visibility of a member determines where you can use or reference that member. There are three visibility keywords used in PHP:

- ◆ **Public:** The member can be accessed from outside of the class code.
- ◆ **Private:** The member can be accessed only from inside the class code.
- ◆ **Protected:** The member can be accessed only from a child class (we'll talk about that a little later).

The Product class example declares all of the members as public, so you can reference them anywhere in your PHP code.

The buyProduct() method uses an odd variable name in the function:

```
$this->quantity
```

The $this variable is a special identifier that references the current class object. In this example, it points to the $quantity property of the class. Notice the removal of the dollar sign from the quantity variable when referencing it this way. This helps PHP know that you're referencing the $quantity variable from within the class.

Now, let's take a look at how to create an actual object using the Product class.

Secret

Between PHP versions 4.x and 5.x, PHP vastly changed the way to define and use classes. The use of the code in this lesson follows PHP version 5 standards. If you're using a PHP version 4.x server, please consult the PHP online manual for how to create and use classes.

Creating Objects

PHP code uses the class definition to define objects but not actually to create the object itself. *Instantiating* is the process of creating an object using a class definition. Once you instantiate a class into an object, you can use the object within your application code to reference properties and methods.

To instantiate an object in PHP code, you use the following format:

```
$prod1 = new Product();
```

This creates the object called $prod1 using the Product class. Once you instantiate an object, you can access the public members of that class from anywhere in your application:

```
$prod1->description = "carrot";
$prod1->price = 1.50;
$prod1->quantity = 10;
```

This code sets values for the properties of this object. Notice that you must use the -> symbol to reference the property of the object. The $prod1 variable now contains these values for the properties, and you can use them anywhere within your application code to reference these values.

The same applies when you need to use a public method of an object:

```
$prod1->buyProduct(4);
```

This calls the buyProduct() method, passing the value 4. Because the buyProduct() method alters the $quantity value in the object, the next time you reference $prod1->quantity, it'll have the value 6.

Writing OOP Code in PHP

Let's write an example program using the Product class so that we can see OOP in action. Just follow these steps:

1. Create a file called example1.php in the /var/www/html folder.

2. Open the file in a text editor and add the following code:

```php
<?php
class Product {
public $description;
public $price;
public $quantity;

public function printProduct() {
echo "Product: $this->description<br>\n";
printf("Price: $%.2f<br>\n," $this->price);
echo "Quantity: $this->quantity<br>\n";
}

public function buyProduct($amount) {
$this->quantity -= $amount;
}
}

$prod1 = new Product();
$prod1->description = "Carrots";
$prod1->price = 1.50;
$prod1->quantity = 10;
```

```
echo "Just added product:<br>\n";
$prod1->printProduct();
echo "<br>Buying 4 carrots…\n";
$prod1->buyProduct(4);
echo "Quantity is now: $prod1->quantity<br>\n";
?>
```

3. Save the file and exit the text editor.

4. Open your browser, and go to the URL http://localhost/example1.php.

When you view the example1.php web page, you should see the web page shown in Figure 30-6.

Figure 30-6: The output from the example1.php code.

This example defines the Product class, which contains the four properties we discussed, plus two class methods: the buyProduct() method you've already seen and the print-Product() method.

The printProduct() method is a quick way to print the property values of the Product object. You can use this method any time you need to display the object values in your application.

Expanding on OOP

The simple OOP example we created isn't necessarily the best way to create a class and use it. In that example, you created all of the properties using the public classification, which means that any application that uses the Product class can directly access the properties and modify them with whatever values it wants. That could be dangerous, and it's somewhat frowned upon in OOP circles. What if a wayward application set the price property of a product to a negative value? OOP allows you to code your classes to help prevent accidents like that.

The preferred way to handle properties in a class is to make them private so that any external code can't change them. It then creates public methods that allow programs to set and get the property values. You can control exactly what happens to the properties in those public methods. Let's create another example that demonstrates this technique:

1. Create a file called example2.php in the /var/www/html folder.

2. Open the file in a text editor and add the following code:

```php
<?php
class Product {
private $description;
private $price;
private $quantity;
public function setDescription($value) {
$this->description = $value;
}

public function getDescription() {
return $this->description;
}

public function setPrice($value) {
if ($value > 0)
$this->price = $value;
else
$this->price = 0;
}

public function getPrice() {
return $this->price;
}

public function setQuantity($amount) {
$this->quantity = $amount;
}

public function getQuantity() {
return $this->quantity;
}

public function printProduct() {
echo "Product: $this->description<br>\n";
printf("Price: $%.2f<br>\n," $this->price);
echo "Quantity: $this->quantity<br>\n";
}

public function buyProduct($val) {
$this->quantity -= $val;
```

```
    }
}

$prod1 = new Product();
$prod1->setDescription("Carrot");
$prod1->setPrice(1.50);
$prod1->setQuantity(10);
echo "Just added product:<br>\n";
$prod1->printProduct();
echo "<br>Buying 4 carrots...\n";
$prod1->buyProduct(4);
echo "Quantity is now: " . $prod1->getQuantity() . "<br>\n";
?>
```

3. Save the file and exit the text editor.

4. Open a browser and go to the URL http://localhost/example2.php.

You should see the same output as for the example1.php code. Notice that the new methods set the property values inside the class. Only those methods are allowed to access the properties directly. If you try using the code

```
$prod1->quantity = 10;
```

in your application, you'll get an error message, because the properties are now private. This safeguard provides a basic level of protection for your data. You can put any type of checks in the methods that set property values. The setPrice() method demonstrates this feature by checking the value that the program code assigns to the price property.

There's one downside to protecting your class properties, though: It's somewhat of a pain to create a new class object, because you have to use the individual set methods to define each property value. Fortunately, PHP provides an easy way to solve this problem.

Class Constructors

Most OOP languages provide a special method called a *constructor.* The constructor allows you to automatically define property values when you instantiate an object. PHP uses the special method __construct() to define the constructor:

```
public function __construct($name, $value, $amount) {
$this->description = $name;
if ($value > 0)
$this->price = $value;
else
$this->price = 0;
$this->quantity = $amount;
}
```

The constructor for our Product class uses three parameters to assign values to the three class properties when you instantiate an object. To create a new Product object, you must use this format:

```
$prod1 = new Product("Carrot," 1.50, 10);
```

You can now use a constructor to force the program code to set the class properties when it instantiates the object. If you choose, you can also block any properties from changing by not providing methods that change the values. That's a lot of control over your code!

At the beginning of this section I mentioned that OOP programming allows you to use your classes in any application. The key is to create the class constructor as a separate program file. Try out this example:

1. For the `Product` class, create a file called `Product.inc.php` in the `/var/www` folder and add this code:

```php
<?php
class Product {
private $description;
private $price;
private $quantity;

public function __construct($name, $value, $amount) {
$this->description = $name;
if ($value > 0)
$this->price = $value;
else
$this->price = 0;
$this->quantity = $amount;
}

public function setDescription($value) {
$this->description = $value;
}

public function getDescription() {
return $this->description;
}

public function setPrice($value) {
if ($value > 0)
$this->price = $value;
else
$this->price = 0;
}

public function getPrice() {
return $this->price;
}

public function setQuantity($amount) {
$this->quantity = $amount;
}
public function getQuantity() {
return $this->quantity;
}

public function printProduct() {
echo "Product: $this->description<br>\n";
printf("Price: $%.2f<br>\n," $this->price);
```

```
echo "Quantity: $this->quantity<br>\n";
}

public function buyProduct($amount) {
$this->quantity -= $amount;
}

public function addProduct($amount) {
$this->quantity += $amount;
}
}
?>
```

Now you can use the Product class in any program you need it. All you must do is use the include() function to include the Product.inc.php code to define the class before you try to use it in your program.

2. Create a file called ProdTest.php in the /var/www folder and add the code:

```
<?php
include("Product.inc.php");

$prod1 = new Product("Carrots," 1.50, 10);
echo "Just added product:<br>\n";
$prod1->printProduct();
$prod2 = new Product("Onions," 2.00, 15);
echo "<br>Just added product:<br>\n";
$prod2->printProduct();
echo "<br>Buying 4 carrots…\n";
$prod1->buyProduct(4);
$quant = $prod1->getQuantity();
echo "Quantity is now: $quant<br>\n";
echo "Buying 3 onions…\n";
$prod2->buyProduct(3);
$quant = $prod2->getQuantity();
echo "Quantity is now: $quant<br>\n";
echo "Adding 10 more carrots…\n";
$prod1->addProduct(10);
$quant = $prod1->getQuantity();
echo "Quantity is now: $quant<br>\n";
?>
```

The Product.inc.php file contains the class definition code for the Product class. Putting the class definition code in a separate file is a common practice that allows you to use the class in any PHP program you want.

Figure 30-7 shows the output generated from this code.

Naming the class file the same as the class name isn't necessary, but it sure makes life easier! All you have to do is use the include() function to bring the class definition code into your application code. Once you include the class definition, you can use it to create as many class objects as you need to handle your data.

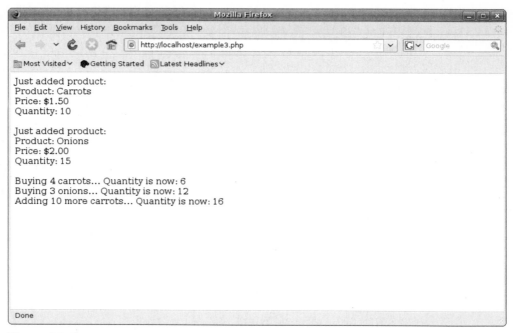

Figure 30-7: The output from using the Product class in a program.

PECL and PEAR

Because PHP is an open-source project, sharing is at its core. There are two great clearinghouses for PHP features:

♦ The PHP Extension Community Library (PECL)

♦ The PHP Extension and Application Repository (PEAR)

PECL provides a great place for finding PHP extensions to perform specific tasks, such as interfacing with a POP3 mail server. Extensions provide additional functions to the PHP language.

PEAR provides a repository for posting actual applications. Most of these applications are posted as object-oriented objects, so using them is as easy as including the source code in your project and using the object methods. There are packages posted to cover many exotic functions, such as producing interactive calendars and sending email through a remote SMTP server.

Summary

Ubuntu provides a full PHP development and production environment in the LAMP setup. This chapter discussed how to ensure you have the LAMP setup installed, then it walked through the basics of the PHP programming language. PHP provides all of the standard programming features that you'd expect, plus some extras. It provides functions to interface your database with your web pages, allowing you to submit SQL queries to the database and retrieve the results. PHP also provides more advanced object-oriented features for professional coding projects. The PECL and PEAR sites are clearinghouses that allow you to share your clever PHP creations with others—and benefit from others' hard work. You can create a complete dynamic web application with just a few lines of PHP code added to your web site.

Thanks for joining me on this journey through the Ubuntu Linux system. I hope you've enjoyed working with Ubuntu and have learned lots of new things you can do with your system. But don't stop your Ubuntu education here. New versions of Ubuntu are released every 6 months. There's always something new to explore in each new version. Stay in touch with the Ubuntu community, and follow along with the new advances and features.

Index

servers. *See* servers
software packages and, 316
sound generation in, 281
updates. *See* updates/installs
upgrading, 75–76, 319
versions, 22–23, 27, 319, 769
web site, 26
workstations. *See* workstations
Wubi project and. *See* Wubi project
ubuntu (home folder), 40
UDP (user datagram protocol), 361, 478, 481, 483. *See also* TCP
ufs, 11
umsdos, 11
unallocated, 56
uniform resource identifier. *See* URI
UNIX mbox spool directory, 232
UNIX mbox spool file, 232
UNIX operating system. *See also* CUPS; GNU
    GNU utilities. *See* coreutils
    Linux filesystems and, 11, 111
    Linux kernel and, 4
updates/installs (Ubuntu), 315–336. *See also* installation process
update (apt-get command), 334
Update Download Progress dialog box, 321
Update Manager applet, 76, 82, 86, 319–322, 336
Updates tab, 318, 319
upgrade (apt-get command), 334
upgrading Ubuntu, 75–76, 319
URI (uniform resource identifier), 84, 137, 262, 371, 372
.us, 471
USB memory sticks, 22
    F-Spot and, 269
    LiveCD and, 41
Usenet news, 231
user accounts. *See also* groups
    adding, 408–411
    deleting, 413–414
    /etc/passwd file, 418–419
    /etc/shadow file, 419
    modifying, 412–413
    in MySQL, 600–602

    in PostgreSQL, 602
User Administration tool, 408–413
user commands, 420–421
user datagram protocol (UDP), 361, 478, 481, 483
user files, 418–419
User Name plug-in, 141
user setting, 582
User Switcher applet, 86, 93
user variables, 613–614
user.log, 431
/usr, 63, 112
/usr/local, 63

V

V4L2 (Video4Linux), 199
van den Berg, Stephen, 553
van Rossum, Guido, 652
/var, 63, 112
variables
    array, 642, 753
    dictionary, 656
    environment, 448, 612–613
    global, 683
    hash, 642–643, 724–725, 753
    list, 655
    local, 683
    Perl and, 641–644
    PHP, 751–754
    Python, 654–656
    scalar, 641–642, 654, 751–752
    shell scripts and, 612–614
    tuples, 655–656
    user, 612–614
versions (Ubuntu), 22–23, 27, 319, 769
vfat, 11
VFS (virtual file system), 11
video cards
    monitors and, 388, 401–403
    3-D, 50, 388, 403–404
    Ubuntu installation and, 14, 50
    X Windows and, 388–389
video clips, web, 302–307
video codecs, 296, 297, 298
video display, 387–405
    Compiz Fusion features and, 396–401

video display and, 388–394
XFree86, 390
X.Org, 390–394
XPM/XBM file types, 260
X Windows display manager protocol
   (XDMCP), 218
Xandros, 20
XBM, 260
XDG menu specification, 91
XDMCP (X Windows display manager
   protocol), 218
xfce, 18, 24
XFree86, 390
xfs, 11
.xls format, 173, 174
.xml format, 168, 174
xor function, 651, 658
X.Org, 390–394
xorg.0.log, 431
x.org.conf configuration file, 390–394
XP. *See* Windows XP
XPM, 260

XSane application, 376
   document scan with, 379–380
   image file types, 383
   scanner detection with, 376–378
   work area, 380–383
Xubuntu, 24

Y

y command, 146
yanking, 146
YouTube, 302, 304
YouTube browser, 300

Z

z shell (zsh), 13, 623
Zend Framework, 742
zone DNS server, 486
zones (subdomains), 471
Zoom buttons, 117, 118
zoom levels, 122–123
zsh (z shell), 13, 623